Doing Social Research

Doing
Social
Research

SECOND EDITION

THERESE L. BAKER
California State University, San Marcos

McGraw-Hill, Inc.

New York   St. Louis   San Francisco   Auckland   Bogotá   Caracas
Lisbon   London   Madrid   Mexico City   Milan   Montreal   New Delhi
San Juan   Singapore   Sydney   Tokyo   Toronto

This book was set in Times Roman by The Clarinda Company.
The editors were Phillip A. Butcher, Marian Provenzano, and Sheila H. Gillams;
the production supervisor was Louise Karam.
The cover was designed by Carol Couch.
New drawings were done by Hadel Studio.
R. R. Donnelley & Sons Company was printer and binder.

Acknowledgments appear on pages 485–487, and on this page by reference.

Doing Social Research

This book is printed on acid-free paper.

3 4 5 6 7 8 9 0 **DOH DOH** 9 0 9 8 7 6 5 4

ISBN 0-07-003492-3

Library of Congress Cataloging-in-Publication Data

Baker, Therese L.
    Doing social research / Therese L. Baker.—2nd ed.
        p.   cm.
    Includes bibliographical references and index.
    ISBN 0-07-003492-3
    1. Social sciences—Research.   I. Title.
H62.B286   1994
300' .72—dc20   93-4267

*T*herese L. Baker is one of the twelve founding faculty members, and professor of sociology, at California's newest university: California State University, San Marcos, founded in 1989. She currently serves as program director in sociology and in social science. Born and raised in Minneapolis, she received her undergraduate education at Cornell University and graduate education at the University of Chicago. For eighteen years, she was a member of the Sociology Department at DePaul University in Chicago, where she held positions at various times as chairperson of the Sociology Department, director of the Chicago Area Studies Center, and director of the Urban Studies Program. In 1987 she was a visiting scholar at the Institute for Research on Women and Gender at Stanford University. In 1989 she joined Standord's Office of Planning and Management, before accepting the founding faculty position at CSU San Marcos.

Her principal research interest is in the changing ways gender and ethnic differences affect the educational and career aspirations of American youth. She has been an advisory editor for *Contemporary Sociology, The Sociological Quarterly, The American Sociologist,* and *Gender and Society.* Professor Baker has taught social research methods since 1975.

FOR KEITH

CONTENTS IN BRIEF

CONTENTS

PART TWO
The Design of Social Research   89

PART THREE
The Methods of Social Research   *169*

PART FOUR
The Analysis of Social Research Data   *313*

*T*his second edition of *Doing Social Research,* like the first, could never have been written had I not taught social research methods for years. It has grown out of my own experiences of delivering the hows and whys of doing social research to college students. In the interim between the publication of the first edition and the preparation of the second, I left the institution at which I had formed my career, DePaul University in Chicago, and traveled west to become a founding faculty member in Sociology at the newest public university in California, California State University at San Marcos, in North County, San Diego.

We took our first students in 1990—juniors and seniors—and, in the Spring of 1991, I offered the first Social Research Methods class at CSU, San Marcos. At that point, we were on a temporary campus, an industrial park off a southern California freeway. But there were a makeshift computer lab and an emerging library facility, and I had 17 eager students, many of whom had been out of college for years. Drawing on *Doing Social Research,* the class designed for its final project a survey of the attitudes of the residents of San Marcos to the development of a new state university in their community. We got some good local coverage on that survey, and the town's mayor even invited a few of the students to make a presentation to the town council. Clearly it was feasible to be "doing social research" in San Marcos!

In writing the book, I have been guided by several principles. I am convinced that the way to get students interested in social research, and to recognize what it involves, is to think seriously about some of the exciting social research studies that have already been done. To consider carefully what researchers did in carrying out their studies, and what they found out, is to begin to understand not only the techniques of social research, but also the motivation for doing it. In other words, by trying to share the experience of doing social research with previous researchers, a student can come to know why people are committed to this enterprise.

This doesn't mean that every research methods student has to do a study. But I would like every student who reads this book to know what it would feel like to do social research and to move in the direction of wanting to do it. So I have also tried to encourage students to ask themselves, "Couldn't I do a study? What would I have to do to be able to take a question that I find tantalizing and turn it into a research project?"

I have also aimed to make this book eclectic in the wide range of methods discussed. Of course, most individual social researchers tend to specialize, using a relatively small range of methods almost exclusively. And many instructors may prefer to emphasize some methods rather than others. But a text should give broad options and encourage students to explore the rich universe of social research. Although research styles and preferences may differ, each of the methods described in this text has in the hands of some researchers produced studies of real fascination and value. In considering how they might generate a study of their own, students are invited to decide if one type of method or another would be appropriate to their interests.

Finally, I wanted the tone of this book to encourage a sense of commitment to doing social research. Other texts adopt a more humorous tone, or remain neutral and technical. Neither of these has seemed right to me. Naturally, working on a research project has its humorous moments, and nothing can be accomplished without appropriate techniques. But these do not capture the essence of social research. Students need to see—and will be more generally engaged by—the choices, the challenges, and the excitement of trying to study some piece of social action. And since the object of this book is to welcome students into the social research enterprise, students are encouraged to think that they *can* become social researchers, and that this is an activity, a way of thinking and working, that requires and is worthy of commitment.

In this second edition, several earlier sections have been substantially revised. Interviews with three of the authors of studies described in Chapter 1 are presented as a way to personalize the experiences of doing social research. Chapter 2 includes new discussions of theory building and testing, and of determining causality in social research. The meaning of measurement is more fully developed in Chapter 5, which includes new discussions of validity and reliability, and in Chapter 16 on scaling. There are descriptions of currently available datasets, such as the General Social Survey (Chapters 4, 6, and 10), the National Longitudinal Surveys (NLS), the Panel Study of Income Dynamics (PSID), the National Health Interview Survey (NHIS), and the American National Election Study (all described in Chapter 10). New computer hardware and software options for the 1990s are presented in Chapter 12. Appendix A offers an updated guide to the use of libraries for social research purposes highlighting the use of computer searches using CD-ROM or online databases, as well as the most recent bibliographical materials, handbooks, and encyclopedias available for social research topics.

In response to users' suggestions, new topics have also been developed for this edition. These include focus groups (Chapter 7), case studies as a form of research and their use in program evaluation (Chapter 11), linear and multiple regression (Chapter 15), the need for triangulation and the use of multiple methods (Chapters 9 and 10), and data management programs for data entry (Chapter 12). There is also an expanded glossary at the end of the book in which all of the Key Terms which appear at the end of chapters are defined.

The book in both its editions has been the outgrowth of suggestions from reviewers from other universities and colleges who have told me how they teach research methods, what they think should be covered, and what they aim to accomplish in their own courses. For the second edition, I particularly want to thank Russell K. Schutt, University of Massachusetts, Boston, who again offered valuable advice on many parts of the text. In addition, I benefited from the reviews of Brian C. Aldrich, Winona State University; Karen E. Gilbert, The University of Georgia; Stephen Green, North Adams State College; Robert Moore, St. Joseph's University; Donald Stull, University of Akron; Ira M. Wasserman, Eastern Michigan University; and Kevin A. Wilson, University of Saskatchewan, Canada. In addition, I received helpful advice from my former colleague Judith Bootcheck at DePaul University and Ray Hutchison from the University of Wisconsin, Green Bay.

Jacqueline M. Borin, librarian at California State University, San Marcos, did a splendid job of revising and updating Appendix A on the use of libraries for social research. Winston M. Turner of Harvard Medical School prepared very useful additions for Chapter 12 on current computer hardware and software and the use of data management programs. Three of the scholars whose research studies are highlighted in the first chapter—Professors Elijah Anderson, Matina Horner, and Travis Hirschi—agreed to be interviewed about their experiences in doing field research at Jelly's Bar (Anderson), the "fear of success" experiment (Horner), and the landmark study of the causes of juvenile delinquency (Hirschi). I am very appreciative to them for their insights.

This edition would never have appeared without the help and advice of Phillip Butcher, the Sociology editor at McGraw-Hill, who has been supportive of this project from its earliest planning stages. In preparing the second edition, I was assisted by Marian Provenzano in myriad ways; her high spirit and warmth have made working on this project very enjoyable. Finally I wish to thank Sheila Gillams who has done a marvelous job at supervising the editing of the book.

This second edition, developing as it did in the early years of my new life in California, has benefited from the support I have received from my new colleagues at Cal State, San Marcos: my dean and associate dean Victor Rocha and Patricia Worden, my close colleague friends Isobel Schon and Trini Melcher, my new sociology colleagues Bob Roberts and Linda Shaw, as well as from close friends in both my new home in Palo Alto: Muriel Bell and Sue Bell, and my former home in Chicago: Roberta

Garner and Judy Mandel. But the strongest support of all has come from those three men to whom I am the closest, my sons Julian and Felix, and my husband, Keith Baker. Now that my sons have grown up, with Julian moving to New York to become a banker and Felix staying in California to complete an M.D./Ph.D., they have passed from the needs of parenting to their new role as advisors to their parents. As before, Keith has lent his clear insights, his literary grace, and his stellar advice to my revising efforts on this text. To him, I dedicate this second edition.

Therese L. Baker

Doing
Social
Research

PART ONE

The Form and Purpose
of Social Research

W hat are the reasons for doing social research? What types of subjects have social researchers addressed? What problems and issues have motivated individuals to carry out social research? The first part of this textbook examines the context of social research. In the Introduction, we consider ways in which topics for social research may emerge from our everyday ideas and thoughts. Subjects for social research may arise from what C. Wright Mills defined as *the sociological imagination,* that is, the effort to understand the relationship between an individual's experiences and the complex flow of actions of others in our social environment. Or an originating question for social research may stem from curiosity about a *social fact,* as Robert Merton suggested.

Since subjects for new social research projects often grow from earlier efforts to study similar problems, reading well-crafted research studies can be useful in formulating new subjects for study. Methods of social research have also evolved from the earlier efforts of researchers to develop ways to study different subjects. Chapter 1 examines a number of classic social research projects done in the past, using three of the primary social research methods: survey research, experiments, and field research.

Chapter 2 asks what it is that makes social research scientific, even though it may appear that the scientific method could not be properly applied to the study of social phenomena. We will examine the empirical and logical-rational character of social research; the role of observation, measurement, and theory building and testing; the conditions under which causality can be established; and the degree to which social research follows a fundamental model of science. Lastly, we will consider what it really means to do science, that is, to carry out scientific research as a human activity. Science emerges from the unsolved problems of earlier research; it is subject to more or less agreed-upon sets of values, and it strives to be more than a mere collection of facts.

Like any human endeavor, social research can lead to negative, as well as positive, consequences. For example, certain types of social research may require a degree of manipulation and deception of subjects, which may raise serious ethical questions. In Chapter 3, these ethical concerns are juxtaposed with the social and intellectual utility (the rationale) for doing social research. From the Introduction and Chapters 1 to 3, you will have a foundation for thinking about social research—its origins, its accomplishments, its scientific character, and its purpose. You should then be ready to start doing your own social research.

Subjects for Social Research

Why do social research? Most of you reading this textbook would probably answer, "To fulfill a course requirement for my major." But let's ask, more broadly, "Why have people set out to systematically study human society and behavior?" We need to subdivide our question into two parts. First, we should ask what *subjects,* what aspects of human society have motivated individuals to want to study them. Second, we need to know what *methods* have been developed to carry out systematic studies of human society.

This book is really about the second part of our question: the methods of social research. But it is essential to ask as well about the subjects of social research, for after all, if you don't have a subject for research, knowing about methods of research will not be useful. Hence, let's begin by considering what types of subjects have motivated people to carry out social research.

YOUR TROUBLES AS SOURCES FOR SOCIAL RESEARCH SUBJECTS: THE EXAMPLE OF C. WRIGHT MILLS

Subjects for social research often grow out of things that trouble people in their own lives. We want to know how these troubles take shape in the society around us, and in the organized social systems that coordinate and affect our actions. The effort to understand the tension between our own individual lives as we experience them and the complex flow of the experiences of others whom we deal with, both directly and indirectly, lies at the heart of the *sociological imagination* as it was defined by C. Wright Mills (1959). At the base of the sociological imagination lies a need to understand how one's individual life mingles with that of the wider society while at the same time one

tries to distinguish oneself within that society. Mills wanted to remind us that we all live out our own lives in a particular society and during a specific period of history. Thus, the features of that society and the character of that period of history naturally affect how each individual acts and reasons. Mills was concerned with the interrelatedness and interdependence of the components of society, such as social classes, basic forms of work, major socializing forces (the structure of families, education, social organizations), and rules and forms of social control that organize a society.

Mills likes to call a problem that is defined in individual terms a *personal trouble.* Once a problem involves a large number of individuals, however, it can no longer be considered only a personal trouble and becomes a *social issue.* Take the example of unemployment, which Mills uses to show how public issues are more than merely the aggregate of personal, individual troubles. One person unable to find a job is an unemployed person. However, when one-third of a nation's inhabitants are unemployed (as was true in the Great Depression of the 1930s),

> that is an issue, and we may not hope to find its solution within the range of opportunities open to any one individual. . . . Both the correct statement of the problem and the range of possible solutions require us to consider the economic and political institutions of the society, and not merely the personal situation and character of a scatter of individuals *(1959, p. 9).*

But what about an 8 to 10 percent level of unemployment, the level which roughly characterizes the United States in the early 1990s? Is that the basis of a social issue? Everyone would agree that for the individual unemployed person, whatever the overall unemployment rate, being unemployed is a personal trouble.

But at what point do these aggregate personal troubles become a social issue? The Democrats and the Republicans often disagree about the meaning of the unemployment rate. Their very disagreement makes unemployment a public issue.

DEVELOPING AN APPRECIATION FOR SOCIAL COMPLEXITY

The sociological imagination grows best in minds that are open to complexity, in minds that are able to examine an issue from various points of view—some of which may seem less familiar and "natural" than others. We all know that everyone else does not see the world exactly as we do, but the sociologically imaginative person must ask, "Am I not able to view a problem from totally contradictory vantage points?" This does not mean that you must forget or disregard your values, but rather that you can place your values in a framework where they compete with contrary values. Learning to ap-

preciate the complexity of social situations can be enjoyable and profitable, for it can add to your repertory of understanding; it can enable you to deal with future events more effectively.

Most jobs require you to deal with people and changing circumstances with understanding and flexibility. Although only a few students may end up as professional researchers, everyone can profit from developing a sociological imagination which can be applied both to work and to personal life. You must cultivate your natural interest: first, in your own troubles; second, in social settings and organizations with which you are familiar; and third, in events beyond your life's setting that strike you as intriguing, puzzling, and edifying.

The tone of social research is that of genuine concern for the subject under study. This is easy if you study what genuinely concerns you. Such an attitude is not incompatible with the style of research we call scientific. Science does not mean that creative, spontaneous interest in a subject must be squeezed out of the researcher. On the contrary, committed interest in social issues can be expressed in—indeed, is indispensable to—a scientific and disciplined style of investigation.

PROGRESSIVELY FORMULATING A SOCIAL RESEARCH SUBJECT: THE EXAMPLE OF ROBERT MERTON

In an article on problem finding in sociology, Merton suggested "three principal components in the progressive formulation of a problem" (1959, p. xiii): (1) an originating question, (2) a rationale, and (3) the specifying questions. Chapter 3, on the uses of social research, discusses developing the rationale for a study. Much of the rest of this textbook addresses various ways to specify research questions by developing concepts, types of measurement, research designs, samples of subjects to study, procedures for data collection, etc.—all of which make explicit what the research will in fact be.

The originating question, in Merton's view, often stems from a social fact, that is, some observation of a condition in society that can be measured and is subject to change. He gave as an example increasing rates of mental illness in the United States (1959, p. xiv). A current social fact is that people are changing their beliefs about how a society should treat those with AIDS or those who are homeless. Factual evidence can be ascertained about these issues, and then a question can be posed in relation to these facts. Merton also suggested that originating questions can grow from considering the relationship between a certain social act and the society as a whole—for example, asking what it is about a certain type of society that determines the types of crime that occur there (1959, p. xv). For Merton, problems for social research do not come "out of the blue" but are grounded in factual evidence.

Mills placed the sociological imagination at the intersection of the investigator's biography and the historical context in which he or she is living. Merton also recognized the centrality of the individual in defining research problems. Noting that a prominent historian once stated that while everyone might like to be his or her own historian, few feel they have sufficient knowledge of the past to do so, Merton argued that this is not the case with sociologists: everyone in the society feels confident that he or she understands it well, and we all develop firm opinions about how it works. Of course, our assumptions about society may be wrong, and "getting the facts" may force the social researcher to reconceptualize a research problem.

LEARNING ABOUT SUBJECTS AND METHODS FROM EARLIER RESEARCH STUDIES

An essential characteristic of scientific research is that it is interactive. From study to study, research methods and strategies are progressively refined, research subjects are redefined and transformed, new ideas are sparked by earlier findings and changing concerns. The methods you choose to carry out a research project will be driven to some degree by the questions you pose and the problems that intrigue you. But these components will also be affected by your choice of a research style. For this reason, Chapter 1 will introduce you to six classic research studies that utilized quite different styles of research to explore a varied array of subjects. Consideration of these exemplary studies will give you some sense of the range, the depth, and the texture of the sociological imagination.

RECOMMENDED READINGS

1. Berger, Peter L.: *Invitation to Sociology: A Humanistic Perspective,* Anchor Books, Garden City, N.Y., 1963. Berger's stress on sociology as a pastime and as a form of consciousness offers many ideas for subjects of social research. A very readable book.
2. Frost, Peter J., and Ralph E. Stablein (eds.): *Doing Exemplary Research,* Sage, Newbury Park, Calif., 1992. In this collection, senior and junior scholars reflect on their research experiences, emphasizing the research process.
3. Gross, Ronald: *The Independent Scholar's Handbook,* Addison-Wesley, Reading, Mass., 1982. Rich with examples of how independent scholars practice their craft and survive, the discussion in this handbook on how to turn "messy beginnings" into serious research inquiries is one of the best available. In addition, Gross offers highly practical advice about such matters as locating resources and seeking out fellow researchers.
4. Merton, Robert K.: "Notes on Problem-Finding in Sociology," in Robert K. Merton, Leonard Broom, and Leonard S. Cottrell, Jr. (eds.), *Sociology Today,* Basic Books, New York, 1959. In this short essay, Merton suggests which ingredients are necessary to the makeup of a sociological problem. He also discusses the conditions that are likely to lead to the discovery of new sociological problems needing research.
5. Mills, C. Wright: *The Sociological Imagination,* Oxford, New York, 1959. Mills's vibrant work includes marvelous chapters on grand theory and empirical work in sociology. However, the part of the book that will probably be the most helpful in your efforts to initiate a research project is the appendix on "intellectual craftsmanship."

Varieties of Social-Scientific Research

LOOKING AHEAD

This chapter compares and contrasts six classic research studies—two surveys, two experiments, and two field studies. It presents current reflections of three of the researchers who did these studies, and it examines commonalities and creative and scientific components of these studies.

INTRODUCTION

*T*o do good research, you need to know what good research is. To whet your sociological appetite, you need delicious sociological studies to chew on—studies with exciting, vivid, memorable designs. This chapter will describe six such studies, which are characteristic of many of the most interesting carried out in the last 20 years. These studies will be described in enough detail so that you will develop some level of familiarity with them. In later chapters, examples from these studies will be used to explain various aspects of research design and analysis.

These six studies were selected because they represent a broad array of social research methods. The researchers in each of these studies maintained a certain intensity of engagement in their research projects, so the studies have a liveliness and a sense of personal commitment that make them memorable. I should add that some of these studies are particular favorites of my own.

The studies discussed here are examples of three of the major methods currently used in social research: survey research, experiments, and field work. These are not the only three social research methods, as this text will clearly show. They are, however, three central types of social research, which represent very different styles of research method. To begin by contrasting these types will help you to appreciate the range of ways in which a social researcher can choose to study a subject. Let me offer a brief and summary description of these three types.

Survey research can *describe* the attitudes and behaviors of a population of people by selecting in a representative way a sample of individuals and soliciting their responses to a set of questions. Such descriptive surveys are familiar to you in the form of polls. Social researchers, however, often use survey research to attempt to *explain* phenomena, not merely to describe them. In such cases, hypotheses (that is, problems that an explanation suggests) are set up to be tested by relating responses to different questions to one another.

Experimental research attempts to *explain* how a specific part of a social unit operates when it is stimulated by an experimental device. This method involves setting up controlled conditions in which individuals being studied, the experimental group, are subjected to the experimental stimulus. Their reaction is compared to that of the control group, another set of individuals not subject to the experimental conditions. By randomly assigning subjects to the experimental or control groups, the experimenter controls differences between the subjects in the two groups that might affect the outcome of the experiment.

Field research attempts to *understand* how an entire social unit like a group, organization, or community operates in its own terms. Researchers using this method usually immerse themselves in the day-to-day life of the entire social unit, trying not to alter the environment by their presence. Then they carefully observe what is going on, take notes on their observations, and try to develop an understanding of the meaning of the social environment.

You can see from these brief descriptions that each of these methods of research involves very different activities and requires different skills and sensitivities. Field studies, for example, are usually carried out to explore some segment of the human scene. The scene to be studied may be very unfamiliar to the researcher, as is often the case with anthropologists studying exotic cultures, or it may be a very familiar environment where the researcher hopes to gain a new perspective. Field research usually begins with open-ended questions, with wide-eyed eagerness to take in all that can be observed. The researcher must be very observant, but not intrusive; very open to understanding other and unfamiliar situations, but not easily misled.

On the other hand, experimental designs are quite different; in such studies the researcher starts with trying to understand a small piece of behavior, a reaction, by constructing a carefully planned situation (or stimulus) which should produce the reaction. The "if . . . then" proposition which states how the stimulus will lead to the reaction is a *hypothesis* (for example, "If teachers praise their students, then the students will have higher self-esteem."). In other words, in an experiment, the focus is narrowed to the testing of specific hypotheses. Here the researcher as an experimenter is very much in charge; he or she creates the experiment and tries to keep it under control so that what the researcher thinks is being tested in the experiment actually is what is being studied.

Survey research may also test specific hypotheses, but it usually has other aims as well, such as describing the characteristics of a select sample and evaluating the presence and effects of various factors. A survey researcher has a carefully designed set of questions (a questionnaire), a specific group of individuals to be studied, and a plan for how these questions will be studied in order to accomplish the researcher's purpose. The survey researcher must be highly organized, matter-of-fact, and impersonal when collecting the answers, combining (or aggregating) the answers from the entire sample, and analyzing the findings.

How, you may wonder, do you pick a method to use? Your choice may depend upon your particular stage in formulating and conceptualizing the problem. One or another method may be more appropriate at a particular stage of a project, or one or another method may be appropriate to the particular theoretical assumptions on which the project is based. If you are at an early stage in thinking about a problem and are trying to "generate concepts" about a social environment, then becoming a participant observer in the social environment might enable you to clarify what seem to be the important issues, the significant types of social action which characterize the setting. In other words, at this early stage of conceptualizing a problem, field research may be the best choice.

In fact, field research may produce concepts which can then be tested more specifically in a laboratory experiment. To design an experiment, you must already be at a point where you can be very precise about exactly what you want to study. This demands a narrowing of focus to a small number of testable questions. A particular research question, however, may seem to require a broadening of focus, a testing of how far what has been observed in one social setting can be generalized to a wider social environment. At this stage, a survey may be called for.

Your choice of method may also depend upon your particular theoretical commitments. One researcher may believe that certain methods are preferable to other methods because of an underlying outlook on how to explain things social. Another may look askance at certain methods as being largely useless. While this is a rather subtle point and I don't want to confuse you, let me offer a few examples.

Some social researchers believe that participant observation, the method of field research, is *the* method of choice because it puts the researcher where the action is. An example of social researchers in sociology who generally hold this view would be those who call themselves *symbolic interactionists*— those who think that the meaning of social behavior can best be captured through careful observation of the ways in which individuals interact one with another. Such researchers think that if you want to understand the social world around you, you must look at it directly, unimpeded by a variety of research contraptions (such as experiments and questionnaires).

Other social researchers have very different beliefs about what is needed to explain social situations. For some social scientists, the point of social research is to look at broad patterns of social life; in their view, sitting around in a bar taking notes or observing life in an organization will never give you the right picture of things. For such individuals—Nicholas Mullins (1973) described them as Standard American Sociologists—survey research is *the* method; field research may be *suggestive* of concepts and hypotheses, but they would not consider it a complete method in itself.

Another set of social researchers find both field and survey research too casual, too uncontrolled, too messy. They demand the precision that can be better achieved in an experimental study. An experimentalist will argue that it is only when you can control (block out) all the extraneous occurrences going on in a social environment that you are able to focus on the behavior relevant to the idea you are testing. Naturally, field researchers may find experiments much too contrived and artificial; survey researchers may find experiments too narrow and unrepresentative.

Assuming that you do not have a commitment to a theoretical point of view, your selection of a method will depend both on the type of problem you want to study and the stage of your thinking about it. Let me add one other criterion that I think helps to determine what type of method a researcher might select: that is the type of research which actually seems to appeal to the researcher personally. Some may think it would be great fun to go somewhere and submerge oneself in a *real* social environment, that is, to do a field study. Others may consider it exciting to design a questionnaire and go out and interview different people on the same set of questions. Still others may think it more challenging to develop a clever experiment to test an idea in a very careful way. As you read through these studies, try to envision what it must have been like to *do* each piece of research, what was the stage of conceptualization of each problem. Naturally you can't ask the researchers whether they were totally committed to a particular theoretical form of studying society, but reading these studies may help you see that different methods enable researchers to reach different types of explanations.

Finally, note that many social researchers do not collect their own data. Instead, they design studies to reanalyze data that have already been collected. The first study to be described here was based on a large national survey which has since been reanalyzed by many other researchers. This kind of research is referred to as *secondary analysis* and is one of the most common forms of social research being undertaken today in the social sciences. Its methods will be discussed in depth in Chapter 10. We will here concentrate on three very different types of study designs where the data were being collected by (or for) the researcher, in order to show you the complete process of doing social research. Keep in mind, however, that many of the study questions you might pose could be addressed as effectively (or often more effectively) by utilizing a set of already collected data.

The first studies to be described are surveys, the most popular form of social research in sociology.

SURVEY RESEARCH

A survey often begins by identifying a number of individuals considered representative of the group to be studied (what is referred to as a sample) and deciding what questions they should be asked. Let me add here that individuals need not be the focus of study (what is often called the unit of analysis) in a survey. Instead the focus might be groups, organizations, or even whole societies. In these cases, responses to surveys of members of the larger units would be drawn together (or aggregated) to represent these units. For beginning researchers, however, survey research generally focuses on individuals.

Surveys can be used to test accepted explanations, or *theories,* and to develop new ones. They can lend support to a theory by indicating that a relationship that is postulated actually occurs among the group studied, or they can throw doubt on the applicability of a theory by offering little evidence that the relationships suggested by the theory actually exist. If the sample is statistically representative of a larger population, then the findings can offer greater support, or greater denial, of the theory.

Surveys must, however, be limited to the study of questions to which people can, in fact, give answers. Thus they focus on attitudes, opinions, pieces of information about the conditions of life, and the categories that define and differentiate individuals. The object of a survey is to determine the variation in the responses; each item of information in the survey represents one *variable,* that is, a measure by which the differences in response can be established. For example, surveys generally ascertain the sex of each respondent. In this case the variable, sex, can have only two possible responses: male or female. If a survey were carried out among males only (say, a study of the inmates in a men's prison), then sex would not be a variable in the survey but a *constant.*

Surveys may be largely descriptive, for example, to study voting preferences or to determine how people voted in the last election. A survey that asks which candidates individuals plan to vote for is measuring attitudes; one that asks, following an election, for whom the voter voted is measuring behaviors (assuming, of course, that voters tell the truth about how they voted). A survey may measure the variation in attitudes about some issue, for example, support for a nationalized health care system. Or surveys may be designed to determine the relationship between one variable and another, for example, "Are husbands of wives who work outside the home more helpful in the household than husbands of wives who do not?" Because the causes or results of what is being studied may be so various, surveys often include numerous sets of questions (in other words, questions which will measure many different variables) to explore a number of possible explanations for a specific relationship.

The two surveys to be described here both addressed important social issues. The first, a study of the achievement of tenth- and twelfth-grade high school students, assessed whether public or private schools were better able to offer conditions conducive to high achievement. The second, a study of the causes of juvenile delinquency, focused on three different theories of why delinquency occurs.

High School Achievement: The Second Coleman Report

Perhaps one of the best-known social science surveys was undertaken by the sociologist James S. Coleman in the mid-1960s. This survey, mandated

by Congress to determine how far the schools in the United States were segregated racially and what effects this racial segregation had on the achievement of American students, led to a renowned report, *Equality of Educational Opportunity* (1966), which came to be known as the Coleman Report. Coleman and his associates had designed a study of a number of schools chosen to represent the full range and diversity of schools in the United States (in other words, a representative sample). In this study, students from several different grades in these schools were surveyed and tested, in order to examine the characteristics of segregated and integrated schools and the differences in educational performance among students in these different school environments. The Coleman Report used the results to describe the state of racial segregation in the American schools and to explain its effects. The study was widely challenged. But the end result, after repeated analysis of the data, was largely to confirm what Coleman and his colleagues had originally found, that the characteristics of schools had little effect on students' achievement, though the qualities of students' peers had some effect.

The first Coleman Report also showed that survey research could be used to address broad issues of social policy. By combining large amounts of information about particular students (their responses to questions about their backgrounds and attitudes about themselves and measurements of their abilities based on tests) and the schools they attended (which were representative of schools across the nation), the researchers could assess how far schools varied in terms of the outcomes of their students and what aspects of a school were more or less important in determining students' achievement.

In the 1980s, Coleman again used a nationwide survey of American schools to address a different, but equally compelling, question about American education, namely whether public or private schools were doing a better job at educating American high school students. Most private schooling in the United States was church-supported (most was Catholic schooling). One thing that was known about Catholic schooling was that it cost less to "deliver" than public schooling. While this was to some extent the result of the contributed services of nuns and other faculty from religious orders, it was also the case that private schools often tended to have older facilities, less fancy science labs, fewer curricular options for students, and many other qualities that made them less costly as institutions. Yet there was increasing evidence that students who attended private schools achieved at a higher level.

High school achievement had also become an important issue because of a sense that America was beginning to suffer a technological lag, especially in comparison to certain other countries, such as Japan. There was increasing evidence that American students did not perform as well as students from many other countries. This was of concern in a society that was undergoing great technological changes, where many unskilled and semiskilled jobs were disappearing because of automation. If Japan was outstripping the United States in the *new* industrial revolution, perhaps it was because its work force was better disciplined to learn and better prepared in subjects like mathematics and science that were relevant to the development of the new technologies.

Now, there are two possible general explanations for why private school students might achieve at a higher level in school than public school students (at least on the average). One is that better students may go to private schools in the first place; this is referred to as a selection effect. What this means is that even if it is shown that private school students perform at a higher level, the private schools are not themselves responsible for this achievement if they begin with higher-achieving students in the first place. Hence, a *selection effect* means that the differences noted between organizations occur not because of what the organizations did, but because of who was selected into the organizations in the first place. A second possible explanation is that private schools actually are able to teach their students more ef-

fectively because the schools have qualities which enable them to do a better job.

The first Coleman Report had convinced the researchers that school facilities (those things which cost money, like science labs and libraries) were not the critical determinants of student achievement, and the qualities of teachers were not of overriding importance either. Instead, they had concluded that students' home backgrounds were the critical determinant of students' academic performance. However, other studies in the 1970s had shown that schools do have an important effect on students' achievement (particularly some studies that had compared how little students learn over the summer, when they are not in school, with how much they learn during the school year). As a result, Coleman came to be interested in studying a new set of factors characterizing the educational climate of a school that might foster learning.

The survey Coleman and his associates used was an ambitious one, begun in 1980, of a representative sample of high school sophomores and seniors in both public and private schools (*High School and Beyond,* 1980). This large survey was carried out by the National Opinion Research Center (NORC), a survey research organization associated with the University of Chicago. The first problem was to get a sample of all American high school students. To do this, a list of all high schools in the United States was needed. This may sound easy, but it is more difficult to get a complete listing of private schools than of public schools, since they may appear and disappear with little notice. Then a sample was drawn to represent public and private schools, as well as a dozen high-performance public and private schools. Once schools were selected, students in the tenth and twelfth grades were sampled. This produced a final sample numbering more than 30,000 sophomores and 28,000 seniors, about 4,000 of whom at each grade level attended private schools (Coleman et al., 1982, pp. 9–12). This was a big survey!

This second Coleman Report addressed itself to four main questions about the differences between public and private high schools in the United States: the distribution of students among them, their comparative resources, how well they functioned, and how well their students performed.

In this study the importance of how effectively a school could function, rather than the strength of its resources, was closely examined. Coleman and his associates found that Catholic high schools are characterized by much stronger discipline and much higher student attendance rates than public schools. Students in private schools take more academic subjects, and more advanced academic subjects, than those in public schools. Private school students also report spending more time on homework and less time watching television than public high school students. Table 1-1 presents the percentages of students in the different types of high schools who spent varying amounts of time on

homework. (See the box on how to read Table 1-1.) This table suggests that the private schools had, on the average, students who were better prepared and more involved in meeting the educational requirements imposed by the school. Clearly, students who have completed their homework help to make classes function more effectively.

Higher achievement in private schools could be accounted for since these schools usually have students with higher abilities in the first place (the selection effect referred to above). In trying to analyze how far private and public schools help their students to achieve, given the level of the students who enter, Coleman and his associates had to find a way to see how effectively public and private high schools taught students with the same level of ability. Because they had data from only a single year (1980), the researchers could not measure

TABLE 1-1

AVERAGE TIME SPENT ON HOMEWORK BY SOPHOMORES AND SENIORS IN PUBLIC AND PRIVATE SCHOOLS: SPRING 1980

| Time Spent on Homework Each Week | U.S. Total Grade | | Major Sectors | | | | | | High-Performance Schools | | | |
| | | | Public Grade | | Catholic Grade | | Other Private Grade | | Public Grade | | Private Grade | |
	10	12	10	12	10	12	10	12	10	12	10	12
No homework assigned	2.3	3.6	2.4	4.0	0.0	0.6	1.7	1.0	1.3	0.7	0.0	0.0
None	4.5	4.0	4.7	4.2	2.3	2.3	2.4	3.8	2.2	2.3	0.6	1.9
Less than one hour	14.1	16.3	14.9	17.1	6.3	9.9	6.3	8.0	7.5	8.0	0.9	2.2
One to three hours	28.3	30.3	29.2	31.2	20.3	24.8	17.6	17.8	16.3	19.5	3.5	4.5
Three to five hours	24.0	21.3	24.0	21.0	24.9	25.1	22.5	22.8	23.2	22.8	12.0	6.8
Five to ten hours	20.5	18.0	19.4	17.0	32.8	27.1	29.8	27.3	36.8	27.2	35.2	29.0
More than ten hours	6.4	6.4	5.4	5.6	13.3	10.2	19.8	19.3	12.7	19.6	47.9	55.6
Average[a]	3.9	3.7	3.7	3.5	5.6	4.9	6.0	5.8	5.6	5.7	9.1	9.5

[a]Calculated by assigning 0.5, 2.0, 4.0, 7.5, and 12.5 to the last five categories in the table, and 0 to the first two.
Source: James S. Coleman, Thomas Hoffer, and Sally Kilgore: *High School Achievement: Public, Catholic and Private Schools Compared,* Basic Books, New York, 1982, p. 104.

HOW TO READ TABLE 1-1

Notice first that the column on the left-hand side of the table presents the different categories of *Time Spent on Homework Each Week*. These categories range from *No homework assigned* (that would be some high school!) to *More than ten hours*. Note that the very last item in the list, *Average*, refers to the average number of hours per week studied; footnote *a* informs you that this is computed by converting the categories of time spent into actual number of hours.

Reading across the top of the table, you see the different types of schools: first, all the schools combined—*U.S. Total;* then the three *Major Sectors—Public, Catholic,* and *Other Private;* second, the two sets of *High-Performance Schools—Public* and *Private.* Under these types of schools are percentage distributions for tenth- and twelfth-grade students. Each column adds down to 100 percent (remember to leave off the average figure at the bottom, since it is not a part of the percentage distribution).

Let's compare tenth-graders in public and Catholic high schools. Twice the proportion in public schools claim they do no homework (4.7 percent to 2.3 percent); nearly a third (29.2 percent) of the public school students claim they do "one to three hours of homework" a week; a third (32.8 percent) of the Catholic tenth-graders claim they do "five to ten hours" a week of homework.

Examine the row for "more than ten hours"—this would refer to the most studious students. What you see is that much larger proportions of Catholic school students than public school students, and of Other Private school students than Catholic, do more than 10 hours per week. When you consider the high-performance high schools, the public ones are similar to the Catholic and private regular high schools, while the private high-performance schools are much higher than any other type of school. Or consider the average hours in the bottom row. There is a steady increase as one moves across the table from left to right.

changes in students' achievement over time. Nevertheless, by comparing sophomores to seniors in the same schools, some estimates could be made. Greater growth in vocabulary and mathematics was found among students in the private schools; but the evidence regarding reading was less clear.

One of the most interesting discoveries was that "achievement difference between students from advantaged backgrounds and those from disadvantaged backgrounds is considerably less in Catholic schools than in public schools" (Coleman et al., 1982, pp. 194–195). And this was the case in comparing white students with black or Hispanic students, or in comparing students whose parents had different levels of educational attainment. This suggested to the Coleman team that public schools did not match their image as "common" schools in which a wide mix of students become more similar in their talents over time.

How far the private schools are responsible for the greater achievement of their students remains difficult to answer. But Coleman and his associates were able to show that private school students are more engaged in their education. (Consider the evidence on homework in Table 1-1.) There is also consistent evidence that the behavioral climate of a high school is related to the academic achievement levels of students; and private schools are less characterized by fights, students threatening teachers, and other disruptive activities.

The second Coleman Report, like the first, created much controversy. Coleman and his associates had again addressed a major issue in American education using survey data, challenging policymakers and other social researchers to consider their findings. Since a follow-up survey is being administered to the same initial students every other year (this is called a *panel study,* a form of a longitudinal survey in which respondents are resurveyed at one or more later points in time), additional evidence will become available regarding the long-term effects of attending public or private schools.

In order to obtain useful data from a survey, you have to know what you want to ask, you must be able to think up clear questions, and you must be able to collect the data. In the analysis of the data, you must reduce the problem being studied to a very simple statement that was asked in the survey. The answers from all the respondents must be aggregated to make generalizations for the whole sample. Let me stress that surveys on the scale Coleman has done them are not simple. You will probably not be able to do a survey of this size unless you are able to work with a large survey team or organization.

Coleman and his associates used the survey technique to evaluate the effectiveness of public and private high schools, which are important social institutions. They were carrying out the type of research referred to as *policy research.* Findings from a survey such as this can be used to defend or refute various educational policies at the national and local level. Coleman recognized that when research evidence indicated defects in social policies, this evidence was often used to undercut the programs or policies being studied. In fact, the results of policy research often appeared to be more advantageous to opponents of a policy (the outsiders) than to its proponents (1980, p. 79).

We will now examine a much smaller survey that was done in the 1960s to address an equally critical social issue—the causes of juvenile delinquency.

The Causes of Delinquency

One of the most difficult questions in any society is why some of its members break its rules—in other words, why some people commit crimes. In our society, responses to this question often begin with the developmental consideration of how a person becomes delinquent in behavior. For this reason, the study of delinquent behavior among youth becomes a focus for trying to understand the causes of criminal behavior in general. If an understanding of how a youth becomes a delinquent can be achieved, then there is some hope that the conditions which bring this about can be altered or ameliorated.

We all have some notions about why we think young people become delinquents: for example,

they come from "bad" families, they are not supervised, they hang about in gangs, or they feel they have no chance to be successful through legitimate avenues. These notions are based on different underlying assumptions about why a person might break laws and how a society is constructed so as to minimize the number of people who will do so. In very simplistic terms, two different views (or theories) of society have been posed to explain the occurrence of delinquency. According to one theory, a society is assumed to be cohesive and unified, with those actions which are beneficial to its optimal running widely supported by most people. From such a perspective, delinquency results from cracks in a unified whole, areas where the cohesiveness of the society has been strained. According to this conception, delinquent behavior is aberrant, that is, it goes against the natural and widely held norms of the society as a whole.

The contrary theory on why delinquency develops is based on a different view of the natural state of society, one in which society is assumed to be fragmented and divisive. According to this view, the primary effort of the society must be to control the largely selfish interests of individuals so that the society can function even minimally. From this perspective, delinquency is a natural occurrence which can only be precluded by a rigorous system of social controls. When such restrictions are lax or when they do not exist, delinquent behavior will naturally break out. Thus delinquent behavior is to be expected, and the society must continually ward it off by reinforcing its systems of social control. These different conceptions of society, and the different explanations of delinquency they suggest, are *theories.* In other words, they offer tentative explanations as to why a set of conditions leads to a number of effects.

It was to test such theories that Travis Hirschi, a criminologist, set out to discover the "causes of delinquency." Hirschi's research has a classic survey design. It begins by identifying contradictory theories; it then sets out a research design to test the theories; it then presents the relevant data, analyzes the data, and comes down in support of one of the theories. In this research, the first theory of delinquency (in which society is assumed to be co-hesive) was called the *strain theory*. For Hirschi, this theory assumed that humans are moral, that we desire to obey the rules and conform to the norms of society (1969, p. 5). Those who break laws are therefore motivated by their inability to fit into the normal, cohesive order. They are "discontent," "frustrated," "deprived" (Hirschi, 1969, p. 6). These negative tendencies grow "from a discrepancy be-tween aspirations and expectations" (1969, p. 8) for opportunities and success, and may explain why delinquency is much more prevalent among the lower classes where adverse social conditions serve as the source of delinquency.

Thus the strain theory seeks to answer the question "Why do people *not* obey rules of soci-ety?" Its opposite, which Hirschi called *control theory,* tries on the other hand to answer the ques-tion "Why *do* people obey rules of society?" The search for the source of people's motivation to commit crimes is therefore less important in con-trol theories of delinquency. Instead, the sources of control which keep most people—but not all—from delinquency are what need to be carefully examined. For, when these controls are lacking, individuals commit crimes.

Hirschi set these two opposing theories against a third way of explaining why individuals commit deviant acts: the *cultural deviance theory.* This theory assumes that deviant behavior does not, in fact, exist; rather, behavior is called deviant only by those with sufficient power and authority in the society to label it in this way (Hirschi, 1969, pp. 11–12). In short, people may break the standards established by others, but they cannot break their own standards. Such a theory suggests an extreme form of relativism according to which each person operates with his or her own cultural values and learns deviant as well as nondeviant behavior within the natural confines of his or her own cul-tural milieu. For the cultural deviance theorists, neither the strain theory (with its emphasis on mo-tivation) nor the control theory (with its emphasis on social restraint) has the right focus. Instead, cultural deviance theory stresses a phenomenolog-ical explanation, which states that perspectives on what is and what is not delinquent behavior vary widely and preclude establishing a precise defini-tion of delinquency.

What Hirschi set out to do was to test these three theories of the causes of delinquency—strain, control, or cultural deviance—on data from a larger survey, the Richmond Youth Project. The sample for this survey was drawn from public ju-nior and senior high school students in western Contra Costa County in the San Francisco–Oak-land Bay area in 1964. Approximately 12 percent of the area's population was composed of African-Americans with some Asian and Mexican-Ameri-cans as well; the rest were white. Before question-naires were administered to the students, written permission from parents was required. Question-naires included items about the student's family situation (characteristics of parents, nature of in-teraction within the family, attachment to parents) and attitudes and opinions (sense of opportunities for social mobility, positive self-image, attitudes toward minorities). In addition, information from school records (general demographic characteris-tics used to establish the sample and grade point averages and achievement-test scores) and police records (number and type of offenses, date of most recent offense, age of youth at time of offense) were also collected.

In a survey, the manner in which you ask the question determines how the ideas you are study-ing will be measured. Hirschi had to decide what would serve as an adequate measure of delinquen-cy: he selected delinquent acts (reported by the re-spondents) as the factor to be measured. He asked his subjects a series of six questions about whether they had ever taken things that did not belong to them, wrecked some property that was not their own, or beaten up anyone (not counting their brother or sister) (1969, p. 54). The responses to these questions were then added up to form an index of delinquency (described in Chapter 2, p. 42).

Who would report more delinquent acts? To answer this question, Hirschi needed to know various characteristics of those studied: their sex, race, social class, and ability levels. The first characteristic, sex, he eliminated after determining that very few girls in the sample had reported delinquent acts. Thus he confined his analysis to boys (sex became a *constant* in this survey). Race differences were much greater than social class differences. But Hirschi also found that lower academic aptitude (revealed in tests on verbal ability) was related to delinquency. Since the minority-race students more often had lower academic aptitude, this factor helped to account for the noted differences in delinquency between the races.

Since strain theory and cultural deviance theory both expect large differences between social classes and races in delinquency rates, Hirschi moved in the direction of control theory as the more plausible explanation of his findings. Thus Hirschi explored the attachment of youth to parents, to school, and to peers. How closely did the parents supervise their son? How much did the son identify with his father? How intimately did the son communicate with his father? Not surprisingly, Hirschi found "that the closer the child's relations with his parents, the more he is attached to and identifies with them, the lower his chances of delinquency" (1969, p. 94). This was the case regardless of the race or class of the father and son. Obviously, this finding did not lend support to the cultural deviance theory, which suggests that some lower-class parents might actually support deviant behavior. On the contrary, it made the strength of attachment to parents, whatever their social class, a positive predictor of nondelinquency.

Having thus considered the link between delinquency and attachment to parents, Hirschi next explored the relationship of delinquency and attachment to school. He found that a general dislike of school, a disdain for what teachers think of students, and the belief that the school had no right to supervise personal behavior (such as smoking) were all related to higher levels of delinquency. In short, the more attached the boy was to the school environment and its norms, the less likely he was to be delinquent. Hirschi found a similar relationship between attachment to peers and nondelinquency.

But what about the case of a boy attached to peers who are themselves delinquent? Both strain theory and cultural deviance theory hold that the influence of peers is central to the development of deviance. Both contend that a youth subculture contrary to the law-abiding adult culture is the seedbed of delinquency. Both therefore suggest that a boy attached to delinquent peers would be more likely to be delinquent himself. In fact, Hirschi found that the evidence was more complicated: delinquent boys were more likely to have delinquent peers; but boys attached to their peers (whether or not the peers were delinquent) were less likely to be delinquent. Thus the most delinquent boys had delinquent peers to whom they were not particularly attached; the least delinquent boys had nondelinquent peers to whom they were attached.

Hirschi had found the strongest support for the control theory of delinquency, modified to incorporate some influence of delinquent friends (cultural deviance theory). His findings offered little support for strain theory, in which social class influence is deemed of central importance. However, his study also did not strengthen the notion that delinquency must be learned in a subcultural setting, which is characteristic of cultural deviance theory. Box 1-1 presents a recent interview with Hirschi on this study.

Some Characteristics of Surveys

Coleman and his associates used the survey technique *to evaluate* the effectiveness of public and private high schools, which are major social institutions in the society. Hirschi used a survey *to test competing theories* of the causes of delinquency. In each case, major social issues were studied by gathering large numbers of responses to a set of questions. In the Hirschi survey, the sample was selected from a single county in California; in the Coleman survey, it was selected from the nation as a whole. The findings from the Coleman Report

BOX 1-1

INTERVIEW WITH TRAVIS HIRSCHI ON *CAUSES OF DELINQUENCY*

Travis Hirschi, a Regents Professor of Sociology at the University of Arizona, was formerly a professor at the State University of New York, Albany, and at the University of California, Davis. This research project was carried out when he was a graduate student at the University of California, Berkeley.

Was the study of delinquency the primary concern of the researchers who did the Richmond Youth Project (RYP) survey, or was it your particular interest while other researchers mined the survey for other analyses? That is, was the delinquency analysis a secondary analysis from that dataset, or would you say that it was a primary analysis?

The study of delinquency was not the primary concern of the RYP. The study was, as I recall, funded by the Office of Economic Opportunity, and it reflected concern for the educational and occupational prospects of lower-class youth. If a delinquency theory could be found in the study proposal, I suspect it was the strain theory of Cloward and Ohlin. My delinquency study was a "tack-on" project, made possible by the generosity of Charles Y. Glock and Alan B. Wilson. Because I was involved in instrument design and data collection, and had major responsibility for the delinquency component, I would certainly describe the analysis as primary, however.

What role would you say that the Causes of Delinquency *book played in establishing control theory in criminology? Why has the theory stood up so well?*

I am not sure of the role played by *Causes of Delinquency* in establishing control theory in criminology. It helped in some ways, but it may have hurt a little as well. Once in a while I think that *Causes* more or less absorbed several excellent theories and left the control tradition less vibrant than it was before. In my view, the theory has stood up as well as it has because its origins are in the kinds of data delinquency research traditionally produces—data on family functioning, school performance, and the like.

Why do you think strain theory and cultural deviance theory have had a continuing impact in the study of crime?

I think strain and cultural deviance theories have deep roots in the social science disciplines and for that matter in American culture. Fortunately, they appear to be especially vulnerable to analyses that focus on the nature of the criminal act, and I am optimistic that in due time they will get their comeuppance.

In your (and Michael Gottfredson's) recent book, A General Theory of Crime *(1990), you also address economic, psychological, and biological theories of crime. Why didn't you address these theories in* Causes of Delinquency?

Economic, psychological, and biological theories of crime were (or appeared to be) much less important when I wrote *Causes* than they are today. I am not sure, however, that if I were doing *Causes* today I would pay much attention to them.

I selected your analyses from Causes of Delinquency *because they were comprehensible to a beginning undergraduate research methods student, set up to test the theories you had presented, and cogently explained and defended. This is no mean feat. At the time you did the study, did it occur to you that the study might serve as a classic piece of empirical sociological research?*

I don't think it did occur to me. Recall that when I was working on *Causes* I was also finishing a book called *Delinquency Research,* a book critical of the research of others. This was a source of considerable strain. There I was, holding others to standards I was unlikely to be able to attain myself. But there was more to my modesty than this: I assumed that work subsequent to *Causes* would quickly move beyond it—that better data and more sophisticated analysis would quickly reveal its shortcomings. That this may not have happened, at least as clearly as it should have happened, is a sad commentary on the depth of our commitment to the task of understanding crime.

Finally, did you think at the time you were writing Causes of Delinquency *that it would have such a long-term impact? Did it have an impact in areas (and on groups of people) which you hadn't expected?*

My guess is that *Causes* is cited for essentially four reasons: (1) as an example of control theory, (2) as a research report containing particular "findings," (3) as a source of information on the Richmond Youth Project, (4) as an example of how to do, or how not to do, survey research. It is difficult for me to imagine the book having much of an impact with any of these elements missing or radically modified. The theory is cru-

cial, but so are the findings. The widespread, immediate availability of the Richmond data for secondary analysis did not hurt. The least important element would appear to be the data analysis. I much enjoy the use of *Causes* as an example of how to do analysis, but such uses are few and far between. I continue to believe, however, that the mode of tabular analysis I employed was essential to the book's integrity. I was complaining about the new techniques of analysis even before they took over the field. And I am still of the opinion that they often merely muddy the waters.

I have been pleasantly surprised by the book's reception outside sociology.

were representative of a whole society (this is called a *national sample*) so that the survey could address a national situation.

Although both surveys addressed social issues of major national concern, Hirschi, working in the 1960s when large-scale national surveys were only just beginning, used a locally based survey to try to study a national problem, while Coleman and his associates, working in the 1980s with a survey based on a national sample, were carrying out the type of research referred to as *social policy research*. Findings from a survey such as this would be used to defend or refute various educational policies at the national and local levels. Coleman recognized that when research evidence indicated defects in social policies, this evidence was often used to undercut the policies. In fact, the results of social policy research often appeared to be more advantageous to opponents of a policy (the outsiders) than to its proponents (1980, p. 79).

The first important factor, though, was whether the policy research would lead to correct answers. Here the quality of the survey as designed would be critical. The responses to the questions formed the different variables comprising the data. For this reason, the whole success of the study hinged on whether the questions were clearly posed and

whether they actually measured what they were intended to measure (which is referred to as their *validity* as measures of the attitudes, characteristics, and behaviors being studied). Once the answers to these questions were accumulated, the range of attitudes, characteristics, and behaviors could be established, and significant variations could be identified by looking at the proportions of respondents who answered particular questions in different ways. Furthermore, the variables could then be related to one another in a way that would show how change in one variable (say, tighter disciplinary control in a high school) would be associated with a change in another (say, higher achievement scores of students in such high schools). Precise analysis of the relationship established between the variables thus made it possible to test hypotheses identified at the very beginning of the study.

EXPERIMENTAL RESEARCH

There is a sharp contrast between the design of large surveys where many people are asked the same questions and the design of an experimental study. The latter involves setting up precisely controlled conditions to which the individuals or groups being studied (usually referred to as the *subjects*) must react. It is their reaction which forms the central focus of an experimental study. Experimental studies can take place either in laboratories or in natural settings. In a laboratory, researchers can more precisely determine experimental conditions, but it may be difficult to make laboratories mirror typical human situations. Experiments in natural settings may not be able to control extraneous events, but the advantages of studying a real environment may outweigh the greater difficulties encountered in not being able to focus as narrowly on the specific subjects under study. In this section, two experimental studies will be described, one with a laboratory setting, the other with a natural setting.

A Laboratory Experiment

Like much experimental social research, this study took place at a university and involved a group of students as subjects. In some experimental studies, the researcher wants to try to substantiate or challenge a general explanation (a theory) of why something occurs. In other studies, however, the researcher is looking for evidence upon which to build a theoretical statement of why various factors may relate to one another. In the course of extensive research on achievement motivation, McClelland, Atkinson, and others (1953) had developed a theory to explain why some individuals are motivated to succeed at various tasks while others are much less likely to want to achieve. Achievement motivation had been measured by subjects' reactions to obscure pictures (called projective tests). Using this technique, evidence had been gathered widely on subjects of different ages and backgrounds, both in the United States and in other countries. Yet little evidence had come to light about achievement motivation in women. In fact, the findings on women's achievement motivation were considered so contradictory that they had been largely ignored until in the 1960s a student of Atkinson's, Matina Horner, decided to develop a new technique to explore how far women were motivated to achieve (1968).

First, Horner developed a new theory to explain the evidence on women's achievement motivation. It had been shown that women seemed to want to avoid competitive situations in which they might have the opportunity to achieve. The reason given for this desire to avoid situations which might lead to success had been that women supposedly were afraid to fail. Horner posited a different explanation for women's avoidance of achievement-oriented situations, which placed more emphasis upon their fear of success than upon their fear of failure (1968, pp. 15–16).

This theory, which came to be referred to popularly as the *fear of success* theory, needed to be tested in an experiment in order to establish whether or not it was a reasonable explanation of women's achievement motivation. Horner's experiment involved college student subjects attending two evening sessions. In the first, they were given the opening lines of a number of stories in which the primary character was female, for the women subjects, or male, for the men subjects. Each of the subjects was then asked to complete the story. One of the opening lines (the cues given the subjects, which were supposed to stimulate a response) was

> After first term finals John (Anne) finds himself (herself) at the top of his (her) med school class *(Horner, 1968, p. 39)*.

This cue was to measure sex differences concerning competitive achievement situations and to tap anxiety about success, in other words, the fear of success. In addition, the subjects took a test measuring anxiety about achievement and a few ability tests. In the second session, subjects were assigned to three experimental conditions: noncompetitive, mixed-sex competitive, and same-sex competitive. In each situation, subjects were given different tasks (verbal and arithmetic problems, anagrams). In this way, Horner could study which subjects performed best under different experimental conditions. In Horner's initial study of 90 women and 88 men, 59 women and 8 men wrote stories that included imagery expressing the motive to avoid success in response to the John (Anne) story. Women who scored high on fear of success performed worse in competitive situations (especially mixed-sex competitive situations) than those scoring low, and better in the noncompetitive situations.

One type of response that women offered in reaction to Anne's success in medical school was based on fear of social rejection. In this type, the subject expressed concern for the potential loss of friends, dates, and the ability to attract a husband:

> Anne will deliberately lower her academic standing the next term while she does all she subtly can to help Carl. His grades come up and Anne soon drops out of med school. They marry and he goes on in school while she raises their family (*Horner, 1970, p. 60*).

Another theme is apprehension over femininity and normality, a concern for sexual identity and emotional stability. One story filled with such anxieties is the following:

> Anne is completely ecstatic but at the same time feels guilty. She wishes that she could stop studying so hard, but parental and personal pressures drive her. She will finally have a nervous breakdown and quit med school and marry a successful doctor (*Horner, 1970, p. 61*).

Or the story might present a sheer denial of the fact of Anne's success:

> Anne is a code name for a nonexistent person created by a group of med students. They take turns taking exams and writing papers for Anne (*Horner, 1970, p. 62*).

Taken as a whole, this evidence served to confirm the theory that women's need to be desired by, and affiliated with, men may account for their fear of succeeding in competitive situations—especially those in which men are involved. This explanation struck a resonant chord in the late 1960s

as a much-sought-after reason why women had been less successful than men in achievement situations. Horner's findings found a ready audience among psychologists and other social scientists trying to redress the failure to study women in the past. Experiments which followed usually varied some aspects of the experimental design: the cues were changed so that the environment for success was feminine (a nursing school rather than a medical school) or less specified ("Judy/Peter is looking at the sunset"); the types of individuals studied changed and were younger or older, less educated, or non-American. While many of the studies inspired by Horner's research on fear of success challenged her theory (see Tresemer, 1976, for a review), the original study exemplifies how a cleverly designed experimental study can create whole new ways of explaining human behavior and open up vast new areas for research. Box 1-2 presents Matina Horner's current reflections on this experiment.

An Experiment in a Natural Setting

Many situations in the real world require experiments in order to be studied properly. This is particularly the case when programs have been designed and implemented and it is not known whether these programs are having their intended effects. This type of research—experiments to determine the effectiveness of social programs—is one of the most common forms of *evaluation research*, which will be the subject of Chapter 11. As in a laboratory experiment, an experiment in a natural setting requires setting up conditions so that an experiment can be run: an experimental and control group, a stimulus and a measured response, and a test to see if the stimulus leads to the response. Recall that an experiment involves exposing an experimental group to a stimulus and then comparing their reaction to a control group which has not been so exposed.

One of the most important forms of social welfare in the United States has involved financial support to those without adequate means or ways

BOX 1-2

INTERVIEW WITH MATINA HORNER ON THE FEAR OF SUCCESS RESEARCH PROJECT

Matina Horner carried out her research on Fear of Success and Gender Differences in Achievement Motivation as a graduate student at the University of Michigan. Dr. Horner served as the President of Radcliffe College and as a Harvard faculty member from 1972 to 1989. She is now an Executive Vice President with TIAA–CREF.

Thinking back to how you originally got interested in the subject of your research, had you had any personal experiences that led you to this interest in achievement motivation and the motive to avoid success?

Well, if you asked me at the time whether I had had moments of fear of success, I probably would have said (as did many of the subjects) "No, that's not rational." In retrospect, however, as I think back to situations in which I thought I was making rational decisions, or moments in which I felt particularly anxious but inexplicably so by any rational explanation, I would have to say that fear of success was the only rational explanation. For instance, at one point in the early part of our graduate careers when my husband was having technical trouble with his equipment in the physics lab, so that the pace at which I was getting closer to my degree was ahead of his, it seemed impossible to find any baby-sitter who would suit me. My husband couldn't figure out why nobody seemed suitable to me. As soon as his experimental equipment came in and his work got going again, then the next person I interviewed [to be a baby-sitter] was perfect. If you had asked me at the time what was wrong with all those other 25 people I had interviewed, I would have had some excuse for my decisions. But it's just very interesting that as soon as his work was back on track, the next candidate seemed perfect.

The John (Anne) cue was so memorable—perhaps because it put women into an environment, medical school, where so few had ventured, and then it placed Anne at the head of her class. How did you come up with this verbal cue?

We wanted a situation in which achievement was expected, in which there were some elements of competition as well as the potential for gaining power and respect in a male-dominated society. In fact, the Ann/John cue gave us what we were looking for. In that era, in the 1960s particularly, women tended to marry doctors instead of going into medicine themselves. This was in contrast to an earlier period in the 1900s when if a woman chose to become a doctor, it was a lot easier than it was in the 1950s and 1960s. Those two decades were the low point for women entering the medical profession.

Given that there are now so many more women in medical schools, what kind of environment might have the same impact today?

I think it was in the 1970s and 1980s that the financial community and Wall Street had similar challenges. For a while, law and then business had followed medicine in attracting women in sizeable numbers to the professional schools and then to the profession. The scientific community, especially in several key disciplines, resisted women's entry longer.

How far do you think women still harbor fear of social rejection if they compete successfully against men? Would this occur in medical school?

Right now going to medical school is a normative thing for women to be doing—about 40–50 percent of medical school classes are now women—thus the resentment against women's presence in medical school has diminished dramatically. But in some more recent work with physicians doing their internships and residencies, negative expectations for some women begin to have some relevancy. In other words, fear of social rejection or recognition of other costs of success in the profession tends to occur later on for women doctors as they get closer on the road to their ultimate professional goal.

What about concerns about normality and femininity? Do women who achieve successfully against men still have these concerns?

Interestingly, these concerns are coming back in new terms, as in the case of women who postpone having children until later in life, for those who chose to marry. The question about "If I want children, at which time can I have them?" In fact, there is no or very little time for a social or personal life during medical training, even to get to know anybody. It is extremely difficult to balance personal and professional objectives. Some women will ask themselves if it is worth it, even though medicine is a career they feel committed to.

All kinds of things happen that make women do the cost-benefit analysis: "Is the flack that I get on the job worth it?" I hear a lot now about women having their "fear of success" in a tennis match.

Relations between the sexes seem to have changed a lot since the 1960s, career opportunities for women have expanded, the age at first marriage for college-educated women has increased, and larger proportions of women do not marry at all. Do you think that each of these factors, or other ones, might affect the level of fear of success among young women today?

I think it both affects and constitutes the content of the fear, the points at which it would be aroused. Remember if there are no negative consequences for you, fear of success won't be aroused and will not affect your behavior. Some of the people in our original study were followed through many years later, and one of the interesting things that Lois Hoffman found was that several alternative things happened to high-achievement women's fear of success: (1) they either took time out and let the significant other get ahead; (2) they had a baby and gained confidence in their "womanhood"; (3) some women found that they needed a change in their relationship and found another significant other,

married somebody else who was not threatened by them and could be more supportive.

But then, five years after that, we found the high-achievement people persisting in their achievement goals despite their fear of success which was no longer aroused because fear of negative consequences was gone. There are different ways of resolving anxiety when it comes up, depending on the cause. Once you resolve it, you can go forward.

Is there anything else you have concluded from your fear of success research project which you would like to pass on to students learning to do social research?

I think that one of the things that is very important—that came out of the study—is that science and politics mustn't get confused. I was fascinated with the number of people who wanted to use this study to justify the fact that they didn't promote women. In addition, other people picked up on the fear of success idea and thought they could make reliable predictions. This can't be done unless you use the appropriate measures and consider the impact on behavior in a given context. Fear of Success does not operate in isolation from other motives in the framework of achievement motivation theory.

The other thing that happened—I think because of the political excitement generated by the women's movement—was that about 18 different measures appeared, each allegedly measuring "fear of success," each of them interesting in their own terms, but they were not in fact really measuring the same thing at all! Being true to the theory and disciplined in measurement of the concept was the only way in a very dynamic period to understand the complex issues that were evolving.

to support themselves. This is the basis of social welfare programs which have been in existence since the 1930s. Such programs have taken the form of giving people either jobs or income. In either case, the objective is to support individuals temporarily until they are able to secure their own employment and/or increase their earnings. Yet

the problem inherent in social welfare programs of this kind is that giving financial assistance may create a disincentive to work, since the need to secure greater income lessens when government programs provide assistance.

Since the 1960s, there have been several attempts by the government to assess how various types of income maintenance programs alter the working patterns of those who receive the support. In the 1970s, a number of major schemes to support the income levels of poor Americans were instituted and subsequently studied. One such scheme operated like a negative income tax. It had three features. First, family incomes would be set at a level below which they would not be allowed to fall. If the income of the family did not meet this guarantee level, a cash transfer from the government was given to the family to raise their income to this level. Second, the tax rate applied to the income earned by the family would be controlled so that the family wage earners would not be discouraged from working, believing that all the money they earned from work would only be taxed away. Third, a cutoff or break-even point was set so that if the family's earned income

reached this point, the cash transfers would cease. (See the box about how such a plan works.)

Clearly, one of the problems for the government is to figure out the right mix of guarantee level and tax rates to reduce the costs to the government and strengthen (or at least maintain) the recipients' incentives to work. To study this problem in the early 1970s, an experiment was set up in New Jersey and Pennsylvania in which both the guarantee levels and the tax rates would vary. In the design of the experiment, a sample of families was drawn from the poorest areas of cities in the two states. Some of these families were randomly assigned to the experimental group and others to the control group. The experimental families were placed at four different guarantee levels and three different tax rates. The control families were given no cash transfers. The central object of the experiment was to see whether work behavior would be different between those receiving cash transfers and those not. Additionally, the evaluators wanted to know which guarantee level–tax rate combination would reduce work least and whether this would vary depending on the race of the person receiving the payment.

The experiment, which took place over three years, involved interviewing members of the two groups on a quarterly basis to find out about their work behavior and other sociologically interesting information. It was found that there were very few differences in the work behavior between the experimental (cash transfer) recipients and the control (non–cash transfer) recipients and that there were very few race differences as well. What were the implications of this finding? It was argued that since the income maintenance made no difference in the work incentive of those who received it, there was sufficient evidence that it was a good program and the "disincentive" to work did not occur.

As social scientists, the researchers also wanted to try to explain their findings more deeply. Was there some reason why those receiving income transfers would continue to work about the same amount as those not receiving payments?

HOW AN INCOME MAINTENANCE PLAN WORKS

Suppose the guarantee level for a family of four is set at $12,000 and suppose that the tax rate for those on income maintenance plans is 50 percent. If the family earned $5,000, what would the cash transfer need to be? Here's how you figure it out—the family would be taxed at 50 percent of their earned income; that is .50 × 5,000 = $2,500 which they would not pay in taxes, but which would in fact be subtracted from the $12,000 guarantee level, meaning that they would need to receive $9,500 as a cash transfer. Their actual income would therefore be the $9,500 cash transfer plus the $5,000 they earned, which would total $14,500. If they earned $10,000 their cash transfer would be reduced to $7,000 and their total income would equal $17,000.

Source: Sonia R. Wright and James D. Wright: "Income Maintenance and Work Behavior," *Social Policy,* 6: 24–32, 1975.

With this question in mind, they had collected other information as well as the work behavior in the quarterly interviews. (Here you can see that survey techniques have been combined with an experimental design.) First the researchers examined other characteristics of the members of the experimental and control groups to see if they were equivalent to begin with. In terms of such factors as median levels of education, age, type of jobs, and labor force histories prior to the experiment, the two groups were very similar. Then they tested a well-known theory that might account for differences in the way that poor people respond to financial aid.

This was the theory of the *culture of poverty,* which the anthropologist Oscar Lewis (1959) had developed to describe the despair and helplessness of the poor. This theory seemed to suggest that many among the poor would not have the psychological strength to raise themselves up from poverty; they would therefore be unable to convert the economic support of an income maintenance program into a form of self-betterment for themselves. The poor were beyond redemption because they did not feel that the rules of society applied to them (they suffered from a sense of anomie), they had no sense that they could change their world (they were fatalistic), they had a low sense of personal worth (psychologists and sociologists call it negative self-esteem), and they were too oriented toward the present time—that is to say, they lacked an orientation to the future which would propel them to work toward long-range goals.

These psychological characteristics were measured by responses to sets of questions grouped to form indexes or scales (see Chapter 16). For example, anomie was measured with items which asked respondents their reactions to statements such as "Everything changes so quickly these days that I often have trouble deciding what is right and what is wrong." Fatalism was measured by reactions to such views as "Planning only makes a person unhappy since plans hardly ever work out anyhow." And present-time orientation was measured by re-

sponses to a set of statements which included "The present is more important to me than the future."

An analysis of the relation between these anomic characteristics and the work responses (in terms of earnings and hours worked) showed that among even the most psychologically weak of the experimental group, receiving a cash transfer had not stopped these individuals from working. However, among those who were stronger psychologically, there was some evidence that receiving income maintenance may even have increased the incentive to work. The poor who did not suffer from the culture of poverty were better able to benefit from social attempts to lift them above poverty. Here experimental evidence allows hope that economic support can help address major social problems without creating new problems (that is to say, a disincentive to work) in its wake.

Some Characteristics of Experimental Studies

These two experiments were selected to illustrate the ingenious ways in which social behavior can be studied through experimentation. In the Horner study, the researcher began with a theory. Then that theory was tested by carefully setting up a condition to produce a stimulus. To measure the reaction to the stimulus, a fear of success, an opening lead sentence was used as a projective measure urging the respondent to react to its meaning in whatever way she or he wanted to. In the income maintenance experiment, the stimulus was the cash transfer payments; the response to be studied was whether the subject would alter the number of hours worked or the amount earned on a job in a period of time after receiving the cash payments. In the fear of success experiment, the performances on the tests in the competitive and noncompetitive situations were used to measure whether women who harbored a fear of success would achieve less well under competition, particularly competition against men. In the income maintenance experiment, the effect of the cash payments was expected to be a lowering in hours worked and income earned.

The environments in which the two studies took place were decidedly different. Horner's study was at a university in a carefully planned, contrived setting. This is considered to be a "laboratory" environment. The income maintenance experiment had a "natural" setting. Such a setting can be a difficult environment for an experiment because the researcher cannot hold constant all the possible conditions which may occur during the course of the experiment. But some efforts must be made to control or reduce the effects of extraneous factors that could alter the outcome of the experiment. Otherwise it may be impossible for the experimenter to figure out whether the experimental stimulus causes the result or whether the outcome is brought about by some unexamined factor. (For example, the tax rates of those receiving cash transfers were altered so that the benefit of the added income would not be lost by pushing the welfare recipients up into higher tax brackets.) Another way to reduce the significance of extraneous effects on the experiment itself is to randomly assign subjects to the experimental or control group. When this is done, the possible effects of such outside factors on the experiment are assumed to be randomly distributed between the two groups.

The careful precision of an experimental design is intended to make such studies replicable by others able to recreate highly similar conditions. Thus social-scientific experiments of this type have many similarities with natural scientific experiments, except that the topic to be observed in a social-scientific study is usually the social behavior of people rather than a phenomenon of the natural world. The two experiments described here studied different human behaviors: the motive to avoid success (noted chiefly in women) and the disincentive to work (noted among the poor). These reactions had been seen in ordinary life situations, but an experimental design helped to isolate their existence so as to better study their effects. What is impressive about these two experiments is that fairly simple ways were found

to study these complex behaviors. This is consistent with the scientific style, in which simplicity and clarity are valued because they foster the understanding and acceptance of findings.

FIELD RESEARCH

Some social scientists believe that the only meaningful way to study human behavior is to become a participant in a particular social setting. Studies that focus on the whole of a social unit, in which the researcher seeks to understand how the unit operates in its own terms (rather than to measure qualities that are of predetermined interest to the researcher), may require that the researcher become immersed in the day-to-day life of the social unit.

This type of research is characteristic of anthropologists. At first, anthropologists carried out their studies chiefly among unfamiliar and exotic peoples. Later, the same principles of study were applied to the study of more familiar groups. Many sociologists as well do field research. Field work was characteristic of the earliest American sociologists who studied urban life, and it has remained a way to study such topics as neighborhoods and ethnic groups, as well as institutions (such as schools) and organizations. Some sociologists think that field research is now very uncharacteristic of the discipline and would point to the fact that few sociological journals publish studies based on field research. Other sociologists remain committed to this type of research, and studies of various segments of the social scene regularly form the basis of full-length books and whole chapters within books. Wherever you and your instructor stand on this issue, an examination of field research offers an excellent contrast to the more quantitative and controlled methods represented by survey research and experimental studies.

In field studies, the role of the researcher is of critical importance. For it is the vantage point (that is, the particular focus and perspective) of the researcher that will determine what is observed and what is reported. To go as a North American social scientist to study a primitive tribe in the South

Pacific offers no possibility for posing as an insider. Here the researcher as an outsider—an appraiser of the culture, a seeker of a greater understanding of the values and meanings of the life in a foreign environment—is the only role available to the researcher. But studies in the United States offer the possibility of varying degrees of assimilation with the group being studied. Obviously such assimilation depends on the common qualities of the researcher with the people being studied. The techniques for studying a social unit may be purely observational; they may involve the researcher joining into the life of the social unit; or they may be based on some other set of services which the researcher is performing, services which enable him or her to accomplish observation as a sideline to a different, but central, activity. An example of the latter could be to serve as a lecturer for an adult education course in a prison while at the same time observing prison life (Cohen and Taylor, 1972).

The social environment to be studied may be highly formal and structured, like a corporation, or it may be a much more casual place where people "hang out." It may be an organization with clearly defined boundaries, as a result of which those who are employees belong to the organization in ways that those who only use its services do not. Or the social environment for study may have much looser boundaries, as in a bar, where those who belong are much more difficult to delineate. Where the boundaries are vague, the researcher must establish the confines of the study more arbitrarily and seek to characterize the whole environment as exemplified by the part which he or she has chosen to study.

The field studies to be described vary in terms of the environments being studied and the nature of the researcher's role in the environment. In each case, however, the researcher came to know the social unit over a long period of intense observation and interaction in the social environment. In each case, the researcher was guided by a set of general concerns, a desire to crack through the veneer of the social world under observation to gain

a true and accurate understanding of why it was the way it was.

What to Look for When Reading a Field Study

While the object of this chapter is to give you summaries of some interesting studies and have you recognize, on your own, qualities of their designs, this may be more difficult when reading a field study than an experiment or a survey. This is because field studies are the least intrusive and artificial means of studying a social environment, and therefore they read more like stories. So while you read (and hopefully enjoy) the two field studies I will describe, keep in mind the following questions:

1. Why did the researcher choose the particular setting?
2. Does the researcher begin with a refined set of hypotheses or a set of vague orienting questions?
3. What are different means of gaining access to a research site?
4. What is the researcher's degree of involvement or immersion in the setting?
5. What constitutes the data (the observations which the researcher takes away from the field)?
6. How does the author begin to develop generalizations from the data? (This is the hardest skill: moving from observation to generalization.)
7. How elaborate was the preplanning to determine how the study would be carried out? (In other words, what was the design of this field study?)
8. Can you anticipate ethical problems in doing this kind of research?

As you read the studies, use these questions as cues for assessing the studies.

Jelly's: A Study of a Hangout

Elijah Anderson's study of a liquor store and bar—Jelly's—on a Chicago South Side street corner set out to "sort out and focus on those items that make up the local status system at Jelly's and on the ghetto streets generally" (1978, p. ix). He wanted to discover the "rules and principles under which these men operate," the structure of the social hierarchies, and the nature of social interaction on the corner. In this way, Anderson aimed to determine who had status on the corner or, as he said, to find out what it takes to be "somebody" (1978, p. ix).

Anderson presented himself as he was: a young black graduate student from the University of Chicago. He would go to Jelly's, order a beer and some potato chips, and just sit and observe the scene. One of the first persons Anderson spoke to was a visitor to Jelly's who asked Anderson what he did for a living. Anderson told him he was a graduate student at the University of Chicago. The other man responded, "When you get out of there, they got to treat you like a white man" (1978, p. 8). Anderson thought the other man seemed both suspicious and a bit proud of his being at the university (1978, p. 8). He then began to tell Anderson about his life, his lack of success, his regrets, and his appraisal of higher education:

> You know, Eli, sometimes I regret I didn't finish high school and go to college. See, I didn't get no education. You got a good chance, you gettin' yourself educated and all, you gon' make something out o' yourself. Hell, get all you can, while you can. Don't be like me. Hell, I wish I could be in your place, goin' to school and all. But I tell you something else. You know, too much education is a bad thing. You can mess around and become a cranium. You ain't no cranium, are you? *(Anderson, 1978, p. 10)*

Anderson's frankness about his role had not turned the other man away; in fact, getting a higher education was something that most of the men at Jelly's wished they had been able to attain.

Anderson learned that the regulars at Jelly's were more likely to hang out in the liquor store than in the adjoining bar, so over time he began to go to the liquor store also. It was here that he developed an easy, friendly relationship with Her-

man, a "regular" at Jelly's. Herman, a 45-year-old janitor, became Anderson's primary contact at Jelly's. Again, when Herman asked him about his occupation, Anderson introduced himself as a graduate student. Herman's response was "That's nice." As Anderson states, "On the ghetto streets and in ghetto bars friendly students are not to be feared and suspected but are generally expected to be 'square' and bookish" (1978, p. 13).

Anderson's openness with Herman encouraged a reciprocal sharing of information on Herman's part. Herman became proud of his relationship with Anderson and began to introduce him to others as his cousin. Anderson accepted this form of familiarity, which in the social milieu of Jelly's was understood for what it actually implied—a person one would be proud to have as a blood relation. At Christmastime, Anderson accompanied Herman to a party at Herman's place of work.

Having a regular job, as Herman did, was not considered in a fully favorable light. Since those like Herman who held regular jobs usually held only low-status, dirty jobs ("cleaning up for the 'honkies'"), having a steady job brought forth only ambivalent responses from those who were unemployed. Yet few of the men who hung out at Jelly's were able to get jobs with higher status than Herman's. The significance of having regular work lay more in its implications for the man's ability to be self-supporting (and, in some cases, to have financial responsibility for members of his family) than in the respect that the job itself gave to the man who held it. Those men whom Anderson came to designate as the "regulars" at Jelly's were often characterized by their having a legitimate job. They were contrasted to the "wine heads" and the "hoodlums" who were unable to hold steady jobs and therefore found illegal means of support.

Herman's love life was also a source of insight into the social rules of the men at Jelly's. Herman lived with a common-law wife, Butterroll. While she never came to Jelly's as a regular (women rarely did), the other men recognized Herman's dependence on her. When she had an operation, they watched Herman succumb to depression and a lack of concern for himself. When Herman took up with one of his earlier girlfriends, Bea, the other men disapproved because they feared that Bea would not treat Herman well and thought that the relationship would weaken his tie with Butterroll. The men had little regard for Bea and reported her lack of faithfulness to Anderson. According to the men at Jelly's, Bea was only after Herman's money and would tire of him quickly. Yet they covered for Herman when Butterroll would call the liquor store in search of him. Few of the men had permanent, formal relationships with women, that is, long-standing marriages. Rather, they had more casual relationships, which would break off and resume (as was true with Herman and Butterroll) or which continued in a nontraditional manner.

Anderson's field study encompassed a period of time when Jelly's was closed down by the city for supposed violations. During these months, the men hung out on the corner. The regulars believed that Jelly's had been closed down because the owner had not paid off the right people: "Jelly just couldn't drop that iron on the man," which meant that he was unable or unwilling to make payments to the "right people downtown" (1978, p. 42). Within a few months, the liquor store reopened. With this break in the field setting, Anderson was able to assess how the men viewed their relationship to Jelly's, how it structured their activities.

A study of Cleo, an elderly regular, brought out the depth of feeling that the men held for each other. When he was asked why he came to Jelly's, Cleo would say, "I live up in here. All these here people you see are my chill'un" (1978, p. 181). The men at Jelly's knew of Cleo's poor health, and if he wasn't seen for a few days, someone would go around to his kitchenette to see if he was all right. If he stayed at Jelly's late, someone (even a hoodlum or a winehead) would volunteer to walk him home.

Many evenings Cleo would come to Jelly's and sit around on the radiator looking out the window, gaz-

ing at the traffic. Then, for no apparent reason, he would begin to cry almost uncontrollably. "I don't want to die. I don't want to leave y'all" *(Anderson, 1978, p. 181).*

One evening Oscar moved closer to Cleo and put his arm around him: "Hey, man. It's a'right. It gon' be a'right. Just take it slow and easy. You hurtin' anywhere?" (1978, p. 182). Such concern and caring convinced Anderson of the strength of the ties that Jelly's fostered.

The blend of friendship and emotional support that Anderson offered the men, in exchange for the view of their social world that he gained, suggests that the subjects of this study had benefited from their interaction with Anderson. Of course, Anderson shared with his subjects one critical characteristic—he was black. In addition, he was a male, and this was a male environment. It would be difficult to imagine a white man or woman (even a black woman) being able to gain the kind of easy access to Jelly's which Anderson was able to achieve. He set out to comprehend the status system of a ghetto bar, to learn how someone was judged as a somebody in the world of Jelly's. The study he produced gives the reader a keen sense of the structure of social relations among the men at Jelly's, as well as an appreciation of what these men valued. For insight into Anderson's research experiences, see Box 1-3, which reports on a recent interview with him.

Indsco: A Study of a Multinational Corporation

Sociologists have long studied large corporations, using the theories of organizations to guide their research. Yet corporations are not easy environments to study. People in such settings act in very goal-directed ways: they may not be willing to spend the time or otherwise take the risks to elaborate on the conditions of their work environment. After all, the organization is the source of their economic security. For this reason, field research turns out to be one of the best means to come to

BOX 1-3

INTERVIEW WITH ELIJAH ANDERSON ON *A PLACE ON THE CORNER*

Elijah Anderson is the Charles and William Day Professor of sociology at the University of Pennsylvania. The study of Jelly's Bar became Anderson's dissertation research project. He began this work at the University of Chicago under Gerald Suttles, then completed it with Howard Becker at Northwestern University while Suttles left Chicago.

Once you decided to do a field study in an informal setting such as a bar, how did you specifically find and select Jelly's?

I went around the South Side (of Chicago) visiting place after place, each of which seemed not quite compatible with me. I just happened upon Jelly's. I sat down and had a drink and it seemed comfortable . . . the people at the counter and in the bar were friendly, and open, and warm. I went back to my dorm room at the University of Chicago and wrote field notes. Then I returned the next day and I hung around. I had a good experience then too. I showed my notes to my professor [Suttles] and he liked them. During this time of returning again and again to Jelly's, I was becoming more and more invested in doing this study, in realizing that this setting could be the basis for a good study.

At what point did you develop some orienting questions for your study?

Typically in a field study, you go out and experience the setting and you write extensive field notes about this experience. You begin to look for certain behavioral patterns; they may emerge, they may not. But that is not something that you become immediately concerned about. The main thing is to write representative notes of what is going on in the setting. Over time, as you read your field notes, you do begin to see certain patterns; and these patterns appear then to provoke certain questions.

Thinking about Herman as your primary informant at Jelly's, would you say it is essential in field research of this type to develop a primary contact?

I think it is very important that one develop this main informant. Almost every field researcher who does a significant project talks to somebody who becomes that "main person" for them. For Whyte [William Whyte in his study *Street Corner Society* (1955)] it was Doc. This person becomes your friend and helps you get into the group, becomes your eyes and ears, and begins to alert you to certain things, to fill you in about certain things that happened when you weren't there.

When did the central theme about studying status on the corner emerge in the course of your field work?

One significant thing that happened after being in the scene for a couple of months, the bar side of Jelly's closed. (There was a liquor store on the other side that stayed open.) I thought the study was over, but Herman continued to call me and say, "Let's go to Jelly's." We would stand around on the corner outside and talk and have a beer, and the guys would share cigarettes, and it was a nice little social scene there.

The props for identity and status were all of a sudden gone because the establishment itself, the seating, the "who can stand where," were gone. So we had to renegotiate something else. Just seeing how people distanced themselves from certain kinds of people, how people "put people down," or "put people up," was intriguing. All this jockeying was going on. The issue of "status" became clearer to me outside the bar than it had been within. I could see that the men cared about status very much, and I became very interested in ranking and status and identity. That's what often happens in a crisis—the social situation begins to reveal itself more clearly.

How did you come to group the men at Jelly's into three types, the regulars, the wine heads, and the hoodlums?

These were the terms that really did surface during the closing. People called people wine heads, or hoodlums, or regulars. These were their terms. The wine head was a low-life person in the mind of the person using that term. People didn't call themselves wine heads! People called themselves regulars. When I asked people, "What's a hoodlum? What's a wine head? What's a regular?," everybody I spoke with said, "I'm a regular!" I became puzzled. I began to ask people about other people. I then mapped out the settings so that I could see the hoodlums, I could pick out the wine heads, I could spot the regulars. Once I had these categories, I could begin to trace the behaviors that were appropriate to each category.

I could also see that to some extent the term *wine head* or *hoodlum* was really a matter of labeling and name-calling. But at the same time, certain people really did behave like "wine heads." When a person was reminded of their place as a wine head, through talk or through action, the person (who really was a wine head) would accept that place. That became intriguing to me and led to other thoughts. I began to map out what I called the "extended primary group." On the one hand, the study is of black street corner men. That's clear. But at the same time, it's a study of how people come together and create and recreate an informal stratification system. The concept of extended primary group is really a concept about the making and remaking of informal stratification systems. It's somewhere between the primary group that Cooley wrote about and his concept of the secondary group.

Did you anticipate any ethical problems, and did any ethical dilemmas emerge in the course of the study?

I was very concerned when I began the study. I was feeling at the time that so much of what had been written did not do justice to the "corner," did not do justice to the lives of men like these. I had the sense that doing this study was a legitimate thing to do. As I began studying these people, I found myself asking, "What are they going to get from it?" I felt it was important to pay back in any way I could for the help they were giving me, by helping them, advising them if I could, running errands for them, driving them places. I thought that was a way to pay back, and it made me feel that I wasn't exploiting the people I was studying.

Is there any other special advice that you might give a student now who was setting out to do a field study?

I think the most important thing would be to read other field studies. But I think you learn to do this work by doing it, by going through the trials and tribulations of everyday experiences in the field and having a real desire to learn about the situation—to empathize with people, and to truly understand what is going on.

understand a large corporation, since it takes immersion in a large company by the researcher before he or she can discover the underlying rules that govern organizational life.

One way social scientists gain access to corporations is in the role of consultants. Recognizing that social scientists who have studied organizational behavior and structure can offer interesting and valuable advice to company executives, large companies often hire such individuals as consultants to study and then report on various aspects of the firm. As consultants, social scientists are in a position to observe the organization from a social-scientific viewpoint in order to gain information and ideas necessary for offering advice and consultation to the company.

It was in the role of consultant that Rosabeth Kanter (1977) first entered the headquarters of the Industrial Supplies Company (Indsco), a multinational corporation. Over a period of five years, she consulted, collected materials, read, and observed in various sectors of the central office of Indsco, gathering information to address her concern "with individuals and their work experiences" (1977, p. 4). Kanter used both quantifiable and qualitative data in her study. One feature of her study is that she used a wide range of methods to collect data. Thus the subject of the study is examined with different sources of evidence from various angles. This is called *triangulation*. Kanter obtained information through (1) surveys, including a mail survey of a sample of male sales workers and managers and a survey of office employees (primarily women) on their attitudes toward promotion; (2) interviews and discussions with the first 20 saleswomen to join the company and with a small group of informants whom she came to know well over her years observing at the corporation; (3) group discussions with workers concerning male-female relationships and other problems in the work setting, with managers about management problems and techniques, and with groups of wives and husbands about relations between home and work; (4) attending meetings and training programs; and (5) examining written materials, including company documents, publications, and performance appraisal forms completed by clerical workers (Kanter, 1977, pp. 293–296).

By these rather complex means, Kanter was able to build up a picture of "life" at Indsco. Her analysis begins with an overview of the people in the corporation and with the setting itself. She then looks at the various work roles of managers, secretaries, and managers' wives who, though they have no formal function at Indsco, are nevertheless called upon by the company to serve in various socially supporting roles and must be prepared to move their homes and alter their social lives in order to accommodate the company's needs. Finally, she focuses on organizational structures and processes—the opportunity ladder, the power structure, the significance of "numbers" in the creation of minority and majority types in the organization. Kanter concludes by reintegrating her empirical observations into a theoretical framework for understanding how organizations work (and fail to work) effectively.

A simple observation of any large corporation in the United States would quickly turn up the evidence that few women hold positions of authority or power in such organizations and most women employed in them are secretaries or other types of office workers. One of Kanter's objectives was to come to understand women's roles in major corporations and how some women were able to scale the male hierarchy into managerial positions. Such women, Kanter believed, served as *tokens:* they took on an importance as symbolic representatives of a group or class of persons that went beyond their personal standing as individuals. As such, they were affected by the perceptual reactions that tokens call forth: they got attention, their differences were exaggerated, and their characteristics were altered so as to fit generalized perceptions of what women are supposedly like. In other words, they were stereotyped (1977, pp. 210–211). Women managers often responded to these perceptual reactions in a way that fulfilled the expectations imposed upon token women: they either overachieved, accentuated their female differences, or became as socially invisible as possible. Here Kanter suggested that fear of visibility may be the source of what others have called fear of success.

Kanter found that underlying their strictly formal roles within the organization, women managers were encapsulated in a set of four stereotyped informal roles that allowed them to interact with their male colleagues in ways which were meaningful and easily understood by the men:

> Two of the roles are classics in Freudian theory: the "mother" and the "seductress." Freud wrote of the need for men to handle women's sexuality by envisioning them either as "madonnas" or "whores"—as either asexual mothers or overly sexual, debased seductresses. . . . The other (types), termed the "pet" and the "iron maiden," also have family counterparts in the kid sister and the virgin aunt *(Kanter, 1977, p. 233).*

The woman manager as "mother" was one to whom the other men could turn with their problems: she was the nurturant woman whom the men could depend on for advice and encouragement.

She was even expected to come to the rescue if a button needed sewing. The woman manager as "seductress" was less likely to interact closely with several men, since she ran the risk of being considered morally loose (whatever the reality of her behavior). Instead, she was more likely to develop a single sponsor among the male managers who would shepherd her through situations. Such a man would need to have a high enough status in the group that the other men would keep their distance from the woman.

The third type into which women managers were sometimes cast in their informal roles was the "pet." Women who were so fussed over often lacked real authority in the organization. Men reacted to their efforts by considering them as either "precious or precocious—a kind of look-what-she-did-and-she's-only-a-woman attitude" (1977, p. 235). Finally, a woman who refused to be the compassionate listener, to be responsive to sexual innuendoes, or to be coddled was considered "tough" and unapproachable. She was treated with exaggerated respect and a sense of distance. Such "iron maidens" were, in Kanter's observations, the most successful in the managerial role, though they paid a price in terms of appearing to be more rigid and standoffish than they actually were.

Thus, by means of her diverse field techniques, Kanter was able to conceptualize how women "lived" in large corporations and what were the causes of their problems. By comparing observations made at different points in time and in different sectors of the corporation, she was able to build up a picture of how women and men interacted in the setting and how each person was enabled or disabled through this interaction to achieve organizational objectives.

Some Characteristics of Field Research

How does Kanter's field study compare to that of Anderson's? Kanter's setting for her research was more formal—that is, the boundaries between what she was studying and what she was not studying were clearer. Anderson also selected a fixed setting, but it was one in which no one (except, perhaps, Jelly himself) was a full member; rather, people came and left at will, though Anderson recognized that the "regulars" had a special relationship to the hangout that was different from those of others who came only on occasion.

Yet while their research took place in different settings and therefore required somewhat different techniques, both researchers present their findings in substantially similar ways. In each case, the central qualities of the social environment are developed so that the reader can get a clear picture of the forces that are operating. People are not mere numbers in such studies but, rather, their situations exemplify the roles within the social structure. At points, the Anderson study reads like a novel; the characters are so finely developed that the reader would probably recognize Herman or Cleo in Jelly's. In comparison, the characters are not developed so individualistically in the Indsco study. Each author seeks out types of individuals either to exemplify specific role patterns or to distinguish groups in the setting. Anderson develops the typology of the "regulars," the "wine-heads," and the "hoodlums." Kanter delineates the informal roles into which women managers slip—the "mother," "seductress," "pet," or "iron maiden."

As to the conduct of the researchers, neither researcher did anything to deceive those under observation. Anderson presented himself as a graduate student; Kanter served as a paid consultant to the corporation during the time of her research. Anderson developed very close acquaintances who served as primary informants on the environment being studied and who helped to legitimate his role as a researcher. Kanter developed more formal ties with certain people she encountered repeatedly whom she also found to be highly informative about the corporation under study.

In each case the researcher tried not to intrude on the scene. The object was to see the social environment as it is, not as the researcher might presuppose it to be. Thus the field researcher must be somewhat unobtrusive; that is, the investigator must not make his or her presence too forceful, but rather blend in with the others in the social setting so as to gain their trust and not make them self-conscious. In addition, the researcher must hold a natural sympathy for the environment being studied. He or she must be understanding and able to encourage frankness among those being studied. In this sense, the field researcher must be a very fine informal interviewer gaining the confidence of those interviewed so as to elicit introspective considerations and evaluations of life within the environment being studied.

Furthermore, a field study has a certain openness in its design. Rather than entering the setting with very specific, fixed questions, the researcher usually begins with a few general questions, a vague sense of direction, and then lets the experiences direct his or her course of research. This is very different from the highly contrived and prearranged design of an experiment or the precision and definitiveness of a questionnaire. The course of a field study may vary depending on what happens in the field. If Anderson had not met Herman and entered into his close confidence, what he would have learned about life at Jelly's might have been quite different. Kanter's research was more formally carried out, using a wider range of data-gathering techniques besides observation and person-to-person conversations, yet she also notes that the informal conversations were among her very best sources of information on life at Indsco (1977, pp. 296–297).

The choice of a field setting must also represent a case considered to be typical of a group of other cases. Jelly's could be a bar in any black ghetto area; Indsco is a characteristic multinational corporation. Thus while field studies center on the unique, the single setting, their aim is to tell a tale of many settings. In order to do this, the social scientist must turn the particular into the universal, the personal experience into a role experience. The specific events must be understood as representing regular patterns of happenings.

However, many social scientists would challenge the contention that field studies are representative of the environments and individuals they portray. A critic might ask, "How would we know if the men at Jelly's were characteristic of bar people in the ghetto in general? And even if they were representative of bar clientele, how representative would they be of ghetto residents in general?" Since field settings consist of a particular environment, their typicality can often be questioned.

The challenges are serious, but field researchers would probably claim that their purpose is less to represent a common phenomenon than to uncover the deeper meaning of the particular situation being studied and gain an appreciation of some human social setting. The reader of a well-done field study usually feels closer to—and warmer about—the environment, more understanding of the situation, more desirous of gaining additional insight into the world being examined. Field research is not a cold, microscopic view of an environment, but rather a keen, sensitive appreciation of some fragment of the human picture.

CHARACTERISTICS OF SOCIAL-SCIENTIFIC STUDIES

Commonalities

This chapter has examined characteristic studies using three types of research methods, as a means of exemplifying the major aims and features of social science research. We can now ask what characteristics they have in common. First we can say that they all seek *regularities*. In field research, the confusion of evidence must be sorted out to form patterns to help understand the interconnectedness of activities in a particular setting. At Jelly's, the regulars were designated in contrast to the nonregulars, who were then defined in terms of their differences (not having "legitimate" jobs) from regulars. In the experiments, the reactions studied—fear of success and work patterns of those receiving welfare—were regular responses to a prearranged stimulus. In such studies, it need only be shown that a large enough number of subjects respond in a certain fashion to support the regularity of the reaction. Finally, the surveys used a large number of respondents to determine regularities in relationships between various factors. Thus regularity is gleaned from particular situations in field studies, inferred from common responses in experimental studies, and extracted from extensive evidence of similar characteristics and relationships in survey research.

The second common quality of social research studies is that they examine individuals and social units *representative* of wider numbers of individuals and social units. Surveys do this most clearly by using probability samples to represent statistically the populations on which they are drawn. Experiments assume that the reactions of individuals serving as subjects are representative of human reactions in general; and by randomly assigning subjects to the experimental and control groups, researchers minimize the possible effects of unique individual characteristics affecting the experimental outcome. Field studies select sites that represent typical social settings and human situations of wide social interest.

Third, these studies all develop concepts, or apply existing concepts, to express the regularities noted among the representative subjects. Anderson developed the concepts of regulars, wine heads, and hoodlums to differentiate those who came to Jelly's. Kanter explained the effects on women promoted to marginal positions in management in terms of the concept of tokenism. Hirschi studied delinquency by operationalizing it to mean delinquent acts either formally recorded as violations or informally self-reported by the youths. Coleman defined the level of discipline in the high schools in terms of students' responsibility to the school for property damage, rules about student dress, and measures of the strictness and fairness of discipline in the school.

Anything that varies or is prone to variation can be studied as a *variable.* Studies single out specific variables for consideration. For Kanter, the major variables studied at Indsco were role positions and forms of accommodation to such positions. Horner measured variations in levels of the "motive to avoid success." In addition, variation was built into her study in the competitive-noncompetitive experimental conditions. Coleman used large sets of variables to represent each component in the possible determination of a student's achievement in high school: the student's home background; qualities of the student's school (its curriculum and disciplinary climate); and the student's course selection, extracurricular activities, and ability level. However, once the variables were initially examined, the analysis concentrated on those most strongly related to educational achievement.

Each study begins, on the other hand, with certain *constants.* These are common features that tend not to vary in the study. Anderson's subjects all went to Jelly's. Kanter's subjects were employed by (or were wives of employees of) Indsco. Horner's subjects were all college students.

Each study either built upon or helped to test a *theory,* an explanation for a set of coordinated occurrences or relationships. The experimental studies had explicit theories defined initially: fear of success and the culture of poverty. The field researchers developed theories out of their observations: Anderson concluded that the strength of the social relations established at Jelly's Bar helped to sustain the precarious social existence of the often-unemployed, vagrant men who "hung out" there. Kanter developed an explanation for women's relative lack of career success in the management hierarchies of large corporations on the basis of their scarcity in such positions (which meant that women who did move up to managerial positions were treated, and thereby came to act, as tokens). The delinquency survey tested three possible explanations for delinquency. The Coleman survey addressed a public policy issue about the relative merits of public and private high schools. However, the authors stated that its "greater long-range contribution is likely to be on the more general question of what characteristics of schools affect achievement, and the question of what is the appropriate way of organizing education" (1982, p. xxx).

Each study followed a preconceived design. A research design is both a plan and a strategy. As a plan, it encompasses a set of steps to follow and a kind of ideal model of what should occur. As a strategy, a research design must search out the potential obstacles to the study and consider ways to avoid or confront these obstacles. The strategy aspect of a research design suggests the "active" quality of developing a project, the need to make things happen, to make requests of others, to gain support, to possibly intrude on the privacy and work of others to carry out a research objective. The experimental studies had the most precise designs: every step was prearranged, carefully ordered and controlled. The expected results were considered in the design, and variations were set up in the experimental procedures to elicit differences in response. The surveys were the next most heavily predesigned. Questions were written so as to represent all phases of the analysis to be carried out. The field studies were the least tightly designed. But the field researchers did not go into the field blindly: sufficient preplanning was necessary to prepare the observer to know what to look for and to whom to talk. Furthermore, in a field study the design (the plan and the strategy) evolves over the course of the research.

Creative Components of the Studies

Each of the studies we have considered bears the mark of its researcher. Of course, the field studies may seem to be the most dependent on the qualities of those carrying them out. Because they began with less fully preconceived designs and because the course of the research altered as the researcher proceeded with the project, the special interests of the researcher guided the course of the study. Clearly, Kanter's interest in women's changing roles in corporate organizations gave a direction to her efforts. Her intuitive insight into the meaning of being a token member of an organization enabled her to discern subtle differences in behavioral reactions to tokenism.

Anderson uncovered a corner of black ghetto life by immersing himself in a specific context where he could develop insight about the forms, strengths, and constraints of ghetto life. Such insight requires taking down the protective covering which insulates the observer from the observed, approaching strangers openly without preconceived notions. Such a process is both shocking and eye-opening. It loosens fixed ideas, shakes up the givenness of beliefs, and makes situations appear to be more susceptible to change. Generally, a person is more open to what is familiar. The danger is that we can be so familiar with a situation that we are unable to see it with "fresh eyes." Whether an insider or an outsider is more perceptive in understanding a social environment is debatable. An outsider enters an unfamiliar environment with a desire to understand it so as to account for what appears to be surprising or unusual. Anderson spent many evenings in a ghetto bar in order to come to know the patrons so closely that he became a trusted confidant. He was an outsider turned insider.

Both experiments had creative qualities. Horner's cues to elicit reactions to achievement imagery were created to capture the interest and imagination of college students. The influence of this created stimulus was to be determined by measuring its supposed effects. The crux of the creativity in this study was in the believability of the experimental design. The income maintenance experiment used a set of psychological scales to try to determine the pathologies of poverty that might have overpowered the individuals being studied. The recognition that financial assistance may weaken the work motivation of some, while strengthening that of others, showed a creative awareness of the meaning of poverty.

The surveys may seem the least creative. Following the old dictum "If you want to find something out, ask," the survey tries to be explicit and largely unambiguous. Yet the selection of questions, the wording of questions, the combining of different items to measure more complex concepts (such as Hirschi's set of questions to tap delinquent behavior or Coleman and colleagues' questions on the disciplinary climate of high schools) all suggest areas where creativity has played a part in the design of specific questions and of sets of questions.

Field studies allow for spontaneity on the part of the researcher to change directions in reaction to some aspect of the study. This spontaneity makes the field study appear more imaginative. In experiments and surveys, however, the creativity must be built into the study design. Neither method depends on spontaneity. Instead, consistency is the hallmark of both good experiments and good surveys.

Scientific Components of the Studies

What is scientific about the six studies described? First, the meaning of the term *science* must be clarified. You may think of science as a body of knowledge, as something more or less fixed that could be learned. I would prefer you to think of science in more dynamic terms as an activity, a means of finding things out. To carry out scientific activity means that the scientist must do something. There are two primary characteristics of scientific activity. The first is that what is studied needs to be observed. Science, in other words, is *empirical research*. It is based on observable evidence (what the field researchers saw, answers to questions, reactions to experimental stimuli) which has been carefully recorded and presented so as to make it as close to the actual observation as possible. This attention to recording and presenting the observations carefully and precisely is a part of the effort to make these studies scientific.

Science depends on a *logical and rational* system of rules for thinking and using language; therefore, precision in the measurement of what is being studied and clarity in the presentation of the data are both necessary. Much of this book will be about the different kinds of rules appropriate for the various kinds of research methods to be described. The cardinal rule is to make the means appropriate to the ends of a study. Thus definition is a critical part of science. What is being studied must be clearly defined in order to determine whether a finding has been made.

The purpose of each study is to seek to know something better, more deeply, more clearly, by applying rational, logical rules of analysis to the empirical evidence gathered through observation. In some cases, these rules were already defined in the *hypotheses* set prior to carrying out the study. In the fear of success study, for example, those with higher levels of fear of success were expected to do less well in competitive situations than in noncompetitive situations. This study exemplifies the *deductive method*, in which a hypothesis is derived from a theory in order to test the theory against specific evidence. In other cases, an explanation is built out of the accumulated evidence. In the field study by Kanter, a theory of how tokenism operates to weaken the effectiveness of minority persons in managerial roles was developed out of the range of observations made at a multinational corporation. This *inductive method* uncovered behavioral patterns (such as detailing the responses of women in management) which indicated that what first appeared to be ineffective and self-destructive forms of exercising authority were, in fact, quite adaptive (though often counterproductive). Thus the inductive approach is one in which the researcher reasons from particular cases to more general, ideal cases, from a few instances of a class to all members of the class.

Each study zeroed in on specific phenomena which were subject to variation under certain conditions. These selected *variables* became the central focus of the study. How the variables were measured is emphasized in great detail in the studies, for if the variables are inadequately measured, the validity of the study, that is to say its ability to represent what it claims to represent, is jeopardized. The ultimate challenge to such studies is to argue that the effect being studied is not really the effect at all. Was Hirschi's operationalization of delinquency as self-reported delinquent acts valid? And if it was, did the set of questions on committing delinquent acts serve as a valid indicator of delinquency?

Finally, the association between variables, how one variable related to another—sometimes approaching a cause-effect model—serves as the primary plan for analyzing the results of the study.

This is central to the scientific method. In most cases, there are no cast-iron findings. Because social occurrences are so complex, it is difficult to find single causes which are inalterably necessary to bring about certain effects. In the Coleman study of public and private schools, for example, where students' achievement (that is, their cognitive abilities as measured by test scores) was defined as the desired outcome of schooling, the object was not to discover one cause of educational achievement but to determine among various possible predictors (or causes) which were the ones that were most highly associated with differential educational results.

One of the simplest means of determining whether a study has scientific qualities is to ask whether it could be replicated by another person in the expectation of reaching similar results. How can you know if a study could be replicated? First, it has to be described carefully enough so that someone else could reproduce the design. Second, the conditions of the study must not be so unusual or esoteric that they could not be reestablished. Yet there is a distinction between a study that is actually replicable (that is, that someone else would carry out an exactly similar study, a replica of the first study) and one that can be described as if it were replicable (so that it might be comparable to other studies). This ability to replicate or make comparable is a key to the scientific quality of a study. Once the study is replicated, those findings which support the original findings are then shown to be generalizable. If they can be generalized to a second test, they should then prove to be generalizable to a third, a fourth, or a fifth test.

Having picked out the scientific qualities of studies like those described here, we will turn in the following chapter to a more comprehensive consideration of the science of social research.

REVIEW NOTES

- Surveys may be used to describe attitudes and behaviors, to explain relationships that test hypotheses and challenge theories, or to evaluate institutions and programs.
- Survey data are gathered through interviews or using questionnaires, carefully designed sets of self-administered questions.
- Social experiments may be set up in laboratories or organized in a natural setting.
- An experiment is based on manipulating a stimulus to produce a response, which is then measured. Generally the subjects who receive the stimulus (the experimental group) are compared to those who do not (the control group). To measure the effects of the stimulus, tests are often taken before the experiment (pretests) to be compared to those taken after the experiment (posttests) in order to determine the amount of change.
- Field studies attempt to understand an entire social field in its own terms.
- Field researchers must immerse themselves in the field but must remain aware of their particular vantage point. They must try not to have an impact on the field they are studying—that is, they must be unobtrusive.
- Social-scientific research studies regularities in social life by examining representative individuals, groups, and institutions.
- The creative aspects of social research can be seen in the imaginative qualities of a research design, a data-gathering instrument, an analysis.
- The scientific activity of a social researcher includes gathering empirical evidence (what is observed) and applying logical and rational rules to this evidence to test a predicted outcome.

KEY TERMS

constant
deductive method
empirical research
evaluation research
experimental research
field research
hypothesis
inductive method

policy research
regularities
secondary analysis
selection effect
survey research
theory
triangulation
variable

STUDY EXERCISES

1. Consider the following six research questions and select which of the three methods (survey, experiment, or field research) would best be employed to study each of them. Justify your selections.
   a. Has the Medicare program (providing financial support for medical care to older Americans) improved the health of the elderly?
   b. What is it like to run a marathon, and why do people do it?
   c. How are attitudes toward drinking alcohol related to attitudes toward use of illegal drugs?
   d. Do high school athletes more often aspire to go on to college than nonathletes?
   e. How do residents living in a public housing project feel about their living conditions?
   f. Are men or women more persuasive?
2. Which of the six studies described in this chapter do you think would have been the most difficult to carry out? Why? Which would have been the most interesting for you to have worked on? Why did you make this choice?

RECOMMENDED READINGS

1. Burgess, Robert G.: *Investigating Society,* Longman, New York, 1989. The contributors, who are British sociologists, relate experiences of doing research on a wide array of social topics to broader issues in sociology.
2. Denzin, Norman: *Sociological Methods: A Sourcebook,* Aldine, Chicago, 1970. This selection of readings contains many very important articles that have addressed problems in doing social research, including Herbert Blumer's "Methodological Principles of Empirical Science" and Ralph Turner's "The Quest for Universals." Issues in survey research, experimental design, and participant observation are covered.
3. Hammond, Phillip E.: *Sociologists at Work: Essays on the Craft of Social Research,* Basic Books, New York, 1964. Includes 12 contributions from major social researchers reflecting on their experiences doing research.
4. Riley, Matilda White: *Sociological Research: A Case Approach,* Harcourt, Brace & World, New York, 1963. This excellent methods textbook combines selections from significant research studies with commentary on the methods and analyses used in the studies.

The Science of Social Research

LOOKING AHEAD

This chapter examines the empirical and logical-rational character of science, discusses how theory is developed and tested, and considers the role of causality in social research. It offers a total model of science, presenting deductive and inductive research. Finally, it considers what kind of activity scientific research is.

INTRODUCTION

Ｗe will begin by considering what is scientific about social research. The scientific character of social research is both empirical and logical-rational. It involves an observational activity, in which phenomena are accurately and precisely observed and recorded as measures, and theory building and testing, in which explanations of the relationships between measured observations are generated and appraised. We will also address how far causality can be determined in social research. We will consider in detail a scientific model covering inductive scientific inquiry (which moves from observations to generalizations as a means of developing theories) and deductive scientific inquiry (in which hypotheses are deduced from theories and tested against observations). We will then consider how this model seemed to guide the designs of some social research studies discussed in Chapter 1.

We will then ask where science starts. What is it about human inquiry that can make it qualify as "science"? To answer this we will consider the meaning of scientific paradigms and see how they guide the direction of scientific activity. Doing social research involves a range of scientific practices, values, and models. We will also consider how far scientific activity is governed by a set of rules functioning as a scientific ethos, and to what degree social research is positivist, that is, striving to accumulate facts as the sole means of establishing explanations.

THE EMPIRICAL CHARACTER OF SCIENCE

At the end of Chapter 1, we examined the scientific aspects of six studies. Here we will examine much more carefully the components of scientific research as they apply to the study of social questions.

Science is *empirical* because it is based on the study of observed evidence. This means that science as an activity is an advanced form of *seeing*. Science is the effort to observe how the real world works. If we could directly *see* into a living cell, *see* the force of gravity, or *see* how juveniles become delinquent, scientific activity would be much simpler. However, since our unaided eyes cannot see all these things, we have devised scientific instruments and scientific methods to enable us to better observe the world.

Empirical Science Is Based on Observation

The primary work of science is careful observation. To observe a cell too small to see with the naked eye, the biologist needs the assistance of an instrument, the microscope. To observe the invisible force of gravity, the physicist must devise tests (such as the pendulum) to prove its existence. To observe delinquent acts when most occur out of public view, the social researcher needs to develop a method for detecting this behavior.

Note that if we ask, "What is delinquency?," no immediate answer is obvious. We might say that delinquency is the committing of actions that are illegal, and that a juvenile delinquent is a youth who commits such illegal acts. But how can we know who *is* a juvenile delinquent? This is what Travis Hirschi tried to figure out in his landmark study, *Causes of Delinquency* (1969).

To observe delinquency, first he had to decide what he would accept as a definition of delinquency, and then he had to come up with a way to measure this quality among a group of youths. Hirschi could have used police records of official acts of delinquency as evidence of delinquency. Or he might have disguised himself as a delinquent youth (or hired an assistant to do so) and tried to infiltrate youth groups so that he might be able to directly see delinquent acts being performed. However, he decided to use a set of survey questions to measure delinquency.

If a large number of youths would truthfully respond to a set of questions by reporting on whether they, personally, had engaged in delinquent behavior, Hirschi would be able to observe who was (and who was not) delinquent. Hirschi developed a set of six questions, each describing a delinquent act, which together formed the index of delinquency that served as his measure. This set of questions could then be asked of a group of youths to find out who was delinquent. Thus the Index of Delinquency was the instrument Hirschi developed to assist him in "observing" delinquency.

Observation Must Be Accurate and Precise. The biologist observing a cell must carry out observations accurately and precisely, never haphazardly. Such observations must be made under the best conditions—where the lighting is good, the technician is trained to know what to look for, the equipment is properly handled and maintained. Then the observations must be carefully recorded. Such care applies to the observation of social phenomena as well. For example, techniques for measuring delinquency attempt to observe and record

delinquent acts accurately, and each technique can be evaluated in terms of the credibility of the observations made.

Let's consider more fully the observation technique that Hirschi used to measure delinquency, namely, the Index of Delinquency. The questions aim to measure acts of thievery, vandalism, and assault. Clearly, if the respondents refuse to answer questions 67 to 72, or if they lie, then Hirschi will not have produced an accurate observation. But note that the questions are posed in a nonthreatening way. The researcher does not want to arouse fear in the respondents, which might discourage them from answering truthfully. Furthermore, the survey questions are placed within a wider series of questions on a number of different subjects rather than being singled out as a specific measure of delinquency.

Measures Are Developed to Record Observations

The Index of Delinquency was developed as a way to record the incidence of delinquent behavior. In essence, it was designed as a *measure* of delinquency.

INDEX OF DELINQUENCY QUESTIONS FROM THE RICHMOND YOUTH PROJECT SURVEY

67. Have you ever taken little things (worth less than $2) that did not belong to you?

68. Have you ever taken things of some value (between $2 and $50) that did not belong to you?

69. Have you ever taken things of large value (worth over $50) that did not belong to you?

70. Have you ever taken a car for a ride without the owner's permission?

71. Have you ever banged up something that did not belong to you on purpose?

72. Not counting fights you may have had with a brother or sister, have you ever beaten up on anyone or hurt anyone on purpose?

USE THESE ANSWERS NOW

A. No, never
B. More than a year ago
C. During the last year
D. During the last year and more than a year ago

Source: Travis Hirschi: *Causes of Delinquency,* University of California Press, Berkeley, Calif., 1969, p. 256.

As a measure, it could be evaluated in terms of how closely it seemed to assess the concept it was trying to quantify—namely, delinquency. This need to develop "good" measures raises two issues: does the measure really measure what it purports to measure (is it valid?), and is the measure consistent (is it reliable?), so that the same respondent would answer it in the same way if the question were asked again? Measurement, validity, and reliability are dealt with in greater detail in Chapter 5. Here, we want to stress that social science research aims to develop valid and reliable measures of the things it is trying to observe.

Measures Record Variation Across Repeated Observations.   The natural scientist (the biological researcher, the physicist) makes repeated observations of the natural phenomenon being studied. Each observation is not identical to the previous one; rather, there are variations. Measures such as the Index of Delinquency are set up to indicate the degree of variation in responses. Examine the Index of Delinquency shown in the box. Note that the first three questions in the index ask whether the respondent has taken things of greater and greater value. This is both to differentiate more minor from more major delinquent acts, and in more general terms to measure variation.

One of the central qualities of scientific observation is the study of variation. Note that the Index of Delinquency offers a range of four possible responses to each question ("no, never" to "during the last year and more than a year ago"). This again will provide variation in response. Variation needs to be observed because it characterizes all things. Human behavior (delinquent acts), gravity, cell compositions all vary.

The aim of scientific observation must be to capture this variation across *repeated observations.* The biologist examines many cells, looking for the same phenomena. Hirschi carried out repeated observations by having his questions included in a large survey which was administered to numerous young people. A central characteristic of scientific research involves taking repeated observations so as to determine the degree of variation.

Variables Serve as the Recorded Measures of Variation of Specific Phenomena

In Hirschi's study, delinquency is one of the primary variables. This means that it is a measure on which differences in response can be established. Naturally, delinquent behavior varied among the respondents to the study. Even those who answered "no, never" to each of the six questions in the Index of Delinquency could be recorded in terms of the delinquency variable as "not delinquent." Those who answered positively, at a more frequent rate, to a greater number of the items could be considered more delinquent than those who responded negatively or those who responded positively to fewer items, at a less frequent rate.

Variables, such as delinquency, become the building blocks of a scientific study. When Hirschi goes on in his study to relate delinquency to social class, to attachment to parents, etc., what he is doing concretely is to associate the variable of delinquency to the variables of social class, parental attachment, etc. Each of the variables represents a set of observations recorded using some form of measure, which has been classified and named as a variable. When you carry out your study, you will discover that working with your variables is the very heart of your research project. That is why definition and accuracy is so important in measurement of variables. Once your variables are set up, it becomes much easier to direct and make progress on your project.

Let's summarize what we have said about science being empirical. This means that scientific research is based on observation, that the observation must be accurate and precise, that measures are developed to record observations accurately, that the observations must be measured repeatedly and variations recorded, and that the recorded measures are classified into variables which become the building blocks of scientific study.

THE LOGICAL AND RATIONAL CHARACTER OF SCIENCE

Scientific research is not a method for proving or disproving revealed truths. Hence, science is different from religion, which is based on truths that are believed to have been revealed from divine sources. Science is the effort to understand the natural and social world by applying reason to careful observations. As we said above, it is based on observation. But to move from observation (however precise that observation may be) to understanding requires that the observations be rationally explained. In other words, the scientific researcher is not merely an observer and recorder of phenomena. Instead, the scientist must apply reason and logic to these observations in order to try to understand their character and significance. We will return to the issue of just how rational science (and, in particular, social science research) is after we have explored the characteristics of science and the scientific model.

Patterns and Associations Among Variables

In the scientific quest to understand observed phenomena, we seek to uncover the patterns in the data collected, and the associations that exist among variables. Here is where we apply logic to the scientific enterprise. The object is not only to isolate and measure separate observations, but to associate—relate—different observations with each other. Furthermore, since we record observations as variables (which vary), we need to examine how a change in one variable might be associated with a degree of change (an increase, a decrease, no change) in another variable.

In Hirschi's study, for example, the aim was not just to measure delinquency (though that was important and not easy to do!), but to determine what other variables were associated with high levels of delinquency. We described in Chapter 1 how Hirschi related delinquency to a number of other factors he had measured in the survey. For example, attachment to parents and social class background were both considered to be variables that might be strongly associated with delinquency. Recall that Hirschi found that delinquency was associated with low levels of attachment to parents but was not strongly associated with social class. In other words, Hirschi found that the likelihood of delinquent behavior depended upon the presence and strength of other variables. Thus, in the Hirschi study, delinquency was the dependent variable, and attachment to parents and social class were independent variables.

Dependent and Independent Variables

Dependent and independent variables are most easily envisioned in a scientific experiment (Chapter 8 describes such experiments in detail). The *independent variable* in an experiment (sometimes called the *stimulus*) is the variable that brings about the effect or *dependent variable* (sometimes called a *response*). The general model of an experiment is to test whether the independent variable led to (brought about, increased the likelihood or occurrence of, or caused) the dependent variable.

The object of the experiment is to try to block out the influence of (that is, "control for") other factors which might produce change in the dependent variable. In this way, we can isolate and examine the effect of the independent variable on the dependent variable. However, in most social research projects, experimental designs are not feasible. It is not possible in relating an independent to a dependent variable in a survey (such as Hirschi's delinquency survey) to totally control for the effects of all other variables. Instead, the researcher looks for the strength of association between two variables such that when the independent variable changes (increases or decreases), the dependent variable also changes.

In the delinquency study, Hirschi was able to say that the stronger the attachment of a boy to his father (an independent variable), the less likely the boy was to be delinquent (the dependent variable). Moreover, he was able to say that the social class background of a youth—whether the youth was from a lower social class rather than a higher social class—was *not* strongly related to self-reports of delinquency. In this case, social class is the independent variable, delinquency the dependent variable.

On the face of it, the first association he found seems to us to be logical. However, the second seems to go against our notions of what might be related to delinquency (we might well have expected lower-class youths to be more delinquent). To make sense of these potential arguments, we need to develop explanations for possible relationships. In the delinquency study, Hirschi tested a number of potential explanations. This is another quality of the rationality and logic of scientific research—its effort to test or build explanatory theories.

THEORY DEVELOPMENT AND TESTING

The object of science is to move beyond observation, beyond the development of measures to record observations, and beyond the study of the associations between recorded variables to the task of putting together explanations for associations—in short, to build theories. A *theory* is a proposed explanation for a set of coordinated occurrences, or relationships.

The aim of science is to establish theories and then to prove (or disprove) them. In other words, theories are logical arguments that try to make sense of empirical data. Theories are not fixed; rather, they are probable explanations which we formulate and reformulate in an attempt to make sense of a body of evidence. And the work of science is both to *build theories* which will explain relationships noted among variables and to *test existing theories* with new evidence.

The Role of Theory in Social Research

As we saw in Chapter 1, theories may play a central role, either explicitly or implicitly, in nearly all social research. The arguments put forth to explain or defend a theory need to have some rational basis, generally stemming from widely accepted commonsense notions or from empirical evidence that has been accumulated and tested. In short, theories must follow the rules of logic so that they are convincing and cannot be easily refuted.

We have noted that scientific studies need to be formal and explicit. Many critics of the social sciences argue that these qualities do not sufficiently characterize theory development in the social sciences. Instead, they argue, theoretical ideas remain inexplicit, or somewhat vague and underdeveloped, in many studies. Many social research projects, however, do not have explanation as an explicit goal; instead, they are exploratory. Let's return to some of the examples from Chapter 1 and consider how far theory either directed, informed, or was generated by these studies.

The Role of Theory in Hirschi's Research on Delinquency.

This study had a classic deductive style: Hirschi posed theories and deduced hypotheses from these theories; then he tested the hypotheses in order to see which received the most support. Where did the theories come from? Most directly from earlier research on juvenile delinquency. For example, strain theory and cultural deviance theory were widely used in the study of juvenile delinquency in the 1960s, when Hirschi carried out his study. But before trying to develop and test his own control theory, Hirschi needed to understand the underpinnings of all theories. Let's consider the steps Hirschi took to make sense of and substantiate the theories he would be testing.

First, he looked for the underlying assumptions and presuppositions upon which these various theories rested. He recognized, for example, that strain theory—the view that the social order is whole and beneficent and that delinquency is a result of "strain" in a cohesive system—is based on assumptions very different from those underlying control theory—the view that society is fragmented and conflicted and that delinquency is a natural occurrence which must be regularly precluded through control. However, as the interview with Travis Hirschi made clear (see Box 1-1), in the decades following the publication of *Causes of Delinquency,* criminologists and other investigators began to focus on psychological and economic motivations for criminal behavior, in addition to the factors Hirschi had examined. Thus, Hirschi also examines these theories in his and Michael Gottfredson's recent book, *A General Theory of Crime* (1990). In other words, theories about the causes of delinquent behavior altered over time; scholars used different assumptions and presuppositions, which led to a shift in disciplinary trends. (We will discuss change in scientific perspectives when we describe Thomas Kuhn's work on scientific paradigms.)

Second, Hirschi noted that the theories accounting for delinquent behavior also stemmed from commonsense notions ordinary people hold about why young people break laws and misbehave. A delinquent act such as stealing is commonly thought to be the result of a lack of discipline (in short, a lack of "control"), or the result of a response to unfairness (a "strain" which demands to be righted), or the result of "hanging out with the wrong crowd" (mixing with a "culturally deviant" group). Note that these different commonsense notions are not compatible with one another. But each can serve as the basis for an explanation, a theory, from which hypotheses can be deduced and then empirically tested.

Third, Hirschi noted that each of the proposed theories offered a logical explanation in that if A were true, then B would follow. For example, if a particular youth lacked strong ties to his or her society (in other words, had weak attachments to family and other institutions), then he or she would not have sufficiently incorporated the norms to be law-abiding; therefore, given the chance, the youth would break laws. Furthermore, given that the outcome of the lawbreaking might benefit the youth (give him or her material benefits), a delinquent act such as stealing would be a rational behavior. Thus each theory presented a *rational* explanation as well. Hirschi developed each

of the three theories with precision in order to test them accurately in his study. In other words, he offered a formal and explicit presentation of the three theories. By making clear their presuppositions, considering commonplace notions about them, and developing the theories in clear and unambiguous terms, Hirschi was able to develop means for measuring the underlying concepts of the theories by creating variables to represent them. Once this operationalization was completed, Hirschi could test the hypotheses he had posed.

The Role of Theory in Anderson's Study of Jelly's Bar.   This field study began at an empirical level with observations at a neighborhood bar. Anderson did not take any well-formulated theories with him to the bar. Rather, he had a broad familiarity with field studies of "hangout" environments (such as William Whyte's *Street Corner Society*) and a hunch that Jelly's environment might be sufficiently hospitable and sociologically interesting to form the subject of a social research project. This is a much more inductive approach, in which the researcher initiates the project with observations, then interprets these observations to explain the meaning of the social environment. If these explanations can be posed in more formal and abstract terms, they become theories that can be applied to other, similar social environments.

For example, when Jelly's Bar closed down for a time and the men retreated to the street corner and the next-door liquor store to "hang out," Anderson began to figure out how the status system operated to differentiate the men and give order and meaning to their relationships. The types of social differentiation he observed among the men at Jelly's led Anderson to develop the idea of a social status system to explain the behavior of men in similar "hang out" environments. Thus the theoretical explanations grew out of the observations.

Building Theories by Trying to Falsify Existing Theories.   Bernard (1990) has argued that social research is not sufficiently engaged in the effort to test theories. In the widely researched area of criminology, he argues, very little effort is invested in building or testing theory while a great deal of effort is expended in generating research without theoretical links. Most social scientists consider theory development to be an arduous task. But it is not always necessary to develop a comprehensive new theory.

Bernard makes the case that building theory should be carried out more routinely by attempting to falsify existing theories. If a theory cannot be falsified, then progress will have been made through support of the theory; if a theory is falsified, progress will also have occurred. This emphasis on theory building through testing earlier theories stems from the influential writing of social theorist Karl Popper (1968).

Bernard prescribes five steps for verifying or falsifying theories. First, new theories must set out falsifiable (or testable) propositions. In other words, theorists must state what set of research findings would disprove the theory. The problem, as Bernard sees it, is that many theories in the social sciences are not designed in such a way that they could be falsified. Second, researchers must analyze existing theories to discover falsifiable propositions within them. Third, social researchers must distinguish between theoretical concepts and propositions about under what conditions hypothetical relationships exist. Fourth, they must analyze the relations among existing theories to see if comparative tests could support or falsify each theory. And fifth, researchers must eliminate value orientations from theories because they make testing for verification or falsification impossible.

Consider this last point. Many theories, such as Hirschi's control theory, are based on value orientations. Underlying the explanation offered by control theory is a conception of society in which human beings are naturally at war with each other. From this presupposition, control theory holds that when there is a breakdown of social controls, crime will occur. The problem here is that the premise that humans are naturally at war with each other cannot be tested, and thus it cannot be falsified. Instead, as Bernard states, "Hirschi's expla-

nation of crime as a breakdown of social controls . . . impl[ies] a nonfalsifiable vision of an ideal society in which . . . human nature has been fully controlled through social forces" (1990, p. 340). Hence, falsifiable propositions cannot be developed for control theory, and thus control theory cannot be theoretically challenged and tested.

Bernard laments that social scientists are not taught to be theorists the way they are taught to be research methodologists. Nor is the academic profession as supportive of theoretical work as it is of research:

> The requirements and opportunities for learning to be a researcher are not matched by comparable requirements and opportunities for learning to be a theorist. Students are required to *learn about other people's theories,* just as they are required to learn about other people's research. But where this is the beginning of their education on research, it is the end of their education on theory. There are no required courses on *how to be a theorist,* that is, how to engage in theorizing as a scientific activity *(1990, p. 342).*

Bernard wants students to learn how to falsify existing theories, how to compare existing theories so that equivalent tests of these theories could be designed, how to construct formal statements of the definitions and propositions in an existing theory, and how to eliminate value orientations in theories (1990, p. 331).

Can social scientists actually eliminate value orientations from their theories? Don't all theories that derive from the study of human society (such as Hirschi's control theory) involve assumptions about human nature which can never be tested? Surely, it is one thing to say that such theories involve value assumptions which cannot be fully tested and another to say that such assumptions can be eliminated. Developing and testing theories are not easy tasks, and (as Bernard has suggested) the goals may not be fully attainable. However, pursuing these efforts might make the components of such theories more explicit. Thus, it is useful to consider Bernard's advice: the science of social research cannot be accomplished if only empirical research is conducted. Instead, for social research to be scientific, theory and empirical research must be mutually enriching.

CAUSALITY

The careful observation and logical explanation characteristic of scientific research are necessary for the purpose of determining causality. This is one of the primary goals of science. But is it one of the primary goals of social science research?

Recall that in Hirschi's delinquency study, strain theory, control theory, and cultural deviance theory all postulated that qualities of the social order produced, or caused, delinquency. This is the kind of rational, logical explanation with which we are all familiar. "Smoking causes cancer," "Gravity causes the pen to fall to the ground," "Hanging around with the wrong crowd causes delinquency": these are all causal statements which state that variable A (smoking, gravity, or hanging around with the wrong crowd) causes variable B to occur (cancer, objects falling, delinquent behavior). In scientific terms, this means that the presence of an independent variable (smoking, gravity, or hanging around with the wrong crowd) is associated with the occurrence of a dependent variable (cancer, objects falling, delinquent behavior).

Conditions Required to Establish Causality

To establish causality, three conditions must be satisfied. *The first condition is that a change in the independent variable must precede (in time) a change in the dependent variable.* This makes simple sense if we consider the association between smoking and cancer. If a person had cancer before he or she began smoking, it would be illogical to argue that smoking caused the cancer. This simple logic is generally more difficult to apply to social phenomena. It seems logical to argue that hanging around with the wrong crowd

may cause a youth to become delinquent. But it also seems logical to argue that a youth who is delinquent may be more likely to hang around with a "bad" crowd. In other words, it is often difficult to decide which variable is really the dependent variable in terms of the issue of time. So the first challenge for the social researcher who wants to establish causality is to try to ascertain the temporal order of the variables he or she is measuring.

In some cases, this is easier because one can simply determine that the influence of one factor must have preceded another. For example, in testing the strain theory, Hirschi selected social class membership as the independent variable predictive of delinquency. Here he could assume that the influence of family social class (in terms of the financial and cultural resources more available to a youth from a higher-class family than a lower-class family) had an impact prior to the time the youth committed a delinquent act. Thus, while he could not precisely date the onset of "social class" influence (as you could the onset of smoking), he could assume that it preceded the occurrence of the delinquent behavior.

The second condition for establishing causality is that there must be a high correlation between the independent and dependent variables. This means that a change in the independent variable corresponds to a change in the dependent variable, such that an increase in the independent variable is related to an increase (or decrease) in the dependent variable. This related change (the correlation) can be measured statistically, as we will describe in Chapter 15.

Let's return to the smoking example. This second condition for establishing causality requires that among a large group of people, there must be a relationship between which people smoke and which ones get cancer. In addition, higher levels of smoking should be more likely to cause cancer than lower levels of smoking, and people who have smoked for longer periods of time should be more likely to develop cancer than those who have smoked for shorter periods of time.

The relationship between delinquency and mixing with the wrong crowd is more difficult to think through. Young people who mix with members of the wrong crowd should be more likely to exhibit delinquent behavior. We also expect that those who are more frequently involved with members of the wrong crowd, those who have a greater number of "wrong crowd" friends, and those who hang out for longer periods of time with such friends would be more likely to be delinquent (and to have committed more delinquent acts) than those who had hung out with "wrong crowd" friends less frequently, who had fewer such friends, and whose association with these friends had been shorter in duration. In sum, there should be a high correlation between measures of associating with the wrong crowd and performing delinquent acts.

Finally, the third condition for establishing causality is that other, competing variables (other independent variables) must be shown to have little influence on the dependent variable. For example, perhaps people who smoke are more likely to be anxious. If so, it could logically be argued that anxiety, not smoking, causes cancer. But we can control the effect of anxiety on the original relationship ("Smoking leads to cancer") so that we can examine this relationship without being influenced by the factor of anxiety. First, we need to measure anxiety (much more difficult to measure than smoking). Once it was measured, we could determine in the group of people being studied which ones had high anxiety, which ones had moderate levels of anxiety, and which ones had low levels of anxiety. Then we could look at the association between smoking and cancer *within* these "anxiety" groups. In this way we have controlled for the influence of anxiety, so we can examine whether there is a causal relationship between smoking and cancer.

In the delinquency study, Hirschi found that attachment is strongly related to delinquency; he needed to control for that factor when he examined other potential independent variables. So, in testing the cultural deviance theory, Hirschi controlled for the attachment of the youth to his peers

and found that only if a youth were weakly attached to members of the wrong crowd was this affiliation related to delinquency. In fact, youths who were strongly attached to their peers, even if these peers were themselves delinquent, were less likely to be delinquent. This suggested to Hirschi that the "wrong crowd" variable was a much weaker causal factor in influencing delinquency than was attachment. This goal of trying to establish causality is not the aim of all types of social research. However, the strategy of moving back and forth between the observational, empirical side of science to the explanatory, theoretical side is generally the way that science is carried out.

Causal Models in Social Research

Many social research studies start with causal models to represent the theoretical contentions of the study. Such models identify the variables in the theory, establish the time precedence between these variables, and set up the grounds for testing the model. Hirschi set up causal models for the three theories in his study:

> *Strain theory:* a person is forced into delinquency because of legitimate desires that cannot be met otherwise;
>
> *Control theory:* a person is free to commit delinquent acts because of the weakness of ties to the sources of conventional social support which would discourage delinquency;
>
> *Cultural deviance theory:* a person who commits delinquent acts is merely conforming to a different set of rules supported by a subculture within the society *(Hirschi, 1969, p. 3).*

One of the major tenets of strain theory is that lower-class youths will be more likely to commit delinquent acts than higher-class youths. Social class is the independent variable, number of delinquent acts the dependent variable. This relationship is depicted in Figure 2-1. Very simply, the figure shows that a person's social class is related to (may cause) the likelihood of the person engaging in delinquent acts. It also implies that variations in

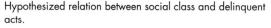

FIGURE 2-1
Hypothesized relation between social class and delinquent acts.

social class are related to variations in delinquent activities. To study this relationship, Hirschi compared the rates of delinquent acts for boys from lower-class families with those of boys from higher-class families. In other words, he moved from stating a theory, to setting up an analytic model of how to test the theory, to testing the theory with empirical evidence.

One of the major contentions of control theory is that youths who are attached to their families, schools, or peers (the independent variables) will be less delinquent (the dependent variable) than those who are less attached. Recall that this would be the case if delinquency were the result of a divisive society, where conflict would naturally occur unless individuals were firmly attached to social institutions and relationships. Figure 2-2 shows a model of how attachment to a father relates to delinquency. To study this relationship, Hirschi compared the rates of delinquent acts by boys with stronger and weaker levels of attachment to their fathers.

The cultural deviance theory sought to explain delinquency as the result of differences in values among different subcultural groups. Thus, it predicts youths who are members of delinquent subcultural groups (the independent variable) are more likely to be delinquent (the delinquent variable) themselves. Another factor, however, is how important it is for the youth to conform to the gen-

eral (or conventional) values of the society. Hirschi hypothesized that those in a delinquent subcultural group who had a "high stake in conformity" to the general values of the society at large would have difficulty deciding whose values to follow, those of the delinquent subgroup or those of the wider society.

The model Hirschi offered for this relationship is depicted in Figure 2-3. To study this relationship, Hirschi needed to compare the rates of delinquent acts for boys who had many delinquent friends *and* were low in conformity to the general norms of the society with boys who had many delinquent friends but were high in conformity. In this instance, the number of delinquent friends is the independent variable, the rate of delinquent acts the dependent variable, and the level of conformity a control (or test) variable. (Chapter 14, on trivariate analyses, explains the role of control variables and how three-variable relationships can be examined.)

For each of these theories the first condition for establishing causality holds: the occurrence of the independent variable precedes (in time) the occurrence of the dependent variable. For the strain theory, social class is determined before the youth commits any delinquent acts. For the control theory, attachment to a parent precedes delinquent acts. And for the cultural deviance theory, number of delinquent friends can be empirically observed

FIGURE 2-3
Hypothesized relations among stakes in conformity, delinquency of companions, and delinquent acts. (From Travis Hirschi: *Causes of Delinquency,* University of California Press, Berkeley, Calif., p. 153.)

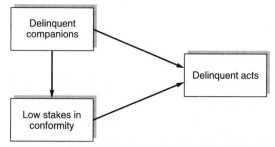

FIGURE 2-2
Hypothesized relation between attachment to father and delinquent acts.

prior to determining the number of delinquent acts.

The object of Hirschi's analyses was to determine whether the second and third conditions for causality could be met. First, he needed to know whether there was a correlation between the independent variables from each theory and the dependent variable, delinquent acts. Hirschi prepared cross-tabular analyses in which reported data on each respondent's delinquent acts were matched with reported data on social class background, attachment to the father, etc. Let's examine a few of these relationships for two of the theories Hirschi was testing.

For the strain theory, Table 2-1 cross-classifies delinquent acts (measured by self-report) and father's occupation (the social class measure that was used). This table presents the percentage of boys from families in which the father had different levels of occupation who had committed "none," "one," or "two or more" delinquent acts. Thus, 62 percent of boys from the lowest-class families had not committed any delinquent acts, compared to 61 percent of boys from the highest-class families. When we examine the columns

from lowest-class occupation to highest, we do not see that higher-class boys report fewer delinquent acts. The only difference between these distributions is that among those reporting delinquent acts, a larger proportion of the highest-class boys report a single act, while a larger proportion of the lowest-class boys report more than one delinquent act. In short, Table 2-1 does not offer strong evidence that increases in delinquent activity are strongly related to social class.

Table 2-2 offers evidence to test the control theory. It cross-classifies self-reported delinquent acts (the dependent variable) and intimacy of communication with the father (the independent variable representing parental attachment). Table 2-2 shows a pattern of steady increase in reported delinquent acts among boys with weaker levels of attachment to their fathers; conversely, boys who are closer to their fathers tend to avoid delinquency. Comparing the boys who have the lowest and highest levels of attachment to their fathers, we note a very large difference in terms of reporting no acts (39 percent vs. 73 percent).

Comparatively, Table 2-2 offers much stronger support that lack of attachment to fathers is related

TABLE 2-1

**SELF-REPORTED DELINQUENCY BY FATHER'S OCCUPATION—
WHITE BOYS ONLY**
(In Percent)

	Father's Occupation[a]				
Self-Reported Acts	**Low** **1**	**2**	**3**	**4**	**High** **5**
None	62	53	56	49	61
One	16	26	25	28	25
Two or more	23	21	19	23	14
Totals	101	100	100	100	100
Number of cases	(151)	(156)	(390)	(142)	(282)

[a]1 = Unskilled labor; 2 = Semiskilled labor; 3 = Skilled labor, foreman, merchant; 4 = White collar; 5 = Professional and executive.
Source: Travis Hirschi: *Causes of Delinquency*, University of California Press, Berkeley, Calif., 1969, p. 69.

TABLE 2-2

**SELF-REPORTED DELINQUENCY BY INTIMACY OF COMMUNICATION
WITH FATHER**
(In Percent)

Self-Reported Acts	Little Intimate Communication			Much Intimate Communication	
	0	1	2	3	4
None	39	55	55	63	73
One	18	25	28	23	22
Two or more	43	20	17	15	5
Totals	100	100	100	101	100
Number of cases	(97)	(182)	(436)	(287)	(121)

Source: Travis Hirschi: *Causes of Delinquency,* University of California Press, Berkeley, Calif., 1969, p. 91.

to delinquency than Table 2-1 offers for the relationship between lower social class and delinquency. This means that Hirschi found more convincing evidence to support the control theory than the strain theory for explaining delinquency. Because this study examined one independent variable at a time, it is more difficult to make the case that influence from other explanatory variables that might have affected the original relationship has been blocked—in other words, to make the case that the third condition for causality has been met. Instead, Hirschi successively examined the effects of one independent variable after another and compared them as to which had the greatest influence on number of delinquent acts.

The Hirschi example has been presented here to show you how one investigator attempted to show causality in a social research project. One of the most common reasons for doing social research is to evaluate a social program. Evaluation research, which is described in detail in Chapter 11, is often concerned with determining the reason some aspect of a program succeeded or failed. Box 2-1 presents a four-model approach to designing a program evaluation which expands on the normal causal model, taking into account the pragmatic goals of evaluation research aimed at changing or improving social programs.

Next, we will turn to a more general discussion of the scientific model to see how theory, observation, data collection, and hypothesis testing can be viewed as a cycle of research activities. Different studies work through the cycle from different starting points.

THE SCIENTIFIC MODEL

A model of science must include both theories and observations, both conceptualizing and data gathering, and both generalizing and specifying. The process of science is usually thought to be either inductive or deductive. By *inductive,* we mean that the scientist develops generalizations based on a limited amount of data about a class of events. By *deductive,* we mean that hypotheses are derived from a generalized explanation (that is to say, a theory). In practice, it is difficult to fully separate these two procedures. The researcher usually has a prior logical-rational model, with a set of hypotheses (or propositions about the relationship between two or more factors) guiding the design of the study which has been developed prior to the data gathering. This model, however, usually undergoes change as the evidence is brought to bear on the problem, and the formal testing of set hypotheses gives way to a reformulation of hypotheses

BOX 2-1

A FOUR-MODEL APPROACH TO PROGRAM EVALUATION

Much social research is carried out in order to evaluate social programs. Such applied research is set up to address specific questions that the program's sponsors need to have answered. A standard theoretical model which identifies independent and dependent variables and the causal relationships between them may not be very useful in designing research for program evaluations.

The typical social program is set up as an "intervention" designed to "break into" a social problem (for example, drug abuse) and try to alter its course and its effects. Such a program may not easily be studied with a traditional theoretical model. The impetus for doing the evaluation research may, in fact, be to identify a problem (such as a "performance gap"). In this situation, the problem's definition and the potential solutions to it may be found in the special insights of those working in the program (the practitioners or clinicians). Researchers studying social programs need to ask, "Does an intervention work?" Practitioners working in the program may need to know "Will this intervention help my practice?"

Bauman, Stein, and Ireys (1991) have offered a four-model framework for considering the range of ways in which theory may inform the design of a program evaluation:

1. A theoretical model describes outcomes and predictors of outcomes and how an intervention might alter an outcome.
2. A conceptual model describes in detail the components of the theoretical model, streamlining the variables to include only those that might alter the success of the intervention, that could be manipulated by the intervention, or that distinguish the closest (or proximal) from the farthest (or distal) outcomes.
3. An operational model presents the pathways through which the intervention works. It generates hypotheses, describes ideal-type interventions, and sets out how the program is to achieve its aims.
4. An implementation model gives a detailed description of the day-to-day operations, organization, and activities of the program, including characteristics of the program (e.g., complexity, timing, length, relevance to clients), the population (background characteristics, cultural norms), and the site (size of organization, skills and nature of staff, resources).

which require a better test. Such a research process has often been viewed as a cycle in which the various phases are interdependent and the beginning point is left indefinite. Walter Wallace's (1971) model of the scientific process has been widely used and adapted to depict the research cycle. It will be described here to help you to gain a fuller conception of the scientific enterprise. Then some of the studies which were presented in Chapter 1 will be considered in the light of this model.

Figure 2-4 shows the Wallace model. It contains what Wallace called "five principal information components whose transformation into one another are controlled by six principal sets of methods" (1971, p. 16). The information components are the basic elements of science: observations, empirical generalizations, theories, and hypotheses; the methods are the ways of moving from one stage of the scientific process to the next. Before describing this model in some detail, let me state that researchers may not go through every stage of this process in a single research project. In one study a researcher may only move from observation to an empirical generalization. Over a series of studies, a researcher may move through the entire cycle. Given the traditional emphasis on hypothesis testing, most researchers begin on the de-

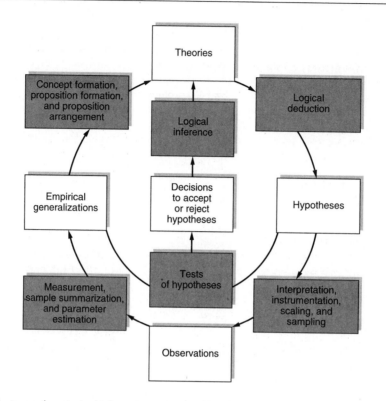

FIGURE 2-4
Wallace's model of science: the principal information components, methodological controls, and information transformations of the scientific process. Informational components are shown in white rectangles, methodological controls are shown in shaded rectangles, and information transformations are shown by arrows. (From Walter Wallace: *The Logic of Science in Sociology*, Aldine, Chicago, 1971, p. 18.)

ductive side, starting with a hypothesis and working out a research plan to test it. The object in taking you through the entire cycle is to see how the scientific process works across time and many projects, not to suggest the steps that each project must go through.

The Inductive Half of the Research Process

Wallace chose to discuss the cycle beginning at the bottom of the circle with *observations,* a principal information component. Not that he believed that this was necessarily the beginning of the research process, but rather that one could start at any point. Wallace recognizes, as I have argued

above, that observations cannot be made independently of ideas, hypotheses, ways of thinking established earlier. Yet scientists often try to control the amount of prior influence that may be imposed on their observations so that they are not blinded by their past impressions and opinions. You as a researcher could go to a neighborhood bar and see what you have been programmed to see, or you could go there to discover how far what you see is consistent with hypotheses and assumptions explicitly set up and recognized in advance.

Keep in mind that starting with observations and moving toward hypotheses, the inductive process, is perhaps somewhat *messier* and more difficult than beginning with a hypothesis and testing the hypothesis through observation. It may well take a kind of imagination or creative leap to move from generalizations derived from observations to concepts themselves. There are different kinds of observations. Some are more clearly created than others. In a field study, you observe what is happening around you. In an experiment or a survey, you create what you observe. In the field, you must be open-minded enough that what you see can modify your views. In an experiment or a survey, you help to produce what you observe much more directly.

A great deal of care and clarity of purpose must go into the creation of a questionnaire or the selection of an experimental situation. In the income maintenance experiment and the laboratory fear of success study, the observations were based on responses to certain stimuli. In the surveys, the observations are the responses to the questionnaires, the data generated from written records. Note that in this case the nature of the questions asked will determine what observations will be produced. Say, for example, the survey researcher forgot to ask the respondents their sex; then sex would go unreported and therefore be unobserved and unknown. But let's assume that the researcher has the names of the respondents; on the basis of these names, the gender of most of the respondents could be deduced (but are Leslie and Terry males or females?).

Thus, what is observed will be determined by (1) what the scientist sets out to observe; (2) how effective the scientist is at observing what he or she is trying to observe (here the scientist's lack of ability to perceive, to see accurately, to discern, may dramatically alter what is in fact observed); and (3) how favorable the context being observed is to this observation process. Note here that, in surveys, if respondents skip some of the questions, this will alter the observations; or, in a field setting, if those being observed deliberately conceal things or distort their environment so as to make a certain impression on the researcher, then the observations will not be representative of the environment.

But observations must be presented in the form of measurements. Here we can distinguish the form of the measurement (its scale) and the taking of the measurement (which is virtually the same as the observation itself). A scale of measurement is based on a system in which different symbols (usually numbers) are given to different observations of the same thing. The way in which observed measurements are summarized is also a very important part of the measurement in any study. In a survey, each response is, in and of itself, only a part of the findings to the degree that it represents the sample being studied. It is presented in a summary form representing the aggregation of the responses of the members of the sample. So, for example, the average age of the respondents to the sample may be 20.6 years, or 62.5 percent of a sample may agree that the president is "doing a good job."

It is necessary to reduce the data to manageable proportions by using summarizations, but the strength of the summarizations will depend on the quality of the scales being used. In addition, these summary measures must be appraised in terms of the plausible limits for that measurement. What range of values could be expected? Against what standard are the measured observations in this study high or low, common or unusual? Statistical tests may be employed in certain cases to help make these determinations. In Chapter 15, we will discuss in more detail how this is done. In certain instances a single observation may serve as an estimate: this would be true in a case study (see Chapter 11 for a discussion of case studies). Clearly, it is more difficult to base a generalization on a single observation; replication is preferable (Wallace, 1971, p. 41).

In this quarter of the cycle, during the inductive effort, the scientist is moving from seeing to knowing, from observing to naming, from taking in the variety and range of sights to sorting these out into the patterns that make the variety comprehensible. The one certain relationship between observations and generalizations is that the scientist is looking for regularities. This was the first commonality which (I suggested in Chapter 1) was shared across all the studies described. Even in a single case study such as that done at Jelly's, it was the regularities Anderson saw in the men's behavior in the bar that indicated the nature of their social world; and there were many regularities. In the experiments, the regularities were the common reactions to stimuli; in the surveys, they were the common responses to questions. However, the process of moving from observation to generalization is only part of the inductive process. The next quarter of the cycle moves the scientific process from generalizations to theories.

As Wallace recognizes, it is more difficult to explain how one moves from empirical generalization to theories. He describes two different views of the procedure (Wallace, 1971, p. 50). In the first view, which has been developed by philosopher Karl Popper, theories do not automatically follow from generalizations. On the contrary, they require a kind of imaginative leap, a creative or irrational element which does not spring from empirical evidence or from the generalizations derived from the evidence (1968).

According to the second view, which is represented by Merton (1968) and Kuhn (1970), the inductive process is much more central to the development of new theories, which spring from anomalies—unanticipated observations and surprising exceptions to generalizations that occasionally occur in the course of scientific research. This confrontation with anomalies has been called the *serendipity factor* and will be discussed below. Suffice it for now that coming up with the unexpected, in the process of observation, forces the scientist to bring new ideas to the forming and understanding of theories—in short, to alter and possibly create new theories.

To the degree that generalizations lead to the creation of theories, this is accomplished through the formation of concepts and propositions. Kanter's generalization about what she saw happening to women as they climbed up the managerial ladder in a large corporation was conceptualized as tokenism, an idea that not only made sense of Kanter's data but could also be extended to the position of any member of a minority group operating in a majority situation. This process of naming generalized observations may be based on a greater or smaller number of actual observations as well as on unobservable factors.

Following the development of concepts, propositions can be set up in the "if . . . then" form [if a woman manager in a "token situation" can "segregate conflicting expectations and has strong outside support groups with which to relax, then perhaps a potentially stress-producing situation can be turned into an opportunity for ego enhancement" (Kanter, 1977, p. 240)]. This hypothesis sets down conditions under which Kanter's theory of the effects of tokenism may not have negative individual effects. However, Kanter stresses that most individuals in token positions do not have such outside support groups, and therefore her theory of tokenism holds up. In essence, once a theoretical proposition has been established by a researcher, it takes on a definitiveness and permanence which may make it resistant to change.

Theoretical propositions are also ordered into a system following the rules of logical deduction. Once this is accomplished, theories can be used either to *explain* empirical observations or to *predict* future observations (Wallace, 1971, p. 57). The token theory was used to explain the behavior of women in management positions, *and* it was used to predict the likelihood that similar effects would continue to occur in the future. In addition, a theoretical concept applied in one area of observations may be predicted to be applicable in a slightly different arena. Kanter began by indicating the evidence for the effects of the many on the few in her earlier studies of Israeli kibbutzim, where sex equality was espoused but where the scarcity of women tended to force them into the traditional positions of child care, cooking, etc. (1977, p. 208).

As Wallace stresses, theories have two primary functions. They help to isolate the variables to be observed; in other words, they prepare for the observation phase of research. They also structure how the findings will be expressed for the purposes of generalization. Taking the fear of success theory developed by Horner, we can see that the theory both set up new variables (such as fear of success) measuring behaviors which had been widely observed among women (what Wallace calls the preresearch function) and provided a comprehensive explanation of various findings which were already available (the postresearch function of a theory) (Wallace, 1971, p. 58).

The Deductive Half of the Research Process

This half of the research process starts with theories at the 12:00 position on the research clock and moves through the process of deduction back to observations. This is the phase of the cycle in which already developed theories are used to generate hypotheses that can then be tested with new observations. The first steps which Wallace suggests are (1) to scrutinize the theory for its own consistency, (2) to compare it to other theories in order to determine whether it is preferable to them, and (3) to analyze the consistency of the empirical generalizations which led up to the development of the theory with hypotheses that seem to flow from the theory (1971, p. 63). Note that these efforts at scrutinizing theories are very much what Bernard suggested. Once there is confidence in the theory, the deductive process may begin.

Generating hypotheses is a form of setting predictions. But Wallace argues that hypotheses in social research are more important for determining the precise observations to be made than for predicting the actual outcome of such observations. Imagine Horner making deductions about the implications of the fear of success theory. The implications of the theory are such that she can arrive deductively at the following hypothetical chain:

If . . . (1) Men with high levels of achievement motivation tend to perform better in competitive situations than women with similar levels of achievement motivation; (2) fear of success is higher in women than in men; (3) women higher in achievement motivation will be higher in fear of success;

(4) fear of success is more likely to be aroused in competitive than in noncompetitive situations.

Then . . . Women with high fear of success will perform better in noncompetitive situations; women with low fear of success will perform better in competitive situations *(Horner, 1968, pp. 31–35).*

The importance of this hypothesis is not simply that it predicts an outcome but that it specifies the measurements to be carried out in order to test the theory. The process of developing instruments to make these measurements is not an easy one. Horner needed an instrument to tap a subtle psychological dimension—fear of success. Because of reported problems with the uses of pictures in this kind of research, Horner decided to use verbal rather than pictorial cues. A statement ["After first term finals John (Anne) finds himself (herself) at the top of his (her) med school class," Horner, 1968, p. 39] was given to the subject, who was asked to complete it. The topics of the verbal cues had been derived from ones which Horner's mentor, Atkinson, had developed with pictorial cues; and the methods for scoring the content of the stories were also derived from a system used by Atkinson (1958). In this type of study, the respondents are not forced into a set scaling procedure, usually the case with survey questions; rather, the scaling of the scores comes after the responses have been read and scored by a number of judges. (Let me add that there are some who are highly doubtful about the meaning of such *projective* tests, who would challenge whether fear of success had been measured by responses to the verbal cues.)

The choice of the sample on which the hypothesis will be tested is also a critical part of the methodological procedure. The researcher must first decide on the population to be studied, that is, the group about which one wishes to make generalizations. A sample must then be selected according to procedures that will make it representative of that population. We will consider issues of sampling more fully in Chapter 6.

This process of moving deductively from theory to hypotheses and then operationalizing the hypotheses for the purposes of research will be illustrated again by going through the steps Hirschi used in his study of delinquency. You will remember that Hirschi began with three contrasting theories of delinquency: strain theory, control theory, and cultural deviance theory.

Next, Hirschi sought to identify the conditions that followed logically from each of these theories and those that were incompatible with them. For example, in considering the logical implications of strain theory, Hirschi noted that the theory had been used to explain the apparently irrational aspects of crime in terms of its relationship to frustration. Desires that cannot be met through legitimate means lead to frustration which can only be relieved by finding other (illegitimate) means to fulfill them. Such a theory can help to explain why disadvantaged groups may turn to crime to achieve success goals which other less disadvantaged groups might be able to accomplish through law-abiding means.

But Hirschi also had to point out what was logically incompatible with this theory: If frustration is the primary source of crime, why does delinquency also occur among those from advantaged classes? Here the more general deduction that it is the discrepancy between aspirations and expectations which leads to delinquency can be used to explain middle-class delinquency as well as lower-class delinquency. The hypothesis that youths with a greater discrepancy between their aspirations and their expectations will be more likely to turn to delinquency can be tested by translating the concepts into scalable variables. In doing this, the researcher may only be able to approximate the variable that he or she actually desires to measure. For example, Hirschi could measure the gap between aspirations and expectations, but he had no way of telling whether the discrepancy between them makes a youth feel deprived (1969, p. 9).

Testing Hypotheses

The final step in the research cycle is to test the hypotheses in order to determine whether they should be accepted or rejected, and then establish the implications of these tests for the theory upon which the hypotheses depend. If the research findings conform with what was expected on the basis of the hypothesis, then it is supported. However, as Wallace stresses, some hypotheses are more amenable to testing than others:

> A hypothesis is highly testable in principle when it can be shown to be false by any of a large number of logically possible empirical findings and when only one or a few such findings can confirm it *(1971, p. 78).*

Even when a hypothesis is testable in principle, it must also be testable in practice; that is to say, the necessary data from observations must be obtainable and thus the methods to collect these data must be known and feasible for the researcher.

Once the hypothesis has been tested, it must be accepted or rejected by a process of determination in which an assessment of the original theory, how the hypotheses were formulated, and the methods used to test the hypotheses are all scrutinized to decide if the testing of the hypothesis can be considered to be fair. Once a hypothesis is accepted or rejected, the implications of this conclusion must be brought to bear on the theory. There are a number of ways in which the test of the hypothesis may bear on the theory. It can

1. *Lend confirmation to the theory* by not disconfirming it;
2. *Modify the theory* by disconfirming it, but not at a crucial point; or
3. *Overthrow the theory* by disconfirming it at a crucial point in its logical structure, or in its competitive value as compared with rival theories *(Wallace, 1971, p. 82).*

In addition, since any test of a hypothesis has been carried out on some sample, the representativeness of the sample must be considered before accepting that the test is applicable to the population to which the theory applies.

Finally, this process of appraising the results of testing a hypothesis may also stimulate the creation of new hypotheses (or new theories) which were unanticipated in the study design. As mentioned above, Robert Merton called the potentiality for unexpected outcomes of this kind the *serendipity factor* in scientific research:

> Fruitful empirical research not only tests theoretically derived hypotheses; it also originates new hypotheses. This might be termed the "serendipity" component of research, i.e., the discovery, by chance or sagacity, of valid results which were not sought for *(Merton, 1968, p. 157).*

Such findings may occur in the scientific process as "*unanticipated results,* when the test of one hypothesis yields an unexpected observation which bears upon theories not in question when the research was begun" (Merton, 1968, p. 158). Such an observation is also "anomalous, surprising, either because it seems inconsistent with prevailing theory or with other established facts" (1968, p. 158). Finally, Merton contends that the surprising fact must be *strategic* such that the observer can relate such an observation to some universal explanation. Merton gives the example of Freud, who took the occurrence of "slips of the tongue" as evidence of repressed, subconscious states. In other words, Freud strategically applied the evidence of slips of the tongue to expand a theory he was developing. In short, serendipity explains how tests of hypotheses stemming from one theory can in some cases lead to the development of new, even seemingly quite unrelated, theories.

Merton offers an example from his own research on a suburban working-class community called Craftown. Merton and his colleagues discovered that many of the residents belonged to more voluntary associations in Craftown than they had in their previous place of residence. In addition, this increase in membership was especially noteworthy for those with small children. This seemed surprising since having young children would seem to make such participation more difficult. When young parents were asked how they managed this, they claimed that the presence of many teenagers in the community made getting a baby-sitter easier. However, Merton and his colleagues discovered in studying the census data for the community that there were not a large number of teenagers in the community; rather, Craftown was full of young adults and small children. In fact, the proportion of teenagers in Craftown was decidedly lower than it had been in the communities from which most of the residents had come.

How could Merton and his colleagues explain such an anomalous finding? Their conclusion—the "strategic" leap they made—was described in the following way:

> It is not that there are objectively more adolescents in Craftown, but more who are *intimately known* and who, therefore, *exist socially* for parents seeking aid in child supervision *(1968, p. 161).*

Craftown was the kind of community where "reciprocal intimacies" were more easily developed than in the urban settings from which most of the residents had moved. Such a finding then was applied by Merton to the more general theory that "social perception is the product of a social framework" (1968, p. 162). In other words, an unexpected finding (that parents of young children were particularly active in voluntary associations) demanded an explanation. The residents offered an explanation (the availability of teenagers) which could not be substantiated with factual evidence. This created an anomalous finding which needed to be understood by relating it to broader theories of the social process.

HOW RATIONAL IS SCIENCE?

The model of the research cycle stresses that science is a *rational* activity. What is meant by this? For science to be rational, it must have a goal toward which scientific activity is directed (to develop true theories which have high explanatory powers or which are useful for making predictions, Newton-Smith, 1981, p. 4). In addition, there must be some agreed-upon rules which can be used to determine whether one theory is superior to another. The issue of the rationality of science has been of great concern in recent years. Some scholars have criticized Kuhn's concept of the paradigm (explained more fully below) on the grounds that it suggests that scientific theories are largely constructed and then replaced through the operation of nonrational factors. But many sociologists of science have tended to support a view that science is nonrational, at least in some respects. Mulkay argues that since facts cannot be independent of theories, theories cannot be proved by an assessment of the facts. Rather he stresses the relativism of the understanding of facts, which may mean different things not only to scientists and laypersons, but even to members of different sectors of the scientific community (1979, p. 35).

Newton-Smith (1981) has tried to counter the arguments about the nonrationality of science by reminding us of its relatively limited aims. While the ultimate objective of science is the discovery of truth, he has argued, science can be considered rational if its theories only get *nearer to the truth.*

> For a theory to have explanatory power it must latch on to something about the world. In the long run the ultimate test as to whether one theory has more successfully latched on to a facet of the world than another theory is their relative observational success *(Newton-Smith, 1981, p. 223).*

What Newton-Smith means by observational success includes two factors: the ability of the theory to generate "novel predictions" and its ability to "account for known observations" (1981, pp. 223–224). According to these criteria, Newton-Smith contends that science has produced many good theories, and he concludes that science is based on a temperate rationalism which is gradually capturing more truth about the world.

But while Newton-Smith's conclusions about the virtues of "temperate rationalism" may be well suited to the natural sciences, do they square with the present state of the social sciences? Perhaps social scientists, rather than "capturing more truth about the world," are positing numerous social worlds about which there are a great variety of often contradictory truths. For truth is an assessment of the value that an answer gives to a question. As questions are revised in the course of re-

search, what might earlier have been considered a truth may no longer satisfy the new question. In short, different questions will seek out different "truths." The theoretical differences between social scientists will affect the types of research questions they pose and the types of truths they seek to uncover.

From examining the character of science, the scientific model, and the rationality of science, we see that the scientific process can begin at any stage of the research cycle, and it can involve a range of activities which may not always appear to be rational. How, then, does the social researcher know where to start? Even more fundamental an issue is, where does the social researcher get the background to begin a scientific research project? Finally, what types of rules govern the conduct of researchers as they perform their work? To answer these questions, we will consider scientific research as an activity.

SCIENCE AS AN ACTIVITY

Where Science Starts

When you think about doing social-scientific research, the question that comes to mind first is, "How do I start?" Do you need to develop your own theory to test? Should you design an experiment, collect a set of facts, go to the library, or what?

In thinking about this question, you should remember that scientific work never starts from scratch. The scientist doesn't just discover some exciting facts in the laboratory. Instead, the very work that is done in the laboratory rests on *already developed assumptions* which are widely shared (though possibly contested) as well as on established ways of studying certain subjects and of presenting the findings both orally and in writing. These shared assumptions and ways of knowing form what the philosopher-historian of science Thomas S. Kuhn (1970) has called a scientific *paradigm.* In general terms, paradigms are "universally recognized scientific achievements that for a time provide model problems and solutions for a community of practitioners" (1970, p. viii).

The precise meaning of Kuhn's concept of paradigm, its utility as a general description of the way scientists think and work, and its particular relevance for an understanding of the social sciences have all been the subject of extensive debate since his work first appeared. Box 2-2 summarizes what Eckberg and Hill (1979) conceive to be three principal meanings of the concept.

The most celebrated aspect of Kuhn's concept of the paradigm in the sciences is his definition of the *exemplar* as "the concrete puzzle solution which when employed as models or examples, can replace explicit rules as a basis for the solution of the remaining puzzles of normal science" (1970, p. 175). He emphasizes that normal scientific activity involves working out the difficulties (the "puzzles") and extending the implications of an already established view of the world rather than thinking of radical alternatives to it. Only in periods of crisis, when paradigms break down and problems appear that simply cannot be solved within the structure of rules and assumptions upon which the paradigms depend, does normal science give way to a "scientific revolution" that eventually introduces a new paradigm to replace the old.

Relatively few historians and philosophers of science are now inclined to accept Kuhn's initial view of scientific change as involving revolutionary shifts from one paradigmatic world view to another. Few scientific disciplines have the kind of unitary paradigm that Kuhn at first seemed to envisage as the foundation for normal science in any field, and many of them appear to have been shaped by a process of continuous interaction among several competing paradigms rather than by a succession of revolutionary shifts from one paradigm to another.

Scientific Practice

How far is science, as it is practiced, guided by a set of rules based on deeply held values? Robert Merton, the eminent sociologist of science, has specified a set of norms or *institutional imperatives* which form a *scientific ethos* protecting the integrity of the scientific enterprise (1973, pp.

270–278). While many would argue that the four principles making up the scientific ethos as defined by Robert Merton are ideals that scientists may aspire to rather than rules that are normally applied, it is useful to consider them in regard to social science research. Let us examine these four norms and how they should ideally operate among scientists.

Universalism, in contrast to particularism, refers to the principle that ideas and knowledge in science must be evaluated on the basis of their merit, not on the basis of the status of the persons who establish them. Similarly, scientists should themselves be evaluated solely on the basis of meritorious achievement, and any other factors should be considered wholly irrelevant. Scientific findings must be tested on a purely impersonal basis; no sets of findings are favored or above refutation.

Communism indicates that knowledge is not knowledge unless it is shared by a relevant community. Creating knowledge is therefore a *public* act; knowledge cannot simply be the property of one person. On the other hand, people claim a right to their ideas in terms not of property but of priority. This would explain the claim of a scientist to recognition as the first to make a particular discovery or to formulate a particular idea. Thus communism in science implies the common availability of scientific work on the condition of recognition of individual contributions.

Disinterestedness refers to the principle that scientific activity must proceed with a sense of neutrality: the scientist must be able to be impartial and receptive to any unexpected observations which might occur and to be open-minded in considering the work of others.

Finally, unlike religion, science fosters the norm of *organized skepticism:* what has been accomplished is not the goal of science but only a way station to be left behind when new findings supersede old ones. Everyone's work must be scrutinized and challenged. Scientific authority must be regularly reappraised.

While most scientists believe that these values are important to protect the integrity of scientific

BOX 2-2

THE THREE PRINCIPAL MEANINGS OF KUHN'S SCIENTIFIC PARADIGM

Eckberg and Hill (1979) have conceptualized what seem to be the three principal meanings of Kuhn's concept of *paradigm* as it applies to science:

1. In the broadest and most abstract sense, a paradigm can be understood as a set of *unquestioned presuppositions* underlying any scientific activity. These comprise the metaphysical and philosophical foundations upon which that science rests. In the social sciences, presuppositions about the true nature of human behavior—for example, whether life in society is thought of as ultimately reducible or not reducible to essentially individual, psychological processes; or whether human beings are assumed to be basically rational or irrational in their social interactions—come under this most general sense of paradigms as metaphysical assumptions.

   Recall that Hirschi's control theory rested on the presupposition that humans naturally are in conflict with each other, while strain theory presupposed that society is, by nature, cohesive, with people desiring to obey rules and live harmoniously. Paradigms as unquestioned presuppositions help determine the kinds of questions to be asked about social life, the kinds of answers to those questions accepted as serious or true, and the kinds of methods that social scientists are expected to follow in their search for such answers.

2. A second way to understand the idea of a paradigm is to think of it as a *disciplinary matrix*—the body of assumptions, theories, ideas, models, test cases, and values shared by a particular community of scientists working in any particular field. In this more sociological sense, then, a paradigm includes all the habits of thought and practice that scientists in a given field take for granted, the customary ways in which researchers interact with one another as members of a single disciplinary community, the things that any newcomer to the field would have to learn in order to become a practitioner of that particular discipline.

   Several different types of shared understandings are distinguished within the broad disciplinary matrix. First, there are the theoretical assumptions Kuhn describes as *shared symbolic generalizations*. This means that the language, the terms, the mathematical symbols an individual scientist uses are already largely established within the particular discipline. While the outcome of the scientific work could challenge, refute, or redefine these generalizations, they are already present and taken for granted at the start of any scientific endeavor. Second, scientific work in a specific field usually has an agreed-upon model which guides the design and execution of any new scientific project. Such models may be analogies to other commonly known systems. Third, scientists must share certain values as to what makes a specific theory "good." These values include the requirement that a scientific theory or explanation be (as far as possible) accurate, consistent, broad in its scope, simple, and fruitful. Scientists working in different fields might have quite different ideas about how to apply a particular theory.

   The disciplinary matrix helps individuals entering a particular field to learn what kinds of problems established scientists in the field regard as the most difficult and important. Further, they learn how to proceed appropriately in carrying out their own work and presenting their theories and results to their colleagues. How do they learn these things?

3. The third and most concrete meaning of paradigm is associated with the idea of an *exemplar*. Exemplars are the "concrete accomplishments of a scientific community" (Eckberg and Hill, 1979, p. 926), the classic studies or experiments that young scientists are taught to admire and emulate, and the

ways of thinking that go along with them. It is from the study of exemplars that young scientists learn how to do research in their field. Textbooks are full of exemplars: often, for example, they describe the solution to a particular scientific problem and then prescribe a series of exercises (or problem sets) for students to work on until they have mastered the specific principles and procedures involved. By showing the problems that have already been solved in a particular field, the textbooks are also in effect defining the outstanding problems that remain to be solved and the kinds of procedures that may be available to solve them.

investigation, careful studies of scientific activity have shown, as mentioned above, that scientists often operate quite differently. For example, Ian Mitroff (1974), in a study of the Apollo moon scientists who were the first to examine the materials brought back from the moon landings, found that the principles guiding the behavior of the scientists were often counter to those which Merton had described as normative. Mitroff found that rather than being *disinterested,* neutral seekers of the truth, none of the scientists interviewed over a $3^1/_2$ year period changed their positions; instead, most became even more committed to their "pet" hypotheses (1974, pp. 586–587). Furthermore, there was great secrecy among the scientists, counter to the norms of communism (according to which ideas should be shared) and universalism (according to which ideas are independent of the statuses of those who have developed them). Mitroff concluded that these counter-norms to those prescribed by Merton were most evident in areas of science where the problems being studied were "ill-structured," and therefore open to challenge. However, in areas where the research was better defined, the classic norms were more often practiced (1974, p. 594).

Avoiding Brute Empiricism

What you should have concluded from the discussion in this chapter is that you can never simply collect raw facts in an unplanned manner and hope that by piling them up you will arrive at something called a finding. The act of accumulating facts and information as if this material were the sole means of establishing an explanation—what C. Wright Mills called *abstracted empiricism* (1959, pp. 50–75)—is neither possible nor profitable in science. To think otherwise is the error of the *positivist* who seeks only empirical evidence (the facts) unimpeded by prior theoretical notions. We know from everyday life that there can be no facts without interpretation of some kind.

Take, for example, what we call mental illness. What facts would you gather to prove a case of mental illness? Suppose you say being overly suspicious of others (paranoid) is one fact supporting mental illness. But a police officer may be trained to be suspicious of others as a protective stance on the job. What might be used as a fact of mental illness in one case would not be construed in this way for a police officer. This shows that facts can mean all sorts of things depending on the interpretation they are given in particular instances.

In a study of psychiatric wards, discussed in greater detail in Chapter 3, Rosenhan and his colleagues (1982) posed as mental patients (by claiming, among other things, that they heard voices). They were admitted to a psychiatric ward and were fully accepted as mentally ill by the staff. This suggests that even among those working most closely with the mentally ill (those with expertise in mental illness), the ability to discriminate false facts about mental illness was not evident. Instead, the staff applied such facts as hearing voices to fit an already constructed diagnosis of schizophrenia; they did not question the credibility of the facts presented to them. Again, this suggests that facts generally take on their meaning within some interpretative scheme or framework.

A *hard positivist* might argue that it is only the present state of our imperfection which makes it difficult to directly comprehend the facts. The *antipositivist* argues, on the contrary, that empirical evidence (the facts) are predefined in terms of some theoretical notions. In other words, for the antipositivist, all facts are socially constructed. This is a particularly important consideration in social research, where the phenomena studied usually consist of the actions of thinking, interpreting beings. While we will talk about ways to gather facts, you must start with the recognition that the facts themselves are not the ultimate goal of social research. It is by interpreting these facts, recognizing their complex meanings and relationships, and understanding the way facts are created in social life that we produce social research. This position does not deny the importance of carefully obtaining empirical evidence, but it continues to stress the significance of the interpretation of the facts.

REVIEW NOTES

- Science is empirical: it is based on the study of accurate and precise observations, which are recorded as measures classified as variables.
- Science is logical and rational. Its aim is to look for patterns and associations among variables, to determine independent and dependent variables.
- Theory development occurs when theories are built to explain relationships among variables; theories are tested when hypotheses generated from theories are tested against new empirical evidence.
- It has been argued that there would be more development of theories in the social sciences if efforts to falsify existing theories were encouraged. However, in order for theories to be testable, they must include propositions that are subject to falsification.
- Causality can be established if a temporal order can be determined in the relationship of the independent variable to the dependent variable, if

there is a high correlation between the variables, and if no other variable causes the association between the two variables.
- Wallace's circular model of science includes an inductive half, moving from observation to empirical generalizations to theories; and a deductive half, moving from theories to hypotheses to observations.
- The serendipity factor in scientific research explains how tests of hypotheses from one theory can sometimes lead to the development of quite unrelated theories.
- Merton's scientific ethos is based on four principles of scientific behavior: universalism, communism, disinterestedness, and organized skepticism. There is much evidence that these principles serve more as ideals than as established practice.
- The ultimate goal of social-scientific research is not to seek empirical evidence (facts) alone, as the positivist would do, but to interpret the facts.

KEY TERMS

brute empiricism
empirical generalizations
hypotheses
observation
paradigm
positivist
scientific ethos
scientific model
serendipity factor
theories

STUDY EXERCISES

1. Look through three issues of the *American Sociological Review* or the *American Journal of Sociology* and find (1) an article that closely links empirical research with theory, (2) an article that presents the findings from an empirical research study with little reference to theory,

and (3) an article that is solely theoretical (and presents no empirical data). Which type of article was the most difficult to find? Which was the easiest to find?

2. Why should you avoid brute empiricism?

3. Take one of the studies discussed in Chapter 1 and try to give examples of how each of the four principal informational components in Wallace's model (Figure 2-4) occurred. For example, you might start with observations or theories.

RECOMMENDED READINGS

1. Barnes, Barry: *Scientific Knowledge and Sociological Theory,* Routledge & Kegan Paul, London, 1974. The influence of scientific thinking and models on sociology and social research.

2. Kuhn, Thomas S.: *The Structure of Scientific Revolutions,* 2d ed., University of Chicago Press, Chicago, 1970. This influential work on the human activity of science focused great attention on the role of paradigms in the development of science.

3. Ritzer, George: *Contemporary Sociological Theory,* 2d ed., Knopf, New York, 1988. This text overviews the contributions of all the major classical theorists and covers a broad array of modern theorists.

4. Ritzer, George: *Sociology: A Multiple Paradigm Science,* Allyn and Bacon, Boston, 1975. Ritzer examines how far, and in what ways, paradigms can be applied to sociological research.

5. Stinchcombe, Arthur L.: *Constructing Social Theories,* University of Chicago Press, Chicago, 1968. This not-too-easy volume explains scientific inference; different forms of causality; and theories based on power, environmental effects, and the structure of activities.

CHAPTER 3

The Uses and Abuses of Social Research

─────── LOOKING AHEAD ───────

This chapter examines reasons for doing social research and considers ethical problems that have arisen in the practice of social research.

INTRODUCTION

*I*f you are reading about someone else's research, you may notice that the purpose of the research project is usually taken for granted. Furthermore, the ethical issues raised in carrying out a research project are rarely mentioned when the research is written up. When you place yourself in the role of the researcher, however, you may be forced to confront both the potential uses and the possible abuses that *your* research project may engender. This chapter will consider you to be a practicing researcher, whether or not this is yet (or ever will be) the case, in order to compel you to think more deeply about the purposes and ethics of social research.

So let's assume that you have begun a social research project. Somewhere along your way in researching a project, you will ask yourself, "Why am I doing this study?" or "Who needs this research project?" You may not easily find a very persuasive answer. Yet research requires a reason for why it is being done. At one level, your purpose may be that you are carrying out a study to meet the academic requirements of a course. But why this particular piece of research? Why this subject? To answer these questions, you need a *rationale* for your effort, a sound reason why this particular subject of study and this particular method of carrying out the research may have some value and purpose beyond the grade it will help you to get in a course.

This is simply a way of saying that, as a researcher, you will want to have some sense of the actual or potential use of the research you are carrying out. However, you should also have some sense of the possible abuses to which it might be subject. Social science research has frequently been criticized as unethical or as completely worthless, and charges such as these demand a serious assessment of the uses and abuses of social research. Of course, it is often easier to attack than to defend practices. Further, it is important to remember that the right to carry out research is a form of the freedom of thought and expression—one of the basic rights of citizens. Yet in exercising this right to carry out research, social researchers must be careful to weigh other rights which are equally important and which may be subverted or come into conflict with one another in the course of a research project—the right to privacy as opposed to the right of the public to be informed about the activities of public agencies and officials, for example.

Social researchers, moreover, want more than their right to practice their profession. They demand to be taken seriously. They want their work to be understood as contributing to the advancement of knowledge and social progress, and they would like their actions to be free from continual attack based on ethical objections. They cannot expect this to occur without continuing attention on their part to the challenges posed by the uses and abuses of social research.

THE USES OF SOCIAL RESEARCH

A number of broad criteria may be used to determine the rationale of a study, that is to say, whether the study has a valid purpose. To seek to understand the purpose of a study is, in itself, a valuable effort, for it pushes you to explain your interest, to clarify why you are curious about something. In seeking an explanation as to your purpose, you are already beginning to think of ways to address your question, to establish a re-search design to get at the evidence. Or, alternatively, you may conclude that your research topic lacks sufficient purpose and value to make it worth your time and effort to study.

Robert Merton (1959), in writing about how to start a research project (discussed in the Introduction), stated that the development of a *rationale* was second only to posing the originating question. Since the sociological imagination is so broad, research topics can be based on any aspect of human affairs. Your reason for doing a particular study may be that you wish to know the answer to a question for its own sake [this is a purpose which Merton recognized (1959, p. xx)]. Yet the knowledge generated may be relevant to other aspects of the social sciences. Merton states that

> The scientist may regard his deep interest in a question as reason enough for pursuing it. But sooner or later, if the question and its answers are to become part of the science rather than remaining a personal hobby, they must be shown to be relevant to other ideas and facts in the discipline *(1959, p. xx)*.

Here, Merton's rationale for research is that it contributes to systematic knowledge in the discipline. This type of research is referred to as *basic research.*

But Merton presents a second rationale, which is that the study may have some practical use (1959, p. xxi). Merton stresses that many social research topics have double relevance; they have import to both systematic knowledge and practical use. Where practical use is an outcome of a research project, it would be an example of *applied research.* An example he gives is in studies of people in particular professions (teachers, physicians, the clergy). Preparing individuals to fulfill roles to serve social objectives is a practical necessity in any society; at the same time the study of this process—that is, the study of adult socialization—is of theoretical import in the social science disciplines (Merton, 1959, pp. xxi–xxii). Many social scientists claim that the purpose of their research is to accomplish both ends—that their work will add to the body of knowledge in the discipline and that it has practical aims as well. Most social research has some practical import.

For social research to be held in esteem, its social value should be made clear in any research project. Here are four broad questions that might be used in considering whether a proposed study has a useful function in the continuing development of the social sciences and/or in the society. Clearly, they do not suggest the *only* possible rea-

sons for deciding whether a project might be useful, but they will serve as a good start. You can then add to the list some reasons of your own.

1. Does the study offer evidence about the changing nature of society?

Most social research studies focus on the present time, leaving to historians the study of the past. Yet what is current today is, by tomorrow, history. So the social researcher is always trying to grasp the present in order to understand the contributions of the past and speak to the probable conditions of the future. It is this dynamic aspect of social existence which is critical to an understanding of the social mechanism. Sociologists refer to this as the study of social change. Subjects that lend themselves to the study of the changing nature of society include social processes undergoing revision (e.g., race relations, cross-sex relations), social institutions which appear to be undergoing radical change (families through divorce, small businesses through consolidation and bankruptcy), and effects of new political and social rules on social structure (e.g., affirmative action, legalization of abortion or pressure to rescind it, desegregation, gun control legislation).

The study of change always highlights the timeliness of the subject: a study should be grounded in a clear time frame, and the researcher must pay heed to the significance of this time frame. The 1990s is not necessarily a typical decade; rather it both expresses the results of earlier years and foreshadows new problems and new ways of living which in prior years were of less concern. For example, the current concern about AIDS sprang forth only in the late 1980s, though the disease had been diagnosed in 1981. Public attention to AIDS was magnified with the announcement in 1991 by basketball star Magic Johnson that he had HIV, the viral precursor to AIDS. Social researchers as well have turned their focus to the study of the social implications of this epidemic. It is by addressing issues which are timely in the ever-changing pattern of social existence that social research attains a clear relevance.

2. Does the study address a subject on which social policies are (or may be) developed, or on which decisions must be based?

Social organizations and institutions devise policies to order and control social events. These policies usually aim to bring about specific objectives of the organization. Often, social organizations formally require and establish research procedures to evaluate the effectiveness of some new policy or social program. For example, the federally funded income maintenance experiment, discussed in Chapter 1, was an evaluation of the effects of cash transfer payments to try to understand under what conditions welfare payments might reduce or support the incentive to work. The federal government generally requires that programs funded with government monies have an evaluation component, so that the "results" of spending tax money for a specific purpose can be determined. (Chapter 11 will describe how evaluation research is carried out.) A lot of privately planned research also appraises the effects of social policies and procedures.

Furthermore, social research may address some aspect of the social structure or social behavior on which judgments will be formed (legislation enacted, referendum supported). Whether your state will build additional prison facilities may depend on how far the voters are convinced that overcrowding in prisons fosters further crime. Suppose you, as a social researcher, are hired by your community government to carry out a study to determine whether an environmental protection organization is having any positive effect in your community. You would need to consider the objectives and strategies of the organization. You would also try to determine who was being influenced by the organization and what changes in policies and practices in protecting the environment occurred as a result of the activities of the organization. In short, you would have to develop

some way to measure the group's effectiveness. This second purpose signifies research which may alter policies and judgments.

3. Does the study seek to develop a better and fuller understanding of some unusual social event or social practice, a less familiar group, or a group whose characteristics and activities have undergone change?

Studies that bring into view aspects of one's own society which are unfamiliar in the dominant consciousness, studies that analyze groups which are in a marginal position, or studies that delve into the makeup of foreign societies enable the researcher and the readers of the research to gain a fuller understanding of human society and social practices. In American society, because of the wide diversity of ethnic and racial groups, there has been an emphasis on ethnic studies and minority relations. Cross-national research has offered an opportunity to compare more familiar (often American) beliefs and practices to those of less familiar cultures. Single case studies of specific foreign or less familiar American cultural groups have also served to uncover aspects of other cultures which shed light on our practices and beliefs.

Sociologists have been fascinated with social groups that break with conventional norms (nudists, members of communes) or that impose on their members requirements which appear to be punitive or restrictive (religious cults). There are difficulties in studying unfamiliar groups, because they may resist being studied. On the other hand, the study of groups without their knowledge through covert means is open to charges of unethical practices, which will be discussed in the next section of this chapter. However, many less familiar aspects of our culture are easy to observe and study: the rationale and practices of vegetarians, the role relations of parents who are employed by their grown children, the social status of a male nurse—subjects such as these would pose little threat to anyone.

4. Does the study make use of experience you have had or particular knowledge you have gained, so as to capitalize on your potential for making unique contributions to social research?

Here you may think that as a novice you have nothing original or special to bring to a research project. You are wrong! Each of you has a wealth of knowledge about family life, your ethnic or religious group, your city or neighborhood, or your job that can be used as a starting point for a research subject. If you are able to develop the subject for the study so that you can relate your depth of experience to some specific research question, you may be able to generate unique and valuable perspectives on this topic. Here the ability to reflect on your own experience, to view your life from different perspectives, or to step outside yourself and look at your affiliations or your beliefs from some distance will enable you to extract the significance of your experience from your memories and perspectives.

This potential for the inclusion of self-analysis differentiates the social and the natural sciences. Those who can focus on what they know best with both insight and disinterested objectivity can make special contributions to the overall understanding of human society.

THE ABUSES OF SOCIAL RESEARCH

Since social research can have as its subject any facet of the study of human society and behavior, a social research project may lead to abuses in various ways. By delving into the social experiences of individuals, groups, or organizations, social researchers might threaten or harm those they are studying. For this reason, there has been widespread insistence in the past decade that social researchers consider, prior to carrying out a research project, all the aspects of their research which may possibly raise ethical questions.

For students who have not yet done any social research, such a discussion may seem overly cautious and premature. As a student, you will probably carry out a study in which the subjects are at little, if any, risk. Or you may reanalyze already collected data, in a study, where you are yet a further distance from the subjects under study. In this book, however, the emphasis is on the doing of research; and as a modern, up-to-date beginning researcher, you must be prepared to consider all the possible ethical issues raised by your study that the most experienced social researcher would be required to consider. Furthermore, in the 1990s, social researchers must consider the ethical aspects of their studies and decide whether their research plans need to be altered or radically changed to meet ethical standards before they proceed with their projects. For this reason, we are discussing research ethics in an early chapter of this text.

The following sections address (1) the primary types of abuses, (2) the ethical considerations required to evaluate and avoid research abuses, and (3) specific guidelines offered by professional associations to curtail abuses.

Primary Areas of Possible Abuse in Social Research

You may be familiar with certain studies in sociology where very private behavior, such as homosexual encounters or nude bathing, has been observed. You may even have been asked to participate in a survey, as I was as an undergraduate, to reveal very personal information about your life. You may have wondered whether such research is legitimate. In the context of the survey on sexual experience in which I was asked to participate, I wondered whether I should give information honestly. Questions ran through my mind: "Should I answer the questions at all? Why is this person doing the survey? Do I risk any harm to myself by cooperating with this request?"

Perhaps this is all new ground to you. If so, you will find some of the most important types of abuses described here, and examples of studies that have been subject to charges of abuse will be detailed. The object is not to point a finger of blame at specific researchers, for where abuse has been charged, there have always been counterarguments supporting some aspects of the method of research which would justify the possibly abusive activity. However, I do want to sensitize you to some of the primary concerns which different types of research methods pose, and in order to do so, it is necessary to give some examples of studies that have raised ethical questions. Whether you think the charges are fair will ultimately be your decision.

There are three types of research procedures which raise ethical concerns: covert research, which usually entails some forms of deception; studies in which there is coercion of subjects to participate in certain ethically questionable practices as a part of the study; and research that is considered an invasion of privacy.

Covert Research. In principle, any area of social life, any group of individuals, is open to study by a sociologically imaginative researcher. However, there are social institutions whose activities are considered so important that social scientists have wanted to uncover more fully the nature of social interaction and influence in such environments, even in institutions where open study would clearly affect their proper functioning. (A jury, with its special emphasis upon the closed and confidential character of the jurors' deliberations, is a very good example of an institution like this.) It is with an interest in studying such social phenomena that social scientists have undertaken covert methods of observation. *Covert research* involves carrying out the research without the knowledge or consent of those being studied; it may involve the researcher misrepresenting his or her role as a researcher in order to enter the environment to be studied as an actual participant.

Kai Erikson has argued "that it is unethical for a sociologist to deliberately misrepresent his identity for the purpose of entering a private domain to

which he is not eligible; and, second, that it is unethical for a sociologist to deliberately misrepresent the character of the research in which he is engaged" (1967, p. 373). The first concern is relevant to field studies where researchers have entered environments as full participants. The second is also implied in covert participant observation studies but may apply as well to surveys or, especially, to experiments. Here are some examples of studies about which issues of the legitimacy of covert research have been raised.

On the psychiatric ward. Covert research often takes the form of giving false information to or about subjects so as to deceive them into believing something for the purpose of studying their reaction. In a study of mental hospital wards, for example, Rosenhan and seven other researchers posing as patients entered mental hospitals in various parts of the United States (1982). Each pretend patient called the hospital for an appointment and arrived with the same story of having had a hallucination of hearing voices that were "empty," "hollow," and like a "thud." False names and employment status were also given. Beyond these deceptive pieces of information, all other details of the pseudopatient's life and experiences were truthfully given, including the quality of interpersonal relationships with family, attitudes, and desires. All eight were admitted to psychiatric wards with a primary diagnosis of "schizophrenia." In each case, while one or two senior members of the hospital staff knew the real identity and purpose of the pseudopatient, the staff of the ward did not. In every case the ward staff gave the same treatment to the pseudopatient as to the other patients; and in no instance did a staff member uncover the sanity of the pseudopatient (though fellow patients often questioned their insanity).

In this covert role, Rosenhan and the other pseudopatients were able to carefully observe the behaviors on the psychiatric ward—the frequency of interaction between the staff and patients and the quality of care and compassion for the patients. By this means, Rosenhan determined the high degree of powerlessness of the patients and the depersonalized manner in which the staff related to them.

> A nurse unbuttoned her uniform to adjust her brassiere in the presence of an entire ward of viewing men. One did not have the sense that she was being seductive. Rather she didn't notice us *(Rosenhan, 1982, p. 33)*.

The staff's inability to recognize sanity attested to the "stickiness of psychodiagnostic labels" (Rosenhan, 1982, p. 22). Once the pseudopatients were labeled as "schizophrenic," there was nothing they could do "to overcome the tag" (1982, p. 22).

Could this finding have been established without the use of covert methods? Were the rights of the mental hospital staff infringed upon by the covert activities of the researchers? Did the entry of the pseudopatients into the world of the mental ward alter the environment in such a way that an accurate observation of its workings could not be made? These were the questions that Rosenhan and his fellow researchers were obliged to address by their critics.

In the classroom.   In their study of psychiatric wards, Rosenhan and his associates misrepresented their identity as researchers and offered false information regarding their mental state. In other cases, covert research has not misrepresented the identity of the researchers as such, but it has involved their offering a false account of their projects. An example of this type of study is the one carried out by Robert Rosenthal and Lenore Jacobson (1968) in a grade school in Massachusetts. The researchers wanted to test the theory of how a self-fulfilling prophecy might operate in a classroom, particularly in relation to minority students. They falsely described a standard, but unfamiliar, IQ test as a Test of Inflected Acquisition—a test that could supposedly determine which pupils might be expected "to bloom" within the next academic year. Under this pretext, the test was administered to students throughout the school in the spring of the school year.

The following autumn, the teachers were given a short list of names of pupils in their current class who had supposedly received scores on the Test of Inflected Acquisition indicating their propensity to bloom. The names on these lists were, in fact, selected purely at random and bore no relation to abilities measured in the test. Furthermore, the test was not a measurement of potential to bloom, for such a measure does not exist and educational psychologists have no evidence that such a propensity even exists in human behavior.

Was this deception harmful to the teachers who received the false lists? Was it harmful to the pupils whose names were randomly left off the lists, thereby implying that they would *not* be bloomers? Rosenthal and Jacobson's finding that such a false prophecy actually raised the test scores of those pupils on the list above the expected gains, when they were retested the following year, led the researchers to conclude that the teachers had unknowingly helped the listed pupils to fulfill the false prophecy of intellectual growth. If teachers could be influenced to alter pupils' behaviors by slips of papers with names on them from a research team, how much more might they be influenced by deeply held prejudices and assumptions about how certain types of students might perform?

This study prompted not only attacks of ethical questionability, but also the charge that the contrivance of the study distorted whatever processes might have been occurring in the classroom. How could the researchers even isolate the influence of the list of names? Was the cost of deceiving teachers worth the benefit of studying a prophecy which might have been largely meaningless to the teachers? Those who saw the study's findings as very problematic thought the benefits were clearly not worth the costs. Others disagreed.

On the jury.   In the 1950s, with the full approval of the judge and lawyers, hidden microphones were placed in a jury room in Wichita, Kansas, as a means of studying jury deliberations. The jurors, however, were not informed that their discussions were being recorded. The social scientists and law professors who were carrying out this research were interested in the human behavior of jurors as they interacted during their deliberations. They believed that such knowledge would lead to a greater understanding of the legal system. The researchers also took extreme precautions to hide the identities of the jurors and to handle the tapes with care. However, once this research became known, a Senate subcommittee held public hearings on the ethics of taping juries, which led to the passage of a law forbidding the recordings of deliberations of juries. (For a detailed presentation of the differing positions in this case, see Katz, 1972.) While jury proceedings are essential to our system of public justice, and the precise nature of their operation is therefore a matter of considerable potential interest, can it be said that this interest is more important than maintaining the principle of absolute confidentiality regarding jury deliberations? The forced termination of this project implied that it is not.

Summary. In the mental hospital study, the role of the researcher was covert and deceptive; in the classroom study, the teachers were deceived about the significance of test scores; in the jury study, the jurors were deceived not by telling them a falsehood, but rather by withholding from them the information that they were being taped during the jury deliberations. In none of these studies did the researcher foresee any major harm to the subjects. Moreover, in all three cases, the presumed benefits of greater and closer understanding of socially important contexts (mental hospital wards, classrooms, jury deliberations) seemed to outweigh any potential costs to those being covertly studied. Critical discussion of these and similar studies has raised concerns about the "costs" of covert research. Some would point out that there is no clear penalty for doing covert research and that many such studies (including a number of the above) have been considered classic research efforts. Others have concluded that such research should be avoided.

Coercion of Subjects. Another major procedural technique that raises ethical questions in social research is the coercion (either explicit or implicit) of subjects to participate in a specific study, to engage in behaviors that might lead to psychological or physical harm. Subjects who are in some ways "captive," such as prisoners, children, or mental patients, may not be able to withhold compliance from an authority figure who requests them to cooperate. Such helpless subjects may believe, whether or not they are so informed, that favors may be granted to them for compliance. In other cases, even where subjects are not in a powerless position vis-à-vis the researcher, they may, nevertheless, be pressed to participate in a research project or to comply with the researcher's requests during a study. Subjects are often persuaded that the benefits of the study (for society as a whole, for the researcher's career, for some group) far outweigh any inconvenience to themselves or other subjects as individuals.

Stanley Milgram's research on obedience (Milgram, 1965) will be described here as a classic example of a study that has raised questions about the ethical problem of coercion of subjects. Out of the experience of the Holocaust in Germany and other atrocities of World War II, there grew the belief that many, if not most, people would obey orders given by a superior to carry out atrocities against innocent people. Furthermore, they would justify these actions on the grounds that they were ordered to carry them out, thereby refusing to accept personal responsibility for their actions. Evidence from the history of the atrocities of Nazi Germany suggested that it was not difficult to get people to follow orders of any kind. Milgram's study of obedience was set up to test this notion. If individuals could be easily made to harm others as a result of complying with authority, could this be tested in an experimental situation?

Milgram brought adult men from various backgrounds to a laboratory setting where they were asked to participate in an experiment on learning. Each subject drew lots with a "confederate" researcher posing as another subject for the study, to see who would be "pupil" and who would be "teacher." The true subject always drew the teacher assignment. The teacher was placed in front of a control panel and told to read word pairs to the pupil. If the pupil made an error, the teacher was instructed to administer an electric shock by turning on switches on the control panel that graduated from "Low" to "Danger—Severe Shock." At the same time, the pupil was taken into the next room and strapped into a chair where electrode devices were attached to the wrists.

The teacher would begin reading the word pairs. Each time the pupil made an error, a light on the control panel would light up: the teacher was then expected to administer the shock, beginning at the "Low" level and gradually progressing toward the level of "Danger—Severe Shock." The confederate pupil always carried out the same set of behaviors, including screaming for mercy, begging for the experiment to end, kicking the wall, and finally making no sound at all. All these reactions were, of course, faked by the confederate pupil. The electric control panel was merely a piece of scenery. However, the subject acting as the teacher did not know this.

In the first experimental setting which Milgram established, two-thirds of the subjects carried out the instructions of the researcher to shock the pupil when he was wrong and continued doing so through all the levels of shock up to the highest. A much smaller proportion, 12 percent, refused to administer any more shocks once the pupil began kicking the wall. When the experiment was over, the subjects were told that they had in fact not been administering real shocks, and they were given an explanation as to the true purpose of the study. Some subjects stated that they had actually felt the pain themselves; some experienced a high degree of tension following the experiment; and a few had uncontrollable seizures.

Covert methods had been used in this study to disguise the identity of the pupil and conceal the purpose of the study; and, more importantly, subjects had been successfully coerced, in many cases

without much pressure, into "harming" an innocent person. The ethical issue raised by this experiment included the morality of duping a subject and then persuading him to comply with an experimenter's wishes, even when the possible price of such compliance was harm to the psychological well-being of the subject. Of course, all the subjects had to do to protect themselves from the negative feelings which many of them experienced was to refuse to go on with the experiment. Milgram argued that the knowledge thereby gained had been worth the costs to the subjects, which, though temporarily painful, had no lasting effects. Others disagreed.

Invasion of Privacy.   At some level, every study with human subjects can be considered as invading someone's privacy. Yet certain areas of life are generally regarded as more private than others. In the United States, the question "Where were you born?" is rarely considered an invasion of privacy; yet were this asked of an illegal alien, it might be a threatening question. The question "Are you a homosexual?" would widely be considered as addressing a private matter, not something that a person would expound upon to a stranger. Yet such behavior became the subject of a study that has been widely viewed as raising ethical concerns. In the mid-1960s, Laud Humphreys became a covert observer of male homosexual liaisons in men's public restrooms (1970). Since such encounters are illegal as well as illicit and yet are carried on in public places, the consenting pair depend upon a third person acting both as a voyeur and a guard to warn them if others are approaching. Humphreys took on this role (called a "watchqueen" in the lingo of the homosexual world) and thereby observed the pattern of homosexual activity in this context.

In addition, Humphreys noted the license plate numbers of the men he observed. With this information and the cooperation of the police, who gave him access to license registers (though without their knowledge of his purpose), he was able to ferret out the names and addresses of most of the individuals observed. Then, as part of another study on general health issues in which he was involved, he disguised himself and went to interview these men, among others, on matters relating to their health, career, and family. In this way, he discovered the very "normal" and wide-ranging backgrounds of the men he had observed in the restrooms.

While the identities of the men were never made known, and Humphreys believed that none had recognized him from his earlier role as a watchqueen, one can ask whether social scientists should practice such deception in order to observe very private behavior of this type. Was this not ethically dubious conduct (both as a threat to the privacy of the individuals and as a questionable activity in itself) for a scientist to be engaged in? Defenders of the study argued that though the behavior observed was private in nature, it had occurred in a public place. Moreover, the researcher had taken on the watchqueen role and carried out the services such a person would regularly carry out were he not a sociologist, without any intention of harming those he observed by divulging their names.

But even if it were legitimate to observe this private behavior in a public arena, was it acceptable to copy the license numbers with the intent of determining the identity of the participants observed? This is clearly the type of data that could *not* have been gathered with the consent of the participants. Further, Humphreys could not have remained an overt outsider and also be permitted to observe the encounters. Was the benefit of learning about the backgrounds of those who engage in casual homosexual encounters worth the risk (however unrealized) of potentially exposing these men's private behavior?

Matters such as the nature of sexual behavior, religious beliefs, attitudes toward minority groups, or the sources and amount of one's income are frequently considered private and rarely detailed to casual acquaintances (though there are great variations among people of different social statuses and life stages as to their propensity to divulge such

information). A college professor might easily ask how much an undergraduate earned on a part-time job (this might be considered an expression of the professor's concern for the student's economic well-being). On the other hand, an undergraduate asking how much a professor earned as a part-time consultant would not be construed in the same light. Rather it would appear as intrusive, and not the business of an undergraduate. Why is this so? Because the status of the professor vis-à-vis the student is such that the income that a professor might be able to earn because of his or her special expertise must remain unknown, part of the mystique of the person of knowledge. Requesting this information would imply a lack of deference toward the professor on the part of the student, an intrusion on the professor's private domain.

Tampering with Results and Plagiarism.   Ethical issues also arise in the reporting of social research. Cases have come to light where the handling of scientific data has been questioned. In the well-known research on IQ and heredity, Cyril Burt's evidence on the correlation between IQ scores of identical twins reared apart as compared to identical twins reared together had been used by numerous other researchers as the foundation for arguing that hereditary factors are more important than environmental ones in determining intelligence. After Burt's death, other psychologists looking at Burt's evidence more carefully came to question it. Burt had first reported on 21 pairs of twins reared separately in 1955; in 1958, he published evidence on over 30 pairs of twins separately reared; and in 1966, he had located 53 pairs of identical twins reared apart. What was peculiar was that in every case the correlation he found between the IQ scores of the twins was .771. Yet it would be highly improbable statistically to arrive at the exact same correlation (Chapter 15 explains correlations) using different sets of data. There were a few other strange factors about Burt's material. One was that he gave very little other information about the twins he had studied (their sex, age when tested) or the type of IQ test he had given them. In addition, some of his work was coauthored by two women, Margaret Howard and J. Conway, who did not seem to exist.

Sir Cyril Burt was a famous and prominent British psychologist. Why would he have tampered with results? Two possible explanations were offered. The friendlier explanation was that Burt, as he grew older, became careless and inattentive to details. Perhaps the correlations were misprints, or perhaps he had merely carried over

the findings from earlier studies to the newer ones. Were the unknown collaborators pseudonyms for Burt himself? The "less friendly" view was that Burt's work was a fraud. As Leon Kamin, the psychologist who had first detected the peculiarities of Burt's work, proclaimed: "[The evidence on the IQ scores of twins] was a fraud linked to policy from the word go. The data were cooked in order for him to arrive at the conclusions he wanted" (Wade, 1976, pp. 916). Box 3-1 describes a cur-

BOX 3-1

WERE THE DATA FRAUDULENT OR NOT?

A case which gained great attention in the scientific community in the last few years involved charges that immunologist Thereza Imanishi-Kari, an assistant professor at Tufts University, had included falsified data in a research paper, published in 1986 in the renowned journal *Cell* jointly with Nobel laureate scientist David Baltimore, then a professor at the Massachusetts Institute of Technology. The paper showed that a gene transplant into mice had a greater impact on the animals' immune systems than scientists had predicted. The charges of fraud were raised by a postdoctoral researcher in Imanishi-Kari's laboratory who claimed that some of the experiments referred to in the paper had not been performed.

A series of investigations ensued, by the universities where the research was performed; by the Office of Scientific Integrity Review of the National Institutes of Health (NIH), which had funded the research; and by a few congressional committees. Research data tapes, secured by the Secret Service working with the NIH, appeared to have been subjected to tampering. The NIH report stated that documents supporting the experimental results appeared to have been made long after the experiments were done.

A forensic expert hired by Dr. Imanishi-Kari, however, charged that the Secret Service evidence was erroneous. Her attorney, claiming that his client had been unable to see her research notebooks, which had been seized by the government, stated that "fundamental fairness dictates they give those who are accused the evidence so they can respond." In July, 1992, charges were dropped when the U.S. attorney ruled that while the evidence was persuasive, the case was too complex to win in court.

Dr. Baltimore, who had previously requested that the paper be retracted, then stated, "I will write to *Cell* and tell them I consider the paper a valid contribution to the scientific discourse and there is no longer any reason to doubt it. I see no reason why the scientific community should consider this a retracted paper any more." On the other side, Congressman John Dingell, who chaired one of the investigating committees, stated, "The decision not to prosecute does not change the fact that the *Cell* paper was retracted because of serious, and extensive, irregularities. Nor does it change the fact that the experiments in question have not been replicated."

Data from *"Researcher Accused of Fraud in Her Data Will Not Be Indicted,"* The New York Times, July 14, 1992, p. B6; and "U.S. Attorney Will Not Seek Indictment of Researcher Accused in 'Baltimore Case,'" *Chronicle of Higher Education,* **38** (46) July 22, 1992, p. A7.

BOX 3-2

THE WORK OF THE OFFICE OF SCIENTIFIC INTEGRITY REVIEW

By 1991, the Office of Scientific Integrity Review of the National Institutes of Health had investigated 174 allegations of scientific misconduct and had levied penalties on fourteen scientists charged with scientific misconduct. Six were barred from receiving federal contracts or grants; the other eight were given lesser penalties. The charges involved misrepresenting the status of research subjects, misrepresenting oneself as the developer of a training program which had been developed by another researcher in a different institution, plagiarism, falsifying data, and altering experimental results. Lyle Bivens, director of the Office of Scientific Integrity Review, believes that the integrity of science is impaired more by the falsification of data than by plagiarism.

Data from "U.S. has Barred Grants to Six Scientists in Past Two Years," *Chronicle of Higher Education,* **37** (42), July 3, 1991, pp. 1, 6–7.

rent scientific misconduct case which gained widespread attention.

The desire to have the evidence match the preconceived hypotheses and notions of the researcher is naturally strong. In some cases, the career of the scientist may seem in jeopardy unless the results turn out as he or she had expected. Researchers may feel pressured by the agencies who fund their research to produce "exciting" findings. That is how people become established as scientists. Yet no other unethical activity threatens the sciences as much as this. The federal Department of Health and Human Services has established an Office of Scientific Integrity Review. Box 3-2 explains its activities. If scientists commit fraud, if they flagrantly disregard the scientific ethos discussed in Chapter 2, not only will the public lose confidence in the value of science, but the institution of science itself may suffer serious damage itself. "Because intentional creation of error is so antithetical to the aims of science, effects (of fraud) may be beyond loss of confidence to a sense of disorientation and despair" (Weinstein, 1979, p. 648).

Closely related to altering the results is the incorporation of someone else's work into your own without proper acknowledgment. This is the act of *plagiarism,* which occurs infrequently in the writings of social researchers. It is also an unethical activity known among some students. Students' reasons for plagiarizing are usually different from those of social researchers. In the case of students, the action is usually a shortcut to meeting the requirements for a course without actually doing the required assignment. Students often do not realize that using someone else's work (their writing, their ideas, their point of view) without acknowledging that they are doing so destroys their integrity as students and undermines the trust that must be at the basis of the relationship between students and teachers. If a researcher is suspected of using someone else's material without citation or of cheating in the collection or presentation of data, that person's career can be irreparably damaged.

The Right to Privacy vs. the Public's Right to Know

By focusing on the protection of individual rights, are we confining social research to the study of those who have nothing to hide or to those who lack the power to refuse to be studied? Consider how journalists operate. Their primary value is the public's right to know. They have secured their right to search for information on people in public positions and public organizations. The courts have decided that those who serve the public may be subject to greater scrutiny than others. The Watergate story was uncovered by the press. By using unnamed informants and other tactics to get at the story, reporters made those in power accountable. Galliher (1980, p. 303) warns that the study of those in power should not be left solely to journalists, for "social science offers a unique type of interpretation of events not usually found in . . . American journalism."

Yet powerful individuals and institutions have means for warding off the intrusion of those seeking to study them. Corporations protect their privacy carefully, and to uncover information in a corporation requires that the social researcher provide a needed service to the organization and establish trust among those with whom he or she deals. Remember that Kanter was successful at studying Indsco because she was performing consulting services for them and because she was able to establish a relationship of trust with a number of individuals in the organization who served as her major informants and supporters. It has more often been the case that social researchers have studied those with lower status than themselves rather than higher. Indigent and poorly educated people do not have the resources or knowledge, the lawyers, or the "I'm too busy" excuses to fend off social researchers.

Whatever the status of the person or group under investigation, if there is potential harm to the right of privacy of those being studied, that harm must be considered in relation to the right to know. As Cassell (1978) puts it, the risks of doing the research must be weighed in relation to the benefits. In research involving deception, both those being studied and the researcher confront risks. The research project itself may be threatened if the subjects suspect that they are being deceived. In field studies, subjects may also suffer emotional risks in their relation to the researcher: if the researcher has developed "friendships" among those being studied, his or her departure may be painful for the subjects. On the other hand, benefits may be gained by the subjects in a study. Cassell suggests that there may be material benefits (help, money), intellectual benefits (an opportunity to understand more about one's social circumstances), and emotional benefits (the pleasure of talking to someone interested in your social world, your attitudes and opinions) (1978, pp. 137–139).

So please keep in mind as you read this discussion of ways of reducing abuses in social research that this concern should not result in choosing to carry out studies only on "safe" subjects (that is to say, on those with little power). In addition, you should treat all your subjects fairly and uniformly, regardless of their status.

Means for Ensuring the Protection of Subjects

In survey research, there are various approaches to ensuring the protection of the respondents. Questionnaires often elicit information regarding attitudes toward minority groups, religious beliefs and behaviors, level of income, and sexual activities (commonly requested in population studies). Survey researchers have long recognized that such questions may deter some respondents from completing the instrument. Yet, depending on the objectives of the survey research, such information may be vital. Remember that information on specific individuals is not the goal. It is the aggregate data representing the entire sample that interests the researcher. What John Doe earned in 1980 is of little interest, but the median income of employed males in the United States is of substantial interest.

Most potential respondents would not be concerned about having information about their income (or even their sexual activity) used to help establish a norm for a larger group. But how can their privacy be guaranteed? Three principles can be used to help establish such privacy: anonymity, confidentiality, and informed consent.

Anonymity.   Granting information to someone who promises that you will remain completely anonymous is the maximum assurance you can receive that your privacy will not be invaded. Anonymity implies that no one, not even the researcher, could connect your name with the information about you. Thus *anonymity* is an assurance that subjects' identities will not be disclosed in any way. How can this be done?

If questionnaires are mailed to respondents who return them without any form of code or identifying information on them, then they are completely anonymous. (This assumes, of course, that the respondent's handwriting cannot be identified by the researcher, because the researcher is not familiar with it or because machine-readable forms are used rather than handwritten replies.) Yet if a questionnaire remains completely anonymous, the researcher will be unable to determine who has and who has not answered; therefore no follow-up surveys can be sent and no patterns of nonresponse can be established. Thus, while anonymity in survey research can be achieved, it is usually given only in certain circumstances, such as when questionnaires are administered in groups. Instead, researchers prefer in most cases to offer confidentiality as the safeguard for the protection of subjects.

Confidentiality. *Confidentiality* is a promise to keep the identities of the subjects known only to the researcher and perhaps selected members of his or her staff and to minimize in any available way the possible exposure of a subject's identity. This is often done by the use of code numbers on surveys or of pseudonyms for persons and places that might be identifiable. Sometimes the code lists and their corresponding names are held at locations distant from the site of the research, and access to this list is strictly limited to the researcher alone. Also, a list of code numbers may be destroyed when it is no longer needed.

In field research, interviews, or experimental studies where subjects have been directly seen by the researcher, confidentiality can again be guaranteed by procedures to store the data on subjects under codes and fictitious names. In some field studies where confidentiality has been promised, the resulting published studies may nevertheless make it possible for subjects and others to identify

specific people and places in the study. Such a situation developed after the publication of Arthur Vidich and Joseph Bensman's study of a small town, *Small Town in Mass Society,* in 1960. Some of the principal individuals in the study were quite easily identifiable to members of the community. This was a case in which confidentiality had been promised but not maintained. While names and obvious identifying characteristics had been altered, roles and situations made it quite easy for subjects to be identified by others. Thus when you conduct a study, you may want to warn participants that although confidentiality is the goal, under certain conditions the identities of certain persons and places may be recognized. Such a warning might form a part of an informed consent statement.

Informed Consent. At the heart of the whole issue of social research and infringement of privacy stands the concern for whether the subject has knowingly agreed to the research in which he or she is participating. *Informed consent* is achieved if the subject knows what the study is, understands his or her level of confidentiality in the study, comprehends the objectives of the study, and agrees to cooperate. Under such conditions, the onus of invasion of privacy is lifted and the problem of coercion avoided. In such a case, the participation is voluntary. What is crucial here is that the subject be truly informed. First, the researcher should give the subject accurate and complete information as to the nature and purpose of the study and the part the subject will play in it. In a mail survey, subjects are often asked to respond and complete the entire questionnaire at the same time that they are explicitly informed that they need not do so unless they choose. The quality of *voluntariness* must be clearly recognized by the subject in order for it to be acted upon.

Second, informed consent also presupposes that the subject is capable of understanding what he or she is consenting to and has been given a clear explanation of what that is. College students, adults with a college education, and many others may well be able to understand the nature and purpose of a social research project. Others may not. In these cases, greater care must be taken to explain the study in a comprehensible fashion. (In the case of studying children, informed consent is often solicited from parents). As mentioned above, people with lower status and less power are often less capable of refusing to be studied. They may not understand the meaning of the informed consent statements, and they may think that they have no option but to agree to a request by a higher-status, educated social scientist. Naturally, the social researcher does not want to emphasize too emphatically the potential dangers or inconveniences of the study. The social researcher cannot tell a person that he or she is incapable of understanding whether or not to participate. The only sensible course of action seems to be to develop an informed consent statement appropriate for the intended audience.

ETHICAL CONSIDERATIONS

The ethical considerations raised in this chapter can be reduced to a simple question. Whose rights are more sacred, those of the scientist, those of individuals or institutions who might be studied by scientists, or those of the public to learn from the research? In this section, these rights will be compared.

The Scientific Right to Study Any Subject of Interest

The right of social scientists to study whatever they deem to be of scientific interest is fundamental in a free society. This right, however, carries with it the responsibility that the research conform to scientific rules and that these rules include the protection of human subjects. We will here consider both the importance of maintaining high standards in carrying out research and the need for full disclosure.

Use of High Technical Standards. Anything may be a possible subject of study, but topics must be studied according to the highest technical standards of the methods available to the researcher to obtain the necessary data. To maintain high technical standards, researchers must be familiar with both the range of types of research already available on a given topic and the methods used to study this topic. They must know which studies have been most successful in gaining the desired information, and they must understand precisely the procedures by which these studies have been carried out.

A researcher with technically high standards not only knows how to do what he or she is doing but can be critical of his or her own method. In other words, a researcher must consider the possible alternative ways of carrying out the study in order to appreciate the advantages and disadvantages of the method chosen. In this text, acceptable standards for each method will be detailed. However, no formal set of procedures can ever cover all the possible contingencies that may arise in setting up a research project. There will always be situations where the researcher will need to exercise discretion in implementing any method. It is precisely within this area of discretion that ethical considerations may arise.

Full Disclosure. Science requires that all evidence generated and analyzed be made available to the relevant scientific community. This means that all aspects of a research project must be open for the inspection and understanding of others. In cases where confidentiality has been guaranteed, this somewhat reduces the full measure of disclosure. Usually, however, the information that is guaranteed to be confidential (names and addresses of subjects) is without scientific interest anyway.

Full disclosure of method and findings requires that negative and insignificant as well as positive findings be presented. The objective must be to make the procedures and findings of a study fully enough available to the reader that he or she could replicate it. In Chapter 2, in the discussion of the scientists who studied the evidence from the Apollo missions, it was suggested that this scientific norm was often not followed and that secrecy and lack of full disclosure was characteristic of much scientific activity. Thus it would seem that while full disclosure is an ideal of scientific researchers, and that social researchers should aim to disclose whatever they find, this goal is not always characteristic of scientific research as it is practiced. Beginning researchers should design and carry out their research with the intention of making all their research available. In this regard, it is important to keep careful records of all steps of a research project so that you are later able to disclose it fully.

The Rights of Human Subjects

Human subjects have the right not to be physically or psychologically abused. They have the right of privacy and protection of their reputations. While the right to protection from physical abuse seems self-evident, the case for the protection of privacy is more complex. A substantial case can be made for the rights of privacy of individuals. However, this concern can lead to practices which are overly cautious. Now that institutions in which most scientists do their work require that all research on human subjects be approved by an *institutional review board,* and all grants received from the government must also go through such an appraisal, there is fear that the concern to protect the rights of individuals may have turned into an obsession with privacy precluding many important areas of research. Again, as in so many of these ethical areas, there are trade-offs. The ethical issues arise where the choices need to be made.

Whose Rights?   Many would contend that the rights of individuals to privacy and to freedom from harassment and harm supersede the rights of scientists to seek knowledge. They therefore pre-

clude the practice of covert research in which the researcher deceives subjects by misrepresenting his or her role. They preclude experiments that coerce subjects to react in ways that may be detrimental to their sense of well-being. Further, they preclude research that invades areas of individuals' lives that are a part of their private domain, unless, of course, the individual freely and knowingly gives up this right. [For an eloquent defense of the individual's right to privacy, see Shils (1982).]

As we stated above, however, some people are "more equal" than others. Social scientists should not limit their research only to those who are unable or unconcerned to protect their interests (real or perceived). There are many important aspects of social life in which the participants may resist being studied for various reasons, and the researcher will need to think seriously about the research strategies that might be available to counter such resistance. There may be instances in which it is necessary to study individuals without their explicit permission, in order to secure the public's right to know. Perhaps the best middle ground is to try to gain access to "difficult-to-enter" organizations and situations by serving in a role different from that of researcher.

Unfortunately, there are real losses to social research when all research that may require covert activity, coercion, or an invasion of privacy is barred. The studies, such as Rosenhan's study of the treatment of mental institution patients or Milgram's classic study of obedience, offered keen insights into important institutions and forms of human behavior that might not have been gleaned by another method. Covert research methods have enabled researchers to study socially undesirable behaviors. Some would argue that without such techniques, the investigation of what Erving Goffman (1959) called "backstage" human interaction is seriously constrained.

Some social scientists have devised ways of studying the problems and topics in which they are interested that have avoided the potential abuse of deception. For example, in studies where research as a covert insider may seem to offer the only practical means of gathering data, the researcher should consider the alternative possibilities: (1) acting as overt outsider, frankly stating one's role as a researcher (as Rubinstein, 1973, did in his study of the Philadelphia police force) or (2) acting in the role of a covert outsider, as Cohen and Taylor (1972) did in serving as lecturers for prisoners' courses as a way of observing prison life (see Bulmer, 1982, for a discussion). Neither of these roles requires that the researcher pose as some individual he or she is not. Instead, one either accepts the overt role of the researcher (many claim, with Rubinstein, 1973, that doing so makes little difference to insiders, once their trust has been gained) or takes on another valid role as an outsider that is compatible with the conduct of the research as a secondary activity.

The Importance of Trust

Since social science is an interactive human activity, meaning that it requires the scientist to act in relation to other human beings, it creates its own behavioral by-products. This chapter has pointed out that some of these by-products may be, or appear, unethical. The accumulation of too many of these negative by-products could make it difficult for social researchers to continue their activities. The work of social scientists, like that of any other professionals whose work involves human subjects, depends ultimately on the trust of those with whom it deals. One covert researcher might be able to collect data surreptitiously on a specific group, but will the public evidence of this foreclose or limit the research possibilities of later researchers?

Better that each researcher establish a level of trust among participants necessary in whatever social environment is being studied, such that those being studied understand that their rights are being protected and find their participation in the study beneficial. Most individuals are fascinated with their own lives, with their own social memberships and social environments. To share this

knowledge with an interested and sympathetic outsider whom they have come to trust is, for many, a rewarding experience.

It may not be possible for you to establish the trust necessary to study every topic you find interesting, but you should select an environment for your research that allows you to be forthright about who you are, what you are up to, and why someone else should accept involvement in your study as beneficial. In addition to being less problematic or painful for your subjects, such a study will be easier for you in the long run as well.

GUIDELINES

Many colleges and universities have institutional review boards which set ethical guidelines for research carried out in, and by members of, the institution; they also evaluate research proposals in order to ensure that the rights of human subjects are protected. These boards may review student projects as well as faculty-initiated research. One of the primary responsibilities of a professional association is to proctor the activities of its members so that they are not accused of acting in disreputable ways detrimental to the profession. In short, professional associations try to monitor the behaviors (read, reduce the misbehavior) of their members so as to protect or enhance their profession in the public eye. Social scientists have never been as fully in the public limelight as, say, doctors, yet their misbehaviors have often brought them to public attention more than their accomplishments. For this reason, the establishment and maintenance of public trust is a more pressing concern now among social scientists than it has been before.

Numerous professional associations have revised their codes of ethics to address the major moral concerns of their disciplines. Box 3-3 presents the first section of the Code of Ethics on the practice of sociology approved by the membership of the American Sociological Association in 1989.

BOX 3-3

SECTION ONE OF THE CODE OF ETHICS OF THE AMERICAN SOCIOLOGICAL ASSOCIATION

I. THE PRACTICE OF SOCIOLOGY

A. *Objectivity and Integrity*

Sociologists should strive to maintain objectivity and integrity in the conduct of sociological research and practice.

1. Sociologists should adhere to the highest possible technical standards in their research, teaching and practice.

2. Since individual sociologists vary in their research modes, skills, and experience, sociologists should always set forth *ex ante* the limits of their knowledge and the disciplinary and personal limitations that condition the validity of findings which affect whether or not a research project can be successfully completed.

3. In practice or other situations in which sociologists are requested to render a professional judgment, they should accurately and fairly represent their areas and degrees of expertise.

4. In presenting their work, sociologists are obligated to report their findings fully and should not misrepresent the findings of their research. When work is presented, they are obligated to report their findings fully and without omission of significant data. To the best of their ability, sociologists should also disclose details of their theories, methods and research designs that might bear upon interpretations of research findings.

5. Sociologists must report fully all sources of financial support in their publications and must note any special relations to any sponsor.

6. Sociologists should not make any guarantees to respondents, individuals, groups or organizations—unless there is full intention and ability to honor such commitments. All such guarantees, once made, must be honored.

7. Consistent with the spirit of full disclosure of method and analysis, sociologists, after they have completed their own analyses, should cooperate in efforts to make raw data and pertinent documentation collected and prepared at public expense available to other social scientists, at reasonable costs, except in cases where confidentiality, the client's rights to proprietary information and privacy, or the claims of a fieldworker to the privacy of personal notes necessarily would be violated. The timeliness of this cooperation is especially critical.

8. Sociologists should provide adequate information and citations concerning scales and other measures used in their research.

9. Sociologists must not accept grants, contracts or research assignments that appear likely to require violation of the principles enunciated in this Code, and should dissociate themselves from research when they discover a violation and are unable to achieve its correction.

10. When financial support for a project has been accepted, sociologists must make every reasonable effort to complete the proposed work on schedule, including reports to the funding source.

11. When several sociologists, including students, are involved in joint projects, there should be mutually accepted explicit agreements at the outset with respect to division of work, compensation, access to data, rights of authorship, and other rights and responsibilities. Such agreements may need to be modified as the project evolves and such modifications must be agreed upon jointly.

12. Sociologists should take particular care to state all significant qualifications on the findings and interpretations of their research.

13. Sociologists have the obligation to disseminate research findings, except those likely to cause harm to clients, collaborators and participants, or those which are proprietary under a formal or informal agreement.

14. In their roles as practitioners, researchers, teachers, and administrators, sociologists have an important social responsibility because their recommendations, decisions, and actions may alter the lives of others. They should be aware of the situations and pressures that might lead to the misuse of their influence and authority. In these various roles, sociologists should also recognize that professional problems and conflicts may interfere with professional effectiveness. Sociologists should take steps to insure that these conflicts do not produce deleterious results for clients, research participants, colleagues, students and employees.

B. *Disclosure and Respect for the Rights of Research Populations*

Disparities in wealth, power, and social status between the sociologist and respondents and clients may reflect and create problems of equity in research collaboration. Conflict of interest for the sociologist may occur in research and practice. Also to follow the precepts of the scientific method—such as those requiring full disclosure—may entail adverse consequences or personal risks for individuals and groups. Finally, irresponsible actions by a single researcher or research team can eliminate or reduce future access to a category of respondents by the entire profession and its allied fields.

1. Sociologists should not misuse their positions as professional social scientists for fraudulent purposes or as a pretext for gathering intelligence for any organization or government. Sociologists should not mislead respondents involved in a research project as to the purpose for which that research is being conducted.

2. Subjects of research are entitled to rights of biographical anonymity.

3. Information about subjects obtained from records that are opened to public scrutiny cannot be protected by guarantees of privacy or confidentiality.

4. The process of conducting sociological research must not expose respondents to substantial risk of personal harm. Informed consent must be obtained when the risks of research are greater than the risks of everyday life. Where modest risk or harm is anticipated, informed consent must be obtained.

5. Sociologists should take culturally appropriate steps to secure informed consent and to avoid invasions of privacy. Special actions may be necessary where the individuals studied are illiterate, have very low social status, or are unfamiliar with social research.

6. To the extent possible in a given study sociologists should anticipate potential threats to confidentiality. Such means as the removal of identifiers, the use of randomized responses and other statistical solutions to problems of privacy should be used where appropriate.

7. Confidential information provided by research participants must be treated as such by sociologists, even when this information enjoys no legal protection or privilege and legal force is applied. The obligation to respect confidentiality also applies to members of research organizations (interviewers, coders, clerical staff, etc.) who have access to the information. It is the responsibility of admin-

istrators and chief investigators to instruct staff members on this point and to
make every effort to insure that access to
confidential information is restricted.

8. While generally adhering to the norm of
acknowledging the contributions of all
collaborators, sociologists should be
sensitive to harm that may arise from
disclosure and respect a collaborator's
wish or need for anonymity. Full disclosure may be made later if circumstances
permit.

9. Study design and information gathering
techniques should conform to regulations protecting the rights of human subject, irrespective of source of funding as

outlined by the American Association of
University Professors (AAUP) in "Regula-
tions Governing Research On Human
Subjects: Academic Freedom and the In-
stitutional Review Board," *Academe*,
December 1981: 358–370.

10. Sociologists should comply with appropriate federal and institutional requirements pertaining to the conduct of
research. These requirements might include but are not necessarily limited to
. . . [obtaining] proper review and approval for research that involves human
subjects and . . . [following] recommendations made by responsible committees concerning research subjects,
materials, and procedures.

Source: American Sociological Association: *Code of Ethics,* Washington, D.C., 1989, pp. 2–3.

USES AND ABUSES RECONSIDERED

This chapter has raised issues of central concern
to the social sciences. It has offered suggestions
as to how to determine the rationale or use of a
study, and it has presented points of view on the
ethical issues confronting social research. Clearly, it is not the purpose of social research to
trample on the rights of individuals, and this
chapter has tried to make you think seriously
about these rights. However, it has also raised
the issue of the accountability of people in public positions and the need for those doing social
research not to shy away from studies of the
powerful who have much greater means of maintaining their privacy.

Some social scientists feel a moral need to reveal how power is exercised in order to maintain
privilege and the status quo. If they cannot gain
access to the organizations where power is held,
they feel morally justified in gaining information
through whatever means are available. In cases
such as that, where a researcher seeks to study individuals or organizations who resist being stud-

ied or who will not willingly consent to being
studied, the risk-benefit dilemma becomes most
acute. Does the value to be gained from the study
(either to the advancement of knowledge in the
discipline or for practical reasons) outweigh the
risk to the subjects, the relationship of the social
researcher to subjects, the maintenance of trust
between the field of social research and the society it seeks to study? Social researchers should
not veer away from a subject simply because they
think it may raise some ethical issues or difficulties. But it is important to make sure that you
think through those issues and difficulties thoroughly before you proceed. Social researchers
need not be so timid and so deferential that any
challenge to their plans sends them running. Instead, if it is your project, talk to others about
it—your professors, the review board at your institution, those whose opinions you value. Think
through the uses of the study; consider the potential abuses. Then decide whether the value of the
study is worth its risks. Research demands not
only caution but courage as well.

REVIEW NOTES

- A rationale for a research project is a sound reason for selecting the particular subject and method for carrying out the research based on some value or purpose.
- Merton's two rationales for research are that the study will contribute to systematic knowledge in a discipline (that is, basic research) or that it will be of some practical use (that is, applied research).
- Four criteria that may guide you in developing a rationale are whether the study offers evidence about the changing nature of society; whether the study addresses a social policy topic; whether the study will broaden knowledge of an unusual or unfamiliar topic; and whether the researcher has particular knowledge or expertise which may enable him or her to make unique contributions in the research effort.
- The three types of research procedures that raise ethical concerns are covert research methods, research which involves coercion of subjects, and research procedures that may be considered an invasion of privacy.
- Unethical practices that may arise in the reporting of social research are tampering with results and plagiarism.
- In the study of persons in public positions and public organizations, the right of privacy must be balanced against the public's right to know.
- Measures for ensuring the protection of subjects in a research study are anonymity, confidentiality, and informed consent.
- Many institutions and professional associations that sponsor research have drawn up guidelines to follow in ensuring the rights of human subjects.

KEY TERMS

anonymity
applied research
basic research
coercion of subjects
confidentiality
covert research
full disclosure
informed consent
institutional review board
invasion of privacy
plagiarism
rationale
rights of human subjects
tampering with results

STUDY EXERCISES

1. Add one more use to the four uses given that seems to you to be an important rationale for deciding whether to do a specific social research project.
2. Select two of the studies described in Chapter 1 and decide which of the uses is best exemplified in each study.
3. Which of the studies mentioned in this chapter as being "charged" with abuses seems to you to bear the greatest ethical problems? Why did you make this choice?

RECOMMENDED READINGS

1. Bulmer, Martin (ed.): *Social Research Ethics,* Macmillan, London, 1982. This collection of essays includes both appraisals of covert participation observation studies and considerations of the ethical issues raised (invasion of privacy, academic freedom, restrictions on research).
2. Kimmel, Allan J.: *Ethics and Values in Applied Social Research,* Sage, Newbury Park, Calif., 1988. This volume addresses the value issues confronted in doing research for organizations and agencies. A useful guide.
3. Lewis, George H.: *Fist-Fights in the Kitchen: Manners and Methods in Social Research,* Goodyear, Pacific Palisades, Calif., 1975. This very lively reader includes considerations of ethical issues in experi-

ments, the rights of subjects, and Irving Louis Horowitz's exposé of the government-sponsored Project Camelot.

4. Sieber, Joan E.: *Planning Ethically Responsible Research: A Guide for Social Science Students,* Sage, Newbury Park, Calif., 1992. This useful volume explains how to prepare a protocol for an institutional review board and how to handle issues of confidentiality, privacy, deception, and consent.

The Design of Social Research

The first section of this text was intended to provide you with a broad understanding of the foundations for the social research enterprise. Here in Part Two, the components of a research design will be laid out. Chapter 4 will examine how a topic can be turned into a problem for social research; and it will outline a plan covering all the components of a research project. Chapter 5 is concerned with concepts, measurement, and operationalization. Once a topic is selected and the research plan is proposed, a careful consideration of precisely what concepts will be studied and how they will be measured is necessary. When the major concepts in the study have been determined, the research project must conceive of a way to make these concepts observable—in other words, to *operationalize* the concepts. Once the concepts have been operationalized, the issue of concern moves to finding an appropriate set of subjects (people, events, institutions, or whatever) to observe or question. The selection of these subjects requires a knowledge of the principles of sampling, which will be the subject of Chapter 6.

Defining a Researchable Topic and Preparing a Research Plan

LOOKING AHEAD

This chapter offers help in selecting a research topic and lays out the eleven steps in carrying out a social research project.

INTRODUCTION

*T*o start a research project, you first need to develop a clearly defined research topic. Then you must set out the necessary steps that you will follow to produce the final research report; that is to say, you need a detailed research plan which may form the basis of a written *research proposal.* The first objective of this chapter is to help suggest ways of finding topics and turning them into researchable problems. It will suggest sources of topics, offer criteria to be used in selecting a topic, indicate ways to intensify knowledge about a topic, delineate how a topic of interest can become a researchable problem, consider the rationale for doing the study, discuss the subjects to be studied, and set the time dimension required.

The second objective of this chapter is to propose a plan to follow in doing your research project. Once a research problem has been formulated and subjects for a study have been determined, the actual means for carrying out the research project must be delineated. This is the proposal-writing stage of the research process, when the overall plan for the project must be set out in logical order.

SOURCES TO USE IN SELECTING A TOPIC

In the Introduction, I emphasized that what is going on in your own life and in the social world around you, what troubles you, what interests you, what your life experiences are—all these areas of concern are full of possibilities for social research projects. Follow C. Wright Mills's notion that for a social research project to be sociologically imaginative, you need to draw upon your personal resources to relate issues in the society to your own experience. What Mills was stressing is that social research is not just a matter of dry numbers and charts, or even of careful descriptions or intricate theories; instead, social research should have a relevance, a depth of concern that raises it above what is mundane and uninteresting to a level of intellectual commitment. However, you cannot begin to get committed to a project until you have selected a topic for study. Besides your own experiences and ideas, there are many sources to which you may turn in trying to identify a research topic. Social research topics need not derive from your own experiences and interests; they can come from more formal efforts at finding a topic. To find a topic, you must expose yourself to some potential sources for ideas. These sources might be already published materials, other people, or research projects which are in progress.

Printed Sources

The studies described in Chapter 1 were examples from the vast literature on social research that is already published. Such studies can provide many ideas for projects. But where can you find these published sources? The results of many research projects have been published in book form. For example, the Coleman study on public and private schools became the basis of a book, *High School Achievement* (1982). Coleman and his colleagues also disseminated their findings in a number of articles in academic journals, and their results were noted in popular magazines and newspaper articles.

A large study reported in a book holds many ideas for smaller projects. Consider the Coleman study. You might want to consider only one of their findings: that private school students do more homework. In that case, you would want to glean from the Coleman study what role homework played in the students' lives, what they associated it with. (It was introduced in a section on Involvement in School under the larger heading of Student Behavior.) The time spent on homework was presented first, followed by a table showing the time spent watching television and one showing the percentages of high school students who claim to be "interested in school" and to "like working hard in school." In other words, Coleman and his associates used time spent on homework not as a measure of student ability, but as a measure of student commitment to school. You may or may not conceptualize homework in this fashion. The important point is that reading the work of other researchers and figuring out how they designed their study, measured concepts, etc., should help you to formulate your project.

In the Kanter (1977) study you might find the subject of the careers of secretaries in large corporations of interest. How are their careers tied to their bosses? How do their roles mimic those of the wives of their bosses? How does a secretary's role change if her boss is a woman? Or if the secretary is a man? You might read Kanter's study with your question in mind and try to find (1) if she speaks directly to your interest or (2) if her findings might suggest a slightly different topic. Take the issue of how having a female boss might change the role of a secretary. While Kanter does not directly discuss this, it is clear from her study that the kind of "emotion-laden relations of individual loyalty" (1977, p. 101) which characterize a secretary's relation to her boss might be altered if the boss were a woman. What significance is there, for example, in the fact that in a session during which secretaries and their bosses discussed "expectation exchanges," one secretarial supervisor "insisted that, in her words, 'The *girl* is there to serve the man'" (p. 80)?

There are so many already published studies that for any idea which you might think of, numerous other researchers will have already been at work on it. Don't feel discouraged by this. No two researchers ever produce the same study. An area in which there has been a lot of research is by definition an important area. Juvenile delinquency would be a good example of a heavily studied area. New approaches and new points of view, however, can generate valuable new findings, and new findings will be more valuable if they have been informed by earlier studies (such as Hirschi's 1969 classic study on delinquency carried out more than 20 years ago).

Appendix A offers a detailed description of how to use a library in order to look for a topic or to intensify knowledge about a topic once it has been selected. We will now turn to a different source for finding a topic, namely, connecting your efforts to an ongoing project.

Ongoing Social Research Projects and Available Data

One way to discover a topic is to find a project currently under way; talk to the people doing the project and see if they can suggest some aspect of the project that you might study further or some aspect from which you might develop a researchable idea. Alternatively, you might look for already collected data which you can use for your purposes.

Finding an Ongoing Project.   How can you find ongoing projects? First you might find out what kind of research your professors are conducting or what graduate students are studying. Another very good way to hear about current research is to attend a scholarly meeting in sociology, education, political science, psychology, or whatever discipline you think most likely would address your interests. Such meetings have printed schedules giving the titles of all the papers, their authors, and the times and places they will be given. Remember that you need not attend a national meeting. Many regional associations have conferences and there are special interest groups that hold meetings (the Law and Society Association, Women's Studies Association, etc.). Individual universities and research centers often sponsor meetings where papers are delivered or where round table discussions are held, which may be directly of interest to you.

Never assume that you would be unwelcome. While there are a few exclusive conferences which only invited participants may attend, they are very rare. Generally, students are welcome at professional meetings, and usually there are special registration fees for students allowing them to participate at reduced rates. Don't feel shy about asking a question either during the discussion following the presentation of the paper or after the session has formally ended. Nothing makes a researcher happier than finding other people interested in his or her research project. Many professional meetings make available photocopies of papers which have been delivered. These may be purchased at the meeting, or you might write directly to the author and request a copy.

Finding Available Data. A topic for a social research project may stem from an available dataset. You may be surprised that a topic for a study could grow from a set of data already produced. But nationwide surveys (like the one Coleman used in his public school–private school study) are usually so broad and may include so many items that a multitude of projects could be produced from a single dataset. Don't think that simply because a book has already been written which was based on a national survey, all the data must have been analyzed. Most survey datasets are vastly underutilized. Even the same sets of questions may be analyzed in so many different ways that no two researchers are likely to produce identical analyses. (It is, of course, legitimate to replicate an earlier study with different data; but most replications usually add new twists to the earlier design.) Many social research projects rely on data that were collected for other purposes. Chapter 10 specifically examines studies that use already collected data sources and provides additional suggestions. Here I will suggest where to find some of these existing sources.

Government-collected data. The most obvious source for data is the government. For an index to statistical material, see the *American Statistics Index: A Comprehensive Guide and Index to the Statistical Publications of the United States Government,* which is published annually with monthly supplements. This index is also available *online,* which means that you might be able to carry out computer searches using this index if the library you are using has the necessary facilities.

Census data can be used as the basis for many social research projects. Remember that census data include information covering the nation as a whole or many subsections of the nation. To get some idea of the types of data available, consult the *Statistical Abstract of the United States.* This book will show you tables that represent a wide range of subjects on which the Census Bureau has data. If you want data for a specific city or community, consult the *County and City Data Book: A Statistical Abstract Supplement.* The Census Bureau also compiles data on smaller areas within cities. For example, in Chicago, data are available on the city, on Cook County, and on community areas within the city.

The Census Bureau also has comparative historical data which you can find in *Historical Statistics of the United States, Colonial Times to 1970.* The United Nations offers data yearly on countries throughout the world in the *Statistical Yearbook.*

The Bureau of Labor Statistics regularly publishes statistical material and interpretations on topics concerning workers. For example, there are numerous published reports on subjects such as women workers, minority workers, and unemployment data. Crime statistics are regularly available from the U.S. Federal Bureau of Investigation in *Uniform Crime Reports for the United States.*

Nongovernmental datasets. Besides data collected expressly by the federal government, there are many sources of data produced for various social research projects which are now available to the public. Probably the best-known set of survey data available is that generated by the *General Social Survey (GSS),* which is carried out yearly by the National Opinion Research Center (NORC). Box 4-1 describes this widely utilized dataset. The data from these yearly surveys may be purchased for use on a wide range of different types of computers. Most large datasets from surveys funded by a federal agency ultimately become available to the public. To take an example already discussed, Coleman's study is based on a nationwide survey of high school sophomores and seniors of 1980 who were followed up biannually over a six-year period. The data from this NORC survey, *High School and Beyond,* can be purchased and used for different types of analyses. Another data set on high school students, the *National Longitudinal Study of the*

High School Class of 1972, followed up 1972 high school seniors five times during the 1970s and then again in 1986. Many of the questions included in these 1970s surveys were repeated in the 1980s *High School and Beyond* surveys. The data tapes for this survey are available from the Center for Statistics of the U.S. Department of Education.

Many universities have large survey datasets available to students, such as the *General Social Survey.* In other cases, you may read about a dataset that has been used for a particular study and which you realize might meet the needs of your study. While some datasets may not be available to you or may be too expensive to obtain, don't get easily discouraged, for many datasets are not very expensive and are readily available.

BOX 4-1

THE GENERAL SOCIAL SURVEY

The *General Social Survey (GSS),* which began in 1972, has been administered nearly every year since that time to a national sample of the adult, English-speaking household population of the United States. (See Box 6-8 for a description of the sample design of the *GSS.*) The data collection method is interviewing.

The questionnaires were designed and reviewed by teams of sociologists and social scientists. They include permanent questions repeated yearly, rotating questions, and a few occasional questions. Information is regularly gathered on occupation, income, religious preference, ethnicity, region, and city size, along with educational, marital, and family histories. Since 1972, certain attitudinal items have been included on a regular basis, such as support for free speech or support for legal abortion under certain conditions. In the late 1970s, sets of questions on current topics of interest began to be added. In 1977, for instance, questions on race relations, feminism, and abortion were added. In 1984, questions on the military, including citizenship obligations, recruitment, and training, were added. Since 1985, a

topical module has been added annually. In 1985, the topic was social networks; in 1986, the feminization of poverty; in 1987, sociopolitical participation; in 1988, religious socialization, behaviors, and beliefs (Davis, 1988, p. 3).

Since 1982, the *GSS* has collaborated with western European data collection centers; specific topics are covered in all participating countries (the United States, Great Britain, Germany, Italy, and Austria). In 1985, the topic was the role of government; in 1986, various types of social support; in 1987, social inequality (including social mobility, intergroup conflicts, reasons for inequality, and perceived and preferred differences in income between occupational groups) (Davis, 1988, p. 3).

Cumulative datasets and specialized datasets are available through NORC or the Roper Center for Public Opinion Research at the University of Connecticut at Storrs. Your institution may possess *GSS* datasets or be affiliated with a consortium that has access to this rich source of data for social research.

Box 4-2 offers three criteria to consider in determining your topic.

HOW TO INTENSIFY KNOWLEDGE ABOUT A TOPIC

Once you have selected a topic, you will need to get more information about it. There are many ways to do this.

Using the Library

Both the above discussion and Appendix A address how to use a library to find a topic. Very similar methods are used to intensify knowledge about a topic, once you have chosen it. The major difference is that in this stage of the project, you must be more selective. You cannot look at everything that has been written on this topic. Instead, you must continually make choices about

BOX 4-2

CRITERIA TO USE IN MAKING THE FINAL SELECTION OF A TOPIC

There are three major criteria to keep in mind when selecting a topic.

THE TOPIC SHOULD BE FEASIBLE TO STUDY

If you can't carry out the project to study the topic, then however fine the topic, it is not the right choice. Some people approach research projects pessimistically. They may feel that no one will give them permission to study what interests them, that no one will agree to being interviewed, or that they could never get the money or the help they need to carry out a project. Others are overly optimistic. They may be sure that everyone will be fascinated with the project, that people will rush to participate, or that support will be easy to obtain. The truth about most research projects is probably somewhere in between: you can generate the interest of others and their help in your project, but you will not be able to get the support of all. Some resources you may want may not be available. Some individuals may refuse to help you or may not be able to provide you with the help you need. The bottom line for most research projects is that you must be inventive; you must adapt your methods if certain plans do not work out. Feasibility must therefore be considered in terms of time, cost, efforts, and skill. Each of these must be available in sufficient amounts to make the research project achievable.

THE TOPIC SHOULD BE OF GENUINE INTEREST TO YOU

So many things can be studied effectively that unless you are doing a commissioned study or working on someone else's project, you should carry out a study on a topic which really interests you. I have argued that this sense of involvement in a research project is what differentiates social research from plain old fact-finding or routine, lifeless studies. The Introduction to this text was written to encourage you to explore your own interests and get in touch with what excites you as a way to begin thinking about a social research project.

YOUR RESEARCH SHOULD ENHANCE OUR UNDERSTANDING OF SOCIETY

While this may sound overly ambitious to some, your study should be designed to offer some new insights or perspectives on the topic which may positively contribute to the body of social research. While you may feel embarrassed to state that your study will enrich our understanding of society, you should keep this in mind in designing your study, for it will tend to push you toward the more relevant aspects of the topic, to ground your study in the "real world" of social realities, social problems, and the search for solutions.

what to look up, what to scan, and what to read in detail.

Let me describe how, in preparation for designing a study, I "reviewed the literature" on the topic of how attending a predominantly white college affects black students. The studies on African-Americans in predominantly white America were numerous. Since my subject concerned black students in predominantly white educational institutions, I needed to look at studies of African-Americans in mixed racial environments, in educational settings, and in institutions that people had entered to enhance their opportunities. Some of the earliest works I found were studies done early in this century on the experiences of individual black students at particular institutions. Since I planned to study two universities in a large northern city which had always had some black students, I would not really be looking at institutions where enforced integration had taken place. Nevertheless, I decided that studies on the effects of integration might suggest how black students reacted to an environment in which their sensitivities to the meaning of entering a predominantly white environment were heightened. What I was doing at stage one was to look at other studies that addressed similar research topics.

At this point in the project, I did not know what type of effect I would be looking for. I began by looking up studies, books, articles, and data related to a few subtopics of the project, with the vast expansion of colleges and universities in the 1960s, the subject "College Effects" had been very popular. Such research came under the general disciplines of social psychology (the effects of college were usually measured in terms of some attitude change) or of education (in this instance the subfield might be higher education or the sociology of education). I needed to consider two things: one was which effect I would study, and the second was which potential causes of the effect I might be interested in studying. The causes include such things as the influence of significant others, the types of activities and behaviors of the students, the background characteristics of the students, and their abilities and aspirations for being at college. The effect to be studied would be the dependent variable, the causes the independent variables. Here at stage two, I was determining the dependent and independent variables in the study.

In the course of my reading, I found in a number of studies a scale which had been used to measure the effects of college on students, often in conjunction with a number of other scales. The scale which appealed to me was called the *Autonomy Scale* (Heist and Yonge, 1968). I thought the items which composed the scale were measures of the types of attitudes that I wanted to study in black students. My advisor was more suspicious of this scale. He wanted to know more about it. This took me on a very interesting search for the origins of this scale. It turned out that the Autonomy Scale was a great-granddaughter of the famous *F-Scale of authoritarianism* (Adorno et al., 1950), though it was a measure of its converse, nonauthoritarianism. Finding out about the concept of authoritarianism and how it was measured by the F-Scale (which will be described more fully in Chapter 5) led me back through a fascinating history of how this concept had developed and how it had been operationalized. With a much firmer grasp of what the Autonomy Scale was actually measuring, I felt more confident in using it. Now at stage three, I selected a means for measuring the dependent variable.

For the search I have described, I used a university library to look up books and articles. I also used a collection of different types of tests, available in a research library, to select the Autonomy Scale and to look at its earlier versions. I also ordered a few earlier dissertations on topics similar to my own, which were available on microfilm from University Microfilms at Ann Arbor, Michigan.

Using Integrative Research Reviews

In many areas of interest in the social sciences, reviews of current and past research in specific fields have been prepared. Such *integrative research reviews* offer excellent groundwork for the beginning researcher. For example, Maccoby and Jacklin's (1974) two-volume review of studies on sex differences both provided a foundation for the rapid rise in research in that area and helped researchers push beyond questions of sex differences to consideration of other gender-relevant concerns in the social sciences. Academic journals often offer review articles.

These integrative articles, referred to as meta-analyses, may simply compare findings of research on similar topics, or they may assess the theoretical contributions of comparable studies (Cooper, 1989). Integrative reviews help the beginning researcher by scanning the literature, noting the most common directions taken by research on a particular topic, and summarizing the cumulative knowledge gained. Finally, reviews often delineate which areas of a field remain to be explored.

Carrying out an integrative research review is itself a form of social research. Cooper's book *Integrating Research: A Guide for Literature Reviews* (1989) overviews the methods for carrying out such literature reviews and offers numerous examples of effective reviews.

Using Written Records and Documents

You can investigate many topics by examining the records or documents prepared by an organization for its own purposes. Suppose you plan to study an organization. Let's say it is a neighborhood community organization. Well, such an organization will probably have minutes of its meetings; it may have some founding charter under which it was organized; it is also likely to have a clipping file of articles that appeared in the local newspapers; it may well have a newsletter describing its activities; it will have files of correspondence, memos sent between different members of the organization. There may also be copies of studies that the organization, or others, have done about some aspect of their work. Can you get access to these materials? The best way to find out is to ask. Minutes from meetings may be considered public or

private. Probably records from the past will be more available to see than current records.

Many researchers need to gather information from government documents. Specific laws may need to be examined, proceedings of Congress, policies of government agencies. Various bodies of the government collect data and analyze them for many reasons. Some of these were suggested above in the discussion of government data. If your subject touches a professional field—say medicine, law, or teaching— you may want to look at materials from the professional associations of these organizations, such as the American Medical Association, the American Bar Association, or the National Education Association. Organizations such as these tend to have research departments which carry out various studies; they often have newsletters or other informational publications which will mention the ongoing research.

Talking to Informed Others

One of the best ways to intensify your knowledge about a topic is to talk to "people in the know." But who are these people? There are three categories to consider. The first group are relevant researchers, those who have studied topics similar to your own. The second are insiders, participants in the very field which you are studying. The third are intellectual comrades, people with whom you talk easily and fruitfully about your ideas.

Relevant Researchers. Many students move into areas of research similar to those of the professors with whom they study. This is a logical thing to do. In graduate school, students generally choose to work with faculty members whose ideas interest them. As an undergraduate, you may select courses, attend lectures, and try to get to know professors whose ideas you find exciting and stimulating. If you know a professor who has done research in the area of your topic for study, go speak to her or him. (Let me repeat how receptive most faculty members are to talking to students interested in their research.) If you can read an article by the faculty member, or hear a lecture about the research before speaking to the person, you will be a better conversationalist. Remember, researchers may get ideas from students as well. Don't feel shy to try out your ideas on the faculty member. Does the topic sound plausible? What problems might you run into? Are there particularly important studies that you should look up? If the conversation goes well, you might ask the professor whether you could show him or her your proposal for the project once you have it drafted.

Insiders.   If you will be investigating a topic that may require a field study or if you plan to study an organization, an institution, a neighborhood, a special event, or an ethnic group, you should seek out members of your subject group to see if they are willing to give you the "inside scoop." These informants can provide you with a basic knowledge about the nature of life in that institution, or wherever. Now, as you know, insiders do not necessarily have an accurate picture of things, but they do have some picture, however slanted or biased. You will want to consider what they tell you in terms of who they are and what their role is in the social environment.

Recall from Chapter 1 how Kanter (1977) got some of her most salient information from certain people at Indsco who served as special confidants to her. In a formal setting, such as a business organization, you will need to be very discreet with the information which an insider offers to you and not pass it on to others. In short, you must generate trust in others in order for them to want to talk to you, and to get insiders to continue to talk to you, they must see you as trustworthy.

Intellectual Comrades.   All of us know people with whom we talk easily, people with whom we can discuss our ideas, our work. You should select one such person and pour out all your ideas about what you are planning to study and why, and let the person react however he or she might. Often such a discussion is best held in a casual environment, over a cup of coffee (or whatever). Tell this

person your major worry—why you think the study might fail. Then see if the person tries to reconvince you that your topic is a sound one. He or she should know you well enough to sense whether the topic sounds feasible given your abilities, your motivation, your other commitments. The very process of talking your ideas through with someone you are close to, someone who is creative and whose judgment you respect, will help you to formulate your ideas better. Because social research almost always involves *doing* something in the real world, the very processes of thinking about it are often enhanced through interaction, that is, talking it through with others rather than simply thinking it through on your own. Remember, talking about it is not a waste of time; it is the beginning of doing the research. And the most valuable talking you can do is with those with whom you talk most effectively.

TURNING A TOPIC INTO A RESEARCHABLE PROBLEM

Social research topics don't come neatly packaged as clearly defined subjects. Your very interest in the topic may lie in its complexity, in the myriad ways in which you can think about it. The best way to begin exploring a topic more systematically is to narrow it down to a researchable question or group of questions. This process of turning ideas into questions, and then refining these questions until you have a research problem, involves a lot of trial and error. I will suggest the course you might follow in doing this.

First: Consider the Most Problematic Aspects of the Topic

Think of all the most troubling aspects of your topic. Where do the roadblocks seem to lie? Don't be afraid to immerse yourself in the problems of the topic until you think the topic seems the most "undoable" you could imagine. Then, try to pull out the central problem that underlies the whole issue. In the study I carried out on the effect of college on black students, I had felt beaten down by a whole variety of concerns. For example, could I study this if I were not black? What was I really trying to find out?

The central issue that came forth was: What, in fact, were black students getting from their efforts to achieve a higher education? I felt convinced (perhaps naively) that the real goal of a college education was more than a credential, more than a lot of information which you learned. It was the development of a kind of self-consciousness, an ability to reflect on yourself, your world, so that you could think, read, talk about ideas with a freshness, an openness, a sophistication not characteristic of those who have not been asked to consider ideas carefully. I found this an interesting question to pose about black students in white colleges, because there seemed to be several possible outcomes of that experience. On the one hand, they might be disadvantaged in achieving this autonomy if, as outsiders, they were unable to fully partake of their college environment. On the other hand, the potential culture shock which a predominantly white college might create for them could help to develop the kind of self-consciousness and ability to see things from a multiplicity of viewpoints which is the essence of autonomy.

Second: Define the Aim of the Project

The aims of a research project will vary with what can be accomplished by the study. Babbie (1992, pp. 90–92) suggests three general purposes of any research project. Many field studies map largely unknown territories. There may be very few guidelines in pursuit of such a problem, though there is usually a lot of advice. When a project addresses largely uncharted areas, its aim is to *explore*. A good exploration of a topic may provide a wealth of material for others to think about. When a project seeks to carefully detail evidence so that a clearer picture can be seen and therefore a firmer understanding of its topic can be gained, its aim is to *describe*. When a project sets out to test some specific idea—to see under

what conditions a phenomenon will increase or decrease, whether it will matter more or matter less—its aim is to *explain*.

One way to tell what your aim is in studying a topic is to think about what you would like to be able to report on once the project is completed. Do you want to say why something occurs (to explain)? Do you want to carefully and thoroughly show the state of the situation you are studying (to describe)? Do you want to uncover some new knowledge or some new idea which may excite or surprise others (to explore)?

Third: State the Topic as a Series of Questions

Jot down all the questions that your topic poses. It is best to express these concerns in the form of questions, because questions demand answers. And thinking of your study as a question (or a set of questions) to be answered will propel you to the next stage of thinking, namely, how you will go about answering your questions. Once the questions have been set down, try to write an answer to each one. This is, in a way, both the beginning and end of a research project. The methods apply to the middle. For each question posed, indicate what would need to be known (what data would need to be collected and analyzed) to try to answer the question.

Now look at the different questions. Which one do you think the study you envision would be best able to address? Is there a second question which the study might also pose? Could it be combined with the first question and thereby strengthen the focus of the study?

Fourth: Set Up a Hypothesis Based on One Alternative Answer

If the aim of the study is explanation, a research question can usually be the basis for establishing a number of hypotheses. Each hypothesis sets out one possible answer to the research question as the stated expectation to be studied. For example, the research question

Do commuter students participate less in extracurricular activities on campus?

could be the basis for this hypothesis:

If commuter students spend less time on campus than residential students, then commuters will have lower rates of participation in campus extracurricular activities than students living on campus.

The hypothesis sets up a prediction to be tested which is logically derived from the research question. The research question merely poses the subject of interest.

In the study of black college students, the research question was

Are black students from segregated high schools (susceptible to experiencing culture shock in a predominantly white college) more likely to undergo a change in attitudes than black students coming from integrated high schools?

One of the potential answers to the research question is used to form the hypothesis:

If black students are in a more racially diverse environment in college (a potentially culturally shocking environment) than they were in high school, then they would be more likely to have changes in attitude (as a result of their culture shock) than black students coming from racially diverse high schools.

The variables here are the differences in racial composition of the high school and college and the attitude change occurring over a period of time at college. More simply, the hypothesis would state:

Black students from segregated high schools would be expected to have greater attitude change in a predominantly white college than those from integrated high schools.

Note that once a hypothesis is formulated, the agenda for the study is determined: the researcher has clarified what data will be needed and how the variables will have to be related. In short, the direction of the study is established by posing a hypothesis. It should be added that studies are often guided by many different hypotheses or by alternative hypotheses. Recall that Hirschi's study of delinquency compared three alternative theories of delinquency by testing different hypotheses derived from the theories.

REASONS FOR STUDYING THE TOPIC

Once your topic is selected, and the research question (or hypothesis) has been posed, you should consider your rationale for the study. Looking back to Chapter 3, you might think over what purpose will be served by the topic of the study. Now that the research question is defined, you are able to think through the research design and determine what you will try to accomplish by carrying out this study.

As stated above, the aims of social research are generally of three types: exploration, description, or explanation. If you are helping to clarify a largely undefined area, your aim is exploratory. Your observations and analyses of these data should add to earlier, related efforts of study. If your study is descriptive, it may expand the body of work in this area. Your study may repeat an older study, in which case it is referred to as a *replication study*. This is a very honorable practice in all the sciences, and one you might consider. Replication studies can also test hypotheses. If your study is based on a hypothesis, the object of your study is to test this hypothesis. Thus, studies based on hypotheses have as their aim explanation. Since a hypothesis is based on a theory, or explanation of some relationship, hypothesis testing can either add to a theory or challenge it. Explanatory studies may develop or alter theories. Descriptive and exploratory studies may also add to or detract from theories. While the evidence from an exploratory field study may not be able to fully refute a theory, it may offer data that could seriously challenge a theoretical explanation. Finally, social research projects may lead to the forming of new theories. In such a case, if the study can account for why a relationship occurs, then this explanatory study is building theory.

WHOM OR WHAT TO STUDY— THE UNITS OF ANALYSIS

Generally, before a topic is fully clarified, the researcher has in mind the type of subjects he or she will need to study. Most commonly, social researchers take individuals as their subjects. Remember, however, that people are not the only subjects of study in social research. You may study groups, programs, organizations, larger communities (states, nations), artifacts, as well as individuals. These social entities whose social characteristics are the focus of the study would be the units of analysis. They are the collection of "things" that will be studied. Box 4-3 gives examples of studies that would be based on each type of unit of analysis.

Depending on the research question posed, a more or less specific set of subjects may be suggested. Some research questions can be answered only with a probability sample representative of the population of subjects to whom the findings refer. For example, if your research question is to ask whether auto accident deaths in the United States are largely caused by drunken drivers, then your data must represent those auto accidents nationwide. A study of the auto accidents in your community would not answer this question, nor would the driving patterns of teenage youths in a local high school. Note that data from these two examples might be able to address interesting research questions, but they would not provide evidence bearing on the question as posed above.

Often there needs to be an act of balancing the kinds of subjects you can feasibly study against the research question you wish to address. In some

cases, the question may need to be restated. However, don't restrict your scope too much in considering a set of subjects for study. Start by defining the very best set of subjects you could imagine in the best of all possible worlds (that's the world in which everything is possible!). That way, you will have the characteristics of the sample which are both desirable and necessary fully laid out. Now ask yourself which of these characteristics are absolutely essential to you in answering your research question. Are there some qualities which would be a bonus to your study but which would not be absolutely vital to its success? In short, separate the clearly essential from the advantageous but nonessential qualities.

Remember that if you use already collected data (census data or survey data), you should read the materials that explain how these samples were formed to be sure that they represent the populations you want to address. (Chapter 6 will address sampling techniques and strategies in detail.) Even if you plan to carry out a field study of a single case, you will in effect be studying some sample of some population. The problem here is that the definition of the sample and of the population may never be fully clear. You must ask yourself who the people you observe represent. In Jelly's Bar, described in Chapter 1, the men represented black, largely unemployed, urban residents. While they were observed in Chicago, they might well have been characteristic of similar men in other large metropolitan areas. Although this study was clearly of a particular bar, the choice of the bar was seen as somehow representative of bars and city hangouts in the ghetto areas of large cities in general.

My study of black college students in predominantly white colleges included only two colleges (ones to which I had access). I clearly could not assume that my findings would be generalizable to the nation as a whole. I had to recognize the particular qualities of the colleges studied. They were both in an urban area. One was largely a commuter college, the other residential. One was a state institution, the other private. I also needed to consider the proportion of black students in each

BOX 4-3

EXAMPLES OF DIFFERENT UNITS OF ANALYSIS

INDIVIDUALS

Most studies in the social sciences address individuals. Hirschi's study of delinquency took as its primary units of analysis delinquent and non-delinquent boys. Even when individual measures are aggregated to form group scores, the units of analysis would be individuals.

GROUPS

Social researchers are often interested in studying groups such as gangs. A study comparing the type of leader-member interaction or the degree of centralization of leadership would use a measure of a group process as a characteristic of the group. These would be different from Hirschi's effort where individual delinquency acts were the primary unit under analysis.

PROGRAMS

Evaluation research (to be discussed in Chapter 11) generally has programs as the units to be analyzed. The income maintenance experiment described in Chapter 1 had individuals as the units of analysis. However, if a study had compared a number of different income-maintenance programs in terms of their financial advice services, and the financial services were measured by funds spent on financial counselors, the units of analysis would be the programs themselves.

ORGANIZATIONS OR INSTITUTIONS

In Coleman's survey of public and private schools, when comparisons were made on students within schools, the units of analysis were individuals. When comparisons were made of qualities of the schools (resources), the units were the schools. The important thing to remember here is that if the variables being analyzed from the organization are based on aggregated data of individuals, the units of analysis are individuals. It is when the variables are based on measures of the organization or institution that are not reducible to individuals (such as resources, finances, or physical and structural characteristics of the organization) that the units of analysis will be the organization.

COMMUNITIES, STATES, NATIONS

Political scientists are likely to use communities, states, or nations as their units of analysis. In their classic cross-national study of political participation and attitudes, Almond and Verba (1963) compared Italians, Britons, Germans, Mexicans, and Americans in terms of such factors as their levels of political information, membership in voluntary associations, and a subjective sense of "competence" (when an individual believes that he or she can have political influence, p. 181). Using nation-states as the units of analysis, Almond and Verba were able to show the distinctiveness of the American and British sense of political competence.

ARTIFACTS

Content analysis, to be described in Chapter 10, often takes artifacts as its units of analysis. Artifacts may be analyzed at the individual or aggregate level. What this generally refers to is that cultural items (such as pictures, newspaper articles, songs, television advertisements, short stories) are selected and their contents compared using a set of criteria.

---

college: Was it higher or lower than the national average for black students in colleges? Did it differ appreciably from the proportion of black residents in the areas studied? In the nation as a whole?

It was also important to assess how representative the particular black students I studied were of black students at the colleges studied (in terms of social background, academic aptitude, earlier educational experience—especially whether their prior education had been in segregated or integrated schools). Then I could also see where the black students I studied fit among black students nationwide. Were they unique in some ways? Were they quite typical of black students attending colleges with few black students? This kind of thinking, which tries to place the subjects you plan to study in a larger framework in order to understand who they represent, must be done in the early stages of the project design.

The Twin Traps: The Ecological Fallacy and Reductionism

Although data representing individual units of analysis can be aggregated into group units if this is desired, once the units of analysis have been determined for a particular analysis, it is important to fix them clearly in mind as the analysis progresses. Often there is a tendency to move from one unit of analysis to another. This is a particular problem in the analysis stage when the findings of the study are discussed. Nevertheless, it is essential to consider these potential traps when you are designing your study so that you can select a unit of analysis which will meet your later analytic requirements.

Let me give you an example. Suppose you want to be able to discuss the causes of illegal drug use. You have the rate of drug use by state, and you have the per capita income level. Let's say that you note that those states with the higher rates of drug use also have higher per capita income. Aha! You conclude this to mean that rich people are more often drug users. Such a conclusion would be an example of the ecological fallacy. You do *not* have evidence on the incomes of the individuals who use drugs, which would be required to draw a conclusion like this. It could well be that it is the poor people in the "richer" states who are more frequently drug users. You have committed the ecological fallacy by taking data analyzed at the state (or group) level and applying these findings to the individual level. Hence, an *ecological fallacy* occurs when evidence from a group level of analysis is used to reach conclusions about individuals.

Let's take another example. Suppose you are studying high school dropout rates. You find that dropout rates are higher in school districts where there are lower proportions of intact families. Can you conclude that children from single-parent families are more likely to be high school dropouts? No, not on the evidence you have. Doing so would be another example of the ecological fallacy, because it could be that in areas that have fewer intact families, it is the students from homes with both parents who drop out. You cannot reach conclusions about individuals (in this case, dropouts) using evidence from a group level (in this case, family patterns in communities). In short, data based on group-level units of analysis should never be used to reach conclusions about individuals, because such a practice may lead to incorrect conclusions.

Reductionism (the tendency to reduce complex social phemomena to a single cause) is in some cases the reverse of the ecological fallacy, since it may involve drawing conclusions about the behavior of groups on the basis of evidence regarding individuals. A common example of reductionism is to use individual personality measures to explain the behavior of groups. Consider these conclusions: (1) Nazism took over in Germany because German boys hated their fathers; (2) The stock market crashed in 1929 because of the sexual looseness of people in the 1920s; (3) American women have attained so few elected offices because they have lower self-esteem than men. In each case, a group-level occurrence is being reduced to an explanation at the individual level. Complex phenomena like the rise of Nazism, the stock market crash, and the election of officials in the United States probably cannot be reduced to the effect of an individual attribute (hating fathers, sexual behavior, or women's self-esteem), even though such an attribute might be a factor in explaining them. There are surely other factors that need to be considered.

Explaining social phenomena solely in terms of individual psychological characteristics is a kind of *psychological reductionism*. Another common form of reductionism is *economic reductionism,* or the tendency to explain social phenomena purely in economic terms. In this case, Nazism might be explained as the result of inflation in post–World War I Germany, the stock market crash as the result of capitalist accumulation without reinvestment, and the sparsity of female elected officials as the result of the economic dependency of women. While these may or may not be important factors in explaining the particular phenomena, it is overly simplistic to reduce such phenomena to a single cause or to try to account for all phenomena in terms of a single kind of explanation.

TIME DIMENSION OF THE STUDY

Once a research topic is defined, you need to determine the time frame in which the study will be carried out. The first set of questions to be considered are: What period of time does the study question address? Will a present time frame be sufficient? Does the study need to make projections into the future? Does it need to take into account material from the past? The second set of questions concern the time period over which you will do the study: Will all the observations be carried out during roughly the same period? Or will you plan to make observations at different points in time?

Period of Time Addressed by the Study

Almost all social research projects take into account some elements of the past. What you are now studying was probably not established the first day you showed up on the project. Thus there is a general need to get some background information about the setting (the group, the organization, the neighborhood) you are studying. All social researchers must also in some ways be historians. As such, they must abide by the norms of historians which require that they respect the past and try to interpret it accurately. (Chapter 10 will describe historical research methods.)

If you are studying an organization, there are records, as mentioned earlier, which can be used to offer evidence of the past. Of course, informants may also be interviewed. But, generally speaking, written records made at the time that is under consideration are more accurate than the memories of those who were there. (This, of course, is not always the case; records may have been written to be deliberately misleading, and some individuals have very good memories.) It must be kept in mind that any source of information regarding the past will have some biases. An individual's memories will tend to revolve around his or her participation in the event, and as a result, the person may see that area as more central. Written records may be biased by the views of the recorder or by those of the person in power who may have gone over the minutes (or the newsletter copy) to edit out materials that were considered harmful to the purposes of the organization. Thus it is important to keep in mind that materials from the past must not be taken as pure facts; they are also interpretations made at the time, and they may also include some distortions and half-truths. One of the best ways to get a fuller understanding of the past is to see different types of records or to interview several persons who played different roles in the organization you are studying. This diverse data gathering may help to build up some elements of a picture about which there is a lot of agreement.

If your subjects are individuals, they have pasts as well. Almost all surveys elicit information about some aspects of the respondents' pasts. The information sought is usually about the family of origin (its socioeconomic status, the number of siblings in the family, the region of the country in which the individual grew up, religious affiliation, etc.); but it may also include evidence about schooling, peers, or activities engaged in during childhood and youth.

A content analysis study (to be described in Chapter 10) may have as its dataset a collection of magazines (or other materials) from different periods of time, from which the researcher hopes to extract patterns of meaning. Such studies have clear historical time frames. A study of current television commercials, however, would have a present time frame. For the study to have any lasting relevance, the researcher should offer some introductory general description both of the time in which it was carried out and of what was happening in the society during this time which might help to explain these advertisements.

Time Frame in Which the Study Is Carried Out: Cross-Sectional or Longitudinal

There are two major ways to set a study in time. From one point of view, the study may be considered as occurring in a single period of time (though it rarely is completed in a day or even in a week). Such onetime studies are referred to as cross-sectional studies. The other possibility is that the study has two or more data collection periods which are set at different times for the specific purposes of studying changes that may or may not have occurred between these points in time. Such multiple-time studies are referred to as longitudinal studies.

Cross-Sectional Studies. In a *cross-sectional study,* whatever is being studied is being observed at a single point in time, as if a section of time were being cut out for observation. Perhaps a good comparison would be with a medical procedure such as a biopsy or an x-ray. These diagnostic procedures are done at a specific point in time to discover the state of the body at that moment (from which it is possible to infer what has happened to the body previously to bring it to its current state). It is possible, of course, that they may detect signs that help predict what may happen in the future.

A cross-sectional study can accomplish the aim of exploration or description. It can also be used for explanatory studies since background information and retrospective data can be related to current statuses, and current statuses to future expectations and aspirations. Studies that aim to describe the current state of something—the reading abilities of eighth-graders in a city, for example—

usually have a cross-sectional time frame. (However, it is very characteristic of such studies to compare these scores with those of last year, which then gives them a longitudinal time frame.)

Longitudinal Studies. In a *longitudinal study,* data are collected at more than one point in time. There are three primary types of longitudinal study designs: *trend studies,* which compare data across time intervals on different subjects; *cohort studies,* which compare data on subjects across time whose age differences parallel the time intervals (so that 15- to 19-year-olds in 1960 are compared to 25- to 29-year-olds in 1970); and *panel studies,* which compare changes in the same subjects as they occur across time. Let's consider as an example a national survey of drug use. The simplest design would be to survey people once and report on these findings; this would be cross-sectional. The three longitudinal designs would be characterized by the qualities described below.

Trend study. The data from this year's national survey of drug usage could be set against data from the last 5, 10, or more years. In this way, comparisons could be made across time. This is the basis of a *trend study,* in which similar data collected in different years (and on different subjects) are compared. However, the national sample selected for study this year would not be the same as that selected last year, 5 years ago, or whenever. Thus if there were a reporting of higher drug use this year, we could not say for certain that this was due to an increase in drug usage, because it might only mean that our sample this year tended to draw disproportionately on drug users. Such changes may come about because of the effects of factors such as migrating and mortality, which produce differences in samples across time. Nevertheless, data from more than one time point can, across time, offer strong evidence of changing trends.

Cohort study. A cohort is a group of persons who were born within the same time period. A *cohort study* is one in which the subjects are grouped by their ages for comparative purposes. Sometimes we refer to such groups as generations. We would refer to those born in the 1930s as depression-era babies. We also often refer to groups who participated in a historical event; those who were young men and women during World War I are part of the war generation. Note that in this example, such war generation individuals would have been born approximately 20 years before the war.

We are also familiar with referring to the 1960s as a special era. But *who* was the generation of the 1960s? Those born in the 1950s, who were growing up in the 1960s; those born in the 1940s, who were young adults in the 1960s; or those born during the 1960s, who are the 1960s cohort? Probably we consider those born in late 1940s and early 1950s, who were young adults and teenagers in the 1960s, as being most characteristic of the 1960s generation.

Cohorts are usually studied not in the time period in which they are formed, during their birth years, but at a future time. Furthermore, they are usually studied comparatively with an earlier or later cohort. But what should form the confines of a cohort? Often instead of specifying the birth years to form a cohort, age groups are used.

Returning to the example of a study on drug users, the data for such a study would probably be given within age groups. Let's say it was reported in terms of age groups: 15–19, 20–24, 25–29, 30–34, 35–39, etc. Assume that a similar study was done five years ago: those who were in the 15–19 age group five years ago would now be in the 20–24 age group, those in the 20–24 age group five years ago would now be in the 25–29 age group, and so on. If comparisons were made within these age cohorts, there would be somewhat greater evidence upon which to base conclusions about change. Remember, however, that the 20–24 age group cohort is *not* made up of the same individuals as the 15–19 age group studied five years ago.

Assume that five years ago, 10 percent of the 15–19 age group reported using cocaine, but now 15 percent of the 20–24 age group report such usage: this suggests that among that age cohort of the population there has been an increase. (Now, there could still be various explanations for this. Perhaps the older group has more access to the finances needed to buy this expensive commodity. However, you still could not be sure whether the earlier users were continuing their habit and being joined by others or whether the earlier users had dropped it and the current group consisted of earlier nonusers.) Cohort studies emphasize qualities of age groups over time.

Panel study. One of the best ways to measure change is to study the same people over time. You first sample a group at one point in time and then return at a later time to ask the same questions again. Then by bringing together the responses of the subjects, you can see whether a characteristic or attitude continues or whether it is taken up, and dropped, over time. This is a *panel study,* one in which the same group of respondents is followed up over time. You are in a much stronger position to try to relate this pattern (a change or a continuation) to other qualities of the individual. Panel studies lend themselves to much more rigorous forms of analysis than other types of studies.

In considering a panel study on drug use, data from a sample of junior high school students might be collected, then the respondents to this sample might be followed up both during and after high school. Following such a sample of respondents would not be easy. You might need access to school information to find out if the junior high school students you were looking for were currently in a particular high school. You would also want to ask the respondents themselves to provide their home addresses during the first survey so that you could locate them for later surveys.

The dataset that Coleman and his associates used for the public school–private school study was the first *wave* of a longitudinal panel study. It was a national sample of high school sophomores and seniors in 1980. These same students were then followed up in 1982, the second wave of the study, when the 1980 sophomores were then seniors and the 1980 seniors were two years beyond high school. A third follow-up was carried out in 1984 and a fourth in 1986. Note that by 1984, those 1980 seniors who had gone directly to college and stayed would be graduating; and by 1986, those 1980 sophomores who had gone to college in 1982 would be graduating.

Responses to the various surveys must be linked so that the responses from Mary Jones, who was a sophomore in 1980, are paired with her responses in 1982 when she was a senior, with her responses in 1984 when she completed a community college, and with her responses in 1986 when she was employed in a large organization. As stated above, such linked data on individuals provide excellent material for the study of change. One can study changes in attitudes and aspirations for the same persons over time as the individuals are exposed to different experiences and statuses across the course of life. In fact, a whole new interest in sociological research in the "life course" often depends on the analysis of panel datasets (a few of which have followed the same individuals from childhood to old age). Individual researchers rarely collect their own panel data, because it is time-consuming, expensive, and difficult to do. However, many fine panel datasets have been made available to researchers at modest costs.

PROPOSING A RESEARCH PLAN

Once a research problem has been formulated and subjects for a study have been determined, the actual means for carrying out the research project must be established. This is the proposal-writing stage of research when the overall plan for the project must be set out in logical order to see if it makes sense. For many researchers, the object of this proposal writing is to try to obtain a grant to cover the expenses of the study. Whether or not you are applying for a grant, writing a *research*

proposal should be useful. Using a method similar to one developed by Julian Simon (1969), I will lay out a series of stages that you must move through in order to complete a project. In describing how you will carry out each stage to meet the objectives of the research project, you write the research plan or proposal.

THE ELEVEN STEPS IN A RESEARCH PROJECT

Step 1: Define the Topic

In your proposal the research topic should be posed in such a way that it is clearly grounded in the general social field relevant to it. If you are studying alcoholism, you need to put your research question into a framework which suggests that you know something about alcohol consumption and abuse. If you are studying the effects of using computers in elementary schools, you should offer some preliminary information about the prevalence of such equipment in the schools and what it is used for, etc. In short, topics must be grounded in some already known factual information which is used to introduce the topic and from which the research question will stem.

Step 2: Find Out What Is Known about the Topic

The beginning of this chapter has suggested ways for you to immerse yourself in material relevant to the topic you want to study. Social research topics are usually embedded in so many different kinds of materials that the researcher must be careful to select the best materials to examine. While everyone goes down some blind alleys, you need to keep the central meaning of your topic in mind to guide you through your search of the literature in the field. It is also important to examine different types of materials where relevant—quantitative data interpretations, studies using various methods.

For the research proposal, you should refer to the most salient findings you have uncovered which seem to raise significant questions or which offer suggestions for avenues for you to follow for your project. You must be able to draw out these findings from the studies in which they are embedded and summarize them succinctly in such a way that someone unfamiliar with the study can easily grasp their meaning and importance. To help you to do this, you should look at the background literature review sections which generally come at the beginning of published research articles. Most of these reviews are very condensed; they extract a few salient points from numerous studies, summarizing them in a way that is relevant to the study in question.

Step 3: Clarify Concepts and Their Measurement

This will be the subject of Chapter 5. The discussion of the language of science in Chapter 2, as well as the conceptual stage of the research model developed in that chapter, are relevant to this step. Precision in conceptualization is critical in the social sciences, and it is not easy to achieve. Concepts like alcoholism, autonomy, juvenile delinquency, and tokenism may all seem to be familiar terms. However, the precise meanings you attach to these concepts must be defined, and then an appropriate way to measure concepts must be found or devised.

In the proposal, a clear definition of the main concept or concepts must be given. The general question of measurement should be discussed so that it is clear that the potential problems in measuring the concepts have been thoroughly thought out. These include two critical issues: *validity,* that is, whether the measurement of a concept in fact produces a result that truly represents what the concept is supposed to mean; and *reliability,* that is, whether the measurement would lead to consistent enough outcomes, were it to be repeated, that one could have some confidence in the results.

Step 4: Establish an Appropriate Data Collection Method

Chapter 1 considered a number of fine studies representing three primary means of data collection in the social sciences. Chapters 7 to 9 are devoted to explaining these methods in detail so that you can use them to design and carry out a survey based on questionnaires or interviews (Chapter 7), experiments in laboratory or natural settings (Chapter 8), and field methods using different types of observation techniques (Chapter 9). Chapter 10 describes different forms of what might be called data selection procedures for using data that have already been collected. In reading these chapters, remember that the same topic may often be studied with a variety of methods, and that the use of multiple methods is desirable in social research.

Kanter's study of Indsco was an example of a research project that used more than one method (questionnaires and interviews, as well as participant observation) in its design. In addition, she examined certain company records and other already available materials (company newsletters).

For the proposal, you must describe how you will collect data and which sources of available data you will actually use. Issues of access to the data are important to discuss. After all, you must be able to get the data you propose. If you anticipate problems in securing the desired data, these problems should be discussed and possible alternative sources of data might be suggested. Most studies have one central type of method to be used (a survey, an experiment), though they may also draw on a few other data sources to widen their scope.

You must also plan how you are going to analyze the data. Do you intend to compare women with men, to contrast one drug rehabilitation program with another, to explore the length of time spent in a shopping mall by the average shopper in terms of whether there is a difference between covered and out-of-doors malls? Such intentions require that the planned contrast be set into the sampling design. Will you have comparable samples of women and men? Which drug programs will you study? What shopping malls should be selected?

In addition, you need to consider which variables you plan to relate to one another. In Hirschi's study, he knew that he would need to measure sets of variables to test each of the theories he posed. So he had to select a data collection method that could get the data he needed.

Step 5: Operationalize Concepts and Design the Research Instruments

This refers to the "nuts and bolts" of the study. In a survey, the questionnaire or interview schedule is the operationalized survey. In an experiment, the operationalization of the independent variable is the actual stimulus. In field studies, this process of operationalizing occurs rather differently. It often must wait until the field notes have been gathered. Then the researcher may find evidence that suggests certain meanings, at which time conceptualizations are formed to describe and explain observations. To test whether the researcher is accurate, he or she may go back to the field to see if another instance of this operationalized concept occurs. Chapter 5 will address this subject.

Concepts are sometimes better measured using more than one indicator of the concept. Chapter 5 will also describe how measuring multiple indicators of a concept can strengthen your study. Developing indexes and scales to measure complex concepts, a topic to be addressed in Chapter 16, can help to accomplish this goal.

In a survey, how the concepts are operationalized in the questionnaire will determine what will be produced from the survey. If the concepts are poorly operationalized, the best national sample and the fanciest statistical routines will not make something useful of the data. In the proposal, the actual way that the concepts will be operationalized should be spelled out. If a survey is to be carried out, it is usually appended to the proposal. In addition, the critical questions that measure the most important concepts in the study should be discussed and their level of adequacy addressed.

Step 6: Select a Sample of Subjects to Study

The selection process for deciding what or whom you will study rests on a large body of thought about the nature of sampling. This subject will be addressed in Chapter 6. Remember that even if you study your parents, the residents of your block, or the dog next door, all of these represent elements in some type of sample. Many researchers want to be able to generalize their findings to subjects beyond those studied. When probability samples are used, it is possible to determine how representative your sample is of all the others out there (the population) who might have gotten into your study. Sampling plans may be very complex or quite straightforward. When the rules of probability are not followed and you merely select a sample of subjects who seem to fulfill the needs of your study, you have a nonprobability sample. For many studies, such a sample is sufficient; and for some, it is the best that can be achieved. Whatever the design of your sample, it needs to be explained in detail in your proposal. It should be so precise that someone else could generate a similar sample by following your procedures.

Step 7: Consider the Purpose, Value, and Ethics of the Study

Once the topic, the background, the clarification of concepts, and the major methods of data collection have been presented, it is time to address the purpose, value, and ethics of the study. In this book, discussion of these kinds of questions was deliberately presented early (in Chapter 3), before the discussion of concepts, measurement, or types of methods. This was done to help you think through how you would justify your study in terms of both its rationale and the ethical issues that it might raise. But in a proposal the study design must be presented before the rationale and ethical issues involved can be discussed. Remember that the rationale for doing the project will be accomplished only if the study is done well. By showing that you have devised a plan to study your topic that looks plausible and seems feasible, you reinforce the sense that the purpose will be achieved. The value of the project lies not only in what it alone will produce, but also in how it may add to or challenge other research in the area.

The ethical issues are often confronted in data collection, for example, in maintaining the confidentiality of the data, in gaining access to the field, and in avoiding deception as to the role of the researcher. If these will be major issues in your study, they should be addressed. Many universities and colleges require students to have their projects reviewed by a human subjects review committee. In any proposal seeking public funding, potential ethical issues are of great importance, and researchers who ignore such subjects may be penalized. Often it is necessary to complete special forms concerned with protection of human subjects. (This may be true for already collected data that you plan to use as well as for data you will collect.)

Step 8: Collect the Data

The separate chapters on the different methods (Chapters 7 to 11) will give many different types of procedures that might be followed. Each form of data collection has its special concerns which need to be considered fully before doing the study. This is why pretesting is so valuable, because it helps you to find and address potential problems before they enter your study and cause bigger problems.

For the proposal, the plans for collecting data should be described carefully. In a field project, it is always more difficult to be precise, and you may need to make changes once the field is entered. Nevertheless, it is better to have a clear plan that can be altered as you go along than only some vague ideas that subsequently you cannot be sure you have followed. For an experiment, data collection procedures can usually be described very precisely. This is also true of a survey. Mail surveys tend to have multiple stages in

the data collection procedure to increase the response rate. If you are using already available data, you need to describe at this stage how you will obtain the data.

Step 9: Process the Data

Once the data are collected, they must be put into a form which will enable them to be analyzed. If they are quantifiable data, you usually have to prepare them for the computer. If they are field notes, they must be organized and categorized. The chapters on the different methods each describe preliminary forms of data handling. Chapter 12 will examine how quantifiable data are processed.

In the proposal, a concise statement may be included to address this subject. It may describe what type of computer facilities are at the disposal of the researcher, what possible sources of assistance are available, and what efforts are being made to increase accuracy in the handling of the data. There are now some technological advances in data gathering which speed the process from data gathering to data entry. An example is the CATI (computer-assisted telephone interviewing) method—to be described in Chapter 7—now becoming quite common for telephone surveys. Interviewers call from a computer terminal, and answers to the questions are directly entered into the computer by the interviewer as they are given.

Step 10: Analyze the Data

How you plan to analyze the data must be thought through carefully while the study is being designed. It is true that once the data are collected, there may be some changes in these plans. Nevertheless, it is better to have a strategy that can be adapted than to end up with piles of data for which you have no organized plan. There are numerous analytic tools for studying quantifiable data. A number of these will be described in Chapters 13 and 14.

The proposal should indicate the analyses planned; it may suggest that some analytic strategies will depend on how earlier ones turn out. In a field study, only very preliminary plans will probably be possible.

Step 11: Present the Results

The data for an entire study may be collected, but the research is not complete until the results of the study have been written up. For research projects which are funded, final reports must be written. Most social research projects become the basis for articles, books, chapters in books, or unpublished papers offered at professional meetings. A single study may lead to many and varied types of publications and presentations. Chapter 17 will review how the results of a research project are assembled for presentation.

REVIEW NOTES

- Sources for finding research topics include printed sources (books, journals, magazines, newspapers), ongoing research projects, and already available datasets.
- Three criteria to use in making a final selection of a research topic are that it should be feasible to study, it should be of general interest to the researcher, and it should contribute in some way to a greater understanding of society.
- To intensify knowledge about a topic, consult a library, use other written records or documents, and talk to informed others.
- Other persons who may help to intensify knowledge about a research project are relevant researchers, who have worked on such projects; insiders, who are familiar with a field or subject; and intellectual comrades, who are the persons with whom the researcher can most easily and profitably talk.
- The four steps for turning a topic into a researchable problem are (1) consider its most problematic aspects, (2) define the aim of the project, (3) state the topic as a question (or series of questions), (4) develop a hypothesis as one (among many possible) alternative, hypothesized answer to the research question.
- The possible reasons for studying a topic are to explore a largely undefined area, to describe a social phenomenon, or to explain a hypothesized relationship. A study may be a replication of an earlier study to see whether the findings can be verified.
- The units of analysis in a study are the subjects to be studied. They include individuals, groups, programs, organizations and institutions, larger communities (states and nations), and cultural artifacts.
- Studies in which the data are gathered at a single point in time are called cross-sectional studies; those which gather data at multiple points are longitudinal studies.
- The three types of longitudinal studies are trend studies, in which data are compared across time points on different subjects; cohort studies, in which data on subjects from one age cohort (that is, individuals born within a certain period of time) are compared at different points in time; and panel studies, in which the same subjects are compared across time.
- The eleven steps of a research project are:

  1. Define a topic.
  2. Intensify knowledge about the topic.
  3. Clarify concepts and their measurements.
  4. Select a data collection method.
  5. Operationalize concepts and design the data collection instruments.
  6. Select a sample.
  7. Consider the purpose, value, and ethics of the study.
  8. Collect the data.
  9. Process the data.
  10. Analyze the data.
  11. Write up the results.

KEY TERMS

cohort studies
cross-sectional studies
ecological fallacy
longitudinal studies
panel studies
reductionism
research proposal
trend studies

STUDY EXERCISES

1. How might you turn the topic of college varsity athletes not graduating from college into a researchable problem for study? Go through the four steps: (1) list problematic aspects, (2) define your aim, (3) state your problem as a researchable question, and (4) develop a hypothesis.

2. Assume that you have defined a researchable topic to be that urban police are less satisfied with their jobs than police working in the suburbs. Briefly write out how you might carry out the next six steps (steps 2 to 8) of the research project.

3. What would be the best time dimension to use in designing (1) the college athletes study? (2) the police study?

RECOMMENDED READINGS

1. Bart, Pauline, and Linda Frankel: *The Student Sociologist's Handbook,* 2d ed., General Learning Press, Morristown, N.J., 1976. This very useful guidebook discusses library research and sources of data. Includes a glossary of statistical terms.

2. Cooper, Harris M.: *Integrating Research: A Guide for Literature Reviews,* 2d ed., Sage, Newbury Park, Calif., 1989. This volume defines integrative research, lays out the methods for carrying out such research, and offers many current examples of integrative reviews of social science research projects on varying topics.

3. Menard, Scott: *Longitudinal Research,* Sage, Newbury Park, Calif., 1991. Presenting longitudinal research designs in a nontechnical manner, this volume addresses common problems in data collection. Comparisons with cross-sectional designs are offered.

4. McMillan, Patricia, and James R. Kennedy, Jr.: *Library Research Guide to Sociology,* Pierian Press, Ann Arbor, Mich., 1981. A practical guide for finding and using resources in the library for a social research project. Includes very well developed illustrations of how to use particular reference works.

5. Reed, Jeffrey G., and Pam M. Baxter: *Library Use: A Handbook for Psychology,* American Psychological Association, Washington, 1983. This work considers how to define a topic, use psychology abstracting services, search for materials (including carrying out computer searches), and locate and appraise psychological tests and measures.

From Concepts to Operationalization to the Measurement of Variables

---
LOOKING AHEAD

This chapter tackles the central issue in the social sciences—measurement. The challenge has been to develop ways for measuring the abstract concepts which describe the human situation. Such measures become the variables in a social science study. Once measures are developed, it is necessary to establish that they actually measure what they purport to measure (that is, to determine their validity) and that they are consistent and repeatable (that is, to determine their reliability). The chapter clarifies differences between categorical and numerical variables, describes the four different levels of measurement, and presents variables that illustrate these four levels of measurement.

INTRODUCTION

*T*he object of this chapter is to introduce you to the central intellectual effort required by social research: How to move from abstract concepts to operational definitions and from operational definitions to the specification and measurement of variables. Once this process has been described in general terms, it will be illustrated and elaborated in some detail by an examination of how two very different abstract concepts came to be measured by social researchers. The reason for concentrating on a history of the development of the two measures is to help you to see what kinds of strategies may be employed when trying to develop operationally defined measures for abstract concepts. The two concepts were selected because (1) they represent different starting points in conceptualization (one, happiness, is a simple everyday term; the other, authoritarianism, a constructed term) and (2) because the types of instruments developed to measure these two concepts represent contrasting solutions to the measurement problem.

We will then move from this more specific discussion to a more general consideration of measurement, describing the central ways to assess the quality of measurement, namely, validity and reliability. In the course of the discussion on reliability, brief attention will be paid to classical test theory which underlies its meaning. Subsequently, the four different levels of measurement will be compared and explained. Finally, the measurement characteristics of six commonly used social research variables will be presented.

CONCEPTS

We use concepts all the time in everyday life. They are the abstract terms we employ to explain or make sense of our experience. Take a term like *happiness*. We learn at a relatively early age that happiness means the state of being happy. We also learn to use this term in evaluating experiences and phenomena which we perceive as making us happy (or unhappy). Thus, the term *happiness* represents a concept, or abstract idea, which we apply to particular situations.

But wait a minute. What is happiness? When did you last see it? Who has it? Where do you get it from? Can you get rid of it? How can you use a concept all the time that seems so vague and so difficult to define that it is not easy to think about it carefully? What would be a satisfying definition of this concept? John Stuart Mill, the English philosopher, suggested this kind of problem when he remarked that in asking ourselves whether we are happy we immediately cease to be so. In fact,

the happiness that we refer to all the time is not a concept which we could easily define.

In everyday life, of course, we rarely need to ask ourselves exactly what a concept like happiness means in general terms. It is usually enough for us to say (with Snoopy), "Happiness is . . . [a particular thing]"; in short, we don't often ask what happiness is apart from the things that make us happy. We simply use the term to describe or evaluate particular situations. While happiness is a psychological term related to a state of being or feeling, it is generally used to describe the results of social relationships among individuals or between individuals and groups or organizations.

This means that happiness is often the result of sociological occurrences. Our understanding of the concept develops as we improve our ability to relate it to particular phenomena. To say "I am happy" or "This makes me happy" refers to a specific piece of experience. It only makes sense, however, to describe particular experiences in this way because the idea of happiness logically implies the possibility of its opposite, namely, un-happiness. At the same time that we apply the concept to particular, concrete experiences, we are also relating it in an abstract way to other concepts. If happiness were not defined logically in relation to other concepts, it would simply make no sense for us to use it. In other words, a concept involves logical relations.

Now let's consider a more unusual concept, that of *authoritarianism.* This is not a term we use in everyday life. Instead, it is a concept that was developed by social scientists to explain a phenomenon which came to be recognized after World War II: the state of mind that disposed individuals to accept the kind of authoritarian regime that appeared most dramatically in Nazi Germany. In this case, a number of beliefs and opinions, which appeared to be logically connected to one another and to the kind of behavior the social scientists were trying to explain, were drawn together to form a single concept—authoritarianism.

The effort to make sense of things by deliberately constructing general concepts (which seems to be the correct way to describe the development of the concept of authoritarianism) may seem in some respects to be the converse of the way in which the concept of happiness is used. Happiness may seem to be part of our basic repertory of ideas, which can be singled out and applied in specific instances where appropriate, while authoritarianism may seem to be a much more technical and artificial invention. Remember, however, that in developing the concept of authoritarianism, social scientists were not just drawing their ideas out of thin air. They were reflecting on other related concepts and on the applicability of these concepts to particular phenomena in everyday life in order to develop a new concept which would more accurately capture the complex nature of the appeal of antidemocratic ideology.

OPERATIONALIZING DEFINITIONS

Our concern about whether we could define happiness occurred because happiness is a concept which refers not to a specific thing that can be seen or heard, but to an abstract idea that is not easy to put into general terms. In the philosophical study of the meaning and use of definitions, three types of definitions have been isolated: real definitions, nominal definitions, and operational definitions.

The aim of a *real definition* is to capture the ultimate or essential nature of the actual phenomenon in question. One example of a real definition might be the mathematical definition of a triangle as a three-sided figure. Outside the abstract realm of mathematics, however, philosophically real definitions may be sought after, but rarely achieved. We could, for example, define happiness as a feeling of well-being, but that would tell us very little about its ultimate nature or essence. From this perspective, Snoopy's definition of happiness—"Happiness is . . . [whatever]"—is an ironic commentary on the fact that a real definition of *happiness,* taken in the abstract, always seems to elude us.

When nineteenth-century English philosopher John Stuart Mill said, "By happiness is intended pleasure, and the absence of pain; by unhappiness, pain, and the privation of pleasure," he was providing not a real definition but a *nominal definition,* one that specified the meaning and components of the term for the purposes of rigorous philosophical inquiry. In practice we often think of happiness in positive terms, on the one hand, as the pleasure resulting from some form of good fortune and in negative terms, on the other hand, as an absence of problems (or pain). Both these aspects could be embraced in a definition of happiness as a feeling of well-being. If we decided to use Mill's definition, we would have established a nominal definition of happiness. Note that we would not have defined the essence of what happiness is, but we would have moved toward a working definition which is reasonably clear and precise.

As social researchers, however, we would not only want to develop a nominal definition of happiness. We would also want to develop a way of studying it. In other words, we would want to "operationalize" our definition; that is, we would want to develop an operational definition. How could we do this? One thing we could do would be to go back to our observation that there might be two qualities of happiness, the pleasurable feeling resulting from good fortune and the absence of problems (note that these are not the converse of each other, but two separate qualities). We would call these two different qualities the *dimensions* of the concept of happiness. How could we then explore these dimensions more fully? What empirical observations could we make in order to study the experience of happiness? In answering these questions, we would be trying to develop an *operational definition* of happiness—a definition that specifies ways of measuring the concept.

Let's take an example of a situation illustrating the positive dimension of pleasure resulting from the presence of good fortune. We might assume that someone who won a lot of money in a state lottery would have been presented with "good fortune." Suppose we see on television a group of people who have shared a large lottery prize. They are smiling, throwing their arms around each other, and they seem to be quite elated. Naturally, we assume that these winners are happy. But what if we wanted to measure *how* happy they are? What could we look for that would indicate their degree of happiness? We might observe the degree of their smiling, hugging, or other behavior indicating the *depth* of their happiness. Or we might question them and find out just how much they think their winnings will matter in changing their economic situations (in altering their fortunes). From efforts like these, we might conclude that the winners were very happy, or quite happy, or not so happy. Of course, in making this judgment, we would in effect be comparing their behavior with the behavior we would expect from similar winners in similar situations.

Notice that in observing these winners, we have identified a number of actions or behaviors that we are prepared to accept as *indicators* (that is, measurable evidence) of how happy the winners are. In social research terms, we have operationalized the good fortune *dimension* of our definition of happiness by identifying indicators of it. We have used variations in these indicators, such as the degree of smiling, as measures of the winners' degree of happiness, and we have done so by implicitly comparing what we have seen in this case with what we would expect to have seen in others. Of course, there might be some variation among the winners in their degree of happiness, and if we observed other winners of big lotteries, we might find more or less similar reactions, which we would then label as indicators of happiness.

If some winners are ill or have some other personal problems, for example, they might be unable to respond to winning the lottery with as much happiness as winners without such problems. To appreciate more fully how happy the lottery winners are, we might also want to ask them about the absence or presence of problems in their lives. These indicators of the second dimension of happiness (the absence of pain or problems) would reinforce our sense that what we were labeling as happiness *really* was happiness. In such cases, if we had evidence on both the presence of good fortune and the absence of problems, we would have *multiple indicators* of happiness. (Later in the chapter, when we discuss reliability of measures, we will see that multiple indicators make the measurement instrument more likely to have higher reliability or consistency.) The more complex a concept is, the more desirable it is to have multiple indicators, since they are more likely to cover all the dimensions of the concept.

Let's recapitulate our discussion of the concept of happiness. First, we started with John Stuart Mill's definition of happiness as the presence of pleasure and the absence of pain (a nominal definition). Then, we recognized that this definition distinguished two separate dimensions of the concept of happiness. Next, we operationalized the definition by taking each of the dimensions of the concept—the feeling of pleasure deriving from good fortune, and the absence of pain or problems—and looked for actions or behaviors to serve as indicators of them. (Of course, concepts do not necessarily have two dimensions. They may be unidimensional—they may have only one dimension—or they may be multidimensional—they may have a number of dimensions.)

Finally, we observed variation in the measurement of the indicators which suggested that happiness occurs in varying degrees. In social research terms, this means that we moved from happiness as a concept to happiness as a *variable*. Let's say that we wanted to go one step further and ask what other differences there were between winners who appeared to be "very happy" (as measured by our indicators) and those who appeared to be "pretty happy." In that case we would be using happiness as a measured variable, and we would be asking how variation in this variable might be related to variation in another variable (which would have to be defined and measured by the same process of *operationalization*).

OPERATIONALIZATION AND MEASUREMENT

In considering how one might operationalize the concept of happiness, we have talked about the example of a group of people winning a lottery. We suggested that if one were to do a study of lottery winners like this, one might try to measure such indicators as the expression of their joy and the absence of overriding problems. This would be a pretty good way of measuring happiness if one were only interested in studying lottery winners. Social scientists, however, would probably want to look for a more general way of operationalizing the concept of happiness, one that could apply to a wide range of particular circumstances. For this reason, I would now like to turn from the hypothetical example we have been using to a real attempt to operationalize happiness in a social-scientific study.

Measuring Happiness

When Norman Bradburn and David Caplovitz at the National Opinion Research Center (NORC) undertook a project in the mid-1960s to measure

the concept of happiness in a survey, their efforts were met with some ridicule. At some level, the idea that social scientists can measure a concept like happiness seems ludicrous. How could one possibly measure so "personal and subjective a phenomenon"? Bradburn and Caplovitz decided upon a very straightforward approach: to ask people directly how happy they were.

They did not join the scores of philosophers who have pondered the true meaning of the concept of happiness. Instead, avoiding the potential hang-up of trying to think through precisely what happiness is, they took a shortcut through the philosophical discussion to find a way of getting at a measure of happiness. In the language which we have used so far, Bradburn and Caplovitz first decided to use a respondent's self-report as an indicator of happiness. Then they had to work out a way of measuring variation in that indicator. They did this by devising a series of categorical responses to the question "Are you happy?" (Actually they dressed the question up a little bit by asking, "Taking all things together, how would you say things are these days?"). Then they simply gave the respondents the option of replying that they were "very happy," "pretty happy," or "not too happy."

Once they had happiness measured, the researchers could examine the other qualities of those who were more or less happy. In other words, Bradburn and Caplovitz were able to relate the response to the happiness question, their dependent variable, to a host of other factors. In the discussion of validity later in the chapter, the efforts taken by Bradburn and Caplovitz to validate their measure of happiness will be considered.

Measuring Authoritarianism

Earlier in this chapter, I talked about authoritarianism as a concept developed by social scientists to try to make sense of the appeal of antidemocratic ideas. The concept was formulated by members of the Institute for Social Research established in Frankfurt, Germany, in 1923. Forced into exile with the rise of Hitler in 1933, the researchers came to the United States and continued their work, first at Columbia University in New York and later at the University of California at Berkeley. Their efforts led to a series of studies of prejudice (anti-Semitism and ethnocentrism) conducted by T. W. Adorno, in collaboration with a team of psychologists and social scientists at Berkeley. This research culminated in the well-known work *The Authoritarian Personality* (1969; originally published in 1950).

In thinking about prejudiced attitudes such as anti-Semitism and ethnocentrism (the dogmatic tendency to glorify one's own group and cast aspersions on other groups), the authors thought they saw a common feature in all the different types of prejudice they studied: a more general, unquestioning belief in authority, to which they gave the name *authoritarianism.*

What were the dimensions of this new concept? The researchers came to define nine attitudes as the *dimensions* of authoritarianism. Defining these dimensions involved thinking about a whole series of attitudes that might be associated with the concept and examining their relationship to one another. This process would enable the researchers to establish a comprehensive operational definition of authoritarianism which logically seemed to fit the abstract concept of authoritarianism.

Having identified the dimensions of their new concept, the researchers next had to develop ways of measuring them. A group led by Daniel J. Levinson, a psychologist on the research team, prepared a series of statements expressing the attitudes in each dimension, so that respondents could be asked to express their level of agreement or disagreement. Different groups of statements therefore served as the *indicators* of each dimension. Take the statement "Young people sometimes get rebellious ideas, but as they grow up they ought to get over them and settle down." Under which dimension do you think it would fall? Since it refers to the giving up of rebellious or unpopular ideas as the proper thing for a mature person to do, it suggests approval of giving in to those in control.

THE DIMENSIONS OF AUTHORITARIANISM AS MEASURED BY THE F-SCALE

The nine dimensions include:

1. *Conventionalism:* Rigid adherence to conventional, middle-class values.
2. *Authoritarian submission:* Submissive, uncritical attitude toward idealized moral authorities of the group.
3. *Authoritarian aggression:* Tendency to be on the lookout for, and to condemn, reject, and punish people who violate conventional values.
4. *Anti-intraception:* Opposition to the subjective, the imaginative, the tender-minded.
5. *Superstition and stereotypy:* The belief in mystical determinants of the individual's fate; the disposition to think in rigid categories.
6. *Power and toughness:* Preoccupation with dominance-submission, strong-weak, leader-follower dimension; identification with power figures; overemphasis on the conventionalized attributes of the ego; exaggerated assertion of strength and toughness.
7. *Destructiveness and cynicism:* Generalized hostility, vilification of the human.
8. *Projectivity:* The disposition to believe that wild and dangerous things go on in the world: the projection outward of unconscious emotional impulses.
9. *Sex:* Exaggerated concern with sexual "goings-on."

Source: T. W. Adorno et al.: *The Authoritarian Personality,* Harper & Row, New York, 1950 (Norton, 1969), pp. 255–257.

Thus agreement with this statement was considered an indicator of *authoritarian submission.*

Similarly, agreement with the statement "A person who has bad manners, habits, and breeding can hardly expect to get along with decent people" was seen as an indicator of *conventionalism.* Notice that the statement was written in a way that placed a high value on getting along with other people and gave this desire for conformity a moralistic quality by using such loaded terms as "bad" and "decent." (It may seem a little humorous to you, because attitudes like good breeding are no longer taken as seriously as they were in the 1950s, but think about how brilliantly the statement was devised in order to tap underlying attitudes without making them too explicit. I will say more later on about the art of devising good items like this.)

Working in this way and testing the effectiveness of different statements as they went along, the researchers eventually agreed upon a set of statements for each dimension to represent the overall concept of authoritarianism. The respondent's level of agreement or disagreement with each statement was measured on a seven-point scale from +3 (strongly agree) to −3 (strongly disagree). The total score, based on averaging the scores for all the statements, then became the measure of the respondent's degree of authoritarianism.

This way of operationalizing and measuring authoritarianism was called the *F-Scale* (Fascism Scale) by its inventors. It became one of the most widely used and most influential attitudinal measures ever developed. One of the fascinating things about the F-Scale is that it played such a large role in the development of other measures of complex concepts in social psychology. Unsatisfied with certain aspects of how the concept of authoritarianism had been operationally defined, a stream of other researchers moved out to develop new measures that reflected variations from or refutations of the original concept. In this continuing process of operationalization, the concept itself was refined and redefined.

Comparing the Measurement of Authoritarianism to the Measurement of Happiness

If we compare the efforts to measure authoritarianism with those to measure happiness, we see a

very interesting contrast. Happiness is a commonplace concept that everyone uses all the time and no one bothers to define. In fact, happiness is such an abstract concept that it would be extremely hard to define it in any satisfactory way. What did Bradburn and Caplovitz do with this abstract concept? They merely took the concept as largely given, and operationalized an indicator by asking persons to report how happy they were. In other words, they greatly simplified the concept-to-operationalization phase and moved swiftly to the operationalization-to-measurement phase.

In comparison, the operationalization of the concept of authoritarianism was a much more complex matter. Adorno and his colleagues virtually invented the concept of authoritarianism (which was not used in everyday life) as a means of measuring the underlying dynamics of prejudice. They then defined the concept operationally by developing a set of indicators to represent what they had defined as the various dimensions of authoritarianism. This operationalized concept, developed first as a measure of the potential for antidemocratic ideology, came to be applied more widely and diversely to different types of social situations and experiences. Thus, for Adorno and his colleagues, the concept-to-operationalization phase was central to their efforts. The operationalization-to-measurement phase was a secondary, though very important, effort.

This contrast is also representative of two of the most important trends in the development of measurement in the social sciences. The efforts of Bradburn and Caplovitz to measure happiness are characteristic of the relatively simple and straightforward (and somewhat nonphilosophical) means that survey researchers have developed for measuring concepts, by devising simple questions that require self-reports. The efforts of Adorno and his colleagues are highly characteristic of the more ambitious (if never fully satisfactory) efforts by social psychologists to operationalize complex psychological concepts by developing scales.

THE MEASUREMENT OF VARIABLES

Measurement is the central concern of all sciences. As we saw in Chapter 2, measurement appeared in Wallace's scientific process model between observations and empirical generalizations in the inductive half of the model and between hypotheses and observations (defined as instrumentation and scaling) in the deductive half of the model. This formulation suggests that measurement is not so much the end, or goal, of science, but rather the means to that end. Without good measurement, the goals of scientific research are unattainable. In social research, the researcher must use variation to make comparisons and to test hypotheses, two of the central tasks of social research. For the social researcher, the art of good measurement is to capture variation in an operationally defined variable. This section will discuss what is at stake in trying to do this.

As shown in the previous section, measurement requires the identification of variables. *Variable* is a term used to describe something that varies. One result of this definition of a variable is that the term can be applied to anything that is measured in a social-scientific study. For example, in the happiness study, the question "Taking all things together, how would you say things are these days?" produces measurable variation by offering the response categories "very happy," "pretty happy," and "not too happy." The question (with its set of possible responses) is therefore thought of as a variable. In the authoritarianism study, each of the separate statements might also be considered a variable, since they too are capable of capturing the measurable variation in the responses to them. However, the whole authoritarianism scale (the F-Scale) can also be considered a variable because the measured responses can be combined into a single measure of variation.

DEFINING MEASUREMENT

The most common definition of measurement presented in the literature is one first offered by S. S. Stevens:

Measurement is the assignment of numbers to objects or events according to certain rules *(1951, p. 22)*.

Let's look at this definition carefully. It contains two parts. First, it indicates that measurement is a *doing* activity—assigning numbers—which involves performing operations sequentially. Second, it specifies that what you are doing must follow certain rules or a model which lays out the principles of the measurement system (Borgatta and Bohrnstedt, 1980, p. 151).

There is also a third quality of this activity which is implied in this definition: that the rules that guide measurement have to do with establishing a correspondence between what is observed and the number it is given. In other words, measurement is carried out according to *rules of correspondence* in which certain phenomena (or types of phenomena) are designated by a particular number (Bohrnstedt, 1983, p. 70).

Here's an example. Suppose you are measuring the variable educational attainment. You decide to use "number of years of education completed" to represent the variable of educational attainment. A person finishing elementary school would be assigned an 8 (for eight years of schooling); a person who dropped out of high school in tenth grade would be assigned a 9; a graduate of a two-year college would be assigned a 14; a holder of a master's degree would be assigned an 18.

Now let's go over the steps in this measurement process:

1. You define a phenomenon, educational attainment, as a variable which includes different levels at which education is terminated to which you assign corresponding numbers according to the number of years of education completed.
2. You observe that a particular subject has a particular educational attainment level.
3. You select the number representing the educational termination point which corresponds to

the educational attainment level. That is a measurement!

However, in the social and behavioral sciences, many of the variables that interest us (as we saw with happiness and authoritarianism) are not as readily convertible to a numerical scale as is educational attainment. In fact, many are not at all the "objects and events" that Stevens spoke of. Carmines and Zeller state the problem with Stevens's formulation very clearly:

> Phenomena such as political efficacy, alienation, gross national product, and cognitive dissonance are too abstract to be considered "things that can be seen or touched" (the definition of an object) or merely as a "result, consequence, or outcome" (the definition of an event). In other words, Stevens's classical definition of measurement is much more appropriate for the physical than [for] the social sciences (1979, p. 10).

In place of this definition, they offer another definition of measurement as an "explicit, organized plan for classifying (and often quantifying) the particular sense data at hand—the indicants—in terms of the general concept in the researcher's mind" (Carmines and Zeller, 1979, p. 10). What has changed here is that "objects and events" have been replaced by "the general concept in the researcher's mind," and "numbers" have been replaced by "indicants." In other words, measurement is the process by which empirical data are organized in some systematic relationship to the concept being studied. This definition of measurement fits better with the kind of activity in which social scientists engage when studying phenomena that are not directly observable.

Let's give an example here of trying to measure an abstract concept which has no clear observable indicator. Suppose that we are carrying out a door-to-door survey and are required to determine the happiness of the families being interviewed. Now, how will we link our concept of family happiness to some empirical evidence in these households? It could be the case that when

you go to the Jones's door, Junior Jones has just thrown a frying pan at his sister, and Mrs. Jones is shouting at Mr. Jones, who is crying. In this instance, our ability to link the behavior we observe to our abstract concept of family happiness would be quite straightforward. But this is not what we could expect to find at most households.

What indicators could we use that would fairly measure happiness from one household to the next, and would these indicators be truly linked to our concept of family happiness? Suppose we had decided to adopt Bradburn and Caplovitz's measure of happiness and change it slightly to refer to *how* happy a family was. Now what if we went to the Jones's house (with the frying pans flying) to interview Mrs. Jones, and she claimed that the family was "pretty happy"? Would we believe her? Wouldn't this response introduce error into our careful measuring process?

All measurement leads to some error. Measurement theory contends that, however precise our instruments for measuring (and in the social sciences our instruments are generally quite crude) and however careful our efforts of observation, there will always be some error introduced into our measurement. In fact, the central formulation of measurement theory states that an observed measure (or score) is equal to the true score plus the error—above or below the true score—necessarily occurring in the process of observing the phenomenon. In short, all measurement contains some degree of error, called *measurement error*. Even though it is impossible to abolish all error, the aim is to reduce it as much as possible.

The most important criterion of the goodness of a measure is its validity, that is, whether the measure is measuring what it intends to measure. It is also important that a measure be consistent, such that when it is repeatedly used, it will lead to the same results. This consistency in measurement is referred to as reliability.

VALIDITY

Put most simply, *validity* addresses the question "Am I measuring what I think I am measuring?"

The validity of the previously discussed F-Scale of authoritarianism has been challenged repeatedly. In developing instruments to measure abstract concepts, the issue of validity is critical. The questions that are designed to tap an abstract concept must do precisely that.

The validity of a measure depends upon the correspondence between a concept and the empirical indicators that supposedly measure it. In short, validity is a property of a measuring instrument that you want to test for. While reliability addresses the consistency in measurement, validity addresses the even more critical issue of the "crucial relationship between concept and indicator" (Carmines and Zeller, 1979, p. 12). It should also be recognized that validity is not synonymous with reliability. It is possible for a scale to be reliable (i.e., it repeatedly produces similar responses in similar situations) and still not be valid. As mentioned above, a reliable but invalid measure would be worthless. There are a number of methods to test for validity by determining the association between a concept and the empirical indicator(s) chosen to measure it. The three methods described here test for content validity, criterion-related validity, and construct validity. (See the American Psychological Association, 1974.)

Content Validity

The most basic method of testing for validity is to carefully examine the measure of a concept in light of its meaning and to ask yourself seriously whether the measurement instrument really seems to be measuring the underlying concept. This form of careful consideration and examination is a method of establishing *face validity* (or what is sometimes called "armchair" validity). In some instances, an instrument may need to appear to be measuring what it purports to measure, even if another instrument which looked less relevant—but actually was valid—could be used. For example, Allen and Yen (1979, p. 96) suggest that in a test used to screen applicants for a job, it may be essential (for purposes of public relations) to have

questions that seem to be relevant to the job even if other types of questions would be just as good for selecting the best applicants. However, face validity is not an adequate test of the content validity of a measure.

Another method of testing for *content validity* asks whether the empirical indicators (tests, scales, questions, or whatever) fully represent the *domain of meaning* of the underlying concept being studied (Bohrnstedt, 1983, p. 98). In this sense, "content validity concerns the extent to which a set of items taps the content of some domain of interest. To the degree that the items reflect the full domain of content, they can be said to be content-valid" (Zeller and Carmines, 1980 p. 78). A simple way of understanding this type of content validity is to consider the example of an achievement test. Suppose we are developing a college board achievement test in American history. The issue is whether the test items fairly represent the range of topics and ideas that should be covered in American history courses throughout the country. A test that has content validity would be one that samples fairly (selects without bias) from each of the different parts of the domain of meaning covered by the study of American history, or that is truly representative of the full content of this subject taught in high schools and presented in high school textbooks. This form of content validity is often called *sampling validity,* because the object is to sample accurately from the various domains. It is used widely by educational psychologists and test developers. Carmines and Zeller stress (1979, p. 21) that for purposes of establishing sampling validity, it is always preferable, in test development, to create a greater number of items for each part of the content domain since it is easier to discard items than to add new ones once the test is formed.

When the concept to be measured is more abstract (as in the example of authoritarianism), it is much more difficult to establish content validity. This is true because the full domain of content of such concepts has usually not been as fully agreed upon. In addition, even when the domain is fully laid out, it is much more difficult to develop a pool of items large enough to represent each part of the content domain. Without a sufficient number of items in each stratum, sampling from each stratum cannot take place. For these reasons, sampling validity is rarely tested for in validating measures of abstract social science concepts.

As Zeller and Carmines concede, there is

> no agreed-upon criterion for establishing whether, in fact, a measure has attained content validity. In the absence of well-defined objective criteria, Nunnally (1967, p. 82) has noted, "Inevitably content validity rests mainly on appeals to reason regarding the adequacy with which important content has been sampled and on the adequacy with which the content has been cast in the form of test items" (1980, p. 79).

The ultimate problem with testing for content validity is whether there is acceptance for the universe of content defined by the variable being measured (Cronbach and Meehl, 1955, p. 282, as discussed in Zeller and Carmines, 1980, p. 79). For a test of American history as presented in our example, it might seem at first glance to be fairly easy to establish some "acceptance" for the universe of content. However, educators do not agree about what *is* the appropriate and important content of American history. This is similarly the case for many social-scientific concepts (alienation, self-esteem, etc.), for which the acceptance of what comprises the universe of content is usually exceedingly difficult to establish. For this reason, content validity is not very useful in trying to validate social-scientific concepts.

Criterion-Related Validity

Why are college board examinations given? One reason is so that admissions offices can select entering students. But how does the admissions staff know that the college board exams are measuring anything relevant to a student's success in college? The answer is that college boards have been shown to be highly related to students' academic success in college. This is an example of *criterion-related validity*. In other words, the validity of the college board examinations can be established by showing that their results are highly associated with a particular outcome, academic success in college, which serves as the criterion of their validity.

In such cases, two measures need to be taken: the measure of the test itself (the set of empirical indicators) and the criterion to which the test is supposedly related. The usual procedure is to use a correlation (to be described in Chapter 15) between the measure and the criterion to determine the criterion-related validity. In the example given, the criterion—academic success in college, usually measured by college GPA—would be measured subsequent to the original measure of college academic potential (the college board examination). In such an instance, the criterion-related validity is referred to as *predictive validity*, for the test scores purport to predict future academic performance.[1]

In other cases, a criterion may be measured at the same time as the concept. Bohrnstedt offers the example of measuring religiousness in terms of the seriousness of commitment to religious beliefs and relating it to the frequency of attendance at church (or other place of worship). In this case, a measure of the attitudes expressing a person's religious commitment is related to a piece of evidence about a person's religious behavior (attending church). Because these are measured at the same time, they are said to have *concurrent validity*.

Another example offered by Bohrnstedt uses a technique for testing for validity based on membership or affiliation with a *known group*, that is, a group known to support certain values, beliefs, and practices (1983, p. 98). Suppose you develop a set of questions to measure antiabortion attitudes. The validity of these questions might be established by relating the responses to membership

---

[1]Carmines and Zeller warn that since the sole reason for accepting the criterion-related validity of a concept is the strength of the correlation between the test and the criterion, even a nonsensical criterion (if it could be shown to be related to the test) would be proof of criterion-related validity (1979, p. 18).

in right-to-life organizations or fundamentalist religious groups.

The problem with criterion-related validity for much social-scientific research is that it is often not possible to determine a relevant criterion. Remember that the criterion must represent not just some outcome that might logically be related to the concept, but rather evidence that can serve as proof that the measured concept (or test) represents what it claims to represent. It is because of the difficulty in determining criteria for theoretical variables that construct validity has been developed to address this need.

Construct Validity

Criterion-related validity is based on getting some empirical evidence (such as college grades) to serve as the basis for judging that what is being measured (college board exams) really measures what it is supposed to measure (ability to succeed in college). This is an empirically based form of validity, in which some observable evidence can be used to confirm the validity of a measure. However, when there is neither a criterion nor an accepted universe of content that defines the quality being measured, then criterion-related and content validity cannot be used to test for validity. With more theoretical concepts, the form of validity testing itself must become more theoretical. This is what characterizes *construct validity.*

Construct validity is based on forming hypotheses about the concepts that are being measured and then on testing these hypotheses and correlating the results with the initial measure. Zeller and Carmines clarify the purpose of construct validity as

> the assessment of whether a particular measure relates to other measures consistent with theoretically derived hypotheses concerning the concepts (or constructs) that are being measured . . . [hence] it is impossible to "validate" a measure of a concept in this sense unless there exists a theoretical network that surrounds the concept. For without this network,

it is impossible to generate theoretical predictions, which, in turn, lead directly to empirical tests involving measures of the concept *(1980, p. 81).*

Then they describe the steps required to test the construct validity of measures:

> First, the theoretical relationship between the concepts themselves must be specified. Second, the empirical relationship between the measures of the concepts must be examined. Finally, the empirical evidence must be interpreted in terms of how it clarifies the construct validity of the particular measures *(1980, p. 81).*

Clearly, according to Zeller and Carmines, construct validity is "theory-laden," though this does not mean that only concepts linked to fully developed theories can be tested with construct validity.

> What is required is only that one be able to state several theoretically derived hypotheses involving the particular concept *(1980, p. 82).*

Carmines and Zeller offer a fairly easy example to describe this. Suppose you have a measure of self-esteem which you want to validate. You might begin by developing hypotheses that set up expectations about what self-esteem might be likely to vary with. If you hypothesized that self-esteem would more likely be high among students who participated in extracurricular activities at school than among those who did not, then you might correlate the self-esteem scale with participation rates in school activities as a means of gathering one kind of evidence that the self-esteem scale was measuring what you believed to be a part of the theoretical construct of the meaning of self-esteem (Carmines and Zeller, 1979, p. 23).

Bradburn and Caplovitz tried to validate their measure of happiness. Their efforts to relate responses to *feeling states* (feeling bad and feeling good) to their measure of happiness is an example of aiming for construct validity. By hypothesizing how their happiness measure should relate to another measure, and subsequently by seeing how

VALIDATING THE MEASURE OF HAPPINESS

To strengthen the evidence that their measure of happiness was valid, Bradburn and Caplovitz related it to statements designed as "more detailed measures of well-being." One set of statements was devised to measure "subjective feeling states which were conceptualized as having positive and negative poles" (Bradburn and Caplovitz, 1965, p. 15). Simply put, this means that Bradburn and Caplovitz developed a series of statements, the responses to which would serve as indicators for feeling good about something, on the one hand, and feeling bad about something, on the other hand. The following categorical responses (Bradburn and Caplovitz, 1965, pp. 16–17) were offered in answer to the question "How are you feeling?"

FOR THE POSITIVE SET:

> Pleased about having accomplished something
>
> Proud because someone complimented you on something you had done
>
> On top of the world
>
> Particularly excited or interested in something
>
> That you had more things to do than you could get done

FOR THE NEGATIVE SET:

> Vaguely uneasy about something without knowing why

So restless you couldn't sit long in a chair
Bored
Very lonely or remote from other people
Depressed or very unhappy

Responses to the items in each set were combined to form an index (a form of measurement to be described more fully in Chapter 16). This produced a *positive feelings index* and a *negative feelings index*. Bradburn and Caplovitz were then in a position to compare respondents' scores on each of these indexes with their responses to the happiness question. They found that it was the balance of these positive and negative feeling indexes that was related to the responses to the happiness question. When the positive feelings index was higher than the negative feelings index, more of the respondents claimed to be "very happy." When the negative feelings index was higher than the positive, more respondents stated that they were "not too happy." When there was a balance between the two indexes, so that there were roughly equal levels of positive to negative feelings, the respondents were more likely to report being "pretty happy." They believed that the importance of the balance in positive and negative feeling states in determining one's general level of happiness could help explain why some people who seemed to have many problems were nevertheless generally "pretty happy," while others who seemed to have very few problems reported being "not too happy."

Source: Norman M. Bradburn and David Caplovitz: *Reports on Happiness,* Aldine, Chicago, 1965, p. 21.

far this turned out to be the case, Bradburn and Caplovitz were able to strengthen confidence in their own measure of happiness and to offer evidence of construct validity for the measure. In the course of trying to establish the validity of their measure of happiness in this way, they came to

better understand the meaning of the concept (or construct) of happiness itself.

Naturally, you could offer greater support for construct validity if you tested a greater number of measures that you hypothesized to be related to the concept in question. Construct validity increases as numerous researchers correlate different measures based on hypotheses about the probable relations of a concept. In some cases, of course, these correlations may turn out to be negative. Over time, such negative evidence (if it is based on theoretically sound hypotheses and carefully developed measures to test the hypotheses) may challenge the construct validity of a concept.

> If [the measured concept, the scale, or whatever] behaves inconsistently with theoretical expectations, then it is usually inferred that the empirical measure does not represent its intended theoretical concept. Instead, it is concluded that the measure lacks construct validity for that particular concept *(Carmines and Zeller, 1979, p. 27)*.

Construct validity can also be strengthened if more than one empirical indicator is being used to measure the underlying concept. When this is the case, each of the indicators can be correlated with the external variable being used to test for construct validity. If the two indicators relate in different ways to the external measure, this suggests that the two indicators are not in fact measuring the same underlying concept (Carmines and Zeller, 1979, p. 26). In summarizing the various types of validity testing for their effectiveness in social research, Zeller and Carmines conclude that construct validity is the most useful and applicable to the social sciences:

> It not only has generalized applicability for assessing the validity of social science measures, but it can also be used to differentiate theoretically relevant and theoretically meaningless empirical factors *(1980, p. 100)*.

RELIABILITY

Put simply, *reliability* is defined as the degree to which a procedure for measuring produces similar outcomes when it is repeated. Why might a carefully constructed question measuring a variable not produce the same measured response each time it is given to a particular respondent? Let's

say that you had a very short questionnaire which asked people only two questions: "What is your age?" (for which a specific number of years was to be given) and "What is your opinion about the effectiveness of the President?" (to which the measured responses were "very effective," "somewhat effective," "not too effective," and "not at all effective"). If you worked for a polling organization and went door to door on a particular street to ask individuals their age and their opinions about the effectiveness of the President and then returned at intervals over the next 6 months to ask the same question, how likely would it be that each person you surveyed would give the same response to the two questions over and over again?

Consider first the variable of age. This is a factual question for which the only expected change might be that a person's birthday might have occurred and therefore the person would be a year older. This would not of course be an example of unreliability. However, you might find that some individuals gave quite varying responses each time you asked. Some elderly individuals might be unsure of their ages as a result of confusion or forgetfulness. Other individuals may be struggling between the "socially desirable" urge to sound younger (or, if young, older) and the realistic urge to state a fact as one knows it. These examples suggest that respondents' feelings may change their answers in ways that will affect the reliability of the responses.

For the question about presidential effectiveness, one would expect greater variation over time because the question measures an attitude (which is often subject to change) in comparison to a fact (which should be less subject to change). For staunch supporters of the President or, conversely, for staunch opponents of the President, responses would be expected to be at the extreme level and changes would be less likely to occur with changing events. In other words, those with stronger attitudes toward a subject should be less susceptible to change. However, for those with less strong commitments for or against the President, changing political events might alter attitudes over time.

This would reflect actual changes in respondents' attitudes and would not be evidence of unreliability in the measuring instrument. If attitudes shifted from one day to the next, this would be greater evidence of unreliability than if they shifted over a month's or over six months' time.

What if the question had been about attitudes toward the effectiveness of the secretary of the interior? Such a question would raise greater worries about unreliability. Many individuals would not know who this secretary was or what he or she was responsible for, let alone whether the secretary was performing adequately. A question such as this would lead to unreliable responses because many respondents would not want to admit lack of information to answer the question, and would just offer some answer. Because the answer was not based on any factual knowledge, or on any developed opinion, it would be unlikely to remain stable over time.

If a question is irrelevant to a respondent, or if it is too complicated or likely to be misinterpreted by the respondent, it is likely to produce highly unreliable responses. Thus, the aim of developing measured variables is to produce ones that present material understandable to the respondent on topics which should be familiar to the respondent, rather uncomplicated, and easy to interpret. The researcher should be careful on questions that may encourage a respondent to respond in what might seem a socially desirable manner.

As stated above, there will always be some error, however carefully the measurement procedures are carried out. Nevertheless, there are ways to reduce measurement error. In assessing reliability, the problem is to determine the degree of random error, rather than systematic error. Because the effects of random error tend to cancel each other out if a greater number of indicators are being measured, it is preferable to have a composite measure (one with numerous indicators) than a single measure in developing reliable measures for social science concepts (Zeller and Carmines, 1980, p. 75). For example, as mentioned in the section on authoritarianism, if you use more than one indicator for each concept, that is, if you collect data on *multiple indicators* for each abstract concept, you can develop more reliable measures of the concept. (Note that for the F-Scale of authoritarianism, numerous questions were developed to measure each of the scale's dimensions. It was the combined score on the set of items that determined the level of each dimension.)

Why should multiple indicators produce greater reliability than single indicators? Any observed (or measured) score is equal to the "true score"—the "hypothetical, unobservable quantities that cannot be directly measured" (Carmines and Zeller, 1979, p.29)—plus the error. Since we can never be sure that our observed score is equal to the true score, the best that can be achieved is to retest the measures over and over again (an "infinite number of repeated measurements," 1979, p. 30) and use the response given most often as the true score. The assumption made about measurement error is that in repeated measures of the same phenomenon, the errors will sometimes be higher (more positive) than the true score and sometimes lower (or more negative), but over time they will cancel each other out and thereby produce an average error score of 0. For this reason, the measurement error is referred to as *random measurement error,* or simply *random error.* The theory of random error forms a central part of what is called *classical test theory.* As Zeller and Carmines (1980, p. 7) explain, the

> main body of statistical theory . . . . that has been used to estimate the reliability (and indirectly, the validity) of empirical measurements is classical test theory . . . which begins with the basic formulation that an observed score, *X,* is equal to the true score, *T,* plus a measurement error, *e.* To state this idea as a formula:

$$X = T + e$$

However, they later go on to say, "in classical test theory, it is assumed that all measurement error is random." While this idea may be justified in strict experimental designs in the social sciences, it is not justified in sample surveys, in observational studies based in the field, or in more structured environments (1980, p. 11). In surveys, for example, respondents' tendencies toward yeasaying and naysaying, and in responding in a socially desirable fashion, may produce systematic error (p. 11).

In addition, classical test theory is not very good at determining the validity of a measure, or at clarifying the relationship between validity and reliability (Zeller and Carmines, 1980, pp. 11–12). In a reformulation of classical test theory, Zeller and Carmines show that "the difference between reliability and validity is entirely dependent upon systematic error" (p. 14). If there were no systematic error, validity would be equal to reliability; conversely, if there were a fair degree of systematic error, validity would be less than reliability (p. 14).

The preceding discussion has described repeated measurements of the same phenomenon on single individuals. It could also apply to repeated measurements across different individuals on the same measure. In this case, you would need to look at the range of scores in relation to the overall mean from all the scores. This is called *variance* (to be described more fully in Chapter 6). Two general procedures can be used to reduce the amount of random error and improve the reliability of a measure: measuring for stability and measuring for equivalence.

Measures of Stability

Reliability tests that determine how much change will occur in the responses of individuals from one testing time to the next are measuring the stability of the measurement instrument. This is often called *test-retest reliability*. There are different possible explanations for unreliability from one testing time to the next. As described in the above examples, unreliability may be due to the varying states the individuals are in when the measure is taken: They may be more or less alert, healthy, concentrating, etc. Or, unreliability may be due to weaknesses in the measuring instrument: respon-

dents may be uncertain as to what is being asked and yet offer an answer to avoid appearing unintelligent. Under such conditions, reliability may be weak from one test to the retest. On the other hand, changes could occur during the period between the tests: then the different answers given at each test do not signify lack of reliability, but true change. An example of such true change could be found in achievement tests, where the individual actually learns more between the testing times.

Measures of Equivalence

Another way to test for reliability, instead of comparing scores on tests given at different times, is to compare parallel items at the same point in time. This provides an on-the-spot form of test-retest. If one has two indicators of the same concept, comparisons of these items can help to determine the reliability of the measure. For example, let's assume you are trying to measure the concept of *anomie,* meaning normlessness. You decide to select two items from Srole's Anomia Scale (1956) (a scale to be discussed at greater length in the final section of this chapter) which are two of the five indicators of anomie which Srole defined (see Miller, 1977, pp. 375–377 for the scale). The two items are (1) "In spite of what some people say, the lot of the average man is getting worse," and (2) "These days a person does not know who he can count on." You test these items on a sample of respondents. The responses to the two items are equal to the same *true* score; the differences are the result of random error. Therefore, the correlation (a statistical procedure to be described in Chapter 15) between the two items measured at the same time offers an estimate of the reliability of the scale. It also follows that since the random errors will cancel each other out, the more items tested, the better the estimates of reliability.

TYPES OF VARIABLES

One essential feature of measurement is that it depends upon the possibility of variation. Another way of saying this is that measurement requires the identification of *variables,* a term that we have defined before as something that varies. One result of this definition of a variable is that the term can be applied to anything that is measured in a social-scientific study. Variables can be measured in two general ways: they are either categorical or numerical.

Categorical Variables

A *categorical variable* is made up of a set of attributes that form a category but do not represent a numerical measure or scale. Many of the most significant variables defining our social existence can be described only as sets of attributes belonging to a category. For instance, a teacher, a Catholic, a man, a Republican are all primary defining characteristics of a person. Each represents one attribute within the categorical variables of *occupation* (teacher, plumber, salesperson, etc.), *religion* (Catholic, Jew, Protestant, Muslim, etc.), *gender* (man, woman), and *voting preference* (Republican, Democrat, Independent). These variables are made up of sets of categories (or attributes) which must follow two rules. In the first place, the categories must be distinct from one another; that is, they must be *mutually exclusive.* This means that no respondent should be able to place himself or herself into more than one category. Let's say that, for the variable of religion, you included the following categories: "Catholic," "Protestant," "Christian," and "Jewish." In this case, your categories would not be mutually exclusive, because the term "Christian" would subsume both "Catholic" and "Protestant," and a choice among them would be meaningless.

In the second place, the categories of a variable must be *exhaustive.* This means that they should cover all of the potential range of variation in a variable. In other words, even respondents with a very extreme position on one variable should be able to place themselves comfortably within one of the categories. In the religion example, you would need to add the categories of

"other" and "none" to Catholic, Protestant, and Jewish in order to have an exhaustive list appropriate to an American sample. When a variable has a potentially different or extreme response, there should be a catchall category at the end to pick up extreme cases (for example, "favor none of the above candidates" might be the final choice in a candidate preference variable).

In order to incorporate categorical variables into a quantitative study and computerize the data, it is usual to assign numbers to the categories. For example, for gender, males may be designated by a 1, females by a 2. This use of numbers, however, does not imply that the categories represent numerical quantities that can be manipulated mathematically. The numbers are merely used as a way to code the categories for analysis on a computer. (Chapter 12 will describe coding.) For analyzing categorical variables, the primary forms of arithmetic that can be used are simple counting and percentages.

Numerical Variables

Numerical variables, as distinct from categorical variables, are broken down into units in which the numbers used to represent each unit of the variable carry mathematical meaning. For example, achievement test scores, personality scale scores, age, and labor force participation rates are all variables in which the numbers represent not merely category labels, but mathematical measurement of the variable. In other words, they represent a scale.

The numbers represented by a numerical variable may be either *discrete* or *continuous.* If the variable is number of children, its range of numbers are discrete (1, 2, 3, etc.), which is to say that they cannot be broken down continuously into smaller and smaller fractional quantities. For example, consider the discrete variable number of children. While no family has 2.35 children, average family sizes are often presented in this manner. In many statistical reports, discrete variables such as average family size are treated as though they were continuous. However, if the variable is weight, the measurement it represents is unambiguously continuous. The weight may be 2.35 or 2.36 pounds. To better conceptualize the differences in the measurement of variables, let us here consider the types of graphs which are used to depict the range of responses to different types of variables. This should help you to visualize the differences between categorical and numerical variables.

Bar Graphs, Histograms, and Frequency Polygons.

A *bar graph* is a graph on which categories of a variable are presented on the horizontal axis and the frequency of this category is presented on the vertical axis. Then a bar the height of each frequency is drawn. These bars have gaps between them on the scale. Figure 5-1 gives a bar graph of the religious affiliations of students at a hypothetical college.

A *histogram,* sometimes mistakenly called a bar graph, is used to depict the frequency distribution of a numerical (preferably a continuous) variable, such that the bars have at their centermost point the value being presented. The edge of each bar is halfway to the next centermost value, and therefore it touches the edge of the bar next to it. A histogram of the weights of students in a class could be made. Histograms are often used to represent discrete numerical variables as well. For example, if the discrete variable number of children

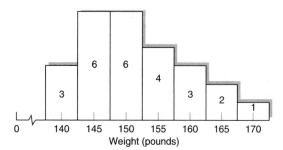

FIGURE 5-2
Histogram of weights, using a continuous variable. (From T. W. Anderson and Stanley L. Sclove: *Introductory Statistical Analysis,* 2d ed., Houghton Mifflin, Boston, 1986, p. 45.)

is used, the bar representing one child would actually depict .5 to 1.5 children, the bar for two children would cite from 1.5 to 2.5 children, etc. Figure 5-2 shows a histogram for a continuous variable, weight, and Figure 5-3 shows a histogram for a discrete variable, number of children per family.

Consider the histogram of weights. In order to form a graph from these weights, you would first need to group the weights into classes: 137.5–142.5, 142.5–147.5, 147.5–152.5, etc., as you can see in Figure 5-2. Then you would find the midpoints of these groups (140 and 145, etc.) and build a graph with the midpoints. In each class of weights you would count up the students who fell into that class and register them on the vertical axis.

A *frequency polygon* is another type of graph

FIGURE 5-1
Bar graph of religious affiliations.

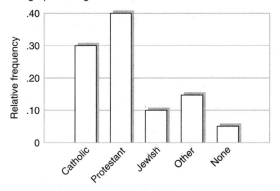

FIGURE 5-3
Histogram of number of children per family, using a discrete variable.   (From T. W. Anderson and Stanley L. Sclove: *Introductory Statistical Analysis,* 2d ed., Houghton Mifflin, Boston, 1986, p. 39.)

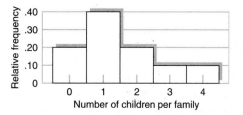

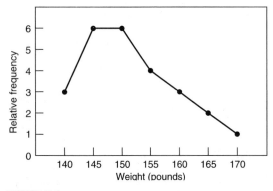

FIGURE 5-4
Frequency polygon of weights in Figure 5-2.

that can represent the same thing as a histogram. However, instead of presenting bars with the center-most point for each value on the horizontal axis, the centermost point is where the top of the bar would be, and the bar is not drawn in. Such a dot graph makes it easier to draw lines connecting the points that indicate the shape of the distribution. Figure 5-4 presents a frequency polygon for the weights in Figure 5-2.

The distribution of continuous variables can be described by a fuller range of statistical measures such as the mean and the standard deviation, which will be described more fully in Chapter 6 on sampling and in Chapter 15. Discrete variables can be described by a narrower range of statistics, such as the median and mode, although many analysts employ the mean as well in describing the distribution of a discrete variable.

LEVELS OF MEASUREMENT

In the social sciences, four types of scales for measuring a variable (two types for categorical variables, two types for numerical variables) have been delineated. These scale types (or *levels of measurement,* as they are usually called) are useful in helping to classify and catalog variables in a study, as well as in designing questions to measure variables.

It is often possible for a variable to be measured at different levels. In deciding how to set up the variable (that is, how to "operationalize the variable"),

you are also making the relationship between your measured variable and the underlying concept more precise. Of course, your choice of measurement categories will also determine the quality of the response data you get. Both the reliability of a variable and its validity will depend on the operational decisions made in the design of the variable. If the measurement of the variable is not a good fit with the underlying concept you are trying to measure, then the data gathered on this variable will be invalid. If the variable is imprecise or unclear, it will not produce reliable responses. In short, poorly measured variables will produce meaningless data, which will in turn make your analysis a waste of effort. Once your data have been produced, it will be too late to decide that your measurement categories should have been quite different. Therefore, you should apply the principles of measurement in designing your data-gathering instruments.

Figure 5-5 gives a diagram of the four scales or levels comprising the classification of variables. Two of the levels (nominal and ordinal) are used for categorical variables; two (interval and ratio) are used for numerical variables.

Nominal Measurement

A variable with a *nominal level of measurement* consists of a set of distinctive categories that imply no specific order. Consider the variable of gender (or

FIGURE 5-5
Classification of variables: the four measurement levels. (From T. W. Anderson and Stanley L. Sclove: *Introductory Statistical Analysis,* 2d ed., Houghton Mifflin, Boston, 1986, p. 29.)

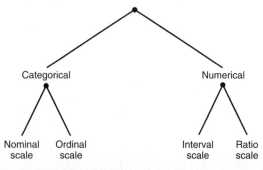

sex). This variable can take only two forms, male or female. There is no real order between the categories; respondents must simply be one or the other. Or take the variable of religion. Here in the United States there are three major categories. But note that it would make no sense to place them on a type of scale from high to low, because they are just different choices with no particular rank order among them. (For religion, not only would the major religious groups be given, but also a catchall category for other religions would need to be included, and a category for none.) In summary, a nominal variable must have at least two categories (but may have as many as are needed), and these categories must be characterized as having no prescribed order.

In sociological research, many of the variables we are most interested in studying—race, sex, religion, nationality, for example—are expressed in terms of nominal measures. For this reason, we must understand this type of measurement and recognize how to handle such variables properly. Chapter 15 on statistics will offer specific statistical tests that can be used in studying relationships between nominal variables.

Ordinal Measurement

Variables that have two or more categories with an inherent order among them are measured at an *ordinal level* of measurement. Consider the variable of social class. However many categories are used, they suggest an order. Even a two-category breakdown of "high class" and "low class" implies an order from high to low. For most purposes, of course, two categories seem too few for the variable of social class. The simplest form of ordinal scale generally used to measure social class has three points: "upper class," "middle class," and "lower class." But more complicated nine-point scales have been created, by identifying three categories within each of the initial three groups ("upper-upper," "middle-upper," "lower-upper," "upper-middle," "middle-middle," "lower-middle," "upper-lower," "middle-lower," "lower-lower").

How many categories you use in setting up your variable will depend on how much variation you expect to find out there among your respondents, and how far these differences interest you in terms of your research. If you wanted to study the fine differences between the upper-upper classes (those perhaps with "old money") and the middle-upper classes (those with "new money"), these categories might be very important. If, however, you were only planning to use the variable of social class in fairly broad terms in your study, then the three-category variable might be preferable.

Although many variables cannot be converted into ordinal scales, a great many can. In some cases, ordinal measures can be joined together with nominal measures to intensify an understanding of a concept. Take the concept of religion. To find out someone's religious affiliation, a nominal variable is needed. To find out how religiously observant a person is, however, an ordinal measure should be used, such as "Do you attend religious services: daily, weekly, a few times a month, monthly, a few times a year, yearly, less often than once a year, never?"

The most common forms of ordinal variables are attitudinal items to which level of agreement is assessed. For example, an index (that is, a combined set of variables added together; see Chapter 16) of Job Satisfaction might include this item: "I consider my job rather unpleasant," to which the respondent must select one of the following: "strongly agree," "agree," "undecided," "disagree," "strongly disagree" (from Brayfield and Rothe, 1951, in Miller, 1977, pp. 368–370). These categories are generally given code numbers of 1 to 5. These numbers imply order of agreement but suggest nothing about the distance between the numbers (is "strongly agree" further from "agree" than "agree" is from "undecided"?)

Attitude scales such as the one described above are ordinal scales. However, they are often treated as continuous variables such that the *average* score of all respondents to the item might be given as 2.3. Or, as in the case of the Job Satisfaction Index, a set of items is summed, and then the average scores and measures of variation among the scores are computed. In this way a variable with an ordinal scale of measurement is actually treated like an interval scale. This practice has raised some questions about the meaning and utility of ordinal measurement.[2]

Interval Measurement

To picture an interval scale, think of a thermometer. It has lines marking off points on the scale to register the changing temperatures. However, there is no true zero point—no point at which there would be *no temperature*. If it is a Fahrenheit thermometer, the zero on the scale will be at 32 degrees below the freezing point of water; if it is a centigrade thermometer, the zero on the scale will be at the freezing point of water. In neither case, however, will the zero refer to a point where there is no temperature. An interval scale is a created scale that has clearly defined intervals between the points on the scale, and it has order; but it has no true zero point.

An example of an interval scale would be a scale of test scores, such as an IQ score. The SAT examination has scores ranging from 200 to 800 (again no true zero point); the ACT is also an interval scale, but with a very different number range of scores. What happens with these tests is that the raw score achieved by an individual on a test is converted into a test score based on test norms developed from knowledge about how others have scored. In some cases, parts of a test are weighted more highly than others.

Because the scores from social-psychological scales, such as the F-Scale of authoritarianism, are generally treated as continuous measures, such scales are often considered as interval scales. Some methodologists would disagree and classify scales of this type as ordinal scales, since they are based on an accumulation of ordinal items—items to which the respondent usually offers a level of agreement.[3] Scores for the F-Scale are computed by cumulating the levels of agreement (+3 to −3) for the 38 items. Since it is not possible to have a zero on the F-Scale, ratios cannot be established. Thus it is inappropriate to describe one person as twice as authoritarian as another because the score is twice as great.

In summary, interval scales are created devices which assist us in ordering things quite precisely. An *interval level of measurement* has separate categories, like nominal scales, and also has ordered categories, like ordinal scales; but in addition, the distance between the points on an interval scale can be determined mathematically and precisely. Interval scales are used for continuous variables that can register very small differences between categories. Most mathematical operations that are carried out in statistics (see Chapter 15) can be done with interval-level measures. The lack of a true zero point is not usually regarded as a critical deterrent to carrying out many statistical tests.

Ratio Measurement

A ratio scale encompasses all the qualities of the earlier forms of scale: it must have more than one category; it must have an implicit order; it must be able to determine the exact distance between the intervals. In addition, however, it must have a true zero point. Think of variables such as income, age, number of children, or cost of housing. Note that

---

[2]Borgatta and Bohrnstedt have strongly argued that ordinal measures are really weak forms of interval measures, in which the information on the distance between the intervals has been "lost." Since ordinal variables are generally described with statistical measures that assume continuous numerical scales, Borgatta and Borhnstedt think it makes much more sense to treat ordinal variables as imperfect interval variables (1980, pp. 153–160) than as separate levels of measurement.

[3]Some methodologists would not consider psychological scales of this type as true interval-level measures, because they are based on an aggregated set of ordinal measures. However, as footnote 2 states, other methodologists consider all ordinal scales to be weak forms of interval scales. Suffice it to say that there is controversy in interpreting the meaning of ordinal and interval measures.

the *ratio level of measurement* can be applied to either continuous or discrete variables. However, strictly speaking, in the examples given and in most other social research variables with ratio levels of measurement, the variables would be discrete. Income cannot be broken down further than to cents; age is usually given in years. Questions about these variables could be answered on a scale with a true zero point. Your income could be nothing; your age before you were born was zero; you might not have children; your rent could be free. For these kinds of questions, a ratio scale is appropriate.

While there are advantages to using a ratio scale, in fact variables (like income) which could be expressed by a ratio scale are often converted into ordinal scales by grouping possible categories of income: e.g., "0 to $4,999"; "$5,000 to $9,999"; "$10,000 to $14,999." Ratio scales are most commonly used in converting ratio-level variables into *rates.* Examples of these will be given in the following section.

Comparing the Measurement Levels

Box 5-1 describes how information about viewing soap operas and attitudes toward such programs can be collected using variables measured at different levels. Box 5-1 has used the different levels of measurement and presented different types of questions.

If your analyses were to be based largely on two-variable, or bivariate, tables for cross-tabular analyses (to be described in detail in Chapter 13), then it would be better to have a ratio variable converted into a categorical variable (either at the nominal or ordinal level). For a multivariate analysis, where you planned to use a form of analysis such as multiple regression (where variables need to be at least at the interval level), then it would be preferable to have interval or ratio-level variables.[4]

Some variables can be converted into different types of levels of measurement which might be se-

---

BOX 5-1

SOAP OPERA VARIABLES: EXAMPLES OF MEASUREMENT LEVELS

RATIO
How many television soap operas did you watch last week?

INTERVAL
Estimate the IQ score of the hero or heroine of your favorite soap opera.

ORDINAL
How true to life are the soap operas you watched last week?
  Very true, somewhat true, not too true, not at all true.

NOMINAL
Which of the following types of soap operas do you watch?
  Medical themes, household dilemmas, etc.

---

lected depending on the type of analysis you hoped to do. An example might be educational attainment. For cross-tabular analyses, it would be better to present the variable in ordered categories (less than high school, high school graduate, some college, college graduate, etc.). For other types of

---

[4]One thing that you should keep in mind about nominal variables is that any concept that can be operationally defined into a variable can be measured by a two-category nominal level of measurement. The first category would represent the presence (or possession) of the quality. The second category would represent the absence (or lack of possession) of the concept. In research analysis, setting up a variable in this either-or method is referred to as creating a dummy variable. In the case of religion, this variable would usually be measured in terms of a series of categories representing different religions. However, for some purposes, it might make sense to have a variable for religion that had only two categories, for example, "Catholic" or "non-Catholic." Or you might take the variable on voting preference for a specific candidate and have either-or categories: "favor Republican candidate"; "not favor Republican candidate."

analyses, it might be preferable to convert this variable into number of years of schooling completed, which would be a ratio variable.

MEASURING SIX COMMONLY USED SOCIAL RESEARCH VARIABLES

As a social researcher, you need to learn how to select, work with, and develop variables for studies you are doing. Because so much social research has already been carried out, you rarely need to start from scratch. Generally you can find ways of measuring concepts that have been tried out by others. Always remember, however, to determine carefully whether your measure is actually measuring what you want it to measure (the validity issue), whether your measure is sufficiently clear that it is likely to produce consistent results (the reliability issue), and whether the scale of measuring the variable is appropriate and best suited for your needs.

In the next section, we will examine six commonly used variables in social research which represent different levels of measurement. You will find that there are a number of different ways to measure some variables, and you must choose the one that best serves your particular research purpose. For other variables, there may be only one agreed-upon way to measure them. When, for example, a variable measures a phenomenon defined by law (say, crime rates), it must meet the specific criteria laid down in the law. In other cases, social researchers have over the years developed certain ways of measuring social indicators that have become widely accepted. For example, the unemployment rate is determined in a precise way, and you could not just come up with what seemed to you to be a good way to determine an unemployment rate and use yours instead.

Two Nominal Variables

Marital Status. This is a nominal variable which generally includes five categories: "single,"

"married," "widowed," "divorced," or "separated." Often the last three categories are grouped together, creating a three-category variable measuring "never married" (single), "currently married" (married), and "previously married" (widowed, divorced, or separated). Even in this latter case, there is no clear order among the categories.

Type of Housing. Housing types are designated by the United States Census Bureau as (1) public housing, which refers to housing units owned by a local housing authority or other public agency and operated as public housing; (2) private housing, which refers to all other housing units; and (3) subsidized housing, which refers to private housing in which the occupant pays a lower rent because a federal, state, or local government program pays part of the cost of construction, building mortgage, or operating expenses (U.S. Department of Commerce, *Social Indicators III,* 1980, p. 574). One might see these three categories as characterized by some order from "wholly private," to "partially private/partially subsidized," to "wholly public." However, such a variable would best be categorized as a nominal variable.

One Ordinal Variable

Occupational Status. Identifying the job a person holds is the main way we determine that person's social status. If someone tells you that she is a bank president, or a garbage collector, or a shoe salesperson, you fit this person into some sense of the overall social hierarchy of the society. Without ever having had a course in sociology, you probably thought that bank presidents had more status than garbage collectors and that shoe salespeople had less status than bank presidents but more than garbage collectors. How did you arrive at these conclusions? Probably because you connected a number of other factors to the meaning of a specific occupation: that it suggested a certain level of education and that it carried with it different rewards in terms of income, prestige, benefits. In short, the measure of occupations—which could consist merely of a set of job titles (a nominal variable)—also suggests more complex, ordered measures.

In the first place, to use the simple nominal level of job titles leads to numerous problems. There are so many job titles that you would need to use some system in order to group people with the same types of jobs in the same categories. A usual source for job titles is that used by the Census Bureau, which lists numerous job categories under six major occupational groups:

Managerial and professional specialty

Technical, sales, and administrative support

Service occupations

Precision production, craft, and repair

Operators, fabricators and laborers

Farming, forestry and fishing *(U.S. Department of Commerce, 1992.)*

These categories, and the job titles encompassed by each, have an inherent order; those in the top categories imply higher levels of education, and higher rewards, than those in the lower categories, though the final group does not clearly belong at the bottom of the order. Therefore, if you subdivide occupations into these six groups, you have an ordinal scale. However, greater differentiation is often preferred so that actual job titles can be given a rating to distinguish them as either higher or lower than another job title within the same general category.

Fortunately for the social researcher, few variables have received more attention, in terms of developing measures and scales, than occupation. Occupational prestige scales (based on the relative ratings of occupations) and socioeconomic indexes (based on income and education data, as well as in some cases on prestige ratings) have been developed to "measure" occupation. These occupational scales will be described in greater detail in Chapter 16 on indexes and scales. It will be

enough to say here that these scales and indexes enable the researcher to collect job titles from a study and score the jobs on a selected scale or index (an interval measure). This scale or index can then be used to determine the mean and range of occupations, etc. If you use an occupational prestige scale or a socioeconomic index, the variable of occupational status will be measured at the interval level.

One Interval Variable

Srole's Anomia Scale. This scale, which was referred to earlier, is presented here as an example of the many social-psychological scales available in the literature. (Refer to footnote 3, which discusses the reservations which some methodologists would have in considering this a true interval scale.) Srole defined this scale as representing "the individual's generalized pervasive sense of self-to-others belongingness at one extreme compared with self-to-others distance and self-to-others alienation at the other pole of the continuum" (Miller, 1977, p. 375). We have already suggested above that the F-Scale of authoritarianism and occupational prestige scales are treated as interval-level measures. Srole's Anomia Scale, which is also an interval scale, consists of five items (see Miller, 1977, p. 376):

1. In spite of what some people say, the lot of the average man is getting worse.
2. It's hardly fair to bring children into the world with the way things look for the future.
3. Nowadays a person has to live pretty much for today and let tomorrow take care of itself.
4. These days a person doesn't really know who he can count on.
5. There's little use writing to public officials, because often they aren't really interested in the problems of the average man.

The respondent either agrees or disagrees with these five items; the responses are cumulated. Validation studies have shown that this scale correlates quite highly with the F-Scale of authoritarianism

($r = .47$) and with measures of socioeconomic status ($r = .30$). (See Chapter 15 for an explanation of the correlation coefficient, Pearson's *r*.)

Two Ratio Variables

City Size. This is the first variable given that would be unlikely to be self-reported by a respondent. In other words, it would be based on a group (a city) unit of analysis. The size of the city, town, or rural area would be determined by the most recent census figures. Note that these sizes might be used to set up ordinal-level variables of this type: cities of more than 1 million, cities of 500,000 to 999,999, cities of 100,000 to 499,999, etc. Or such a measure could be the basis of forming another type of ordinal variable: large cities, moderate-sized cities, small cities, towns, rural areas. When it is based on an actual estimate of the number of residents of a city, it is a ratio variable. Again the type of measurement level a researcher would choose to use would depend on various factors: the types of analyses planned, how important it was to be able to make fine discriminations between respondents in terms of the sizes of their cities of residence, etc.

Labor Force Participation Rate. This is a measure determined from the work status of individuals. It is a ratio measure, with a precise, agreed-upon definition as to how it must be measured. The labor force participation rate is based on the number of persons in the civilian labor force per 1000 persons (16 years old and over) in the civilian noninstitutional population (*Social Indicators III,* 1980, p. 576). It is often reported separately for men and women, for different ethnic groups, and for those from different regions of the country or from different cities.

Variables: The Tools of Social Research

Note that for all these six variables, as for all others, it is important that definitions are established

and used consistently throughout your study. If you are doing your own study and are gathering your own data, your measures may be your own. Even in this case, you need to follow common procedures for defining variables (though there are often choices that can be made). If, on the other hand, you want to use an established rate or a population figure, you must get that information from the appropriate source (as described in Chapter 4) and be certain that you are using the official definitions. A study that uses established variables in a way that does not conform to accepted definitions of those variables will not be taken seriously.

Many of the six variables offered could be transposed into different levels of measurement. Take employment. If it is set up in terms of a rate (labor force participation rate), it is at the ratio level; if it refers to an ordered set of work involvement ("work full time," "work part time," "not work"), it is an ordinal variable. This work of measuring variables is one of the primary tasks of the social researcher. You need not start from scratch, for there are many good examples to use. However, you must be certain that the variables you choose and measure follow the accepted procedures and serve your needs.

REVIEW NOTES

- The measurement of concepts is a major challenge in social research. It proceeds from defining terms, to developing operational definitions, to preparing instruments which can measure the variation in the concept.

- Social research concepts can be commonplace or very abstract. They can have one or many dimensions. Single or multiple indicators of these dimensions need to be isolated in order to develop an effective instrument to measure the full domain of the concept.

- Measurement involves assigning numbers according to rules of correspondence between definitions and observations.

- The validity of a measure is determined by tests of correspondence between the concepts underlying the measure and the empirical indicators. Content validity, criterion-related validity, and construct validity offer different means for assessing this correspondence.
- The reliability of a measure is determined by whether repeated measuring procedures produce similar results.
- The measurement of categorical variables assigns numbers to distinct categories that must be mutually exclusive of one another and exhaustive of the range of possible meaning. The numbers assigned carry no mathematical significance.
- Numerical variables assign numbers to units which have mathematical meaning. These numerical scales may represent discrete data based on whole numbers (e.g., number of children) or continuous data which has a continuous range of values (e.g., weight).
- Variables are classified according to four commonly defined levels of measurement: nominal, for distinct categories with no order; ordinal, for ordered categories; interval, for numerical scales with mathematically defined intervals between points on the scale, but no true zero point; and ratio, for numerical scales with mathematically defined intervals and a true zero point.

KEY TERMS

bar graph
categorical variables
classical test theory
concurrent validity
construct validity
content validity
continuous variables
criterion-related validity
dimensions
discrete variables
exhaustive categories
face validity
frequency polygon

histogram
indicators
interval level of measurement
measurement error
mutually exclusive categories
nominal definition
nominal level of measurement
numerical variables
operational definition
operationalization
ordinal level of measurement
predictive validity
random measurement error
ratio level of measurement
real definition
reliability
sampling validity
validity

STUDY EXERCISES

1. Consider the concept of educational aspirations (which is different from educational attainment).
   a. Give a nominal definition of this concept.
   b. Now develop an operational definition of this concept.
      (1) Determine how many dimensions it has, and what they are;
      (2) Develop an indicator for each dimension;
      (3) Turn the indicators into a variable which can measure the concept.
2. Considering the educational aspirations variable,
   a. How could you determine its criterion-related validity?
   b. How might you set up a test of predictive validity?
3. Give one example of a variable common in social research that would be measured at the nominal, ordinal, interval, and ratio levels. (You might consider variables presented in the surveys or experiments described in Chapter 1.)

RECOMMENDED READINGS

1. Allen, Mary J., and Wendy M. Yen: *Introduction to Measurement Theory,* Wadsworth, Belmont, Calif., 1979. The authors describe this textbook as an attempt to bridge the gap between a "cookbook" on measurement and a mathematically rigorous discussion of measurement theory. It can be quite easily followed with some mathematical background.

2. Burgess, Robert G. (ed.): *Key Variables in Social Investigation,* Routledge & Kegan Paul, London, 1986. Essays on 10 commonly used variables, reviewing their underlying concepts and how they have been operationalized.

3. Carmines, E., and R. Zeller: *Reliability and Validity Assessment,* Sage, Beverly Hills, Calif., 1979. A brief and clear presentation of the meaning of and tests of reliability and validity; an explanation of classical test theory.

4. Hoover, Kenneth R.: *The Elements of Social Scientific Thinking,* 5th ed., St. Martin's, New York, 1992. This highly readable book has an excellent discussion of levels of measurement.

CHAPTER 6

Sampling

LOOKING AHEAD

This chapter identifies different kinds of probability and nonprobability samples and describes how to design them.

INTRODUCTION

Sampling refers to systematic methods of selection. In social research, it is used to select subjects to be studied. For a survey, sampling methods are used to select respondents; for a content analysis, a sample of materials (or "content") is selected to be analyzed. The reason for sampling is to expand the representativeness of the subjects studied.

The chapter begins with an example of why probability sampling is advantageous. If a sample is selected according to the rules of probability (if it is a *probability sample*), then it is possible to calculate how representative the sample is of the wider population from which the sample was drawn. This chapter will first cover the principles governing probability sampling and then describe different types of probability sample designs (simple random sampling, or SRS; stratified sampling; systematic sampling; multistage cluster sampling; and PPS, or probability proportionate to size sampling). Sample designs used in two of the exemplary studies from Chapter 1 will be given.

In some studies, probability samples cannot be set up. In such cases, samples must be designed on the basis of rules other than probability; such samples are referred to as *nonprobability samples.* The major methods of nonprobability sampling (convenience, purposive, quota, and snowball) will be described, and examples of studies requiring such sampling designs will be given.

THE MERITS OF GOOD SAMPLING

On election day, November 3, 1992, a national poll of 13,471 voters in 300 randomly selected precincts in all states and the District of Columbia was carried out by Voter Research and Surveys (a polling organization created by ABC, NBC, CBS, and CNN News) as the respondents left the voting polls. This election day exit poll of 13,000 estimated the final presidential vote to be:

Clinton	43%
Bush	38%
Perot	18%

nearly exactly the true proportion of the vote actually cast by nearly 78 million Americans. How could this poll based on the voting preferences of 13,000 so accurately predict the votes of 78 million? The answer to this question is that the polling organization had a very good sample. Box 6-1 describes pre-election polls estimating the voting preferences of samples of "likely voters" carried out in the week prior to the 1992 election.

How, exactly, did they get such accurate predictions? To learn how they were so accurate requires an understanding of probability

sampling. For it was by following the principles of probability theory that the Gallup pollsters were able to make such accurate guesses about the voting behavior of American voters. These guesses are referred to as *inferences,* and the object of probability sampling is to be able to make accurate inferences from evidence gathered on a relatively small sample to a much larger population.

Why didn't the Gallup organization survey the entire population of American voters? On the one hand, it would have been very time-consuming and costly to do so; and, on the other hand, it is likely that if they had tried, their findings would have been less accurate than they were from drawing a probability sample of the voting population. The following discussion will explain why this is so.

This chapter will begin by explaining the basic principles of probability sampling. It will offer an explanation of why probability samples are representative of the populations from which they are drawn. It will discuss how you can determine the representativeness of a sample. Then it will describe different methods for drawing a probability sample. The final section of the chapter will describe the principles and methods of nonprobability samples, often called judgmental samples.

BOX 6-1

THE 1992 PRESIDENTIAL PRE-ELECTION POLLS

Polling prior to American presidential elections has gained great momentum in the more than forty years since the early polling organizations wrongly predicted in 1948 that Thomas Dewey would defeat Harry Truman. In the week preceding the 1992 presidential election, seven national polls made predictions on the presidential election based on national samples of "likely voters." The sample designs and the days on which the polling occurred varied slightly. However, of these seven polls, two predicted Clinton would receive 44 percent of the vote, three predicted 43 percent, one predicted 42 percent, and one predicted 41 percent. On election day, Clinton received 43 percent of the vote. Clearly, political polling strategies have come a long way since 1948.

Let's consider more closely three of these polls. The Gallup CNN/USA Today poll was carried out on October 30–31 of 1,579 likely voters; the ABC News poll of 1,369 likely voters was completed between October 29 and 31; the Harris Poll of 1,695 likely voters was conducted from October 30 through November 1. Note that the sizes of these samples were quite small (about 1,500 respondents being selected to represent a voting population of nearly 78 million). Hence, it is essential that the sampling design be so carefully conceived that the small number of "likely" voters sampled will be truly representative of the very large number of American voters.

Their results were as follows:

	Bush	**Clinton**	**Perot**
CNN	36%	43%	16%
ABC	37	42	17
Harris	39	44	17
Three-poll average	38	43	17

These predictions are estimated to be accurate to within three percentage points of the actual outcome. Given that the vote on November 3, 1992, was Bush, 38 percent; Clinton, 43 percent; and Perot, 18 percent; these pre-election polls made very accurate estimates of the actual vote.

HOW PROBABILITY SAMPLES WORK

A *probability sample* is one designed according to the rules of probability, which allows a determination of how likely it is that the sample members are representative of the population from which they were drawn. Suppose you are working in a cookie store.[1] Your store sells three types of cookies which you and your coworkers prepare, bake, and then (hopefully) sell. The cookies for sale are chocolate chip, peanut butter, and co-

conut. The cookies are supposed to be of roughly equal weight since you sell them at a set price per pound, and customers like to think they are getting a fair number for their money. One day the boss comes in and weighs the 15 cookies that are currently for sale on the counter. Table 6-1 presents the weights the boss finds for these cookies.

A Consideration of the Statistics in the Example

Arithmetic Average (Mean). Table 6-1 shows us a number of things. It gives all the weights for each type of cookie, the total weights for each type,

---

[1]The cookie store example is modeled after a different example offered by Slonim (1966).

the average weight of each type, and the grand total weight and grand average weight of all the cookies. The average weight is the arithmetic average (or *mean*) for each type. (You probably recall that an average is determined by adding up the quantities of each unit and then dividing by the number of units.) The average weight of the chocolate chip cookies was 2.9 ounces; the peanut butter cookies, 3.8 ounces; the coconut cookies, 4.75 ounces. The grand average of all the cookies was determined by summing all the weights and dividing by 15 (55.5/15 = 3.7 ounces per average cookie.

The findings of Table 6-1 show (1) that the coconut cookies are on average the heaviest (4.75 ounces) and the chocolate chip the lightest (2.9 ounces); (2) that the heaviest cookie (No. 14) weighs 6 ounces and the lightest (No. 3) 2 ounces; and (3) that the peanut butter cookies tend to be more representative of the average cookie in weight than the other two types. These findings describe both which type of cookie was more likely to be near the mean weight and which types were further away (at a greater range) from the mean. This subject of the *range* or dispersion of the weights from the average weight is measured in terms of variance.

Variance.   *Variance* is a way of measuring how far different units which have been used to establish a mean vary from the mean. The principle is that you take the difference between every measure and the average measure, square these differences, sum them, and then divide this sum by the number of measures considered. Thus, in Table 6-1, you would proceed in this fashion:

$$\text{Variance} = \frac{(2.5 - 3.7)^2 + (3 - 3.7)^2 + \ldots + (6 - 3.7)^2 + (3.5 - 3.7)^2}{15}$$

$$= 1.29$$

Sampling the Cookies

Suppose that the boss said it would take too much time to weigh all 15 cookies, that you should select only 5 of the cookies and determine the average weight from the 5. You know that your selection should not be affected by any personal biases, that it should be random. Therefore, you number every cookie from 1 to 15 (as you see in Table 6-1), write down numbers 1 through 15 on index cards, shuffle the cards, and then draw five cards

TABLE 6-1

WEIGHTS OF A POPULATION OF 15 COOKIES

Chocolate Chip		Peanut Butter		Coconut	
Cookie No.	Weight, oz	Cookie No.	Weight, oz	Cookie No.	Weight, oz
1	2.5	7	5	12	5.5
2	3	8	2.5	13	4
3	2	9	4	14	6
4	3.5	10	4.5	15	3.5
5	4	11	3		
6	2.5				
Total	17.5		19		19
Average	2.9		3.8		4.75
Grand total		55.5			
Grand average		3.7			

and select the cookies represented by each number. (We will consider this selection method below, but first let's consider the sample you actually draw.) Table 6-2 presents your selection.

You can see that the average from the sample of 5 cookies (Nos. 2, 6, 7, 11, and 14) is slightly higher than the total average for the 15 cookies. Naturally, had you selected a different set of 5 cookies you would have gotten a different average weight.

Sampling Error

The difference between the mean you determined from your sample of 5 (3.9) and the mean of the population of 15 (which was 3.7) is .2. This .2 is the *sampling error* of your sample. Thus sampling error is not the result of mistakes you have made, but is a measure of the variability of the sample from the population. Sampling error must be distinguished from *nonsampling errors,* which are due to other types of mistakes that may be made in a study. In the cookie study, if a cookie is weighed inaccurately or if your method of selecting the sample is somehow faulty, these mistakes will produce nonsampling errors. We will come to see that the larger your sample is, the more likely are your sampling errors to be small. However, larger studies (in which larger samples are generally drawn) can create more possibilities for nonsampling errors. This could occur if resources were too limited to allow effective follow-up of the entire sample, in which case there would be more bias due to nonresponse. (It's better to have a somewhat smaller sample with a higher response rate.) Nevertheless, it is important to point out that from the standpoint of sampling theory, larger samples are better! Researchers must decide how confident they want to be statistically in their findings, and then procure the resources to allow them to draw a sample of the requisite size.

Drawing Repeated Samples from the Same Population

The terminology used here should be made precise. We are considering the 15 cookies as the *population* of cookies with which we are concerned; the 5 selected cookies are a *sample* drawn from this population to be representative of the cookies, that is, a sample using methods to randomize the selection of the cookies, which will be discussed in detail below.

We could repeatedly select 5 cookies from the 15. Because there are so many different combinations of five numbers within the 15, we would be able to get thousands of different samples (for example, we could select Cookies 1, 2, 3, 4, 5 or 1, 2, 3, 4, 6, or Cookies 1, 3, 5, 7, 9 or 11, 12, 13, 14, 15). Each sample of 5 cookies would produce a different average weight for the cookies and a different range from the heaviest to the lightest cookie. Examine Table 6-3, which presents two other possible samples (Samples L and H). In Table 6-3, we see that the average weight of a cookie in Sample L is 2.5 ounces, while an average cookie in Sample H is twice the weight, 5 ounces. Now look back to Table 6-1 on the average weight of the 15 cookies, which was 3.7 ounces. Clearly, if you had drawn Sample L as your sample, the average weight would have been too low by quite a bit (3.7 − 2.5 = 1.2 ounces); and if you had selected Sample H, the average cookie weight would have been too high (3.7 − 5.0 = −1.3). In short, neither of these two samples would have been very representative of the population. Each would have had a substantial sampling error.

TABLE 6-2

WEIGHTS OF A SAMPLE OF 5 COOKIES

Cookie No.	Weight, oz
2	3
6	2.5
7	5
11	3
14	6
Total for sample	19.5
Average for sample	3.9

TABLE 6-3

WEIGHTS OF COOKIE SAMPLES L AND H

	Sample L		Sample H	
Cookie No.	Weight, oz		Cookie No.	Weight, oz
1	2.5		5	4
2	3		7	5
3	2		10	4.5
6	2.5		12	5.5
8	2.5		14	6
Total weight	12.5			25
Average weight	2.5			5

But in Table 6-2, we saw that the sample we drew first was much closer to the actual average of the 15 cookies (3.9 as compared to 3.7). Would we be more likely to draw one sample rather than another? Not if we use a random method of sampling. On any one trial, any of the thousands of possible samples could be selected if we use a random method. However, if we did repeated samples, we would tend to have more samples for which the average was closer to the grand average than to the extreme averages seen in Samples L and H.

Suppose we draw 100 samples of 5 cookies from the 15 cookies and determine the mean for each sample. Then we set up a graph in which the horizontal axis represents the average weights of the 5 cookies in each sample and the vertical axis represents the number of samples, or frequency, at which that average weight appears in a different sample. (Recall that there are many different combinations of cookie numbers that could produce the same average weights, since some of the cookies are of the same weight and many combinations of cookies would equal the same total weights.) For each of the average sample weights, we enter a narrow column or bar on the horizontal axis where it belongs. Each time we find another average weight of the same magnitude, we must extend the height of the bar upward to represent the frequency of the samples with that weight. What

we are producing in this graph is a histogram (as described in Chapter 5) which figuratively presents the array and frequency of average weights in the sample.

The Sampling Distribution of the Sample Mean

Figure 6-1 represents what the distributions of the means for repeated samples from the cookie population would hypothetically look like. An understanding of this distribution of the sample mean is

FIGURE 6-1

Histogram of cookie weights.

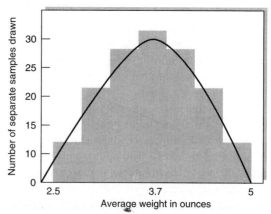

"the fundamental concept in sampling theory" (Williams, 1978, p. 57). This is true because from this distribution, the range and frequency of the sample mean (which determine the variance of the mean) can be studied. The square root of this sampling distribution mean, the *standard deviation* of the sampling distribution, is called the *standard error*. This standard deviation of the sampling distribution has no necessary relationship to the value of the population mean. Of course, this theoretical distribution is not actually observed (being composed of infinitely many samples), so its standard deviation cannot be calculated directly. The standard error (as calculated from one sample) estimates the standard deviation of the sampling distribution. When the sample size is large, 100 or more, this estimate will be very good indeed.

The size of this standard error is very important. If it is small, then the distribution will be narrow and crowded around the grand mean, and the likelihood of your sample mean being close to the population mean will be high. If the distribution is wide, the likelihood of your sample mean being close to the population mean will be lower, and the standard error will be larger. This graph based on samples measuring a continuous variable (the weights of cookies) comes to look like a bell-shaped curve (or what is called the *normal curve*), the greater the number of samples that are drawn.

How representative your sample is of the population from which it is drawn is important when you want to use the findings from your sample to infer to the nature of the population. If you compute a mean, a variance, or a standard deviation from a sample, these numbers which describe the central tendency and distribution of the sample are referred to as *statistics*, that is, summary descriptions of particular variables in a sample. (Statistics will be discussed in greater depth in Chapter 15.) If the sample was selected according to the rules of probability, a statistic (such as the average of a particular variable) will be an estimate of the true mean of that particular variable within the population, which would be called a *parameter*. In most cases, since only the statistic (such as the average of a particular variable) from the sample is known, it must be used to make estimates of what the parameter really would be in the population.

The Normal Curve

The distributions from continuous variables (like the cookie weights) approach the normal curve as samples are repeated or as the sample size increases.[2] What is useful about the normal curve is that it makes it possible on the basis of probability theory to calculate what proportion of the sample statistics (the estimates from each sample drawn) will fall within a given distance from the mean of the population (the mean parameter).

This distance from the mean—the difference between the average measured weight of several different samples of cookies and the true mean of the entire population of cookies—is the standard error of the sampling distribution (that is, the standard deviation of the sampling distribution mean). Thus within one standard error, just over 34 percent of the sample estimates will occur. If you consider one standard error in each direction from the mean, then 68 percent of the sample estimates would likely occur. Two standard errors above and below the mean would account for 95 percent of the sample estimates; three standard errors above and below the population mean would account for more than 99 percent of the sample estimates.

What you can infer from this, in the case of a single random sample, is that your sample mean has, for example, a 99 percent chance of falling within three standard errors of the population parameter, a 95 percent chance of falling within two standard errors of the parameter, and a 68 percent chance of falling within one standard error of the population parameter. These are the *confidence levels* that a researcher can use.

---

[2]The sampling distribution of a binomial variable (one with only two categories: success or failure, yes or no, support or no support) also approximates the normal curve as the sample size increases.

So, for example, you might claim to be 68 percent confident that the mean from the sample drawn is within one standard error of the mean of the population.

The size of the standard error is affected both by the variance of the population and by the size of the samples drawn. The larger the sample size, the narrower the sampling distribution will be, and, thus, the better the normal curve will approximate the sampling distribution of means. (This follows mathematically from what statisticians call the *central limit theorem.*) Since the variance of each sample mean is divided by the sample size, the bigger the sample size, the smaller the variance. In a sampling distribution, the standard error decreases as the sampling size increases. We will examine how the size of the sample affects results again when we consider various types of sample designs.

What we want to know, whenever we draw a sample, is how much confidence we can have that the mean of that sample is reasonably near the mean of the population (or, in other words, that the sampling error is not too large). However, it is usually the case (1) that we do not know the population mean and (2) that we have not drawn numerous samples from the population in order to determine the sampling distribution. This is where the normal curve comes to be useful.

We can replace the population mean with the sample mean and the standard deviation of the sampling distribution with the standard error of the sample. To calculate the standard error from the sample data, divide the sample's standard deviation by the square root of the number of cases. Within three standard errors above and below the mean, we could be 99 percent confident that our sample mean was within three standard deviations of the mean of the population. This would be the *confidence interval* we were using.

Or, more narrowly, the interval within one standard error above and below the mean would represent the 68 percent confidence level. The *normal curve* graphed in Figure 6-2 represents a sampling distribution of differences from the mean as

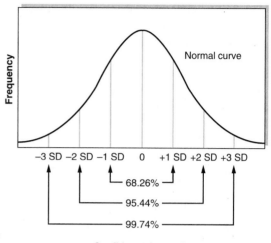

Confidence intervals

FIGURE 6-2
The normal curve, standard deviations (SD), and confidence intervals.   (From Jack Levin: *Elementary Statistics in Social Research*, 3d ed., Harper & Row, New York, 1983, p. 129.)

a probability distribution. We can choose the confidence interval that satisfies us. If we want to be 95 percent confident that our sample mean falls within a specific distance from the population mean, then we must move out two standard deviation intervals away from the sample mean in each direction to achieve that certainty.

SAMPLING TERMINOLOGY

A *sample* is a selected set of *elements* (or *units*) drawn from a larger whole of all the elements, the *population.* This population may be fully enumerated or it may only be hypothetical. An agricultural researcher . . . could sample a set of tomatoes from a population of "all tomatoes" or "all tomatoes raised on Farm X." In neither of these cases could the population of tomatoes be actually enumerated. You simply cannot draw up a completely accurate list of all tomatoes on Farm X.)

The enumeration of the population (that is, the "list" of the population) is the *sampling frame.* A small population might be precisely enumerated, but many large populations could never be completely enumerated; there will always be some names left off, and some on the list who should not be there. Therefore, the sampling frame is the best attempt that can be made to enumerate the members of the population. In short, the frame is the empirical representation of the population. What this means is that the sampling frame (the list) is what is used to represent the population empirically (the known, observed, listed members of the population). When a sampling frame is prepared, the sample is a subset selected from this frame.

If the sample is to be drawn directly from the sampling frame, without considering subgroups of elements within the population, then every unit is considered at each selection of the sample members. If the units are to be grouped first, then the groups would be the first or *primary sampling units* and the individual elements within the groups would be the second or *secondary sampling units*.

POPULATIONS, SAMPLING FRAMES, AND SAMPLES

The quality of a sample, however carefully it is selected, can be no better than the sampling frame from which it is drawn. If the sampling frame is not truly representative of the population it supposedly enumerates, then the sample cannot be representative of the population. In fact, samples are only really representative of sampling frames. Therefore, in designing a sample, you should consider the possible mismatches of sampling frames to populations.

As I will discuss in Chapter 7 on surveys, telephone directories, which may seem to be good sampling frames, are notoriously weak sampling frames for city residents. Poorer people are much less likely to have telephones, and many people in large cities have unlisted numbers for reasons of security. In rural areas, telephone directories are considered to be much more representative of households and therefore can be used more effectively as sampling frames.

Any list that is used as a sampling frame should be given careful scrutiny. Suppose you want a list of all the students at your college. That seems unproblematic. But what should be the criteria used to determine the list? Is the student population at your college based on all students registered for courses in a particular term? Do these students need to be degree-seeking? Or would nondegree students be included as well? Are students who have not paid their tuition for that term excluded from the list? Most colleges can generate different lists of their students, depending on the criteria requested. But in drawing your sample, and in discussing your findings, you need to keep these criteria in mind.

A sampling frame of students at a college is like a membership list. It represents an association which is of fairly long duration. Membership lists of this type often make the easiest and best sampling frames. Let's consider the characteristics of some other lists prepared to record the participation of individuals, which may lead to better or worse sampling frames.

For example, a sampling frame could be based on a list of persons who came to a particular type of institution in one state (say, a blood bank in Texas), who ordered a certain product (tulip bulbs from Holland), who participated in a single event (the 25,000 who attended an antiabortion rally held in Kansas on August 25, 1991, and heard Pat Robertson speak). Let's consider the problems inherent in each of these lists, which would need to be considered in deciding if such lists could be used effectively as sampling frames.

For the blood donors, we would first need to get a list of all blood banks in Texas so that we could select at random a number of blood banks that would be representative of the whole group (the technique for doing this will be discussed later). Then we would need to get from these blood banks the names and addresses of all persons who had donated blood during a particular period of time. We would need to consider the possibility that these blood donor lists might not include all the persons who donated blood at the selected banks during that period of time (in other words, we would want to know the match between the sampling frame and the population). Since blood banks would be unlikely to let persons give blood without recording this information, you might expect that blood bank lists would be composed of an accurate compilation of donors.

A list of those who order tulip bulbs would also probably be quite a good one, since such orders would require paying for them and this would generate names and addresses, etc. Marketing firms use such lists to generate more customers for other products. The issue with these lists would be whether these buyers represented some definable larger population. Would it be appropriate to assume that such a list comprised a representative sample of tulip lovers? Were orders for these bulbs a response to an advertisement? Where did the advertisement appear? (Was it in a regional publication? Did it appear in a special-interest magazine?) In other words, were certain types of people more likely to have been exposed to this ad than others? In this case, the list of tulip bulb customers might be an accurate list of those who ordered bulbs, but it is not apparent whom, exactly, these customers might represent.

Finally, let's consider the antiabortion rally participants. What type of list might be available? It is unlikely that the names of those who attended would have been written down and registered in any manner. However, lists of members of antiabortion groups in Kansas and elsewhere might be available. But one could make no assumptions as to which members attended the rally.

Much of the issue of the relationship between a population and a sampling frame is that the frame must be truthfully described. But in many sampling situations, no sampling frame can be established. Here's an example. Suppose you want to sample people who have gone to Disney World. You fly down to Orlando and interview people there for a few days. Clearly you have not drawn their names from any sampling frame, for a list of all people who go to Disney World does not exist. This is not to say that there is no population of

Disney World attenders; it only means that there has been no effort to keep records of their names. There is obviously some record of who goes to Disney World maintained by marketing companies, and this may give you some ideas as to what types of people (by age, sex, race, geographical residence) they are. You might then be able to use this information to select a quota sample (to be explained later) representing these different types of persons. However, since this sample has no sampling frame, it is not a probability sample, but a form of nonprobability sampling, to be described below.

DESIGNING A PROBABILITY SAMPLE

Suppose you plan to carry out a survey of students at Gungho College (GC) concerning their satisfaction with their extracurricular activities. In this hypothetical sample design, as in an actual survey, the design for the sample must correspond to the characteristics of the survey itself. As Leslie Kish states in his definitive text,

> The survey objectives should determine the sample design; but the determination is actually a two-way process, because the problems of sample design often influence and change the survey objectives *(1965, p. 4).*

Let's say that there are 5,000 students at GC, and you decide to select a sample of 100. Now you need to do three things: (1) you must define who the population of students will include (all students registered in the current term, full-time students only, degree-seeking students, or whatever); (2) you must secure a list of these students; and (3) you must select a method for sampling these students so that your sample is truly representative of the population.

You have to think hard about the nature of the population of students you will be studying in relation to the survey you plan to carry out. If you consider what factors might affect students' attitudes toward extracurricular activities, one question seems very important: Do students live on campus (or stay around campus) in such a way that they are exposed to extracurricular activities and to other students engaged in such activities? This question implies that there may be groups of students characterized by their living arrangements or by their on-campus presence who may be more likely to be exposed to extracurricular activities. In terms of living arrangements, it would seem important to consider whether students live on campus or off. In addition, it would seem relevant to know whether students are employed during the school year. Those employed would probably have less time for extracurricular activities. These group differences could be measured by two variables: the living location (1 = "on campus"; 2 = "off campus") and whether the student works during school year (1 = "yes"; 2 = "no"). Now you are ready to consider different types of sampling methods.

METHODS OF SELECTING PROBABILITY SAMPLES

Simple Random Sampling (SRS)

Simple random sampling (SRS) is a method of sampling in which the elements in a sampling frame are numbered and then drawn into the sample if they match the random numbers which have been selected. Suppose that you are able to get a list of the 5,000 students registered spring term at Gungho and that you decide to ignore the subgroups of students we have mentioned. You might number the students on the list from 0001 to 5,000, and then use a *random number* series to select your sample. This would be *simple random sampling (SRS)*. Today there are numerous computer programs, such as SPSS[x] (which is described in Appendix C), that will generate random numbers for you (after you have specified the range within which these numbers should be drawn) and select a sample based on these random numbers. Box 6-2 describes a method for devising your own computer program to generate random numbers,

using BASIC. If you decide to use SRS, you might use one of these methods, or find out if your computer center has a different method for generating random numbers.

The more traditional method of selecting random numbers has been to use a random number list. There are books printed with as many as a million random numbers (Rand Corporation, 1955). A single page from such a book is included in Appendix B. Box 6-3 describes how to use a random number list.

Whichever method you use to select the random numbers, every number has an equal chance of being chosen. Each time you select a number, the corresponding student on the numbered list is drawn into the sample. However, the feasibility of carrying out a simple random sample may depend on the type of sampling frame that can be provided (a consecutively numbered one is most helpful). For this reason, it is less commonly used than systematic sampling.

Systematic Sampling

A more common form of selection for a probability sample is to select every *n*th person once you have made a random start—this is *systematic sampling*. This method is simpler if you are working by hand. Let's say you want the sample of 100 from a population of 5,000. In this case, you simply pick every fiftieth name after beginning with a random start. How do you select where to begin with your list of names? Since you want one-fiftieth of the names to appear in your sample, you should start somewhere among the first 50 names and then consider the list continuous, so that when you reach the bottom you will go back to the top. In this way, every element on the list will have an equal chance of being selected.

You might select a number randomly between 1 and 50. Let's say it's 23. You will take the 23rd name on the list, then count down 50 more and take the 73rd name, the 123rd name, the 173rd name, etc., until you have selected 100 names.

Remember that the sampling frame list must

BOX 6-2

HOW TO GENERATE RANDOM NUMBERS FROM A COMPUTER

GETTING RANDOM NUMBERS FROM A COMPUTER*

Most home and larger computers use a language called BASIC, which has in it a pseudo-random number generator. A program such as the following will provide random digits, one at a time, between specified limits. The same string of random digits will be given unless a different starter digit is given.
   Check your computer's BASIC manual on how to enter and use the following program.

```
10 PRINT "******** RANDOM NUMBERS ********"
15 PRINT
20 PRINT "GIVE ANY STARTER NUMBER";
25 INPUT N2
30 PRINT "HOW MANY RANDOM NUMBERS";
35 INPUT N1
40 PRINT "RANGE = (LOWEST)";
45 INPUT N3
50 PRINT"        (HIGHEST)";
55 INPUT N4
60 SEC=VAL(RIGHT$(TIME$,2))+N2
65 FOR I=1 TO SEC
70 DUMMY=RND(1)
75 NEXT I
80 FOR I=1 TO N1
85 NO=RND(1)*(N4-N3)
90 NO=INT(NO)+N3
100 PRINT "PRESS ENTER";
105 INPUT X
110 NEXT I
115 PRINT "MORE NUMBERS";
120 N$=LEFT$(R$,1)
125 IF N$ = "Y" THEN 10
130 END
```

Note: Omit lines 100 and 105 if you do not want to press the Enter key to get each random number. BASIC on some computers may use slightly different commands. Check your BASIC manual.

*D. McTavish and H. Loether: *Descriptive and Inferential Statistics*, 3d ed., Allyn and Bacon, 1988.

not be ordered in a way that sets up systematic intervals. If there is some fixed, repeated interval in the list (such as a sergeant always listed prior to every 100 privates) then such a list would not produce an unbiased sample. Usually lists are alphabetical and present no problems.

Stratified Sampling

Stratified sampling is a variation on the forms of sampling discussed above. In *stratified sampling*, the sampling frame is divided into one or more *strata*, based on sex, region, grade, etc. Then the sample is drawn from each of the strata. The rea-

BOX 6-3

SELECTING A SAMPLE FROM A RANDOM NUMBER LIST

Assume that there are 5,000 students on the list, numbered from 0001 to 5,000. You want a sample of 100. Look at the random number list in Appendix B. Note that there are sets of five 2-digit numbers in columns and rows. Since you want to select from among 4-digit numbers ranging from 0001 to 5,000, you must decide to combine two 2-digit numbers to form 4-digit numbers.

But how to start. You must first determine which sets of two 2-digit numbers to use, where to begin on the table, and which direction to move in. It makes no real difference what choices you make as long as you make a *random start*. You could close your eyes and merely point to a place on the table; you could throw dice to determine how many sets to move down or over; etc.

Let's say you decide to use the last four numbers in each set (2,533 would be the last 4 digits in the first set of 5 two-digit numbers), to begin three whole—5 two-digit numbers across by 5 two-digit numbers down—sets down and four whole sets over (with 3,433), and to move down the column in making your choices. Since 3,433 is lower than 5,000, you would select the student numbered 3,433 for your sample. The next number down is 4,201, which is also within the range, so you would select that student. Then you would likewise select 0610. The next number down is 6,493; since it is higher than 5,000, it is skipped.* The next number, 1,368, would be selected, but the next two numbers, 7,186 and 8,253, would need to be skipped. When you reach the bottom of one column, you would merely continue to the top of the next column. You would proceed in this fashion until you have selected 100 students.

*This example describes random selection *without replacement*. Many statisticians consider random sampling *with replacement* to be purer.

son researchers often want samples stratified on demographic or social characteristics, such as sex or region, is that such factors might influence responses. Stratified sampling can be used in conjunction with either simple random sampling or systematic sampling (the more usual choice). For our hypothetical study at Gungho College, we might order our sample first by whether students live on or off campus. In effect, we would make two lists from the sampling frame. One would be for on-campus students, the other for off-campus students. From each of these lists, two sublists would be drawn up—one for those with jobs, the other for those without jobs. As a result, the original sampling frame would have been broken down into four lists (the box, Stratifying a Sample, depicts how this could be set up). Thus your sample would be of 80 on-campus students, 25 of whom work, and 55 of whom do not; and 20 off-campus students, 15 of whom work, and 5 of whom do not.

To get the same proportions in the sample as are in the population, you merely need to group the names together by category, and by categories within categories. With one continuous list broken down as shown, you could use the same procedure as for a systematic sample and select every *n*th name in each category. This would produce the desired one-fiftieth (.02) of the population from each subcategory. Or, if you set up four separate lists, you could employ simple random sampling techniques until you had a sufficient number from each subgroup.

Stratified sampling sets up *homogeneous groups* and then selects within these groups to the proportions in which these groups are represented within the sample. Box 6–4 describes the type of stratified sample Hirschi used in his juvenile delinquency study, presented in Chapter 1. Box 6–5 offers Hirschi's current reflections on the sampling techniques used in that study. If you desire to make the groups even in size once the sample data are collected, this can be done by weighting.

STRATIFYING A SAMPLE: COLLEGE STUDENTS' SATISFACTION WITH EXTRACURRICULAR ACTIVITIES

A. Sampling frame = 5,000 (based on a list of all students at Gungho College, fall 1992)
   Desired sample size = 100

B. First stratum:

Location of Residence	**Desired Sample Size**
On campus = 4,000	80
Off campus = 1,000	20

Second stratum:

Work Status	**Desired Sample Size**
Work = 2,000	40
Do not work = 3,000	60

C. Desired sample sizes for stratified sample:

Residence On Campus		**Residence Off Campus**		
Work Status	**Desired Sample Size**	**Work Status**	**Desired Sample Size**	**Sample Totals**
Work = 1250	= 25	Work = 750	= 15	40
Do not work = 2750	= 55	Do not work = 250	= 5	60
Sample totals	80		20	100

Weighting for Disproportionate Sampling

Many probability samples employ a *weighting* technique to give subgroups their fair share of weight in the analyses. (In mathematical terms, all samples are weighted: if the sample sizes are used directly, they are weighted by 1.) Suppose you are doing a study comparing the academic performance of foreign students and American students at American colleges. Naturally there are many fewer foreign students than American students. Let's say you plan to select 50 American students per campus. You may decide for purposes of comparison to select 50 foreign students as well. However, at a college of 1000 students, where 100 are foreign students, you would give the foreign students a 50 percent chance of being selected for the sample, but the American students a 5.5 percent chance of being selected. In this case, a subgroup would have been "oversampled" in order to get a large enough number to study from an underrepresented group in the population. This method might

well be a good strategy if you compensate in the analysis stage of the study by weighting the findings.

The foreign students in this example are just over nine times as likely to be selected for the sample as the American students. Since the Americans make up nine-tenths of the students and the foreign students one-tenth, you could determine the weights by multiplying this fractional proportion times the number selected from each group. Thus at the college described, the findings from the 50 foreign students would be multiplied by one-tenth, and those from the 50 American students by nine-tenths. This means that in weighted terms 5 foreign students were equivalent to 45 American students. This would be the same as simply weighting the American sample by 9. Most computer package programs allow for simple procedures to weight a sample or parts of a sample. Or you might compose tables separately for the foreign students and the American students and then multiply the American data by 9.

BOX 6-4

HIRSCHI'S STRATIFIED SAMPLE IN THE DELINQUENCY STUDY

In Hirschi's (1969) study of juvenile delinquency, described in Chapter 1, the sample was drawn from the population of 17,500 students entering the public junior and senior high schools in western Contra Costa County (across the bay from San Francisco) in 1964. This population was stratified according to race, sex, school, and grade. Certain subgroups were sampled more heavily than others (85 percent of black boys, 60 percent of black girls, 30 percent of non-black boys, 12 percent of non-black girls). This form of *disproportionate sampling* (described below) was carried out to ensure that sufficiently large numbers of key subgroups would be available for analysis. This procedure produced a sample size of 5,545 students.

Let me mention at this juncture that Hirschi's actual (or realized) sample ended up only three-quarters the size of the intended sample. This reduction was due to losses of members in the selected sample, which is termed *attrition*. The attrition occurred for several reasons. The school system required parental permission for a stu-

dent's participation in the survey. Letters seeking approval were sent to parents, and if there was no response, a follow-up letter was sent. Finally, a field worker would visit the parents who still had not responded. Despite these efforts, 6.5 percent of the parents refused permission and 5.5 percent could not be contacted.

Another cause of attrition was due to the time lag between when the sampling frame for the survey was put together in the fall of 1964 and when the survey was administered in the spring of 1965. During this period, 6.2 percent of the students chosen for the sample either had transferred out of the county or had dropped out of school. Another 7.1 percent were absent during the administration (and follow-up administrations) of the survey. Once the surveys were completed, a screening indicated that 1.2 percent had to be excluded because of invalid responses on the answer sheet. All in all, 26.5 percent of the original sample was "lost" through these various forms of attrition.

Source: Travis Hirschi: *Causes of Delinquency*, University of California Press, Berkeley, Calif., 1969, pp. 35–37.

Hirschi's (1969) sample for the delinquency study used a form of disproportionate sampling for the different race and sex subgroups in the study. Each black girl in the sample represented about 8.0 other black girls, whereas each black boy represented only 1.2 other black boys (Hirschi, 1969, p. 37). (You may recall that the delinquency rates for the girls in the sample were so low that they were ultimately excluded from the analysis, even though they had been a part of the sample design.)

Weighting may also be used to cancel out the effects of differential response rates from different subgroups. Considering the response rates of the various subgroups—recall that this refers to the proportion of those sampled who responded— Hirschi used the following weighting procedure. If white girls had an overall average response rate of

65 percent in all of the schools and in a particular junior high school they responded at a rate of 70 percent, the excess responses from the particular junior high school would be selected randomly and discarded from the analysis (Hirschi, 1969, p. 38). In schools with lower response rates from white girls, the responses would be weighted to become the equivalent of a 65 percent rate.

Multistage Cluster Sampling

Cluster sampling differs from stratified sampling in that strata are homogeneous groups created for the purpose of sample selection, while clusters bring together *heterogeneous groups* that are usually already formed as established groups, for example, organizations (such as schools) or residen-

BOX 6-5

HIRSCHI'S REFLECTIONS ON THE SAMPLE DESIGN FOR THE RICHMOND YOUTH PROJECT (RYP)

What comes to mind is how sensible Alan Wilson's (the principal investigator of the RYP) research plan really was. He designed the sample the way samples should be designed, taking into account the needs of analysis, the greater interest of the project in some groups than in others, the need ultimately to make estimates for the population as a whole. (The contrast case is the general population sample in which every case has an equal chance of being selected, and where meaningful analysis of important subgroups is usually next to impossible.) And he kept very good track of the ways in which the final sample of respondents differed from the population from which they were drawn. As I note in *Causes of Delinquency,* the RYP carefully documented its departure from the ideal sample. As a result, as I predicted, it has occasionally attracted utterly unfair criticism. I remain convinced that such documentation, whatever qualms it may produce, is better than the optimistic ignorance that often pervades descriptions of sampling procedures.

Source: Adapted from a written response of Travis Hirschi to the query: "Is there anything particularly memorable about the sample designs of the Richmond Youth Project that would help social researchers today in thinking about how they might design a research study?" (Spring 1992).

tial locations (such as blocks). Characteristics of individuals are often the criteria for the strata (sex, race, etc.); social organizations of comparable types are often the basis of the clusters. Thus in *multistage cluster sampling* we first establish heterogeneous clusters (e.g., schools), then select members of the clusters at a second stage.

What is most important about cluster sampling is that the list of all elements required for the final sampling units need not be available in the beginning, but only the list of all clusters. Usually the clusters are sampled first, and then the units within the clusters. The National Opinion Research Center sample drawn for the *High School and Beyond* survey (see Chapter 1), which Coleman and his colleagues analyzed for their private school–public school study, had multistage cluster design, described in Box 6–6.

As was true in the *High School and Beyond* sample, cluster sampling is often combined with stratified sampling: in this case, clusters are sampled first, then subgroups (strata) within the clusters, and then individual units within the strata. A common form of multistage cluster sampling with stratification is used when researchers want to carry out surveys of areas (cities, states). This is what you could do to sample a city:

1. Get a list of all the census tracts in the city. (Census tracts are the subdivisions the Census Bureau develops to collect the census.)
2. Using either SRS or the systematic method, select census tracts.
3. Get a list of all blocks in each census tract selected.
4. Select the same number of blocks from each tract.
5. Get a list of each household on the selected blocks. (This may require going out to the blocks.)
6. Select households within each block.
7. Get a list of the members of each household. (This would probably be done during the interview itself.)
8. Select a member of that household to interview, using some random method. (Usually there will be definitions of what types of household members can be selected for the final sampling units. For example, they may have to be age 18 or older.)

When there are so many selection stages, errors are likely to increase. Since the members of a cluster tend to be more like one another than like members of other clusters, it is usually better to sample a greater number of clusters (as was done in the *High School and Beyond* sample) and a smaller number of elements within each cluster. However, this is a more time-consuming and costly method of sampling, since each different cluster requires a new sampling procedure within it.

PPS: Probability Proportionate to Size Sampling

When clusters to be selected for a sample contain greatly varying strata within them, the *PPS sampling method* can be employed to select strata proportionate to their size within clusters. If you want to sample households in a city, you might first draw a sample of city blocks. If the city has 5,000 blocks, and you select a sample of 100, you will have given every block a 2 percent chance of being selected.[3] However, there may be great diversity within the blocks in terms of the number of households. Some blocks may be made up of high rises with hundreds of families in a building, others of large single-family homes with only one family per building. Let's assume that there are 200,000 households in this city and that you want to select 10 households per block.

To enable every household to have an equal chance of being drawn into the sample, blocks should have a probability of being selected into the sample proportionate to the number of households on that block. This means that a block with 500 households should have a five times higher chance of being selected into the sample than one with 100 households. PPS is a sampling method that will first select clusters proportionate to size, and then give the strata within the clusters a chance of selection proportionate to their number.

This is a two-stage process. Returning to our example, let's say that in a city with 5,000 blocks and 200,000 households, we want to select 1,000 households (100 blocks selected at the first stage,

and 10 households per block selected at the second stage). Here is how we can be assured that every household will have an equal chance of being selected.

First we need to select the 100 clusters (blocks). To determine the probability of any particular block being selected, divide the number of households on that block by the number of households in the city and multiply this by the number of blocks to be selected (100). If Block X has 50 households, the following formula would determine its probability of being selected from the 200,000 households in the city:

$$100 \times \frac{50}{200,000} = .025$$

In this equation, 100 represents the number of blocks to be selected, 50 the number of households on Block X, and 200,000 the number of households in the city.

If Block X is drawn into the sample, then each of its 50 households would have the following probability of being selected:

$$\frac{10 \text{ (selected from each block)}}{50 \text{ (households on Block X)}} = .2$$

If you multiply the probabilities for the block being selected (.025) by the probability of a household on the block being selected (.2), you get the overall probability of each household on Block X being selected (.025 × .2 = .005) as 5 in 1,000.

It turns out to be the case that whatever the number of households on a block, the PPS method will produce the same probability of each being selected. For example, on Block Y there are 200 households. Here the probability of Block Y being selected for the sample would be

$$100 \times \frac{200}{200,000} = .1$$

In this equation, 100 is the number of blocks to be selected, 200 the number of households on Block Y, and 200,000 the number of households in the city. The probability of any particular household on Block Y being selected would be

---

[3]The example here is similar to one used by Babbie (1992, pp. 223–225).

BOX 6-6

MULTISTAGE CLUSTER SAMPLING IN THE *HIGH SCHOOL AND BEYOND* SURVEY

As you may recall, Coleman's study (described in Chapter 1) was based on a large, national survey of high school sophomores and seniors in 1980, called *High School and Beyond* (HSB). The National Opinion Research Center (NORC) wanted to develop a sample of students for HSB from whom one could generalize to all students in the country. But how does one go about finding such representative students? One logical way to find high school students representative of the nation as a whole is to begin by finding high schools representative of the country. But according to what principles do you select the high schools? And from what source do you get a list of the high schools?

Let me restate what I have just said, using the terminology of sampling given before. The NORC researchers wanted to produce a *probability sample* of high school sophomores and seniors, representative of the *population* of all high school sophomores and seniors in United States high schools in the spring of 1980. The *elements* of their sample would be individual students; but they would need to select these elements at three stages. First they would select schools (the clusters that would form the *primary sampling units*) ; then they would select sophomore and senior students within schools (the strata that would form the *secondary sampling units*) ; and then they would select the individual students within those schools and those class levels (the *tertiary sampling units*).

The list of all schools would make up the *sampling frame.* Thus the first step in constructing the sample was to find a list of all high schools in the United States to serve as the sampling frame from which the sample could be drawn. Where would the researchers find such a list? It would be fairly easy to find a list of all public schools, for each community would have such a list. Remember, however, that NORC wanted *all* schools, including private schools. Private schools are not necessarily part of some central system. Some are religiously affiliated (mostly Catholic); some have no religious affiliation; some serve very specialized types of students

(schools for ballet dancers, schools for the children of foreign diplomats). Where would a list exist that might include all private high schools?

Finding a list is often the major chore of sampling. If only every "whole" were printed out on some easily accessible list, then sampling would be a snap! Here's how the NORC researchers put together their list of all schools. They created what they called a *school universe file* (that is, a composite list of all the sampling units from which the sample might be drawn). To develop this file, they relied on lists which had been created by others. A common procedure in sampling is to track down lists prepared by others which may be relevant for your sampling design. This universe file was based on two lists of public and two of private schools prepared by different organizations (Coleman et al., 1982b, *High School Achievement,* pp. 15–16). On the basis of these lists, NORC built a cumulative list representative of all schools named on any of the lists.

In addition, NORC wanted a *special* subsample of high-performance public and private schools. This was developed in somewhat different ways for the public and private schools. For the private schools, the 11 high schools with the largest proportions of National Merit semifinalists were chosen from those in the private school file (but no more than 1 school was selected from a single state). For the public schools, once the initial sample was drawn, a subsample of 12 high-performance public schools drawn on exactly the same criteria (percentage of National Merit semifinalists and no 2 schools from the same state) were selected (Coleman et al., 1982b, pp. 9–10). (Note that these two subsamples are not completely comparable—the private school subsample was drawn from the sampling frame representative of the population of all private high schools; the public school subsample was drawn from the selected sample of the public high schools and was therefore representative of the sample, but less directly representative of the population from which the sample was drawn.)

Every sample has some problems. The important thing is to recognize what they are and to state them in describing your sampling design. Coleman and his colleagues identified the following as one of the major problems with their sampling design. It was difficult to generate a really good list of private schools, because of the nature of such schools. Non-Catholic private schools are particularly diverse in quality and status. They range from elite, long-established schools to casually run schools that may arise and disappear with little notice.

Whenever an element was selected which turned out not to be a school or which appeared to be an unacceptable school, a replacement had to be selected from the same category of schools. A further complication was that some schools refused to participate. Where this occurred, substitutions were made. Once a school was selected, the sophomores and seniors in that school became the population from which the student sample was drawn. Approximately 36 sophomores and 36 seniors were sampled from each of the two classes in each of the 1,122 schools (Coleman et al., 1982a, "Cognitive Outcomes in Public and Private Schools"). The strategy here was to sample many clusters, but only a few units within the clusters. If students were unavailable, because of continued absence from school, they were not replaced. Most of the nonresponse among the students was due to continued absence, not to refusal to participate.

Table 6-4 shows the sample sizes, the re-

TABLE 6-4

SAMPLE OF SCHOOLS FROM THE 1980 *HIGH SCHOOL AND BEYOND* SURVEY
Sample of Schools as Drawn Corrected Through Replacement, and as Realized, and Sample of Students as Drawn and as Realized

Item	Total	Public	Catholic	Other Private	H.P.
1. Total numbers of schools represented	20,316	15,766	1,571	26,966	12
2. Initial sample size	1,122	984	88	38	12
3. Number of eligible schools	1,019	893	86	28	12
4. Number of eligibles after replacing ineligibles	1,118	982	88	36	12
5. Final realized sample size	1,015	893	84	27	11
School Response Rates					
6. Among initial eligible schools (row 3)	.71	.70	.79	.50	.75
7. Final rate neglecting substitution (row 5/row 4)	.91	.91	.95	.75	.92
Number of Students					
8. Total eligible students	70,170	62,027	5,965	1,387	791
9. Sophomores eligible in final school sample	35,338	31,241	2,975	727	395
10. Seniors eligible in final school sample	34,832	30,786	2,990	660	396
11. Sophomores in final sample	30,280	26,448	2,831	631	370
12. Seniors in final sample	28,450	24,891	2,697	551	311
Student Response Rates					
13. Sophomores (row 11/row 9)	.86	.85	.95	.87	.94
14. Seniors (row 12/row 10)	.82	.81	.90	.83	.79

Source: Coleman et al., *High school Achievement: Public, Catholic and Private Schools Compared,* Basic Books, New York, 1982, p. 12.

sponse rates, and the differences between the types of schools. An eligible school was a four-year high school, operating in 1980. An eligible student was one listed as a sophomore or senior in that year who was still present at the school. The *response rates* (to be discussed in greater detail in Chapter 7) are estimated by dividing the actual number who participated in the survey by the eligible number. Note that the response rate for the schools was highest from the Catholic schools (79 percent), lowest from the other private schools (50 percent). Among students, the response rates were highest, again, for the Catholic school sophomores (95 percent), lowest for the high-performance private school seniors (79 percent). Because of the differences in the quality of the sample among the various sectors, the sampling error varied across the groups (Coleman et al., 1982b, pp. 10–13).

$$\frac{10}{200} = .05$$

In this equation, 10 is the number of households to be selected from each block and 200 the number of households on Block Y. Hence if Block Y is selected, every household on it has a 5 percent chance of being drawn into the sample.

Thus the overall probability of the two-stage process (.1 × .05 = .005) leads to the same result. In short, the overall probability of any one house being selected from the larger Block Y (the block with more households) is just as good as any one house being selected from the smaller Block X (the block with fewer households). This is because the larger block has a higher probability of getting into the sample, but a lower probability of any one household being selected on the block. On the other hand, the smaller block has a lower probability of being selected in the sample, but if it is selected, the households on it would have a higher probability of being selected at the second stage.

Mathematically, this occurs because the number of households on each block serves as the numerator in the first equation and the denominator in the second equation. Therefore the differential number of households per block is canceled out. Thus, the overall probability for a household being selected in a city of 200,000 households, where 100 blocks and 10 households per block would be selected, would be

$$100 \times \frac{10}{200,000} = .005$$

Because blocks tend to have similar-type housing on them, they tend to include homogeneous households. For this reason, it is not necessary to sample too many households on any one block. Instead, it is preferable to sample a greater number of blocks.

Deciding What Type of Sample to Employ

If you wish to do a survey in which the responses to your questionnaire can be generalized to some more widely defined population, then you must develop a probability sample. You cannot generalize your findings to some wider group without a probability design. In addition, many statistical tests (some of which will be discussed in Chapter 15) assume that the data have been collected from a sample selected according to the rules of probability. This means that some statistical tests will be meaningless if they are applied to findings from a nonprobability sample.

Survey research is often based on probability samples. Content analysis (discussed in Chapter 10) may also use a sampling design for choosing contents to examine based on the rules of probability. Experimental designs and field research rarely use probability samples to select subjects for study. Subjects in experiments are usually volunteers.

However, data from experiments can be tested with statistical measures if the subjects have been assigned to the experimental and control groups by a process of randomization (see Chapter 8 for a broader discussion of this). In field research, probability samples are virtually never employed.

The design and objectives of the study will determine what type of sample is needed. Coleman wanted his findings on public and private high schools to be representative of all such schools in the United States. Thus he required a national sample which would be representative of schools and the students within them (this led him to a multistage cluster design). Naturally, he needed a probability sample; otherwise he would not have been able to claim that what he found in his sample was representative of high schools in general.

Hirschi, on the other hand, was studying the correlates of self-reported delinquency among youths. A national sample might have been desirable, but a smaller area survey was regarded as sufficient, on the grounds that a representative local sample of urban youths, wherever they were from, might exemplify the factors related to committing delinquent acts as well as any other. However, Hirschi did utilize a probability sample (a stratified sample) in order to be able to relate his evidence to delinquency records in the area.

In any study, two important factors in determining what type of sample to employ are feasibility and cost. Probability samples require finding or developing a sampling frame. When such lists are unavailable and unobtainable, then probability sampling may not be feasible. In addition, large-scale sampling efforts may be very expensive and may be beyond the reach of many researchers.

Because of the great expense in generating a national probability sample, many researchers reuse data that have been collected in national surveys by large survey organizations. Box 6–7 describes the evolving national probability sample design used for the *General Social Survey (GSS)* described in Chapter 4. Using an already collected dataset for a new study is called secondary analysis and will be discussed in detail in Chapter 10. Secondary analysis has become one of the most common forms of research currently done in sociology, precisely because it enables the researcher to work with data based on a high-quality sampling design that the individual researcher would be unlikely to be able to collect personally. In short, secondary analysis allows many researchers to work with data based on very good samples.

When the researcher wants to collect his or her own data, and it is not feasible to draw a probability sample, there are a number of nonprobability techniques that can be used. Such samples often have serious limitations because those selected into the sample are not representative of the population from which they are drawn. Thus, researchers should always try to develop a probability sample if at all possible. Nevertheless, nonprobability samples may be satisfactory for many types of study designs and objectives.

NONPROBABILITY SAMPLING

In many instances probability sampling is simply not feasible. A sample that does not follow the rules of probability sampling is a *nonprobability sample.* Although many statistical tests require probability sampling, in certain cases nonprobability samples are the best that can be achieved. It is important that you understand whether you can select a probability sample, and that, if you cannot, you consider the best means for developing and explaining a nonprobability sample. Many groups might be interesting to study, but, for various reasons, no sampling frame could ever be developed for them. Imagine that you want to do a study of prostitutes. Certainly there is no list available (or unavailable) of individuals who engage in prostitution. However, you might be able to draw together a sample useful for your purposes by using a form of nonprobability sampling.

The rationale for using nonprobability sampling is that it is the best form of sampling that you can use for the study you are designing. While

BOX 6-7

THE *GENERAL SOCIAL SURVEY SAMPLE*: ITS EVOLUTION

The sample design used from 1972 through 1974 was a modified probability sample. The primary sampling units (PSUs) were Standard Metropolitan Statistical Areas (SMSAs) or non-metropolitan counties, which were stratified by region, age, and race before selection. The secondary units were block groups (BGs) and enumeration districts (EDs), which had also been stratified by race and income before selection. The third tertiary sampling unit stage was blocks, selected with PPS (probability proportionate to size) sampling or, when blocks were not clearly designated, estimated by field counting.

At the block level, the original sampling design reverted to a quota sample requiring equal numbers of women and men. The proportions of employed and unemployed women were to be proportional to the district levels; the proper proportion of men under 35 years of age was also required.

In 1975–1976, sufficient funds were available to establish a full probability sample with predesignated respondents. The sampling frames changed between 1970 and 1980. The 1970 sampling frame used percentage of black residents as a stratifying variable, while the 1980 frame relied on geographic control variables. In 1982, an oversample of black respondents was carried out in order to obtain a national probability sample of black Americans.

The GSS has three different types of weighting that users can employ (for example, the oversample of African-Americans can either be included or excluded). The GSS samples have been studied in comparison to Census Bureau samples. Certain sample biases have been recognized, and ways to alter them have been carried out where possible. For example, the underrepresentation of Mormons was addressed when the 1980 sample frame put a primary sampling unit in Utah. There seemed to be some underrepresentation of 18-year-olds, since there were proportionately fewer in the sample than in their population cohort. However, since respondents had to have reached their eighteenth birthday before being interviewed, and since the interviewing occurred around March, only those born in the first quarter of the calendar year were included. An extensive bibliography on the sample designs is presented in the *Cumulative Codebook* (Davis, 1988).

---

a study based on a nonprobability sample has disadvantages (especially the fact that its findings cannot be generalized to a definable wider population), it nevertheless can be an excellent way to study a particular sample of interest. Nonprobability samples are often used for pretests of large surveys where the cost and effort of selecting a probability sample may be considered unnecessary for the purposes of the pretest.

Nonprobability sampling may also be effectively used in studies that seek to explore ideas that are still undeveloped. In such exploratory studies, the object may be to generate theories or hypotheses that might then be studied using a probability sample. Here a few commonly employed types of nonprobability samples will be described.

Convenience Sampling

Assuming that you have little access to a sample of prostitutes, you might change your design and try to study attitudes toward prostitution. Now it would seem to be easy to find a sample of respondents prepared to give you answers to such a study. (You could, of course, design a probability sample and include in your survey a question on attitudes toward prostitution.)

But let's assume that you need your information quickly, so that designing a probability sample is out of the question. In other words, you need "warm bodies" willing to answer your questions without too much hassle. Try your college cafeteria. If you survey whoever you happen to come upon in your college cafeteria, the sample you will get will be a *convenience sample*. A college instructor who requests a college class to complete a survey for his or her research is using a convenience sample. A *convenience sample* is merely an available sample which appears able to offer answers of interest to your study.

Naturally, a convenience sample cannot be composed of just anyone. It would probably not be a good idea to stand on a street corner, stop people walking down the street, and survey them on their attitudes toward prostitution. Many would feel that answers to such questions are too sensitive to be given to a stranger on a street corner. In other words, it is always better to consider carefully whether the people you plan to use as respondents are likely to comply with your request and give careful consideration to your questions.

Purposive or Judgmental Sampling

Assuming that you are still trying to do the study on prostitutes, you might decide to go to a certain street or to a particular bar and try to interview persons who seemed to you to exemplify the typical prostitute. This form of sampling generally considers the most common characteristics of the type it is desired to sample, tries to figure out where such individuals can be found, and then tries to study them. Another method is to look for the untypical, or deviant, individual. Responses from untypical respondents allow a comparison with typical cases. A *purposive sample* is a form of nonprobability sample in which the subjects selected seem to meet the study's needs.

A student of mine once wanted to study the characteristics of Beatles fans. Although many individuals fit this description, the problem is to know where to find them. The student came up with a good strategy. A national Beatles fan conference was going to be held. He went off to this conference armed with 250 questionnaires and found a ready set of respondents. Although this sample would not represent the *average* Beatle fan, it would be a group highly motivated to respond to this survey.

Quota Sampling

Quota sampling is a form of nonprobability sampling that is often mistaken for stratified probability sampling. This is because there is an attempt to select certain-sized subsamples from clearly defined groups. The difference is that in quota sampling, sampling frames from which to select the sample are not set up. Rather, the groups are defined, and the sizes specified, and then individuals who fit these descriptions are selected to fill the quotas wherever they can be found. Hence *quota samples* are nonprobability samples in which subsamples are selected from clearly defined groups.

Quota sampling generally begins by setting up a matrix of the characteristics desired: sex, age, race, etc. Let's say you want to do a survey of the student body at your university in order to find out whether students would prefer to change to a trimester system (or if you are already on one, to a semester system). You recognize that such opinions might vary for those in different colleges, for those in different years in college, and for those with (or without) jobs off campus, etc. You would begin by trying to get from the administration the percentages of students (1) in each college, (2) in each year, (3) who work off campus. Let's say that you find out that 65 percent of the students are in liberal arts and 35 percent in business. Considering the next variable, you find out that 30 percent are first-year students, 20 percent are sophomores, 25 percent are juniors, and 25 percent are seniors. Considering the third variable, you discover that 40 percent work off campus and 60 percent do not. Now you decide to get a sample of 100 students. Of these 100, 65 should be from liberal arts and 35 from business; there should be 30 first-year students, 20 sophomores, 25 juniors, and 25 seniors; 40 should work off campus. Be sure to remember that these divisions overlap. Thus, of the 65 liberal arts students selected, 35 percent should be first-year students, 20 percent sophomores, etc., and 40 percent should be employed off campus. By setting up a matrix, as seen in Table 6-5, you can set out all the various subgroups that you need.

TABLE 6-5

MATRIX FOR A QUOTA SAMPLE OF COLLEGE STUDENTS

Year in College	Liberal Arts & Sciences Students (65%: N = 65)		Business Students (35%: N = 35)		Total N
	Work Off Campus (40%)	Do Not Work (60%)	Work Off Campus (40%)	Do Not Work (60%)	
First year	30%	7.8 (8)	11.7 (12)	4.2 (4)	6.3 (6)	30
Sophomore	20%	5.2 (5)	7.8 (8)	2.8 (3)	4.2 (4)	20
Junior	25%	6.5 (7)	9.75 (9)[a]	3.5 (4)	5.25 (5)	25
Senior	25%	6.5 (6)[a]	9.75 (10)	3.5 (3)[a]	5.25 (6)[a]	25
Total N	100%	26	39	14	21	100

[a]Rounded numbers in parentheses designate the actual numbers to be sampled. They must sometimes be rounded up or down to produce the needed row and column totals.

The procedure for quota sampling, once the quota sizes are determined, is simply to go out and fill the quotas. Since you see in the matrix that you need 5.2 (5) sophomores who are liberal arts students and who work off campus, you merely seek out 5 such students. You do the same for the 7.8 (8) sophomores who are liberal arts students and who do not work off campus. Note that you figured the first-mentioned quota by multiplying the 65 liberal arts students by .40 (40 percent work off campus), which equals 26; then multiplying these 26 off-campus workers by .20 (20 percent sophomores), which equals 5.2, and rounding to 5.

Don't be fooled into thinking that this will get you a probability sample. You may remember hearing about the famous polling error made at the time of the 1948 election by the Gallup organization, which predicted a victory for Thomas Dewey over Harry Truman. That poll was based on quota sampling. Because the subgroups are not selected from sampling frames representing the population of all members of the subgroup, the selected subgroups do not establish a known probability of every member in the subgroups being included in the sample. This means that the selection of cases within the quota groups can be biased. As a result, you cannot make valid inferences to a wider population from a quota sample.

Snowball Sampling

In snowball sampling, you first find a few subjects who are characterized by the qualities you seek; you interview them; and then you ask them for names of other people whom they know who have the same qualities or other qualities that interest you. In this manner, you accumulate more and more respondents by using each respondent you get as a source of new names for your sample. A *snowball sample* is built from the subjects suggested by previous subjects.

This approach might be a way to select subjects for the prostitute study. If you were able to find a few prostitutes willing to talk to you, you might ask them for the names and locations of others they know who might also be willing to be interviewed. Sampling of this type has often been done in studies of elite groups, either those in power in a community or members of upper classes. In community studies, there has often been the sense that only those in power really know who else has power. Because there is no sampling frame listing all those who are powerful (as there would be a listing of all those who hold office), a snowball sampling technique might lead you from one power holder to another.

DESIGNING A SAMPLE TO MEET YOUR RESEARCH NEEDS

The object of this chapter has been to give you some help in understanding the meaning of probability and nonprobability samples, the proper terms to use to describe your sample, and the methods of drawing a decent sample. As mentioned earlier, the design and objectives of your study will determine the type of sample you need. Perhaps the best way to begin to design a sample to serve your purposes is to draw up a design of the ideal sample you would like to get if you had all the resources possible. Of course, you will be unlikely to be able to actually draw that sample, but at least you will understand the ideal characteristics of a sample that would meet your highest purposes. You can then think about which parts of the sample design might be most feasible (and least feasible) to achieve. Finally, you can begin to redesign a sampling model that can meet your most critical needs, even if it abandons some characteristics of your ideal design. Remember that another strategy is to consider using an already collected dataset, which may be based on a very fine and very ambitious sample that you would not be able to carry out yourself. This is the approach of the secondary analyst, which will be discussed in detail in Chapter 10.

However, if you do carry out your own sample, whatever the design you ultimately implement, remember to keep careful records of exactly what you do. It is essential to your final research report that you be able to explain exactly how your sample was drawn. Note how forthright Coleman and his colleagues were in providing their own criticism of the weaknesses of their sample. This commitment to careful explanation of your sample design and of the problems you may have in implementing your design is a crucial part of the sampling process itself.

REVIEW NOTES

- Data gathered from probability samples make possible accurate inferences to the larger population from which the sample was drawn.
- Probability samples are based on the rules of probability theory, which allow a determination of how likely a particular sample is to be representative of its population.
- Simple random sampling (SRS) is a form of probability sampling in which computer-generated or published lists of random numbers are used as the criteria for selecting sample members from a sampling frame.
- Systematic sampling is a form of probability sampling in which every nth member on a sampling frame is drawn into the sample, assuming that the list has no biased order and the first selection is based on a random start.
- Stratified sampling involves stratifying the sampling frame into separate homogeneous subgroups based on characteristics of interest (such as gender) prior to selecting a sample within the subgroups using SRS or systematic sampling selection procedures.
- Multistage cluster sampling selects heterogeneous clusters (such as schools) and then selects members of the cluster using a random selection procedure.
- Nonprobability sampling does not follow the principles of probability theory. The various types of nonprobability samples include convenience samples, judgmental samples, quota samples (not to be confused with stratified sampling), and snowball samples.

KEY TERMS

attrition
confidence interval
confidence levels
convenience sample
disproportionate sampling
element
heterogeneous groups
homogeneous groups
inferences (inferential statistics)
judgmental sample
mean
multistage cluster sampling
nonprobability sample
nonsampling error
normal curve
parameter
population
primary sampling unit
probability sample
probability proportionate to size sampling (PPS)
purposive sample
quota sample
random numbers
sample
sampling distribution of the sample mean
sampling error
sampling frame
secondary sampling unit
simple random sampling (SRS)
snowball sample
standard deviation
standard error
statistics
strata
stratified sampling
systematic sampling
unit
variance
weighting

STUDY EXERCISES

1. Consider the kinds of samples that you might use to carry out the evaluation of the basic writing course (or some other first-year program) in your college. If you decide to use a probability sample of all sophomores in your college representative of every major field within the college who began at this college and never attended any other college,

    a. What is the population of this sample?

    b. Describe the sampling frame you would need to select this sample.

    c. What would the primary and secondary sampling units be for this sample?

    d. Describe the elements of this sample.

2. Let's say that for the above sample, you decide to carry out a stratified sample using the principles of systematic sampling to select each element. Describe carefully and fully what you would need to do to accomplish this.

3. Now reconsider this sampling design for the first-year writing program and set up a non-probability sample. If you decide to use a quota sample, describe what you would need to do to get a sample of sophomores as defined in question 1.

RECOMMENDED READINGS

1. Kish, Leslie: *Survey Sampling,* Wiley, New York, 1965. The most widely referenced work on sampling in the social sciences. Includes all the mathematical formulas for the sampling principles described in this chapter as well as comprehensible discussions of the relative advantages and appropriateness of different types of sampling.

2. Henry, Gary T.: *Practical Sampling,* Sage, Newbury Park, Calif., 1990. A very readable guide to developing samples, with four practical sample designs included.

3. Slonim, Morris J.: *Sampling,* Simon and Schuster, New York, 1966. A brief and colorful exploration of how probability sampling works. A discussion of sampling and nonsampling errors, desired sample sizes, types of probability samples.

4. Stephan, Frederick F., and Philip J. McCarthy: *Sampling Opinions: An Analysis of Survey Procedures,* Wiley, New York, 1963. A classic on the principles of designing samples for surveys. Discussion of how sampling and measurement are interdependent.

5. Williams, Bill: *A Sampler on Sampling,* Wiley, New York, 1978. A readable, but serious discussion of the principles of sampling. Beginning with examples of "bad samples," Williams goes on to give very lucid explanations of the normal curve, types of probability sample designs, common types of bias in sampling, and a final how-to chapter.

PART THREE

The Methods
of Social Research

This section of the text will introduce you to the major methods used in social research. We will begin in Chapter 7 with survey research, the most widely used method, and examine the range of ways in which surveys can be designed and delivered. Chapter 8 presents experimental methods. Because these methods follow scientific rules, a careful examination of the criteria needed to perform social experiments and of the challenges to the validity of experiments is given. Since social research questions often cannot be studied using a true experimental design, preexperimental and quasi-experimental designs widely used in social research will be examined. Chapter 9 raises issues in the designing and carrying out of field research projects, with many suggestions on methods and approaches for observing in the field and how to turn the evidence gathered into a research report. There is also a discussion of the field of visual sociology.

Studies based on a range of methods that utilize already collected data are the subject of Chapter 10. Examples of studies and ways of doing secondary analyses, content analyses, analyses of unobtrusive measures, historical research, and analyses of existing statistics are given. Finally, Chapter 11 addresses evaluation research and case studies. Evaluation research is not a method but a purpose for doing research. Both experimental and nonexperimental evaluation projects are described. A description of case studies—how they are designed and how they can be used for evaluation—is included. The use of social indicators for large-scale evaluations of national trends is presented.

Survey Research

—— LOOKING AHEAD ——

This chapter covers how to design surveys using questionnaires or interviews (either face-to-face or by telephone) and describes focus groups as a means for generating survey ideas and developing survey questions.

INTRODUCTION

*S*urvey research is a method of collecting data in which a specifically defined group of individuals are asked to answer a number of identical questions. These answers form the dataset of the study. Survey research is the most common type of social research, probably for both the right and wrong reasons. As the old dictum states, "If you want to find something out, ask!" There is something simple and straightforward about seeking information through questions. Yet we all know that to many questions there are no answers, that answers to questions may be wrong, and that a question may be incorrectly asked so that it cannot elicit the desired information. All these possible problems, which frequently confuse everyday forms of communication, also confront surveys. Furthermore, many topics cannot be properly studied by simply asking questions. Many researchers may also find it difficult or impossible to set up a survey which will meet the basic requirements for a respectable survey.

In Chapter 1, we looked carefully at two surveys in order to give you some idea of what a good survey might accomplish. In Chapter 5, we considered how to operationalize variables, which are the building blocks of a survey. Selecting the group of individuals to be questioned was the subject of Chapter 6, in which sampling techniques were discussed. In this chapter, we will first consider the creative and scientific dimensions of a survey. Next the components of a survey will be laid out. The major types of survey research will then be presented and compared. Focus groups are presented as a way to generate ideas and questions for surveys. Finally, we will consider various ways of determining whether a survey is the best means to study your intended topic.

THE ART AND SCIENCE OF SURVEYS

Creative Aspects of Surveys

On the face of it, a survey may not seem to be terribly creative. After all, you may think, anybody can put together a set of questions. That may be true, but not just anybody can put together a set of questions which (1) get as precisely as possible the information the researcher wants, (2) are clearly understood by all the respondents to mean the same thing, and (3) constitute a unified whole (that is, a questionnaire or an interview schedule) that is pleasing enough to the respondents that they are willing to spend the time to complete it and sufficiently engaging that they will not give superficial or misleading answers. To be able to produce a survey that meets these criteria is, first of all, an art.

The most vivid and direct forms of communication are produced by artists. Great art is art that touches and moves many people deeply; it is a presentation which forces one to react. Now don't think me strange if I argue that a superb questionnaire should also be irresistible to the respondent.

He or she should feel that these questions must be answered. If the questions are given by an interviewer, the presentation of the questions should also be so inviting that the respondent again feels fully engaged in the process of answering. In interviewing, the relationship between the questions as written for the interviewer and the questions as presented to the respondent resembles the relationship between the score of a symphony and the symphony as played. The score (or the set of questions) must be wonderful if the symphony (or the survey) is to be wonderful. But a wonderful symphony can be massacred by a poorly rehearsed, badly trained orchestra; and a wonderful survey can be destroyed by bad interviewing.

Let's first consider the questions themselves. They must be worded so carefully and unambiguously that the questions measure the concepts which the researcher intends. If they do, they are valid measurements of the concepts being studied. If they do not, they are useless. Thus, the designing of questions is a critical phase of the survey. This design of questions requires creativity so that the gap between what the researcher wants to measure and what the questions produce for measurement is as narrow as possible. [See the box that presents Hirschi's (1969) survey questions to measure self-reported acts of juvenile delinquency.]

QUESTIONS TO MEASURE SELF-REPORTED DELINQUENT ACTS

When Hirschi (1969) wanted to measure delinquency, he created a set of questions which together formed an Index of Delinquency. These six items were:

1. Have you ever taken little things (worth less than $2) that did not belong to you?
2. Have you ever taken things of some value (between $2 and $50) that did not belong to you?
3. Have you ever taken things of large value (worth over $50) that did not belong to you?
4. Have you ever taken a car for a ride without the owner's permission?
5. Have you ever banged up something that did not belong to you on purpose?
6. Not counting fights you may have had with a brother or sister, have you ever beaten up on anyone or hurt anyone on purpose?

Hirschi was actually trying to tap whether youths had committed crimes. Since many people would be reluctant to tell you whether they had committed any crimes, the questions describe the acts without any intimation that the writer of the question disapproves of these acts or regards them as very serious. Notice how stealing a car is described as "taking a car for a ride without permission." This is a euphemism for "stealing a car." Furthermore, it may more closely represent the way in which the delinquent teenager considers the act: as an essentially harmless activity in which the youth was merely having a bit of fun.

This ability to create questions to tap ideas that may be on the surface undesirable to answer, or lacking in interest, requires an artistic touch. But this touch can be fostered by carefully re-creating the best types of questions which one has used in everyday life. We don't often ask people outright, "Are you a car thief?" Instead, we pose questions in such a way as to generate the information we desire without unduly upsetting or annoying the persons asked. So, too, in a survey. While we don't know the people whom we are surveying, we must, in many ways, design our survey as if we did.

Finally, the way in which the survey is presented, either in spoken form as an interview or in written form as a questionnaire to be answered by the respondent, must be creative. Interviewers must be engaging, but not to the point that they would strongly affect the responses given. Note that I haven't said to the point where they would have no effect. This is because it is impossible for an interviewer not to have some effect on the types of responses generated. We will discuss the style of the interviewer below. For the moment, it is enough to remember that an interviewer will always affect in some ways the meaning and interpretation of the questions being asked, through his or her personal style.

A questionnaire, too, expresses a certain style. It may look crowded and wordy, or uncluttered and inviting. The type of printing may look official and precise, or it may be a mimeographed copy which looks more like the work of an amateur. Remember that a questionnaire which appears to have been prepared by an amateur may arouse less suspicion and more cooperation than a study which seems more formal and authoritative. Further, because a questionnaire is an object, its appearance will also determine how it is treated.

Scientific Aspects of Surveys

In the research model considered in Chapter 2, the design of a survey would fall into the phase of the research process after hypotheses have been formulated. Wallace refers to it as *instrumentation*

(1971, pp. 68–69). The two forms of instrumentation which he defines are those based solely on "human sensory organs" (such as "seeing" things) and those based on "technologically augmented sensory organs." The first type would be best represented by participant observation, in which the researcher's primary instruments are his or her eyes or ears. The second type would be best represented by a survey in which a questionnaire or an interview schedule supports the basic sensory data collectors.

Matilda White Riley explains the differences between the data generated from participant observation (which we will consider in Chapter 9) and that from questionnaires in the following way:

> Data from observation reflect the network of actions and reactions among group members—the objective properties of the system. Data from questioning reflect the subjective network of orientations and interpersonal relationships—the underlying ideas and feelings of the members, their dispositions to act toward the others and to define and evaluate these others in various ways (*1963, p. 184*).

For example, while observing the behavior of people on a city street corner, an observer may see someone ask another person a question. Judging by the behavior of the two people, the observer might interpret that the question concerned soliciting a geographical direction. But the field researcher would not know what question was asked or why it was asked. Questions in a questionnaire or in an interview try to get at the underlying attitudes and dispositions (the orientations) surrounding a piece of information. Surveys generally go beyond merely asking people *who* they voted for or *what* their religion is to asking *why* they voted for a particular candidate and *how* religiously observant they are.

Does this make survey data more or less scientific than data based solely on observation? Surveys are more focused and planned. They go after very specific pieces of information, or, in an interview situation, they may probe around an issue—but always with the intent of embellishing a specific piece of information. On the other hand, surveys may be very badly designed such that they are ambiguous and produce misleading data. When this is the case, the scientific value of the study is undermined.

Surveys also may be based on much more precise samples than an observation study. As we saw in Chapter 6, probability samples enable a researcher to relate findings based on a specific sample to a much wider population. Much of the popularity of surveys and polls rests on the ability to generalize the findings so widely. Finally, survey questions can be developed so that their reliability levels are quite high. This means that questions will tap the same responses from people if repeated again and again.

The analysis of survey data rests on a form of scientific logic based on relationships and changes in relationships associated with the introduction of new factors. In certain types of surveys—those based on panel data, where the same respondents have been surveyed at more than one point in time—a clear time dimension can be established, and certain types of casual analyses may be carried out. Chapter 14 will describe how survey data may form the basis of scientific analyses.

GENERAL COMPONENTS OF SURVEY RESEARCH

Modes of Eliciting Information

There are two primary modes of doing a survey: using questionnaires or giving interviews. Both methods are based on a set of questions. In the *questionnaire,* these questions are written down and the respondent reads them and gives written answers. In an interview, the interviewer asks the questions as they are written in an *interview schedule* and then records the respondent's answers either by writing them down or recording them electronically. Interviews may be face to face, or they may be carried out on the telephone.

Modes of Selecting Respondents

In Chapter 6, we discussed the various types of samples that might be used for a survey. The first consideration in choosing among them is whether a potential set of respondents will be able to give answers to the types of questions to be asked. The relevant issue here is, what is the appropriate population to which your questions apply? If you are doing a study of farm abandonment, you will probably want to survey farmers, ex-farmers, and others who live in rural areas. If you want to survey college students about attitudes toward the Reserve Officers Training Corps (ROTC), then you will want only students, probably more male students than female, and you may want to concentrate on those students who have been in ROTC.

Second, it will be important to design a survey which will be appropriate for this sample. It should include questions which such a group could and would answer. That is, the questions must be presented in language familiar to the sample and phrased so that members of the group will understand them. The questions must also be acceptable to the sample; they cannot probe into subjects which the respondents would refuse to consider because the questions make them look socially undesirable or stupid. If the questionnaire will be received in the mail, it must have an appropriate cover letter designed to encourage the respondents to participate. If an interview is to be given, the opening remarks must also encourage participation and mollify any concerns which a potential respondent may have. In short, the mode of eliciting information must support the selection of respondents.

Modes of Returning Information

Once a questionnaire is completed, there must be clear instructions as to how it is to be returned. In most mail surveys, return self-addressed envelopes—which are usually stamped—are included with the questionnaires. In this case, the questionnaire need contain very few instructions about

its return. Interviews, once terminated, need to be fully converted into information which may be processed as a part of the study. Usually, the interviewer completes an interview schedule which is basically like a questionnaire. In certain cases, interviews may be taped. When this occurs, the information on the tape must be transcribed. The sooner this is done following the interview, the more accurately the interviewer will recall the exact details of the interview.

This brief review of the general components of surveys is set up to make you aware of the whole scope of surveys. Before we take them apart and examine them carefully in detail, let me go over the general issues in administering surveys using examples from four surveys which had different types of data-gathering procedures.

ADMINISTERING SURVEYS: FOUR EXAMPLES

Administering a survey is the fourth step in the research process. The first step, defining the problem, was discussed in the Introduction and in Chapters 4 and 5. The second step, selecting an appropriate sample, was addressed in Chapter 6. The third step, designing the questionnaire or interview schedule, will be the subject of this chapter. The fourth step, survey administration, will also be described here; and the fifth step, analyzing the data from the survey, will be presented in Chapters 13 and 14.

There are two primary ways of administering a survey: using questionnaires or giving interviews. Questionnaires may be administered to a group or sent to individuals to be filled out on their own; interviews may be carried out in a face-to-face exchange between the interviewer and the interviewee, or they may be given on the telephone. Whether to use a questionnaire or an interview and how to carry it out will depend very much on the circumstances of the particular project you are designing. Four actual surveys each using a different type of data collection technique will be presented here for purposes of comparison.

Example 1: A Questionnaire Administered to a Group

In order to study the effects of ability grouping on the social status of high school students, I gained the cooperation of two large suburban high schools which had different types of ability grouping practices. In North High, students were rigidly placed into ability groups on the basis of test scores with little chance to select a different group or to change groups if they thought they had been misplaced. Furthermore, ability grouping was practiced in almost all academic subjects. In South High, grouping was much less rigid. Students could select different classes with advice from teachers, and certain academic subjects had no ability grouping at all.

With the support of the school administration, I administered the questionnaire to the entire senior class of South High during a senior assembly, a regular gathering held weekly at that school. In North High, where senior assemblies were not held, questionnaires were distributed in senior homerooms by the homeroom teachers using the same instructions I had used for the group administration.

Example 2: A Mail Survey

To determine whether attending a predominantly white college increased the autonomy of black students as compared to white students, I surveyed black and white students attending two different predominantly white colleges. The questionnaire included a set of questions from an autonomy scale which was used as an indicator of autonomy. The survey was a panel study, in that the respondents answered more than one questionnaire over a period of time, and the data from the questionnaires were linked to each respondent. This study had two questionnaires which formed the "two waves" of the data collection procedure: the first questionnaire was sent out at the beginning of the first year of college, before the effects of college could have occurred; the second, at the end of the first year. Information at more than one point in time was needed so that any changes in level of autonomy (the hypothetical result of being at college) could be measured.

Since one of the institutions to be studied was a large state university, I knew I could not survey the entire first-year class. I therefore needed to select a sample of students that would include a sufficiently large number of black students. However, since the university did not have lists of students identified by race, there did not seem to be any way for me to draw up my two samples. Finally, I discovered that there was a listing of which high schools the students had attended. Since most came from local city high schools, I could get a reasonable number of black students by sampling students from all-black high schools; and I could balance these with a sample of students from all-white high schools. Since I also wanted to have black students in the study who had attended integrated high schools, my third sample could be drawn from racially integrated high schools. The final designation of race could be determined by self-report on the questionnaire. In the other university, a directory with photographs of first-year students was available, and I was able to select students by race from this directory.

Selected first-year students were sent questionnaires through the mail shortly after the fall term began. The first mailing included a letter explaining the survey, the questionnaire itself, and a stamped return envelope. Those who did not send the questionnaire back within two weeks received a postcard reminder requesting them to complete the form and return it. A third mailing, to those who had not returned the questionnaire within a month's time, included a different cover letter urging the person to complete the survey, another copy of the questionnaire, and another return envelope. A second questionnaire, which included the same measure of autonomy, was sent at the end of the spring term to every person who had completed the fall survey. Again, two follow-up requests were sent to those who did not return the initial questionnaire.

Example 3: A Face-to-Face Interview

A civic organization, hoping to address some of the causes of youth unemployment in a major city, acquired the services of the Northern Illinois University Public Opinion Laboratory, then headed by political scientist Jon Miller. Miller and his colleagues were to gather information on this subject from face-to-face interviews with youths aged 17 to 24, representative of those with the greatest degree of unemployment. Interview schedules were prepared that included questions about the youths' education and skills, aspirations and plans, job searches, and work experiences.

The public opinion laboratory drew a sample of 50 blocks in the city, representing the lower half of the income distribution of the city. Interviewers were selected, hired, and trained from among college students on summer vacation who were roughly similar to those being interviewed in age and race. Teams consisting of a few interviewers and a supervisor went to the selected blocks to interview every youth between the ages of 17 and 24 currently residing there. They also tried to secure appointments with youths on the block who were away at the time of their visit. Blocks were revisited three and four times over the month period of interviewing. The material from the interview was recorded on a schedule by the interviewer during the course of the interview.

Example 4: A Telephone Survey

Sociologist Steven Klineberg and his undergraduate students at Rice University have been carrying out annual telephone surveys of residents of Houston to measure their attitudes toward the changing conditions of their rapidly expanding city. To elicit views representative of all adult Houstonians, the group had to be sure that it had a representative sample. In the first year of the survey, a total of over 1,400 Houston-area telephone numbers were randomly selected (using random-digit dialing, to be discussed later in the chapter); of these, nearly 700 numbers were business or disconnected lines or were unworkable

for other reasons. For the workable numbers, the number of adults over age 18 living at the residence was ascertained, and then one of these adults was randomly selected to be the person to be interviewed on the telephone.

Over a three-week period, the telephone interviews were carried out with the selected individuals (numbers often had to be recalled a number of times in order to reach the particular person needed for the sample). The undergraduate interviewers recorded the interview information on schedules.

In each of these four surveys, the collected data were entered into a computer, and analyses of the aggregate findings were prepared. Thus, in each of these surveys, the researcher ended up with sets of answers to the same questions. The differences in these surveys lay in terms of how the data had been collected. These brief descriptions of surveys that vary in their style of administration have been offered as an overview of the primary forms of surveys.

How to choose the appropriate form of administration for your survey will depend on the type of problem you are studying, your access to a sample to study, your resources, and your personal preferences. We will now carefully go over how to design and prepare questionnaire surveys for in-person and self-administration questionnaires, and we will then describe interview surveys for face-to-face and telephone situations. You will need this information if you decide to do a survey; it will help you select the most appropriate type of survey for your particular circumstances.

DESIGN OF QUESTIONNAIRES FOR GROUP OR SELF-ADMINISTRATION

General Rules of Questionnaire Construction

1. Include only questions which will address your research concerns and which you plan to analyze.

2. Make the questionnaire as appealing as possible to the respondents.
3. Keep the questionnaire as short as will suffice to elicit the information necessary to analyze the primary research concerns. Be sure, however, to include questions on all aspects of the research problem that you will need to address.
4. If the questionnaire is self-administered, keep the instructions brief, but make sure they contain all the information required to complete and send back the questionnaire.
5. Consider in advance all the issues that a respondent might raise when he or she receives this instrument. Be sure that the questionnaire addresses these issues.

General Format of a Questionnaire

A questionnaire should include a cover letter, brief instructions on how to complete the questionnaire, the questions, a clearly defined space and method for the respondent to register answers to the questions, possibly codes for transcribing the data onto a computer once they are collected, instructions on how to return the questionnaire (as well as a stamped, addressed return envelope), and a final thank-you to the respondent for the time and effort expended.

Cover Letter.   The primary objective of a cover letter is to tell the respondents the purpose of the questionnaire and to request that they participate. The purpose of the study should be stated clearly and simply. There are often two different types of purposes in a study: the first is the more general purpose of collecting information to address specific research questions or hypotheses; the second is to accomplish the objectives of the researcher, who may be a student carrying out a study in a methods course, a graduate student seeking data for thesis research, a government researcher collecting data for reporting, a marketing researcher who is exploring the tastes of potential clients, or an academic researcher who is collecting data on some topic.

Whoever is doing the study wants those who receive the questionnaire to complete it. Will the potential respondents be more likely to complete the instrument if the cover letter stresses the importance of the research project itself (its contribution to scientific understanding) or if it stresses the importance of the needs of the researcher as a person? In the first case, you are trying to convince the respondents that valuable information can be gained through survey research and that by participating in this study he or she may be helping to do science. This has been called an egoistical approach because it assumes that a respondent who consents to participate has been convinced that participation will better society as a whole, the state of scholarship, and thereby, indirectly, the respondent also. In the other case, where you are stressing your needs as a researcher, you are banking on the altruism of the respondents to motivate their participation. If the respondents are convinced that their help is really vital to the study, then out of a sense of generosity they may volunteer the time needed to complete the survey. Usually the significance of the study is also stressed. Further, if the researcher is a student and makes an earnest request for help with the study, respondents may be encouraged to assist.

Whatever the pitch of the covering letter, the researcher must decide how it will sound to potential respondents. Sometimes a very matter-of-fact letter succeeds. If respondents have very little time (for example, if they have high-pressure jobs), it may be wise to stress both how important the data are for studying the subject and how short a period of time it will take to complete the form. It is important that the suggested time of completion be reasonably accurate. Ethical issues should also be considered. The letter should describe how the protection of human subjects will be accomplished (whether anonymity or confidentiality will be offered).

Instructions.   In a self-administered questionnaire, all the information necessary to complete the form accurately and completely must be given. The following issues might need to be addressed in the instructions:

1. How and where does the respondent give his or her answers? (Check the box, circle the correct response, etc.) In this case, the questionnaire should be consistent so that all the answers can be given in the same way.

2. If there is a separate answer sheet which is machine-readable, clear instructions must be given about how to move from reading questions on the questionnaire to providing responses on the answer sheet. If a special kind of pencil is required, this must be made absolutely clear. Generally, separate answer sheets are not desirable for a self-administered survey because of the possible problems of confusion and error in using them. Questionnaires themselves may be printed on machine-readable forms; this simplifies the processing of the data, without sacrificing the ease of having respondents place their responses right next to the questions. (Of course, some groups, such as college students, probably have had extensive experience at taking tests where the responses must be filled in on machine-readable forms, but other groups may not have had much experience at filling out such materials.) The most appropriate way of administering a survey using machine-readable forms is to a group. Then not only may the use of correct pencils be clearly stated by the administrator, but the pencils themselves may be made available.

3. Clear instructions for contingency questions (described below) where respondents are allowed to skip certain questions or specifically answer certain questions must be given throughout the instrument as they are needed.

4. Clear instructions for returning the questionnaire are also necessary. These may be given in three different places: in the cover letter, at the end of the survey, or at the beginning of the survey. The best policy is to have the instruc-

tions on the survey itself. If the cover letter is, in fact, the top sheet of the survey, the method of returning the questionnaire may be mentioned in the letter. If the letter is on a separate sheet of paper, however, it may accidentally be disposed of before the respondent finishes the survey. Thus the return instructions are best printed on the survey form itself.

Developing Appropriate Wording for Questions

As Shakespeare knew, the word's the thing! In a written questionnaire, the words that make up the questions are the basis for your study. Hence, the survey designer must develop unambiguous, clear, and simple questions which serve the purposes of the research study. Here are a set of rules developed from suggestions offered by de Vaus (1986, pp. 71–74), which you should go through for every question you prepare for your survey:

1. *Are the words that make up this question, and the meaning of the question, simple and clear?* Avoid words that are known only by experts in an area (i.e., jargon), and avoid overly complex and unfamiliar words. Carefully consider the sample who will be answering the questionnaire and ask yourself whether the questions will be fully understood by the likely respondents. This means, of course, that if the respondents have some particular expertise—for example, if they are pharmacists—then you could include words experts in that field would know. Remember that on certain questions respondents may honestly not have a response; therefore, ask yourself whether a "don't know" or "not relevant" category should be offered as an option.

2. *Could the question have an alternative meaning to some respondents?* This addresses the issues of ambiguity and possible group differences in interpretation. You may not see the question, or words within it, as ambiguous;

however, others might. Sometimes members of particular ethnic groups or occupational groups use words differently from the conventional way. The best assistance you can get on this problem is to show your questions to others and to pretest the questions on a broad range of individuals who share the characteristics your sample will have.

3. *Word questions in such a way that respondents are not likely to give false information to make themselves look more socially desirable or prestigious.* People want to make themselves look good. Your questions must discourage this bias toward *social desirability* by trying to elicit honest answers on years of education, income, number of friends. Ask yourself whether the question easily lets the respondent report, for example, a low income, a low level of education, or a few friends while experiencing as little shame as possible about revealing this information. One method used is to not ask people to give an exact income or education level, but to place themselves within grouped categories, which are more neutral.

4. *Avoid negative questions.* The use of negatives in questions—for example, "AIDS cannot be prevented through safe sex practices: Agree or Disagree?"—is confusing. It is always better to word questions positively and then give the respondents a chance to respond positively or negatively.

5. *Avoid double-barrelled questions.* Any question that subsumes more than one response is ambiguous. For example, "Do you like San Diego and San Francisco? Yes/No" cannot be easily answered by a respondent who likes one of these cities but not the other.

6. *Check for bias in your questions!* Leading questions encourage respondents to answer in a certain way. Questions such as "Do you agree with Chief Justice . . . " or "If the X welfare program is bankrupting the state, what do you think the state should do with the program?" are biased in favor of one answer.

7. *Should the question be posed directly or indi-*

rectly? Questions that touch on more personal matters are often best posed, or moved toward, indirectly ("Many people have tried marijuana . . . " or "Do you know other people who have tried marijuana?"). Then it is easier to ask whether the respondent has tried it. However, you must be careful that indirect questions do not seem too coy or contrived.

Types of Questions

Chapter 5 gave some examples on how variables were operationalized in terms of developing questions. Here we want to consider the different types of questions which a questionnaire might contain.

Closed-Ended and Open-Ended Questions. *Closed-ended questions* force the respondent to select a single response from a list (for this reason they are often called *forced-choice questions*). Such lists of responses must cover the entire range of possible answers; that is to say they must be exhaustive. A question that includes a broad enough range of responses so that every possible answer to the question can be fit into a given response has *exhaustive categories.* For example (as noted in Chapter 5), if you ask about religion, you might offer as possible responses "Catholic," "Protestant," "Jewish," "other," and "none." This would determine the major religious groups in the United States. Or you might want to include specific smaller religious groups such as "Hindu" or "Moslem." Even in this case, however, you would still want to keep the "other" category for anyone who did not feel that they could comfortably place themselves in any specific category. For an attitudinal item, such as "How good a job do you think the secretary of state is doing?" where the range of choices is "excellent," "very good," "good," "fair," and "poor," you would want also to include "don't know" or "no opinion" for those who are actually unsure.

One other condition which must be met in a closed-ended set of responses is that those responses must not overlap one another in such a way that a respondent might think he or she should appropriately select more than one category. This requirement means that responses must be *mutually exclusive.* Using the example of foods, if the categorical choices offered were "meat," "fruit," "vegetables," "bananas," "dairy products," and "grains," then "bananas" and "fruit" would overlap. In other words, since a banana is a subcategory of fruit, it is being measured twice in this list. Be sure that the terminology you use clearly distinguishes one category from another. (Of course, in certain instances, multiple answers may be allowed: e.g., "What are your favorite sports?")

Open-ended questions state a question and leave room for the respondent to write out an answer. If a specific number of lines are left, a suggested length for a response is more precise than if only an amorphous space is left. It is also possible that handwritten responses might be clearer if lines are printed on the questionnaire. On the other hand, if, in the opinion of the respondent, too many or too few lines are left, he or she may be more likely to skip the item.

Closed-ended questions with forced-choice responses are more likely to be completed by respondents than open-ended questions. Questionnaires with numerous open-ended questions are often returned with many questions left blank. Remember, it takes much more time and thought for the respondent to generate a written response than to merely check an offered response (see the box that contrasts closed- and open-ended questions). Furthermore, open-ended questions are much more difficult to code (see Chapter 12 on this subject). However, there may be certain questions to which only an open-ended response seems reasonable.

Contingency Questions. Questions which depend on the responses to earlier questions are referred to as *contingency questions.* If you want to ask a person how many cigarettes he or she smokes a day, such a question should be contingent on an earlier question ("Do you smoke

cigarettes?"). The box shows how such a series of questions might be set up.

Matrix Questions. *Matrix questions* allow for the answering of sets of questions with similar types of responses. Usually the questions are similar—for example, a set of attitudes with which the respondent is asked to either "strongly agree," "agree," "disagree," "strongly disagree," or "have no opinion." Matrix questions help conserve space in the questionnaire and make it easier and quicker for the respondent to give answers. The fear with matrix questions is that the respondent will start to answer questions in a pattern, for example, checking "strongly agree" to every item. This problem, which is called *response set,* can be minimized by clearly reversing the meaning of some questions so that consistency in response requires agreeing with some questions and disagreeing with others. See the box that presents a matrix question.

CLOSED- AND OPEN-ENDED FORMS OF THE SAME QUESTION

OPEN-ENDED QUESTION

How much does your job as a program manager *challenge you*—in the sense of demanding your skills and abilities?

CLOSED-ENDED QUESTION

How much does your job as a program manager *challenge you*—in the sense of demanding your skills and abilities?

[ ] Completely demands my abilities
[ ] Demands most of them
[ ] Demands about half
[ ] Demands some of my abilities
[ ] Demands very few of them

Source: Donald P. Warwick and Charles A. Lininger: *The Sample Survey: Theory and Practice,* McGraw-Hill, New York, 1975, pp. 135–136.

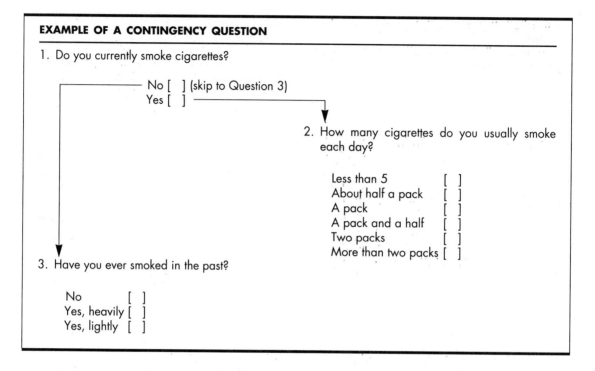

EXAMPLE OF A CONTINGENCY QUESTION

1. Do you currently smoke cigarettes?

   No [ ] (skip to Question 3)
   Yes [ ]

   2. How many cigarettes do you usually smoke each day?

      Less than 5   [ ]
      About half a pack   [ ]
      A pack   [ ]
      A pack and a half   [ ]
      Two packs   [ ]
      More than two packs [ ]

3. Have you ever smoked in the past?

   No   [ ]
   Yes, heavily   [ ]
   Yes, lightly   [ ]

Ordering of Questions. There are two simple rules to remember. In a self-administered questionnaire, the first questions should be interesting so that the respondent is encouraged to begin (and hopefully complete) the questionnaire. (In an interview, the early questions often ask for simple, nonthreatening demographic information such as "How many adults over the age of 18 live here?") The other rule is that questions which the respondent may be reluctant to answer (on income or race, for example) should come near the end of the questionnaire. This is to discourage respondents from refusing to complete the form.

Questions on the same subject are generally grouped together to keep the respondent thinking about the same material. In some cases, a set of questions on a specific topic (let's say, educational background) may be set off in a separate section.

Pretesting the Questionnaire

Once you have a draft of the questionnaire, you should *pretest* it to determine its effectiveness and

its problems. This preliminary pretest might be with friends or acquaintances who will agree to take the questionnaire. The questionnaire form might be typed with large margins and spaces between questions. Ask the respondents to go through and answer the questionnaire as if they had received it from someone they did not know. Then ask them to go through the questionnaire again and point out (possibly by writing comments adjacent to the questions) any problems they noted with questions. Were there some questions that they did not understand? Did some of the questions seem particularly stupid?

After going over the responses of your preliminary pretest and making changes that seem advisable, it is time to have your formal pretest. For this pretest, you should try to have a trial administration that is as similar as possible to the actual survey administration. If you are planning to mail out your surveys you should mail your pretest to a small sample of individuals who might have been selected for your actual study (but were not). If you plan to administer it to a group, find a similar

---

EXAMPLE OF A MATRIX QUESTION

How far do you agree with the following statements about your community? Do you "strongly agree" (SA), "agree" (A), are you "uncertain" (UN), do you "disagree" (D), or "strongly disagree" (SD)? (Circle one response on each line.)

	SA	A	UN	D	SD
This community is a good place to raise children.	1	2	3	4	5
I feel safe in this community.	1	2	3	4	5
The cost of food in this community is about the same as anywhere else in the city.	1	2	3	4	5
If I had a chance to move out of my community, I would move.	1	2	3	4	5

Note: In this question, for some statements the "agree" answers suggest positive attitudes toward the community; in other cases they suggest negative attitudes. Any person reading the items carefully would be unlikely to circle, for example, all the 1s.

---

group and see if you can administer it to them. This pretest questionnaire should look precisely the same as your actual questionnaire will look. In a group administration, you might ask them following the completion of the questionnaire to write comments on it or to discuss with you any problems they found with it. In this formal pretest, be sure not to tell the respondents that this is a pretest until it is over.

The main purpose of the formal pretest, however, is to examine patterns of response. For this reason, you will want to have a sufficiently large pretest sample. Look for the following types of responses: (1) questions that many people have skipped (Were they parts of contingency questions? Should they have been skipped?); (2) questions that everyone seems to answer alike (if there is no variation in response to an item, it will not prove to be very useful in the analysis); (3) open-ended questions that have been answered ambiguously (for example, the answers to "What is your occupation?" may often be very imprecise); and (4) "response set" to matrix-type questions where

the respondent seems to have merely circled all the same numbers without seeming to have read the items carefully.

Revise your questionnaire on the basis of the preliminary pretest and the formal pretest. The revised form might be given again to a few friends to be sure you haven't inserted new questions that have problems. It is worth spending the extra time to carry out the pretests and consider the comments and patterns of response. Remember that once you send out the final questionnaire, it is too late to fix any problems in the questionnaire design.

Questionnaire Distribution

On-Site Administration. There are various precautions to consider in administering a questionnaire to a group. The atmosphere of the session must be sufficiently serious that respondents complete the questionnaires objectively. Sometimes, with a student audience, an amusing question or a joke by the administrator may touch off a mood of frivolity. The light mood could have serious effects on the results of the questionnaire. A researcher must always consider whether an instrument has been filled out in jest. Thus the manner of the person administering the questionnaire should be matter-of-fact and serious.

An explanation of the purpose of the survey must be given. This should be brief and neutral: "Today you will be participating in a survey about college students' attitudes and interests." Again, the researcher must decide what pitch to use. When the sample group is already present, it may not be as necessary to try to sell the benefits of participating. It is much more difficult in a group environment for a respondent to throw out the questionnaire or refuse to participate.

The instructions for completing the surveys must also be given. If the survey researcher will not be giving the instructions, then she or he must be certain that the person(s) administering the questionnaire is (are) properly trained.

Mail Questionnaires. Most *mail surveys* contain the survey itself, a cover letter (which may form the top page of the survey), and a return envelope which is addressed and stamped. If the survey is to be printed, the return envelopes may be printed as well. The size of the return envelope should adequately hold the completed questionnaire. The envelope in which the survey is sent may either be stamped and sent first-class or printed with a bulk-rate permit. Bulk-rate mail must be ordered by zip codes and must include at least 200 pieces. You should check with your local post office for any changes in mailing regulations.

Getting an Adequate Response Rate

Various conditions affect the number of respondents who complete and return a questionnaire. The *response rate* is the percentage of returned questionnaires [the proportion of those sent (or given) out that are returned].

Appearance of the Questionnaire. The appearance of a questionnaire will have an effect on the

respondent. A potential respondent will react to a questionnaire initially in terms of its overall appearance. Crowded questionnaires, which look wordy and squeezed together, generally draw fewer responses than a slightly longer questionnaire which appears more spacious. This does not mean that all mailed questionnaires must be professionally printed. In fact, a questionnaire that looks less official may serve certain purposes better. What is important is that the audience for the questionnaire be carefully considered.

If the questionnaire is being prepared by a student, a well-typed questionnaire that is then photocopied may be perfectly adequate. Such a homemade survey must be neat and well spaced, with every word correctly spelled. A sloppy-looking survey will turn off most respondents. ("If the researcher can't prepare a better-looking survey than this, why should I bother to fill it out?") However, a clear, accurate, but amateur-looking survey may encourage certain respondents to complete the survey thinking that the data will be used primarily to help a student complete an educational project. Now that word processors are quite widely available, you may be able to use one to prepare your survey. With different print formats, right alignment, and other features, a questionnaire prepared on a word processor may incorporate many of the features characteristic of printing. If you have access to a laser printer, its copy can hardly be differentiated from actual printing.

In some cases, a more professional-looking printed survey may seem preferable. When the survey is quite long, a printed form will conserve space, thereby making the survey seem shorter. Printing also allows for variation in type. Italics can be used for emphasis. Separate sections of a questionnaire may be printed on different-colored paper for emphasis. As discussed above, printing will make the form appear more official; typing and reproducing will make it look more the work of an amateur. The reason to do it one way or the other will be based both on cost and on a consideration of whether printing will enhance the response rate. However it is produced, neatness and spaciousness are important.

Nature of the Request to Respond. To encourage a potential respondent to respond is a critical aspect of survey design. The best-looking questionnaire which does not lead to a strong response rate may have been harmed by a lack of careful consideration on how to request cooperation from respondents. As described above, the cover letter is generally used to ask the respondent to answer the instrument. You might decide to keep your explanation very simple, expressed without social-scientific jargon. Here are a few examples:

- This survey is being carried out to try to discover what the residents in your community think are the most serious local problems.
- College students need adequate financial support to complete their studies. This survey asks how students get this support.
- What are the attitudes of parents to various child-rearing practices? The purpose of this survey is to ask parents their views.

Personal appeals. As stated before, the survey researcher may appeal to the potential respondents for assistance in order that the study will be a success. Such an appeal is probably more effective when the researcher is a student and the audience receiving the questionnaire can be assumed to be familiar with, and sympathetic to, the needs of students. If they are not, appeals of this type could backfire.

Sponsorship. If the study is being *sponsored* (paid for) by some organization, funding agency, or other group, this should be told to the respondent. An alumni association of a university, a marketing research firm, a government sponsorship for research—all suggest different objectives for the study. The stationery used for the cover letter may indicate the source of sponsorship. Researchers should always consider what the title of the sponsor may mean to the respondents. If respondents are unlikely to know or understand who the sponsor is and why the sponsor is supporting this project, an explanation should be given. The box presents some brief examples of how such explanations might be presented.

Other inducements to participate. The purpose of a study should never be stated falsely. Every objective of the study need not be mentioned. The major aim, however, should be stated clearly, and respondents might be told that if they would like more information about the survey, they may contact the researcher "at the following address or telephone number." In relation to the full-disclosure aspect of surveys, respondents are often told that they will be sent (automatically or upon request) a summary of the survey's results. Such promises should be given only if the researcher fully plans to make good on them.

Financial inducements are sometimes sent with a questionnaire to try to encourage a respondent to reply. The argument for such a plan is that many respondents will feel more compelled to complete a questionnaire if it comes with such an inducement. In some cases, $1 has been enclosed and the respondent told that $5 would be sent once the questionnaire was returned. In other cases, a larger sum (say, $2) has been sent initially. Of course, some respondents may merely keep the money and discard the survey. However, the position favoring financial inducements is that respondents who are disinclined to complete the questionnaire may feel guilty keeping the money and

---

EXAMPLES OF SPONSORSHIP DESCRIPTIONS

The Center for Public Broadcasting is interested in finding out whether American college students regularly watch television news discussion shows.

The Alumni Association of Happiness College wants to know to what degree graduates of Happiness have found their education beneficial to their careers and personal lives.

This study is being supported by the National Institute of Child Health and Development in the interest of furthering an understanding of the effects of family size on the careers and personal lives of parents.

will therefore complete the questionnaire in order to reduce this feeling. On the other hand, some respondents may be angered at the small amount of the inducement, feeling that their time is worth more than the token amount of money sent. Financial inducements must therefore be considered in relation to the type of people being surveyed. Young people may be more likely to appreciate a small fee than older people. People with higher incomes may be more annoyed with a small fee than those with lower incomes.

Anonymity and Confidentiality. Surveys usually ask some questions which are personal in nature. They almost always ask about attitudes which a respondent might not want to make public. Respondents therefore may not want to divulge their identities. If the survey asks for no identification and includes no code number, then when it is returned it will be completely anonymous. A survey can offer *anonymity* to potential respondents if the researcher is not able to identify the respondents. Naturally, this means that the researcher would not be able to determine which respondents had completed the questionnaire and which had not. In such a study, no follow-up materials could be sent to the nonrespondents and no study of nonrespondents could be made.

For this reason, most researchers do not want to have respondents completely anonymous. They prefer to have the questionnaires coded so that returned forms can be checked off against a list of names and follow-up efforts directed toward the nonrespondents. Also, if the survey is a panel study, where it will be necessary to get back to the respondents and the questionnaires from the different surveys will need to be linked, then the researcher must know which questionnaire belongs to which respondent.

In such a case, a researcher can promise respondents that the data from the questionnaire will be confidential. In this instance, *confidentiality* can be offered to the respondent if no one other than the researcher will be able to associate the respondent's questionnaire and name, and if once the fol-

low-up efforts are complete the list of names will be destroyed. Whatever the respondent is told should represent what the researcher actually plans to do.

Studies have shown that respondents are usually not worried about confidential handling of the questionnaires. In some cases, questionnaire forms request that the respondent sign the form. Many respondents do not object to this. In other cases, a detachable postcard is attached to the questionnaire. Respondents are asked to detach it, to fill in their names and addresses, and to send the postcard back separately from the questionnaire. This enables the researcher to know who has responded, without being able to associate the respondent with a particular questionnaire.

Attempts to hide the coded number (for example, with invisible ink or as a phoney room number on the return envelope) raise ethical issues if they are accompanied with a promise of anonymity. I once knew a student researcher, desperate to increase her response rate, who wrote the code number in invisible ink under the stamp on the return envelope with the plan of steaming off the stamps of the returned questionnaires. One respondent discovered this method and wrote back furiously to object. Such deception is inadvisable.

Type of Enclosed Material for Return Mailing.
A return envelope which is addressed and stamped should accompany every survey. These envelopes may be printed with business-reply postage which will be charged only if the respondent sends it back. Some believe that stamped envelopes are preferable to business-reply envelopes, possibly because the respondent may be less likely to discard an envelope with an actual stamp (especially if it is an attractive, commemorative one). It is not a good idea to use a metered postage marking because it is dated and if a survey is not returned quickly, the post office may refuse to deliver it.

Type of Mailing Procedure. The type of mail delivery and the timing of the mailing may affect the response rate. Many researchers have found that surveys mailed special delivery are more likely to be answered. First-class postage seems to improve the response rate over bulk-rate mail (possibly because some people are likely to throw away nearly all material sent bulk rate). Here the relative costs must be weighed against the relative benefits. As with the return envelope, a prestigious-looking stamp on the outgoing envelope may stimulate the interest of respondents and discourage them from throwing away the survey without opening it.

When to send out a survey should vary with the intended audience. General rules would suggest not sending them near major holidays, especially Christmas, when people are often inundated with mail. Beginning of school and end of school periods may also be undesirable if the respondents are students or teachers. As for the day of the week, the respondents should be taken into account. Studies have found that surveys to organizations are better received early in the week, but those to home addresses may be better received nearer the weekend, when there may be more free time to fill them out.

Follow-up Procedures. Nearly all surveys which are serious in nature *follow up* the initial questionnaires with two or three additional mailings as well as telephone calls to increase the overall response rate. Generally, the second follow-up occurs two to three weeks after the initial survey was sent out; sufficient numbers of surveys have usually been returned by then to allow the researcher to make up lists of nonrespondents. Second follow-ups generally do not include another copy of the questionnaire. In some cases, a postcard is used to remind the person to complete the questionnaire and return it. In other cases, a letter is sent reexplaining the purpose of the study and reiterating the importance of having every respondent reply to the survey in order to make it a representative study.

Third follow-ups often include another request letter and a copy of the questionnaire, which may be assumed by then to have been discarded or misplaced. Third follow-ups are sent out a month to six weeks after the original survey. Telephone reminders may come before or after the third follow-up; and these calls may be used to find out why the survey was not returned (it was misplaced or thrown out, the respondent refuses to answer it, the respondent would be happy to answer it as soon as time is available, etc.). Some surveys have had as many as six follow-ups. Generally, it is found that the first follow-up will increase the response rate by one-fifth to one-fourth. Each additional follow-up brings in proportionately fewer respondents (even though the pool is narrowing as the follow-ups continue).

Assessing the Response Rate. What is a respectable response rate for a survey? There is disagreement on this point. With a carefully selected sample, a researcher would hope to have 70 percent respond in order to feel confident that the respondents were largely representative of the sample (though the researcher might try to determine whether respondents are representative of the sample by gathering some information on the nonrespondents and comparing them to the respondents). Even a 70 percent response rate could produce an unrepresentative sample if the 30 percent nonrespondents included a large proportion of the types of respondents desired for the study. (For example, a survey of delinquency could get a much lower response rate from delinquent youths than nondelinquent youths.) Surveys without follow-ups are unlikely to surpass 50 percent response rates. Of course, different types of surveys and, more particularly, certain types of individuals sampled will yield different response rates. A survey sent to a group of people who are professionally concerned about the results may yield a high rate. For example, a survey in a university to study the effectiveness of graduate programs yielded a much higher response rate from the faculty in the program than from the graduate students. Possibly the questions addressed issues the students did not think they could judge yet. And probably the faculty more than the graduate students perceived ad-

BOX 7-1

FOCUS GROUPS

Focus groups, sometimes called group depth interviews, consist of a small number of individuals drawn together to express their views on a specific set of questions in a group environment. This research strategy is often used as a starting point for developing a survey. The researcher is able to get a better idea of how respondents talk and think about topics, which could help with the design of the survey instruments. Focus groups also help when a researcher needs to get background information on a topic. Such group interviews can stimulate new ideas and concepts, reveal potential problems in a research design, or help interpret evidence generated from a quantitative study.

A focus group generally includes 6 to 12 people, selected by the researcher, who are knowledgeable about a specific subject because of their experiences or who can represent the views of some group of interest. The members of the group gather at a specific site; questions are prepared in advance; there is a moderator; and the group session allows all the participants to air their views.

As Stewart and Shamdasani (1990,

pp. 16–17) report, there are several advantages to using focus groups: (1) they provide quick and inexpensive sources of information that can be set up in a wide array of settings with a great range of respondents; (2) the researcher has the opportunity to talk directly to the respondents in order to clarify, elaborate, and better understand ideas; (3) respondents have the chance to develop their reactions to, and build upon, the responses of other participants in the group, and this may create a dynamic, "synergistic" effect; (4) they offer a way to gather information from individuals who are usually more difficult to study, such as children or those with very low levels of education; and (5) successful focus groups can be carried out through teleconferencing even when the individuals in the group cannot be physically drawn together in a specific place.

Fewer than 12 questions are generally posed in a focus group session. The moderator often leads into a topic with less structured, usually open-ended questions to elicit the broadest and most original responses, then moves to more structured questions to draw out more specific information. However, the moderator must be

ministrative pressure to provide evaluations of the graduate program.

The best response rate is the largest one that you can produce given your time, your finances, and your persistence. Many researchers have been able to get response rates in excess of 90 percent. In such cases, the analyses are greatly strengthened because the researcher can rest assured that the responses are truly representative of the people sampled

DESIGN OF FACE-TO-FACE INTERVIEWS

The difference between *face-to-face interviews* and paper-and-pencil questionnaires is simply that conducting an interview involves having one person address questions to another. The spoken responses are then recorded by the interviewer. In the self-administered questionnaire procedure, the respondent first reads the questions and then writes responses. This difference must be kept in mind when designing an *interview schedule* for an interview. Because the interview involves two people, the nature of the relationship developed between these two people before and during the interview will have a great effect on the success of the interview obtained. Box 7-1 describes a group interview technique, the *focus group,* which is an excellent preparatory method for developing a survey. Whether the interviewer is the actual researcher or someone else may affect the outcome careful not to lead the respondents so fully that she or he is providing the response (Stewart and Shamdasani, 1990, p. 64). Many different types of questions might be included in a focus group session: (1) main research questions direct the purpose of the session; (2) leading questions push for a deeper level of meaning; (3) testing questions rephrase a respondent's words to get the group to reiterate or challenge an answer; (4) steering questions guide the group back to the main subject; (5) obtuse questions allow members to discuss uncomfortable questions by addressing them in terms of other people's feelings or reactions; (6) factual questions allow group members to address nonrisky subjects and can be used at points when the discussion is getting too emotional; (7) "feel" questions allow the expression of personal feelings (however, the moderator cannot let anyone discount another group member's personal feelings); (8) anonymous questions often begin by asking group members to write out an idea that immediately comes to mind when they think of a specific issue; and (9) silence lets the moderator simply wait for a response, resisting filling in the pause in the conversation (Stewart and Shamdasani,

1990, p. 83, based on Wheatley and Flexner, 1988).

A variety of potential problems can confront a focus group. One way to avoid problems is to select group members carefully. Stewart and Shamdasani (1990, pp. 96–98) suggest friends should not be members of the same focus group because friendships distort the anonymity of the group. The researchers also advise moderators to control the participation of legitimate experts, who may inhibit responses from others in the group; self-appointed experts, who may intimidate other members and who may be more difficult to move to a genuine helping role; and hostile group members, whom the moderator may need to ask to leave, possibly after a short break.

In the early stages of a survey research design, a focus group can assist in formulating questions for the survey, in relating other topics to the primary research issue, and in generating research hypotheses. Later, when the survey data have been collected and analyzed, a focus group can help a survey researcher to better understand the results by facilitating a fuller interpretation of the survey data.

of the interview. Box 7-2, which discusses the effects of hired-hand interviewers, should be kept in mind in considering seeking assistance with interviewing

Preparing the Interview Schedule

A structured interview schedule is very similar to a questionnaire. A questionnaire may be converted into an interview schedule and vice versa. An interview schedule should be prepared in accordance with these rules:

1. Instructions for the interviewer to follow must be clearly given.
2. Questions should be worded so that they can be easily read out by the interviewer without dis-

torting the response which will be given. (They should offer no threat and should be totally neutral.) Furthermore, the response categories should be carefully considered so that they offer a meaningful range of possibilities but are not so vague that the respondent cannot easily select a category.
3. Questions ought to be ordered so that the respondent is quickly engaged in the interview and so that interest is maintained throughout.

Instructions. An interviewer needs clear and precise instructions about how to give the interview. While many instructions may be spelled out during practice sessions, the interview schedule should include all of the basic rules that the interviewer needs to follow in order to carry out the

BOX 7-2

HIRED-HAND INTERVIEWERS

Roth (1966) warned of the possible effects of hiring interviewers to collect data. Roth gives his own experience doing *hired-hand research* as a case in point:

> One of the questions on the interview schedule asked for five reasons why parents had put their child in an institution. I found most people can't think of five reasons. One or two—sometimes three. At first I tried pumping them for more reasons, but I never got any of them up to five. I didn't want (the director) to think I was goofing off on the probing, so I always filled in all five (1966, p. 191).

Cheating of this type occurs, Roth argues, because persons hired to carry out interviews rarely hold the "dedicated-scientist" (p. 191) norms that the original researcher holds. Instead, a hired interviewer would tend to do his or her work much like workers in most other settings [by shaving down the job bit by bit to "just enough to get by" (p. 192)]. Roth also cautions that this type of slacking off is not a moral issue; "rather, it is expected behavior of workers in a production organization . . . [and] there is no reason to believe that a hired hand in the scientific research business will behave any different" (p. 192).

The best safeguard against this, Roth contends, is to tie hired hands as firmly into the research project itself as is feasible. If those working on a project feel committed to its execution, they are less likely to behave like ordinary hired help.

serve as the basis for including or excluding individuals from the survey: these may request information on residence, age, membership, or other factors. Interviewers should be informed as to how to end an interview quickly with a person who does not meet the requirements for the study.

Instructions on how the interviewer should proceed through the instrument must be given. When there are contingency questions which do not apply to the respondent, the interviewer should be able to see at a glance where to move for the next question. The form should include places for responses such as "don't know," "no opinion," or "no answer." Naturally, the interviewer should encourage respondents to give an opinion or a response when they seem to have one that would apply. Usually the interviewer does not offer "don't know" as a selection category to the respondent; rather, it is recorded only when the respondent cannot pick a response from those given.

Wording. Questionnaires and interview schedules often read somewhat differently. Interview schedules may include short transitional expressions to make the interview proceed smoothly: "Now, I wonder if you could tell me . . . ," or "We would like to know what you consider . . . ," "Please tell me . . . ," "We are interested in how. . . ." This last expression could be used to introduce an assessment of financial security: "We are interested in how people are getting along financially these days." This could then be followed by the question: "Compared to your financial situation five years ago, are you (better off, worse off, or about the same)?"

Types of Closed-Ended Questions. In order to have respondents select from a group of possible responses, choices must be made available. There are a number of different techniques for doing this: rating scales, rank ordering, paired comparisons, semantic differentials (some of which will be described in Chapter 16 on scales). The card sorting method can be used only in a face-to-face

interview successfully. (If you plan to do your own interviewing, you should apply these suggestions to the instructions you write for yourself.) The form should ask for information regarding the time the interview began, how long it took, where it occurred (if this varies), and on what day of the week the interview was held. Early questions may interview situation. In this case, numerous cards with different statements (measuring attitudes) are given to the respondent, who is asked to sort them into piles which signify different levels of agreement or disagreement. A variation on this method may also be used to get respondents to select a category from a list printed on a card, which the interviewer hands to the respondent after a question is asked. Consider the income question asked in two forms in the box.

Each of the ways of asking the respondent about income avoids the personal question "Tell me how much?" In the first method, the interviewer reads off income categories and the respondent tells the interviewer when to stop. In the second, the respondent selects an income category from a card. This second method, developed by the National Opinion Research Center (NORC), is probably less intrusive and easier for an inexperienced interviewer to handle (Bradburn and Sudman, 1979, p. 182).

EXAMPLES OF QUESTIONS ON INCOME

FORM 1

Please tell me approximately where your annual household income fell in 19—, before taxes; that is, the income for all members of the household. Stop me when I reach the category that includes your household income. *(The interviewer then slowly reads the various income categories, beginning with the low end).*

FORM 2

For the purposes of our survey, we need to have a rough indication of the income of your family. In which of these groups . . . *(The interviewer hands the respondent a card with the various categories of income delineated in a column, each preceded with a letter)* . . . did your total family income, from all sources, fall last year, in 19—, before taxes? Just tell me the letter of the group.

Social Desirability. Questions that address potentially threatening topics or raise the possibility that the respondent is being asked to divulge something personal and derogatory may be answered by the respondent in such a way as to make the individual look better. Such responses often tend toward offering the normative response. Sudman and Bradburn found this was more often the case when the respondent did not relate strongly to the topic being addressed, that is to say, when the respondent knew less about it and was less affected by it (1974, pp. 36–39).

If your interview will include potentially threatening questions about criminal activity, sexual behavior, or personal habits which may seem negative, it will be important to prepare such questions carefully in order to make them as nonthreatening as possible to your respondents. If you do not do so, your respondents may answer in ways that appear to make themselves look socially acceptable. Techniques have been developed for asking very sensitive questions in interviews (see, for example, the Random Response Model of Bradburn and Sudman, 1979).

Minimize Use of Open-Ended Questions. When open-ended questions are asked, the interviewer should write down the answers. Obviously, there is a potential for shifts in meaning and emphasis between what the respondent says and what the interviewer writes down. Open-ended questions should be worded to encourage brief responses and a greater degree of precision. Interviewers are not psychoanalysts who know how to interpret the deep thoughts of respondents.

Use of Quantifying Words for the Responses. The response categories often contain quantifying adverbs which may be vague. Bradburn and his colleagues found that choices such as "very often," "pretty often," and "not too often" may mean quite different things to different individuals (Bradburn and Sudman, 1979, p. 159). When the events referred to occur more frequently on the average, the responses are higher for everyone; when the responses refer to a more positive event, they also tend to be higher than for a negative event. You should try to see in pretest interviews whether responses seem to be skewed in this way. You may want to add one or more quantifying categories or, possibly, delete one.

Ordering Questions in an Interview Schedule. An interview should try to capture the initial interest of the respondent; therefore, the interview should begin with a question which tries to engage the interviewee. Demographic questions, especially those of a personal nature, should come at the end of the interview. Many interviews start with a question or two to determine whether the person being addressed meets the criteria for being interviewed in terms of age; voter registration; residence in a community, city, or household; or whatever. Actual questioning sometimes commences with an open-ended question which seeks a global response to the major issue of the study: "What would you say is the major problem confronting people in your community?"

One advantage to an interview as compared with a self-administered questionnaire is that the interviewer can lead the respondent through the questions in exactly the order they are presented, whereas in a self-administered questionnaire the respondent may jump around the survey or skip sections completely. Interviewers should be encouraged to present the interview exactly as it is ordered. This will help to standardize the interview situation from one interview to the next and among different interviewers.

The Interview Experience

An interview is a piece of social interaction with one person asking another a number of questions and the other person giving answers. Everyone has, in a number of different situations, been an interviewer. Small children are always interviewing adults: "Mom, why do I have to go to bed?" "Why do you have to go out tonight?" "Why does Mary get a new toy and not me?" As we mature,

we tend to become more leery of asking people too many questions and may consider people who seem too inquisitive to be nosey, intrusive, and certainly not cool. On the other hand, our world would come to a standstill if we were unable to ask anyone anything. We must ask people questions in order to carry on with our lives.

Now, this general type of questioning is different from a formal interview, but not entirely different. We have all learned that to find out what we need to know requires *asking the right question.* This means that we need to think through what our question will mean to the other person in order to be able to phrase the question so that we can expect the respondent to give us the answer we need. Furthermore, we must ask it in a way that will not confuse or turn off the person to whom we are speaking and therefore produce an invalid answer.

This is not so different from the situation in a formal interview, a situation you probably all have encountered. Many of you have had job interviews, interviews with college admissions people, or others. In such cases, we are generally trying to put our best foot forward and look good so that the person interviewing us will be impressed. Yet we all know that if we brag about ourselves too much, if we try to make ourselves sound too wonderful, we may not seem very believable and the interviewer may conclude that we are insincere and shallow. Thus we have all developed some techniques for answering other people's questions about ourselves, our interests, our attitudes, our characteristics so that we appear to be honest and forthright.

Some of you may have been interviewed in a survey. The major difference between interviews for a job, for admission to a college, and for a survey is that the interviewer in the survey has nothing to offer to, or withhold from, the respondent. If the respondent thinks that the interviewer cannot affect his situation, cannot do something for the respondent, she or he may conclude that giving all these answers is a big waste of time. The reason why so many individuals agree to being interviewed is that the interviewer *sells* the interview effectively (Downs, Smeyak, and Martin, 1980, p. 364). The interviewer must convince the respondent that it is in her or his personal interest to participate. As Downs and his colleagues state (1980, p. 364), the tactics offered to motivate interest include telling respondents that

    (a) A neighbor or friend has participated,
    (b) A person's opinion is really sought,
    (c) The report is important enough to be published or to be used in making important decisions,
    (d) You really need the person's help.

Stressing the usefulness of the answers in the aggregate for the study of some subject may ease the respondent's fears of exposure, but the interview situation itself may bring back unpleasant memories of earlier interviews. Such interview experiences, possibly for a job, may have been threatening and anxiety-producing; it is this situation that the prospective respondent may recall when considering whether to let the interviewer proceed. Thus, the interviewer needs to fully consider how to make the request for an interview nonthreatening and the experience of being interviewed as enjoyable (and even as enriching) as possible.

The Desirable Interviewer. Sociologist David Riesman once described the ideal interviewer as the person who could adapt the standardized questionnaire to the unstandardized respondent (1958, p. 305). This ability to handle a two-way conversation under varying conditions, without losing the central meaning of the survey in any of these conditions, is *the art of interviewing.* There seems to be a certain schizophrenic quality about the advice given as to how to be a good interviewer. Interviewers are technical specialists, but ordinary persons; they must be prudent in widely varying situations, but they may also need to be persistent to the point of being annoying in order to get the responses they need; they must probe, but remain neutral; they must be interested in what the respondent says, but seem oblivious to the implications of what it may mean.

This ability of the interviewer to respond to the answers given with a kind of "friendly obliviousness" (Converse and Schuman, 1974, p. 32) sets up a mood of nonchalance in which the interviewer seems not to be shocked, surprised, or amused or to react in any strong way to the respondent's answers. The cardinal tenet of interviewing, state Converse and Schuman, is to restrain prejudice, to suppress one's own opinions (p. 12). If the answer is incomplete, the interviewer must probe for greater depth and clarity in the response, but without seeming to be personally concerned. Interviewers must veer away from becoming too emotionally involved with the respondent; this is what Converse and Schuman refer to as "overrapport" (p. 54). Box 7-3 gives an example of a situation where an interviewer found it very difficult to remain impersonal.

BOX 7-3

THE NEED FOR NEUTRALITY IN INTERVIEWING

This account of an interviewer's experience, offered by Converse and Schuman, is an example of how interviewing may require much self-restraint on the part of the interviewer:

> When the respondent said, "Women shouldn't go past the first grade; then they couldn't take jobs away from men," I [the interviewer] failed utterly to subdue my feminist spirit. I said, "What if she never marries or what if her husband dies or deserts her and she has children?" I lapsed instantly into silence. I had biased the interview, in that I had revealed myself even more thoroughly to be the kind of female the respondent most objected to: not only was I working—I was in favor of women working!

Source: Jean M. Converse and Howard Schuman. *Conversations at the Randon:Survey Reseach as Interviewers See It,* Wiley, New York, 1974, pp.12-13.

Converse and Schuman offer four reasons why many people are happy to be interviewed. The first is that most people enjoy telling their opinions to a good listener. Interviewers are terribly good listeners (they even take notes!). Second, interviews tend to be about a person's personal experiences and attitudes (their career, their family, their political attitudes)—all topics about which most people spend a lot of time thinking to themselves and talking to those to whom they are close. Thirdly, an interview costs the respondent nothing. Whether the respondent thinks he or she is doing a favor for the interviewer or whether the respondent gives the information to conform to the interviewer's request, the interview is free: the only cost is the time spent. Finally, interviews can offer fresh insights and can be stimulating (Converse and Schuman, 1974, pp. 55-56). Most people do not normally converse with strangers about their attitudes; but then, strangers are rarely interested in your attitudes! In the interview situation, these attitudes may be explored in ways that open up new ideas to the respondent.

As the Survey Research Center (SRC) at the University of Michigan tells its interviewers, interviewers must be both diplomats and boors. They must be able to make the most difficult situation seem comfortable. However, they may not let the respondent feel so comfortable that he or she is allowed to skip pertinent questions. Rather, the good interviewer must be ready to elbow his or her way into whatever questions must be asked (Converse and Schuman, 1974, p. 31). The SRC manual states that the interviewer must be both a human being who "builds a permissive and warm relationship with each respondent" and a "technician who applies standard techniques and uses the same instrument for each interview" (reported in Converse and Schuman, 1974, p. 30).

Whatever the situation, the interviewer must get his or her questions answered by everyone. This may in some cases lead to what Converse and Schuman refer to as "the comedy of questions." Consider this example:

You sit in a lady's living room, look through cracked, broken-out windows at blocks and blocks of gutted "has-been" homes. You walk across a sagging creaking floor, and look into narrow eyes peering at you from beneath a dresser. Not a dog, nor a cat—no, a child. Now you ask the big question in the neighborhood problem section: "Have you had any trouble because of neighbors not keeping up their property?" *(1974, p. 27)*

The very rationality which is sought in interviews may, Converse and Schuman think, lead to its own biases. Because the interview asks for *opinion,* it denies feelings. Questions have tended to be worked up in such a way as to filter out emotion. The one-to-one experience denies the more normal effects of others beyond this dyad. There is a stripping away of spontaneity by the formality in the wording of the questions. The very ultrareasonableness of the interview makes it a little artificial (Converse and Schuman, 1974, pp. 73–74). This distortion seems to be the price that must be paid to accomplish the social survey interview.

How to Become a Good Interviewer

Five basic rules must be followed in order to become a good interviewer: (1) understand the interview material, (2) make a commitment to complete the interview, (3) practice enough to feel confident and comfortable with the interview, (4) try to reduce the effects that your personal qualities might have on the interview situation, and (5) use common sense in dealing with potentially difficult situations.

Rule 1: Understand the Interview.   Naturally, the interviewer needs to know what the interview is about. If you are to be doing the interviewing, you should know why the questions being asked are included. To know this means that you have a solid understanding of the purposes of the research. If you designed the study, you will be more likely to know why questions are included than if you are working on someone else's project.

However, there is a tendency to throw in questions which may seem obvious to include, but even you, the designer of the project, are not sure why they have been included.

An interview should not seem to be a fishing expedition where any material that might possibly appear interesting is included on the chance that it might be used. If the study is seeking alternative explanations of a phenomenon, then you should understand why one set of questions—very different from an earlier set—has been included. The reason the interviewer needs this self-understanding is that if the respondent asks why a specific question is being asked, the interviewer can quickly explain its importance to the overall survey. It is not acceptable to say that the question might prove useful or that it is interesting. Every aspect of the interview must be considered vital to the study.

Rule 2: Make a Commitment to Complete the Interview. Interviews may occur at inconvenient times. In some cases, an interviewer may try to reschedule a session. However, whatever the nature of the situation in which the interview occurs, whether there is a baby crying in the background, a dinner burning on the stove, a person about to go out, once the interview has begun, the interviewer must persist and try to complete the interview. This can be more easily accomplished if the interviewer remains comfortable. Clearly, short interruptions may need to take place. The interviewer should be gracious, but should stress the importance of completing the interview.

One problem in trying to complete total interviews is that respondents may give incomplete answers. In this case, the interviewer needs to probe for more information and clarification so that the response is fully understandable and useful. This tendency to give less than fully developed answers parallels everyday speech. Nevertheless it is also very common in everyday conversation to try to get the person with whom you are talking to flesh out what he or she is saying.

Converse and Schuman (1974, p. 50) suggest

the following types of responses to incomplete answers, which appear exactly as they might in everyday conversation:

Could you tell me a little more about that?

This question is requesting additional information, an expansion of the material that has been given.

How do you mean, exactly?

This is a request for clarification, for a better explanation of what was said.

Why would you say you feel that way?

This is a way to seek out an elaboration of the answer given.

In examples like these, the technique of the interviewer is not to be satisfied with incomplete answers. If you don't think you fully understand what the respondent means, if there might be multiple meanings, if the answer is confusing at the time of the interview, it will mean even less at a later point when you are trying to code and analyze the data. That is why the interviewer must get full and complete information that will be clear and fully interpretable later on.

Rule 3: Practice the Interview. Interviewers must practice by reading the interview and administering it to others. In the first step, the reading should identify any areas of misunderstanding which the interviewer has. Here the adequacy of the instructions for the interviewer will be made evident. The first practice might be to interview yourself, as Converse and Schuman (1974, p. 18) suggest. This should help sensitize you as to how you might react to the interview. This is a way to explore your own personal attitudes and see whether you have biases that might be aroused if the respondents reply in certain ways.

The second practice might be with a friend or fellow workers with whom you feel completely comfortable. Genuine pretesting of the interview with the types of respondents to be studied should also be carried out. Depending on the size and complexity of the interview, you should pretest the interview on a few people and in a few situations representative of the prospective respondents and situations. These practice interviews (which should not be announced as practice sessions) will inform you as to what problems are likely to confront you in the interviews.

Rule 4: Minimize the Effects of Your Personal Characteristics. Your sex, age, race, accent, dress—all of your personal characteristics and styles will, in some way, affect the interview situation. Although you cannot change your sex, age, or race, you should be aware of the possible effects that they may have on respondents. (For example, studies have shown that black respondents often give different answers to black and to white interviewers.) You should consider your appearance and grooming. Different types of interview situations may make certain types of attire desirable. In a formal door-to-door interview, a businesslike appearance may be best; however, college-student attire (jeans) may be fully acceptable for many types of interview settings.

Rule 5: Always Use Common Sense. This is a quality that everyone needs to have ready to be used when difficult situations arise. It is especially important for interviewers. If the interviewer realizes that the situation is becoming dangerous, perhaps that the respondent is making menacing remarks, the interviewer must use good judgment about whether to discontinue the interview. No one wants to endanger oneself simply to get an interview. However, common sense can often tell you when a situation is just a little doubtful and when it is truly ominous. Moreover, the friendly neutrality of the interviewer may often serve to defuse a difficult situation. A household in which a family fight is in progress may calm down when the interviewer arrives. Whatever the event, the in-

terviewer must always rely on common sense as the ultimate factor in deciding what to do.

This brings us to the point of stating how to end an interview. Naturally, the respondent should be thanked for the time and effort put into the interview. If results are to be sent out, this should be explained to the respondent. Try to end the interview in a positive, upbeat fashion so that the respondent doesn't end up with negative feelings about the experience. Remember, another researcher may want to interview this respondent in some future survey.

DESIGNING A TELEPHONE SURVEY

There are two primary tasks in organizing a *telephone survey*. One is to design the survey instrument itself. The other is to select a set of respondents.

Telephone Interview Schedules

Telephone interview schedules are not so different from in-person interview schedules. In both cases, the schedule must include instructions to the interviewer on how to proceed with the interview and questions which the interviewer is to read off to the respondent. The language of the telephone interview schedule may need to be a little different from the in-person interview schedule. It may require a few more verbal clarification statements, such as "OK?," "Did you understand?," "Is that clear?," or "Can we continue?," interspersed throughout the conversation; these are less necessary in the face-to-face situation, because the interviewer can see the respondent's reactions.

Questions that depend on visual cues presented on cards, as described above, can be adapted to a telephone format. Groves and Kahn offer two primary ways to accomplish this: the unfolding method and the numbered-scale method. The boxes that follow give examples of each of these methods.

In the unfolding method, the respondent is led along to more specific questions on the basis of responses to earlier questions. This makes it less necessary for the respondent to remember too much at one time and reduces the presentation of irrelevant material to the respondent.

In the numbered-scale method, the respondent is asked to think of a scale of numbers and register where on the scale his or her response would fall. In Groves and Kahn's "thermometer" scale to rate

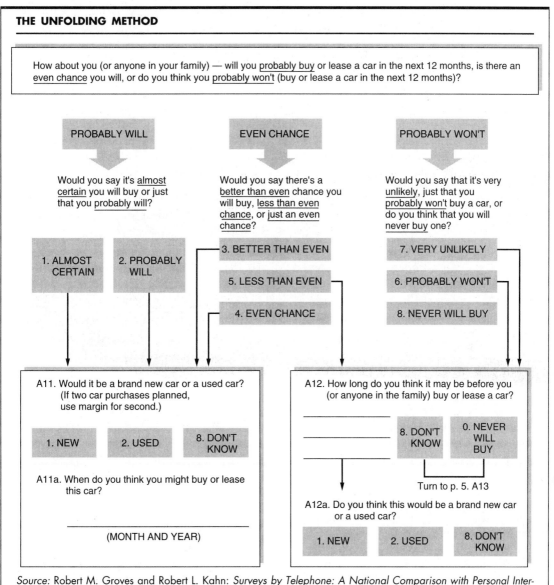

THE UNFOLDING METHOD

How about you (or anyone in your family) — will you <u>probably buy</u> or lease a car in the next 12 months, is there an <u>even chance</u> you will, or do you think you <u>probably won't</u> (buy or lease a car in the next 12 months)?

PROBABLY WILL   EVEN CHANCE   PROBABLY WON'T

Would you say it's <u>almost certain</u> you will buy or just that you <u>probably will</u>?

Would you say there's a <u>better than even</u> chance you will buy, <u>less than even chance</u>, or <u>just an even chance</u>?

Would you say that it's very <u>unlikely</u>, just that you <u>probably won't</u> buy a car, or do you think that you will <u>never buy</u> one?

1. ALMOST CERTAIN   2. PROBABLY WILL

3. BETTER THAN EVEN
5. LESS THAN EVEN
4. EVEN CHANCE

7. VERY UNLIKELY
6. PROBABLY WON'T
8. NEVER WILL BUY

A11. Would it be a brand new car or a used car? (If two car purchases planned, use margin for second.)

1. NEW   2. USED   8. DON'T KNOW

A11a. When do you think you might buy or lease this car?

_____
(MONTH AND YEAR)

A12. How long do you think it may be before you (or anyone in the family) buy or lease a car?

_____
_____
_____

8. DON'T KNOW   0. NEVER WILL BUY

Turn to p. 5. A13

A12a. Do you think this would be a brand new car or a used car?

1. NEW   2. USED   8. DON'T KNOW

Source: Robert M. Groves and Robert L. Kahn: *Surveys by Telephone: A National Comparison with Personal Interviews,* Academic Press, New York, 1979, p. 233.

THE NUMBERED-SCALE METHOD

Now I'd like to get your feelings toward some political leaders.

Imagine a thermometer going from 0 to 100 degrees. Give a score on the thermometer that shows your feelings toward each person I mention—0 to 50 degrees if you don't care too much for the person, 50 degrees if you don't feel particularly warm or cold toward the person, and between 50 and 100 degrees if you have a warm feeling toward the person. If you don't know too much about a person, just tell me.

Is it all clear?

| 1. YES | 5. NO |

GO TO B5a

Here is how it works. If you don't feel particularly warm or cold toward a person, then you should place that person in the middle of the thermometer, at the 50-degree mark.

If you have a warm feeling toward a person, or feel favorably toward the person, you would give him or her a score somewhere between 50° and 100°, depending on how warm your feeling is toward that person.

On the other hand, if you don't feel very favorably toward a person—that is, if you don't care too much for him or her—then you would place that person somewhere between 0 and 50 degrees.

Of course, if you don't know too much about a person, just tell me and we'll go on to the next name.

B5a. Our first person is Ross Perot. Where would you put him on the thermometer?

Adapted from Robert M. Groves and Robert L. Kahn: *Surveys by Telephone: A National Comparison with Personal Interviews*, Academic Press, New York, 1979, p. 243.

various political figures, they found that responses to these scales on the telephone tend to be numbers divisible by 10, whereas in an in-person interview, respondents tend to select numbers that are actually given on a thermometer presented on the show card (1979, p. 122). These examples suggest that when visual material is given, the respondent will attend to its cues. Without such material, a respondent on the telephone must utilize other ways to simplify responses.

Open-ended questions tend to be answered more perfunctorily on the telephone. If the interviewer wants multiple answers to a question (such as "What are the most important problems in your community?"), it will be difficult to get more than two responses on the telephone (Groves and

Kahn, 1979, p. 138). Probing in a face-to-face situation may produce more responses.

Selecting a Sample

Getting a Sample of Telephone Numbers. There are numerous ways of selecting a set of telephone numbers to represent the population to be sampled. The method you choose will depend on the size of the area you are sampling as well as the size of the survey.

Using telephone directories. In the early days of telephone interviewing, telephone directories were largely used. In rural and nonmetropolitan areas, where most households are listed in the directory, this list may still serve as an effective sampling frame. In large cities, however, directories may exclude (because of unlisted numbers) more than one-third of the residential telephone numbers. To get around this problem, Sudman (1973) suggested a method according to which only the last three digits of numbers selected from the directory are replaced by randomly selected numbers. This is a two-stage project: first numbers are selected from the directory, then the last three digits in each are replaced with random numbers. In this way, unlisted numbers will have a chance of being selected.

Most localities also have cross-index telephone directories (which are usually available in public libraries). These directories list phone numbers by address or by numerical ordering. Such directories may be especially useful if you are studying a particular neighborhood. They may also distinguish between residential and commercial numbers by, for example, printing the commercial numbers in bold type.

If directories are used, a means for randomizing the selection numbers should be employed. There are computer programs which will select a page number (once you have given the maximum limits), a column number, and a selection number within the column (once you have specified the number of telephone numbers given in each column).

Random-digit dialing. The newer way to select a telephone sample does not use telephone directories at all. Instead, the use of *random-digit dialing (RDD)* obviates the need for the telephone book. RDD uses a computer to select the numbers to be called. If the sample is to represent some regional area of the United States or of the country as a whole, there will usually be a desire to get responses from across the area in a random fashion. This can be done by stratifying the computer's choices, first, on the basis of the area codes (the three-digit numbers that must be used first to call long distance) and, second, on the basis of the three-digit local exchanges or prefixes which precede the last four suffix numbers. At present, there are about 100 area codes in the United States and 30,000 exchanges. The area codes are given in most telephone directories; the exchanges may be selected from telephone directories or obtained from the local telephone company.

If you want to be exact in your sampling design, Groves and Kahn suggest that you also secure the vertical and horizontal (V & H) coordinates, which the phone company uses to determine long-distance charges. By stratifying the choices of area codes, then the exchanges within the area code, and then the V & H coordinates in a rotated fashion so that people with the same exchanges are selected randomly from across their locale, a representative sample of telephone numbers can be drawn (see Groves and Kahn, 1979, pp. 21–30 for a more comprehensive discussion of this method). Once this ordering is done, a systematic sample of every *n*th six-digit number (area code and exchange) is drawn. Of course, for a regional study, many fewer area codes (possibly only one) are needed. The number of exchanges varies greatly within an area code. The final four numbers are selected randomly using a random number generation program or a list of random numbers as described in Chapter 6.

Selecting a Respondent from a Household. A telephone survey will not be random if any person who answers the phone is interviewed. Rather a

BOX 7-4

SELECTING AN INTERVIEWEE AT A TELEPHONE RESIDENCE

Now, how many people living in this household are over the age of 18? Who's the oldest member of the household? (Write in summary box). How old (was that person/were you) on (his/her/your) last birthday? Who's the next oldest person in the household? Etc. (List names in order of age beginning with the oldest, down to age 18).

Line No.	Summary Box Name	Age		Selection Table 1	2	3	4	5	6	7	8	9	0
1			1	1	1	1	1	1	1	1	1	1	1
2			2	1	1	2	2	2	1	1	2	1	2
3			3	3	2	2	1	2	2	3	1	1	3
4			4	1	4	2	3	3	2	1	4	2	4
5			5	5	2	1	1	3	2	4	3	5	4
6			6	1	6	2	6	4	5	3	2	4	5

Now, let's see: That's *(read names listed)*. Is that everybody over the age of 18 who usually lives here? (Have I missed anyone?)

Number over age 18:   1 : 25%
2 : 58%
3-6 : 17%

Now let me see whom I'm supposed to interview next . . .

(From the last number listed in the Summary Box, go to the corresponding row on the selection table. Then go to the column corresponding to the last digit of the telephone number, and draw a line straight down to the row associated with the last person listed. The respondent's number is the one that intersects both lines.)

According to my selection table, the person I need to interview next is (Respondent's Name). [Is (he/she) there? Could I speak to (him/her), please? When do you expect (him/her) to be in? Etc. . . .]

Source: Steven Klineberg, Houston Area Survey, 1983.

selection within the household of individuals who meet certain criteria (usually age) is used, and then among those members of the household, a random choice is made. The model followed is one developed by Kish (1949). Box 7-4 describes how Steven Klineberg in his Houston Area Survey used the Kish table to randomly select one person from each household to be interviewed. To put it more formally, it is a method to randomize selection within households of varying sizes. The first thing the interviewer does is ask how many people there are in the household, listing them in the summary box by age. Then considering the last digit in the telephone number, the interviewer turns to the selection table and selects the appropriate number of the person listed in the summary box to interview. Note that in the selection table the numbers change depending on the number of persons in the sampling unit.

Let's again go over how the selection of the person to be interviewed in the household is made. Say that it was a household of three and that their telephone number was 123-4567. You would go to row 3 and across until you got to column 7. Here you see the number 3. That means you will interview the third person on the list. Now, let's try another one (you would, of course, need a different summary box for each household): say you interview a household of two, whose telephone number was 123-1234. You would go down to row 2 (because there are two persons in the household) and then move across to column 4 (to correspond with the last digit in the telephone number). Here you see the number 2. Thus, you would interview the second person listed in the summary table.

Once the person is selected, that person is the only one to whom the interviewer will speak. In many cases, this requires calling back at a time when the person on the telephone thinks the respondent will be available. If the desired person cannot be reached, he or she is not replaced by someone else in the household.

Telephone and Face-to-Face Interviewing

Advantages of the Telephone Survey. Interviewing respondents over the telephone has become increasingly popular in recent years. It is easier to call individuals on the telephone than to go out to interview them in their homes or on the street. This form of survey has been revolutionized by the more sophisticated means for drawing a sample representative of a specific area that have become available and by computer-assisted telephone interviewing (CATI, to be described below) for carrying out the whole interview over the telephone.

The advantages of telephone interviewing as compared with face-to-face interviewing are primarily three in number: (1) telephone surveys are

cheaper to carry out, (2) telephone surveys take less time and effort, and (3) telephone surveys are more impersonal than face-to-face interviews. When these conditions are deemed to be advantageous, then telephone interviewing may be preferable.

Cost. Estimates of the comparative costs of in-person and telephone interviewing all lead to the same conclusion: telephone interviews are less expensive than face-to-face interviews. In a careful comparative study, Groves and Kahn, of the University of Michigan's Survey Research Center, found that a survey of approximately 1,500 individuals cost more than $84,000 for in-person interviews, nearly $38,000 for telephone interviews. This meant the in-person interview cost about $55 per interview, while the telephone interview cost $23 (Groves and Kahn, 1979, p. 188).

By keeping careful track of the costs in each area, Groves and Kahn found that the costs of selecting the sample were only 2.5 percent of the total budget of the telephone survey, while the costs were 10 percent of the in-person survey. Training and prestudy work for the field staff in the in-person study was twice the cost of the telephone survey (11.2 compared to 5.4 percent). The cost of field staff travel made up nearly 20 percent of the in-person study, while there were no travel costs in the telephone survey. On the other hand, the telephone charges made up 41 percent of the costs of the telephone survey, whereas various communication charges (telephone and postage) made up only 7 percent of the in-person interviews.

Time and effort. Sitting in an office calling respondents saves time and expends less energy than going out to interview in person. Groves and Kahn (1979) estimated that the total hours spent in the telephone survey of 1,500 by all participants equaled 5,419 as compared with 13,522 in the in-person survey. This averaged out to 3.3 hours per interview for the telephone survey and 8.7 hours per interview in the in-person study. Clearly, less time is necessary to contact people by phone than to go out and talk to them, even though it may take many telephone calls to make a contact.

The impersonal quality of a telephone survey. Because the interviewer cannot see the respondent, the respondent may feel more willing to divulge personal information than in a face-to-face encounter. Bradburn and Sudman (1979) found that in a metropolitan survey containing threatening questions (regarding arrests for drunken driving or bankruptcy experience), respondents were more likely to cooperate by telephone than in the face-to-face situation. On the other hand, there is a two-edged problem, as Bradburn and Sudman see it: "overreporting of socially desirable acts [being a registered voter, having a library card] might be highest for the more personal methods, whereas underreporting of socially undesirable acts might be highest for the more anonymous methods" (1979, p. 9). In other words, it seems to be easier to deny to someone on the telephone that an undesirable act occurred than to deny it to someone facing you; but, on the other hand, there is less temptation to try to enhance your image to a telephone interviewer.

Disadvantages of Telephone Surveys. There are three disadvantages to telephone interviewing: (1) Selecting telephone numbers that actually lead to completed interviews involves a large number of tries to achieve a small number of successes. (2) There is less motivation generated among respondents in a telephone interview because of the reduced stimulation of not seeing the interviewer in person. (3) Facilitating certain questions by giving the respondent a list with the choices, cards to sort, or some other cue or form of visual assistance cannot be done in the same manner in a telephone survey.

Getting working household numbers. In the past, telephone surveys usually selected numbers on a random basis from telephone directories. As related above, for many reasons the use of tele-

phone directories for selecting samples is undesirable. Yet the use of random-digit dialing (RDD), described above, produces many telephone numbers that are not residential households. This creates what has been called the *dross rate. Dross numbers* are those which for one reason or another do not lead to households. The ratio of good numbers to dross numbers is about 1:5 (Groves and Kahn, 1979, p. 46). If the first digit of the suffix (the final four numbers in a telephone number) is selected from directory listings as a "used" digit, then it can be assumed that numbers in that set are being assigned. Using only a random choice for the last three digits has led to a ratio of good to dross numbers nearer to 1:2.

Lack of motivation on the telephone. Once an interview has begun, it is much easier for respondents to hang up than to discontinue an interview with the interviewer standing (or sitting) right across from them. Because there is no eye contact in a telephone interview, it is more difficult for the interviewer to assess the interest level of the respondent. Therefore it is necessary for the interviewer to try to keep the telephone conversation flowing so that the respondent doesn't have time to consider whether he or she is bored or too busy. This means that it is more difficult to obtain in-depth information from an open-ended question in a telephone survey.

Questions which depend on visual cues. As described earlier, some questions are well asked by presenting the possible answers to the respondent on a card (for example, income). In a telephone interview, possible responses must be read off to the respondent for a selection. In some cases, where reactions to pictures or other visual cues are desired, the telephone is not appropriate. Most questions, however, can be adapted for a telephone interview (recall the unfolding and numbered-scale methods described above). The advent of the video telephone would probably alter the receptivity of respondents to being interviewed on the telephone. Whether individuals will be more receptive or less receptive to being interviewed on video, however, will have to be seen.

COMPUTER-ASSISTED TELEPHONE INTERVIEWING (CATI)

In the new technique of *computer-assisted telephone interviewing* (CATI), the interviewers sit at a computer terminal with a screen (a CRT). The computer may first generate a list of telephone numbers for the interviewer to call. Once a respondent is reached, the interviewer reads the questions which appear on the computer screen. The answers given are directly entered into the computer by the interviewer, who types them into the terminal. Once an interview is completed, the interviewer calls another number, the questions reappear, and the process is repeated.

By this means, a machine-readable dataset is prepared. The data from the interview are directly entered into the computer without the intervening steps of writing the data down on an interview schedule, coding them, and then transferring them onto a computer disk. You will see in Chapter 12, in the discussion of coding and transferring data to computers, that the CATI method would greatly reduce the time to carry out an interview survey as well as reduce the possible errors which the coding and transferring of data usually generate. Thus the CATI system, which is already being used at some institutions, is a much more efficient system than other forms of interviewing.

DECIDING IF A SURVEY IS APPROPRIATE FOR YOUR TOPIC

Surveys are undoubtedly the most common form of research method in the social sciences. Surveys generate data useful for a great range of study topics and lend themselves to wide-ranging forms of analyses. What they provide the researcher with is a set of responses, often to fixed-choice questions, which in the aggregate can be used to measure the characteristics and attitudes of some definable social group. The substance of the material collected in survey research includes responses to questions, aggregated across many respondents. These responses tend to tap subjective attitudes and orientations, as well as more external indicators of the respondents' personal and social situation. As I suggested in Chapter 1, survey research tends to be the method of choice for those who want to look at the broad patterns of social life or who want to describe widespread social reactions (to candidates or to social policies). If these are your goals in a study, then a survey may be your best choice.

Remember, however, that there are disadvantages as well as advantages to the survey method. As I said in Chapter 1, surveys focus on attitudes, opinions, pieces of information about the conditions of life, and the categories that define and differentiate individuals. But there are other phenomena to study in the social sciences and other ways to study these phenomena. It is not as easy to get a sense of a whole cultural group by interviewing them as it is by living among them. Consider the people of a foreign country. Suppose you decided to do a survey of the Balinese (the people who live in Bali). Would that be a good way to find out all about them? Possibly not. You would probably not know what questions to ask them, what is important to them, or how to question them properly. For such a study, field research would be preferable, though once you understood more about the Balinese, then you might be able to use more formal interview techniques.

Or let's say you wanted to understand under what conditions individuals may become very aggressive toward a stranger. It would be very difficult to get such information from a questionnaire (though you might develop scenarios of aggression-producing situations and ask respondents what they would do); in this case an experimental design might be preferable.

This is not to caution you too much on the use of surveys. They can be used in a myriad of ways to study very many subjects. While surveys may be done very poorly, a well-constructed survey administered effectively is a powerful means for gaining knowledge about the social world around you.

REVIEW NOTES

- Survey research is a method of data collection in which a defined group of individuals are asked to answer a number of identical questions.
- The components of a survey include selecting a sample of respondents and presenting the survey questions to the sample either in an interview or in a self-administered questionnaire.
- Rules for questionnaire design are: (1) include only questions pertinent to the research; (2) make the questions appealing; (3) keep the questionnaire short; (4) have brief, but clear, instructions; (5) preconsider all issues that a respondent receiving the questionnaire might have.
- The format of a mail questionnaire should include a cover letter, instructions on how to complete and return the questionnaire, the questionnaire itself, and a stamped and preaddressed return envelope.
- There are two strategies for soliciting cooperation in a survey: either stress the importance of the research project itself as a contribution to science or stress the needs of the researcher.
- Pretesting of questionnaires should be carried out to determine problems before the actual data collection begins. When reviewing a pretest, look for widely skipped questions, questions that produce little variation in response, open-ended questions that are ambiguously answered, and response set.
- The following factors may increase response rate to a mailed questionnaire: (1) its appearance, (2) the request to participate, (3) personal appeals, (4) sponsorship, (5) other inducements (possibly financial) in the survey, (6) promises of anonymity or confidentiality, (7) type of return mailing enclosures, (8) type of mailing procedure, and (9) follow-up procedures.
- What is considered a respectable response rate

for a mail survey varies, but rates below 50 percent are undesirable. Since few surveys reach a 50 percent response rate on the first mailing, follow-up mailings are advised.
- Successful interviews are highly dependent on the nature of the relationship developed between the interviewer and the interviewee.
- Focus groups draw a small group of relevant people together to discuss a specific issue. Focus groups can help in developing the concepts and questions for a survey, in generating hypotheses, or in understanding findings.
- Interview schedules should have simple instructions for the interviewer to follow, the questions should be worded so that they can be easily read, and the order of questions should quickly attract the respondent and keep her or him interested in completing the survey.
- The cardinal rule of interviewing is to suppress one's own opinions.
- An interviewer must build a warm relationship with each respondent at the same time as applying standard techniques of asking each respondent the same questions in the same way.
- The four rules for becoming a good interviewer are (1) understand the interview, (2) commit yourself to completing each and every interview, (3) practice giving the interview, and (4) use common sense in difficult situations.
- Interviewers may need to probe for deeper and fuller responses.
- Selecting a telephone survey sample from a telephone directory to represent an area is not a very desirable method because so many individuals are unlisted or without telephones.
- Telephone surveys have three advantages over face-to-face interviews: telephone surveys are cheaper; they take less time and effort; and they are more impersonal. The three disadvantages are that they often require many calls to complete a single interview, that there is less motivation to comply or complete a telephone interview, and that fewer facilitation techniques can be used in gathering sensitive or complicated data in a telephone survey.

KEY TERMS

anonymity
closed-ended question (forced choice)
computer-assisted telephone interviewing (CATI)
confidentiality
contingency question
dross numbers
exhaustive categories
face-to-face interview
focus groups
follow-up procedures
hired-hand research
interview schedule
mail survey
matrix question
open-ended question
pretesting
questionnaire
random-digit dialing (RDD)
response rate
response set
social desirability
sponsorship
telephone survey

STUDY EXERCISES

1. Using the hypothesis "Students who commute to campus will participate less in extracurricular activities than those who live on campus," write a short questionnaire to gather the data to test it. Design two *closed-ended questions* to measure the variables mentioned in the hypothesis. In addition to these, include questions to measure sex, means of commuting to campus, time required to commute to campus, and work status of student. Try to set up the three questions concerning commuting as *contingency questions.*

2. If you were administering the above questionnaire to students in a college classroom, you would need a brief set of instructions at the top of the questionnaire to inform the respondents how to fill it out. Write out such instructions.

3. Now assume that you are planning to mail this questionnaire to students. You would need to enclose a cover letter. Compose a cover letter for this questionnaire encouraging students to participate (assume that your reason for doing this survey is to fulfill course requirements for a research methods course).

RECOMMENDED READINGS

1. de Vaus, D.A.: *Surveys in Social Research,* Allen & Unwin, Boston, 1986. This very nice short text on survey research includes a lot of useful designs and hints for constructing questionnaires and building scales. Includes exercises.

2. Dillman, Don A.: *Mail and Telephone Surveys: The Total Design Method,* Wiley, New York, 1978. This volume tries to cover every aspect of these types of surveys. It stresses ways to win respondent participation.

3. Frey, James H.: *Survey Research by Telephone,* Sage, Newbury Park, Calif., 1989. This book covers recent developments, problems of random-digit dialing, how to overcome obstacles to selection caused by answering machines.

4. Marsh, Catherine: *The Survey Method: The Contribution of Surveys to Sociological Explanation,* Allen & Unwin, Boston, 1982. This book presents a history of the use of surveys, and then a very interesting evaluation of what surveys have contributed to the understanding of social phenomena.

5. Merton, Robert K., Marjorie Fiske, and Patricia L. Kendall: *The Focused Interview: A Manual of Problems and Procedures,* 2d ed., Free Press, New York, 1990. This welcome reissue of a classic work addresses the purpose, range, specificity, depth, personal context, and group setting of the focused interview.

6. Schuman, Howard, and Stanley Presser: *Questions and Answers in Attitude Surveys: Experiments on Question Form, Wording, and Context,* Academic Press, New York, 1981. The authors are experts on survey development. Subjects addressed here include question order, open and closed questions, "no opinion" options, acquiescence, and tone of wording.

7. Stewart, David W., and Prem N. Shamdasani: *Focus Groups: Theory and Practice,* Sage, Newbury Park, Calif., 1990. The potential role of focus groups in

survey research and other research methods is discussed. The design and conduct of a focus group, as well as means for analyzing data from focus group interviews, are described.

8. Turner, Charles F., and Elizabeth Martin (eds.): *Surveying Subjective Phenomena,* 2 vols., Russell Sage, New York, 1986. These volumes discuss the central methodological worries which concern leaders in the survey research enterprise. An excellent reference on issues of measuring attitudes, conceptual ambiguity in surveys, interviewer-respondent relations, and the social use (and misuse) of surveys.

CHAPTER 8

Experimental Research

LOOKING AHEAD

This chapter focuses on experimental designs for social research carried out in laboratory or natural settings. It discusses how to recognize obstacles to experimental success and how to design simple experiments.

INTRODUCTION

*A*n experiment based on social phenomena is not unlike an experiment based on natural phenomena. For this reason, experiments in the social sciences most closely parallel the methods of the natural sciences. We will begin our discussion by considering the creative and scientific aspects of experimental methods, including a discussion of causality in experimentation. Because experimentation is a rather difficult form of social research, its methods are perhaps best described by laying out precisely the characteristics and procedures of actual experiments. For this reason, two contrasting experiments on the effects of mass-media violence on aggressive behavior will be described in detail. One of these experiments was carried out in a social psychologist's laboratory, and the other was based on an analysis of statistics reporting real-life occurrences.

The greatest challenges to experimentation in the social sciences (as in the natural sciences) are the obstacles that threaten the validity of experimentation; such obstacles will be closely examined. Then, a simpler example of an experiment, one which a student might devise, will be offered. This example will be used to consider the general components of an experiment and to contrast the major types of experimental designs: true experiments, preexperiments, and quasi-experiments. Finally, the grounds for choosing to do a particular experiment will be considered.

THE ART AND SCIENCE OF EXPERIMENTS

Creative Aspects of Experiments

The choice of an experiment as the method to use for your research will depend on whether the study's primary goal is to examine a specific reaction or effect. Experimental design must focus on that occurrence, that happening, that moment when a cause supposedly brings forth an effect. It is this production (or observation) of an effect which is the experiment, and this production must be created or observationally selected out of ongoing occurrences by the experimenter. As the two experiments described in Chapter 1 indicated, designing an experiment requires manipulating situations (often those which are artificial copies of real situations) to try to bring forth an effect.

In the natural sciences, this situation or experience is called a *stimulus*, and the reaction to it is called a *response*. In the social and behavioral sciences, the causal condition is generally referred to as the *independent variable* (the IV), and what is

supposedly affected is referred to as the *dependent variable* (the DV). The area of experimental design which must be most creative is that part which addresses the design of the independent variable. Thus the types of topics which can be successfully studied with an experimental design are those where the cause-occurrence (IV) and the effect-result (DV) are of primary concern.

This focusing in experiments gives them a narrow, highly specified quality. The researcher must zero in on the central meaning of the subject of study. In contrast to survey research, where variables tend to be numerous, experimental research generally has only two primary variables. With so much concentration on these two variables, their qualities become highly significant. As stated above, the independent variable is the one that requires the most creative effort. This is a variable not only to be measured, but to be productive of something else.

In certain experiments—more often those in real-life settings—the independent variable may be a particular educational program, a social welfare benefit (such as the income maintenance project), a medical treatment, or some other event which is occurring in the real world; and the object of the experiment is to see if this independent variable is having its supposed effect. In other experiments—more often taking place in laboratories—the independent variable must be created so that it will resemble the supposed cause of what the researcher is studying. This creation or isolation of an independent variable which may lead to the effect to be studied is the central problem in the design of experiments.

The literature of social psychology is full of many fascinating (and sometimes objectionable) examples of independent variables for experiments. Stanley Milgram's (1965) research, which was briefly discussed in Chapter 3, simulated a shock machine, a teaching device which was used to stimulate the subjects who gave wrong answers by punishment (a shock). Horner's (1968) experiment, described in Chapter 1, developed verbal cues meaningful enough to the subjects that they were supposedly able to generate fear of success. Rosenthal and Jacobsen's (1968) classroom experiment (explained in Chapter 3) described a phoney test's potential as an independent variable to try to alter teachers' expectations about student performance. Note that in two of these examples, what I have called a highly creative independent variable involved an element of deception. Thus, while the researcher needs to be free enough to try to cook up a stimulating event which can cause the desired effect, the subjects must remain somewhat unaware of the experimenter's strategy or their reaction may not be a genuine response to the independent variable. For this reason, experimental designs often generate difficult ethical considerations.

Scientific Aspects of Experiments

The experiment is the quintessential scientific method. Our stereotyped image of a scientist is a person dressed in a white lab coat working in a laboratory. He or she is pouring some mixture into a test tube, setting it over a fire, watching it change

(color or whatever), and recording these observations. And we have it essentially right. The social-scientific experiment, however far from this chemist's laboratory it seems to be, is essentially following the same scientific model. It is setting up (or isolating for observation) a condition in order to be able to observe how one factor identified as the stimulus, or independent variable (the heat of the fire), will bring about a change in another factor, identified as the response, or the dependent variable (the composition or other characteristics of the mixture in the test tube). Of course, the scientist still has some of the original mixture in another test tube which was not heated so that he or she can compare qualities of the heated mixture to those of the unheated mixture.

This little experiment possesses the three primary qualities of a classical scientific experiment:

Independent and dependent variables
Pretest and posttest
Experimental group and control group

The object of the experiment is to determine what (if any) effect can be identified in the dependent variable as due to the treatment of the independent variable. The reason to have measures taken before the experiment (*pretest*) and compared with measures taken after the introduction of the independent variable (*posttest*) is to try to isolate the specific effects of the stimulus. The reason for making observations on part of the sample which has not undergone the experimental treatment (the *control group*) and comparing them with the part of the sample which has undergone the experimental treatment (the *experimental group*) is to see how different the experimental group is from a group which was not exposed to the experimental treatment. Again this distinction between experimental and control groups helps to isolate the experimental effects.

One of the major differences between experiments of natural scientists and those of social scientists is that social scientists must interact with their subjects while natural scientists need not do so. There is a major problem in experiments where the experimenter must talk to the subjects. What should he or she tell the subjects about the purpose of the experiment? If the full intention of the experiment is described, then the subjects may try either to bring forth the experimental effect or possibly abort it. This means that experimenters are rarely frank with their subjects: some type of deception is a common element of most laboratory procedures in social experiments. This problem of the need of the experimenter to interact with subjects is one of the major confounding issues in social experimentation. This will be discussed at greater length below when we discuss obstacles to validity.

The Rules of Causality

The experimental method, more than any other type of social research method, forces a consideration of causality, which was addressed in Chapter 2. Let's return to the chemistry lab example. How does that simple experiment exemplify general principles of causality which would be likely to apply in any kind of experiment? Recall that in the experiment, the experimenter poured a mixture into a test tube, heated it, and then observed changes that had occurred in the mixture.

One characteristic of this experiment is that it followed a *known time-ordered sequence.* First, the experimenter had a mixture in a tube (and naturally observed the characteristics of it); second, the experimenter placed the tube over a flame to heat it; third, the experimenter observed the mixture after the heating and noted the changes that had occurred. The object of the experiment was to look for changes that occurred as a result of a second factor being introduced after observation of a first factor.

A second characteristic of the experiment is that it tried to establish an *association between the stimulus and the response.* The chemist would correlate the occurrence of this change in the quality of the mixture with the temperature change in the

mixture caused by the heat of the fire; and he or she would be likely to carry out the experiment again and again to show that the association between these factors occurred repeatedly. The chemist would also observe that the unheated mixture did not change, which would also support the selection of heat as the causal factor in bringing about the change (heat is correlated with a change in the mixture; lack of heat is correlated with no change in the mixture). It is the evidence of a constant correlation (though not always the exact same level of correlation) between two factors that strengthens the contention that there is a causal relation between them.

However, an event that precedes a change does not necessarily have to be the cause of the change. It could be that another, unobserved factor is bringing about the change. When this can be shown, then the correlation between the two initially observed factors is considered spurious. (A much more developed discussion of spurious relationships will be presented in Chapter 14 when the elaboration model is described.) Thus, a third characteristic of an experiment is to *search for possible additional (spurious) factors that could explain the observed experimental effect.*

These characteristics of an experimental design follow the rules for determining causality. A causal relationship between two variables means that one variable (the independent variable) brings about a second variable (the dependent variable). Such a relationship is held to exist if (1) there is a time-ordered sequence between the variables so that the independent variable precedes the dependent variable in time, (2) there is a correlation between the two variables so that a change in one variable is related to a change in the other variable, and (3) there is no evidence that the relationship between the independent and dependent variables is spurious, such that when the influence of a third variable is examined, the original relationship disappears.

To apply these rules to a social research experiment, let's consider the income maintenance experiment described in Chapter 1. The independent variable (or stimulus) in that experiment was the cash transfer made to certain subjects (the experimental group). The dependent variable (or response) was a change in work incentives (or hours worked) occurring after this cash transfer. Recall as well that there was a comparison group of individuals, the control group, who were not given cash transfers but whose work behavior was studied.

How were the rules for determining causality followed in this experiment? First, there was a known time-ordered sequence (the cash transfer preceded the observation of work incentives and hours worked, which had been measured both before and after the cash transfer so that changes could be determined). Second, the associations between the giving of the cash transfers and the changes in work incentives using evidence from the many individuals to whom these transfers were given were determined (these are the correlations between the independent and dependent variables). These correlations could then be compared with changes in work incentives for those who were not given cash transfers (the control group).

Third, there was a search for spurious factors that might account for the correlation of cash transfers to changed work attitudes and behaviors. An example here was the study of personality characteristics (culture-of-poverty traits) of the subjects. It was shown that for those characterized as having culture-of-poverty traits, such as a high level of anomie, cash transfers often led to a lowering in work incentive. Conversely, for those with lower levels of factors such as anomie, cash transfers often strengthened work incentive. This indicates an *interaction effect* between the receipt of cash transfers and the personality characteristics of the receiver. Thus an interaction effect occurs when the independent variable's impact varies because of interaction with another independent variable. This means that the effect of receiving cash transfers interacted with the personality character-

istics of the recipients in affecting how they would respond.

These personality traits did not, however, explain away the correlation between cash transfers and work incentives. Had the relationship between receiving cash transfers and subsequent changes in work attitudes and behaviors disappeared when the influence of the personality factors was controlled (that is, when the original relationship was considered under each condition of the third variable) then the original relationship would have been considered spurious. Thus all three rules for determining causality were followed in this social experiment: the time-ordered sequence, the study of correlations between the independent and dependent variables, and the search for, and analysis of the effects of, other variables which might explain the observed original relationship between the independent and dependent variables.

The rules for establishing causality do not apply only in experimental designs, though experiments are usually intended to demonstrate causality and therefore most often follow these rules. Surveys also frequently seek to show causal relationships. This is especially common when survey researchers use panel data in which measures have been taken on the same subjects over a period of time. It is then possible to determine the time order between different observations.

Finally, it should be noted that social researchers are often uncomfortable with the concept of causality because they recognize that observations and measurement of human behavior and attitudes are frequently imprecise and subject to a lot of variation. This means that the correlations between variables may be quite unstable. In addition, it is very difficult to determine, let alone control for, all the possible factors that might influence a correlation between two variables. And the time order between variables may be difficult as well to establish. However, when an experiment is being designed, a researcher should carefully consider whether the experimental design will meet the criteria for determining causality.

TYPES OF EXPERIMENTS

Laboratory and Field Experiments

As we have stated before, experimental research may take place in a laboratory, where extraneous factors can be controlled most effectively; or it may take place in the real world, where some phenomenon not controlled by the experimenter can be examined in relation to its possible effects. Note that in the natural sciences certain types of scientific subjects (for example, chemistry) lend themselves to being studied in a laboratory, while other subjects (for example, astronomy) require real-life settings to be studied. In some cases, a subject can be studied either in the laboratory or in the field. Geology would be an example. One may study the effects of erosion on certain types of rocks in a field setting, or one may take rocks into a laboratory for experimental research. In the laboratory, approximate conditions of erosion may be created to replicate those which happen in nature (falling water, different levels of acidity), and their effects on the rocks may help to explain how erosion occurs. Note that the primary goal here is to be able to generalize the findings noted in the laboratory to those one would expect in the real world.

True and Natural Experiments

In a *true experiment,* the experimenter produces a set of conditions (the independent variable) and then measures its effects (the dependent variable). The variations in the independent variable are expected to lead to differences in the dependent variable. On this point, Anderson states that "the defining characteristic of a true experiment is the presence of an IV (independent variable), that an IV is a variable manipulated by the experimenter, and that manipulation of a variable involves both establishing the experimental conditions and assigning the Ss (subjects) to these conditions" (1971, p. 39).

In the experiment designed by Horner, described in Chapter 1, recall that she manipulated

the fear of success cues (the IV) by asking subjects to complete a story from an opening line cue in which a woman or a man was at the top of the medical school class. In addition, she assigned subjects to different competitive and noncompetitive single-sex and cross-sex game situations in order to test whether women who had a strong fear of success would perform worse in competitive and cross-sex conditions.

A *natural experiment,* on the contrary, would involve no manipulation on the part of the experimenter. Instead, the experimenter would *observe* one condition (the predictor variable) and relate it to another condition (the criterion variable). The major difference between these two forms of experimentation (true and natural) is in the area of controls.

In the true experiment, the experimenter tries to control as many other factors as possible in order to eliminate those factors that might have a possible influence on the dependent variable (DV). The usual procedure introduces changes in one control condition at a time so as to see how this alters the experimental effect. In contrast to this, "the natural experiment begins with a situation in which all variables are free to vary and allows controls to be introduced one at a time" (Anderson, 1971, p. 40). The adequacy of controls in an experiment and the problems addressed in trying to establish sufficient controls without making the experiment hopelessly artificial are the major challenges to experimentation as a method.

One of the primary differences between true and natural experiments is in the problems they confront, that is to say, the types of errors that are likely to occur in these experiments. In a natural experiment, where little is controlled during the experiment itself, certain constant errors may occur and affect the whole experiment. In a true experiment, the experimenter tries to control all potential sources of error. This is done by setting up different conditions of the IV and by assigning subjects to the various IV treatments according to a system of randomization (to be described below) designed to ensure that any special characteristics of subjects which might affect the outcome are randomly distributed across all the groups.

Laboratory experiments have been characteristically used by social psychologists to study specific types of social behavior in a highly focused manner. Sociologists and other social scientists have more frequently used real-life situations and occurrences as the bases for experiments. Sometimes these real-life experiments take place in actual social environments (such as a factory after a strike) where the experimental stimulus is a real social occurrence (the strike) and the experimenter comes in to study the specific effects of this occurrence. Recall that experiments like these, which take place in real settings, are referred to as *field experiments.*

In other cases, some occurrence in social life (such as a regularly scheduled television program) may be isolated and related to some other occurrences (perhaps changes in attitudes). In this case, the experimenter is singling out specific parts of social action to see if there is a causal relationship between the observed social phenomenon and some subsequent event or condition. This type of experimentation is natural. Note that a natural experiment is generally based on real-life occurrences, but it need not take place in a field setting. Similarly, a field experiment may be based on natural occurrences (such as the strike example), but it may also be based on experimentally contrived occurrences. For example, the income maintenance experiment described in Chapter 1 was a field experiment, but not a natural experiment.

Different types of experimental methods can be used to study similar research questions. A laboratory experiment is often used in order to reduce, as much as possible, extraneous factors that might alter the relationship between the experimental independent variable and the specific consequences, the dependent variable. However, the laboratory always has a somewhat artificial quality that challenges the applicability of the findings to wider social spheres. The field or natural experiment, on the other hand, may be affected by other factors in the real world which cannot be suffi-

ciently controlled. Thus it may be more difficult in a nonlaboratory experiment to be convinced that it was the independent variable that brought about the change in the dependent variable, in other words, that there was a causal relationship between the two.

Here we will carefully examine a laboratory experiment and compare it to a natural experiment. Each tries to address a question of great social significance: Can violence portrayed in the mass media lead to actual increases in aggressive behavior?

TWO CONTRASTING EXPERIMENTS

A Laboratory Experiment

Can Aggression Be Aroused by a Film? In a series of laboratory experiments, social psychologist Leonard Berkowitz and his colleagues (1963, 1966, 1967, 1973) used the presentation of a prizefight film as the independent variable to try to arouse aggressive behavior in the subjects being studied. In one of these experiments, Berkowitz and Geen (1967, pp. 365–366) had 90 male subjects (University of Wisconsin undergraduates who volunteered to participate) follow the experimental procedure outlined in Box 8-1.

Note how complex and intricate an experiment this was. Each step of the procedure was engineered to produce the desired effect which the researchers were studying. As you can see, Berkowitz and Geen were trying to study how far aggressive acts seen on a film might translate into aggressive acts in real behavior. The primary independent variable was the prizefight film; the primary dependent variable was the number of shocks administered to another subject after viewing the film. A prefilm mood questionnaire determined the aggressive levels of the subject before seeing the film. This could then be compared to the postfilm mood questionnaire to determine how much the film had altered the subject's moods. Thus the mood questionnaire served as a control in the experiment.

BOX 8-1

THE BERKOWITZ-GEEN EXPERIMENT ON THE EFFECTS OF MASS-MEDIA VIOLENCE

INSTRUCTING THE SUBJECTS ABOUT THE EXPERIMENT

1. Each subject was met by the experimenter and another subject (who was in fact a confederate of the experimenter).
2. The experimenter stated that the experiment was about "problem solving and stress."
3. The subject was told that stress would be produced by receiving mild electric shocks from the other subject in response to how well or how poorly he was able to solve a set of problems (1 shock for a good solution, 10 for a very poor solution).

THE EXPERIMENT

1. The subject was separated from the confederate. He was given a problem to solve (designing a contest for an advertising campaign for a store) while his partner (the confederate) was supposedly watching a film.
2. The solution he gave was then (supposedly) taken to the other subject for appraisal.
3. A shock bracelet was strapped on the subject and he received 7 shocks from the other subject (actually from the experimenter).
4. Then the subject filled out a questionnaire to determine his mood.
5. Now it was the subject's turn to see the film.
   a. Two-thirds of the subjects saw a prizefight scene from a film.
      (1) Half of these were told that the hero (who would be beaten up in the fight) was a bad person. This was the *justified aggression* condition.
      (2) The other half were told that the hero was a good person. This was the *less justified aggression* condition.
   b. The other third saw a nonaggressive film about a track race. This was the *nonaggression* condition.
6. After the film, each subject's mood was measured by a second mood questionnaire.
7. The confederate came into the subject's room saying he had finished his problem.
8. The experimenter asked the two men their names, implying that both were strangers. In some cases, the confederate said that his name was "Kirk Anderson," in others, "Bob Anderson."
9. For those subjects who had seen the prizefight film and had a confederate named Kirk, the experimenter mentioned that it was coincidental that the hero who took the beating in the film was the film actor Kirk Douglas.
10. The confederate then returned to his room.
11. The subject was given the confederate's solution (developing a promotion campaign for a laundry powder) and reminded that he was to deliver the appropriate number of shocks depending on the quality of the solution.
12. The subject was left alone to administer the shocks.
13. A final questionnaire was given to evaluate how the subject felt about the confederate's solution.
14. The experiment was over; the experimenter described the deceptions and asked the subject not to discuss the experiment with anyone else.

Source: Leonard Berkowitz and Russell G. Geen, "Stimulus Qualities of the Target of Aggression," *Journal of Personality and Social Psychology*, **5**:364–368, 1967.

This experiment attempted not only to show that moods may change with exposure to a film but also that aggressive behaviors themselves can be aroused and turned into action as a result of viewing violence. The full experimental treatment was seeing the prizefight film with the "justified" aggression version of the story and learning that the name of the confederate subject in the experiment was "Kirk." The full control treatment was experienced by the group who saw the track race (nonviolent) film. There were also other intermediate control groups (those who heard the "less justified" aggression version of the plot and those who were told that the confederate they were working with was "Bob").

Berkowitz and Geen found that there was a definite correlation between viewing violence in a film and greater aggressive behavior in the viewers. First they saw, by comparing the pre- and postfilm mood questionnaires, that the prizefight film had had little effect on increasing the anxiety, anger, or worry of the subjects. On the other hand, those who had seen the prizefight film administered more shocks to their fellow subjects than those who had seen the track race film. This was especially true for those who had been in the strongest experimental conditions (those who had heard the justified aggression version and who had also been told that their fellow subject was Kirk). From this the authors concluded that a film showing aggressive behavior can trigger aggressive behavior, particularly against those who appear to be similar to the victims portrayed in the film.

Table 8-1 offers the primary results of this experiment. Examine the top row of numbers. It reports on the average (mean) number of shocks administered to the confederate after viewing the

TABLE 8-1

BERKOWITZ-GEEN EXPERIMENTAL FINDINGS
(Mean Number of Shocks to Confederate)

Confederate's Name	Justified Film Aggression	Less Justified Film Aggression	Track Race Film
Total sample[a]			
Kirk	5.87_a	5.13_{ab}	4.13_b
Bob	5.00_{ab}	4.67_{ab}	4.60_{ab}
Omitting 5 most anxious men in each group[b]			
Kirk	6.4_a	5.0_b	4.4_b
Bob	5.8_b	4.3_b	4.7_b

[a]$N = 15$ in each group
[b]$N = 10$ in each group
Note: Cells having a subscript in common are not significantly different at the .05 level.

Source: Data from Leonard Berkowitz and Russell G. Geen, "Film Violence and Cue Properties of Available Targets," *Journal of Personality and Social Psychology*, **3**:525–530, 1966.

film. (The subscripts refer to the number of subjects in each treatment group.) Note that the table presents separate figures for the treatment group who were told that the confederate was named Kirk and the treatment group who were told he was called Bob. In the lower half of the table, mean numbers are given for each of the treatment groups after the five most anxious subjects (determined on the basis of the mood questionnaire) have been excluded. The top row shows that the experimental group, who saw the justified aggression version and who were told that the fellow subject was named Kirk, gave the greatest number of shocks. Note that the name Kirk was more strongly related to increased shocks when the justified version was shown. In the bottom half of the table, which excludes the most anxious subjects—they were excluded on the assumption that the most anxious subjects might inhibit their aggression (Berkowitz and Geen, 1967, p. 366)—the results become even more vivid. In this case, a substantially greater number of shocks were given by those in the experimental group (justified condition and Kirk confederate) than by those whose confederate was called Bob or who saw the less justified prizefight film, or who saw the track race film.

Berkowitz, a social psychologist, had been primarily interested in studying aggressive behavior and had used a mass-media form (a film) to try to elicit aggressive reactions. He and his colleague concluded that "available target persons who are associated with the victim of observed violence receive more attacks from angered individuals than do other possible targets lacking this association" (Berkowitz and Geen, 1967, pp. 367–368).

A more sociological concern is to determine how far violence reported or presented in the mass media may lead to actual violent crimes, the most socially deleterious types of aggression. David Phillips (1983) addressed this issue in his study of the potential effects of heavyweight prizefights on the homicide rates in the United States. Let us carefully examine the very different experimental design he used.

A Natural Experiment

Can Mass Media Trigger Violent Behavior?

To study the widespread social effect of violence experienced through the mass media on violent behavior in the society at large, Phillips selected a particular type of violence depicted in the mass media, namely, heavyweight prizefights—the same type of violent stimulus that Berkowitz and Geen had used—and then related the timing of these fights to changing homicide rates in the United States as a whole. Instead of bringing sub-

BOX 8-2

THE PHILLIPS EXPERIMENT ON THE EFFECTS OF VIOLENCE IN THE MASS MEDIA ON HOMICIDE RATES

1. Using the standard reference work that records prizefights, Phillips selected heavyweight prizefights which took place between 1973 and 1978.
2. He determined the date and day of the week of each fight.
3. He then examined the homicide rate for each of the 10 days following each fight.
4. He used a time-series regression analysis (to be described below) to see whether there was an unexpected rise in homicides following the prizefights, and if so, on which day after the fight it occurred.
5. In this analysis, he established controls for days of the week, holidays, and months of the year (using statistical techniques) because of the known variation in frequencies of homicides by days, holidays, and months.
6. He also compared fights held within the United States to those held in other countries, and those fights which had been discussed on television news with those which had not.

Data from David Phillips, "The Impact of Mass Media Violence on U.S. Homicides," *American Sociological Review*, **48**:560–568, 1983.

jects into a laboratory, he used available information on the dates of prizefights and aggregate crime statistics to do his study. Box 8-2 lays out the steps in this experiment.

Phillips found that there was an unexpected rise in homicides three days after prizefights. Table 8-2 gives the actual number (called the observed number in the table) of homicides occurring three days after each of the 18 fights, then the expected number (based on a statistical prediction of the number of homicides likely to happen on that day). The difference between the observed number of homicides and the expected number is then determined. You can see in Table 8-2 that for

13 of the 18 fights, the observed number of homicides three days after the fight exceeds the expected number. In other words, more murders usually took place three days after a major heavyweight prizefight than would be expected on those days.

Checking the possible "personal experience" hypothesis, that actual attendance at a prizefight might trigger violence more than exposure through mass media, Phillips compared the homicide rates three days after a fight in the United States with those three days after a fight in a foreign country (which Americans were unlikely to have attended). The comparison showed that homicide rates were even higher when the fight took place outside

TABLE 8-2

PHILLIPS' EXPERIMENTAL FINDINGS
(Fluctuation of U.S. Homicides Three Days after Each Heavyweight Prizefight, 1973–1978)

Name of Fight	Observed No. of Homicides	Expected No. of Homicides	Observed Minus Expected	Fight Held Outside U.S.?	On Network Evening News?
Foreman/Frazier	55	42.10	12.90	Yes	Yes
Foreman/Roman	46	49.43	−3.43	Yes	No
Foreman/Norton	55	54.33	.67	Yes	No
Ali/Foreman	102	82.01	19.99	Yes	Yes
Ali/Wepner	44	46.78	−2.78	No	Yes
Ali/Lyle	54	47.03	6.97	No	Yes
Ali/Bugner	106	82.93	23.07	Yes	No
Ali/Frazier	108	81.69	26.31	Yes	Yes
Ali/Coopman	54	45.02	8.98	Yes	No
Ali/Young	41	43.62	−2.62	No	No
Ali/Dunn	50	41.47	8.53	Yes	Yes
Ali/Norton	64	52.57	11.43	No	Yes
Ali/Evangelista	36	42.11	−6.11	No	No
Ali/Shavers	66	66.86	−.86	No	No
Spinks/Ali	89	78.96	10.04	No	Yes
Holmes/Norton[a]	53	48.97	4.03	No	No
Ali/Spinks	59	52.25	6.75	No	Yes
Holmes/Evangelista[a]	52	50.24	1.76	No	No

[a]Sponsored by World Boxing Council; all other fights sponsored by the World Boxing Association.

Source: David Phillips, "The Impact of Mass Media Violence on U.S. Homicides," *American Sociological Review,* **48:** 560–568, 1983.

the United States. Testing a "modeling" hypothesis, that the greater the publicity for a fight, the higher the rise in the homicide rate, he found that those fights covered on network television news were related to much higher postfight homicide rates than those receiving less television coverage.

Another test of the modeling hypothesis is similar to one Berkowitz and Geen employed in their laboratory experiment when they matched the name Kirk, the actor playing the prizefighter who lost in the film, to the confederate researcher. Phillips compared the race (white or black) of the loser of the prizefight to the race (white or black) of young male homicide victims; and he hypothesized that if modeling occurred, homicide victims would more often match the racial characteristics of the prizefight losers (victims). This turned out to be the case. When the prizefight loser was white, there was an increase in *white* male homicide victims; conversely, when the loser was black, there was an increase in *black* homicide deaths (Phillips, 1983, pp. 564–566).

Note that in this type of experimental design (which will be described below as one form of quasi-experimental design), pretests and posttests and experimental and control groups are not set up. Phillips was able to enter a series of controls regarding the fight (for such factors as the day of the week, the month, whether it occurred on or near a holiday, its location, and the race of the loser). However, he had no control at all over the fight itself or how the public might be exposed to it

Is the Prizefight/Homicide Experiment Valid?
In his experimental research, Phillips attempted to show that homicide rates in the United States were affected by the recent occurrence and publicity of heavyweight prizefights. In other words, did public sports violence have an effect on the incidence of violent crimes? In the terminology of an experiment, the stimulus was the prizefight (televised, broadcast and/or reported in the print media); the response was homicides, measured in the aggregate.

Baron and Reiss (1985) challenged Phillips'

findings (and other similarly conceived experiments) by arguing that such research lacked a testable theory of imitation which could (1) clarify the qualities of media stimuli that affect the magnitude and duration of the imitation effect, (2) lay out those behaviors that could be considered as imitation responses, and (3) define the process that brings forth the imitation. Examining the average number (and variance of) homicides occurring on specific days of the week during the years covered by the Phillips study, Baron and Reiss found homicides were more frequent on weekend days and less frequent on midweek days: "of the seven fights that apparently induced substantial amounts of imitative violence, five occurred on a Tuesday or a Wednesday" (1985, p. 357). Thus the three-day lag effect (from prizefights to homicides) may have appeared because Friday and Saturday are the two heaviest days for homicides.

To further disprove Phillips' findings, Baron and Reiss replicated Phillips' analysis of which days, months, and holiday were the highest predictors of high homicide rates for each year in which a major fight took place and for the following year (when no major fight was held). Their design employed this logic: if the imitative effect were an artifact—if the effect appeared because there are more homicides on specific days of the week, holidays, etc.—then homicide rates should remain as high when there had been *no* prizefight three days before. (The only correction they made to the "following year" data was to make the day of the week equivalent from the actual year to the next). They found that in the year after the prizefight occurred, a similar (though slightly weakened) lag effect on homicide rates also appeared. Thus Baron and Reiss contend that Phillips' results were merely an artifact of his research design.

Our interest here has been to consider the research methods of a quasi-experimental design. Controversial experimental designs are always open to challenges. Phillips and his colleague Bollen (1985) carried out further experiments to try to reconfirm their findings, while Baron and Reiss continued to refute the evidence. Researchers commonly replicate others' experiments, with some variations in the design, in order to test the reliability and validity of experimental findings.

OBSTACLES TO AN EXPERIMENT'S VALIDITY

Any errors in experiments are a serious concern. Anytime the dependent variable (or *criterion variable*) in an experiment is affected by anything other than the independent variable (or *predictor variable*) under study, there is experimental error. Naturally, no experimental design can completely eliminate all error. Nevertheless, the object of a good experimental design is to reduce error as much as possible by recognizing how it may occur and by choosing a design that will minimize it. The primary obstacles to scientific validity in experiments have been laid out in very influential works by psychologists Donald Campbell and Julian Stanley (1963) and Campbell and Thomas Cook (1979). Drawing upon their discussions, we will consider how these obstacles were handled in the two experiments described.

Internal Validity

According to Campbell and his associates, internal validity must be the most central concern of the experimenter. To consider internal validity is to ask whether the investigator can be confident that the experiment actually caused what it appeared to cause or whether there were other factors in the conduct of the experiment that distorted the true experimental purpose.

Cook and Campbell isolated numerous types of problems that may occur to challenge the internal validity of an experiment and suggested means of reducing or controlling for their potential effects. (In a broader sense, the internal validity of any type of research design can be challenged, and many of the problems to be considered below would also be problems in other types of research designs.)

The problems to be countered might be grouped in the following ways: obstacles stemming from who is in the experiment, what happens during the experimental procedure (from the pretest, through the experimental treatment, to the posttest), and what problems arise due to time changes or statistical laws (1979, pp. 51–55).

Problems concerning who is in the study:

1. *Selection.* Are there differences between the two groups being compared? In the Berkowitz study, we might ask whether the subjects who saw the prizefight film were somehow different from those who saw the track race film. In a real-life experiment on the effectiveness of a social program (such as a remedial reading program) where the experimental group subjects getting the treatment (the IV) are the ones who need the program and the control group are the ones who do not need it, problems of selection are necessarily present. Recall that in the income maintenance experiment, described in Chapter 1, this potential obstacle was avoided by assigning subjects randomly to groups which either received or did not receive income increments. In such a design, selection effects can be reduced.

2. *Mortality or loss of subjects.* Will all subjects remain in the study? If the experiment occurs over an extended period of time some of the subjects may no longer be a part of the study. In the income maintenance experiment, some subjects dropped out of the program, some moved or died, and others were simply not available at the end of the experimental period. If the subjects who drop out are fundamentally different from those who remain, then the two groups may not be truly comparable.

An example of how such experimental mortality might affect a study might be the case of an experiment intended to cover an entire academic year: the pretest would be given in the fall, the students would then be exposed to some program, and the posttest would be given in the spring. In such a study, students who dropped out of college during the year would not be available for the posttest. This would be a case of *experimental mortality* of subjects. Note that if there were more dropouts from the experimental than from the control group, the comparability of the two groups would be affected.

3. *Rivalry between subjects in experimental and control groups.* If members of the control group recognize that their performance is to be compared with that of an experimental group, they may outdo themselves in trying to show that they can perform as effectively.

4. *Demoralization of subjects receiving less desirable treatment.* When some control groups receive no treatment or an undesirable treatment, they may become resentful and perform differently from the experimental group, not because they lack the effects of the treatment, but because of the negative feelings generated by not being given a treatment or by being treated in a less desirable manner.

   Another problem with the assignment of individuals to control groups is that there may be subtle and unintended cues given to those in the control group that could weaken their potential reaction. Of course, subjects usually do not know which group they are in. However, if those assigned to the control group perceive that they are not supposed to change or that they are supposed to change less than the other group, they may actually fulfill the prophecy. This phenomenon may work in reverse for the experimental group, where individuals who are expected to react may help to bring about this expectation. (This latter phenomenon, which is referred to as the *demand characteristics* of an experiment, will be discussed in a later section.)

Problems concerning the experimental procedure:

5. *Testing.* The effect of what subjects learn on the pretest upon their performance on the

posttest tends to be a problem in experiments where ability or achievement tests are to be used as the dependent variable. If a pretest is given, some subjects may become overly familiar with the test itself and perform better on the posttest. The effects of testing also show up when attitudinal scales or personality tests are used as pre- or posttests.

6. *Instrumentation.* Validity problems due to changes in measurement or to imprecision of the measurement instruments or of the person measuring (or observing or scoring) could result in a false indication of an experimental effect. In other words, an effect may appear to be present when what has actually occurred is a shift in the instrument itself. For example, in the Phillips experiment, if the government were to change its method of reporting homicides (basing the figures on a different type of indicator, such as arrest rates rather than victimization rates), an increase in errors could occur since variables based on different types of rates were being compared.

7. *Imitation of treatment.* In a situation where the control group might become exposed to a treatment or condition similar to the independent variable, it might be impossible to isolate the effect of the independent variable. Cook and Campbell give an example of a study of the effects of legalizing abortion in one state where residents of a neighboring state were to be used as a control group. If residents of the neighboring state could easily go for abortions to the state being studied, then they would not make a satisfactory control group (1979, p. 54).

8. *Compensation to the control group.* In experiments, such as the income maintenance experiment, where the experimental group is benefiting from assets of which the control group is being deprived, there may be a tendency to try to equalize the benefits to the control group. Social programs, which are usually set up to increase equity, often distort the efforts of experimenters who are trying to study how

effective the benefits actually are by providing forms of compensatory equalization to the control group.

Problems concerning time:

9. *Maturation.* Between the pre- and posttests, the subjects may grow older or more experienced, or they may change in terms of intelligence and physical strength. This is more often a problem in an experiment that spans a number of years.

10. *History.* Between the pre- and posttests, events occur beyond the experiment that may alter the experimental effect. (Take, for example, a study of attitudes toward airplane safety in which the stimulus is to be a film on causes of airplane crashes. If a major plane crash actually occurred between the pretest and the posttest, it would be very difficult to determine how far attitudes toward safety were due to the film or to the actual event.)

Problems of interaction of selection with other factors:

11. *Interactions with selection.* These obstacles occur in situations where the selection of subjects affects maturation (a selection-maturation interaction) or history (a selection-history interaction) or instrumentation (a selection-instrumentation interaction). Selection-maturation interaction occurs when the experimental and control groups are maturing at different rates. Selection-history interaction occurs when different groups come from different settings and are thereby exposed to different historical changes. Selection-instrumental effects may take place if the experimental and control groups have sufficiently different means on the test being used as the pretest. A *ceiling* effect may occur when members of one group score so high that it is not possible for them to raise their scores sufficiently in the posttest. A *floor* effect occurs when a greater proportion of the scores in one of the groups are at the lower end of the scale than is

true of the other group (Cook and Campbell, 1979, p. 53).

Problems of statistical regression:

12. *Statistical regression.* There is a tendency for the scores of high scorers and low scorers on a pretest to be more subject to errors than the scores of those in the middle range (which are more likely to be balanced by errors that inflate scores as well as errors that deflate them). Thus, when posttests are given, there is a greater tendency for high scorers (whose earlier scores were increased by error) to move lower and for low scorers (whose earlier scores were decreased by error) to move higher. This regression to the mean of the group by scorers in the extreme will be falsely registered as an effect of the experimental treatment.

Consider an experiment in a social research methods class. Let's say that the instructor decides to regive the midterm exam and offers special preparation sessions to half the class (the experimental group) to see if this will improve their performance. The comparability between this experimental group which gets the special preparation sessions and the control group which does not may be affected by the average scores that the two groups had on the first midterm exam (the pretest).

Let's say that, although the students are assigned to groups randomly, the experimental group has more high scorers from the first test; it is therefore more likely that these subjects' scores were subject to errors that inflated their scores. Therefore, in a second testing, the scores of the experimental group members might be expected to fall. If the control group had more middle-range scores on the first testing, these scores would represent a better balance of scores affected by inflation and deflation error, and in a second testing their scores might change less. In such a case, the results of the posttest may lead to a lowering in the scores of the experimental group with initially high scores (regardless of the effects of the special preparation program) and a slight increase in the middle group. Thus the experimental effect of the preparation session appears weaker because of the tendency of those with more extreme scores to regress to more average scores regardless of the experimental treatment.

External Validity

Obstacles to the external validity of an experiment raise the question of how far an experiment can be generalized to other settings, to other treatments, or to other subjects. In laboratory experiments, there is always the conflict between trying to maximize control over the possibly confounding factors that would distort the treatment effect and trying to minimize the artificiality necessarily imposed in exercising so much control over subjects, over the experimental setting, and over the treatment itself. Problems of external validity arise because of the unintended effects of aspects of the experiment, the time frame within which it occurs, and the treatment (or independent variable) itself. These cross-effects are referred to as *interactions.* The three types of interactions which Cook and Campbell (1979 pp. 73–74) define as possibly reducing the "generalizability" of an experiment are interactions of (1) selection of subjects, (2) setting of the experiment, and (3) the period of history over which the experiment is carried out with the treatment effect.

One problem is that subjects in an experiment are usually aware of the highly controlled experimental environment and may attend very closely to what the experimenter is trying to prove. In this way they may try to be *cooperative* subjects, that is, to "validate the experimental hypothesis" (Orne, 1975, p. 187). Subjects often seem to invest themselves in the experiments they are participating in. For this reason, deception of subjects is widespread in experiments. Yet the very deception on the part of the experimenter may encourage the

subjects even more to try to figure out what the experiment is meant to study.

Orne describes the subject's behavior as "problem-solving" (p. 187) and defines *the sum total of cues that may "convey an experimental hypothesis to the subject" as the demand characteristics of the experimental situation* (emphasis added; pp. 187–188). Naturally, such a predisposition on the part of the subjects invalidates the experiment itself. Orne argues, in sum, that the subject's behavior in an experiment is determined not only by the experimental variables but also by the "perceived demand characteristics of the experimental situation" (p. 188). One way to try to figure out how far demand characteristics have affected an experiment is through "postexperimental inquiry," but Orne warns that experimenters must beware that they don't encourage the subjects to deny that they knew what was going on in the experiment (p. 190).

Experiments done on volunteer college students (as in the Berkowitz experiment) suffer from possible interactions caused by selection of subjects and treatment. Are the students who volunteered characterized by qualities that make their reactions unrepresentative of what the reactions of nonvolunteers might be? Cook and Campbell (1979, p. 73) suggest that one way to reduce the interaction effect of treatment and selection is to make the experiment as convenient (short in time, easy to get to) as possible so that the inconvenient aspects of the experiment do not selectively keep out certain types of subjects and draw other types in.

In the case of the laboratory experiment using the prizefight film, the study might be challenged by asking what the effect of this film would be in a different setting (say, a standard movie theater instead of the laboratory). This challenge to external validity questions an interaction between the setting and the treatment. In the Phillips experiment, the researcher tried to reduce the interaction of history and treatment (by carefully controlling for the day of the week, month of the year, and holidays) because he knew that homicides were more prevalent on certain days. However, Baron and Reiss challenged Phillips' findings by controlling for the year of the experimental effect.

A FILM'S EFFECTS ON ATTITUDES: A HYPOTHETICAL EXPERIMENT ON ATTITUDES TOWARD DRUNK DRIVING

In order to consider carefully all components of an experiment and the different types of experimental designs, let's set up a fairly simple hypothetical experiment (one that a student might easily design) as a model. Suppose you are very concerned about the incidence of drunk driving and automobile accident fatalities and wonder how you might generate greater concern among teenagers. You see an excellent documentary film on television, showing fatal car crashes, which examines the drinking behavior of the drivers. The film also supports strategies to reduce drunk driving. You expect that the film might serve as a stimulus that could change students' attitudes toward drinking and driving (the effect).

Doing the experiment would require the following steps.

1. Define the independent variable as the movie and the dependent variable as the change in attitude toward drinking and driving from that held before viewing the film.
2. Select a sample of individuals, some of whom would watch the film (the experimental group) and others who would not (the control group).
3. Measure the attitudes about drinking and driving before showing the film (the pretest) and after the film (the posttest) among both the experimental and control groups.

What are the critical factors which will determine whether this is a meaningful experiment or not? First, the independent variable, the film, must be considered to be potentially arousing enough so that viewers might be subject to a change in attitude. Second, the questions asked before and after the film must be relevant to the nature of the film

itself and phrased carefully enough to measure attitudes that are potentially alterable by the film. Third, the selection of the groups should not be biased; the groups can be compared only if they are equivalent. Fourth, the administration of the questions to all subjects before and after the film should be done in as similar a fashion as possible (for example, the length of time from the viewing of the film until the posttest should be equivalent). Fifth, the extraneous factors which might interfere between the showing of the film and the response to it should be minimized.

Careful attention to these questions will help to validate the experiment. Recall that the central scientific concern in experiments is whether what is discovered is, in fact, the result of the experiment (whether the experiment has *internal validity*) and whether the experiment itself is representative enough of the real world that what occurs in the laboratory (or even in a natural setting) can be the basis for understanding how this process might occur in the real world (whether the experiment has *external validity*). Remember that the obstacles to internal validity concern the internal qualities of the experiment itself and whether other processes can be occurring at the same time as the experiment which might alter the effects. The obstacles to external validity concern whether the experiment itself creates conditions that necessarily make it unrepresentative of the actual situation which it is trying to study.

Once potential problems of this kind are recognized, they can, in some cases, be controlled. In social research, however, where so many factors—people, organizations, institutions, states—are being studied, it is often difficult to control conditions sufficiently. For example, in presenting the film it would be important to control for the manner in which it was viewed. The experimenter could try to control factors that could alter the impact of the film. The physical condition of the room, the quality of the film and the projection equipment, the statement made by the experimenter at the outset of the film can all affect how the audience will react to the presentation of the film. By getting all of the experimental group to view the film in a single place, the conditions could be held more constant.

Similarly, the selection of the sample for this study would have many potential problems. What if those with strict attitudes toward drinking and driving watched the film and those with lax attitudes did not? However, if the experimenter used volunteer subjects and assigned them to groups randomly to either view or not view the film, then any potential differences between the groups that might have distorted the findings should be randomly distributed and thereby made insignificant.

These issues are raised to suggest the variety of ways in which experimenters must try to eliminate or reduce the conditions which might change the relationship between the independent and dependent variables. The most important way is to fix (or control) as many of the possibly confounding conditions as possible so that the true experiment has a chance to produce an effect. This kind of control is achieved by careful, thoughtful design, anticipating all the possibly contaminating problems before the experiment is carried out. In the next two sections, we will examine, step by step, the components of a true experiment and the range of types of designs for social experiments, those which meet the qualifications of a true experiment and those which do not meet the qualifications for a true experiment but which represent what are referred to as preexperiments and quasi-experiments.

GENERAL COMPONENTS OF AN EXPERIMENT

Independent and Dependent Variables

As I have stated already, the heart of an experiment is to understand a cause-effect relationship. The independent variable must be defined, isolated, and operationalized so that it can be measured. This independent variable is a kind of stimulus which will supposedly trigger some change. Note that if the independent variable brings forth no

change, the experiment will be useless; therefore, it is important to select an independent variable that seems likely to lead to a change.

The dependent variable, which is the central focus of the study, is the condition that should be brought about (at least in part) by the independent variable. This dependent variable should show some change in condition from before the experiment and between subjects who experience it and those who do not. The experimenter must isolate the dependent variable as a natural occurrence which can be observed or must create a measure to call it forth (such as answers to specific questions).

Experimental and Control Groups

To experience the experiment is to be subject to its influence. If the experiment works, then the subjects who go through the experiment will all be affected in some way. However, what if those who do not go through the experiment show the same effects? This would suggest that the observed effect was not caused, or at least not solely caused, by the experiment. To control for this possibility, experiments nearly always include a control group which does not experience the experimental conditions. For the control group to be comparable to the experimental group, the two must be equivalent. The primary means for creating equivalence between control groups in a true experiment is through the process of *randomization in assignment to groups.*

Randomization.   As you recall from Chapter 6 on sampling methods, the rules of probability ensure that bias can be reduced in the selection of subjects for any study if random procedures are used which place people in a sample (or, in the case of an experiment, in the experimental or control group) according to the laws of chance. Such methods might employ techniques such as flipping coins, pulling names from a hat, throwing dice, using a set of random numbers, or using a computerized means to select random numbers. All these methods give each subject an equal chance of being drawn into the sample (or into the experimental or control group). The box describes how assignment to experimental groups by randomization differs from random sampling for surveys.

In sampling for an experiment, the subjects are usually volunteers. In fact, in social experiments, the vast majority of subjects are college students. Thus, they are not randomly selected from the general population, but they can be randomly assigned to either the experimental or the control group. This is done by first drawing together a list of all subjects. Then, by using a system for randomly placing students in the experimental or control groups, the biases that might have occurred if placement had been done in some other way should be controlled. What this means is that the errors that might occur due to assignment to groups should be randomly distributed between the groups by having randomly assigned subjects to either of the groups. It is this process which makes it justifiable to use statistical tests to compare the results of the experimental and control groups.

Matching.   In this method, which is now rarely employed on its own in experimental research, the characteristics of subjects are matched; then, one of the subjects is placed in the experimental group, the other in the control group. According to this procedure, if half the subjects are women, half of the women should be assigned to the experimental group and half to the control group. This is similar to the principles for the nonprobability sampling called quota sampling, which was described in Chapter 6. If the fifth-grade class under study is in a lower-middle-class suburb, the control classroom should be a fifth-grade in a like suburb. However, simple reliance on matching cannot address all the potential differences that these two groups may have. This is because the important characteristics of the subjects that might affect the experiment may not be recognized by the researcher. However, if the groups are assigned on the basis of randomization, these unknown (but significant) factors should be randomly distributed between the two groups.

This is why matching is not generally used alone, though some forms of matching (having equal numbers of male and female subjects) may be paired with the system of randomization to make the two groups comparable. (This is similar

---

ORENSTEIN AND PHILLIPS ON HOW NOT TO CONFUSE RANDOM ASSIGNMENT WITH RANDOM SAMPLING

RANDOM ASSIGNMENT AND RANDOM SAMPLING

Warning: Do not confuse *random assignment* and *random sampling.* When we randomly assign subjects to the treatment groups in an experiment, we are trying to create treatment groups that have a high probability of being similar on all variables. If this is the case, then we can infer that something about the treatments, rather than differences in the people or groups exposed to each treatment, led to differences on the dependent variable. The random assignment of subjects does not insure that the results of an experiment con be applied to any larger group of subjects. When we randomly select or sample respondents from a larger population of respondents, we are trying to create a sample of respondents that has a high probability of being similar to the population on all variables. If this is the case, then we can generalize from the results based on the sample to what would have been obtained if our survey had questioned all members of the population from which the sample was drawn. The random sampling of respondents does not insure that the independent variable of the study, rather than other variables associated with the independent variable, led to differences on the dependent variable.

Source: Alan Orenstein and William R. F. Phillips, *Understanding Social Research: An Introduction,* Allyn and Bacon, Boston, 1978.

to stratified sampling where the sample is first divided into homogeneous groups before selecting the sample randomly.) Another important reason for using randomization rather than matching is that the statistical tests likely to be used in an experiment depend on the groups being randomized.

Double-Blind Experiments. In nearly all true experiments, members of experimental and control groups are not told which group they are in. Furthermore, if the investigator knows which subjects are in the experimental and which are in the control groups, the results may be interpreted differently. To avoid this occurrence, experiments are often set up to be *double-blind* so that neither the subjects nor the experimenter know which subjects are in which group. (Clearly the information must be known ultimately by the experimenter, but it may be possible to conceal this information during the experiment and analysis stages by using a coding system for each subject which leaves out information about group placement. Group placement identification can be stored elsewhere and recovered once the initial results of the experiment have been established.)

Problems Caused by Using Volunteer Subjects. There are problems generated in using volunteer subjects, the most common type of subjects used in experiments. Studies by Rosenthal and Rosnow (1975) of volunteers in experiments show that certain types of people are more likely to volunteer for an experiment. Usually, people who volunteer are better-educated, they come from higher social classes, they are more in need of social approval, and they are more intelligent than those who do not volunteer. The fact that particular types of subjects are attracted could affect the generalizability of the findings.

The Hawthorne Effect. This is a problem generated in many experiments that may require an additional type of control group (that is why we will consider it in this context). In a famous study carried out in the 1930s, it was found that being in an experiment may have an effect whether or not the supposed stimulus is presented. In this study of the Hawthorne plant at Western Electric in Chicago, the conditions of the working environment of those in the wiring room were altered to see if work productivity would increase. While it was found that improving these conditions (for example, by increasing the lighting) improved productivity, it was also discovered that altering the conditions in what would seem to be a negative fashion (such as making the lighting dimmer) also increased productivity. What this suggested was not that workers do better in both bright and dull lights, but that workers do better in experimental conditions—whatever those conditions might be—than in nonexperimental conditions (see Roethlisberger and Dickson, 1939). Thus the *Hawthorne effect* refers to the tendency of subjects in an experiment to respond in the predicted manner whatever the experimental treatment.

To control for this effect, some experiments use two control groups: one of the control groups does not experience the experiment at all; the other is subject to experimental conditions, but not the actual ones being studied (this is the Hawthorne control group). The most common examples of these two types of controls are the ones used in testing new drugs. In this type of medical research, there are nearly always three groups of subjects: the experimental group who receive the actual drug, a control group who receive a placebo (a sugar pill), and a control group who receive nothing. What is usually found is that those receiving the placebos tend to show some of the same effects as those receiving the actual drug (though usually not as strongly), while those receiving nothing at all show no effect. In the Berkowitz and Geen experiment, those who saw the track race film were a Hawthorne type of control group: they experienced an experimental treatment, but not with an independent variable that was expected to affect them. In that experiment, there was no true full control group, that is, one not subject to any form of the independent variable.

Pretest and Posttest

Since the focus of any experiment is on the *effect* of the experimental stimulus (independent variable), it is crucial to prove that the stimulus actually brought about the effect. It is this need to prove the centrality of the stimulus in bringing about the effect that has made the pretest-posttest design so important in experimentation. Thus, what the researcher is looking for is not the after-stimulus effect, but the change in the dependent variable, from a point in time before the stimulus was presented to a point in time after.

Certain problems are generated by giving a *pretest* (as suggested above in the discussion of internal validity) as well as a *posttest*. Subjects may become familiar with the types of questions and interests of the study and may, between the first and second tests, alter their responses to accommodate what they have come to believe is the investigator's interest. Furthermore, the subject may become bored with the test on the second administration and feel less motivated to respond. In addition, a two-test design requires more time on the part of the subject, and there may be a greater number of dropouts in the experiment (mortality) than if the test were given only once. Finally, between the times of the two tests other factors might have changed, either in the subject's own life or in the environment around the subject, that would make the subject react differently (history effects). As a result, the differences between the first and second tests could be due to nonexperimental causes.

EXPERIMENTAL DESIGNS

True Experimental Designs

True experimental designs are those organized in such a way as to meet the criterion for an experiment—that an independent variable be related to change in a dependent variable—and at the same time successfully address the potential problems of invalidity. Such designs tend to be more complete than either the preexperimental or quasi-

experimental designs to be discussed next. The standard true experiment, which is termed the *classical experiment,* follows the pattern shown in Table 8-3.

Let us return to the viewing of the film on the effects of drinking on driving. A classical experiment would have

1. Randomly assigned the subjects into experimental and control groups
2. Given a test (pretest) of attitudes toward drinking and driving to both groups
3. Shown the film (the independent variable) to the experimental group and not to the control group
4. Given another test (posttest) of attitudes toward drinking and driving (virtually a repeat of the first test) following the film

To control for obstacles to validity, the experimenter must be concerned about the period of time covering the testing itself and the time between the tests; these times should be equivalent for both the experimental and control groups and for different members within the groups. If a serious, widely publicized accident involving a drunk driver occurred between the two testing times, this incident could affect the responses to the second test. If the tests are given in groups, different administrations of the tests may vary in quality depending on what the administrator of the test said and what times of day the test was given. Campbell and Stanley suggest that these intrasession problems can be alleviated by testing indi-

TABLE 8-3

THE CLASSICAL EXPERIMENT

	Time 1	Time 2	Time 3
Experimental group	Pretest	Independent variable	Posttest
Control group	Pretest		Posttest

viduals separately (so as to avoid group demonstration differences) and by randomly carrying out the tests at different times for the experimental and control groups (1963, p. 14).

In an experiment where observation or interviewing is the mode of testing, there may be biases. These can be overcome by assigning observers (or interviewers) randomly to subjects. Randomization of subjects to the experimental and control groups will also alleviate the potential problems of statistical regression (those with extreme scores would be randomly distributed between groups). To address the mortality problem of losing subjects between the two testing periods, Campbell and Stanley suggest keeping those who fail to take the posttest in the analyses in order to see if they differ systematically from those who do complete the experiment. (If the groups are comparable, then the loss of some subjects should not alter the experiment; if the groups differ in some definable way—for example, if the dropouts from the drunk driving film sessions all favor strict antidrinking policies—then a distortion is present and the experiment might need to be repeated) (1963, pp. 15–16).

The biases created by retaking the test—due both to the effects of the pretest (on how the subject responds to the stimulus) and the effects of the posttest—can be eliminated with the *Solomon Four-Group Design,* the most comprehensive type of true experiment, which is depicted in Table 8-4. In this more complex design, the problems of the interaction between the pretest and the posttest

and between the pretest and the IV can be controlled by comparing the two experimental groups (Groups 1 and 3) and the two control groups (Groups 2 and 4), where one group has had the pretest and one has not.

Applying the experiment of the drinking and driving film to this design would require the following steps:

1. Assigning the subjects among four groups on the basis of randomization
2. Giving the pretest to Groups 1 and 2
3. Showing the film to Groups 1 and 3
4. Giving the posttest to each group

Comparisons forming the basis of the experimental effect would use Groups 1 and 2. Control for the pretest bias could be seen by comparing Groups 1 and 3 and by the differences in change between Groups 1 and 2 as compared with Groups 3 and 4.

Campbell and Stanley argue that pretests are, in fact, not essential to a true experiment, provided that the groups have been randomly assigned (1963, pp. 25–26). The *posttest-only control group design* is all that is actually needed to have a true experiment. Thus, the posttest-only design is one of the most favored forms of true experiments. It is depicted in Table 8-5. In this design, the pretest is not given to any group. The design includes Groups 3 and 4 of the Solomon Four-Group Design. This simplified design can be fully effective only where there has been assignment of the sub-

TABLE 8-4

THE SOLOMON FOUR-GROUP EXPERIMENT

	Time 1	Time 2	Time 3
Group 1: First experimental group	Pretest	IV	Posttest
Group 2: First control group	Pretest		Posttest
Group 3: Second experimental group		IV	Posttest
Group 4: Second control group			Posttest

TABLE 8-5

POSTTEST-ONLY CONTROL GROUP DESIGN

	Time 1	Time 2
Experimental group	IV	Posttest
Control group		Posttest

jects by randomization and there is no basis for believing that the two groups are not equivalent. It avoids all the problems of the effects of the pretest on the posttest and the problems of how the pretest may alter the way the subject reacts to the stimulus itself.

In the example of the drinking and driving film, the posttest-only design would require these steps:

1. Assigning subjects to the experimental and control groups randomly
2. Showing the film to the experimental group
3. Administering the posttest to the two groups

In this case only one comparison is available (but it is the crucial one): did those who experienced the stimulus have a different posttest effect from those who did not?

Finally, experimental designs which meet the criteria for being *true* may have more than one stimulus, which means that different types of the treatment may be presented to different experimental groups. These *factorial designs* can be extended versions of the three earlier designs presented, where additional stimuli require the same set of experimental and control groups as the design demands (Campbell and Stanley, 1963, pp. 27–31). For example, in the Berkowitz and Geen experiment, there were three different film conditions (the prizefight film with the justified aggression synopsis of the story, the prizefight film with the less justified aggression synopsis, and the track race film) and two different names given to the confederate. Thus, this study had a 3 × 2 factorial design.

Preexperimental Designs

Many experiments carried out do not include all the qualifications for true experiments, and many situations which social researchers might wish to study do not allow for the factors required for a true experiment. In such experimental designs, there are even more threats to internal and external validity. In the simplest cases, a stimulus may be presented to one group and its reaction measured. Campbell and Stanley refer to this type of *preexperimental design* as a *one-shot case study* (1963, pp. 6–7). Using the film example again, a group would see the film and then answer a survey about their attitudes on drinking and driving. If their attitudes support strict enforcement of laws against drunk driving, we might want to conclude that they were affected by the film. However, we do not know what their attitudes were before the film, and we do not know how their attitudes would differ from those of others who never saw this film. Thus it is difficult to assess in this case whether the experimental effect occurred. Table 8-6 depicts this design.

A slightly more elaborate preexperiment would add a pretest. This *one-group pretest-posttest design* addresses the problem (in the case of the film experiment) of the level of attitudes prior to exposure to the film, but it cannot control other factors that might have occurred between the two tests which, other than the film, might have influenced a change in attitudes. Table 8-7 diagrams this design.

Finally, the *static-group comparison,* diagrammed in Table 8-8, is a preexperimental design with a control group but no pretest. In this design, as applied to the film showing, one group would

TABLE 8-6

ONE-SHOT CASE STUDY

	Time 1	Time 2
Experimental group	IV	Posttest

TABLE 8-7

ONE-GROUP PRETEST-POSTTEST DESIGN

	Time 1	Time 2	Time 3
Experimental group	Pretest	IV	Posttest

see the film and answer questions following it, and another group would simply answer questions without seeing the film. In this design, there is a control for possible sources of stimulation beyond the film, but no measure of attitudes before having viewed the film.

The difference between this design and the posttest-only control group design, shown in Table 8-5, is that in the static-group comparison design, there is no random assignment to groups. It is therefore not possible to assume that the groups are equivalent in attitudes. These preexperiments are generally less desirable ways of carrying out a research study, though in some cases they may be the only choice. But Campbell and Stanley strongly favor quasi-experimental designs over preexperiment designs, if these can be arranged.

Quasi-Experimental Designs

Quasi-experimental designs should be employed in situations where the basic elements of a true experiment cannot be set up. For example, in certain cases the experimental and control groups cannot be made to be equivalent through randomized assignment to groups because their natural situation

TABLE 8-8

STATIC-GROUP COMPARISON

	Time 1	Time 2
Experimental group[a]	IV	Posttest
Control group[a]		Posttest

[a]Groups are not randomly assigned.

precludes this possibility. In many educational studies, where classes (or classrooms) are being studied, the comparison group can only be a similar class or classroom (but not a randomly assigned one). Nevertheless, this *nonequivalent control group design* can be effectively used in an experimental design where random assignment to groups is not feasible. In a case where the experimental group represents volunteers (such as blood donors), a comparison group may be selected who are similar to the experimentals. In this design, characteristics of the experimental and control groups can be compared before the experiment; such comparisons might help explain the results of the experiment.

Regression-Discontinuity Experiment.   In most treatment situations, the group receiving the treatment is the group that needs the treatment. Let's take, for example, a remedial math program which a college offers to first-year students to enable them to succeed in fulfilling the natural science and mathematics requirements of the college. Those taking the remedial course will be those who *need* the course, as indicated through a placement or preadmission examination. In this case, the remedial math course is the independent variable. It is offered to the experimental group. Normally, however, it would not be practical to have another group (who did not appear to need the course) take it in order to serve as a control group. It would also not be feasible to refuse the course to half the students who needed it in order to have them serve as a control group. This is a situation in which a *regression-discontinuity design* might be best. In this design, the researcher is looking for differences that occur at the point of the treatment which would differentiate the posttreatment scores of those receiving the treatment from those of the control group not receiving it. Figure 8-1 shows a diagram of this design for the math remediation program.

In this regression-discontinuity design, students with similar preprogram scores are considered a group. In other words, the groups are or-

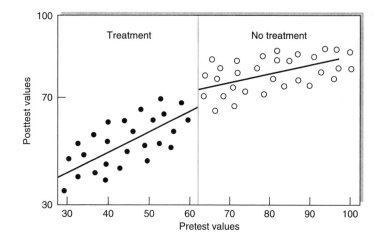

FIGURE 8-1
Hypothetical outcome of a pretest-posttest regression-discontinuity quasi-experiment on the effects of a remedial math program. Preprogram math scores were used to select program entrants (those with scores of 60 and below were selected for the program).

dered in relation to the selection factor. Those below the cutoff line on the pretest are placed in the remedial course; those above it are not. It would therefore be expected that those receiving the treatment (the remedial course) would have a sharper increase in their scores than those not receiving the treatment; but it would also be expected that the scores of the experimental group might remain lower than those of the control group (because they started lower to begin with).

The exposure to the remedial math program (the treatment) serves as the independent variable. The difference between the postprogram math score and the preprogram score serves as the dependent variable. A comparison of the average change in score of groups of individuals who began with similar scores is used to determine whether the treatment had its intended effect. In Figure 8-1, you can see that those who took the remedial course had a sharper increase in their math scores than those who did not; though the math scores of the others did advance, they did so at a more gradual level.

Time-Series Experiment. When there is a large set of already collected data which indicate rates over time, another form of quasi-experimental design may be used. This is the *time-series experiment.* The Phillips (1983) experiment had such a

design. Recall that Phillips was trying to see whether there was an unexpected rise in homicides following a heavyweight prizefight event. This required setting up a type of statistical analysis called a regression analysis to see if and when there was an increased homicide rate. (For a discussion of time-series regression techniques, see Ostrom, 1978). Time-series designs generally use already collected aggregate data (which will be discussed in Chapter 10) published regularly over standard intervals of time as the basis for determining the dependent variable. Then some other event (a law or a social occurrence) is superimposed on this time line data to see whether there is a change at the point (or somewhat after the point) where the independent variable occurred.

For example, certain states have adopted breathalyzer tests to deter drunk driving and reduce serious traffic accidents. In this case, there would already be data measuring the incidence of serious traffic accidents (e.g., those causing serious injury or fatality), perhaps on a yearly basis. The introduction of the breathalyzer test could therefore be treated as a stimulus, or independent variable, the effects of which could be examined in terms of later measures of yearly rates of serious traffic accidents. Figure 8-2 depicts this design for the serious traffic accidents of a state.

As in the regression-discontinuity design, the

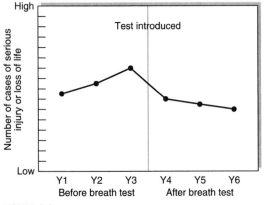

FIGURE 8-2
Serious traffic accidents for years 1 to 6 in State X, be-fore and after the breathalyzer test was introduced (Y1 = year 1).

interrupted time-series analysis looks for sharp changes occurring after the introduction of a new procedure or program (the treatment). In this case the time frame is *longitudinal,* which means that data are collected at more than one point in time, and the experimenter is looking for changes in a particular measurement over time that occur following the introduction of a treatment. (In contrast, observations in the regression-discontinuity design were taken at one point in time.)

The quasi-experimental designs here described may need to be used in cases where the conditions for a true experiment cannot be met. Regression-discontinuity designs are widely used now to assess the effectiveness of new programs and treatments, and the time-series regression design is utilized in studies of how specific social policies (laws) or practices can affect patterns of social behavior across time.

DECIDING IF AN EXPERIMENT IS APPROPRIATE FOR YOUR TOPIC

If the object of your research project is to explain some type of behavior, an experiment might be your choice of method. Remember that an experiment requires very careful preparation. The experimenter may need to contrive a situation in order to study it. For some researchers, this makes experiments too artificial for their taste. Nevertheless, a very carefully organized experiment has the advantage of producing rather specific findings. Further, if you observe a condition in the social environment (a new law or social program), you might design a natural experiment in which you relate this independent variable to changes in some pattern of events. Such studies often depend on aggregated datasets (such as crime rates). In Chapters 10 and 11, we will look again at experimental designs using aggregated data.

Could you develop conditions which would create the behavior you want to study in a laboratory setting? Or would a natural experiment be a better design? Developing the independent variable is one of the most critical parts of an experiment. In some cases, the stimulus is available (like a strike at a factory) and needs only to be utilized by the investigator in an experimental design which incorporates the presentation of the stimulus. In other cases, an investigator may use an independent variable that another experimenter has developed. (Social-psychological literature is full of experimental ideas which you might be able to use for your purposes.) Once you have designed the experimental situation, you need to consider the subjects to be studied. Would you be able to randomly assign them to experimental and control groups? This is the major requirement of a true experiment, and it enables the use of statistical tests to compare the groups. The primary advantage of an experiment is that it is a tightly controlled research method which may be small in scope. Furthermore, once all the planning is done, the experiment itself may not take very long to carry out.

REVIEW NOTES

• In a true experiment, the experimenter manipulates the independent variable and assigns subjects to the experimental condition. In a natural experiment, the experimenter does not manipulate the independent variable, but rather observes it and relates it to other conditions.

- The primary challenge to experimentation is to establish sufficient controls without making the experiment too artificial and thereby invalid.

- A field experiment differs from a laboratory experiment in that the former takes place in a real environment. A field experiment may be based on real-life occurrences (a natural experiment) or on manipulated ones (a true experiment).

- Internal validity addresses whether the experimental conditions actually brought forth the intended effect.

- Problems in the internal validity of an experiment can be caused by lack of comparability between the groups; loss of subjects; rivalry between the subjects in the experimental and control groups; demoralization of subjects; testing; problems with instrumentation; imitation of treatment; compensation to the control group; maturation of subjects between the pre- and posttests; historical events that intervene; effects from the interaction of selection factors of the subjects with maturation, history, or instrumentation; and, lastly, the effects of statistical regression.

- How far the findings from an experiment can be generalized to other settings is the issue of external validity. External validity may be challenged because of the interactions of the experimental treatment with other aspects of the experiment (selection of subjects, experimental setting, and period of history).

- Demand characteristics are the cues that convey the expected hypothesis to the subjects and make the subjects cooperate with the experimenter to bring forth the experimental effect. Such demand characteristics challenge the external validity of an experiment.

- Assignment of subjects to experimental and control groups by randomization is the primary means in experiments of controlling for biases in how the two groups might respond to the independent variable. When the groups have been randomly assigned, statistical comparisons of the outcomes of the experiment can be made.

- In a double-blind experiment, neither the subjects nor the experimenter know which group is the experimental group and which is the control group. This is done to reduce the possible biases that the experimenter might inadvertently introduce if the identity of the groups were known.

- A Hawthorne effect in an experiment occurs when subjects produce the expected experimental effect without being exposed to the experimental independent variable (they are affected by merely being in the experiment itself). To control for this, an experimental design may have a second control group, a Hawthorne control group. This group is exposed to a supposedly meaningless independent variable (such as a placebo, or sugar pill, in a drug experiment); the regular control group is exposed to no independent variable (that is, it is given no pill). It is expected that the Hawthorne control group will have a stronger experimental effect than the regular control group, but not so strong an effect as the experimental group.

- True experimental designs include the classical experiment, the Solomon Four-Group experiment, and the posttest-only control group design.

- Preexperimental designs include the one-shot case study, one-group pretest-posttest design, and static-group comparisons. In all cases of preexperimental designs, there is no random assignment to experimental and control groups.

- Quasi-experimental designs are for experiments with nonequivalent control groups. Comparisons between experimental and nonequivalent control groups can be made using regression-discontinuity or interrupted times-series analyses.

KEY TERMS

classical experiment
control group
criterion variable
demand characteristics

dependent variable
double-blind experiment
experimental group
experimental mortality
external validity
factorial design
field experiment
Hawthorne effect
independent variable
interaction effect
internal validity
laboratory experiment
matching
maturation
natural experiment
posttest
posttest-only control group design
predictor variable
preexperimental designs
pretest
quasi-experimental designs
randomization in assignment to groups
regression-discontinuity design
response
Solomon Four-Group Design
statistical regression
stimulus
time-series experiment
true experimental designs

STUDY EXERCISES

1. Select either the Horner or the income maintenance experiment from Chapter 1.
   a. Explain the experimental design (pre- and
      posttests, experimental and control groups,
      dependent and independent variables).

   b. Discuss the validity issues raised by this ex-
      periment.
2. Explain why an experimenter must be concerned about demand characteristics. How
   might such characteristics affect, for example,
   the outcome of the drinking and driving film
   experiment?
3. Why is it so important for an experimenter to
   use randomization in assigning subjects to experimental and control groups?

RECOMMENDED READINGS

1. Anderson, Barry F.: *The Psychology Experiment,* 2d
   ed., Brooks/Cole, Belmont, Calif., 1971. A small text
   that takes you through all the stages of an experiment, with appropriate statistics presented.
2. Cook, Thomas D., and Donald T. Campbell: *Quasi-
   Experimentation: Design and Analysis Issues for
   Field Settings,* Houghton Mifflin, Boston, 1979. This
   includes Campbell's classic work on types of validity
   problems in experimental designs, and detailed discussions of different types of quasi-experimental designs.
3. Fairweather, George W., and William S. Davidson:
   *An Introduction to Community Experimentation:
   Theory, Methods, and Practice,* McGraw-Hill, New
   York, 1986. This small text describes the reasons for,
   and methods of, carrying out and analyzing experimental research in community settings.
4. Gottman, John M.: *Times-Series Analysis: A Comprehensive Introduction for Social Scientists,* Cambridge, New York, 1981. More advanced than the
   title suggests, this volume gives good, clear explanations of most aspects of time-series analysis.
5. Lipsey, Mark W.: *Design Sensitivity: Statistical
   Power for Experimental Research,* Sage, Newbury
   Park, Calif., 1989. Very helpful to those with limited
   statistical background; points out the potential problems in an experimental design.

Field Research and Observational Studies

LOOKING AHEAD

This chapter presents strategies for successful field work in a variety of settings and discusses various means for recording and analyzing field observations. It also describes the use of cameras for still and video photography.

INTRODUCTION

*F*ield research refers not to a specific method but to a context in which research occurs—the field. The methods used to gather information in the field vary, but they generally center around the direct *observations* of the researcher. As an observer, the researcher may be a member of (or closely involved with) a group being studied; in other cases the researcher may be a stranger to the scene. In some cases, the tools for observation may be highly formalized: they may include video cameras and other recording devices, or they may depend only upon the researcher and a notepad.

In field locations, observation may not be the only method used. Interviews may be carried out, and the verbal interaction may be recorded or categorized using some standardized scheme. But the most usual activity in field research is *seeing* the field—taking it in, soaking it up—to try to understand what is really occurring there. Successful field research requires a high level of creativity to conceive the project and uncover the meaning of what is being studied. Most important, however, is a scientific frame of mind to guide the project and to direct it to its original purposes.

In this chapter, I shall delineate the general components of field research, in which observation and note taking are the primary techniques of data collection. The design of a field study with all its intermediate stages will be developed. Finally, a discussion of the use of film, video, and still cameras to capture social environments (visual sociology) will be offered. Since two fine field studies were carefully described in Chapter 1, I will use these as examples throughout the chapter. Therefore you might want to refer to Chapter 1 and reread the studies of Jelly's Bar and the Indsco Corporation.

Before beginning, I would like to clarify two further points: the first, the distinction between field research and case studies; the second, the role of anthropology in the development of field research.

FIELD RESEARCH AND CASE STUDIES

Some social methodologists refer to group observational studies and field research under the heading of *case studies.* (See Chapter 11 for a more extensive discussion of case studies.) This category usually refers to research done on a single case. Recall the field studies from Chapter 1. Kanter studied a single organization; in other words, she did a case study of Indsco. Jelly's Bar was Elijah Anderson's case study of a ghetto bar. Because observational studies in a field tend to be intensive and time-consuming, the researcher often narrows research down to a single field setting. However, field research need not be confined to single cases, but may compare different social settings. For this reason, field research is a more generic form of research than case studies.

Field studies have the advantage of presenting an in-depth picture of environments. This is why reading a field study of a social organization or environment is more like reading a novel or an inter-esting piece of journalism than reading an experimental or survey study. The focus is narrower. The observations may seem sharper and more intense. Field studies use less technical jargon and fewer contrived methods. As discussed in Chapter 1, field research is for some social scientists the best way to study the problems that interest them. For others, it is not a method they would consider using. Many sociological journals do not commonly publish research based on field studies. However, many sociologists are field researchers, and they often publish their studies as books.

ANTHROPOLOGISTS AND FIELD RESEARCH

In the discipline of *anthropology,* field research is the primary method for study. Anthropologists study (among other things) the nature of human culture. Most characteristically we picture the anthropologist on an exotic island, observing the native peoples. Such field research has a romantic aura about it, if not excitement and glamor (remember Indiana Jones!). Today, however, many anthropologists study modern societies.

The observational work of trying to describe a whole people is referred to as *ethnography.* Ethnographic studies of specific cultural groups have been collected together to form the extensive collection of ethnographies started in the late 1930s as the Human Relations Areas Files (HRAF). This collection has provided the basis for cross-cultural studies which compare different cultures and different cultural practices, as well as comparison of ethnographic studies of the same culture. Later in this chapter, there will be a discussion of how the later ethnographic work on Samoa by Derek Freeman challenged the earlier research of Margaret Mead.

Sociologists, political scientists, and other social scientists use field methods as well. This is because they often share the same central concerns of the anthropologists: to try to uncover the true meaning behind the cultural practices, belief systems, social customs, and taboos of a group of people. To do this requires more than the skills of good description; it also requires the inductive development of theory. Thus, ethnography is a theory-building method; its aim in the study of particulars is to draw out the general themes. The exact methods of field research are not easy to spell out. They are less precise than survey research or experimental design. In what follows, I will examine field research methods and other observational techniques to provide you with a general basis for understanding this type of research.

THE ART AND SCIENCE OF FIELD RESEARCH

Creative Aspects of Field Research

The object of field studies, however they are done, is *verstehen,* to understand social action. We have all been in situations—enjoying the festivities at a wedding, overhearing negotiations in a used car lot,

listening to the cheers at a pep rally, watching a couple in a restaurant argue over dinner—where we say to ourselves, "I know what's going on here" or "I have it figured out." What we mean is that the situation or event epitomizes some quality of the culture which we have always recognized but taken for granted. Let's take a high school football pep rally (as I remember it from the deep dark past) as an example. The cheerleaders are on the stage, the band is blasting away in the pit, the football team comes on stage and everyone goes crazy. Then the coach comes out and makes a few remarks about the importance of the upcoming game, and everyone screams again. But let's stop for a moment. What is everyone screaming about? What is really at stake here? Does it really matter who wins the game? What is school spirit anyway?

The sense of blending in with the euphoria of group excitement is one of the great joys of human experience. There is a losing of a sense of self and with it the sense of worry about problems and responsibilities that are difficult to face. How is this all achieved at a pep rally? Well, what do the cheerleaders represent? Usually, they are attractive young women and men who are "peppy," which means that they are exuberant, outgoing, and inviting. They draw you out of yourself into the group spirit. In a sense, they are rather like primitive rain dancers. They jump around, shouting common calls and focusing the emotions of the group on the common wish—the wish to succeed, to overcome, to defeat another.

In some ways, this wish to succeed (even if only at a football game) is the universal wish of all humans about life: to make it a successful endeavor. Perhaps the big football players represent human force, a factor which may be less vital in modern life in helping people obtain basic needs but which is still the impulse that makes people sense that they can get where they want to go by pushing ahead. Maybe this is the meaning of football. To want to enter into the spirit of this drive for success is to want to live, to push oneself physically, to strive against odds, and to have the emotional support of others in your endeavor.

You may be thinking that I've ignored the sexual aspects: the big male players, the petite females jumping, the padded shoulders, the short skirts. These aspects are also present and may be central to some understandings of the pep rally. A good field study of a football rally would try to come to terms with the sense of the event, to make it come alive to the reader, to build meaning out of what seems to be an ordinary event. Remember that what may seem to be ordinary to you and me could seem very exotic (or at least very strange) to a foreign-born person. The reaction would be even stranger to a person living in the future (imagine someone in 2094 reading your field study of a football rally) or to someone from outer space! What you must keep in mind is that good-quality field work should convey meaning to anyone who might read it.

I have tried to suggest the various meanings which a pep rally might symbolize. Whatever the meanings you seek, you need some methods to know how to see what you are watching, to understand what you are hearing, to figure out what is really happening. The techniques for studying a field must be creative; they must be right for the field being studied. The researcher must remain *open* to the field; he or she must be able to absorb what is happening in the environment without being overwhelmed by it. Thus, the creative steps needed to carry out a field study include (1) choosing the field, (2) selecting the methods to be used in the field, (3) observing in the field, and (4) turning observations into meaning. These steps will be described more fully in the section on design. Here it is important to emphasize that, at each step, being creative means possessing the following qualities:

Insightfulness: Seeing with understanding

Receptivity: Openness and eagerness to enter into the field

Self-understanding: Ability to understand one's own reactions and distinguish them from reactions that others might experience

To achieve self-understanding, a field researcher with divorced parents might (for example) need to recognize that he or she could have quite a different reaction to watching a couple argue in a restaurant than one who did not. Knowing how you are personally affected by what you see and how your reactions might differ from those of others is the kind of sensibility which field researchers need to develop. The social class background of an observer (race, religion, region of upbringing, etc.) is bound to affect personal perspectives. On the one hand, an observer must be cautious not to intrude upon the scene in such a way that the environment being observed is altered. However, a field researcher should not be totally detached. The researcher must experience other situations deeply, as if actually involved, to enter into the world of others and see their world from their viewpoint. Yet the field researcher must at the same time be careful not to get so intensely involved that he or she "goes native" and is no longer objective. There must be a middle ground of "involved detachment."

This ability to become engaged in the human achievements of others (for example, their writings, art, music, acting) is the kind of talent in which those who study the humanities excel. In the social sciences, the material which needs to be appreciated may appear to be simpler—the meaning of a meal, the culture of a gas station, the relationship between a teacher and his or her pupils. However, each of these is also a "human production" expressing the values and cultural traditions and customs of a people; and the more closely we study them, the more complex they appear to become.

Recognizing the importance of insightfulness, receptivity, and self-understanding should give you a good start in field research. In order to set up a good initial design and guide yourself along the way, you also need to carefully consider the scientific aspects of a field project.

The Science of Field Research

Walking into a scene unprepared is not the way to do field research. Remember Elijah Anderson's (1978) study of Jelly's, the Chicago South Side bar (Chapter 1). Anderson did not just wander into a bar (though he probably had done so before he conceived his project). Having decided to study Jelly's, he had also developed a research question which he planned to answer. He had set out to study the status system of a ghetto bar, to find out who was a "somebody" and who a "nobody" in this transient social milieu. His objective was to gather information relevant to his question by working his way into the social fabric of Jelly's. This meant that he had to act in a particular way. He had to follow certain types of leads and build up a rapport with those who patronized Jelly's in order to gather the kinds of material he needed to address his research question. While he was observing at Jelly's, he had to keep his research purpose foremost in his mind in order to direct his research efforts. Field research never seeks to alter what is happening in the environment being studied. Nevertheless, more or less systematic means for observing what is happening need to be utilized.

GENERAL COMPONENTS OF A FIELD STUDY

Whatever the method used to do the observing, certain factors must be delineated which refer to the field.

The Setting

The studies described in Chapter 1 took place in distinctly different settings—Anderson's study was set in a bar, Kanter's in the headquarters of a multinational corporation. Anderson's bar was a small place, Kanter's corporation a large place, but they were both places with walls and you knew whether you were in them or not. Some field study environments (like a neighborhood) have much less clearly defined boundaries.

The settings also differed in terms of who belonged, who were members (or regulars, as at Jelly's) in these settings and who were strangers. In Jelly's there were no formal members, though

Jelly and the bartenders who were his employees were the most regular participants in the bar. Anderson was really interested only in the clients at Jelly's, all of whom came of their own accord, when they felt like it. Some were, nevertheless, regulars, some came much more infrequently, and still others were strangers (as Anderson was when he first came). A bar is the type of setting that is a public place, but people who visit it regularly try to make it into a more private place. It is open to the public, but only a certain subsection of the public would ever consider going there: people who want to drink, people who want to drink in a public place, people who would be comfortable drinking in a largely black bar in a largely black area of a large American city. Those qualifications would not be met by most people. Therefore, although Jelly's was a public place, it was not a place that all members of the public would in fact enter.

Indsco (the corporation Kanter studied, which was described in Chapter 1) was also a public place in that anyone could walk into the building. There were clear differences between employees and nonemployees. Employees went to Indsco to carry out their work; nonemployees went to carry out some transaction with Indsco employees (to order materials, deliver supplies, or get information). There may also, at any time, have been some stray people wandering around Indsco (perhaps who came in out of the cold) who were not supposed to be there. Being at Indsco meant that you had a goal to accomplish, some purpose for being there. The setting was very different from Jelly's in that way.

In summary, settings have various qualities which need to be considered in a field study:

1. Are they public or private settings? Can anyone walk in? Do you need a ticket? Are there guards checking who can enter?
2. Are there regular, permanent members in the setting, or do the people in the setting usually vary? Do some people come more regularly than others? What are the purposes for which

people in the setting come? Are they formal or informal?

3. What are the objects in the setting? Do they seem to belong there? What do they tell you about other characteristics of the people who live or work there?

A General Subject

Field researchers usually have a general or specific subject in mind when they enter the field. At Jelly's, Anderson wanted to understand the social status of the men, what it took to be a somebody at Jelly's. He was trying to discover the social structure of what seemed a structureless place. Kanter was trying to understand the meaning of the roles women play in large corporations, the way they scale the hierarchy of a corporation and the effects of being one of a small minority of women at the top of a corporation.

According to Lofland (1971), an analysis of a social field can pose only three major questions:

1. What are the *characteristics* of a social phenomenon, the forms it assumes, the variations it displays?
2. What are the *causes* of a social phenomenon, the forms it assumes, the variations it displays?
3. What are the *consequences* of a social phenomenon, the forms it assumes, the variations it displays? (1971, p. 13).

Thus suppose we decide to do a study of a hot line for teenagers with problems. In terms of characteristics, we would want to know both the structure and characteristics of the hot-line organization itself and the characteristics of the people involved: who works for it (and answers the calls) and who calls in. Furthermore, we would want to know something about the history of the hot line—who started it and why. Such a subject could form the basis of a field study and would require going to the organization itself, talking to its director and workers, and observing the hot line in action. The researcher might even want to take (or

listen in on) a few calls to understand exactly what occurs during a hot-line telephone conversation (though ethical objections would arise if a researcher posed as a hot-line receiver).

If our study were focused on why young persons call hot lines, we would have a study concerned with causes. For such a study, we might need to concentrate on a specific period of time to see what types of requests were received. Or we might want to examine the records of the hot line to study the nature of the calls during a previous period. Such a causal study might well require data from sources other than observation (such as from records). Finally, if our primary intent were to study what effect calling a hot line has on the teenager—that is, its consequences—we would need to develop some form of evaluation research design (see Chapter 11) to follow up on the youth who had called and received advice from the hot line. We might also measure results in terms of what the staff thought had been accomplished.

Whatever the subject, it is best, as I stated above, to have it very clearly in mind at the beginning of the study. It will serve as a guide to what you look for in the setting. While it is true that field studies tend to evolve over the course of the field research, it is still better to enter the field with a clear understanding of what you would like to discover. Then if what you see and hear leads you toward a different course, at least you will know where you began and how you have altered your plan.

A Time Frame

A field research project may occur in one continuous period (like a structured observational study of interaction) or over a long period of time. Kanter spent nearly five years (obviously not on a full-time basis) observing at Indsco. Anderson did his observing at Jelly's Bar intermittently, over a long period of time.

The order of the visits may be sequential or nonsequential. In a sequential time frame, the visits have a regular order, one regularly following the next, perhaps at a specific time, interval, or daily event (dinnertime). Visits over longer periods of time are usually nonsequential; but they may be timed to coincide with specific occurrences (special occasions such as Herman's Christmas party in Anderson's study or a major family event such as a wedding); with occasions which bring together the important characters in the setting (meetings at Indsco, family dinners, an assembly at a high school); or with specific times of day (such as the opening up of an organization in the morning or 5 p.m. at the bus stop).

The timing of your project will depend on the nature of the project. Some studies must have a short duration because the event takes place over a short period of time (a Fourth of July parade, for example, though there could be pre- and postparade activities which might extend the study time). Other subjects have no clear time frame. When and for how long should Kanter have studied Indsco? Clearly a very short period of time for field study might not have given her the depth of information needed to make her very familiar with the corporation. Timing should also be considered in terms of the researcher. If a limited time frame is necessary, the researcher should try to identify and design a type of study in which it is appropriate to gather data over a short period of time.

Types of Things to Observe

Once you have a setting and a subject, you must still decide what you will observe on the scene. The following are the types of things you should consider.

The Environment.   Any field, be it a street corner or a corporation, has a general environment with a social temperature, a smell, a look, and a feel about it. Being in Times Square in New York City gives one a certain sense of the environment of the place. The weather might be cold, hot, or even pleasant; the odors might include chestnuts, car fumes, or nothing in particular; the look may seem exciting, lively, lurid, seedy, depressing, or

whatever. But clearly Times Square has a certain *feel.* This feel is often what you seek out when you travel somewhere. The Golden Gate Bridge in San Francisco, the River Walk in San Antonio, Palm Beach, Harlem, the Rockies—all have a certain *feel,* but so do less famous places like Filene's basement (a department store in Boston), Wrigley Field (the home field of the Chicago Cubs), and Arthur Bryant's Barbeque in Kansas City. Specific places like these have a particular ambiance about them that settles in on you when you're there.

Most field studies in the social sciences take place in more ordinary places where people work, live, and relax. But in the studies we read about in Chapter 1, Jelly's Bar had a special environment which took some time to get to know. This was a place that a lot of people would not want to visit, but it offered a view into a little-known lifestyle. Indsco was a place with a bureaucratic environment—organized, structured, hierarchical, and orderly—where people were positioned in the environment according to their roles in the organization. Whatever the environment of the field you study, try to take it all in and capture the feel of it.

The environment, or setting, is the widest angle that can be taken for a field study. All field studies take place in some setting, but the environment itself need not be the primary subject of study.

People and Their Relationships.   We tend to notice people more than anything else (probably because we are interested in our own types). Generally, field studies are concerned with studying people. In any field, there are people in it who belong to that field, and others who are only visiting or who are outsiders to it. The most socially interesting phenomenon about people is the complex types of relationships they have with one another. When these relationships are very specific and formal (and governed by quite precise norms), we describe the people as "playing roles." In *role playing,* a father and son are not equivalent to an older man and a boy. Rather, a father and son are as-

sumed to have a value-based relationship, an economic interdependency, strong affective ties, and
long-term commitments to each other, though
these assumptions may be wrong.

People not only relate to others as situations
evolve, but they also set up fairly regular relationships with organizations and institutions. In short,
they become participants as workers, family members, club members, church members, etc. Some
persons come to participate in more unusual and
specific groups (war game players, rock climbers),
or they may participate with "deviant" groups in
special settings for these members (nudist camps,
gay bars).

These forms of participation are characterized
by power differences in the relationships between
persons. It was not hard for Kanter to distinguish
the managers from the secretaries at Indsco. It
might also be interesting to contrast people who
are nonmembers in a field with the members.
Since their relationships with others will be different, the types of interaction that occur between
members and nonmembers should differ. For example, Kanter found that bosses treated secretaries
in particular ways. Comparing this type of relationship to the manner in which a visitor treats a
secretary (and how a secretary treats a visitor) may
help to clarify what is characteristic of the boss-
secretary interrelationship.

Behavior, Actions, and Activities.   The subject
of a field study may be specific examples of behavior. This is the narrowest angle for a study. If
the actions become routinized so that they occur
over and over again, then they become an activity.
An example of this would be going to church. To
go to church once is an action; to go regularly is
an activity because it has a regularity to it that suggests greater commitment and involvement on the
part of the churchgoer.

Let's consider a classroom. Here the observer
may note who raises a hand to answer questions.
(Girls more than boys? Tall students more than
short? Hispanic students more than African-Amer-
ican students? Students sitting in the front of the

class rather than those at the back?) Or a study
which observes the teacher's behavior may consider where the teacher stands. (In front of the
desk, in back of the room, in front of the board?
Does the teacher move about or remain station-
ary?) Or a study on attentiveness in a primary
school classroom might try to determine which
children are attentive by zeroing in on those who
are preoccupied doing other things. (Which ones
are daydreaming or whispering?) These types of
behaviors which are somewhat secretive can be
detected by all of us, though sometimes we may
be wrong. The child who seems to be daydreaming could be concentrating on the teacher's instructions, and the student who seems very attentive could, in fact, be daydreaming.

Clearly a field researcher needs to be very
knowledgeable about the scene under study so that
behavior can be accurately understood. This is not
a new method for any of us; we all interpret the
behavior of others regularly. What may be important in field research is that we understand the field
we are viewing well enough that we are able to
comprehend what we see. This can be done by trying to put yourself into the environment and, in
this case, to experience what it would be like to be
a child in that classroom. In this way, you may be
better able to appreciate the meaning of the scene
you are observing.

Verbal behavior.   What people say both describes and tries to explain what is happening in a
social environment. Thus verbal behavior addresses the meaning of a social field. What is said may
be misleading or inaccurate, but it is someone's
interpretation. If that someone is important to the
social setting, then that person's evaluation or description is a critical source for understanding that
field. Naturally, a field researcher will generally
not want to depend on the comments of only one
person. Instead, the more people whose perspectives can be gathered, the more comprehensive an
understanding can be gained. (Naturally, what different persons say may be contradictory, but the
researcher must try to pick out the dominant pat-

terns while not overlooking the deviant perspectives in drawing together an overview.)

Verbal behavior can be "observed" in two primary ways. You can listen for the content of the conversation and record it in terms of the types of language presentations: questions, answers, statements, affirmations, praise, etc. Or you can view conversation as social interaction and note who talks to whom, who asks questions of whom, who answers questions from whom, and who supports whom. In the first form, the conversation is more salient than the speakers; in the second form, the speakers are more salient than the content. Of course, the two types of observations may be combined. Since verbal behavior is so complex and so full of meaning, it is usually helpful to use a system for categorizing the conversational data which may capture the full extent of the meaning.

In the 1950s, there was great interest in the careful study of interpersonal behavior. A number of schemes to measure verbal behavior, such as Bales' Interaction Process Analysis (IPA), were developed at that time (1951). Bales' IPA divides all verbal behavior into 12 categories. The observer follows the pattern of verbal interaction by designating every member of the observed group with a letter and by taking down the category number of each verbal utterance, associated with each speaker, over a specific period of time. While such techniques are less frequently used today, they still offer comprehensive means for studying small-group verbal interaction in laboratories and in natural settings (see Bales, 1980, for a more recent, three-dimensional coding scheme). One typical environment in which interaction has been closely studied is the classroom. An example of an observational method for coding classroom interaction is Withall's (1952) socioemotional climate index, which evaluates the qualities of teachers' verbal interaction with their pupils.

Psychological Stances.   Psychologists often observe the psychological postures of subjects. Certain stances can be readily observed; others are very difficult to detect. For example, an observer can observe amusement, laughter, or contentment quite easily. It may be more difficult to observe discontent and anger because individuals may more often conceal such emotions. In children, there is usually less concealment; it is more common to see a nursery school child who has been rebuffed cry than to see similar behavior in a company meeting. Observers should know very clearly what they are looking for in terms of psychological reactions.

Histories.   Anthropologists and historians often seek to find out the background of their field through historical informants. In many cases, for example, the immigrant history of a specific family resides only in the memories of a grandparent. Certain stories will have been told about great-grandfather so-and-so back in the old country, about how great-great-grandmother got her passage to America, about how the early settlers chose a region of the country and a specific type of work, about reactions to unusual events such as freak accidents or unexpected success. Often only fragments of the histories remain, but they have been carried down because they reflect the attitude toward important conditions or beliefs of this family, both as it was in the past and as it has evolved into the present. These family stories are not just old tales, but genuine sources of insight into the nature of a family's life. Accuracy may be gone, but the symbolic meaning of the stories remains.

One story I remember being told repeatedly by my mother was about how she would come home from high school every Friday afternoon to help her mother clean the house (especially to wash the kitchen floor) before going off with her friends to have fun. She did this because she felt guilty about the amount of work my grandmother was expected to do as an Eastern European immigrant woman, the mother of five and wife of a very traditional man who expected much of her. Why did my mother stress this story so much? It seems to me that it represented the essence of her life situation as she grew up—an American-born child of immigrant parents, trying to mix socially with her

American friends and to enjoy the ease of American social life but at the same time recognizing the difficulty of her mother's role and the distance at which she was placed from her mother by reason of her American birth. Washing the kitchen floor was in one sense the price of her freedom, but it was also an acknowledgment of her origins. Of course, she may also have stressed this story to me so that I should also feel some guilt (and wash some floors for my freedom) because of what I owed to those (especially my mother) who had raised me.

Anderson (1978) sought the stories of Herman's past, his history of relationships with others. Social researchers may consider themselves students of the present, but the present is continually becoming the past, and to understand it requires a consideration of the past.

Physical Objects. People and human interaction are not the only materials in a field. There are also inanimate objects. In a classroom, there is the regular equipment—desks, chairs, blackboard, maps, students' work, etc. How have these been arranged? If the teacher's desk is in the front of the class, this suggests a leadership position for the teacher in the role of presenter to the class. Sometimes the teacher sits in the back facing the front as the children do. Such a desk position alters the meaning of the teacher's role. It might suggest that the teacher is only being a participant in the class with the students; or it might suggest that the teacher is determined to detect qualities of the students which are better observable from the back of the classroom than from the front (e.g., note passing).

Observing in a person's home offers many chances to consider the types of objects present: plants, art objects, furniture, reading material, musical instruments, basic decorations (paint or wallpaper, carpets or rugs, lighting fixtures or lamps). In addition, the arrangement of objects tells a story. For example, a television centered in the living room suggests the primary purpose of the room. Where is the telephone? Is there a comfortable chair near it, or must one stand to talk (thereby suggesting that calls from that phone are businesslike and brief)?

The Need for Triangulation

In field research, there is a special need for multiple types of evidence gathered from different sources, often using different data collection methods. Unlike the experimenter, the field researcher casts her or his net widely, to gather in a lot of different fish so that the richness, the complexity of human environments can be captured and understood. In *triangulation,* the researcher gathers evidence from multiple sources in order to address the questions at hand from different points of view. Ultimately a researcher needs to narrow down and focus on the subject, but field researchers begin more broadly, deliberately exploring the whole mosaic of a situation so that the research subject is not trivialized. Triangulation is the strategy of casting out broadly for diverse evidence so as to more effectively focus on the study question at hand.

As Fetterman contends (1989, p. 89), this bringing together of different types of evidence in order to test sources of information against each other is a way to determine which explanations are accurate and which ones should be rejected. By triangulating evidence, the researcher can prove, or disprove, her or his hypothesis. In any field study, the researcher can gather comparable pieces of evidence to test whether the conclusions initially reached remain valid as additional pieces of evidence are accumulated.

THE DESIGN OF FIELD STUDIES
The Role of the Observer

One way to differentiate the types of roles an observer may play was first developed by Gold (1969): the observer may become a *full participant* in a field or a partial participant—a *participant-as-observer;* or conversely, the observer may act as a *full observer* or a partial observer—an *observer-as-participant.* The choice among these four types depends upon what the observer decides to do before the research begins. It may also be dictated to a large extent by the nature of the field (if you are studying your own job environment or your own family, then you are already a participant and cannot be solely an observer) and by ethical considerations (remember the issues raised when a researcher participated as a mental patient, or as a "watchqueen" in a public lavatory). Being a sole observer, however, may restrict your range of possible observations because you remain essentially an outsider, a stranger to the field.

The behavior required of these roles varies. Naturally, participants must take part fully in their roles (as workers, residents, members, etc.). For a full participant, the process of observing is secondary. Notes cannot be taken in the field; formal or semiformal interviewing may seem artificial. In some ways, because the full participant in the field has a position to fill which predates the role of researcher, there may be more restraints on research activities than for the observer. The full participant, however, has some types of knowledge about and experience in the field that would be difficult (or impossible) for the observer to obtain. Humphreys (1970), who served as a watchqueen in public lavatories in his study of homosexual encounters (a study discussed in Chapter 3), was a full participant. So also was Rosenham (1982), who played the role of a mental patient in order to study psychiatric wards. But both of these roles involved deception. Cohen and Taylor (1972) were able to observe prison wards by participating as lecturers in the prison (they were participants-as-observers). In this way, they played a role *not* based on deception in order to gain entry to a field and observe what they needed for their study.

The participant-as-observer role requires being a participant but acknowledging that one is an observer as well. Kanter (1977) began her association with Indsco as a consultant. Only later did she decide to use her experiences at the corporation as the basis for a study of the roles of men and women in a large organization. She describes some of her research activities, such as taking part in meetings, as *participant observation.* Kanter explains the basis for her participation at such meetings as follows:

> In one or two cases I was invited to meetings by Indsco managers who were interested in having an outsider present with whom they could later discuss the events of the meeting. Often, beforehand, an informant or the person who invited me would describe the participants to me: their career stage, their present position, and their characteristic style *(1977, p. 295).*

She also served in the capacity of participant-as-observer at training programs or during interviews with staff. In her role as consultant, Kanter recorded much material because "as all good consultants know, it is wise to keep complete notes and collect as much system information as possible in order to be maximally helpful to clients" (1977, p. 296).

Perhaps the most common role for a field researcher to take is that of observer-as-participant. This would seem to describe Anderson's (1978) role at Jelly's. In this case, his role as an observer was more central than his role as a participant, although he did participate. In Anderson's case, the participation was quite easy. He went to the bar—a public place—like anyone else. He ordered a beer and chips and sat around to watch what was happening. A bar is the kind of place where people often spend a lot of their time playing at social research, observing one another. The difference is that Anderson regularly recorded what he observed so that he could build from his observations a set of generalized conceptions of the social system of Jelly's, whereas the ordinary bar client merely compiles a mental picture which may be quickly forgotten.

To be a full observer puts one in a position much more similar to a person doing a survey or carrying out an experiment. Observational studies in a laboratory (for example, using Bales' IPA) have the researcher in the sole role of observer, often behind a one-way mirror. Many field studies which take place in highly unstructured environments, such as a street corner, also place the researcher in the sole role as an observer. It seems more appropriate to be a sole observer either in a highly structured environment like a laboratory, where a lot of control is possible, or in a totally unstructured environment like a street corner. In either case, the presence of the researcher as observer is less threatening than in a semistructured environment with some control, such as an organization, or in an even more weakly structured environment such as a bar.

Field Work Preparation

Whatever role is planned, the researcher needs to prepare for the field before entering it to do the research. This preparation is of two types. On the one hand, information about the field must be sought from external sources. These sources could include books and other printed materials about contexts like the one to be studied (or, if they exist, about the specific field itself). On the other hand, information should be gathered, if possible, from internal sources, through informants who can advise the beginning field researcher about how best to accomplish research aims.

The types of reading materials you peruse should include (1) field studies of similar fields, if such studies exist; (2) studies of persons similar to those you plan to observe in the field; (3) studies using methods such as those you plan to use, regardless of the type of field they were used in; (4) general information material (statistical, historical, geographical, and evaluative) which may give you greater knowledge about what you are studying before you enter the field; (5) literary or journalistic works describing aspects of the field which may help to put you in the proper frame of mind so that you can function effectively in the field. In addition to reading outside source material, it would be good to talk to individuals who may be

familiar with any aspect of your subject (the types of people to be studied, the type of method to be used, etc.).

You should try to get some perspective on the field from insiders who may be able to help you prepare for your entry and decide how to carry out your project. The pre–field entry period—the period before you begin to make your actual observations, to collect notes, and to go regularly to the field—will not be the same in every study. In a highly unstructured field, the prefield period may seem quite disorganized and disjointed. You might not know exactly where to go or whom to talk to.

When William Whyte (1943) set out to study his "street corner," he found little help until he met Doc, the leader of the street corner gang, who became the central character in Whyte's classic field study. In a more structured environment, like a corporation or a school, you would need some insiders (employees) to tell you about the organization and about the people who lead it. Certain individuals who are in key positions in an organization hold a broad view of the organization (secretaries for central figures or employees who have worked for the organization for a long time), but the most valuable informant is one who has insight into his or her surroundings. It is the person who has a sociological imagination.

Entry into the Field

Once the field is selected and the researcher is ready to begin, an initial entry period is begun. Suelzle and Borzak (1981) describe the entry situation as putting the researcher into the role of a stranger. If your field of study is an organization which serves clients (a day care center, a hospital, or a welfare office), your entry phase will not be dissimilar to that of a client initially coming to the agency. Perhaps you can remember your first day in school (kindergarten?) or going to a new school after a move; these impressions often stay very strong. You remember the climate of the place, whether the teacher was warm, whether she (or he) was like your mother (or father), whether you felt you could belong to this environment. Clearly, as we get older, we learn how to belong to all kinds of places. We also learn that even if we are in a place where we would not like to belong, we can act in a nonchalant and casual manner. This is very much the style of entering a new field. Inside you may feel as you did on your first day at school, but outwardly you should act as if the place were "old hat" to you.

Suelzle and Borzak point out that "there may be many subjective responses to the first impressions, both negative and positive" (1981, p. 138), but they warn the field worker that in an organizational setting open-mindedness and a nonjudgmental attitude are essential. Opinions of what is being noted should not be given. If you remain open and innocent, it is much easier for you to ask questions, to ask for advice, to seek assistance. If you sound opinionated or even too informed, you may compromise your position to gain more knowledge about the field.

The newcomer to the field wants to move rather quickly to the role of a guest:

> As a guest you are gradually admitted into interpersonal relationships on a regular basis. You are still a newcomer and are accorded certain privileges: People do not expect you to assume a full share of responsibility. You are still learning the roles, and mistakes are expected and tolerated. Others may be solicitous of your welfare and protective of you *(Suelzle and Borzak, 1981, p. 139).*

Rosalie Wax describes field workers as often awkward and insecure in their first stage of field work. To move beyond this stage requires learning and relearning, socialization and resocialization. Success is measured by the point at which *reciprocal relations* have been established between the field worker and the members of the field.

The researcher's involvement in the field is "circular" and "cumulative," according to Wax. With a growing awareness that the research is

going well, the field researcher becomes less anxious. Wax contends that it is through the support and help of the hosts in the field that the researcher comes to understand what is happening in the field environment under study (Wax, 1971, p. 20). Of course, Wax is describing field environments which are difficult, where people are uncomfortable and aggrieved about their situation, where suspicion about a field worker could be high.

Her own experience was as a field researcher in the Japanese relocation centers set up to confine Japanese-Americans during World War II. This was just such a difficult-to-study environment because of the low level of trust the Japanese-Americans had in others. The Japanese-Americans were forced to label themselves as either "loyal" or "disloyal" to the United States. Wax naturally thought it would be easier to get to know those who were loyal to the United States, but this turned out not to be the case. Rather, it was the disloyal Japanese who had less to lose by confiding in her and explaining their point of view. Many fields may be more accommodating to you as a field worker; but it is always better to be prepared for a difficult situation, which may turn out to be easy, than to be unprepared (remember the Boy Scouts motto!).

Collecting Information

In psychological terms, observations define the reactions of the sensory apparatus to what a person sees, smells, hears, feels (and tastes?). But how does one collect these sensory images? The field worker must use a system that will help the memory to retain these images. By itself, the human memory is hardly a perfect system. Much of the material which we think we have committed to memory cannot be recalled. Psychologists have shown that laying new experiences over old memories tends to bury the old memories. For this reason, it is important that field researchers record what they see before engaging in other activities. The box suggests that data can also be drawn from

LOOKING FOR NEGATIVE EVIDENCE IN THE FIELD

Lewis and Lewis warn that much of what is important in understanding a field setting may be lost or distorted if *negative evidence* is not considered. Negative evidence includes "(1) the non-occurrence of events, (2) an occurrence that is not reacted to or not reported . . . (3) [an occurrence which is reported] . . . in its raw form [but is] distorted in its interpretation or withheld from analysis and report" (Lewis and Lewis, 1980, p. 555). An example of this would be in the study of supposedly powerful elites. When there is no evidence of the intervention of the elite on a specific issue, this may suggest that the elite is not powerful. However, it might "reflect conscious agreement on non-intervention" (Lewis and Lewis, 1980, p. 548). Field researchers also may ignore very interesting aspects of a field because they are not sensitized to recognize them. For instance, Zablocki (1971), in his study of a commune in the 1960s, overlooked the sexism and sex-segregated work situations in the commune environment (Lewis and Lewis, 1980, p. 552). What Lewis and Lewis are suggesting is that what is *not* happening in a field may be an important clue to what is really happening.

Source: George H. Lewis and Jonathan F. Lewis, "The Dog in the Night-time: Negative Evidence in Social Research," *British Journal of Sociology,* **31**:544–558, 1980.

taping. In certain situations, taping may be perfectly acceptable; in others, it may not. It is best to consult with those in the field about this method.

Cameras may also record field situations. Video cameras can offer an excellent means of capturing both the sounds and scenes in a field setting (see the discussion of visual sociology below). Still cameras may also set down views of the field. Those in the field may not object to cameras as long as they do not wish to remain anonymous. Photographs may also help the researcher to remember people and how things looked on a specific day.

Note taking is the backbone of collecting field data. It can be done in different ways. Taking notes in the field itself will depend on the field and on the role of the researcher. If you are a participant in a field, it is much more difficult to take notes because it will not be a part of your participating role, but rather of your role as observer. If you are a full observer, note taking may make you very conspicuous. What, those in the field may wonder, is this person writing down? Thus, while some situations may lend themselves to unobtrusive note taking, in most cases detailed notes will have to be written after leaving the field. In the field, notes will largely consist of casual jottings whose primary purpose is to arouse your memory later when you are writing the more detailed notes. Thus, casual jottings should concentrate on material that will serve to spark your memory once you have left the field. The memory "sparkers" may include

events that do not occur (or are not reported), that is, from *negative evidence.*

In the Field.   What is observed in the field can be recorded in many ways. Tape recorders, video cameras, still cameras, and note taking are all excellent tools. Tape recorders can be used if the people being observed approve of them. It is never advisable (and usually illegal) to record conversations with participants if they are unaware of your

1. The cast of characters in the field during the observation time.
2. Certain details of the physical scene which appear unusual.
3. Verbatim comments that seem critical for describing the situation observed or for capturing the central meaning of what was happening.
4. Incongruent aspects of the scene. In this case you may write yourself questions: Why did something occur? What was X trying to accomplish by doing what he or she did? What did Y

mean by saying that? Why wasn't Z in the field today?

These memory sparkers should help you to add detail and substance when writing up your fuller notes. They should also help you to remember significant moments in the field.

After Leaving the Field   Most field researchers write notes after returning home or the next morning. The general rule is that as much time will need to be spent writing what you have seen as was spent in the field itself. Naturally, this will vary depending on what was occurring in the field. (The more complex and/or significant the occurrence, the more notes are required to describe or explain it.) It is critical that these detailed notes be prepared within 24 hours of the field observation. Writing the notes may be time-consuming, but without them, your ability to write a final report or a paper may be jeopardized.

It is good to take down the notes separately under different headings. For this purpose, sheets of paper or index cards may be used, depending on the type of filing system you set up. It is useful to have multiple copies of the notes so that they may be filed under different headings. You can achieve this by photocopying your notes.

If you have access to a computer, putting your notes in a word processing system file is the most convenient system possible. You can move the notes around, copy them, and use parts of them directly in your final report by transferring them from the note file to the report file.

Types of Note Materials.   Lofland (1971) suggests five types of materials which should be included in your thorough notes.

Running descriptions.   As Lofland describes *running descriptions,* they include "events, people, things heard and overheard, conversations among people, conversations with people" (p. 105). Every time a new person enters the scene or a different scene is encountered, new notes should be taken.

Drawing maps can help to preserve a more exact setting of the scene observed. Lofland stresses that these running descriptions should be *concrete,* that is to say, they should be filled with specific details, devoid of imputation (X was trying to get Y to . . .). Rather the notes should try to include the *raw* actions as they occur. Also, the observer should make distinctions in the notes themselves as to how exact they are, whether they are verbatim quotations from conversations (perhaps these should be in quotation marks), inexact quotations (perhaps in single quotation marks), or merely reworded comments which are not precisely what was said (left without any marks) (Lofland, 1971, p. 105).

Recalled material that had been forgotten.   As you move along in a field project, one day's observations may help you to recall earlier incidents. This recalled material should be put into each day's notes, but clearly labeled as *recalls* of earlier material.

Ideas that interpret the meaning of a situation. Lofland suggests that any notes which offer an analysis of the situation should be set off in square brackets, so that when you go back to them, you will be able to differentiate what you have interpreted about a situation from the raw description of what took place (1971, p. 106). Of course, it is valuable to put your interpretations into your notes as you write them. Early interpretations may vary from those made weeks after an observation. Since you may forget your early interpretations as you forget your actual observations, put into your notes your ideas of what you think is happening in the field.

Lofland suggests that analytical ideas are usually of three different types: they address the central ideas of the project; they concern a major subarea of the study; or they are very small ideas that may add some detail to the final report (Lofland, 1971, p. 106). These analytic themes throughout the field notes will guide you in developing your arguments and setting your position in the final report. Remember, every study has to find something. It has to make some case or state some position. It cannot be only a series of isolated facts. The more analytical your ideas in your notes, the stronger your case will be when you get down to putting it all together.

Personal impressions and feelings. These impressions are the subjective reactions of the observer. They may be emotional states that you go through while making the observations or very personal reactions to a situation (for example, you felt that someone you observed had been mistreated). Again, you must label these personal impressions as such so that you will be able to separate these reactions from other types of notes.

Notes for additional information. The observer may make special notes as a reminder to take an extra look at something, to speak to someone about something, etc. These reminders may be interspersed throughout the notes, but should be gathered up at the end of each note-taking session to guide the next observation period (Lofland, 1971, p. 107).

Organizing the Field Notes

There are many different ways to organize notes. You may arrange them according to people or events, in chronological order, or by ideas. If you have multiple copies of notes, they may be cross-classified under various categories. But you must have a sense of how you yourself typically order and remember things. People who have a very strong sense of chronology may be less dependent on a chronological file. Your system of filing may also affect how you analyze your data. The categories under which you choose to file your notes may form the *taxonomies* (the systems of classification) for your subsequent analysis.

Those with a weak memory for names had better keep a careful record of names. Ultimately, notes are used to develop themes, to build analytic arguments, to make points. The notes, by whatever categories they are organized, are the ingredients

of a study. As the earlier section suggested, if they are rich and informed, they will help to form a better final product. But their order and organization will facilitate putting them into a final product.

A reading of the notes will inevitably suggest "holes" in your research. There will be ideas that are not fully fleshed out; facts that are imprecise; and people whose names, positions, or relations to others are unknown or unclear. These gaps in your notes can be filled by pinpointing them and revisiting the field to ask informants for information. Some evidence will remain unobtainable and this may occasionally require some redirection in the focus of the study.

ANALYZING THE RESULTS

Once all the data are gathered and organized, they must be analyzed. In a field study where notes are the depository of the data, the plan to create meaning out of the material must be carefully structured. Because field research is so varied, only general advice can be offered here. Keep in mind that the task of analysis is to bring order out of the chaos of your notes, to pick out the central themes of your study and to carry them across to your written work. Consider as well that field work is, at its most ambitious, theory building. If you have seen numerous patterns of activity, you may reach for an explanation and in so doing create (or restate) a theory.

Strategies for the Analysis

First, you should look for *repeated patterns* and common occurrences. What is typical about the field studied? This search for general trends, normative modes, and typical patterns may be enhanced by your system of note classification. Second, you should consider the converse. What is unusual, atypical, or rare? Look for the *deviant cases*. The consideration both of what is unusual and what is common should be combined with a careful reconsideration of the primary problem that originally attracted the researcher.

The dominant patterns may reflect the universals, the givens, in this study. The deviant cases, the unusual examples, may be the particulars, the unexpected, in the study. Anthropologists have tried by comparing characteristics of wide-ranging studies to see if there are some behaviors or patterns of social organization which are universal to human cultures. Particulars indicate different forms of adaptation that societies can make; and, in a comparative context, they suggest the great breadth of human expression that is realized.

This suggestion to look for the overall patterns and unique qualities should remind you that field research seeks big answers. Although a careful study of one bar or one corporation may seem to focus on the narrow picture, interpretations from such studies, in fact, generally tend to be broad. Remember that in her study, Kanter (1977) wanted to understand how the sparsity of women in managerial positions affected the role of the woman manager. This was a big question.

Recall that after her observations, interviews, and examination of various written materials, she came to see four types of women managers. The qualities of these four female managerial types were related to types of women familiar in other contexts: the "iron maiden," the "pet," the "mother," the "seductress." This forming of a set of types based on a model (in Kanter's case, a model to explain how minority persons react to situations where they must work closely with and be equivalent to majority persons) is referred to as a *typology.* Anderson developed a typology of the different sorts of men who inhabited Jelly's. Every field will not lend itself equally well to the development of a typology, but when variations on types can be observed, a typology can be a powerful way to express it.

Typologies are very well established in the social sciences. Box 9-1 describes McKinney's (1966) efforts to clarify the development and uses of typologies in the social sciences. McKinney does not see the delineation of typologies as the goal of social research; rather, he sees it as an instrument in reaching the goal—"the establishment of uniformities of explanatory value" (1966, p. 201), which means developing powerful theories. The search for patterns and a way to group such patterns around bipolar ends is the search for typologies. It is not an easy task for a researcher, but consideration of some of the primary factors that differentiate social groups may help you to look for typological characteristics in social settings.

VALIDITY AND RELIABILITY IN FIELD STUDIES

Field studies appear to be the basis for the most valid types of social research studies. Because they actually take place in the field and because they try to capture the true meaning of the social context and understand its nature, field studies attempt to address the most crucial criteria for establishing validity. Reliability, however, is more difficult to establish in field studies. Since field work tends to be so individualized and nonroutinized, it is often difficult for a second field researcher to replicate the earlier work of another. Consider the following example.

A Case of Replicating a Field Study

As noted above, different field workers might well find different trends or different qualities in the field. It is difficult to replicate field studies. In anthropology, there have been very few replications of earlier field work. Recently, however, anthropologist Derek Freeman (1983) challenged the field work that the late renowned anthropologist Margaret Mead carried out in Samoa in the 1920s. Freeman charged that Mead misunderstood Samoan life because she had been sent out by her faculty advisor to find differences from western patterns in adolescent behavior (and had therefore found them). Mead's most prominent findings in the Samoan study were that there was a lack of constraint in adolescent sexuality, that jealousy was rare, and that fidelity in marriage was not highly valued. Freeman argues that these findings were in error:

BOX 9-1

MCKINNEY'S DEVELOPMENT AND USE OF TYPOLOGIES IN THE SOCIAL SCIENCES

McKinney (1966) stresses the theoretical importance of developing typologies in social research. For example, Tonnies' famous gemeinschaft/gesellschaft distinction (between societies or social groups distinguished by primary close relations, and those characterized by contractual, formal, impersonal relations) had powerful effects on the way that later social researchers and theorists studied societies and social organizations and groups. Such typologies generally develop out of a search for polar types. Gemeinschaft and gesellschaft are not exact opposites, but they are at opposite ends of several different continua. Figure 9-1 shows the concepts of gemeinschaft and gesellschaft at opposite ends of a set of continua representing different rules of orientation in social organizations and groups.

The norms of orientation seen in Figure 9-1, which were central in the theoretical understanding of societies as developed by Talcott Parsons (1951), include the continuum from affectivity to affective neutrality (the range from warm emotional environments to cool impersonal ones), from particularism to universalism (the range in environments from the situation where the unique, the favored, the special are served to those where laws and rules require that all are served fairly and without special treatment), from ascription to achievement (the range from evaluating on the basis of inborn qualities to evaluating on the basis of performance), from diffuseness to specificity (the range from a wide-angle concentration on *all* aspects of persons and things to a highly focused, specific, goal-oriented interest in persons or things), from traditional to rational practices (ranging from the use of old and established customs and practices to guide actions to formal rules calculated to maximize objectives for persons), and from familistic to contractual relationships (the range from affective, diffuse, and ascriptive relationships to goal-oriented, fair, unemotional social relations). These norms comprise the primary differentiating characteristics of gemeinschaft and gesellschaft, which have been so important in social-scientific studies about the social environment.

FIGURE 9-1
McKinney's use of the gemeinschaft/gesellschaft typology. *(John C. McKinney, Constructive Typology and Social Theory, Appleton-Century-Crofts, New York, 1966, p. 169.)*

Profiles Typing the Norms of Orientation of Subject to Object in an Action Context

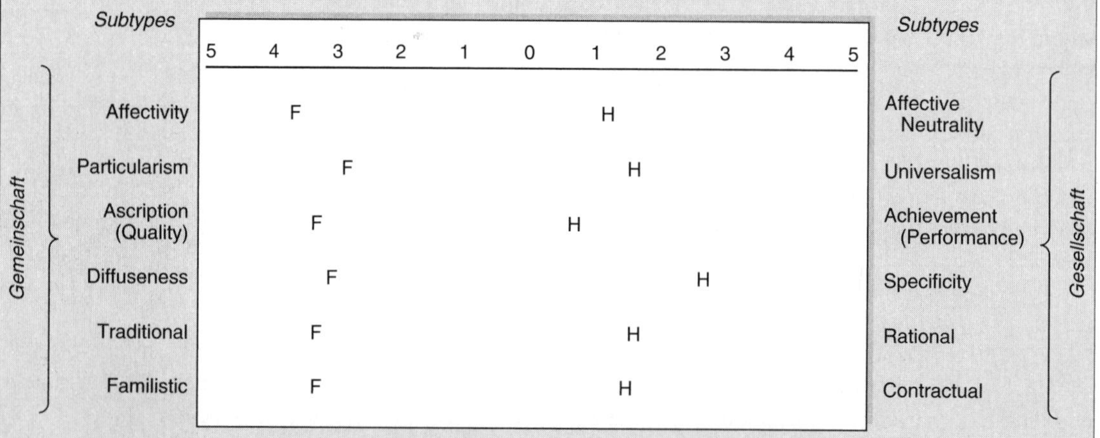

F designates the profile of the relationship of informal community leader and an assistant in a community of family-sized farms.
H designates the profile of the relationship of the manager to an immediate

for example, Freeman insists that Samoans revere virginity and that rape is prevalent.

Freeman's book caused a strong reaction among social scientists. Should his challenges be taken seriously? The debate that ensued (Marshall, 1983) raises many of the issues of concern that a field researcher should consider. Can field work be replicated? Anthropologist Lowell Holmes also had tried to replicate Mead's field work in the 1950s. Although critical of some of Mead's findings, Holmes nevertheless largely supported her conclusions about the gentle, submissive quality of the Samoans (Marshall, 1983). Field work done by different people at different times might well turn up different perspectives. For one thing, Mead was a woman and was therefore excluded from the all-male councils of the Samoan villages. (Nevertheless, as a young woman she may have had access to communication with adolescent girls, which would have eluded Freeman.)

To what extent is field work affected by the general overview of human behavior that is held by the field researcher? (In other words, to what extent does reliability depend not only on shared field strategies, but on shared theoretical predispositions?) Freeman charged that Mead's anthropology ignored evolutionary biology and that she was an extreme cultural determinist. Critics of Freeman have insisted that his critique of Mead is merely a sociobiological diatribe (Marshall, 1983). In other words, Freeman and Mead believe in different theories for explaining human behavior and therefore their field work necessarily reflects what they believe. Field researchers must examine their closely held beliefs and try to free themselves sufficiently from their influence so that such beliefs do not totally control the way in which the field is observed.

If theories and preconceptions dictate (or even shape) what a researcher sees as the facts, perhaps selective perception is inevitable. Perhaps field researchers should sensitize themselves to the way in which theories shape perceptions. In practical terms, this may require sharing initial findings with colleagues, especially with those who operate from different assumptions.

Generalizability

While it is difficult to replicate another field worker's research, it is often good for the field researcher to try to get another viewpoint. The views of an impartial observer, someone who is a visitor to the field for a different purpose and who is familiar with the field but was not present when the observations were made, may help to offer counterviews or to support the contentions of the field researcher. Since the views of the researcher must be subjective, to compare them with those of others is to seek *intersubjectivity*—a comparison of subjective perceptions. If there is a lot of agreement, the researcher may well feel more confident of his or her observations. This will help to establish the study's reliability and validity.

It is also good for the researcher to try to see the field from some other person's point of view. (How would a police officer look at Jelly's? From what stance did the male managers view their wives' roles in relation to Indsco?) By trying to evaluate your information from a number of different angles, you may be better able to determine whether what you found is plausible.

Once you have decided that your ideas about the data are cogent, it is time to see if they can be used to generalize about other situations. Can you develop hypotheses from your field observations which could be tested in similar environments? Can you select what is universal about your observations from what is merely particular to the circumstances you observed? In short, can you make your findings generalizable to other situations? Field studies must aim to move beyond simple description of one small environment to address many similar social contexts. But this cannot occur if the observations and reporting of the field work have not been done with great care.

VISUAL SOCIOLOGY

Photographs accompanying sociological studies were used quite widely in the early years of sociology in America, but following this early period, visual imagery largely disappeared from sociological studies. Its revival, under the name *visual sociology,* in the 1970s created a new speciality in the sociological discipline. Visual sociology generally attributes its origins to the work of documentary photographers or to the use of cameras in the ethnographic work of anthropologists, such as Gregory Bateson and Margaret Mead's study of Bali (Stasz, 1979, p. 119). Visual sociology refers to a way of studying social action that uses technology (cameras) to capture pictures of social environments and the people who inhabit them, attempting to convey sociological meaning to others. Visual sociologists use film, video, and still cameras.

For Curry and Clarke (1977), visual sociologists must address a number of concerns. In the first place, the documentary approach as used by social scientists, especially anthropologists, should be richer in theoretical interpretation than journalistic documentary photography. "The strength of such a film rests not only on its visual appeal, although this is of critical importance, but also on the clarity and insight of its basic propositions" (Curry and Clarke, 1977, p. 16).

The second issue concerns the role that visual methods play in a sociological project. Here the central question is one of conceptualizing the relationship of the visual images to the problems addressed in the particular sociological study. Some research problems easily lend themselves to incorporating visual material; others lend themselves less easily. Proponents of visual sociology think that many more researchers should consider going after visual images. Visual images (pictures) can offer direct referents, and they can show relationships. It is in showing social relationships that "visual thinking becomes an important part of the research process" (Curry and Clarke, 1977, p. 20). The visual language of the photographic images, if separated from a written narrative, can be controlled by the researcher if the symbols and artifacts that make up the images are carefully ordered or presented in sequence so that they create a visual narrative.

Photographs and film enable a researcher to return to the original data, rather than to depend on

recollections (that is why they are popular in field settings), and they help in the defining of sequences. Howard Becker (1974) has argued that a visual image should help to bridge the gap between a concept and its behavioral indicator. Finally, the meaning of visual images (theorizing about images) can advance the theoretical study of society. For example, Cloninger (1974) studied differences in the content, style of depiction, and use of background environments of the photographs by male and female photographers.

The Purpose of Visual Data

For visual sociologists, the object of gathering visual data is to present "typical" arrangements of social and cultural objects, social actors, and social interaction in a social environment so that these visual images can be used for descriptive or analytic purposes. Generally this involves photographing or filming current social phenomena. However, it may also include collecting old photographs and films that address the subject being studied.

Visual sociologists must also learn to build linkages between the different images they develop. Although most visual material is accompanied by some written commentary, it is often desirable not to overload visual images with too much written material, or the purpose of having the visual image carry the message may be lost. The best photographic documentary maintains an integrated and complementary relationship between a visual narrative and a written narrative that clearly specifies the meaning which the visual sociologist intends. The critical issue is that the written narrative should not do the work of the visual communication, or the visual images become redundant. A final point: although visual sociologists are not primarily photographic artists, they must nevertheless be concerned with the aesthetic appeal of their images.[1]

---

[1]This discussion is drawn from a paper delivered by George H. Lewis (1982).

Doing Visual Sociology

The two main types of visual sociology are those based on still photography and on video documentaries. Two of my former DePaul University colleagues are engaged in these efforts. Charles Suchar is working with still photography. He has been carrying out a photography and interview study of a gentrified urban neighborhood. His aim is to contrast the lifestyles and material culture of older and newer residents of this Chicago neighborhood (Suchar, 1988). John Koval is working with video documentaries. He has produced a series of tapes of festivals, which include studies of an agricultural haying festival, an Italian fest in a Chicago neighborhood, and football game festivities (e.g., tailgate parties) at the University of Notre Dame.

Some sociology departments now offer courses explicitly devoted to visual sociology; others include a discussion of its techniques in a qualitative methods course. (For example, Suchar and Koval offer courses in documentary still photography and video documentary, respectively.)

Visual sociologists must learn not only how to use cameras, but also how to develop and edit their films once they are taken. In video filming, editing can be a fairly complicated matter. Those considering the use of video cameras should consult the National Park Service guide prepared by the Project for Public Spaces (1979a). There are also many texts now available on television production, which address most of the technical problems raised by video documentary. For still photography, Wagner's reader *Images of Information: Still Photography in the Social Sciences* (1979a) offers numerous suggestions on the use of still photography in field research.

Students of visual sociology particularly need to learn how to integrate written and visual narratives, in other words, how to do photographic essays. Thus the skills of interviewing (see Chapter 7), taking field notes (discussed earlier in this chapter), and using archival material (see Chapter 10) must be mastered, as well as the photographic skills.

Wagner suggests ways to avoid error in doing visual sociology with still cameras. First, errors in picture taking can be reduced by using several photographers, by photographing from scripts which help to order the pictures, by comparing photographs with other types of available data, and by taking photographs of different subareas within the environment to be studied that have been selected randomly (Wagner, 1979b, pp. 148–152). In order to reduce bias in the analysis of the photographic material, Wagner suggests using several persons for the analysis, studying the photographs in relation to one another and in relation to the impressions prompted by the set of photographs (what he calls "editing analytically"), and examining random samples of photographs (1979b, pp. 152–153). He also offers some suggestions on how to subject the photographs to a content analysis (see Chapter 10), whereby the analyst sets up a coding system to select specific qualities of the photographs. For example, one can note the presence of certain types of things in photographs (cars, persons, open space, vegetation, etc.), the amount or number of things, and the combination of two or more expected features (1979b, pp. 154–155). Such strategies can increase the validity and reliability of photographs as data on a particular social environment or condition.

Proponents of visual methods contend that photographs and film provide a necessary component of the techniques of the social researcher. If you plan to carry out a field study, you should seriously consider the use of such visual methods.

DECIDING IF A FIELD STUDY IS APPROPRIATE FOR YOUR TOPIC

Consider your topic carefully and ask yourself whether a study of a natural environment based on observation will give you the material you need. As suggested in Chapter 1, some social researchers think that field research is mainly desirable for the study of problems that are not yet well formulated—a method appropriate for underdeveloped research problems. Others choose this method as the only true way to study human behavior and society unimpeded by the artificial techniques that characterize other methods. I also stated that personal qualities of the researcher may determine which method to choose. Especially in field work, a person may need to have (or to develop) a certain ability to establish rapport with others, to enter into the worlds of others without imposing too much of the self on the research.

If you think that a field study might be the best way to approach your research problem, you must then consider how to carry it out. You will need to prepare for the field; you may need help in gaining entry to the field. Careful consideration should be made of how you will record the information. (Will you use tape recorders, a camera, a video camera, a pencil and pad?) Going into the field is something like going on a long trip: you need to consider all the possible eventualities before you go, so that you won't find yourself stuck (without something you very much need) at an inconvenient moment. As in planning for a trip, it is useful to make lists of what you need and to go over these plans with another. (In this case, the most useful kind of person to help you is someone who has done a similar piece of field work.) Most of all, remember that even though field work is a "natural" method, with few formal techniques, this does not mean that the researcher can proceed without plans. Even though all your preparations are not of use in the field and even though you may need to devise some new ways of doing things on the spot, it is better to have entered the field well prepared.

REVIEW NOTES

- Field research involves observational study of real social environments.
- Field research generally focuses on a single field setting; such studies are thus referred to as case studies.
- Field research is the primary research method of anthropologists whose observational studies describing whole peoples are termed ethnographies.
- Ethnography, the observational technique of trying to study a whole culture, is a theory-building method attempting to draw generalizations from cultural particulars. Cross-cultural ethnographic comparisons foster the discovery of generalizations.
- Field studies take place in field settings and address general subjects. They are carried out within a specified time frame. Field study subjects generally focus on descriptions of characteristics of the field or on the causes and consequences of a social phenomenon.
- Things to observe in a field setting include the general environment, people and their relationships, actions and activities, verbal behavior, psychological stances, histories, and physical objects.
- The role of an observer may be as a full observer, an observer-as-participant (primarily an observer but participating at some levels), a participant-as-observer (primarily a participant, but observing as well), a full participant (in this role note taking, interviewing, and other formal research techniques cannot be carried out).
- Before going into the field, the researcher must gain information from external sources on the type of environment to be studied and from internal sources for advice on how to accomplish the researcher's goals.
- Field researchers must remain open-minded and nonjudgmental in entering a field. They should not offer opinions.
- Successful field relations have been reached when reciprocal relations between field researcher and members of the field have been established.
- Field notes may include running descriptions, recalled material that had been forgotten earlier, ideas that interpret and examine the meaning of a situation, and personal impressions and feelings.
- Strategies for analyzing field data include looking for repeated patterns; for normative modes; for typical forms; for that which is unusual, atypical, or rare.

- The forming of a set of types based on a model is a typology. Typologies of social groups or systems (such as gemeinschaft and gesellschaft) are often differentiated by the bipolar ends of normative orientations, such as traditional-rational, ascription-achievement, particularistic-universalistic.
- Visual sociology is a way of studying social action with the use of photographic technology to capture pictures of social environments which convey sociological meaning.

KEY TERMS

anthropology
case studies
ethnography
field research
intersubjectivity
negative evidence
observer-as-participant
participant-as-observer
participant observation
running descriptions
triangulation
typology
verstehen
visual sociology

STUDY EXERCISES

1. Suppose you are training students to go out and do field work. You decide to give them a short list of do's and don'ts. Make up such a list.
2. Think about Elijah Anderson carrying out his field work at Jelly's Bar (from Chapter 1). Let's assume that every time he returned from the bar, he wrote field notes. Give examples of what types of *subjects* the notes might have covered. Describe how you think he was able to move from the notes he wrote to the development of the overall themes of the study.

RECOMMENDED READINGS

1. Ball, Michael S., and Gregory W. H. Smith: *Analyzing Visual Data,* Sage, Newbury Park, Calif., 1992. A small volume on how to use still photographs as social data.
2. Collier, John, Jr., and Malcolm Collier: *Visual Anthropology,* University of New Mexico Press, 1986. Reviews the use of still photography in the various phases of ethnographic field work.
3. Fetterman, David M.: *Ethnography: Step by Step,* Sage, Newbury Park, Calif., 1989. An anthropologist's guide to carrying out field studies, from practical advice on equipment to conceptual ordering of the research cycle.
4. Johnson, Jeffrey C.: *Selecting Ethnographic Informants,* Sage, Newbury Park, Calif., 1990. A systematic approach to selecting informants in a field on the basis of theory or data.
5. Lofland, John: *Analyzing Social Settings: A Guide to Qualitative Observation and Analysis,* Wadsworth, Belmont, Calif., 1971. One of the most widely used and respected books on qualitative analysis and observation methods.
6. Strauss, Anselm, and Juliet Corbin: *Basics of Qualitative Research: Grounded Theory Procedures and Techniques,* Sage, Newbury Park, Calif., 1990. How to make sense out of all the data collected in a field study; how to create clear, theoretically sound formulations.

Methods of Analyzing Available Data

LOOKING AHEAD

This chapter describes five methods for analyzing available data: secondary analysis, content analysis, historical research, analysis of unobtrusive measures, and analysis of existing statistics. It presents model examples of effective research, as well as ways to find data and handle them properly. It discusses the advantages of using multiple methods in a study.

INTRODUCTION

*T*his chapter presents a number of different methods of studying data that are already available. Available data can be found in two general ways. In some cases, data that have been collected for one set of analyses are made available to other researchers for new projects. Such formally available data may be either in raw form, so that the second researcher can carry out an analysis (that is, a secondary analysis on a dataset prepared by another researcher), or in statistical form, in which case the researcher can reanalyze these existing statistics.

In other cases, data merely exist in one form or another, but have not been drawn together by anyone. In this situation, the researcher must first decide which data to use for the study. Such data may be in the form of printed materials, visual or recorded materials, or artifacts that are of interest to the researcher. Historical research generally depends on written sources, though oral history based on interview data is being used increasingly as historical data. Content analyses are usually also based on written materials, though artifacts may also be studied. Or researchers may use or develop novel ways to measure things unobtrusively (amount and type of garbage, for example), which could facilitate studying certain subjects. Your first challenge as a researcher of available data is to find some type of data which can address your research problem and to use these data to answer the questions you wish to ask. This implies that you look for available data once you already have a research question defined.

The use of available data for carrying out social research projects is therefore different from the methods described in the preceding three chapters—methods by which the researcher creates and collects new data. What is different between finding available data to analyze and creating and collecting your own is the point of time in the research process when the researcher and the data meet. In an experiment, a survey, or a field study, the initial research effort is to produce or create the data. In almost all cases (the exception may be a field study), the research questions are clearly formulated before the data are collected. When available data are used, naturally this order is reversed: the data have been collected or are available ready to be processed before you, the researcher, come along to pose a research question.

Studies in which you have collected your own data and those in which you use already collected data reach the same point at the research stage of data processing and analysis. One thing that may occur to you is that using already available data should be easier and quicker than collecting your own. In theory this should be the case, since such studies avoid the data collection process. However, the process of finding a body of data relevant to your research problem may be a slow one; and a more difficult and time-consuming effort is often required to code and process the data for your specific purposes. Since they were collected for different purposes, these data must be reconceptualized and manipulated so as to specifically address your concerns. Above all, they must not be used inappropriately! That is to say, issues of validity and reliability become of central concern in studies on already collected data. The researcher must understand the data well and not use them in ways which ignore or subvert their meaning.

There are many types of social research which are based on the analysis of available data. In this chapter, I shall present five different methods not commonly grouped together. They have been gathered together here because they each depend on the use of available data.

THE ART AND SCIENCE OF ANALYZING AVAILABLE DATA

Creative Aspects

It takes a creative idea to link a research problem to a set of available data. Generally, the researcher has a problem in mind, then ingenuity is required to conceive of, and find, an available source of data to address the problem. The way the data are handled may also be quite creative. Schemes for selecting specific objects to study, coding the data, ferreting out patterns within the data—all demand an eye for the unique and unusual.

Appreciation is also a central feature of analyzing available data. You must be able to appreciate the qualities of the data. In historical research, documents and artifacts from the past must be appropriately valued in order to be understood. Appreciating the strengths of an earlier survey (for secondary analysis) or of a collection of pamphlets on a particular theme (for content analysis) both demand a level of understanding which can take into account the qualities of the materials. Studying unobtrusive measures requires the ability to select such indicators to illuminate a problem of interest.

Linking your interests to a set of materials in which these interests can be furthered is also a creative process. One thing to consider in analyzing available data is whether you have a special expertise or knowledge about some materials (knowledge of a foreign language, experience in an environment from which these data were drawn, a hobby which has given you a store of information about a set of objects or an area of interest). Such special knowledge areas may be ones in which you will be able to be more creative.

Scientific Aspects

Analysis of available data also often requires scientific operations and norms. Where the rules and formal procedures of a scientific method are used (as would be common in many forms of secondary analysis, analysis of existing statistics, and even in content analysis), the scientific model would operate. Because secondary analyses begin with a body of data, they are often used in very sophisticated state-of-the-art types of analyses. Sociological research studies in the major journals using the most modern and advanced analytic methods are often based on already collected datasets.

In some studies, inductive explanations may be drawn from the data by examining the patterns among factors and the possible reasons for observed changes. An inductive approach would often guide an analysis based on unobtrusive measures. Deductive analyses can also be carried out on already collected sets of data; in such cases a hypothesis is posed and data are found and analyzed in order to test it.

In an analysis of existing statistics, for example, suppose the hypothesis is that raising the legal drinking age will reduce automobile fatalities. Data on auto fatalities could be compared from states with different drinking ages to see if there is a relationship between these two factors.

The empirical foundation of a social-scientific study has already been laid once the data are collected. You must take care to understand how and why this was done in the original study, for whatever weaknesses occurred in the original study will continue as weaknesses in your own study. Conversely, the strengths will remain as strengths. The scientific method also depends on rules of rationality. Here the purposefulness and logic of your approach will foster the scientific credibility of the project.

SECONDARY ANALYSIS

Secondary analysis, as stated before, is not a specific method, per se; it simply means a new analysis of data collected for another purpose. Hakim defines it as "any further analysis of an existing dataset which presents interpretations, conclusions, or knowledge additional to, or different from, those presented in the first report" (1982, p. 1). Generally, it refers to using already collected survey data to study problems different from those addressed by the original researcher(s). Another reason for carrying out a secondary analysis may be to use already available survey data in the study of a research method. By applying different methodological techniques to the same dataset, for example, much might be learned about a statistical technique.

For your purposes, you should consider secondary analysis if you want to use a dataset larger than what you could collect yourself. When you look for a dataset, you must hold clearly in mind what the essential needs of your study are. Does the survey you are considering have questions that address your needs? Is the sample of the survey adequate for your purposes? Will it allow you to generalize to the population you are aiming to consider?

In short, a set of already collected data offers you a "menu" from which you can pick out what you want to study—that is to say, you can create your secondary analysis. You must be sure your project can be served by that menu and that you like what's on the menu. The menu metaphor also implies that until you've ordered and tasted the items ordered, you will not be precisely sure how much you like them. Naturally, you look carefully over a questionnaire before you decide to use the data generated from it, but often not until you start to work with data do you fully appreciate exactly how effective they will or will not be for your purposes. You will, in addition, need to consider the costs both of purchasing the dataset and of running the necessary computer analyses.

"One advantage of secondary analysis is that it forces the researcher to think more closely about the theoretical aims and substantive issues of the study rather than the practical and methodological problems of collecting new data" (Hakim, 1982, p. 16). This may be one of the reasons that it has become such a widely reputed method.

An Example of a Secondary Analysis

A colleague of mine, Joyce Sween, and I received a federal grant in the late 1970s to study the potentially disruptive effects of childbearing and child rearing on women's career outcomes. The plan was to carry out a secondary analysis of a longitudinal dataset based on a national survey of college graduates of 1961 who were followed up five times across the 1960s until 1968. The longitudinal design would enable us to examine career activities and attitudes both before and after childbearing and to compare these across time. A sample of college graduates was attractive to us because we wanted to examine a group including

some women who would be sufficiently trained for the work force and hold sufficiently high career aspirations for the effects of childbearing on their careers to be of possible consequence to them. (For a paper from this analysis, see Baker and Sween, 1982.)

Acquiring the dataset was relatively easy. For a modest price, we purchased a data tape from the National Opinion Research Center (NORC), which had collected the dataset. It came with a large and complex codebook and a computer printout of the frequencies of responses to every item on the tape. It took some time to familiarize ourselves with this tape and to select all the variables we needed to carry out our intended analysis.

We began, as is often the case, by considering a fairly wide range of variables. However, it is necessary in a secondary analysis to avoid carrying out what is termed a "fishing expedition," where the researcher "fishes" for one variable after another. To narrow our choice of variables, we considered which ones were the best measures of concepts that interested us (which ones had greater face validity). We also prepared many cross-tabulations of potentially interesting independent variables with our dependent variable (career status attainment) to decide which seemed to have the strongest relationships with higher attainment.

We also had to carry out a good deal of data manipulation (to be discussed in more detail in Chapter 12) and index and scale construction (to be discussed in Chapter 16). In order to consider carefully how childbearing affected work patterns and attitudes, we had to develop new measures indicating the patterns of work activity, childbearing, returning to work, etc., which characterized the early adult years of young women. These patterns could then be compared to women with earlier or later first births and to those with higher or lower career aspirations.

In a study such as this, the effort to collect these complex and very detailed data had already been completed by a professional survey research center whose standards for carrying out surveys were very widely respected. Not only would we have been unable to finance such a national survey ourselves, but as only two sociologists we would not have been able to carry it out on our own. We spent the largest amount of time creating new variables from old, selecting the variables for the final analyses, and then analyzing the results.

This is the virtue of secondary analysis. Most of the effort can be placed at the analytic stage rather than at the data-gathering stage. Remember, however, that you can transform variables only so far; you cannot make up data that are not there.

Whether to Use Old or New Data

In the opening section, I mentioned that one factor that distinguishes the analysis of already collected data from studies where the researcher collects new data is time. When data are already available (that is, when they are extant), they represent a period of time prior to the efforts to carry out the new analysis. Some very interesting longitudinal survey datasets were collected in the past, and some excellent datasets are being collected in the present. Here I will first present a brief discussion of how Glen Elder (1974) undertook a reanalysis of a set of data initially collected in 1931. Then I will explain how Karl Alexander and Aaron Pallas (1983) reanalyzed the *High School and Beyond* data (from the Coleman study of private and public high schools described in Chapter 1) in order to challenge some of Coleman's findings.

Children of the Great Depression. In order to study the effects of economic factors on family relations across generations, Elder (1974) utilized a longitudinal dataset, the Oakland Growth Study. This panel of data was developed by the Institute of Human Development at the University of California at Berkeley. It began in 1931 as an intensive study of 167 children who were in the fifth and sixth grades of five different primary schools in one section of Oakland, California. These children were closely followed, using interviews and questionnaires, from 1932 to 1939. In the 1940s, data

collection was continued in 1941 and again in 1948. Another follow-up was carried out during the period 1953–1954, yet another in 1957, and the final contact was made in 1964. Thus these longitudinal data covered a time period of 31 years.

By modern standards, the sample was not a very good one. In many secondary analyses, one of the major attractions of this method is that the quality of the sampling is superior to that which many researchers could afford to do. In Elder's case, however, the attraction of the Oakland Growth Study was the historical length of the dataset and the richness of data on intergenerational family matters. The original sample of 84 boys and 83 girls were all white, children of native-born Americans, and only slightly higher in social class than a more representative sample of Oakland residents from that same period.

The early data collection efforts were deep and broad. They included interviews with mothers and questionnaires administered to the pupils. In the 1930s, families were visited yearly, and a log was kept on each member of the sample. Child-rearing practices, family relationships, and activities of the child with friends were solicited. As the respondents moved into junior and senior high school, questionnaires on social and emotional behavior were administered on seven different occasions. In addition, the Strong Vocational Interest blank which measured occupational interests was used in one survey. Ratings of the family in terms of the closeness of the subject to each parent and the evaluation of the parents by the subject were made using a set of judges.

The follow-up surveys and interviews in the 1950s and 1960s produced a sample of 76 women and 69 men. For these individuals, life histories could be developed based on occupational and family histories across the decades. In these later studies, subjects were given physical examinations, psychiatric assessments, and numerous personality tests. This gave Elder some insight into the mental health of the subjects and its relation to childhood conditions.

Working with old and complex data such as these presents many problems of validity. Whenever possible, Elder searched for multiple indicators, especially to use as dependent variables. Indexes were often formed so that multiple measures might reduce the possible errors that single measures might contain.

Elder also made use of other studies from the 1930s with which to compare his findings. Here the need to have some grounding in historical material from the period covered is important. Elder's interest, however, remained with the individual and with the family across time. Let me offer you one among the many interesting findings of this study. Elder differentiated his sample between those who grew up in deprived families (those in which the breadwinner was unemployed) during the Depression and those who did not. In doing so, he found support for the hypothesis that "family life acquired value through exposure to conditions which made rewarding, secure relationships difficult to achieve and therefore scarce" (1974, p. 226). That is to say, those who had grown up in deprived families in the 1930s had a stronger preference for family activities in the 1950s and 1960s as compared to nonfamily activities such as career, leisure, or community than did those whose families had not been deprived in the 1930s. This finding was especially true for women.

Challenging Coleman's Findings.   One of the great advantages of secondary analysis is that it can allow for a very quick reanalysis of someone else's findings. Recall Chapter 1 when we examined the study by James Coleman and his colleagues about the advantageous educational effects of private high schools. This study was based on the first survey of a large longitudinal study of a national sample of high school sophomores and seniors in 1980 who were to be resurveyed four times, on a biannual basis. This ambitious dataset, referred to as *High School and Beyond* (HSB, described in Coleman et al., 1982), was available to other researchers through the National Center for Education Statistics (now the

Center of Statistics of the U.S. Department of Education).

Alexander and Pallas (1983) wanted to challenge the Coleman finding that private school students performed better on cognitive tests because of their educational experiences in private schools. Since Coleman and his associates had only the 1980 dataset to work with, they had only cross-sectional data on achievement test scores (though they could compare sophomores with seniors, in a cohort-effect design). In order to strengthen their analysis, Alexander and Pallas used not only the *High School and Beyond* dataset from 1980 but also a comparable longitudinal dataset from the 1970s—the National Longitudinal Study (NLS) of the Class of 1972 (Riccobono, 1981). From these data, there was longitudinal evidence on the cognitive achievement of students across time.

If high schools made a difference in affecting students' cognitive abilities, then it was necessary to get some measure of how the students differed in abilities before they entered the school. Perhaps the private schools only drew smarter students who therefore tested higher at the completion of their schooling. Now from what you already know of research design you can imagine what would be needed to test how far high schools actually contribute to the cognitive abilities of their students. You've got it! Pre–high school cognitive ability scores. That's what Alexander and Pallas would have liked to have been able to find: a longitudinal survey with pre–high school test scores. But they knew of no such study. Instead, they settled for a different kind of measure that could serve as a kind of substitute (or surrogate) for pre–high school ability, namely, high school curriculum placement.

Students are placed in high school curricular tracks (college preparatory, vocational, etc.) on the basis of performance in junior high (or elementary) school, as well as parental influence and school policies. These different curricula expose students to quite different subject matter in their high school courses. One easily attainable fact is that a much larger proportion of students in private high schools are in academic, college preparatory tracks than those in public high schools. By comparing public and Catholic high school students "within" curricular tracks, in both the HSB and NLS studies, Alexander and Pallas found (contrary to Coleman's position) that most of the advantages that Coleman had attributed to private schools had disappeared. By reassessing data from the survey *High School and Beyond*, in comparison to data from the NLS survey, and by focusing on a different variable (curricular track), Alexander and Pallas were able to challenge one of Coleman's central findings. This attempt to reassess the important findings of others is one of the functions of secondary analysis.

COMPONENTS OF A SECONDARY ANALYSIS

In theory, you should always know what you want to study before getting your data. In fact, secondary analysis often begins with finding a dataset you think is especially exciting or rich and then devising a problem which can be studied using these data. Here we will examine the components in the "proper" order, but remember that in practice the data may be chosen before the problem is set

Selection of a Topic

A topic for a secondary analysis may be very ambitious. It may be one that only a large national (or even cross-national) dataset could address. Once you have posed a hypothesis or a research question, the operationalization must be carefully considered. What control variables will be critical? Must the dependent variable be measured in a particular way? Usually there is some latitude in your design, so if you find a relevant dataset that does not have every feature you want, you can adapt your study slightly to conform to what is available. In secondary analysis, you need to focus quite precisely on your topic in order to select an appropriate dataset.

Search for Available Data

In Chapter 4, a general discussion of where you might find available data was offered. A researcher with access to a computer can study a vast array of research topics, using datasets from well-designed surveys based on carefully constructed samples. Major survey research centers at universities or government agencies can usually carry out data collection procedures much more rigorously and thoroughly than a lone researcher can. The institution at which you are studying may be affiliated with a social science data archive that stores datasets and makes them available to users for a reasonable charge. Your institution may have its own data archive, or it may be affiliated with a group of universities which hold a collection of data tapes.

The largest and best-known social science data archive, the Inter-University Consortium for Political and Social Research (ICPSR) at the University of Michigan, has thousands of machine-readable data files. These include surveys that have been collected by American centers such as the *General Social Survey (GSS)*, which was described in Chapter 4; the numerous datasets collected by the Census Bureau; and data from foreign sources. Any institution of higher education which includes social scientists can join ICPSR and then have access to vast holdings of datasets. Box 10-1 describes a number of the most widely used databases available from ICPSR. For a broad listing of survey data archives in various states, see Kiecolt and Nathan (1985, pp. 76–79).

There are social science data archives in other countries as well (Kiecolt and Nathan, 1985, pp. 79–80). In Britain, the Social Science Research Council (SSRC) Data Archive at the University of Essex stores hundreds of datasets to which a user can gain access by filling out a very simple application. You can check the SSRC's holdings by examining the *Guide to the Survey Archives Social Science Data Holdings and Allied Services.* The SSRC can also help you gain access to international datasets.

BOX 10-1

MAJOR DATASETS IN THE UNITED STATES

SURVEYS OF NATIONAL SAMPLES ON BROAD-RANGING TOPICS

1. The *General Social Survey (GSS)* has been conducted by the National Opinion Research Center (NORC) yearly since 1972. It samples a national cross-section of noninstitutionalized English-speaking persons 18 years of age and older. In some years, special subsamples have been surveyed (such as black Americans). The *GSS* has measured attitudes toward controversial issues, such as abortion and civil liberties, over nearly two decades, thereby allowing for trend studies. In addition, measures are collected yearly on work and job satisfaction; personal happiness; family relations; and characteristics of the sample subjects, such as age at first marriage, number of children, and educational, marital, and military histories. (See Davis and Smith's *User's Guide,* in the Recommended Readings.)

2. Data collected by the Census Bureau are available in many forms at state data centers. The Public Use Microdata Samples (PUMS) offer different types of representative samples of the decennial census; some of the census questions have been asked annually since 1910. The Current Population Survey (CPS) surveys a national sample of Americans monthly on labor force activity, with background data on marital, fertility, educational, and immunization histories.

SURVEYS OF NATIONAL SAMPLES ON FOCUSED TOPICS

1. Work and income: The National Longitudinal Surveys (NLS), carried out by the joint efforts of the Department of Labor and Ohio State University, provide a rich data source on labor market experience. The NLS surveys have covered panels of young women and men (ages 14 to 24), women ages 30 to 44, and men ages 49 to 59. Respondents were first interviewed in 1966 and were reinterviewed over a period of 15 years. A new survey of young Americans was begun in the late 1970s and has been followed up.

    The Panel Study of Income Dynamics (PSID) conducted at the Institute for Social Research at the University of Michigan has surveyed low-income families, heads of households, and wives of male household heads. Data are available on family units or individuals. (See the *User's Guide* in the Recommended Readings.)

2. Health: The National Center for Health Statistics (NCHS) prepares a catalog of public use data on health. The National Health Interview Survey (NHIS) focuses on specific systems of the body in order to identify diseases, as well as on other health topics such as smoking. The National Health and Nutrition Examination Survey (NHANES) gains its data through physical and laboratory examinations and survey questions. A primary focus is nutrition.

3. Education: The Center of Statistics of the U.S. Department of Education offers a number of datasets. Two we have discussed in detail are the National Longitudinal Study of the High School Class of 1972 and *High School and Beyond,* a longitudinal survey of students who were high school sophomores and seniors in 1980. One of the most extensive longitudinal surveys of school-aged students ever carried out was Project Talent, which surveyed high school students in their first, second, third, and final year in 1960 and then followed them up over a number of years. These data form the Project Talent Data Bank, available from the American Institutes for Research in Palo Alto, California.

4. Politics: The Center for Political Studies and the Survey Research Center of the University of Michigan's Institute for Social Research have been carrying out election surveys since 1948. This American National Election Study assesses political and social attitudes, including appraisals of domestic and foreign policy, reactions to social groups, the mass media, social-psychological predispositions, and voting behavior and party identification. Data from panel studies have been gathered in certain years, as well as extensive cross-sectional data. These data are also available through ICPSR.

Public opinion data are held by the Louis Harris Center (at the University of North Carolina, Chapel Hill Social Science Data Library) and the Roper Center for Public Opinion Research (at the Institute for Social Inquiry at the University of Connecticut). The *Directory of Louis Harris Public Opinion Machine-Readable Data* describes the various surveys covering a wide array of social and political topics. Researchers looking for data on a specific topic can ask the Harris Center to conduct computer searches on the basis of keywords. The Roper Center, the world's largest public opinion data archive, has data tapes from television and newspaper polls as well as the Gallup polls (conducted by the American Institute for Public Opinion), the Harris polls, and surveys from NORC and other survey centers. There are numerous reference guides to the Roper Center holdings, such as the *Roper Center American Collection,* which describes the center's U.S. holdings, and *Data Acquisitions,* which is published biannually.

Data archive centers can usually prepare the type of machine-readable tapes or disks you request for your specific computer system. Codebooks for the surveys are always available. Constructed indexes and scales prepared from the data are often included. Many centers prepare bibliographies of published studies and unpublished reports based on particular datasets. Some data archives will prepare datasets on request based on specific subsamples or statistical tables. The price of datasets is generally quite reasonable. To justify the public expense of data collection funded by the government, there is often an explicit agreement that the data must be accessible to others.

Re-creation of the Data

Once you have acquired a dataset, you must make it meet your research objectives. This requires a few steps. First, you must search out the variables you think you need. Second, you must study them carefully. If you have the frequency counts on each variable, this will intensify your knowledge

of them. (If, for example, a large proportion said "don't know" to a specific question, this is a factor which will be important in deciding whether or not to use the item and how to use it.) Third, you must select a set of variables which will fully address the needs of your study, but which will not overwhelm you. (The typical mistake is to take on too many variables and become bogged down in too many analyses.)

As a secondary analyst, you can re-create much of the data to suit your needs. But you must always be careful not to use the data for a purpose for which they are inappropriate. (You cannot turn a sow's ear into a silk purse, as the proverb goes.) If you create your own indexes and scales, you should take care to give them valid names.

You may also decide to use only subsets of the sample (only the males, only those over age 21, only those born in the southeastern United States, etc.). If you do this, you will need to reconsider the sample design to see what effects your selection will have on the quality of the sample. You will need to consider how representative the subsample of the population was from which it was drawn.

Analyzing the Data and Comparing Results

The major effort of such a study is to analyze the data. Chapters 13 and 14 will explain analytic techniques. Your secondary analysis of a dataset becomes a part of the corpus of analyses of that data. Survey research centers often develop bibliographies of the studies carried out and of the publications prepared using a specific dataset. You may want to compare your efforts to those of others who have used the data and to inform the survey center of your project.

Issues of Validity and Reliability

In selecting a dataset for a secondary analysis, the issue of validity should be your primary criterion. You must be strongly convinced that the data measure what they purport to measure and that these measures in fact are ones that are appropriate for the variables you need for your project. To meet these objectives, the following qualifications should be considered in selecting a dataset: (1) the quality of the data-gathering organization, (2) the purpose of the original researchers, and (3) the extent to which the dataset contains indicators that will enable you to test your research problem—in particular, what will be used for the dependent variable and the primary independent variables.

Because these data have already been analyzed, many questions about their validity have already been addressed. If scales and indexes have been created, validity and reliability tests (as described in Chapter 5) may already have been carried out. Examinations of how variables of interest to you were related to other variables in already prepared analyses from the dataset should help you to see whether the variable seems to be measuring what you would expect it to measure.

Secondary analyses based on highly professional data-gathering techniques often contain measures of higher validity and reliability than a single researcher would be apt to prepare. Because the data have to be analyzed again, the issues of reliability and validity are also raised again. In the selection of such data, the researcher examines and challenges the validity of indicators within the study. These additional efforts to reappraise the data will offer greater information on their value.

DECIDING IF SECONDARY ANALYSIS IS APPROPRIATE FOR YOUR TOPIC

For many social researchers, secondary analysis is *the* preferred method. Some social researchers (and professors who teach social research methods) believe that beginning researchers should be encouraged to carry out secondary analyses because of the quality of the data that can be used. It is, of course, the case that a lot of data will never be fully analyzed by the original researchers. A large survey, such as *High School and Beyond*, contains so much data that many researchers working on many different problems are required to be able to analyze all the material.

If you have a problem that needs to be addressed with a large body of data, and you know of a dataset which contains relevant material for your study, you should consider secondary analysis. Of course, your advisor may want you to collect your own data (for a class project, for a master's thesis, or a doctoral dissertation) and there is much to be learned by doing so. But it is worth bearing in mind that there are so many available datasets still not fully analyzed that it is sensible to consider examining already collected survey data before setting out to do your own data collection. Let me add that even if you want to carry out your own survey, it often makes sense to begin by examining and analyzing earlier survey data that may address the same problem. Finally, every project has its time span and effort span; secondary analysis concentrates that effort on the analysis stage of research by abbreviating the need for data collection and manipulation.

CONTENT ANALYSIS

Some problems can best be addressed through *content analysis*—an analysis of the content of communication. In a review of the varying definitions of content analysis, Ole Holsti (1969, pp. 3–5) found three common requirements. First, content analysis is *objective:* it "stipulates that each step in the research process must be carried out on the basis of explicitly formulated rules and procedures." The researcher needs to develop objective categories for coding the data, which represent objective decisions about this content and not the researcher's subjective ways of seeing the material. Replication tests for objectivity. Would another researcher set up similar procedures, criteria for data selection, and means of interpretation in order to analyze the body of communication for the same research problem?

The second requirement is that content analysis must be *systematic.* According to Holsti, "the inclusion and exclusion of content or categories is done according to consistently applied rules" (1969, p. 4). This means that content which fails to support the researcher's hypotheses must not be left out; categories for data coding must be applied consistently. As Holsti contends, these two qualities (objectivity and systematic application) are necessary but not sufficient to define content analysis, for they could also define indexes and other bibliographical techniques. Holsti's third point is that content analysis must possess *generality,* which "requires that the findings must have theoretical relevance" (1969, p. 5). The goal of content analysis is never just description; rather, the analyzed content must be related to some other factor or factors about the documents, about the persons stating the content, about the intended audience, or about the times in which the content was produced.

In one of the earlier definitions of content analysis, Bernard Berelson stressed that it was a technique "for the objective, systematic, and quantitative description of the manifest content of communication" (1954, p. 489). While quantitative analysis is generally a primary objective in content analysis, it is not necessary to count the frequency of certain attributes in some document. Holsti suggests that studying the presence or absence of an attribute allows for a "contingency analysis" (1969, pp. 7–8). Or documents might be categorized in their totality by major themes. Let's consider an early debate among the Democratic candidates hoping for success in the 1992 presidential primaries. We could take the content of the seven candidates' statements on the December 15, 1991, televised debate, and (1) count how often each one referred to President Bush or to the flagging economy, etc; (2) examine whether reference to the demise of the Soviet Union was present or absent in each of their speeches; and (3) determine the major "message" or theme that each candidate tried to make in his statements.

Berelson's definition also focused on the content being *manifest*—in other words, stressing that what was said or written or shown was what

would be studied. Here Holsti (1969, pp. 13–14) contends that in the coding stage of the research, the manifest material is all that the researcher can appropriately consider. However, at the interpretative stage, latent meanings in the data may well be drawn out, though the researcher must be careful to corroborate interpretations concerning values, motives, and personality characteristics of the communicators.

One of the best ways to get a sense of this method is by considering examples of how it has been used. Since this method analyzes culturally created work, it tends to select "content" that is either "popular" and/or influential or culturally valued. By selecting popular works, the researcher can infer that such works affect, in some ways, large numbers of people; by selecting influential or culturally valued works, the researcher can assume that they represent important aspects of the culture under study.

Content analysis is generally undertaken to test some hypothesis or assumption. Thus the content must be representative of some universe for which a population can be defined and a sample drawn. The content analyses offered below range from legal briefs submitted to the Supreme Court, to the lyrics of rock music, to dramatic prime-time television programs, to family portraits. In each study we will consider the problem posed, the method of coding, the sample drawn, and the types of analyses brought to bear on the data.

FOUR EXAMPLES OF CONTENT ANALYSES

Violence on Television

One controversial subject of social research over the past 20 years has been violence on television and whether this prevalent phenomenon is related to aggressive behavior. In order to do such research, investigators must study the content of television programs to search for the presence and the degree of violence in them. One of the best-known researchers in this hotly contested field is George Gerbner of the Annenberg School of Communication at the University of Pennsylvania. Gerbner's analyses are based on content analyses of television programs.

The programs are videotaped, and then coders analyze the programs searching for a number of qualities. *Prevalence* is the incidence of violence in any program (P). The abbreviation %P is the percentage of programs with violence. *Rate* is the number of "violent episodes" occurring in each program (R/P) and each hour (R/H). *Role* is a measure of characters as "violent" (that is, committing violence) or "victims" (subjected to violence); "killers" or "killed" (1978, p. 181).

From these data, two scores are produced: the *program score,* based on prevalence and rate of violence; and the *character score,* based on the role measures. The *violence index* is then determined by the sum of the *program score* and the *character score.* This explanation has not been as detailed as it would need to be for you to comprehend it fully; the purpose here is to give you some idea of what can be done in a content analysis of television programs. (For more detailed descriptions, see Gerbner et al., 1978, 1980.)

Since 1967, when Gerbner and his colleagues began presenting their Violence Index, showing which types of programs, time slots, and networks feature the most violent shows, the controversy about how violence on TV is measured and what its effects are has increased. For example, Gerbner codes violence as "the overt expression of physical force (with or without a weapon, against self or others) compelling action against one's will on pain of being hurt and/or killed or threatened to be so victimized as part of the plot" (1980, p. 11). This leaves out simple threats, abusive language, and gestures that have no clear violent consequences. However, it includes "natural" and "accidental" violence and violence in comedy or fantasy shows. Some researchers have criticized the inclusion of violence in comedy or fantasy, as well as natural and accidental violence in studies of TV violence (Wurtzel and Lometti, 1984), though Gerbner and his colleagues defend their method (Chaffee, Gerbner, et al., 1984).

Box 10-2 offers a content analysis of violence and sex in advertisements for television programs; this is another way to use content analysis to study the media.

Legal Briefs Submitted to the Supreme Court

In a study of the relationship of the content of legal briefs to the decision-making process of the Supreme Court, Bannan (1984) wanted to show that justices were not affected solely by their ideological positions, but also by the amount and range of legal and other types of evidence brought to

BOX 10-2

ANALYZING THE SEX AND VIOLENCE CONTENT OF ADVERTISEMENTS IN *TV GUIDE*

In a content analysis of the words and images used in advertisements for television programs in *TV Guide,* Williams counted overt visual portrayals and verbal referents to physical violence and sexual behavior. First he selected a sample of issues of *TV Guide* from 1980 to 1985; then he defined the range of verbal referents ("Jessica plays cat and mouse with devious killer!," or "Blackmail in a sex clinic . . . ladies expose their sex lives to uncover vicious criminal") and visual presentations (characters pointing guns, or individuals dressed in swimwear, lingerie, and other revealing clothing) for violence and sex. TV ads were also coded for program type, time slot, network, and size of ad. The analysis related qualities of the advertisements to the ratings of the programs and found "that sex and violence do have a positive impact on a program's rating" (1989, p. 973).

Source: Gilbert A. Williams, "Enticing Viewers: Sex and Violence in *TV Guide* Program Advertisements," *Journalism Quarterly,* **66**:970–973, 1989.

bear in specific cases. She contrasted the legal briefs for the petitioners with the briefs for the respondents in 37 cases brought before the Supreme Court over the "right of counsel to the indigent"— a right guaranteed by the Sixth Amendment to the U.S. Constitution. The petitioners in every case were very poor individuals who had been pleading the illegality of a decision of a lower court on the grounds that they had not been given counsel (which means that they had not been provided with the services of a lawyer). In short, Bannan had selected a sample of Supreme Court cases on the basis of the type of constitutional right being challenged.

For each case, the number of *assertions* (arguments in favor of the legal position) and the number of *supports* for these assertions were estimated. In addition, the "content" of these supports was coded according to its source (official authorities such as constitutions, statutes; unofficial authorities such as social science surveys and law journal articles). From this a cumulative score was derived for the petitioner and for the respondent. Bannan sought to measure both the quantity and range of types of supporting evidence offered, to test the expectation that the legal brief with the superior "cumulative score" would "win" the Supreme Court decision. This proved to be the case in 33 of the 37 cases.

Family Portraits Reflect Family Relationships

In a study of the relationships in families across generations, Fischer (1978) examined the content of 30 American family portraits from 1729 to 1871. Before 1775, all the portraits but one had the father placed above the other family members, the mother seated, possibly with other female adult members of the family below, and the children below the mother. After 1775, this vertical arrangement suggesting the patriarchical role of the father and the hierarchical role of parents over children was superseded by a horizontal arrangement in which all family members were painted on

the same level. Comparing these earlier family portraits with the more contemporary, Fischer found that the horizontal arrangement suggesting more egalitarian roles in the family was superseded in the twentieth century with greater variation in arrangements, in some cases with the children placed above the parents.

Courtship Patterns in Song Lyrics

A number of content analysis studies have taken as their subject the lyrics of popular songs. In a study comparing the changes in the courtship pattern from the 1950s to the 1960s, Carey (1969) drew a sample of songs from the 1960s to compare with an analysis carried out by Horton (1957) a decade before. Following the sampling technique of Horton, Carey selected songs listed in four magazines (*Hit Parader, Song Hits Magazine,* etc.) over two summer months in 1966, identical to the ones Horton had used for his selection in 1955. In addition, the *Billboard* listings of the top 30 songs as well as the top 30 from a San Francisco radio station were also included. This produced a sample of 227 songs including rock and roll (about 52 percent), rhythm and blues, country western, and other types.

Horton had worked out a four-stage courtship pattern which Carey labeled as the courtship stage (or period of "active search"), the honeymoon stage (that is, the "happy stage"), the downward course (the "breakup"), and the isolation stage (where the protagonist was "all alone"). Carey not only examines the number of songs relating to each stage, but also carefully considers the meaning of the content of the lyrics of each type. One quality that Carey found in songs addressing the first stage was that "romantic involvement is not a necessary ingredient" (p. 726). The song "You Don't Have to Say You Love Me" by Dusty Springfield expresses this mood. At the other end of the courtship stage, Carey offered Neil Diamond's "Solitary Man" as an example of a young man's acceptance of isolation. The box presents some lyrics from both songs.

**THE LYRICS OF DUSTY SPRINGFIELD
AND NEIL DIAMOND**

You Don't Have to Say You Love Me

*You don't have to say you love me,
Just be close at hand.
You don't have to stay forever,
I will understand.*

Solitary Man

*Don't know that I will but until I can find me
A girl who'll stay and won't play games
   behind me
I'll be what I am,
A solitary man*

Source: James T. Carey, "Changing Courtship Patterns in the Popular Song," *American Journal of Sociology,* **74**:720–731, 1969, p. 728

From examining such lyrics Carey concluded that there was a reduction in romantic courtship in the 1960s. Springfield's song suggests that relationships can be temporary and lacking in commitment. A commitment to "establishing one's own identity" (p. 728) outside of a relationship and that perhaps the end of a love affair fosters such self-strengthening seems to be the message of Diamond's lyrics. By examining the changing content of lyrics across a decade, Carey had highlighted some of the important changes in social values and interpersonal goals that differentiated the 1960s from the 1950s.

COMPONENTS OF A CONTENT ANALYSIS

Selection of the Content and the Topic

In a content analysis, the selection of the topic must be closely coordinated with the selection of the content to be analyzed. It is desirable to begin with a specific research question and then select a body of material in which this question can be

pursued. There should be some logic to the choice of the content to be studied. Often that logic is obvious: one clear way to study violence on television is to examine the contents of television programming. In other cases, a researcher may select a body of material to study among a number that might have been as useful.

Sometimes, the content seems to create its own research finding, such as the family portraits which show changes in portrait positions that seem to indicate social changes in family positions. Working on the content may refine the research topic as it develops.

Sampling from the Body of Content

When the volume of material available for the study is great, it will be necessary to sample content for the analysis. Of course, the sample design must provide for representativeness. Methods of organizing the content according to some characteristics (for example, by year of publication) might be utilized to create a stratified sample. Once the sampling units are considered equivalent (for example, in the case of a set of documents, each is as desirable to bring into the sample as any other), then the use of a random number table or systematic sampling methods would achieve a representative sample. (Review the sampling strategies in Chapter 6.)

Uncovering the Meaning of the Content

The usual strategy in content analysis is to "describe the attributes of messages, without reference to either the intentions of the sender (encoding process) or the effect of the message upon those to whom it is directed (decoding process)" (Holsti, 1969, p. 27). Often the researcher compares documents generated from a single source. The researcher may focus on two or more variables, looking for them in one or more documents. He or she may use a deductive approach to test hypotheses. A set of documents can also be the basis for an inductive examination. For example, Holsti suggests that the coverage of foreign news in a set of newspapers could be analyzed to develop an index of foreign news coverage, which could then serve as a standard against which to study a particular newspaper (1969, p. 31). Finally, a researcher might use some standard developed by experts in evaluating the content of a set of documents or messages. For example, a group of physicians could set up standards for reporting on a certain disease, let's say AIDS. Then a set of radio broadcasts on AIDS could be analyzed in terms of these standards.

Developing a Scheme to Code the Content

There are as many ways to process the content and to break it down and recombine it into categories of meaning as there are researchers out there to devise them. However coding is devised, it is important to have the coders adequately trained. Each must understand what needs to be looked for, and how it is to be recorded. Each must share with every other coder a common understanding of what the content consists of. This issue of reliability is of critical concern in content analyses. The examples given offer a number of the types of qualities of such codes.

Frequency. One commonly used way to sort out the content of material is to count certain patterns which recur in the content. This was the case in the television violence study where incidents of violence of various types were recorded and cumulated.

Amount. Closely related to frequency of appearance is the amount of each content piece which contains a particular quality. This may be measured in time (for television) and in space (for written material).

Presence or Absence of a Quality. Another way to study the content of a communication source is to look for specific qualities to see how far they are present or absent in each work examined. In the portrait study, it was important to determine whether the father had a dominant position in the painting.

Typology. Another common feature of content analyses is to sort the contents by types. In the popular song study, types of courtship patterns were looked for.

Origin or Source. Sometimes the object is to establish who or what is responsible for a particular aspect of the content. In the Supreme Court study, the sources of support given for an assertion were categorized and recorded.

Degree of Intensity. Content may also be differentiated by how strongly certain elements are present. For example, sexual explicitness in films could be measured in this way.

Analyzing the Coded Content

Once you have coded the content, you need to relate it to your research question. Tables and graphs are often used to present the aggregated patterns in the data. The interpretation of what these patterns mean is the essence of content analysis. If that cannot be done effectively, then all one has is a description of material. The social significance of the study must be inferred from the patterns developed. Remember, however, that the ways in which you sort the content will also determine what you have to analyze. Thus, there is a back-and-forth strategy between devising the coding schemes and figuring out what findings you will produce with the various schemes. What may seem like very fruitful coding strategies may not lead to interesting findings with your body of content. You may then need to alter the coding schemes to characterize evidence that seems to be interesting. Remember that, as in all data analyses, you need variation to have important findings. Ideas for analytic approaches and the types of tables and graphs which might best exemplify your data can be borrowed from others, or you can use an idea seen in one study and then elaborate upon it yourself.

Issues of Validity and Reliability

Content analysis needs to be subjected as well to considerations of whether the method devised is valid and reliable. To increase validity, a careful balance between the content being studied and the questions being asked needs to be considered. Does the content address the problem being studied? Will the coding scheme devised for the content fairly extract the meaning from the content data? This need to get at the specific contents that interest the researcher often requires complex coding and analysis.

Because of the complexity of the coding schemes, the reliability between different coders may not be high. Even a single coder may have trouble remaining consistent in coding data with a complex coding plan. This is a major challenge in content analysis: to devise ways of coding content that are reliable (that would lead to similar results if carried out at different times and by different coders) and to select and use content in ways that are valid (that produce analyses of content that correspondingly address the study's subject).

DECIDING IF CONTENT ANALYSIS IS APPROPRIATE FOR YOUR TOPIC

Content analysis might be the best method for you to use if your problem can be addressed by a study of patterns in various forms of communication. Studies using content analysis often seek to understand cultural values and broad social perspectives as portrayed in the media. The method also allows for studies with varying time dimensions by the examination of a form of media over a selected time span. At times you might have access to a fascinating collection of material. Your college library or some other institution in your immediate area may have an extensive collection of comic books, the complete series of a certain magazine, school textbooks in a particular field, films by a specific director, or the collected letters of some famous person. Such a source may prompt you to create a study in which one of these resources might be used. However, keep in mind that content analysis needs a theoretical framework. It can be an excellent method for testing hypotheses or inductively developing standards.

Content analysis almost always requires developing a somewhat ingenious means of sorting and coding the content to be studied. While coding will be discussed in greater depth in Chapter 12, the ability to handle detailed material carefully and systematically is essential for content analysis.

Content analysis as a method is perhaps the most distant from field research. Rather than going out into a social field to find data, the researcher defines a body of communication as the "social field" and looks within that set of material for descriptive qualities that can be quantified. Thus, content analysis lacks the spontaneity and unplanned qualities of field research. Rather it is a heavily planned method, where the researcher carefully organizes and orchestrates how the data will be treated. Because content analysis uses available forms of communication, it does not intrude on a social environment as is characteristic of field research. It is unobtrusive. In the next section, we will examine the study of other unobtrusive measures.

In many ways, the work of content analysts is also similar to that of historians. In both cases, written materials are usually of central concern. What is specific to content analysis is that quantitative aspects of the communication are central, and the historical chronology of the period is not; in history, on the other hand, interpretation of the deeper meaning of written materials and artifacts is generally sought in relation to the historical period in which they occurred. We will examine historical research following the discussion of unobtrusive measures.

UNOBTRUSIVE MEASURES

In 1966, a book *Unobtrusive Measures: Nonreactive Research in the Social Sciences* was published. Its team of authors, Eugene Webb, Donald T. Campbell, Richard D. Schwartz, and Lee Sechrest, were social psychologists whose stated goal was "not to replace the interview but to supplement and cross-validate it with measures that do not require the cooperation of a respondent and that do not themselves contaminate the response" (1966, p. 2). Earlier (in the chapter on survey research) we discussed the problems of gaining cooperation of respondents and keeping them committed to completing questionnaires and interviews. In discussing experimental studies, I addressed the problems of demand characteristics (where the subjects in an experiment are affected by what they think the experimenter wants from them) and also of the Hawthorne effect (where the occurrence of an experiment, even if it offers what would seem to be a meaningless or negative experimental stimulus, may itself produce an experimental effect). In field studies, too, the researcher needs to consider carefully how her or his role in the field may alter the actual field environment being studied.

The study of *unobtrusive measures* was devised to avoid such problems. As Webb and his colleagues stressed in their influential book, this approach developed as a supplementary method, one that would add to a study and help validate its findings. Another reason for the development of unobtrusive measures as a method was to avoid certain ethical issues. To study a subject unobtrusively is to avoid infringing on anyone else's privacy. As explained in Chapter 3, there are many research strategies that encroach on private aspects of the lives of individuals.

In 1979, one of the authors of the original volume, Lee Sechrest, edited a volume on unobtrusive measurement in which updated studies were described. The editor noted that although the original book by Webb and his colleagues had been very widely read, the actual use of unobtrusive

measurement by social researchers was not great. In what follows, the most influential type of unobtrusive measures delineated in the 1966 volume will be discussed.

TYPES OF UNOBTRUSIVE MEASURES

Webb and his associates defined three broad categories of unobtrusive measures: physical traces, archives, and observations. Here we will consider only the study of *physical traces* as representing a rather unique form of research method which researchers might be able to include in a project.

Physical Traces

Measures of erosion and accretion are certainly the most familiar types of unobtrusive measures. The initial example for an *erosion measure* was in a study of the popularity of various exhibits at Chicago's Museum of Science and Industry. Rather than survey visitors or even observe the size of crowds around various exhibits, the researchers studied the wear and tear on the vinyl tiles surrounding various exhibits. They found, for example, that the tiles around the chick-hatching exhibit wore out very quickly (they needed to be replaced about every six weeks) (Webb et al., 1966, p. 36).

Other erosion examples include the wear on library books (as a measure of their popularity). Obviously, a researcher could determine a book's popularity by checking the library records to see how frequently it had been taken out. In this case, study of the erosion of books would be a way to cross-validate the popularity of the book and suggest that the book was being held and read, not just taken out and left on a shelf! It is also a way to study the use of reference works which are not checked out of libraries (Webb et al., 1966, pp. 37–38).

The most commonly studied *accretion measure*, that is, a measure of something that has been laid down or built up, is garbage. Consumer behavior (such as the use of diet foods) has been analyzed by studying garbage. For example, the weight, volume, and nature of the food consumed can be determined by this method (Rathje, 1979, p. 77). Analyzing garbage in this way is unobtrusive because it has no effect on the producers of the garbage. Other commonly studied accretion measures are graffiti and household possessions.

Webb and his colleagues (1966) also differentiate between *natural* erosion or accretion measures and *controlled* measures. Natural measures are those which occur without any interference by the researcher (all measures described above would be of this type). Examples of *controlled erosion measures* offered by Webb et al. include a before-and-after measure of the wear on children's shoes or having children wear special wristwatches to record their level of activity (1966, p. 43). *Controlled accretion measures* would include such researcher-intrusive strategies as were used in a study of how carefully advertisements were read in a magazine. In one study, small glue spots were used which would not stick together again once the pages were opened (Webb et al., 1966, pp. 44–45). By this means it was possible to tell whether readers had looked at various ads. In short, controlled erosion and accretion measures involve some form of pretest-posttest design or manipulated act by the researcher.

Issues of Validity and Reliability

The primary purpose of unobtrusive measures is to serve as a supplementary, not a primary, source of data. To the degree that unobtrusive measures offer additional means for supporting (or refuting) conclusions drawn from other forms of data, they increase the validity of a study. Recall that there are two forms of validity: internal and external. To the degree that data based on unobtrusive measures from the same subject of study add to other forms of evidence, they help to establish the internal validity of the study. In other words, they provide additional evidence that what was found actually exists.

But unobtrusive measures can also add to the external validity of a study by providing additional evidence that may make findings from one situation applicable to other situations. In short, unobtrusive measures may help to increase the generalizability of a study's findings. Recall from Chapter 6 that using multiple measures tends to reduce the influence of errors occurring in any one measure.

DECIDING IF UNOBTRUSIVE MEASURES ARE APPROPRIATE FOR YOUR TOPIC

If you are carrying out a study using records or other archival resources or if you plan an observational study where you will in no way participate in the field or be known to those in the field, you will be using unobtrusive measures. The unfamiliar types of research suggested by this method are the erosion and accretion measures. If such measures can be devised and used in a project you plan, they may well strengthen your research effort. Erosion and accretion measures tend to be novel and often easy to utilize, but they may not be easy to devise.

One might make the case that a study based on unobtrusive measures is a good choice for someone who is shy since the researcher would not need to confront the subjects being studied. However, it takes a good deal of creative effort to devise such measures and an equal amount of systematic effort to measure them accurately and precisely. This is why it is not a good method for the casual researcher. Think about your topic carefully before deciding whether it can be studied unobtrusively.

HISTORICAL STUDIES

All studies of extant (that is, already collected) data are historical to some degree, because they are based on evidence from and about the past. Historical research, however, is not merely defined as studying anything from the past. It also implies certain methods and points of view that historians bring to the study of material from the past. This section will offer a few general considerations about historical method and present two examples of historical studies of varying types.

History usually refers simply to an account of the past of human societies. Since that is such a vast subject that it can never be recounted, what history consists of is the study of what "can be known . . . [to the historian] . . . through the surviving record." It is what the late historian Louis Gottschalk referred to as *history as record.* This he differentiated from "the whole history of the past (what has been called *history as actuality*)" (1950, p. 45).

"The process of critically examining and analyzing the records and survivals of the past is . . . called *historical method.* The imaginative reconstruction of the past from the data derived by that process is called *historiography* (the writing of history)" (Gottschalk, 1950, p. 48). Historical writing always involves a *re-creation* of the past, not a *creation;* Gottschalk stresses, "These limits distinguish history from fiction, poetry, drama, and fantasy" (1950, p. 49). It is this blending of the study of written records with an interpretation of these materials in the light of other evidence and with the historian's own imagination that produces history.

Let me add at this point that there is currently great interest in *oral history,* that is, history based on verbal accounts instead of written records. It is considered especially useful in the study of historical crises of great magnitude and cultural traditions that seem to be disappearing where the likelihood of finding adequate written records is not considered high. An example would be oral materials from the survivors of World War II concentration camps, recollections of black Americans about what their ancestors related to them about life under slavery, or the experiences of various ethnic communities in the United States.

Written records are, nevertheless, the central sources of data for historians. These sources are generally differentiated into two categories: *primary sources,* which are the records of eyewitnesses to events, and *secondary sources,* which

are written materials which describe and/or interpret some past event either close to the time it occurred or in later years. Naturally, historians are particularly fond of primary sources because such materials would seem to be more accurate and less biased. Yet Gottschalk warns that all historical sources, whether primary or secondary, are written from a particular point of view and therefore organize the past according to certain principles. What the historian must do is to take these materials and try to "get as close an approximation to the truth about the past as constant correction of the mental images will allow, at the same time recognizing that that truth has in fact eluded him forever" (Gottschalk, 1950, p. 47). "In short, the historian's aim is *verisimilitude* with regard to a perished past" (1950, p. 47).

Historical work thus generally centers around the study of written materials. These may be *archival material,* such as records, letters, diaries, or handwritten manuscripts; or printed books, pamphlets, or periodicals. Thus the historian must go to where these materials are, namely, the library, the archives, the museums, the government records office, wherever there are materials relevant to the historian's topic.

For this reason, historical research generally starts with searching for relevant sources and reading very broadly. Some historians will go directly to the archives to search for the surviving records pertinent to their subject; others will read widely in secondary sources about the period under study. One historian related to me that he had been told as a graduate student to go to a large research library and read everything, every written thing in that library, on his general subject. Of course, this is exaggerated advice. Historians cannot read everything in a field, and they don't wait until they have read everything to define a problem. However, it is certainly true that historians would tend to read more widely and deeply about a general topic than might other social researchers. This is at least in part because they tend to be *contextualists;* that is, they try to relate the phenomena they are studying to as many aspects of social life as possible.

Consider the differences between the historical method and that of other types of social research which we have so far presented. The historical approach is somewhat like the approach of field researchers in that its object is usually not to isolate a narrow research topic, a hypothesis to test. Instead the historian tends to put together a multiplicity of contexts, to search for a whole set of reasons why an event occurred. Like field researchers, historians move into a field in search of a richer description of the historical era, the social environment, the material examined. Rather than observing and interviewing the inhabitants of the field, however, the historian must read about this field. One of the objects of this reading of materials from the past is to determine the chronology of events, to understand how the chronological order of events has affected later events.

TWO HISTORICAL RESEARCH STUDIES

The examples to be described here have been chosen in order to show you differences in the foci and in the sorts of evidence used in carrying out historical studies. In terms of focus, a historical study can be very broad and address an entire society or institution over an extended period of years, or it can be very narrow and address the life of a single individual or a single event. The former would be a *macro-level historical* view, the latter a *micro-level historical* focus. The evidence used to prepare the study may be drawn from a wide range of written materials, or it may consist of a very small number of documents (or a single document); conversely, it may be based on quantifiable data from the past which may need to be reexamined or, in some cases, created from other sources of information. The examples have been selected to present a contrast in breadth of focus. The author of the first study is a sociologist; the author of the second study is a historian.

The History of American Journalism

Michael Schudson (1978), a sociologist, wrote a social history of the development of journalism in

the United States. His particular interest was to explore the extent to which the ideal value of objectivity was realized and altered by comparing newspapers of early nineteenth-century America with those of the present day. Schudson's sources are varied. He refers to the large body of previous studies on American journalism, biographies of important American journalists, appraisals of American newspapers by journalists, and newspaper articles, as well as theoretical writings which address ideas of relevance to Schudson's analysis. He also includes some quantifiable evidence on the circulation and price of papers, but such incidental information is used only to fill in details of the broad picture he draws of this central cultural institution.

This type of historical work is both selectively descriptive and analytic. Schudson describes certain newspapers and certain journalists more fully—those which best represent the institution he is studying and those who best exemplify the case he is trying to make. There is no attempt here to select examples representative of the population of all newspapers in the United States. Instead, by examining the changing structure of certain influential American newspapers as institutions and the changing occupational roles of particular journalists, Schudson shows that the value of objectivity which influenced American journalism both reflected and affected the wider values in American society. The belief in the "facts," the relationship of journalism to public relations and propaganda, the growing skepticism about the ability to present the facts objectively—these valuative changes in American journalism are the findings of Schudson's research.

A Case of Adultery in Sixteenth-Century France

If Schudson's focus is broad and comprehensive and his sources varied, Natalie Davis's (1983) history of the "return of Martin Guerre" rests on a single legal case from sixteenth-century France which was decided by a court of appeals in the city of Toulouse. The case can be stated simply. A certain Martin Guerre abandoned his wife and son in 1548. In 1556 he reappeared (from his travels and the wars) and was reunited with his wife. Subsequently he and his wife had a daughter. A few years later, he quarreled with his uncle over his desire to sell some property. The uncle, having heard rumors to the effect that the man who returned was not actually Martin Guerre, challenged the identity of Martin.

The trial that ensued was quite fascinating. In the first trial in a local court, the wife stood by her husband, as did many other witnesses; but others challenged his identity (like the shoemaker who claimed that the earlier Martin had had smaller feet!). The defendant was declared guilty of impersonating Martin Guerre and abusing his wife. The case was appealed to the court in Toulouse. During the second trial, the "real" Martin Guerre returned. Even with this appearance, many of the witnesses (including Martin's four sisters) still claimed that the first man to return was the true Martin Guerre. But now the wife, confronted with both men, recognized her real husband. The imposter was hanged.

Why would a single legal case 400 years old be of interest currently? Because of the strange occurrence surrounding the case, a wide range of evidence was gathered about the nature of Martin's marriage, family relationships, economic and social condition, and reasons for abandoning his wife. Much information was also gathered about the situation and motivation of the imposter. All this information brings to light the quality of life in a peasant village in sixteenth-century France. What is probably of greater interest, however, for an audience in the late twentieth century is what the story indicates about the meaning of marriage and the meaning of male-female relationships and heterosexuality 400 years ago. The most intriguing part of the study is not why the first Martin left or even why the second Martin chose to take on his role, but why the wife accepted the deception. What was her motivation? Here the story of the prepuberty marriage of the couple, of Martin's

early impotence, of the quality of the relationship between the wife and the second Martin suggests something of the true feelings and sexual needs of this woman of so long ago.

But this case not only speaks to the meaning of sexuality in the sixteenth century; it can also be related to other important social developments of that era. Most notably, Davis relates the willingness of the wife to accept an imposter in the place of her long-absent husband to the growing influence of Protestantism in this section of southwest France. For in the newly developed Protestant city of Geneva, an abandoned wife could, after a few years, divorce her husband and remarry—a right not recognized in Catholic France.

In the absence of the actual trial records, there are only two historical sources of information about this case. The *primary source* is that written by Jean de Coras, one of the judges in the Toulouse court, who, following the trial, wrote the account of the case into a book. Davis describes Coras' book as combining a legal case with a literary moral tale (p. 4). The other source, a *secondary source,* is a short history published, like Coras' account, in 1561, written by someone who was not present at the trial. From this scant evidence, enriched with a study of related archival materials and readings about peasant life in that period and with visits to the current village and area, Davis was able to develop a historical account of such modern interest that it became the basis of a feature film.

COMPARING THE TWO STUDIES

These two historical studies indicate the different roles that historical records may play in historical writing. Schudson began with a research question and then found written records to address his question. (Schudson used newspapers mainly, but other materials as well.) Davis began with a single curious record and then asked what that record could tell her about the period in which it was written.

Yet each of these researchers had to figure out the way in which the record was produced and the point of view from which it was written. Schudson read the early American newspapers not to find out what happened at the time, but to uncover in the way that the events were written the newspaper reporters' beliefs about the value of objectivity. In short, Schudson asked, "What does the manner in which newspaper pieces are written over a period of time tell me about the changing values of the reporters who wrote these articles, about the profession of journalism which they were creating, and about the role of newspapers in American society?" Davis had to read her case, first, to question the assumptions of the man who wrote it and, second, to consider what in fact was being said about the meaning of marriage and heterosexual relations in sixteenth-century France.

COMPONENTS OF HISTORICAL RESEARCH

Defining a Problem of Study from the Past

If the problem you select is to understand more clearly an event, an institution, a city, a person, or a group from some earlier period, then you will carry out a historical study. The topic will need to be defined in terms of the types of written materials and other resources (artifacts, individuals to interview) available to you. Part of the historical research may be to determine what materials are available on your topic. In other instances, a set of available materials may trigger the study in the first place, and the specific topic may therefore be more narrowly defined once you know what materials you plan to use.

Establishing and Collecting Sources of Evidence

Whatever the period of time selected, historical research generally requires an appreciation not only of the specific topic, but also of the period in which it occurred. For this reason, historians generally read widely in secondary sources, including other histories of the period they are studying, in order to increase their familiarity with the period. Good university and college libraries tend to have a great deal of secondary source material on modern historical periods in America and Europe. Your library is also likely to have materials on earlier periods and nonwestern societies. For extensive materials on a subject, however, you may need to go to a large research library or a library with extensive holdings on a specific subject. In short, libraries are the obvious place to find secondary sources. Keep in mind that historical work on a specific topic continues to be done. For example, if one selects the history of slavery in the United States, historical interpretations of this institution written while slavery was still legal in the United States, after its abolition, and continuing right up to the present time are available.

Consider also the primary sources. There were accounts of slaves, in the form of diaries, letters, etc. (though because most slaves were illiterate, most could not write). Thus the written records of slaves tend to be from somewhat unusual slaves—those who had been taught to read and write or who had run away. There were also written accounts by those who held slaves (mistresses' diaries) as well as records of the slave trade and records of the slaves of particular plantations: their numbers, their roles, their births, their deaths. Various forms of unwritten records—stories, songs, and tales passed down—form the basis of oral historical material on slavery in America. Finally, artifacts bearing witness to certain practices still exist.

No researcher can examine all the material available. How to select the best sources is important for historical work. You need in some sense to draw up a sample of sources that you feel would represent what you must look at in order to generalize more widely. Since in historical research the full "population" of what is available can never be known, the sample of materials examined must always be a purposive one. What it represents and what it fails to represent should be considered.

Developing Means to Quantify Evidence

Some historical studies include data that may be quantified, such as marriage records. When this is the case, the presentation of the quantifiable data is often made in tables. Usually the forms of quantitative analysis need to be quite simple in historical studies because the data often include many missing elements and the determination of what population the data represent is usually very difficult to make.

Historical Writing

The quality of writing in historical work is of great importance. Ideas and materials must be *synthesized* into a historical narrative that is rich in content and clear in meaning. This is not to say that writing style is irrelevant in other forms of social research. But surveys and experiments, for example, have a kind of formal structure that must be followed, which helps to organize the form of written presentation. In historical work, the structure of the study is usually set out less precisely; rather, the work builds and develops out of varied types of sources.

Issues of Validity and Reliability in Historical Studies

There can be serious challenges to the validity of documents. Recall a few years past that a supposed diary of Hitler turned up; it was examined by historians and deemed to be authentic (in short, it had face validity), but later it was determined to be a hoax. Historians must be attentive to the authenticity of documents and written records which they use. Not only may documents and written records be false, but they may also be highly biased. Historical research must consider historical materials in a broad enough context so that a fair re-creation can be made.

Historians often study subjects that have previously been studied by others. However, a complete replication is virtually impossible to do. Be-

cause historical research involves so much choice along the way as to what to look at and what to ignore, and because there is so strong a need to synthesize the material and put it into a framework, one historian cannot replicate another historian's research design. However, it is very common for subjects of historical interest to be studied over and over again. In each case, the later researchers are expected to be fully conversant with the work of the earlier historians. Thus, while reliability cannot be tested as in an experiment, historical research (both the selection and interpretation of historical material) should be done and documented with great care so that another historian could build another study upon it.

DECIDING IF HISTORICAL RESEARCH IS APPROPRIATE FOR YOUR TOPIC

If you are studying a topic from the past or if you are beginning in a much earlier era and tracing the course of events or developments over time, you will need to use historical methods. Remember that looking at historical material is not the same as looking at current material. You need a strong foundation of knowledge about the period in which the material was written in order to understand the material itself. If you are planning to look at records from the nineteenth century, you should first read broadly about the subject you are studying in that century. What this means is that a great deal of concern must be centered in getting yourself grounded in the field you are studying. You must also make sure that you can get the materials you need. Historians often have to travel to where the actual written materials are available (a library or an archive). Social researchers surely should not avoid historical research. If the subject you want to study is from the past, you will need to become a historian.

THE ANALYSIS OF EXISTING STATISTICS

The analysis of *existing statistics*—that is, statistical data that has already been prepared and reported—is similar to secondary analyses in that the data are already collected, but rather than providing the second researcher raw data to be analyzed, the researcher using existing statistics has "created" data. This is both an advantage and a disadvantage. Existing statistics generally report on large aggregate datasets which might be very time-consuming and difficult for a researcher to prepare on his or her own. Such statistics are often drawn from the census or other very large-scale data-gathering operations. As such, the use of these statistics offers high-quality evidence to a researcher. However, since these statistics are already analyzed, it is often not possible for the second researcher to alter them to suit the new study. Instead, they must often be used as they appear.

One widely used type of study on the analysis of existing statistics is the social indicators study. This will be discussed in Chapter 11 on evaluation research. Here I would like to give you a few examples of how aggregated data have been used by others and suggest how you might use them as the basis of a study or as supporting data in a study.

The wealth of data regularly collected by the government and by other bodies and published in the form of statistics allows for a great range of potential analyses. This form of analysis is used mainly to compare rates of major social factors between large conglomerates, such as nations (for example, rates dealing with health, crime, prosperity), or to compare changes over time using the same indicators as a form of trend analysis. Government planning and decision making may depend on these forms of analysis, and various branches of the U.S. government prepare these forms of statistics regularly.

A Research Project Based on Existing Statistics

Cantor and Land (1985) wanted to understand the relationship between unemployment and crime. They began their work by using existing statistics on the level of unemployment in the United States, and they related these to the level of crime. The

hypothesis that these two factors should be related has been claimed widely and over a very long period of time (1985, p. 317). However, the authors contend that because of the types of quantitative analyses used and the failure to control for certain confounding measures (such as changes in the age structure over time), little of the past research can validly be used to support or refute this relationship. For example, since both crime and unemployment rates are higher for young people, both tend to rise as the proportion of young people in the population increases. It is therefore important to control for this increase.

In a quite sophisticated analysis (which is characteristic of many studies based on existing statistics appearing in the journals), Cantor and Land show that the unemployment rate affected the rates of five of the seven crimes they studied. They used existing statistics on unemployment from the U.S. Department of Labor for the period 1946–1979 and from the Executive Office of the President for the years 1980–1982 (U.S. Department of Labor, 1980). The crime statistics were drawn from U.S. Department of Justice's *Uniform Crime Reporting Handbook* prepared by the FBI (1980), and from studies of criminal victimization in the United States (U.S. Department of Justice, 1981), as well as from the Office of Management and Budget's 1973 publication *Social Indicators.*

Cantor and Land found that unemployment was associated in some of the analyses with increases in certain crimes, and in other analyses with decreases. They stress that this is not surprising given that unemployment may affect crime on the one hand by weakening opportunities for crime (unemployed people are more likely to be at home in a more guarded environment, and also less likely to have access to many settings and activities where crime may be initiated) and on the other hand by strengthening the motivations for crime (particularly property crimes) (1985, pp. 320–321).

Analyses such as Cantor and Land's are built on highly complex analytic models. However, existing statistics may be incorporated into a wide range of studies as corroborating evidence. In this way, they can be quite easily used by anyone carrying out social research. Below I describe my use of a number of existing statistics for a paper I once prepared.

Using Existing Statistics

As a researcher, you may want to incorporate *aggregate data* into your studies or to use sets of aggregate data as the basis of a new analysis. Let me give you an example of how I used current data on the status of American women. In the summer of 1983, I was preparing to attend the Australia/New Zealand Sociological Meetings in Melbourne. I had offered to give a paper on my current research, but the organizer said he preferred that I give a more general talk on the status of American women after the defeat of the Equal Rights Amendment (ERA). Such a paper would, like most papers, need a theoretical argument and some evidence. In terms of data, I needed to show how the conditions of American women had changed from before 1973 (when the ERA was first passed by Congress) until 1982, when the time to gain the necessary two-thirds support of the states for ratification had run out. Since the ERA broadly addressed the social role of women, I needed aggregate statistical evidence on how the role of women had changed in the United States during that precise period of time.

Such data are widely available. The U.S. Bureau of Labor Statistics regularly publishes aggregate data describing the work status of women. These data are presented in relation to other factors such as marital status, presence of children, educational attainment, age, race, etc. Many of the tables compare the labor force participation rates, unemployment rates, income, or other work measures across a period of years so that changes over time can be seen. The bureau publishes monthly reports, compiles special reports, and contributes data to various other statistical abstracts, so these materials are readily available in most libraries. Because I wanted the most recent data possible, I

went directly to the office of the Bureau of Labor Statistics in Chicago (where I then lived). Most of the existing statistical data I used came from this bureau.

The remaining statistical data I needed, such as marital status, childbearing, and head-of-household information, came largely from *Current Population Reports* from the U.S. Census Bureau. Data on the estimated number of legal abortions were available in the Census Bureau's *Statistical Abstract of the United States* and had been gathered by a private institute. With these data I was able to write a section in my paper entitled "A Statistical Portrait of American Women in the 1980s."

COMPONENTS OF AN ANALYSIS OF EXISTING STATISTICS

Determining the Problem

Many research problems require large sets of aggregate data in order to be addressed. Any question that concerns a national trend about a social phenomenon requires such data. Has there been an increase in drug addiction in the United States? Are there more automobile accident fatalities in states where the drinking age is lower? Has cycling become a more popular sport among adults? Questions such as these may be of interest to various bodies. Data on drug addiction might interest social welfare workers, law enforcement agencies, and health planners. Politicians and policymakers are concerned with the drinking-driving relationship, as are the liquor and automobile industries. Cycling trends are of interest to bicycle manufacturers, to sporting goods stores, and to people and organizations who offer services or support physical fitness. Note that existing statistics from aggregate data may be used to evaluate changes that have occurred (they may be the basis of an evaluation research project as we shall refer to it in Chapter 11); but they may also merely monitor change or stability.

If you have a problem which might be addressed by an aggregate data source, you must carefully consider the types of statistical evidence that could speak to it. Remember how I used data on changes in employment rates, on employment rates in relation to marriage and childbearing, and on fertility rates and income data to show that women's employment patterns had altered radically over the preceding 20 years. You might be able to strengthen your analysis by incorporating already available statistics into your study.

Treating the Data

Since aggregate data are established against a defined base, it is often impossible to disaggregate them. For example, if you find the rates of home ownership over the past 50 years, you cannot arbitrarily break these data down between the sexes, if this has not already been done. What you can often do is compare information from datasets based on smaller aggregates, say states or cities. This would allow you, for example, to compare such factors as unemployment rates or rates of home ownership for the 10 largest American cities. Remember that there may be many types of measures that could represent the same social indicator. Try to select the one that is the best measure of the concept you are trying to explore. Don't just take the first thing you find!

One of the primary problems that may occur in analyzing existing statistics is to imply that these findings based on aggregate data can be applied to individuals or subgroups within the dataset. Suppose you are using statistics on teenage pregnancies in the United States and you note that there are higher rates in the northeastern states than in the west. Suppose you also note that there are higher proportions of racial minority groups in the northeastern states. From this you might want to draw the conclusion that teenage pregnancies are higher in one section of the country because pregnant teenagers are more likely to be members of racial minority groups. However, you could be committing an *ecological fallacy* by extending conclusions based on group data to individuals. It could be that the white teenagers in the northeast

have higher rates than those in the west, while the rate for minority teenagers shows no difference between the areas or is lower. Recall the discussion of the ecological fallacy in Chapter 4 when units of analysis were discussed. In any study of existing statistics, the units of analysis are an aggregate group. It is very important to have a clear sense of what that group is and to make inferences from the statistical data only about the group itself.

Referencing Data

The sources of these data must always be referenced and understood. Careful notation of the dates of the data presented, the population base, and the exact type of measurement of the indicator must be clearly recognized. Be sure to take down exactly where a data source came from. You may want to photocopy the table so that you have the source. Often you need to return to the data or to find some supporting evidence. By looking widely and then photocopying the tables you desire, you will be able to select the best presentations for your study.

Issues of Validity and Reliability

One could argue that a good reason for using available statistics is that many of the validity and reliability issues have been handled very well. The measurement of indicators in existing statistics is usually based on widely used and accepted means for such measurement. For example, crime rates or unemployment rates are measures that have been developed, critiqued, and redeveloped over many years. There is a great deal of consensus on the way to measure such variables. However, there is still a high degree of error in such statistics because of the way in which the measurements are carried out, their degree of completeness. In crime statistics, for instance, there are problems stemming from unreported crime and differential arrests of persons of different social class origins. These problems can undermine the reliability of the data. It is important for the researcher to be aware of such problems: the researcher must not uncritically accept the weight of statistical evidence as fact.

To increase validity in using existing statistics, researchers should try to find more than one measure of a finding. Replicating evidence is a good way to increase confidence that the finding is real. It is also important that the researcher find evidence that actually tests her or his theoretical notions. This requires, of course, that there be a logical relationship between the statistics that are used and the hypothesis posed (or research question asked). Remember that studies which use existing statistics that were compiled and presented in order to offer an aggregate picture must be selected and handled carefully when they are being related to another purpose. You must examine the original purpose for which the data were collected to be certain that you are not distorting or falsifying them.

DECIDING IF THE ANALYSIS OF EXISTING STATISTICS IS APPROPRIATE FOR YOUR TOPIC

Since it is generally a very economical way to carry out research, the use of existing statistics should be given serious consideration. Because census data and other large-scale data cannot be developed by individual researchers, these sources offer valuable assets to all those who are trying to study society. In short, using existing statistics has many advantages. The hard work of data collection and preparation of statistical analyses has already been done for you. What you need to determine is whether the evidence you need has been prepared, where it is available, and how it can be presented in your study. Relating such statistics to your research problem may not be easy. You need to use the statistics appropriately, you must be sensitive to the errors they might contain, and you must discuss them in terms of the units of analysis which they represent.

As I have suggested for beginning researchers, existing statistics may best be used for supplementary data in a study. They can serve as an excellent reference for a researcher wanting to gain an overall sense of a field of evidence. In some areas of social research, such as criminology, existing statistics are central. It is probably a good idea, once you have defined a problem, to consider carefully whether there are existing statistics that might be used to study or to supplement your research efforts.

USING MULTIPLE METHODS TO STRENGTHEN A RESEARCH DESIGN

This chapter has presented five different types of research methods which use already existing data. Chapters 7 to 9 offered three primary ways to design studies that would generate their own data. It is highly advantageous to use *multiple methods* to address any problem. Kanter used interviewing, surveys, participant observation, and analyses of documents to develop the comprehensive body of material she used to write her forceful study of Indsco. In many research projects primary research designs involve generating original data, but the projects could be strengthened by also carrying out a content analysis of documents, or a secondary analysis of already existing survey data or statistics, or a study of some unobtrusive measures.

In Chapter 9, it was suggested that field research could be strengthened by using the tactic of triangulation to measure phenomena. In other words, multiple measures, both qualitative and quantitative, more effectively zero in on the meaning of a piece of evidence. However, Brewer and Hunter (1989) suggest that the multimethod approach be applied to all stages of the research design. They stress that the multimethod strategy is "to attack a research problem with an arsenal of methods that have nonoverlapping weaknesses in addition to their complementary strengths" (1989, p. 17). They note the advantage of using more than one major research method (field work, survey research, experimentation, or the analysis of existing data) is that the researcher can more thoroughly test the theories underlying the research. Repeating investigations can strengthen (or undermine) a theory; using more than one method to investigate a problem also offers the advantage of an added investigation and employs the corrective features that one method may have over another (1989, p. 48). Another argument strengthening the case for multiple methods is that often the ideal method for studying a problem cannot be employed for strategic, ethical, or economic reasons. In such cases, using multiple methods may better help to approximate the ideal method, to create realistic alternatives and generalizable evidence, and to avoid researcher biases (1989, pp. 52–53).

PROBLEMS TO CONFRONT IN ANALYZING AVAILABLE DATA

In this chapter, five different methods of social research have been presented. These methods not only share the use of already collected data, but they also require certain common efforts on the part of the researcher regardless of the method. In the first place, the researcher must consider why the data were collected. This issue was raised most directly in historical research, where the data may seem the most obscure. However, it is necessary whenever already collected data are examined that the researcher clearly address the question of why they were collected in the first place: what was the motivation of the person(s) who collected the data?

This is true because all forms of analyzing available data demand a careful consideration of the assumptions underlying the data themselves. Without a consideration of this kind, it will be impossible for you to use the data effectively or to know the limits beyond which they cannot be used. In the case of current survey data, you should ask yourself what to make of all the questions. You must not just accept the data as given

and valuable because they are available. You must look at them with fresh eyes and try to see them as they are in their strengths and their flaws. For content analyses, this task of considering the underlying assumptions must be done before selecting the content to be analyzed. Once the content is selected, these latent concerns give way to a study of the more manifest meaning of the content. In historical research, the examination of the underlying assumptions is often the essence of the historical effort. Finally, in the analysis of existing statistics, you need to consider whether the assumptions of those who built the indicators and set out the statistical findings seem justified.

REVIEW NOTES

- Secondary analyses involve carrying out additional analyses beyond those made by the original researcher on already collected data. In sociological journals, secondary analyses are one of the most common forms of research published.
- In selecting a dataset for a secondary analysis, you should consider the quality of the data-gathering organization, the purpose of the original researchers, and whether the primary indicators you need are measured in these data.
- Content analysis is a research technique used to describe in an objective, systematic, and quantified manner the content of a body of communication.
- Ways to describe the content of communication materials include determining (1) frequencies, (2) amount of specific types of content, (3) presence or absence of a quality, (4) typologies and sorting by types, (5) origins or sources, and (6) degree of intensity.
- Content analyses generally require developing a complex means of sorting and coding data in a careful and systematic manner.
- Unobtrusive measures refer to studies of physical traces, archives, and observations without participation.

- The study of physical traces includes examining the unintentional erosion of products (wear and tear) and the accretion (laying down or building up) of objects of human origin (such as garbage or graffiti).
- The primary aim of unobtrusive measures in a study is to serve as a supplementary source of data.
- Unobtrusive measures avoid errors generated both by the subjects being studied and by the researcher interacting with the subjects.
- The historical method involves critically examining and analyzing records and other surviving materials from the past.
- History may take for its subject broad, macro-level historical topics, or it may focus on a specific event or person with a micro-level historical approach.
- The analysis of existing statistics is a way to study the relationship of different trends in American society, in other societies, or in aggregate bodies within a society.
- The use of multiple methods in a social research project can strengthen its design.

KEY TERMS

accretion measures
aggregate data
archival research
content analysis
contextuality
erosion measures
existing statistics
historiography
history as actuality
history as record
manifest content
multiple methods
oral history
physical traces
primary sources
secondary analysis
secondary sources
unobtrusive measures
verisimilitude

STUDY EXERCISES

1. Give a one-sentence description of each of the five different methods of analyzing available data given in this chapter.
2. Consider the following social issues that emerged in the 1990s.

   a. The crisis in the delivery and costs of health care in the United States.
   b. Whether banning discrimination of homosexuals in the military would weaken the discipline and morale of soldiers.
   c. The incidence of racial tensions and violence in large cities, such as Los Angeles

   Either design a study using one of the analyses of available data methods for one of these issues, *or* select an appropriate method from the five discussed in this chapter for each of the three issues and defend your choice of method in each case.

RECOMMENDED READINGS

1. Brewer, John, and Albert Hunter: *Multimethod Research: A Synthesis of Styles,* Sage, Newbury Park, Calif., 1989. This book makes a strong case for the use of multiple methods in social research projects, addressing its advantages in orienting research and theory to each other.
2. Davis, James A., and Tom W. Smith: *The NORC General Social Survey: A User's Guide,* Sage, Newbury Park, Calif., 1991. This guide makes this dataset very accessible.
3. Gottschalk, Louis: *Understanding History: A Primer of Historical Method,* Knopf, New York, 1950. This is an old but very careful and considered discussion of the methods of historical research.
4. Hakim, Catherine: *Secondary Analysis in Social Research: A Guide to Data Sources and Methods with Examples,* Allen & Unwin, London, 1982. A thoughtful introduction to, and appraisal of, secondary analyses, with extensive suggestions for data sources.
5. Hill, Martin S.: *The Panel Study of Income Dynamics: A User's Guide,* Sage, Newbury Park, Calif., 1991. This less detailed guide presents a clear overview of the survey design and content and data preparation and quality.

6. Kiecolt, K. Jill, and Laura E. Nathan: *Secondary Analysis of Survey Data,* Sage, Newbury Park, Calif., 1985. This little volume has an excellent compilation of sources for locating datasets as well as research strategies for using existing survey data.

7. Krippendorff, Klaus: *Content Analysis: An Introduction to Its Methodology,* Sage, Beverly Hills, Calif., 1980. Written by a professor of communications, this volume covers the conceptualization and design of content analyses, as well as analytic techniques (unitizing, sampling, recording, developing constructs) and issues of reliability and validity.

8. Webb, Eugene J., Donald T. Campbell, Richard D. Schwartz, and Lee Sechrest: *Unobtrusive Measures: Nonreactive Research in the Social Sciences,* Rand McNally, Chicago, 1966. This is the central work in the study of unobtrusive measurement. It includes many fertile suggestions for measures.

Evaluation Research and Case Studies

LOOKING AHEAD

This chapter covers a rapidly expanding area of social research—evaluation research. Human service agencies and social programs are evaluated singly, as case studies, or comparatively. Large social systems (cities, nations) are evaluated using social indicators and quality-of-life measures.

INTRODUCTION

*E*valuation research is not really a different method of doing research; rather, it is research done for a specific *purpose*. The purpose is to evaluate some social activity, usually a social program, which has been set up to address and ameliorate a social problem. The methods used in evaluation research can be any of those described in the earlier chapters, though some form of experimental design is the most common.

The growth of this type of research in the 1970s paralleled the increase in social intervention programs which occurred in the 1960s. These programs set out to alter some negative social occurrence (a disadvantageous social factor) by intervening in the process that seemed to lead from the cause of the social disadvantage to its occurrence. The social program was often meant to strengthen the abilities of the subjects not only to withstand their disadvantage but also to give them a means of overcoming the disadvantage and an opportunity to succeed. Since social programs were costly and often supported by public funds, there was pressure to be sure they were effective. This was the impetus behind the growth of evaluation research. As this form of research developed, it began also to be used to anticipate the effects of social intervention programs before they started *(preprogram evaluation)* and to evaluate their progress while in operation *(ongoing program evaluation)*. It also came to be used to study the effects of the implementation of new laws and other social policies.

The income maintenance experiment described in Chapter 1 is a good example of a preprogram evaluation research project of the most typical kind—an evaluation using an experimental design to compare a group exposed to a social intervention program with a group not so exposed (or exposed to a variant of the program). However, experimental design studies of this type are only one form of evaluation. The survey of public and private schools analyzed by Coleman and his colleagues (described in Chapter 1) was in its way an evaluation study: it tried to evaluate the effectiveness of the public and private schools. Both these studies had important effects on social policy. You might want to look back at those two studies as you read this chapter.

In order to expand your understanding of evaluation research, we will first consider four brief examples of different types of evaluation projects. Then the components of an evaluation research project will be laid out, and the essential aspects of an evaluation research design will be discussed. The definition and design of case studies are discussed, and examples are offered. The analysis of social indicators based on aggregate data will then be described. Finally, the chapter will offer ways for you to decide whether this type of research could help you achieve your research objectives.

FOUR EXAMPLES OF EVALUATION PROJECTS

In order to expose you to the range of types of research which fall under the heading of evaluation research, four different types of evaluation research projects will be described below. These four types exemplify commonly used forms of evaluations: an *ex post facto (after-only) experimental design,* in this case applied to the study of a federally funded preschool program; a *cost-benefit analysis,* here applied to mental health treatment covered by Medicaid in a single state; a *community impact assessment,* addressed to the potential effects of busing in a particular city; and a *time-series analysis,* using aggregate existing crime data to analyze the effects of the federal Gun Control Act of 1968.

An Ongoing Program Evaluation: Head Start

The Head Start program was a federal program initiated in 1965 to offer preschool education to disadvantaged children, in order to help them perform more effectively in school. Numerous evaluations of this program were carried out, but the one that had the greatest effect on social policy-making was the large study developed by the Westinghouse Learning Corporation at Ohio University. The final report of this evaluation, *The Impact of Head Start,* which appeared in 1969, concluded that Head Start had produced only a marginally positive effect on the long-range cognitive abilities (reading readiness, IQ) of the children who had attended full-year Head Start programs, and virtually no effect on those who had attended only summer programs. The researchers also concluded that the long-term effects of the program on affective outcomes (such as improved self-esteem or school behavior) were virtually nonexistent.

How had the evaluators reached these conclusions? Since they had been selected as the researchers to study a program which had been in existence for four years, it was not possible for them to assign the children by means of randomization to participate in the program (the experimentals) or not to participate (the controls). Instead, they were obliged to evaluate the effects of the program on those who had already completed their participation and to compare these effects with the performance of a group of children who might have participated (in that they shared similar characteristics with those who had participated) but who in fact had not done so. (This would be a *nonequivalent control group,* as explained in Chapter 8). Furthermore, the focus was on the long-term effects of Head Start, since children who had already experienced the program and were now in first, second, or third grade were to be studied. This meant that pretesting was not possible; rather the experiment would have an *after-only,* or *ex post facto,* design.

Simply described, the researchers selected geographical regions in which Head Start programs had been set up. They then defined two subpopulations of children: those who had attended a Head Start program and those with similar characteristics who had not. From these subpopulations, a sample of attenders was selected (serving as the experimental group), and a sample of nonattenders was drawn from those children who matched the experimental subjects best regarding a number of specific variables (race, sex, socioeconomic status) and whether the child had subsequently attended kindergarten.

Once the samples were selected, data were collected from a number of sources, including interview material from parents, grade school teachers' observations of the child's behavior, and various tests of the child's cognitive abilities and affective qualities. Since Head Start children from across the United States were studied, this project was large and demanding. There were efforts to systematize the data collection procedures by careful training of the data collectors.

The analyses of the data were complex and varied. The basic objective of these analyses was to try to determine whether the experimentals (those who had attended Head Start) performed better than the controls (those who had not attended Head Start) on cognitive and affective factors. As stated above, the evaluators found modest gains for the experimentals on cognitive factors for those who had attended full-year programs. These gains were greater for black children and for those attending programs in the southeast United States. (Later analyses of these data, however, challenged these interpretations!)

A Cost-Benefit Analysis: Mental Health Care

The influence of economics has been widely felt in evaluation research. As the support for funding expensive social programs came under greater pressure in the 1970s and 1980s, cost-benefit analyses became a much more popular design for social program evaluation. Very simply, a cost-benefit analysis seeks to assess whether the benefit of a program or social strategy is worth the cost. There can be serious problems with measuring costs and benefits which may not make this approach viable for many types of studies. Naturally, it is most feasible to carry out such a study when the costs of the implementation of what is being studied can be measured in terms of dollars (such measurement is often, but not always, the case). It is also useful if the benefits can be measured in terms of dollars as well. Where this is difficult, proxy measures must be developed to operationalize the benefits.

A cost-benefit analysis of mental health care services provided to the poor in Massachusetts under Medicaid used a comparative model according to which Medicaid recipients were compared to non-Medicaid recipients who also sought mental health services (Davenport and Nuttall, 1979). The Massachusetts Department of Public Welfare was trying to determine which of its varied services was most cost-effective—that is to say, which of the services produced the greatest positive effect for the least cost. First the researchers needed to determine the range of services offered, the costs of the various treatments, and their benefits. The range of services was great, though there were some controls on their variation by policies governing different forms of care. For example, the researchers determined the cost of therapy sessions with various types of mental health personnel both in clinical settings where a range of mental health care professionals offer therapy and in nonclinical settings where only physicians can offer therapy (Davenport and Nuttall, 1979, p. 177).

This first aspect of the evaluation study was simply to describe the range in costs of the various services available and to relate them to the services offered (the benefits). These benefits were measured in terms of length of treatment, type of diagnoses, and use of medication. Note that the first of these, length of treatment, could easily be translated into dollars, while the other two could not.

The second aspect of the evaluation examined the impact that changes in state policies had had on the delivery and cost of services. For example, psychiatrists' fees had been cut. Within six months, this led to a drop in reimbursements (amounts paid to doctors) but an increase in claims (more patients were seen). After a year the reimbursements increased and the number of claims

decreased. In another six months the first pattern reappeared. This suggested that the cut in psychiatrists' fees did not bring about the desired drop in the program's costs. Rather, the cut in fees brought about different types of effects (more patients were seen in clinics where the fees were higher; there were some cases of fraud where psychiatrists used less trained personnel for the therapy sessions but billed the state for the psychiatrist-level fees) (1979, p. 179). This second aspect of the evaluation design required an analysis of existing records as part of the design. Box 11-1 de-

BOX 11-1

THE POLICY IMPLICATIONS OF COST-BENEFIT STUDIES

In an experimental study of the cost-effectiveness of community-based health services in Georgia for a sample of low-income (eligible for Medicaid) elderly, Skellie, Mobley, and Coan found that although the experimental group who received the community-based care spent fewer days in nursing homes and lived longer, their care (both Medicaid and Medicare expenses) cost more than that of the control group.

But when the experiment focused only on clients who were more at risk for entering a nursing home (those who were less able to care for themselves), their care cost less than that of the control group. Hence the authors stress that in studies of cost-effectiveness of alternative health services, it is critical that the target population be screened so that those most in need of the services have access to them. For it is when they are provided to this most needy group that such alternative services will be most cost-effective.

Data from F. Albert Skellie, G. Melton Mobley, and Ruth E. Coan, "Cost Effectiveness of Community-Based Long-Term Care: Current Findings of Georgia's Alternative Health Services Project," *American Journal of Public Health,* **72**:353–358, 1982.

scribes the policy implications of a cost-benefit evaluation of long-term care programs.

A Community Impact Assessment: A School Busing Program

The cost-benefit model for evaluation research assumes that containing costs while trying to maximize benefits is in everyone's interest. This would suggest that individuals consider each situation from a *utilitarian* point of view and decide where their benefits lie. Allen and Sears (1979, p. 172) suggest that socialization theory would offer a different view of how people orient themselves to particular social situations. In this view, individuals are affected by values and attitudes which are adopted in childhood and are resistant to change.

Controversial social policies, such as busing to achieve racial integration, require community support. One form of evaluation research, *community impact assessment,* can be used to try to determine what effect a new policy might have on a community. Impact assessment studies are often based on surveys where attitudes of those who might be affected by a program are gathered and related to other characteristics of the respondents.

For example, in a telephone survey of the attitudes of a random sample of Los Angeles residents, Allen and Sears (1979) found that opposition to busing (the dependent variable) was much more strongly related to racial intolerance and political conservatism than to the respondent's specific self-interest. The researchers thereby challenged the notion that individuals respond to social policies on the basis of rational considerations of what they have to gain or lose (1979, p. 175).

A Time-Series Analysis: The Effects of Gun Legislation

Laws are forms of social policies which carry punishments if they are infringed. The problem with some laws is that they are difficult to enforce; in such cases, there is always the fear that if they are widely abused and ignored, contempt for the law

will grow. In 1968, responding in particular to the assassination of Robert Kennedy, Congress enacted the Gun Control Act. Its object was to control the use of handguns by outlawing the importation of firearms except for sporting purposes, to restrict interstate traffic in firearms and ammunition, and to forbid certain categories of persons from using them.

What Zimring (1976) set out to evaluate was whether, in fact, the Gun Control Act had reduced the use of handguns in violent crimes. How could one measure the effects of the law itself? One way to examine the impact of the legislation would be to look at indicators of what should have changed as a result of the new legislation. One example of an indicator Zimring used was the number of guns imported into the United States. He was able to show a sharp increase in the importation of handguns into the United States from 1964 to 1968, followed after 1968 by a drop in handgun imports, remaining quite steady from 1969 to 1973. Since the new law is the independent variable in this study, measures of its short-term specific effects (reduction in gun importation) validate the claim that the law brought about some of its expected consequences.

To study the long-term effects of this legislative initiative requires a focus on what a reduction in handguns might hopefully lead to, namely, a reduction in criminal acts related to the use of guns. Zimring could examine this by using the years before and after the legislation as a measure of the presence of the legislation. Then using a *time-series analysis* of aggregate data from the law enforcement agencies, Zimring examined whether there was a shift in the amount of crime related to handguns after the legislation. (Refer to Chapter 8 for a discussion of time-series analysis as a form of quasi-experimental design.) In order to compare the short-term and long-term effects of this law, Zimring drew up graphs to show the proportion of crime related to handguns and how it altered after the introduction of the Gun Control Act. (It should be noted that firearm assaults include those related both to handguns and to other types of guns, though about 80 percent of the firearms used in assaults are handguns.)

The proportion of crimes (homicides and assaults) carried out with handguns peaked shortly after the legislation was enacted and then leveled off (though it continued to rise very slowly). Zimring offers various suggestions for why the law was not more effective. One factor was that it actually led to the use of other types of weapons ("Saturday night specials"), which came to replace some of the illegal types of guns.

COMPONENTS OF AN EVALUATION RESEARCH PROJECT

Clarify the Purpose

Evaluation research is usually carried out at the request of someone else (who also covers the cost). It is that someone who must define the purpose of the research. However, the decision makers who are requesting the study may not have defined their purpose clearly. Your first job as an evaluator is to help them to do this. Only then can you begin your study.

Carol Weiss (1972, p. 12) suggests a number of reasons why an evaluation may be sought. First, it may be required in order to fulfill a contract or grant commitment. (Many publically funded programs must include an *evaluation component*). Second, the evaluation may be a kind of delaying tactic or a way to shift responsibility or get favorable publicity for the program (Weiss, 1972, p. 11). In other words, the people requesting the evaluation may be interested in having it done not to find out how effective their program is, but rather to use the evaluation effort to alter the political situation in the organization. These ulterior motives can deeply affect a researcher's ability to clarify the purpose of the evaluation.

One good way to get at the purpose is to consider for whom the study is being done. Weiss suggests seven potential utilizers of the results (1972, p. 18): (1) a funding organization, (2) a national agency, (3) a local agency, (4) the project directors, (5) the staff of the project, (6) the program's clients, and (7) researchers and other learned individuals who may use the findings of this project to further research in other studies. Note, for example, that if the primary users are the staff, then the *inputs* to the program (what is being offered) may need to be closely considered; if the clients are the primary users, then the *outputs* of the program may be the primary focus of the evaluation.

One commonly used means for differentiating types of evaluations is that developed first by Scriven (1967) to evaluate educational programs—that is, to differentiate between *formative evaluations,* which set out to study a program in process and where the information will be "plowed back" into the program to reform it as it is being administered, and *summative evaluations,* which summarize the effects of a program after it is completed. What this distinction does is to focus the attention of the evaluator on different aspects of the program being evaluated, to set a timing perspective on the evaluation, and to determine how firm and conclusive the findings of the evaluation can possibly be.

In a formative evaluation, the focus is on the dynamic process of the program itself: it is the study of an ongoing system of social interaction. The time dimension in a formative evaluation is the present. Final conclusions cannot be drawn about the effectiveness of the program; rather, the evaluation must make proposals directed toward improving the ongoing operation of the program (or possibly aborting it). In a summative evaluation, the focus is on the program as a completed entity. The time frame is the past. Conclusions can be drawn. Here the purpose of the conclusions may be to advise others on the effectiveness of this particular program, to suggest its weaknesses and problems as well as its strengths and accomplishments.

Establish the Dependent Variable

As in most types of social research, the evaluator needs to home in on what precisely he or she will be looking for. What should the program have accomplished? What were its ends, its goals? In the Head Start evaluation, the dependent variables were cognitive abilities and affective qualities. The expected variation was that those who had attended Head Start would have made greater gains in cognitive (intellectual) and affective (emotional) readiness than those who had not. In the mental health care study, the dependent variable was based on the services offered (these were measured in terms of number of visits, types of diagnoses, etc.). In the community impact study, the dependent variable was opposition to busing (or its converse, support for busing). In the gun legislation evaluation, there were a number of dependent variables—namely, the number of crimes committed with handguns, the number of handguns imported, etc.

Weiss warns that the choice of the evaluation goals, the dependent variable(s) in the study, should be considered in the light of their practicality, to whom they are important, and whether they are short-term or long-term goals (1972, pp. 30–31). Selecting an impractical dependent variable may make the results of the evaluation of little use. Considering who will use the findings and, among those who will use it, who the most important users are likely to be are ways of addressing the political implications of evaluation research. If the program directors need information on what to do at the present time, then short-term goals are critical. All these considerations require that the researcher work out the final goals, the dependent variables, with those who will be using the evaluation (Weiss, 1972, p. 31).

These dependent variables will generally be the outputs of the program (and in an impact assessment study, they would be the likely impact of a supposed new policy). Although they are rarely easy to define, they may be even more difficult to operationalize. Note that in the mental health study, what would seem to be the true output is improving the mental health of the patients. Since this is so difficult to ascertain, the output indicators become measures of the services themselves (which supposedly are indicators of improved

mental health). In Coleman's study of public and private schools, the dependent variables were cognitive test scores, which were used as indicators of educational achievement. In the busing impact study, the dependent variable was based on a five-item scale of opposition to busing.

If the dependent variable is unreliable or its validity is doubtful, this may throw the whole evaluation into doubt. For this reason, it is of critical importance to be careful in conceptualizing the dependent variable and developing a means of measuring it. Weiss (1972, pp. 34–39) offers some suggestions for developing the outcome indicators (the dependent variables in the evaluation). If the outcomes are attitudes, it may be wise to consider using already developed attitudinal scales which have been tried out in other studies. The track record of such measures will include evidence on the range of probable responses, the likelihood of persons to change their responses easily (an issue of reliability), and the question of whether the measures are actually related to other factors that would seem probable (an issue of validity). Another way to strengthen the measurement of outcomes is to develop multiple measures. As Weiss states, "By the use of a number of measures, each contributing a different facet of information, we can limit the effect of irrelevancies and develop a more rounded and truer picture of program outcomes" (1972, p. 36). When the true goals of what is being evaluated will only be realized in the future, it is difficult to select indicators for measuring the outcome. Weiss suggests that in such cases only proximate measures can be developed (1972, pp. 37–38). Such measures should represent intermediate goals, outcomes which seem to be propitious for the long-term goal.

Determine the Independent Variables

Independent variables are the inputs to the program being studied. In most evaluation studies, what is being evaluated (the social intervention program, for example) is itself the independent variable. In experimental design studies, where a program is being evaluated, being "in the program" is the primary independent variable (this would be true of the income maintenance experiments and the Head Start experiment). It would also be true of the Coleman survey where attending a public or private school was the primary independent variable. When membership in the program is the primary independent variable, operationalization is easy. Even in studies where membership serves as the major independent variable, other qualities and characteristics of the program may also be included as input variables (for example, in the income maintenance experiment there was variation in the amount of income received and the tax rate applied).

In some evaluations, other types of independent variables are used. In the opposition-to-busing evaluation, the independent variables included measures of the self-interest of Los Angeles residents as well as measures of general attitudes toward racial toleration and political conservatism (Allen and Sears, 1979, p. 173). In the mental health evaluation, personal characteristics of the patients (age, sex, race), their location of treatment (clinical or nonclinical), and their ability to pay (Medicaid or private patients) were related to the dependent variables of length of treatment, diagnosis, and types of therapy received (Davenport and Nuttall, 1979, p. 178). Box 11-2 offers Weiss's suggestions for developing input measures for an evaluation research design.

Set Up the Research Design

Once you have clarified your dependent and independent variables, you are ready to lay out the design of your study. In an experiment, you need to determine what type of control group will be necessary (and what type is feasible). Should it be a group which is not exposed to the program, a group exposed to a variant of the program? Do you need to be worried about Hawthorne effects? (If so, you may need two control groups, one exposed to some type of program but not the one you are studying, the other not exposed to any pro-

BOX 11-2

SUGGESTED INPUT MEASURES FOR AN EVALUATION PROJECT

Among possible input measures of the program to be evaluated, Weiss includes the following: (1) *purpose* of the program, (2) *principles* of the program, (3) *methods* used in the program, (4) *staffing* of the program, (5) *persons served* by the program, (6) *length of service* provided by the program, (7) *location* of the program, (8) *size* of the program, (9) under whose *auspices* the program is being offered, and (10) *management* of the program (1972, p. 46).

Weiss goes on to suggest that if persons are being put through the program, and the effect of the program on the persons is of primary interest, then characteristics of the clients themselves can be considered as input variables. She proposes the following 11 factors to be measured regarding the persons being served by the program: (1) age, (2) sex, (3) socioeconomic status, (4) race, (5) length of residence in the community, (6) attitudes toward the program, (7) motivations for participating in the program, (8) aspirations relevant to the general objectives of the program, (9) expectations of what they hope to achieve as a result of participating in the program, (10) attitudes of other family members about the program, and (11) degree of support from other family members concerning the hoped-for outcomes of participating in the program (pp. 46–47).

Finally, Weiss cautions that the comprehensiveness of these lists should not encourage you to go out and measure everything. Analyzing data is time-consuming and demanding. If you have too many variables, you may get submerged in the details and find it difficult to concentrate your evaluation on what is of central significance.

Source: Carol H. Weiss, *Evaluation Research*, Prentice-Hall, Englewood Cliffs, N.J., 1972.

gram.) Are there other characteristics of the experimental or control groups that need to be controlled?

If randomization in the assignment of subjects to groups is feasible (which it often is not), it should be done. The statistical test you will be likely to use to compare the experimental group to the control group can only be used appropriately if there has been randomization in assignment. For an experiment, you need to consider whether a pretest is possible. Remember that the point of a pretest is to determine some baseline against which the effects of the program (the independent variable) can be compared. In many experimental designs for evaluation, a pretest cannot be carried out prior to the experiment. In the income maintenance experiment, you may recall, there were preexperiment measurements of the culture-of-poverty traits against which postexperiment measurements of these traits could be compared.

Specify the Control Variables

If you are carrying out a survey, you will need to consider variables both antecedent to the independent variable and intervening between the independent and dependent variables which may affect the direct relationship between the input and output variables. Drawing a diagram of the potential relationships between all the variables is a good way to try out all the possible design strategies.

A part of the design will be to specify all other factors which you think may affect the evaluation of the program or event to be studied. Can you measure these effectively? You may want both to test whether these other factors make a difference to the outcome measures (does sex or race make a difference) and to control for these other factors by excluding them or making them equivalent between comparison groups. In the evaluation of a social program, you may need to consider situational factors which characterize the environment but are not of primary concern in your study. Might they affect the results? Can they be controlled?

Ethical Implications and Political Impact

Evaluations using experiments where some people are exposed, and others not exposed, to a social program may raise many questions of fairness. Are the people who need the program getting it? In many cases, assignment based on randomization to experimental and control groups cannot be carried out for ethical reasons. In this case (recall from Chapter 8) various types of quasi-experimental designs may be used. Furthermore, the use of records, interviewing techniques, or the treatment of subjects in the study may all raise ethical considerations which need to be planned carefully in designing the evaluation.

Most evaluations have some political impact on those who will use the findings. If you suggest that some changes be made, some will come to a defense of the program and try to have your study ignored. Conversely, others may take up your findings to fight their own causes, which may in cases be ones that your study would not advocate. Box 11-3 describes ways through which evaluations can be resisted. Most people do not like to be evaluated and so you must be prepared to face efforts to contain your research in the beginning and to bury the findings once the study is done. The better the evaluator understands the political situation of the program or agency being evaluated, the better she or he will be able to consider ways of carrying out the evaluation.

The other common drawback with the use of the findings is that they may not be used at all. As Weiss aptly puts it, those who do the evaluations are often academics who may lack appreciation of the mundane considerations that those being evaluated want to know. The evaluator may try to ferret out the most profound and academically interesting findings from the study and ignore many practical aspects of the study which would be of greater interest (and, possibly, of greater use) to the program staff (1972, p. 111). The staff may also need more specific conclusions and suggestions than the evaluator feels confident to make

BOX 11-3

WAYS PROGRAM EVALUATION MAY BE RESISTED

Posavac and Carey suggest nine forms of resistance to program evaluation studies that must be considered in the planning stage of the study so that the researchers will be ready to address opposition. These problems include (1) program directors' expectations that the evaluation will show a "slam-bang" effect, which may make them unreceptive to negative or weak findings; (2) fear that the evaluation of the program will inhibit innovative changes; (3) fear of program termination; (4) fear of information abuse; (5) fear that the subjective benefits of the program will be ignored after the arrival of quantitative data; (6) fear that evaluation costs drain resources; (7) fear of loss of control over the program; and (8) fear that the evaluation will have little impact.

Source: Emil J. Posavec and Raymond G. Carey, *Program Evaluation: Methods and Case Studies*, 3d ed., Prentice-Hall, Englewood Cliffs, N.J., 1989, pp. 39–42.

(Weiss, 1972, p. 111). But without the specific recommendations, the evaluation report may be ignored. The agency may have no one able to fully understand the research findings in the evaluation study (no one who has had a good research methods course!). For this reason, the evaluator may need not only to do the evaluation, but also to *sell* the results to those for whom it was done (Weiss, 1972, p. 113).

DESIGNING AN EVALUATION RESEARCH PROJECT

The types of designs for evaluation research can be loosely grouped as *experimental* designs and *nonexperimental* designs. Whichever type your

study follows, considerations of the time frame of the study and the types of subjects to be studied are important. The design must be considered in terms of its validity: is the *real* effect going to be measured?

Experimental Designs

Chapter 8 offered a comprehensive overview of the types and qualities of experimental designs. Here we will discuss how to determine whether what you are trying to evaluate can be studied by an experimental design. Remember that for a true experiment you need randomization of the subjects between experimental and control groups. The income maintenance evaluation described in Chapter 1 was able to randomly assign subjects to the experimental and control groups; the Head Start evaluation carried out by the Westinghouse research organization was not. Two important factors made randomization possible in the first case, though impossible in the second. In the income maintenance experiment, the evaluation was preprogram. Therefore, the experimental design was set up and built into the intervention program itself. In the Head Start evaluation, the study was retrospective; the experimental subjects had experienced the program two to five years before the evaluation was made. In this case, a comparison group of subjects to serve as controls had to be developed. This meant that the Head Start evaluation was an ex post facto, or after-only, design with a comparison group. (Strictly speaking, then, the Head Start evaluation would not qualify either as a quasi-experimental design, in which data from before the program might be used to study the program effects in a time-series fashion, or as a nonequivalent control group design, in which preprogram measures were available.)

With a true experimental or a quasi-experimental design, selection of subjects and controls before exposure to the program is needed. Usually preprogram indicators are needed (though sometimes they may be available to be measured after the evaluation has begun; for example, prior school grades or earlier test scores might be available for that purpose).

Nonexperimental Designs

These include experimental design studies which fail to meet the criteria for experiments as well as other types of designs. Examples would be surveys which assess the effects of a program or the potential impact of a proposed policy, the analysis of available data related to the imposition of a new law or social practice, or a cost-benefit analysis of the relationship between the inputs and outcomes of a program. In these cases, both the *time dimension* and the *basis for comparison* need to be fully considered.

The Time Dimension. Every evaluation study has a primary focus in terms of time. It may focus on the past (the Head Start project), the future (the busing impact study), or the present (the Coleman survey, the mental health cost-benefit study). Whatever the primary focus, some concern about the relevance of the past needs to be taken into account. In surveys, information about background characteristics is often needed, frequently in terms of family origin (social class, ethnicity, number of parents present, employment status of parents, number of siblings) or other demographic factors such as sex, race, and size and location of hometown (urban, suburban, rural). The validity of retrospective measures must always be questioned. While nearly everyone can indicate their hometown and other basic characteristics of family origin, many cannot fully recall attitudes that may have been held in the past or reactions to experiences undergone.

Projections about the future must also be cautiously weighed. First, there must be a very careful operationalization of variables to measure projections about the future. (For example, in the literature on career aspirations among youth, there is a clear distinction between aspirations, which indicate hopes, and expectations, which imply plans

and more realistic appraisals. In addition, there is variation in the degree of commitment—a measure of motivation—to future hopes and plans.) Second, evaluation projects which conclude with recommendations must focus on the future. But to project suggestions for the future requires not only that you consider what the likely fate of the program you are studying will be, but also that you consider the social and political context in which this program will operate.

A Comparative Baseline. Evaluation studies need some form of comparative basis for determining whether what is being evaluated is a success or a failure. This is a major reason why experimental designs are popular for evaluations, since the control group offers a solid comparative baseline in such designs. (You must remember of course that only control groups in which members have been assigned to the group by randomization offer a true experimental basis of comparison.)

Other types of nonexperimental studies tend to use comparative bases as well. The comparisons are usually between the subjects' experiences: examples from the evaluations we have cited would be attending a public or private school and being on Medicaid or not. Comparisons may also be made in time, from before and after what is being evaluated: the Gun Control Act study was of this kind. Most time-series studies, in fact, use as their primary comparative base a before-and-after comparison in measuring trends thought to be affected by the input being studied.

Probably the weakest example of a comparative base was in the community impact opposition-to-busing study: here comparisons could only be made on the basis of certain characteristics of the sample (such as having or not having school-aged children, which would presumably affect level of interest in the issue). Other background characteristics of subjects, such as age or educational attainment, are also often used for comparative purposes: for example, the busing evaluation found that the age and education of the residents were related to their attitudes. These factors were then used comparatively to assess differences in the potential impact of busing.

Will Your Design Lead to the Real Effect That Must Be Evaluated?

Let's say that you have set out the components of the study and put them into a research design, paying appropriate attention to the time frame of the study and the comparisons which you will be able to make. It is now the moment to review your design and consider seriously whether it will accomplish what you need to do and evaluate what you need to evaluate.

A good way to review this question is to think again about precisely who the persons or organizations are, the effects upon whom you are trying to measure. Weiss (1972, pp. 39–42) delineates four possible *primary recipients* of the effects of what you are trying to evaluate: the persons to be served, the agencies or organizations offering the services, larger systems (such as public education or mental health), and the general public. Let's consider the evaluation studies we have described in terms of who is primarily affected. The income maintenance experiment (from Chapter 1) focused its primary attention on those persons receiving the cash transfers (the persons being *served*). This evaluation was not primarily centered on the social welfare system but on how the recipients of social welfare provisions would be most effectively served. The mental health study in Massachusetts had as the primary recipient the mental health agencies in that state—how effectively (in terms of cost) services were provided, in which types of settings, and with which types of personnel.

The Coleman survey of public and private schools (from Chapter 1) was directed to the larger system of public and private education. With a comprehensive survey of this type, any of the first three types of receivers of effects could be the primary recipients. But Coleman and his colleagues addressed themselves to the larger systems of public and private education, which were studied in

terms of aggregate data from pupils, teachers, and administrators of these different school systems.

Finally, the community impact assessment study of opposition to busing and the Gun Control Act evaluation were both examples of trying to measure effects on the general public. In the busing study, the public is any community which might be ordered to set up a system of busing to achieve racial integration of the schools. The Gun Control Act evaluation, as well, specified the public (that is, anyone who might become the victim of a crime committed with the use of a handgun) as the primary recipient. Once you have decided who or what is being primarily affected in your study, you should go through every aspect of your research design to be sure that what you are planning to do will produce the type of evidence needed to measure how strong the effect is.

CASE STUDIES

A Definition

A case study is not a specific method of social research. Though field studies of specific organizations or social groups or environments are case studies, so are many program evaluations, which often use preexperimental or quasi-experimental designs. Thus a *case study* is a research strategy which focuses on a single organization, institution, event, decision, policy, or group (or possibly a multiple set). Both field studies described in detail in Chapter 1 were also case studies. Elijah Anderson's study of Jelly's Bar was, in fact, a case study of a group of black men who hung out in a Chicago South Side bar; his research purpose was to understand the men's social status system and the forms of commitment and support that existed among them. Rosabeth Kanter's study of Indsco was a case study of a multinational corporation; her primary purpose was to better understand the comparative roles of women and men in that organization. Anderson's research methods were observational. Kanter used numerous methods in addition to observation, such as the study of documents and archives, and surveys of groups of employees.

As Robert Yin (1989, p. 17) proposes, case studies are appropriate when the research question to be addressed asks *how* and/or *why*. This means that a case study often seeks an explanation, as an experiment might. Case studies may be largely exploratory, or they may be descriptive. But often the reason to study a particular case is to try to figure out why a certain situation prevails or how an organization or group has succeeded. Evaluations of programs and organizations are explanatory in their purpose and are a form of case study research.

When the phenomenon to be explained happened in the more distant past, the best method of study may be historical research. Some historical materials may be used when the question addresses a contemporary case, but much of the data will be collected not from accumulated evidence from the past (records, documents, other written sources) but by the researcher through observation, interviewing, and contemporary written materials. Within this contemporary time frame, a study of a single event, group, or organization is considered a case study. Experimental designs are generally inappropriate in a case study because the researcher cannot control the course of action and the types of behaviors which will occur.

Yin (1989, p. 23) defines a case study as an empirical study which (1) "investigates a contemporary phenomenon within its real-life context; when (2) the boundaries between phenomenon and context are not clearly evident; and in which (3) multiple sources of evidence are used." In other words, a case study examines a current phenomenon in its real-life situation, using whichever research strategies are necessary to address the problem at hand.

Designing a Case Study

The first effort, as always, is to set up the research question. Let's take an example. Suppose the elementary schools in your city or town are consid-

ered inadequate in many ways; however, Jones School, in the poorest part of town, is widely considered to be very successful. This could well be a subject for a case study. Clearly the research question would be of the *why* and *how* variety. *Why* is Jones School successful even though it has the same inadequate funding, the same source of teachers, the same ill-prepared students as the other, less successful schools? And *how* does the school manage to get such positive results (test scores, positive attitudes about the school, etc.) when the same set of problems seem to undermine the efforts of its sister schools? The final research question might be more focused: it could be on a specific reading program in the school, on the decision-making strategy employed in the school, or on how decisions are implemented.

Yin suggests that the researcher develop propositions linking the research question to specific things that will be carefully examined in the study. One proposition could be that Jones School is successful because the teachers and administrators have identified ways to meet certain objectives (i.e., improving reading scores); and a second proposition could be that they have perfected a means to work together to achieve these goals. This proposes that the leadership of the school is effective in defining, stating, and getting the teachers to support specific objectives, and it proposes that the teachers and administrators work successfully together to meet their goals.

Yin argues (1989, p. 31) that the way the research question is set up will define the actual units of analysis in the study. In the Jones School study, the unit of analysis depends on the exact nature of the research question. In a study focused on a specific program or programs, the unit of analysis is a program. In a study directed at how decisions are made, the unit of analysis is decisions. In a study of how decisions are implemented in the school to reach results, the unit of analysis is the implementation process.

Next the researcher must collect data that address the propositions. As Yin states (1989, p. 33), this is no easy matter. In a formal experiment, subjects are assigned to treatment conditions which connect the hypotheses to the data. However, in a real-life case study, this type of control cannot be gained. How can the researcher know whether the data to be gathered will really address the proposition? Suppose the Jones School study focuses on the implementation of a strategy to teach reading. The researcher might select several types of information that zero in on how the strategy was implemented (qualities of training sessions for teachers, incentives for teachers to undertake training and implement the strategy, how teachers presented new techniques in class). A researcher who could study various training sessions with different leaders, or watch different teachers incorporating this new method in their classes, might detect patterns in which the implementation seemed to be more effective and might relate these to specific training sessions, specific teaching styles, etc.

This ability to *link the data collected to the propositions* set out for the study is related to the final component needed in a case study research design, the setting of criteria to determine the findings of the study (Yin, 1989, p. 35). In the Jones School study, the criteria would need to differentiate levels of effectiveness of implementation.

Case Study Theory Building

The first step in theory building is setting up propositions to link the data to be collected with the research question. A theory offers a provisional explanation for why certain factors might lead to certain results. In the Jones School study, one theory might be that reading scores improved most when the teachers were given certain incentives for implementing the new program. A rival theory could state that the success was due to a change in the administrative structure of the school, giving teachers more authority and autonomy.

The case being studied is not representative of a sample of similar cases; thus one cannot make statistical generalizations. However, as Yin contends, the case study allows for "analytic general-

izations in which a previously developed theory is used as a template with which to compare the empirical results of the case study" (1989, p. 38). Such generalizations strengthen the explanatory power of the study. Classic case studies in the literature have often enabled researchers studying cases in very different places, and at different times, to find similar processes and similar explanations operating.

Issues of Reliability and Validity

If another researcher studied this same case with the same research question, would the results be the same? Researchers need to design their studies so that the audience will be able to follow exactly what happened. Could another researcher read the case study through its various steps, think through the logic of how to link the propositions to the data, repeat the research effort, and reach the same conclusions? In order to strengthen the replicability of a case study, the researcher must carefully document each step in research design and data collection in a *case study protocol,* described below.

Three types of validity issues arise in a case study. *External validity,* as described in Chapter 8, addresses whether the findings of a study can be generalized to another example. Again, as Yin argues, the issue is not to analogize to some broader population, for a case study is not based on a sample. Rather, as in an experiment, we need to be able to test the external validity of the study through replication. For example, if another school used the Jones School incentive strategy, would it achieve similar results?

The problem of establishing *internal validity* arises when a case study seeks to explain a phenomenon. In such a study some spurious unmeasured factor, rather than the proposed cause, might actually account for the result. A case study, unlike an experiment, does not allow the researcher to even attempt to reduce extraneous factors. But he or she can carefully consider all the possible unmeasured factors and then infer what effects such factors might have.

Yin particularly stresses the need to address the problem of *construct validity* (1989, pp. 41–42): does the operationalized measure of the effect of the study actually measure what the researcher states that it measures? Many case studies examine "change" in the organization, group, or whatever case is being studied; the issue is whether the measure or measures of change actually reflect the kinds of alterations the study is focused on, and whether the types of changes studied closely relate to the original objectives of the study. Yin strongly advises that the case study researcher get multiple sources of evidence and/or try to establish a chain of evidence so that one can pick out the steps that lead to a final effect.

Case Studies as a Method for Evaluating Programs

Organizations and agencies that receive funding from the government to implement programs are generally required to evaluate the effectiveness of these efforts. Thus evaluation research has become a growing industry. In most cases, researchers study the outcomes or processes of specific programs rather than setting up comparative research designs. Thus much evaluation research is in fact based on the study of single cases. In their comprehensive text on program evaluation, Posavec and Carey (1989) use five case studies to exemplify the methods of evaluation research. Box 11-4 describes these exemplary forms for using case studies as the research design for evaluations.

Developing a Protocol for the Case Study

As suggested above, a *protocol* is the major way of establishing the reliability of a case study. The protocol is a written plan, based on a comprehensive outline, of how the study will be carried out. Yin suggests (1989, pp. 70–80) that the protocol have the following sections: (1) an overview of the entire project, which includes its objectives, and the readings that are relevant to it; (2) a description of field procedures, including forms of access,

relevant credentials if needed, sources of information, and various reminders of how to operate in the field; (3) the questions to be answered in the study, which will guide the data collection and suggest sources of information for answering the questions; and (4) the guide for preparing the final case study report. This written protocol will guide the entire research effort, and at the end of the project it becomes an additional document in the final report.

Qualities of Effective Data Collection for a Case Study

Yin stresses three general goals that researchers must strive for in collecting data in a case study (1989, pp. 95–103). First, they must seek *multiple sources of evidence.* Kanter's study of Indsco, described in Chapter 1, relied on a broad array of data collection methods (1977, pp. 293–296). She utilized

Survey research involving sales workers and managers

Secondary analysis of a survey of staff on attitudes toward promotion

Interviews of the first group of women to enter the sales force, along with less structured conversations on specific topics with individuals

Group discussions, which were recorded

Participant observation of meetings

Documents of various types, most of which were public, and some more private memoranda and reports (which Kanter never specifically refers to in her study)

Intensive discussions with individuals in the organization with whom Kanter had established particularly close ties, who could provide background and perspective on various matters she was studying

Second, Yin stresses that the case study researcher develop a *case study database,* separate from the report of the case study. The data, or evi-

BOX 11-4

EXAMPLES OF CASE STUDIES AS PROGRAM EVALUATIONS

Posavec and Carey offer five exemplary case studies to explain the methods of program evaluation. The following brief descriptions of these cases show the range of ways the case study approach serves the needs of evaluation.

CASE 1: REDUCE STRESS OF EMPLOYEES IN A BURN UNIT OF A COUNTY GENERAL HOSPITAL

The evaluation was designed to assess the problems in the work environment, provide feedback to the staff, plan and institute changes, and then reassess the work environment. The intervention strategy was a set of eight group meetings led by a psychiatrist. The study focused on several dimensions of the work environment, including relationships, goal orientation of employees, and system maintenance and change (in clarity of expectations, use of rules to control behavior, level of innovation encouraged, and pleasantness of physical setting).

CASE 2: ALCOHOL EDUCATION PROGRAM AT A STATE UNIVERSITY

An advertising campaign was instituted to try to affect students' attitudes toward drinking. The project focused on two attitude themes: could students resist peer pressure to drink heavily, and would students stop their friends from driving while drunk? The campaign used a variety of carefully timed media efforts (posters, ads in newspapers, a call-in radio show, and information booths) over a 10-week period, and the researchers interviewed students during the intervention to measure their awareness of the themes. In the last two weeks the researchers mailed a survey to find out whether the media effort had been effective.

CASE 3: UNAUTHORIZED ABSENCES AMONG MARINES

The experimental design randomly divided eight battalions into control and treatment groups. The treatment groups were exposed to varying versions of the intervention program, which involved setting objectives, monitoring absence rates, clarifying and communicating commanders' policies, monitoring command actions, providing rewards, and training field commanders about the goals of the absence prevention program.

CASE 4: A COST-BENEFIT ANALYSIS OF TITLE XX FUNDING FOR FAMILY PLANNING SERVICES IN TEXAS

This study was carried out in 1981 to determine the effectiveness of the program and relate it to the costs. The outcome of the study was prevention of unwanted births, but it is difficult to measure what does not occur. The researchers developed at surrogate measure based on the difference between the expected number of births in the population being studied and the observed number of births. In this study, the family planning services themselves are the "intervention." The costs of these services could then be related to the welfare costs saved by the state for the births that were averted. The type of contraception used by each woman studied was the only other data used. The research determined a benefit rate in terms of dollars saved.

CASE 5: FAMILY PRACTICE RESIDENCY PROGRAM

In this university evaluation, no intervention took place. Instead, careful study of the program included an analysis of documents; in addition, key faculty members described and explained the program's goals, a small number of residents were closely observed over a three-day period, and all residents were interviewed. The areas deemed most in need of improvement were those in which there was the greatest discrepancy between the program's goals and the residents' experiences. These areas were comprehensiveness and continuity of care, formal teaching sessions, and quality of clinical teaching and training.

Source: Emil J. Posavec and Raymond G. Carey, *Program Evaluation: Methods and Case Studies,* 3d ed., Prentice-Hall, Englewood Cliffs, N.J., 1989, pp. 289–320.

dentiary, base in a case study is parallel to the computerized dataset of aggregated responses to the questions in a survey. In survey research, as described in Chapter 7, this dataset is fully separate from the written research report or paper that is the end product of the research. Similarly, in a case study, the database must be a separate set of materials. It may include aggregated answers to survey questions (if the case study utilized a survey), responses to specific interviews, notes from observations, case study documents, and tabular materials. In addition, Yin advises that the case study database contain *narratives.*

A case study researcher, using the narrative technique, composes open-ended answers to the questions in the protocol. As Yin states,

> each answer represents an attempt to integrate the available evidence and to converge upon the facts of the matter or their tentative interpretation. The process is actually an analytic one and is an integral part of the case study analysis *(1989, p. 101).*

Yin compares the preparation of these answers to completing a take-home exam in a graduate course, in which certain types of evidence are linked and related to the issues in the study, and citations to other related work are included.

Third, Yin stresses the need to maintain a *chain of evidence.* He compares this strategy to that of a criminological investigation where all the facts need to be gathered, their relevance to the case assessed, and the logical links between facts and other forms of evidence carefully connected and addressed to the problem at hand. The reader of a case study should be able to track the course of the research backwards to where the researcher began and figure out the logical steps in the development of the research project (1989, p. 102).

When Is the Case Study Method Most Appropriate?

Case studies have often been wrongly considered to be easy to carry out. Like other types of research, they require forethought, careful planning,

data collection, analysis, and final preparation for reporting. While they focus on a single social environment or institution, the strategies involved are as comprehensive as in other research methods. Case studies are often the bases of doctoral dissertations. More and more, studies of the degree of success of new policies require multiple case studies. Effective case studies serve as classic exemplars of how social research can be done. They may reach theoretical conclusions which have widespread and long-range implications, both politically and in terms of theoretical developments in a field.

SOCIAL INDICATORS

Definition and Origins of Social Indicators

What are *social indicators*? Quite simply, they are measures of aggregate social conditions that are of interest to a society because they offer a way to evaluate the overall state of that society. As explained by the federal government,

> A social indicator . . . may be defined to be a statistic of direct normative interest which facilitates concise, comprehensive and balanced judgments about the condition of major aspects of a society (*U.S. Department of Health, Education and Welfare, 1969, p. 97).*

For example, the "average life expectancy at birth" given in years is a social indicator of the "health" of a society. It is reported as a mathematical average (a descriptive summary statistic). Such statistics are generally presented comparatively across a number of years so that *trends* can be denoted.

Undoubtedly, the health of a nation is of social concern, and average life expectancy is an indicator of the state of this health. This indicator is normative in that it suggests how various rules and values of the society (as pertaining to health care, hygiene, health education, and public health issues) are affecting the state of health of the nation.

The social indicator must be accurately measured and must be a simple enough statistic, based on sufficiently fair evidence, so that many people will both understand and trust what it supposedly represents.

In the 1960s, interest was generated in the United States to have available a range of easily understood social indicators that would enable policymakers and others to be able to make better decisions about social conditions in America. The early conception of which social indicators to develop, as laid out by the then U.S. Department of Health, Education and Welfare, stressed the *positive output* qualities of the definition. For this conception, a social indicator was "a direct measure of welfare and is subject to the interpretation that if it changes in the 'right' direction, while other things remain equal, things have gotten better, people better off" (Carley, 1981, p. 22). This definition emphasized two factors: that the *outputs* of a social system were critical and that they should be measured in terms of *positive accomplishments,* the betterment of persons, and social welfare (Carley, 1981, p. 23).

Others challenged the normative, or positive, stress on the definition since what was currently a positive social good might become a negative social evil later on (an example here might be the rate of population increase). Social indicators were closely allied to various forms of policy analysis. If the health of poor Americans was getting better, did this indicate the success of the Medicaid program? In other cases, an analysis of social indicators might suggest areas in which new policies needed to be formulated so that new programs and funding might ameliorate social ills.

The Use of Social Indicators

The analysis of social indicators is a form of evaluation that encompasses all of society. It is based on analyzing aggregate data and presenting tables, graphs, and discussions which show social trends over time. The social indicators are generally based on an aggregate unit of analysis such as a

city or a country. The actual data are usually measured in terms of that aggregate unit, though they may be based on data from surveys of individuals which are then aggregated. *Objective social indicators* refer to measures of some actual occurrences (completion of high school, family income); *subjective social indicators* refer to the attitudes and perceptions of individuals about special social conditions (for example, job satisfaction or a sense of well-being). Social indicator analyses often combine both objective and subjective indicators.

Most studies using social indicators present sets of tables and graphs. However, this is not always the case. Box 11-5 describes how John Naisbitt used social indicators in writing what became a very popular book, *Megatrends* (1982). This book was followed by *Megatrends 2000* (Naisbitt and Aburdene, 1990), which projects trends for the 1990s. Other typical presentations of social indicators are for reporting on national trends (what is called national reporting) and in what is probably the main branch of social indicators research, called *quality-of-life* studies.

One of the uses of social indicators is in providing a rich source of information on a nation. In the United States, the first effort to present social indicators for the country was *Social Indicators, 1973* (Office of Management and Budget, 1973), which contained numerous tables and graphs on various aspects of American social life. A second, even larger, volume appeared later—*Social Indicators, 1976* (U.S. Department of Commerce, 1977). During the late 1960s and throughout the 1970s, there was a vigorous growth in research on social indicators. However, with the closing of the Center for Coordination of Research on Social Indicators in Washington, D.C., in 1983, there was a reduction in government support for such widespread statistical reporting (Andrews, 1986, p. xi). At the international level, the Organization for Economic Cooperation and Development (OECD) in Paris also reduced its statistical reporting activities. Other international organizations are currently providing comparative indicators: the

BOX 11-5

MEGATRENDS FOR THE 1980S AND 1990S

In 1982, John Naisbitt published *Megatrends*, which delineated 10 major trends, based on a form of social indicators analysis (a term he does not use), that would guide the 1980s. He projected the following trends for the 1980s:

1. The United States is moving from an economy based on industry to one based on "creating and distributing information"
2. High technology is being introduced side by side with a greater stress on self-help and personal growth (what Naisbitt calls "high touch")
3. The United States is now part of a world economy, rather than being a self-sufficient national economy
4. Planning is being based on longer-term considerations
5. Innovation in the governance of cities and organizations has a high priority
6. Greater reliance on individuals and less dependence on institutions is being stressed
7. Representative democracy is being affected by the mass media and their ability to provide instantaneous information
8. Hierarchical structures are being replaced with more informal networks (especially in business)
9. Population has shifted to the sun belt
10. A wider and wider range of options are being offered to Americans in terms of consumer goods and lifestyle choices.

In *Megatrends 2000*, Naisbitt and Aburdene set out 10 new trends they project will influence the 1990s:

1. A booming global economy
2. A renaissance in the arts
3. The emergence of free-market socialism
4. Global lifestyles and cultural nationalism
5. The privatization of the welfare state
6. The rise of the Pacific Rim
7. The decade of women in leadership
8. The age of biology
9. The religious revival of the New Millennium
10. The triumph of the individual

The sources of evidence supporting these new projected trends are detailed in footnotes, many of which refer to newspaper and popular magazine articles. Note that the trends for the 1990s are often merely catchphrases ("the decade of women in leadership," "the age of biology"). What evidence could show at the end of the 1990s that these trends had not occurred? Or are these propositions so general and nonspecific that they cannot be disproved?

Material from John Naisbitt, *Megatrends: Ten New Directions Transforming Our Lives*, Warner, New York, 1982, p. 13; John Naisbitt and Patricia Aburdene, *Megatrends 2000*, Morrow, New York, 1990, p. 13.

World Watch Institute develops yearly State of the World reports (see Brown, 1991) and the World Bank presents economic data for the countries of the world on a yearly basis on diskette and tapes as well as in print (see World Bank, 1991).

Quality-of-Life (QOL) Studies. In the mid-1970s, numerous studies began to appear that

would report on the average quality of social life in the United States and make projections for future conditions. Terleckyj's (1975) volume *Improvements in the Quality of Life: Estimates of Possibilities in the United States, 1974–1983* was typical. The objective was first to select a series of areas of social concern and then to determine one or more indicators that would represent a measure of this concern (in short, to find one or more social indicators). Box 11-6 presents factors used to measure QOL in metropolitan areas. Liu (1976) emphasizes that to be meaningful, QOL measures must be computed separately for large, middle-sized, and small cities.

Subjective indicators of QOL. There were also hopes of developing an overall indicator of the quality of life as a whole. There were attempts to develop such an indicator by combining a number of objective social indicators into a single measure. However, there were serious measurement and conceptualization problems in trying to devise such overall QOL indicators. Many came to feel that the quality of life, as it was experienced by individuals, was based less on physical qualities (such as the amount of crowding) than on subjective qualities (such as a sense of well-being).

For example, Andrews and Withey (1976) at the Institute for Social Research at the University of Michigan developed a number of measures of global well-being as indicators of the quality of life. A global measure is one that seeks to uncover a very broad perspective, an overview, a general orientation. They began with the contention that

> People's evaluations are terribly important: to those who would like to raise satisfactions by trying to meet people's needs, to those who would like to raise dissatisfactions and stimulate new challenges, to those who would suppress or reduce feelings and public expressions of discontent, and above all, to the individuals themselves. It is their perceptions of their own well-being, or lack of well-being, that ultimately define the quality of their lives *(1976, p. 10).*

The global measure of well-being that Andrews and Withey found to be the best indicator (after carrying out a number of analyses of different types of global measures) was the question "How do you feel about your life as a whole?," to which the respondent was offered a seven-point scale: "delighted," "pleased," "mostly satisfied," "mixed (about

equally satisfied and dissatisfied)," "mostly dissatisfied," "unhappy," "terrible."

Campbell's (1981) studies on the sense of well-being among Americans, based on subjective self-evaluations, analyzed a number of factors including social status, marital status, friendships and family relationships, and job status. Once established, these measures of well-being were then examined nationally, regionally, and among different age and status groups. Throughout the 1980s, interest in the quality of life continued with research on happiness, job satisfaction, marital satisfaction, subjective mental health, social support, intergenerational relations, and lifestyles both in and outside of America (see Andrews, 1986).

Social Indicators as a Form of Evaluation Research

Social indicators research is big-scale evaluation research. It is generally based on data aggregated on a country as a whole, though it may be based on smaller units. Its purposes are for social reporting so that governments can recognize the strengths and weaknesses of social factors in their society. It may also serve as a means for evaluating how certain social policies or programs (say, Medicare or national student loans) are affecting the social conditions of wide numbers of individuals in a society. The great concern with quality-of-life measures stems from the desire to be able to develop a barometer of the state of a nation (or some other aggregate group). Given that most societies have a commitment to progress and social betterment, there is the expectation that life will improve over time. Quality-of-life studies evaluate whether such an improvement can be noted.

Social indicators data can be used by other researchers as background or as comparative data for their own studies. If you are doing a small-scale evaluation of some organization, you might compare, for example, indicators of overpreparation for the job among employees of different sexes and racial groups with national data. As stated in Chapter 10 on the analysis of aggregate data,

BOX 11-6

QUALITY-OF-LIFE INDICATORS IN U.S. METROPOLITAN AREAS

QOL indicators have been used to rank American cities in terms of various qualities. Liu divided cities into three groups based on population size so that comparisons based on QOL indicators would be fair. Otherwise all one would learn is that the large cities have more health facilities, more visual pollution, etc. He focused on five components of the quality of life (economic, political, environmental, health and education, and social) and developed indicators to measure each component. Examples of some of the factors measured for each component follow:

ECONOMIC COMPONENT

    Personal income per capita

    Wealth (e.g., savings per capita)

    Percentage of families with income above the poverty level

    Degree of economic concentration

    Productivity (e.g., sales per employee in retail trade)

    Total bank deposits per capita

    Income inequality index (e.g., central city/suburban income distribution)

    Unemployment rate

    Number of full-time Chamber of Commerce employees per 100,000 population

POLITICAL COMPONENT

    Informed citizenry (e.g., newspaper circulation)

    Political activity (ratio of presidential voting to voting-age population)

    Professionalism (e.g., salaries of government employees)

    Performance (e.g., violent crime rate, percentage of revenue from federal government)

    Welfare assistance

ENVIRONMENTAL COMPONENT

    Air pollution index

    Visual pollution (e.g., dilapidated housing, acres of parks)

    Noise

    Solid waste

    Water pollution

    Climatological information

    Recreation areas and facilities

HEALTH AND EDUCATION COMPONENT

    Health (infant mortality, death rate)

    Education (e.g., median school years completed, percentage of age-specified population currently enrolled in school)

    Medical care availability and accessibility (e.g., number of dentists, physicians, or hospital beds per 100,000 population)

    Educational attainment (e.g., local government expenditure on education, percentage of population over age 25 who completed four or more years of college)

SOCIAL COMPONENT

    Existing opportunity for self-support (e.g., labor force participation rate, percentage of children under age 18 living with both parents

    Maximum development of individual capabilities (e.g., individual health index, persons with less than 15 years of schooling who have had vocational training)

    Opportunities for individual choice (e.g., motor vehicle registrations, local radio stations)

    Individual equality (e.g., ratios of black to white residents; ratio of females in professional employment; unemployment; spatial factors, such as housing segregation index)

    General living conditions (e.g., crime rate, availability of telephones, plumbing facilities, persons per room)

    Facilities (e.g., availability of recreation, commercial areas, services)

    Other social conditions (e.g., births, deaths, sports, cultural events, natural environment index)

Source: Ben-Chieh Liu, Quality of Life Indicators in U.S. Metropolitan Areas, Praeger, New York, 1976, pp. 57–77.

it is always very important to be careful that you understand how the indicator is measured, that you report carefully the group on which it is aggregated, and that you avoid the ecological fallacy of imputing trends seen in aggregate groups to individuals or subgroups within these larger groups (see Chapters 4 and 10 for discussions of the ecological fallacy).

DECIDING IF EVALUATION RESEARCH IS APPROPRIATE FOR YOUR TOPIC

This is generally quite easy to do. If you are carrying out a research project requested by some organization to study its operations, you know you will be evaluating that agency. Since most evaluation research is funded by the agencies seeking the evaluation, it is not difficult to decide in such instances whether evaluation research is the appropriate purpose of the study.

You may, however, carry out many types of evaluations without the funding of an outside source. You might design your own community impact assessment. You might use existing data sources over a period of years to try to carry out a time-series analysis of the effects of some major social change on a set of indicators. You may also be able to study a small program, for example, a new writing course at your college or the effects of a new student activity at your college. In cases like these, you will be able to build a much more effective design if you are able to collect data from students or from those offering the services (faculty or staff) at different points in time, before the program is offered, during the program, and after it is over (or after the individuals you are studying have completed the program). You will also want to consider comparing those who participated in the program with those who did not.

Finally, you should recall the Coleman study as one that was based on a general survey in which the issue of evaluation grew out of the analysis. There are many available datasets, such as the one Coleman and his colleagues used, which have data that lend themselves to the evaluation of many so-

cial factors. It is often more precise to think of such research as *policy research* rather than as evaluation research. This means that the purpose of the research is to address public policies, or issues that the society or some segment of it thinks are important, without necessarily setting out to carefully evaluate precise programs.

While evaluation research must be undertaken with great care, a student researcher can carry off an evaluation study very successfully (even one that has required that compromises be made in the design) as long as he or she understands the quality of the study that has been attempted and is sufficiently humble in presenting what may be partial or only tentative results.

REVIEW NOTES

- Evaluation research is not a separate type of research method, but research carried out for the purpose of evaluating some social program, law, or activity.
- Evaluations of social programs may begin prior to the beginning of the program (preprogram) or during the course of the program (ongoing evaluation).
- Cost-benefit analyses seek to assess whether the benefit of a program or social strategy is worth the cost. It may be difficult to measure costs and benefits. It is easier if the measurement of both costs and benefits can be operationalized in terms of dollars.
- Community impact assessment studies can determine what effect a new policy might have on a community.
- One way to examine the impact of new legislation is to compare indicators that should be affected by the law from before to after its enactment using a time-series analysis design.
- Evaluation projects may be directed to many different audiences. These include funding agencies; local, state, or national agencies; project directors or staff; program clients; and the research community.
- Formative evaluations set out to study programs

in process and feed the findings of an evaluation back into the program; in contrast, summative evaluations summarize the major effects of a program once completed.
- Ways of strengthening the reliability and validity of the dependent variable in an evaluation project are to use an already developed measure or multiple measures.
- In evaluations of social programs, participation or nonparticipation in the program is usually the independent variable.
- Possible input measures include purposes, principles, methods, staff, clients, location, length of service, size, and management of the program as well as under whose auspices the program is being offered.
- The findings of evaluation studies may be "contained" or "buried." Evaluation research is often underutilized because it lacks practicality and specific recommendations.
- Evaluation studies need a comparative baseline for determining the success or failure of what is being evaluated.
- Case studies investigate current phenomena in real-life settings using various research methods. Program evaluations are often case studies.
- Social indicators are measures of aggregate social conditions of social interest.
- Quality-of-life (QOL) studies have attempted to develop global measures of well-being as indicators of the overall quality of life in a society.
- Studies on the sense of well-being, based on subjective evaluations, have been examined nationally, regionally, and among different age and status groups.
- Policy research is a form of evaluation research which addresses the effectiveness of public policies.

KEY TERMS

case studies
case study protocol
community impact assessment

cost-benefit analysis
ex post facto design (after-only)
formative evaluation
nonequivalent control group
objective social indicators
ongoing program evaluation
policy research
preprogram evaluation
quality-of-life (QOL) studies
social indicators
subjective social indicators
summative evaluation

STUDY EXERCISES

You have been hired by North High School to design an evaluation study of their college counseling program.

1. Your first step is to consider the purposes of the program. How would you go about doing this?
2. Having determined the purpose of the counseling program, define one or more measurable outputs of the college counseling program. Be sure that they would serve as measures of the effectiveness of the program.
3. Now define the inputs to the program that you would want to study in relation to the outputs.

RECOMMENDED READINGS

1. Boruch, Robert F., and Werner Wothke (eds.): *Randomization and Field Experimentation,* Jossey-Bass, San Francisco, 1985. Discussions of evaluations of social programs and services in which randomized assignment was carried out in various field settings. The editors conclude with a strong plea for using randomization and present several designs for implementation.
2. Carley, Michael: *Social Measurement and Social Indicators: Issues of Policy and Theory,* Allen & Unwin, Boston, 1983. Social indicators, as measures used to monitor social change, have been developed in various countries. However, there is a general lack of agreement on what constitute measures of social

indicators. The most typical examples are measures from the health field.

3. Love, Arnold J.: *Internal Evaluation: Building Organizations from Within,* Sage, Newbury Park, Calif., 1991. Organizations are increasingly taking the initiative in self-evaluation. This resource book can help in the development of studies evaluating goal achievement, effectiveness, and efficiency in an organization.

4. McKillip, Jack: *Need Analysis: Tools for the Human Services and Education,* Sage, Newbury Park, Calif., 1987. Describing need analysis as identifying and evaluating needs, this volume offers a set of research tools (resource inventories, social indicators, service use, surveys, structured groups) for carrying out such an analysis.

5. Posavec, Emil J., and Raymond G. Carey: *Program Evaluation: Methods and Case Studies,* 3d ed., Prentice-Hall, Englewood Cliffs, N.J., 1989. This thorough and thoughtful text overviews program evaluation, covering program planning and monitoring, evaluations of outcomes, applications of findings, and case studies.

6. Weiss, Carol H.: *Evaluation Research: Methods of Assessing Program Effectiveness,* Prentice-Hall, Englewood Cliffs, N.J., 1972. This very readable book covers the purposes, design, and utilization of evaluation research.

7. Yin, Robert K.: *Case Study Research: Design and Methods,* Sage, Newbury Park, Calif., 1989. A comprehensive guide on how to design, conduct, and analyze a case study.

The Analysis
of Social Research Data

*I*n this final section of the text, we shall discuss various ways of analyzing data. Remember that the primary reason for designing a study and collecting the data is to enable you to establish and present your findings. This requires careful analysis of your data. You begin by carefully setting out and cataloging everything you have collected. Then you must figure out what you have found. This analysis can be done in a number of ways. The data may be rearranged so that those parts of the data which are similar are grouped together. This is normally what is done in survey analysis where variables from each of the cases are aggregated across all the cases. In a field study, where notes have been taken, the analysis may be considered as a sifting process where the relevant materials are sorted out and other material discarded. Whatever the type of data, the object of a data analysis is to turn the amorphous heap of evidence into firmer, more solid findings. These more condensed data, which you have decided to focus upon, then need to be interpreted.

You must examine the findings in terms of the hypotheses or research questions which you originally posed. How far does the evidence support your hypothesis? Are there answers in the analyzed data to the research questions you posed? Data analysis may seem a bit like a game in which the strategy is to see if the evidence fits the case. You look for the strengths in the analyzed data: the clearest patterns among the variables, the strongest associations between particular variables. Then you try to make the best case for what you have found. However, in the analysis of social data, the evidence may *not* fit the case. In such a circumstance you must report that you have not found support (or have only weak support) for your hypothesis. Remember, having evidence to reject a hypothesis is often as interesting as having evidence to support it.

Chapter 12 serves as an introduction to data analysis by discussing the preparation of data. Such preparation will naturally vary, depending on the types of data you have. In the chapter, I concentrate on *quantifiable* data which are generally analyzed with the help of a computer. In order to analyze your data on a computer, you must prepare them to be transferred to a computer through procedures such as coding. Since there are many different types of computer systems, the chapter offers only general guidelines regarding what needs to be done to computerize your data. Even if you do not plan to use a computer in your study, Chapter 12 offers sound principles of data handling which should be considered by any researchers whatever their plans for analysis.

Chapter 13 offers an example of data analyses which will be referred to in all the following data analysis chapters. It is from a data analysis prepared specifically for this text: a secondary analysis of a national survey is developed in order to address an important, but fairly simple and straightforward research hypothesis. The chapter includes presentations of univariate tables, the most elementary form of tables, and two-variable (bivariate) tables, showing how these tables are prepared and how they may be interpreted. Chapter 14 introduces three-variable (trivariate) analyses and the elaboration model of analysis, which is a classic means of interpreting trivariate tables. Again, the data are taken from the study detailed in Chapter 13.

Chapter 15 describes some elementary social statistics and shows when and where to use them, offering examples from the dataset presented in Chapters 13 and 14. Some of the students using this text may already have had a course in statistics. For students with a background in statistics, Chapter 15 can serve as a refresher course in the uses of a few regularly employed statistical tests in social research. For students without any previous background in statistics, Chapter 15 offers some very basic guidelines for the use of statistics in social research and suggests which statistic tests might be good to use with different types of variables and analyses. Chapter 16 offers some basic training in constructing indexes. Creating indexes depends on the use of bivariate analyses, which were presented earlier. Principles of the most commonly known types of scales used in the social sciences and descriptions of some frequently used scales are also presented. Chapter 17 concludes Part Four with a discussion of the steps to be followed in preparing and presenting a final research report.

Data Preparation and Computerization

LOOKING AHEAD

This chapter covers how to code data for quantitative analysis by computer. It also goes through the general procedures needed to enter data into a computer and prepare the data for analysis.

INTRODUCTION

The data that you have collected, whatever your method, will be in the form of *raw data*—that is, data that has not yet been processed in any way. Your first step in analyzing the data will be to prepare these data for the type of analyses you plan to carry out. If you are doing a field study, the major form of analysis may involve organizing your notes to address your primary research question and then writing up these notes into a paper. In this type of analysis, there may be no information to convert into quantifiable categories. Methods used to prepare data for qualitative analyses were described in Chapter 9 on field research.

Most of the other methods which have been discussed in this book require that the initial information gathered (the raw data) be converted into numerical equivalents for the purposes of quantitative analyses and (possibly) statistical testing. This chapter will be devoted to a discussion of how to turn potentially quantifiable raw data into numbers which will represent the range of meanings—the variation—in the raw data themselves. Such a procedure is necessary in order to prepare tables, charts, and graphs that will *describe* the data precisely and in order to *explain* how far the data support your hypotheses. If you plan to test your hypotheses statistically, measures to determine the *strength of relationships* may be established. If your data have been drawn from a probability sample, other statistical tests will allow you to make inferences from the sample to the population from which it was drawn.

Data preparation will be explained in four stages. The first stage, in which the raw data are coded into numbers, is the *coding stage.* The second stage, preparing the coded information to be transferred from written form to a form which can be accepted by a computer, is the *transfer stage.* The third stage, which involves the actual process of entering the coded data into the computer, is the *computer entry stage.* In considering this stage it will be necessary to look at the various types of procedures available for "computerizing" data—which will naturally vary according to the type of computer system available to you. (There are now so many different types of computer systems that it is not possible to give you specific instructions on how to use your equipment. Enough general information will be provided, however, to show what you will need to do to enter your data if you have access to one of the more commonly available types of computer systems.) The fourth stage involves *cleaning the data* once they are on the computer. This means that you need to check the accuracy of the data after they are entered into the computer since errors can be introduced at every stage of data handling.

The data to be discussed in the forthcoming chapters, whatever their source, are made up of the same set of information (that is, the same set of *variables*) on an array of subjects (or what are usually referred to as *cases*). While the type of data considered in this chapter are those produced from surveys, many of the suggestions offered apply as well to data gathered from experiments, from content analyses, or from other forms of data collection.

COMMITMENT TO CARE

Careful attention to the methods and procedures of data preparation described in this chapter is vital to your study. Whatever your form of data, unless you handle them with great care and try to minimize and rectify the errors that occur at each step of your preparation (as they almost always do!), your results may be seriously jeopardized. The data preparation phase of your study is not simply "busywork" that anyone can do. It may be true that anyone could do it, but it is not true that anyone could do it *right!* If you have assistants helping you to code or transfer your data, you must nevertheless stay in command of the situation and check their efforts at every stage. There is no reason to suppose that your assistants will deliberately make errors, but you must assume that their knowledge of the study (however much you have explained it to them) and their personal commitment to its outcome will never be as great as your own.

The fanciest computer program, the largest research grant, and the cleverest statistical routines cannot convert messy, dirty, sloppy data into valid results. Thus the issue of care in data handling is another area where the validity of a study can be challenged. There is a well-known saying about computer analyses: "Garbage in, garbage out!" This means that if the data you enter into the computer are full of errors—if, for example, what is supposed to be the measure of "attitude toward income inequality between the sexes" for the fifteenth case in the sample is mistakenly entered into the computer as the measure of "attitude toward nuclear disarmament," then once the variable of income equality attitude is computed, the mistaken fifteenth case will have distorted the finding. Further, if there are many such errors, the measure of income equality attitude may no longer represent that attitude.

In such an instance, all your efforts at designing the variables so that they would truly get at the concepts you are trying to measure and all your efforts at gathering the data so that the respondents would comprehend the questions and answer them with understanding can be for naught. For, if errors are added into the data when it is put on the computer, the data will be spoiled. Thus, "garbage in, garbage out": If you put bad data into a computer, no matter what is done to them in the computer, you will get bad analyses out of the computer. So think carefully about the suggestions offered in this chapter in relation to your study. Some of the precautions and suggested procedures may not be necessary in your particular study, but a consideration of the reasons for each will help clarify what you must be sure to do and what you must be sure to avoid in the handling and preparation of your dataset. Remember, your data are your most precious resource in your research project, so *treat them with care!*

DEVISING A CODING SYSTEM

General Principles to Follow

Coding the data involves taking the information, the raw data, you have and putting it into a form which can be quantified for analysis. There are a number of principles to keep in mind in organizing a coding system. *The first principle is that coding must resolve issues of definition and ambiguity so that the codes can be applied consistently. It requires making decisions on the basis of how best to code responses to the variables so as to maintain the meaning of the concept which your variable represents.* These decisions can be made on the basis of theoretical and empirical criteria.

In considering these issues in coding, you might look back to the material presented in Chapter 5 on conceptualization and operationalization. Operationalizing a variable is not completed once you have developed a survey question with its categories. For, if you recode that question once the data are collected (if you combine categories or if you rename these combined categories) or if you create an index or scale (to be discussed in Chapter 16), the criteria used to carry out these changes will alter the initial operationalization and thereby change the relationship between the concept and the measured variable. That is why you must do this data handling and coding thoughtfully and deliberately.

Theoretical criteria test whether the scale (or set) of attributes making up the types of variation in a variable has been fairly carried over to a set of numerical codes which accurately represent the range of meaning you wanted to measure in the variable. Such criteria test for the *validity* of the variable. *Empirical criteria* test how far the results from measuring the variable seem to represent reasonable and expected outcomes: in other words, they help you determine how far the respondents understood what was being asked of them and how far they shared the meaning you gave to the question. The essential concern here is whether the respondents would be likely to respond to the item in a consistent fashion, that is, whether you can reasonably expect them to respond to the same question in the same way if they were asked again. In deciding this, you are testing for the item's *reliability.* Note that one difference between the use of theoretical and empirical criteria in making decisions about coding is that theoretical criteria can be applied before data collection begins by the use of precoding (to be described below). Empirical criteria, on the other hand, may only be fully established once the data are gathered and certain patterns evident in the responses can guide coding decisions.

From a theoretical point of view, you must assign codes that represent the range of meaning you want a variable to have. This range must be sensitive to the types of variation possible. Are the responses to the question actual numbers that can be worked with mathematically (such as income, age, number of children)? Do the responses represent an ordering which should be carried over into the coding pattern (attitudes with which respondents can "strongly agree," "somewhat agree," etc.)? Or are the responses merely categories which have no ordered relationship to one another, but are merely different from one another (religious affiliation, race, sex)? In this latter case, it may make no difference which category is given the highest number, what order the categories are in, or what number codes are actually given.

For example, there are theoretical considerations inherent in coding "don't know" responses that can only be solved by thinking through what exactly you meant by offering "don't know" as a response (assuming it was one) or what you had planned to do when respondents gave "don't know" responses when they were not offered. For attitudinal items, "don't know" would seem to be a valid response meaning *no settled opinion;* for information about personal background and history, it could mean *a failure of memory* (e.g., educational attainment of one's father) or *lack of access to the information* (e.g., one's blood type). In each case, you should give consideration to the intended meaning of the question before deciding how to code the variable.

From an empirical point of view, you want to code the data so as to preserve the full variation given by the respondents, but you may also feel justified in combining certain types of responses in certain cases. Remember that *the second general principle of coding is to preserve as much as possible of the actual meaning of the responses and of the variation presented in the data.* This can be understood by reference to an example from open-ended questions. With open-ended items, you may plan on the prospective answers, but final coding decisions must wait until the data are collected. This after-the-fact type of coding is based on what the empirical results came out to be.

Suppose you have asked people to list their favorite pastimes. You might have decided on prearranged categories for (1) sports, both competitive and individual; (2) films, plays, concerts; (3) reading, listening to music, watching television; (4) homemaking activities—gourmet cooking, needlepoint, gardening, etc.; (5) hobbies, collections. What do you do, however, when a respondent cites "washing the dog" or "shopping"? Should you start a new category for "pets"? (Is washing the dog a hobby? Is shopping a homemaking activity?) These are situations where you have to decide how much of the original information you want to preserve. The usual strategy is to code all the data, to avoid discarding any information or collapsing any categories in the course of coding. Instead, it is preferable to leave the process of reducing and recoding the data to a later time. This will give you more options as to how you might use the variables as you proceed with the analyses.

The third general rule is to plan your coding system as far as possible, at the time you design your data collection instrument. Theoretical issues in coding should be carefully considered if you are designing a questionnaire and coding guides can be included on the instrument (see discussion below). *Fourth, the coding system should help to reduce the number of times that the data must be handled,* for every time they are handled additional mistakes may be added. For this reason, coding systems should be clear and precise. *To serve as a guide to the coding system and a record of all the coding de-cisions made, a codebook should be prepared and updating procedures arranged—this is the fifth rule of good coding procedures.* This codebook will be needed not only to guide you in the coding but to refresh your memory as to what a variable really measures as you carry out your analyses.

Prestudy Coding

As stated above, it is a good plan to have your coding system planned out at the time you are designing your study. If questionnaires are to be used, it is best that they include coding information on the actual instrument. This greatly simplifies and speeds up the data transfer procedure itself. If the coding appears on the questionnaires, then the person entering the data into the computer is able to transfer the information directly from questionnaires to the data entry mechanism for the computer. If not, the coding must be written either on the questionnaires or on the coding sheets.

In large studies, coding is often done by persons other than the study designer. When this is the case, as mentioned earlier, the chances of error are increased since an outside coder is less likely to understand the coding system or the intended meaning of a question than the questionnaire designer. Therefore, if you plan to have others help you code your data, you should aim to give them as much assistance as possible; and a precoded questionnaire should help to increase accuracy during coding.

Precoded questionnaires usually have the codes running down the right-or left-hand side of the page. These codes generally include the locations (called *column locations*) on the computer file where the data from this question will reside. This is referred to as *edge coding.* Other types of edge coding simply give the number of the question and the response category to the question. Such codes may also include a questionnaire number, if the survey is longitudinal and if it utilizes multiple questionnaires. The box gives an example of edge coding without computer locations. It is

taken from the National Longitudinal Study (NLS) of the High School Class of 1972.

The athletic participation variable, one of the variables we will consider in Chapter 13, was question 10A in the first of five questionnaires. The edge coding for this question, BQ10A, stands for base questionnaire [that is, the first (1972) survey], question 10, first part (part A). Then the actual codes for the range of responses are to the right of the question (1 = "have not participated," 2 = "have participated actively," 3 = "have participated as a leader or officer"). This was the precoding system devised for the NLS questionnaire data. If you have a large and complex questionnaire, you may be wise to include coding information on the survey instrument.

Codebook Preparation

A precoded questionnaire may serve as a guide to carrying out the coding procedure, but it will not remind you of the decisions you made in setting up the codes as you did, and it will not include the variables you "constructed" subsequent to the data collection. For these reasons, it is important to prepare (and update) a *codebook.*

Defining the Purposes of a Codebook. A codebook is, first of all, a *notation* of what you have decided to call your variables (and the attributes within the variables) and how these names correspond to what was measured by the variable. Secondly, a codebook is a *guide* to where each variable can be found (by its name in the computer file, or wherever, depending on how your data will be processed). Finally, a codebook is a *record of the decisions* which you reached in determining how to set up the variable. Ambiguities in the question, differences in definitions which a question might suggest, must be resolved through coding; and these decisions should be systematically recorded in your codebook so that you remember your rationale for treating a variable in the particular manner you chose to handle it.

EDGE CODING ON THE QUESTIONNAIRE FROM THE NATIONAL LONGITUDINAL STUDY OF THE HIGH SCHOOL CLASS OF 1972

10. HAVE YOU PARTICIPATED IN ANY OF THE FOLLOWING TYPES OF ACTIVITIES, EITHER IN OR OUT OF SCHOOL THIS YEAR?

(Circle One Number on Each Line)

		Have Not Participated	Have Participated Actively	Have Participated as a Leader or Officer
BQ10A	Athletic teams, intramurals, letterman's club, sports club	1	2	3
BQ10B	Cheerleaders, pep club, majorettes	1	2	3
BQ10C	Debating, drama, band, chorus	1	2	3
BQ10D	Hobby clubs such as photography, model building, hot rod, electronics, crafts	1	2	3
BQ10E	Honorary clubs such as Beta Club or National Honor Society	1	2	3
BQ10F	School newspaper, magazine, yearbook, annual	1	2	3
BQ10G	School subject matter clubs such as science, history, language, business, art	1	2	3
BQ10H	Student council, student government, political club	1	2	3
BQ10I	Vocational education, clubs such as Future Homemakers, Teachers, Farmers of America, DECA, OEA, FBLA, or VICA	1	2	3

Setting Up a Codebook. A codebook catalogs each variable first by its formal name and then by the name by which it will be referred to in the computer program. Then it gives the numerical code for each of the values, or attributes, of the variable (for the athletic participation variable, 1 = "have not participated," etc.). In addition, a codebook notes the position on the computer file (to be discussed below) where the variable can be found; this is called its *computer entry form.* Some codebooks (particularly for datasets which have been prepared for secondary analyses) include the actual number of respondents whose answers were coded under each of the code numbers. The box presents the entry for the athletic participation in high school variable in the NLS codebook. The various parts of the coding information will be broken down into the following components, which are typical of many codebooks.

Components of Codebook Entries.   The data to be entered for each variable in a codebook should be consistent from one case to the next. The following are the typical types of information which should be given for each variable in the codebook.

Computer entry position. Column positions should be entered for each variable if a raw data computer file in *fixed format* is being set up. Note that in the second box the athletic participation variable was located in two-column fields given position numbers of 507 (the beginning column, BC) to 508 (the ending column, EC). Can you guess why two columns were needed? (It was because some of the codes—98, 99—had two digits.) I will explain this point in case some of you find it confusing: in each column only one number (or letter) can be entered. Therefore to handle a

two-digit number, you must use two columns; for a three-digit number, you need three columns. When you set up your computer system file (described below) you will need to instruct the computer to relate a certain variable name to a certain column or to more than one column of data. Often data are entered in a free format and column entry numbers can be omitted.

Formal name. Every variable should be given a formal name which will identify what it measures. For example, if the variable is sex, this is such an obvious name that it needs no further elaboration in the codebook. Social class, however, may be too inexplicit to be used as a formal name. It may be better to specify the type of socioeconomic measuring instrument used in the formal name (for example, "Respondent's current socioeconomic status—Duncan Scale," to be described in Chapter 16) might be the formal name given. Note that in the second box the variable of athletic participa-

---

CODING INFORMATION FOR ATHLETIC PARTICIPATION IN HIGH SCHOOL IN THE NATIONAL LONGITUDINAL STUDY OF THE HIGH SCHOOL CLASS OF 1972

A. CODEBOOK ENTRY

CODEBOOK FOR NLS RELEASE TAPE

VAR#	Label	#DEC	BC	EC	Question Label
241	BQ10A		507	508	DO YOU PARTICIPATE IN ATHLETICS?

B. FREQUENCY DISTRIBUTION WITH CATEGORY CODES

VAR# 0241 BQ10A   COLS 0507–0508
    DO YOU PARTICIPATE IN ATHLETICS?

Category Label	Code	Absolute Frequency
HAVE NOT PARTICIPATED	1	11,590
HAVE PART. ACTIVELY	2	7,031
HAVE PART. AS LEADER	3	1,940
BLANK	98	661
LEGITSKP	99	1,430
	TOTAL	22,652

tion was given no formal name by the NLS staff; instead the actual question on which it was based is used as its name. In selecting this variable to use in a secondary analysis (as we will in Chapter 13), however, we would give it a name, say, high school athletic participation, and record the name in the codebook we would devise.

Computer name.   Here there are two common conventions. One is simply to number the variables. This is the strategy used in the second box. The athletic participation variable is VAR241. This is the way the variable is to be identified by the computer and by the researcher as well. But this need not be the case, for most computer programs can handle either numbers or words as designators of variables. For example, if sex is the first variable entered in the computer file, it might be given the name VAR1 (variable 1) or it might be given a *mnemonic,* i.e., a word or set of letters used to recall some specific thing. SEX is a name which is so short it can serve as its own mnemonic. For a variable such as athletic participation in high school, a suitable mnemonic might be HSATHPAR. Thus, the second convention is to give the variable a word name.

Value labels for the attributes of a variable. These are the actual codes for the various categories (or scale numbers) of a variable. In the second box, the codes are 1, 2, 3, 98, and 99. The designation 98 is the code for those who did not answer the question (those who left it blank); 99 is for those who had a legitimate reason for skipping the question. The NLS codebook entry did not include the categories; however, the NLS staff provided the initial frequency distributions which gave the code numbers of the categories of the variables. These frequency distributions served as an additional codebook in which codes given to the categories (or attributes) of the variable were presented.

A variable with an ordinal scale set of responses should be coded in order: for example, 1 = "strongly agree," 2 = "agree," 3 = "undecid-

ed," 4 = "disagree," 5 = "strongly disagree." For a variable with responses representing actual numbers, the codes can be the responses themselves. For example, in the case of age, the categories can simply be the actual number of years the person has lived. (Naturally you would not need to write in the codebook 1 = "1," 23 = "23," etc.) When the numbers are a continuous series with fractional amounts, like weight, the coded numbers will need to be rounded in a systematic and consistent manner.

Case numbers.   As every variable in a study is given a variable name, every respondent to a study is usually given a case number. The primary reasons for doing this are to keep your responses systematic and to make checking for errors (cleaning) easier. If the respondents have filled out questionnaires, the case numbers might be written in on the top of each questionnaire (from, for example, 001 to 250). Then these numbers should be entered into the computer as if they were a variable in the study. Thus the codebook might include the variable ID, which could be described for a sample of 250 as a three-digit code from 001 to 250. Naturally the computer position would be included as well.

Creating a Flexible Codebook.   When preparing your own codebook, consider using a loose-leaf folder that holds 3 × 5 inch index cards with punched holes. Each card can record a different variable. You can then sort the cards in different ways and may insert a card for any new variable (which may often be created from recoding or combining other variables) next to the card for the original variable on which it was based. Such a codebook therefore gives you a lot of flexibility for adding to and rearranging your variables.

Cross-referencing.   One of the helpful techniques you might incorporate into your codebook is to cross-reference variables. For example, from the name of the city, suburb, or rural area in which respondents reside, you might create a new variable entitled urban/suburban/rural. This means that you would have one variable with the name of each place coded and a second variable with only three categories: urban, suburban, and rural. In such a case, when new versions (or constructed variables) of earlier variables have been created, you should cross-reference these variables in the codebook. You might also want to refer to variables that are identical but were collected at different times (SES measures taken in different years) and to variables that measure very similar qualities (number of years of schooling completed, highest degree attained).

Noting reasons for coding decisions.   As mentioned above, it is important to remember why you coded variables as you did. Don't trust memory alone. Brief notes included with the code for the variable will be much more reliable.

Coding Open-Ended Questions. There are three possible strategies in coding open-ended questions. One is to develop in advance the set of categories you think will cover exhaustively all the possible responses to the question, to give these categories codes, and then to classify the answers according to these codes. For many types of questions, you can precode all such responses. For example, you might decide to code responses to a question about occupation into the categories "white collar" and "blue collar." Remember that you must also include the category "other" for occupations which you might not be able to fit into either of the first two categories. (By some definitions, of course, all occupations could be placed in one of these two categories.) Finally, for respondents who failed to give an answer to the question, you would need a "no response" category.

One problem that may arise with the strategy of coding open-ended questions in advance is that some categories may not have any responses falling into them. If that is so, then they are *irrelevant* categories. To minimize this possibility, it may be helpful to try out the open-ended questions in a pretest to see which coding categories should be used and which left out.

Another form of precoding is to separate the possible responses to a single question into different variables. Let's say that you have asked respondents to list their favorite sports. You might have a study where the major sport which interests you is swimming. In this case you might want to look at each sport mentioned, coding the answer as follows: 1 = "swimming mentioned"; 0 = "swimming not mentioned"; 9 = "no answer." Then if baseball is mentioned, it would form another variable, etc. In this case, none of the information would be lost, but a single question would form the basis of a number of variables.

The third common strategy is to develop a set of categories on the basis of the responses themselves. This postsurvey technique is particularly suitable for questions which might generate many different types of answers which you cannot fully predict in advance. For example, suppose you ask people, with an open-ended question, why they voted for a particular political candidate. Since you are unsure of the range of reasons respondents might give, you must begin by looking at the responses and making a list of the types of responses given—the respondent likes the candidate's economic position, approach to foreign policy, social policy, personality, and so on. In listing the types of responses in this way, you will in effect be categorizing them. This means that you must decide on the number and kinds of categories you need.

Take the area of social policy, for example. Do you need only one category for liking the candidate's stand on any type of social policy, or would it be better to have separate categories for the candidate's position on various issues such as abortion, Medicare, social welfare, or whatever? Here the choice you make must depend on what you hope to be able to analyze. If you want to be able to compare respondents who support candidates who are pro-choice or pro-life, for example, then you had better categorize abortion positions separately. If you think that this social issue will need to be considered only in terms of a broader social issues category, however, then you should feel comfortable with collapsing this category and combining it and other social issues responses into a single category.

You may be concerned that, at the coding stage, you will not know exactly what forms of analyses you plan to carry out. In fact, that is often the case. In such situations, it is a good rule to use *more* categories rather than fewer. It is always possible to collapse categories which are not needed (or which contain too few cases) into other available categories, once the data have been coded. Finally, once open-ended questions have been coded, the principles used for doing the coding should be entered in the codebook.

Coding Missing Data.   There are always some data missing in a study. In a questionnaire, respondents may not choose to answer every question, or they may inadvertently skip questions, or they may think that certain questions are not relevant to them. Moreover, answers may be given that are inappropriate to the question: for an open-ended question, an answer may make no sense in terms of answering the question; for a forced-choice question, instructions may not have been followed appropriately (e.g., where "Circle the single best answer" has *three* answers circled). In other cases, open-ended responses may be illegible.

For the purposes of coding, you must still code these responses in some way. Here is where "no response," "not relevant," or some other type of no-meaningful-data-available-for-this-case-on-this-variable response may need to be used. The convention is to code "no response" as a 9. If you can make distinctions between "no response" and "not relevant," and these distinctions seem important to you for your study, then you should give them different codes. Often a questionnaire will include a "don't know" category for respondents to select; this is conventionally coded as an 8. If you are using two-digit codes, the 9 would be 99 and the 8 would be 98.

When analyzing the variables, missing data are often excluded from the analyses. Most computer programs for analyzing data offer easy means to specify data as missing when you have coded them clearly as such. One of the main reasons you want to keep information on missing data is to assess its prevalence within the sample. If a variable has too much missing information, it may not be worthwhile to use in your analysis. If you are comparing the responses of two or more subgroups, you must be concerned that one group does not have a much higher proportion of missing data on a specific variable of interest than another. Knowledge of missing data will be important for you in your analyses, and so you must be sure to code it fully and accurately in your coding procedure.

Using a Blank Questionnaire as a Codebook. It is not wise to use a blank questionnaire as the sole form of a codebook, because it does not have the space to incorporate all the decisions you have made or to include constructed variables or those derived from sources other than the questionnaire. But if the data were drawn from questionnaires, it will probably be useful to *code* a blank questionnaire to accompany your codebook as you carry out the coding. The coded questionnaire form will help serve as a guide.

Types of Coding Strategies

Typical questions usually offer one of five types of response categories. The first type involves answers (often to attitudinal questions) providing a set of ordinal scale responses, such as "strongly agree," "agree," "disagree," "strongly disagree." The second offers answers which are dichotomies: a yes-or-no response is an example, as well as answers that measure whether a quality is present. "Do you play tennis? Yes/No" is equivalent to "Which of the following sports do you engage in? Tennis, Swimming, Boxing, etc." In the latter case, each sport would be the basis of a different dichotomized variable such that those who checked "tennis" would be coded 1 = "plays tennis"; 0 = "does not play tennis."

The third type of response category offers answers which are a set of categories that have no specific order (such as your religion—Catholic, Protestant, Jewish—which have no logical order). The fourth involves questions which can be answered directly by a number (income, age, number of children). The fifth type of question allows open-ended responses, which must be coded one by one on the basis of the content of the answers and which can then be reconverted into numerical categories.

Spot-Checking for Errors

Since coding involves a number of different types of shifts, there is a great potential for error. Most cleaning of data for computer entry is done after the data have been entered into the computer. However, I suggest that you do a spot check of your data before transferring them to the computer. You may discover that one or two questions were particularly susceptible to miscoding. If you can find any patterns in the noted errors, you will have a chance to correct them before transferring the data to a computer-readable form.

If the number of cases in the study is very large, your coding may be done by a team of people rather than only by you, the primary investigator. In this case, there may be even more chances for error or lack of comparability in the coding done by different coders. Intercoder reliability can be checked by testing for how far different coders classify the same data in the same way. This will require monitoring coders over the course of the coding procedures.

TRANSFER PROCESS

Once the data have been coded, they must be transferred to some medium that will allow them to be entered into a computer. There are a number of different ways to do this. Your choice of which to use will depend both on the type of computer equipment that is readily available to

you (and this, in turn, may require a choice between different types of computers and different forms of computer entry mechanisms) and on relative costs.

Final Written Code Forms

The final written code forms are those that are used to transfer the data to the computer. Let me emphasize again how important it is to restrict the number of times the data are handled, in order to reduce errors. For many researchers, this means trying to transfer the data as directly as possible from questionnaires to the computer. Since this is not always feasible, other methods can be utilized.

As discussed above, edge coding on questionnaires is a method of putting the coding information on the questionnaire itself so that the person processing the data need only transfer a response to an often-specified computer column location. (On some questionnaires, answers are to be filled in at indicated edge locations.) In general, edge coding simplifies the coding procedure and increases consistency.

Making Data Machine-Readable

Use of Punch Cards. Until quite recently, the use of punch cards was the most common way of entering data onto computers. In some institutions, this form of entry is still used. In others, it has virtually disappeared. Keypunch machines are similar to typewriters except that instead of entering a typed number or letter, the keypunch machine strikes out a number by punching a hole through it on a special card that has 80 columns and 12 rows. In each row, the numbers 0 through 9 are offered, as well as two additional unmarked rows above the 0 row referred to as rows 10 and 11.

Use of Optical Scan Sheets. Many computers allow for entry of data from optical scan forms. These forms are read into a machine to form a *raw data file* in the computer. Filling out the forms involves darkening spaces on the form which correspond to the coded attributes of specific questions. Some questionnaires are now developed which have optical scan forms as answer sheets, or the questionnaire itself may be superimposed on an optical scan form. If this is the case, the researcher will not need to transfer the data to the forms.

Because optical scan data can be read only if the spaces are darkened sufficiently and if no unintended stray marks are placed on other parts of the form, care must be taken in using optical scan sheets. Highly educated respondents are more likely to be familiar with filling out machine-readable forms; thus, the background of the respondents should be considered in deciding whether to use such forms. Finally, since the forms must be fed into a machine, they cannot be torn, folded, or otherwise mutilated; this requires including warnings on the forms as to their care as well as providing large enough return envelopes so that the forms will not need to be folded.

Direct Terminal Entry. More and more computer systems are moving toward direct terminal entry. For this procedure, you take your coded data (let's say coded questionnaires), sit down at a computer terminal, and enter your data on the keyboard of the terminal, case by case. Once your data are entered, you can get a listing from the computer of what you have entered and check the list with the original coded data.

Computer-Assisted Telephone Interviewing (CATI). Recall from Chapter 7 that computer-assisted telephone interviewing is an increasingly popular way to collect and transfer data. In this method, the questions being asked appear to the interviewer on a computer monitor with the various response categories offered. The answers given by the respondent are immediately entered by the interviewer into a computer. This method dramatically cuts down on the steps in the data transfer process and thereby reduces the errors generated by multiple handling of the data.

COMPUTER ENTRY AND PROCESSING

Let's stop for a moment and consider what computers are. We will describe computers very simply but will include many of the terms you will be likely to confront once you begin working with a computer. Naturally if you are already familiar with computers, this discussion will be superfluous.

Nature of Computer Equipment

Whatever the type of data entry method you select, the computer itself will have certain basic components: *input mechanisms, storage capacities, central processing unit* or CPU and *output mechanisms.* These four components make up the computer machinery, or what is called the *hardware* of the computer. The input mechanisms include the card reader or the computer terminal discussed before. Computer terminals may be *hard-copy terminals,* where the information typed into the terminal is printed out at the terminal (such printout material is often referred to as *hard copy*). Or they may have a screen, like a television screen, where whatever is typed into the terminal appears. These types of terminals are called *cathode ray tube (CRT)* terminals. Most computer systems have both CRTs and hard-copy facilities.

The storage capacities of a computer system allow users to store data, computer files, and other information in ways that can be readily accessed by the computer when they are needed. Such information is generally stored on *tapes, disks,* or *cards* or in the computer itself (where the storage capacity is referred to as *core memory*). Different computer systems allow different types of storage depending on the size of the computer, the types of input mechanisms it has, and issues of cost. The CPU is the computer itself; it is the machine that carries out the commands given to it by the computer program.

The output mechanisms are generally of two types: line printers which produce hard copy, or terminals where the results are displayed on the screen. Many of you will enter your data on a *mainframe computer,* that is, a large computer which can run many different kinds of jobs simultaneously. Often such computers service an entire institution, and you may enter your data at a location distant from the actual machine. This is done through a *remote job entry* facility. The terminal may be connected to the mainframe by a *modem.* In this case, the terminal you are using may have a telephone connection. In other computer facilities, the terminals may link directly to the mainframe, in which case they are said to be *hard-wired.* Many students have access to a mainframe at their college or university through a system of *timesharing,* which allows students access to the computer for specific and legitimate purposes. If you have collected a large amount of data, and certainly if you are carrying out a secondary analysis of a large dataset, you may have to have the help of a mainframe computer to process all your information.

Some of you may carry out your computer analyses on *microcomputers,* which are often also called *personal computers.* These are smaller computers in which the terminal, the screen, and the computer itself are located together in a rather small-sized set of units. Since microcomputers are becoming more widely owned by individuals and since their memory capacities are in some cases very large, the potential for the use of these small computers for data analysis is becoming greater and greater. For example, while CATI is often set up on a mainframe computer system, database management approaches using a microcomputer are also available. Microcomputers can also be used as terminals to mainframes with the help of a modem.

The important thing to find out is what computer facilities are available to you and which ones will best serve your needs, given the size and form of your study. Remember that data prepared for one type of computer can usually be entered into another though certain alterations may need to be made.

ESTABLISHING A COMPUTERIZED DATA FILE

If you are putting your data on a computer in order to produce tables and statistical tests, you will most likely do so with the aid of a computer software program. Recall that the computer equipment itself is referred to as *hardware.* The data will be entered into the computer and form the basis of a *raw data file.* If you are planning to use a software program to process the data, you will need to enter this computer program into the computer, access it, and link your dataset to that program.

Computer Software for Data Analysis

The instructions, or commands, that tell the computer what to do are the *software* of the computer. Software consists of computer programs, which may be either developed by an individual computer user (or *programmer*) for a specific task (using one of the computer languages, such as BASIC, COBOL, or FORTRAN, which can be understood by the computer) or, more commonly, already prepared programs for the use of social researchers.

In Chapter 13, computer output from a dataset using the Statistical Package for the Social Sciences (SPSS[x]) software program will be presented. SPSS[x] may not be the computer program that you will be using. You may, for example, be using SAS, BMD, or possibly the personal computer version of SPSS referred to as SPSS[PC]. Whatever you use, we will try here to explain some of the procedures that software programs of this type can carry out for you. If you are planning to use SPSS[x], there is an elementary description of how to run certain subprograms within the SPSS[x] program in Appendix C. Tables produced by this program will accompany the description of analytic techniques and statistical tests in the following chapters on the analysis of data. Moreover, these tables are not very different from ones you would produce if you used a different software program. Box 12-1 offers an overview of the hardware and software options for social research in the 1990s.

BOX 12-1

COMPUTER HARDWARE AND SOFTWARE OPTIONS FOR SOCIAL RESEARCH IN THE 1990S

HARDWARE

As the cost of owning a personal computer continues to fall, the power of these machines has increased dramatically. A modest investment of under $1000 will purchase more computing power than the best university computing facility could offer 25 years ago. Furthermore, today's personal computer is extremely small and very easy to use. The decision to buy a computer should be weighed carefully, of course. You must consider your current needs (word processing is the most common use of a personal computer) as well as your plans. Major considerations include speed of processing, size of memory, and operating systems. All of these considerations will significantly affect the price of your machine as well as the availability of software programs. There are excellent books and courses available on these topics. Hardware and software resellers also provide useful information. Take the time to become an informed consumer before investing in a computer system.

Most schools now have computer laboratories available to students. These provide wonderful opportunities to try various machines and software packages prior to making your own investment. You may also find that the computer laboratory provides all of the resources that you need, particularly if you have only a short-term or infrequent need for a computer.

SOFTWARE

Today's software programs make using the computer extremely easy. While there are always some commands or instructions to master with each program, they are easy to learn. Once the basics are acquired, the rewards are great. The benefits of speed and editing power make software applications extremely popular. Many of the more sophisticated software packages will interact with each other so that information can be shared between programs. Listed below are several general categories of software programs used in research and a description of their functions.

Word processing: Word processing programs make the computer act like an intelligent typewriter. Documents are created on the computer screen, stored in memory, and then printed on paper. Since the image on the screen is only a copy of the document, the position of words on the screen can be manipulated with ease. Single words, sentences, or paragraphs can be moved to other locations within the document, and the rest of the text moves to accommodate the changes. Furthermore, the document can be saved electronically to a disk where it takes up very little space. Then, in the future, the writer can call the document back from the disk to the screen, where the writer can edit it without having to retype the entire document. Additional advantages include automatic spelling and grammar correction and access to an online thesaurus.

Spreadsheets: Electronic spreadsheets have revolutionized budgeting and accounting functions. The computer screen serves as a very large columnar spreadsheet where not only numbers but formulas can be entered. Working with a pencil and a paper spreadsheet, one had to tally numbers by hand or by using a calculator. Spreadsheet programs allow you to tally numbers automatically on the spreadsheet by entering a formula (e.g., for the total). When you change a number within the column being added, the total changes automatically. For those who do a great deal of budgeting or other accounting functions, spreadsheets are invaluable software programs.

Databases: Database programs perform a function that blends word processing and spreadsheets. Often referred to as *list processors*, databases use a spreadsheet format (columns and rows) but accept letters and numbers into each cell. For instance, you might want to automate your personal address book, with entries for names, addresses, telephone numbers, birthdates, etc. These entries can then be sorted in various ways and special lists can be produced (e.g., birthdays in March). Many of the same functions can be accomplished with either a word processing or a spreadsheet program, but database programs are tailored for list processing and are much more powerful and easier to use for that purpose.

Statistical packages: These packages tend to be extremely specialized and consequently very expensive. They are capable of performing hundreds of statistical procedures which range from simple frequencies to sophisticated analyses. Until fairly recently, these packages were available only in mainframe environments. Smaller versions of the mainframe packages are now available for the personal computer, and files created in either arena (mainframe or personal computer) can be transferred easily to the other as needed. Most statistical pack-

ages will read data that have been entered and stored within spreadsheet or database programs. Statistical packages also require a great deal of computer processing speed and memory storage.

Graphics programs: Charts, graphs, and tables can be created using graphics packages. These specialized programs offer a variety of formats (pie charts, bar graphs, organization tables) and output media (paper, color slides) for displaying data.

Today's research environment has become highly automated. For instance, first a survey can be typed and formatted using a word processing package; then the collected data can be entered into a database program, analyzed by a statistical package, and displayed in a graphics format; and finally, the results can be transferred back to the word processing program for the written report.

Source: This article was written by Winston M. Turner, Ph.D., Harvard Medical School.

A Social Sciences Computer Program. As explained above, once your data have been read into the computer and form the basis of a raw data file, you will probably want to process this raw data with a computer software program, very likely a software program specifically designed for social research analyses. Such a program will have the necessary subprograms to produce the quantitative tables that you want and to generate the statistical tests required for your study. If you know computer programming, you may not want to use such a program, since you will be able to write your own programs to produce tables and to compute statistical tests. Most individuals who do social research, however, do not have (and do not need to have) the programming skills to do this. The software programs available to social researchers are so comprehen-

sive in terms of what they are capable of doing, yet so relatively easy to use, that few programmers could carry out the tasks more effectively or more efficiently.

A software program, such as SPSS^x, enables you to use its simplified commands in requesting what you want from the computer in order to produce the tables, graphs, and statistical tests which you need for your analysis. Such a program is a combination of a cookbook and a translator. As a cookbook, the program tells you what ingredients are needed to produce the quantitative analyses you want. Also like a cookbook, the program manual can actually suggest different recipes—different types of quantitative analyses and statistical tests that might be useful for specific types of data. In short, it can give you a taste of what each subprogram might offer that will help you in making choices as to which subprograms to run.

As a translator, the software program is an intermediary between you and the computer. The program allows you to make your requests in terms of simple statements. In short, you don't need to know a computer language, such as BASIC, to be able to run a program such as SPSS^x. Instead, relatively simple command statements are translated into a computer language by the software program.

Setting Up an Initial Computer Run

A computer *run* involves having the computer carry out the tasks that have been requested—in other words, getting the computer to do its work. The product of this work is referred to as a *job*. Once the computer run is complete, your job will be done. To set up an initial run requires coordinating three things: (1) your raw data, (2) the computer software program, and (3) the computer system you are using. Your data will be in some machine-readable format (cards, a tape, a disk) or ready to be entered directly into the computer at the terminal. You must first access (or call forth) the computer software program on your computer system. The commands you use to link the software program to your computer system will vary from one type of computer to another and from one computer location (or *installation*) to another. You must ask at your computer installation for assistance in accessing your data and selecting the best software program for your purposes. While the procedures described here apply to a mainframe computer system, microcomputers could also be used with slightly modified methods. In addition, this discussion will highlight *batch software programs* (these are programs where first the user sets up one or more command statements and then the computer carries them out) in contrast to interactive software programs (where the user interacts with the software program by putting in commands over the course of

the processing). SPSS^x, SPSS^{PC}, and other statistical software programs offer data entry modules. Box 12-2 describes the use of a database management program for the purposes of data entry.

Once the data and software are accessed, the data must be transformed from a *raw input data* file to a *system file*. This system file will contain both the data you plan to use (from the raw data file) and also all the necessary commands (from the computer software program) needed by the computer to recognize the data accurately and to process it effectively so that statistical analyses can be carried out. In such a file, every variable is named, its position in the data file is shown, and the range of codes to be used for every attribute are given. This system file will also be the file you access each time you want to run another computer job.

For purposes of analyses, the object of your initial computer runs will be to "see what the variables look like." This means that you want to know how many cases can be described by each of the attributes of a variable (if the variable were sex, for example, that would mean how many cases are males and how many are females; if the variable were a math test score, you would want to know how many people attained each possible score on the test).

In addition to knowing how many males and how many females there are in your sample, for example, you would then want to know what proportion of the sample were male and what proportion female. This could be produced by determining the percentage of males and females in the sample. Tables which give you this information are referred to as frequency distributions, since they indicate how the sample is distributed across the range of possible attributes of the variable. For the math test score, which is numerical and can be treated as a number scale, you might prefer to know the mean score and the standard deviation, which would tell you the nature of the distribution of scores.

Cleaning the Computerized Variables

Once you have taken a look at the data, your first step is to clean up variables which look messy or inaccurate. For example, if your cases refer to high school students, and for the variable of age you find a case with an age of 75, what effect would such a strange response have on your findings? Let's say you plan to use student age as a variable in your analyses. The means and standard deviations which are often used for computational purposes would be distorted by even one case in such a high category.

If you conclude that a mistake has been made in the data, there are a number of possible ways of cleaning up this variable. In the example given, you might want to look back to the original data (the questionnaires, let's say) to see if there was a 75-year-old subject. You might decide to recode the age variable into age categories, thereby enabling you to combine that case with the highest category: say, 25 and older. Another choice would be to convert that case to a *missing value* so that it would not distort your findings.

If you find a large number of cases falling into strange categories, then you need to go back to check the variable at earlier stages. To check on what was actually entered into the computer as a part of your raw data file, you should examine your file information (or file info) listing. To go back further will require you to check whatever you used to enter data into the computer. If you entered it into a terminal, then the file information listing would have what you entered. To check back even further, you should go back to the original questionnaires, interview schedules, or whatever were the original forms on which the information was put. This can be time-consuming and discouraging, but it is essential to clean up your variables before you try to use them in statistical analyses. Often you will be able to find a source of error quite quickly. If you cannot find it or if you cannot change it once it is found, then you might consider not using that variable in the analyses (or at least not using it in the most important parts of your analysis).

DATA MANIPULATION PRIOR TO ANALYSIS

Handling Missing Data

Whatever program you are using, there will be methods for handling missing data. The computer must be told which cases to identify (or flag) as missing on each variable so that they can be excluded from the analyses. You often do not want to exclude a case entirely from consideration in a study if only a few variables are missing; rather, you want those variables included which have actual responses and those variables flagged as missing which have no responses. In the language of the software programs, this is called *pairwise deletion* of missing data. You may, conversely, choose to exclude a case from an analysis if there is missing data on any variable being considered for that analysis; this is referred to as *listwise deletion* of missing data. As mentioned before, 9, 98, or 99 are the code numbers conventionally used to designate missing values. Once a value is designated as missing, it will be kept out of the analyses, though the number of cases missing on that variable will be reported on the tables.

Some computer programs, such as SPSS[x], allow you to have a mean number entered to replace a missing response. This means that individuals who skipped a question are assigned the average response for the whole sample as their response. This helps to maintain the number of cases (the *case base*) for each analysis, but it gives cases responses that they did not offer. Don't forget that the treatment of missing data could affect the validity and reliability of a variable. If there are too many missing cases, the aggregate response may not really represent the views of the sample. If the variable with the missing data is being analyzed in relation to another variable, this relationship may also be distorted if there are many missing cases on one of the variables.

BOX 12-2

DATA ENTRY USING A DATABASE MANAGEMENT PROGRAM

The transfer of data from the collection instrument to the computer is a crucial step in any research project. Traditionally, data are transferred from the questionnaires to large spreadsheets or code sheets and then entered into the computer. Database management software programs offer more reliable options for transferring data into the computer for storage and analysis.

Code sheets often consist of endless rows and columns of numbers with no spaces between them. It is very easy for data entry operators to lose their place and enter the wrong values into the computer.

```
47335554092039448112384990
30336683849588838211283928
83746572322211882944728459
20354759409437762324492347
82634782428464634443674854
36412365720400412120242934
67756014676045576634014674
24145758478578568701074734
30564761041647364084673647
16476436434184785745876584
75634315841513447847112340
07413714365451435S
```

Database management programs permit a more structured approach to data entry that reduces the likelihood of making data entry errors. The database management program creates separate *files* for each data collection instrument.

The *structure* of the file is defined first. Each of the variables within the instrument is given a name, a data type (e.g., numeric or character), and a width. Once the structure is defined, the variables are displayed on the screen and data can be entered directly into the file.

The power of database management packages lies in the ability to program them. For instance, each variable can be given a defined range of acceptable values (e.g., 1 through 5), so that erroneous entries (e.g., 7 or J) are impossible. Furthermore, the data collection instrument (questionnaire) can be displayed on the screen with blanks appearing where data are to be entered. Acceptable code ranges can also be displayed. This further reduces the chances for the data entry operator to make mistakes, since they will be less likely to lose their place. Alternatively, subjects could be administered the questionnaire on the computer screen and enter their responses directly into the database.

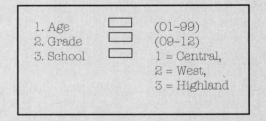

If the research project is particularly complex, involving a large number of data collection instruments, multiple sites, and/or multiple follow-up periods, the process of managing the data

Entry   Schedules   Reports   Mailing List   Exit
⌐ Demogs   ⌐ Individual   ⌐ Facility   ⌐ Alphabetic
├ Activity   └ Monthly   └ Productivity   └ Zip code
└ Attitudes

collection can be further automated using the *menu* capacity of modern database management programs. Menus display several options for the computer user and are easily customized to the researcher's needs. Once a primary option is selected, additional suboptions can be displayed and output can be generated or data entry can begin. For example, the menu bar presented displays a variety of alternative procedures for the computer operator.

> *Entry* selects data collection instruments (Demographic Data, Sport Activity Survey, and Attitudes Toward Sports Questionnaire). Selecting one of these suboptions displays that instrument and allows data to be entered from that form.
>
> *Schedules* prints either individual practice schedules for each study subject or monthly schedules of practice times across subjects for a specified month.
>
> *Reports* prints either a current facility use report or a summary of coaching staff productivity.

> *Mailing list* produces a set of mailing labels for study subjects, sorted either alphabetically by last name or numerically by zip code.
>
> *Exit* exits the menu.

Database management programs allow the researcher to store data from each research instrument and/or testing period in separate files for later analysis. Once the data are entered into their respective files within the database management system, reports can be printed directly from the database program or the data can be transferred to a statistical software package for analysis directly. The statistical software program retains the variable names that were assigned within the database management file structures. Individual data files can then be linked together using common variables (such as subjects' ID numbers) that were placed in each data file.

Source: This article was authored by Winston M. Turner, Ph.D., Harvard Medical School.

Recoding Variables

One of the most common manipulation procedures you will use in setting up your variables for analyses is recoding. The purpose of recoding is generally to reduce the number of categories in a variable to a number more manageable for numerical analysis. If you plan to examine the relationships between two or more variables (a subject to be discussed in Chapter 13), you may want to reduce the number of categories in a variable so that you can see whether the cross effects of two variables upon each other indicate strong or weak trends. Once you have recoded a variable, however, the original set of categories will be permanently altered. To avoid this, it is usually better to create a new variable from the old one, keeping the old one with the original set of categories and having the new one represent the recoded set of categories.

There are two main principles to consider in deciding how to recode a variable. Either it makes sense *theoretically* (i.e., a recoded variable will better represent the meaning of the variable you want in your study—an example here would be deciding to combine all the members of racial minorities in your study into one group because you have decided that the distinction between white and non-white is the only one you are interested in), or it makes sense *empirically* (i.e., you will use the way the respondents answered the question in deciding how to regroup the variable—an example here would be to decide to combine all the minority groups, once you have examined the data, since each minority group is too small in number to be analyzed on its own).

Let me offer a few other examples. Suppose you are doing a study on attitudes toward the federally supported Medicare program. Since people can qualify for Medicare at age 65, and since you think that people's attitudes are likely to vary according to whether they do or do not qualify for the program, it might make sense to recode the variable, age of respondent, into two variables: younger than 65, and 65 and older. This would be a theoretical reason for the recoding, since your decision to recode the variable was based on ideas that you held about how the variable would be best used to support your research question or hypothesis.

Or, take another example: suppose you are studying unemployment and you know the region of the country in which each respondent lives. You might want to combine those living in the northeast and midwest into one group, those living in the southeast and southwest (the sun belt) into another group, and those in the far west, Great Plains, and northwest into a third group. Your rationale here would be that the unemployment rate is different in these sections of the country. Both these examples offer explanations for recoding based on what you already know and think about the subject of your study; and they make sense because they should help to test your hypothesis and highlight and clarify your findings. In these cases, the recoding has been carried out for theoretical reasons.

However, let's say that, in a study of fifth-graders' school achievement, the variable to be recoded is a math aptitude score. Now for many types of analyses which would use the average score as the primary unit for analysis, there would be no need to recode. If, however, you want to know what proportion of students who come from varying racial backgrounds or whose families are at different social class levels did very well or not too well on the test, one procedure would be to calculate the average scores for each of the subgroups of interest. Another way, however, would be to split the data according to *percentiles* (representing ten groups of 10 percent each) or *quintiles* (representing five groups of 20 percent each) or *quartiles* (representing four groups of 25 percent each).

Let's say you decided to use quartiles. You would want to rank the scores from the highest to the lowest. Then you would start at one end of the range of scores and form the quartile groups at the points at which each successive 25 percent of the cases had been accounted for. In this way, the 25 percent of the students with the highest scores would be the top quartile, the next 25 percent would be the second quartile, the next lower 25 percent would be the third quartile, and the lowest 25 percent would be the bottom quartile. Now, rather than having a variable with (say) 50 or more categories based on the actual math test score, you have a new variable with 4 categories based on the math scores ranked in descending order and then grouped into quartiles. In this case you have taken the aggregate findings of the data (the empirical evidence) and used this as the basis for recoding the variable.

Data Preparation in Social Research

The procedures described in this chapter may not have seemed to you to have been very important or challenging. Yet such efforts are at the core of what makes social research scientific. Recall in Chapter 2 that one of the characteristics of scientific research is that it must be systematic, that the language used must be careful and precise so that observations can be accurately recorded and aggregated, one with another. The quantification of data fosters this objective. By turning numerous responses into the same codes which can be analyzed by computers, the systematization of observations is achieved. Although a study in which quantitative data have been systematically prepared for analysis will not necessarily make a contribution to the social sciences, an unsystematic study where the data have been haphazardly treated has no chance of adding to the cumulative knowledge of the social sciences. Careful data preparation is one of the cornerstones of scientific research.

REVIEW NOTES

- Data preparation must be carried out with great care.
- Coding requires solving issues of ambiguity in the definition of variables.
- Coding should try to preserve the actual meaning and range of variation in the variable.
- Precoded questionnaires facilitate later coding and data transfer.
- Codebooks serve as systems of notation for variables, guides to the location of variables (on computer files), and records of coding decisions. Codebooks should be flexible and should allow for cross-referencing.
- Transferring data to computers may be done in various ways, depending on the type of computer facilities available.
- If transferring choices are available, pick the one which requires the least amount of data handling, in order to reduce errors.
- Computer components consist of an input mechanism, a storage capacity, the central processing unit, and an output mechanism.
- Computer software for social data analyses allows you to carry out a wide range of types of computerized data analyses without needing to know how to write your own programs.
- Initial computer runs allow you to check and clean variables, to label missing cases, and to recode variables to facilitate later analyses.

KEY TERMS

cathode ray tube (CRT)
central processing unit (CPU)
codebook
database management program
edge coding
hard copy
hardware
mainframe computer
microcomputer (personal computer)
modem
raw data
software
system file

STUDY EXERCISES

1. Suppose you had a study with three variables: race, tobacco use, and parents' tobacco use. Prepare a codebook for these three variables, creating for each all the information which you would need to include to have a useful and comprehensive codebook.
2. Using appropriate terminology, explain the various ways in which data might be entered into a computer.
3. Suppose you ask an open-ended question of a group of college students: "What is your college major?" You end up with a very wide range of responses and you decide to recode them to reduce the number of categories. Describe one rule for recoding the variable college major that you might follow for combining categories based on theoretical grounds, and another rule you might follow based on empirical grounds.

RECOMMENDED READINGS

1. Jendrek, Margaret Platt: *Through the Maze: Statistics with Computer Applications,* Wadsworth, Belmont, Calif., 1985. A clear and precise discussion of the nature and use of computers with instructions on how to use SPSS^x.
2. Li, Peter: *Social Research Methods,* Butterworth, Toronto, 1981. This small volume has a very useful chapter on data processing.
3. Weisberg, Herbert F., and Bruce D. Bowen: *An Introduction to Survey Research and Data Analysis,* Freeman, San Francisco, 1977. Good sections on coding and computer utilization are included in this text.

Data Analysis I: Univariate and Bivariate Analyses

────── LOOKING AHEAD ──────

This chapter carefully goes through the steps of a data analysis, prepared for this text, on how athletic participation in high school relates to higher educational attainment. One-variable (univariate) and two-variable (bivariate) tables set up for this analysis are developed and explained.

INTRODUCTION

*B*efore you analyze your data, you need to understand what researchers try to accomplish by carrying out an analysis. In other words, you need an overview of what should take place as well as a rationale for it. I have prepared an example specifically for the text and will take you through the steps of a data analysis. We will use the same example in Chapters 14 and 15. Beginning with a simple hypothesis and using an already collected dataset, we will carefully go through the steps for a secondary analysis of the research hypothesis.

Data analysis in the social sciences has become a complex affair now that computers and social science computer package programs are in wide use. The analyses in current social science journals may be incomprehensible to many students. But remember two things: first, researchers currently carrying out data analyses began by learning how to do simpler forms of analyses. And second, even researchers who use complex multivariate techniques usually prepare more elementary tables before moving on to complex analytic techniques.

As a student, you too will want to begin by learning how to carry out data analyses that are relatively simple, clear and logical. You will need to know how to convert computer-generated tables into properly labeled tables you can include in your research report (or whatever final project you are preparing). The analysis in this chapter presents tables prepared on a computer using the SPSS^x software program. We will begin at the most primary point in the analysis, with one-variable, or *univariate,* tables. After we have carefully looked at the distribution of each variable, we will construct and analyze two-variable, or *bivariate,* tables. In Chapter 14, we will progress to three-variable, or trivariate, tables and discuss a model for interpreting trivariate analyses.

TRYING OUT A DATA ANALYSIS OF OUR OWN

Having considered Hirschi's study of juvenile delinquency in Chapters 1 and 2, we have seen that one way to test a hypothesis is to select variables to represent each of the factors in the hypothesis and then set up a table to relate (to cross-tabulate or cross-classify) these variables with one another. For example, Hirschi chose self-reported delinquent acts to represent delinquency, his dependent variable, and intimacy of communication with the father to represent attachment, his independent variable. Then, by examining the relationship between these factors, by preparing a cross tabulation of delinquency by attachment, he could see to what extent those who were more attached to their fathers reported delinquent acts as compared to those who were less attached. This type of cross-tabular analysis is one of the most common and widely used forms of data analysis in the social sciences, and it is the kind of analysis which we will use in the forthcoming presentation.

High School Athletic Participation and Educational Attainment

Defining the Research Problem. In order to move speedily into our data analysis, I will sketch the background to the problem to be studied very briefly (and superficially). Naturally, you would need to do more to substantiate a rationale for a study, but I am going to skip over most of that effort here and move very quickly to an analytic model. Suppose we hypothesize (on the basis of our knowledge and reading) that participation in high school athletics is related to educational attainment beyond high school and, in particular, to earning a college degree. Let's say we think this to be the case because high school athletics foster such characteristics as competitiveness, physical rigor, regularity in schedules, responsibility—all of which we think are important factors in pursuing higher education and completing educational programs.

We begin by looking in the library for similar studies and find a few that have studied this idea before. In particular, we see that Otto and Alwin (1977) found a strong relationship between athletic participation in high school and post–high school educational attainment among a 15-year interval panel survey of 340 males. In their conclusion they make the following statement: "Like an academic curriculum, extracurricular activities provide a forum for developing attitudes and skills from which status goals evolve and upon which future success is grounded" (1977, p. 112). This seems to support our contention by suggesting that the experience of participating in extracurricular athletic activity should help form attitudes and teach skills that may be applied to the pursuit of higher goals, such as a college education.

Setting Up the Analytic Model.   Hypothesizing that athletic participation in high school affects post–high school educational attainment, we set up our basic research model as shown in Figure 13-1. Figure 13-1 states that the independent variable, high school athletic participation, may be related to the dependent variable, educational attainment. What we will try to see is whether those who participated in high school athletics, and especially those who were athletic leaders, are more likely to reach higher levels of education subsequently.

Our reading in this area (as well as our background experience) suggests that there may be a number of other factors that could affect this hypothetical relationship. One of the obvious factors that needs to be considered is sex. Otto and Alwin (1977) ignored this factor by studying only young men. Athletic participation for males has tended to be highly praised and encouraged. For females, the role of athletic competition is less clear. Currently, there is much more support for it; but in the past relatively few women participated competitively in athletics. Nevertheless, athletic competition could be very important for women's pursuit of higher educational goals. Certainly the differences between the two sexes in this relationship seem interesting and socially important. For our study, we decide to examine both sexes.

In addition, the social class origins of the students seem to be another factor that should be controlled. Students from more affluent families may be encouraged to attend and graduate from college, whether or not they are athletes. Students from poorer families may have less encouragement to attend college, and fewer resources to finance a college education. For these students, athletic prowess and the possibility of athletic scholarships at college may make a great difference in determining whether they go to and complete college. For students from middle-class families, the effects of athletic participation in high school on educational attainment may or may not be important. To control for the differential economic base of families, we will want to consider the variable of socioeconomic status (SES) of family in our model.

There is another factor that seems to be missing in the model. Otto and Alwin (1977) stated that extracurricular as well as academic activities should affect future goals. Perhaps it will be a good idea to consider academic performance in high school as well. These three variables—sex, SES, and high school academic performance—will be used for the trivariate analyses to be presented in Chapter 14.

FIGURE 13-1

Hypothesized relationship between high school athletic participation and educational attainment.

Securing the Data.   Convinced that this is a topic worthy of study, we decide to find a dataset on which to test this hypothesis rather than to collect our own data. There are many good reasons for doing a secondary analysis, which were discussed in Chapter 10. One is that while surveys based on national probability samples are very expensive to carry out, they are relatively inexpensive to procure and analyze once they are made available to the public for secondary analyses. Again, by looking at studies that have already been carried out, we come across mention of a longitudinal dataset based on a national sample of the spring-term high school graduates of 1972 who were followed up four more times (1973, 1974, 1976, and 1979). This survey, the *National Longitudinal Study of the High School Class of 1972 (NLS)* (Riccobono, 1981), is available from the Department of Education in Washington. The survey covers a wide range of measures on educational and career attitudes and attainments of these adults.

First we want to acquire the original survey instruments to see whether the variables of interest to us were measured. We can assume that the sex and SES of the family would naturally have been included. Moreover, in a longitudinal study of high school graduates, we can also assume quite logically that information on high school academic performance and on college attendance and attainment would have been gathered. However, we want to be sure that athletic participation in high school had been determined. We contact the government agency in Washington and request the survey instruments. The questionnaires indicate to us that all of the variables needed to study our hypothetical relationship are available in this dataset.

We purchase the dataset in the form of tapes for computer analysis at our institution. Our plan is to select the variables we need to test our hypothesis, use a social science software program (SPSS^x) to produce the tables and statistical tests we need, and then analyze these tables and statistics. Each of these steps will be explained in much greater depth in the forthcoming chapters (and SPSS^x will be described more fully in Appendix

C). In this chapter, we will examine the dataset, select the necessary variables to test the hypothesis, and see how the data are distributed among the categories of each of the variables.

When we receive the dataset, we find that three books of information on the data are sent to us as well. These include a codebook explaining all of the variables (a selection from this codebook was presented in Chapter 12) together with information on the sample, the forms of data collection, and response rates, as well as frequency distributions on all the variables for the total sample. Moreover, constructed variables such as scales, indexes, and various types of recoded variables are explained. (Constructed variables are ones that have been created from the original variables based directly on questions from the survey. Indexes and scales will be the subject of Chapter 16.) By looking through the constructed variables, we see that an SES variable for the family of origin has been created. We also see that educational attainment has been measured several different ways (number of years of education beyond high school, types of degrees attained) and that the NLS staff has constructed some composite measures of this concept using various indicators. We will need to choose which measure of the concept best serves our needs.

Selecting Which Subsample to Study.   The *National Longitudinal Study of the High School Class of 1972* was based on a two-stage, stratified sample in which high schools (both public and private) were sampled at the first stage, and seniors within these high schools were sampled at the second stage. In the spring of 1972, 1,200 high schools were selected and stratified on the basis of criteria such as public or private, geographic region, percent of minority students, and degree of urbanization. Of these, 948 schools actually participated; the others either refused to participate or had no senior classes. Replacement schools were then selected, boosting the response rate to 1,069 schools. A total of 21,384 students were sampled within these schools (approximately 18 per school), and the initial survey was followed up four times between 1972 and 1979. A total of 12,980 students responded to all five waves of the survey. In order to have complete data on each student, we decide to select for our subsample only students who had participated in all five waves of the study.

Selecting the Variables. Our model has five variables in it. After examining the codebook and the constructed variables, we select the five variables for the study. The NLS staff has named the variables using numbers, and we decide to use their numbers for our analysis.

1. *Sex.* This variable was VAR1626. It had (surprise!) two categories: "male" and "female."
2. *Socioeconomic status of family of origin (SES).* This was a constructed variable based on father's education, mother's education, father's occupation, family income, and presence of certain household items (newspaper, encyclopedia, typewriter, two cars, etc.). It was then grouped into three categories: "high," "medium," and "low." It was variable VAR1070.
3. *High school athletic participation.* This variable was VAR241. It included three categories: "athletic leader," "active participant," and "did not participate."
4. *High school grade-point average.* This variable (VAR229) was coded into eight categories corresponding to the responses offered in the first questionnaire: (1) "mostly A," (2) "about half A and half B," (3) "mostly B," (4) "about half B and half C," (5) "mostly C," (6) "about half C and half D," (7) "mostly D," (8) "below D."
5. *Educational attainment.* We decide to use a composite measure which was constructed out of three different questions on the 1979 questionnaire: years of vocational, trade, or business school; highest level of college education; and kind(s) of degrees earned. From these, a new variable was constructed that had eight categories: (1) "advanced degree"; (2) "four- or five-year bachelor's degree"; (3) "two-year de-

gree (or a degree of more than two years), some vocational training"; (4) "two-year degree (or a degree of more than two years), no vocational training"; (5) "less than two years of college, some vocational training"; (6) "less than two years of college, no vocational training"; (7) "no college, some vocational training"; (8) "no college, no vocational training." This is variable VAR3281.

UNIVARIATE ANALYSES

The first step in seeing what your data look like is to examine each variable separately. This can be accomplished by getting the distributions of each variable one by one. Such single-variable analyses are called *univariate analyses,* that is, analyses based on one variable. Frequency distributions offer one type of univariate table. Another type examining the central tendencies of each variable (such as the mean, mode, and median; the standard deviation; the shape of the distribution; and the range of responses with the minimum and maximum values) are usually used only when a variable is based on an interval or ratio scale. In Chapter 16 when indexes and scales are introduced, which are interval-level measures, a univariate analysis presenting measures of central tendency (mean, standard deviation, etc.) will be presented. In this chapter, we will focus only on the frequency distribution.

The computer tables to be presented here were prepared using the computer package program SPSS[x], which was introduced in Chapter 12. The instructions needed to produce these tables using SPSS[x] are explained in Appendix C. If you will be using this software program, you may want to follow these instructions as you examine the tables in this chapter.

Frequency Distributions

The simplest way to see how the data are distributed across the categories of a variable is to set up a frequency distribution of the variable. This will give you the number of cases which fall into each of the categories of the variable and the percentage of the total number of cases they represent. This is the most basic set of information you can generate from your data. It will serve two primary purposes: in the first place, it will provide you with a foundation for understanding this particular variable in your study and help you decide how to use the variable in later analyses; and second, you will be able to use these frequency distributions to *clean* your data further if necessary. Now you can see exactly where the computer "thinks" the data are located on this variable. Even though you may have cleaned the data after the coding procedure and may have gotten your data file "listed" from the computer, examining these initial frequency distributions will be an important final step in the cleaning operation.

Composing Frequency Distributions from the Computer Output. Once the data have been entered into the computer and we have set up an SPSS[x] system file with the sample we want and the five variables we need, we are ready to examine the initial frequency tables to see how the data are distributed for each variable. Tables 13-1*A* through 13-5*A* present the actual SPSS[x] computer-prepared frequency distributions; Tables 13-1*B* through 13-5*B* show recomposed versions of these tables suitable for presentation in a research paper.

Tables 13-1*A* to 13-5*A* give the frequency distributions of the five variables as they appear in the SPSS[x] output. On the basis of the initial examination, we decide to recode certain variables for different reasons. (This would require special data manipulation procedures for recoding which can be easily carried out with SPSS[x]; see Appendix C.) We reversed the order of VAR1070 (making the "high" category equal to 1, the "low" category equal to 3). We also condensed three variables to make them easier to analyze by getting rid of very small categories and combining categories that were similar. VAR229 (high school GPA) was reduced from eight to four categories, and VAR3281 (educational attainment) was condensed into three categories: "college degree or more," "some college," and "no college." Having done that, we first look in these tables for the following qualities:

- How evenly are the cases distributed among the various categories?
- Which categories have the most and which have the fewest cases?
- Are there many missing cases?

Starting with Table 13-1*A* the frequency distribution for VAR1626, sex, we see that there are 6,184 males and 6,796 females. These categories are fairly close in size, but to understand the relationship of the categories to each other, it is best to examine the percentages in each category. Here we see that 47.6 percent of the respondents are

TABLE 13-1A

FREQUENCY DISTRIBUTION FOR SEX—COMPUTER TABLE

VAR1626 SEX

VALUE LABEL		VALUE	FREQUENCY	PERCENT	VALID PERCENT	CUM PERCENT
MALE		1	6184	47.6	47.6	47.6
FEMALE		2	6796	52.4	52.4	100.0
		TOTAL	12980	100.0	100.0	
VALID CASES	12980	MISSING CASES	0			

TABLE 13-1*B*

FREQUENCY DISTRIBUTION FOR SEX[a]
(National Longitudinal Study of the High School Class of 1972, Five-Survey Respondents)

Percentage Distribution of Sex

Sex	Percentage
Male	47.6
Female	52.4
	100.0
	(12,980)

[a]Recomposed table.

FIGURE 13-2
Bar graph of sex.

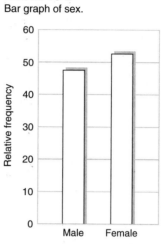

male, and 52.4 percent are female. Table 13-1*B* is a recomposed version of Table 13-1*A*. The table also tells us that 12,980 cases are reported upon (everyone in the sample we are using) and no cases are missing. Figure 13-2 presents a bar graph of the distribution of males and females.

The distribution of parental socioeconomic status (SES), VAR1070R in Tables 13-2*A* and 13-2*B*, shows that approximately half of the sample (48.1 percent) lies in the "medium" category, while the other half is quite evenly divided between "low" and "high." In this table, we discover missing cases: there was no information on SES for eight respondents, and these have therefore

been entered as missing cases. In this instance, the SPSS[x] output gives us the percentage distributions with the missing cases percentaged under PERCENT and with the missing cases excluded under VALID PERCENT. We are more interested in examining the VALID PERCENT column, in which the missing cases have been taken out of the base number of cases.

In Tables 13-3*A* and 13-3*B*, our major independent variable, VAR241R, shows the following distribution: 10 percent of the respondents were athletic leaders, approximately 35 percent were

TABLE 13-2*A*

FREQUENCY DISTRIBUTION FOR PARENTAL SES—COMPUTER TABLE

VAR1070R   PARENTAL SOCIO-ECONOMIC STATUS RECODE

VALUE LABEL	VALUE	FREQUENCY	PERCENT	VALID PERCENT	CUM PERCENT
HIGH	1.00	3178	24.5	24.5	24.5
MEDIUM	2.00	6240	48.1	48.1	72.6
LOW	3.00	3554	27.4	27.4	100.0
	9.00	8	.1	MISSING	
	TOTAL	12980	100.0	100.0	
VALID CASES 12972	MISSING CASES	8			

TABLE 13-2B

FREQUENCY DISTRIBUTION FOR PARENTAL SES[a]
(National Longitudinal Study of the High School Class of 1972, Five-Survey Respondents)

Percentage Distribution of SES	
SES	**Percentage**
High	24.5
Medium	48.1
Low	27.4
	100.0
	(12,821)
No data	(8)

[a]Recomposed table.

athletic participants, and 55 percent were nonparticipants. If we consider both athletic participation categories as athletes and compare them to the nonathletes, we have a 45/55 split. This means that there is a large enough number of athletes to make the analysis possible. Figure 13-3 depicts this distribution in a bar graph.

High school GPA (VAR229R), as seen in Tables 13-4A and 13-4B, presents more uneven categories. Roughly half the sample have B grade-point averages, fewer than a third have A aver-

ages, about one-fifth have C averages, and only 1 percent have D or below averages. When we carry out our analyses, we would have to be careful that there are enough cases in the D category to be able to cross-tabulate this variable with other variables. This suggests that it might be a good idea to consider collapsing categories. However, combining the A and B groups would produce too large a category, and C and D would be too small. Another possibility might be to compare the A category to all others combined, as a non-A category. A final plan would be to collapse the "D and below" category into the C category, making a trichotomized variable. The final strategy is the one we shall follow. Figure 13-4*a* presents a histogram of GPA in the ordinal scale version we will follow. You might want to refer to Chapter 5 for an explanation of histograms. Figure 13-4*b* shows a histogram of an alternative measure of GPA, as a continuous variable on a ratio scale. Note the slight differences in the graphs which occur with the change in the scale of measurement.

Finally, Table 13-5A gives the educational attainment variable in two versions: VAR3281R reverses the original order of the codes, and VAR3281T is a collapsed three-category recode of those without any college, with some college, and with a college degree or higher. In the transposed

TABLE 13-3A

FREQUENCY DISTRIBUTION FOR HIGH SCHOOL ATHLETIC PARTICIPATION—COMPUTER TABLE

```
VAR241R HIGH SCHOOL ATHLETIC PARTICIPATION
```

VALUE LABEL	VALUE	FREQUENCY	PERCENT	VALID PERCENT	CUM PERCENT
PARTICIPATE AS LEADER	1.00	1283	9.9	10.0	10.0
PARTICIPATE ACTIVELY	2.00	4418	34.0	34.5	44.5
NOT PARTICIPATE	3.00	7120	54.9	55.5	100.0
	9.00	159	1.2	MISSING	
	TOTAL	12980	100.0	100.0	

```
VALID CASES    12821    MISSING CASES      159
```

TABLE 13-3B

FREQUENCY DISTRIBUTION FOR HIGH SCHOOL ATHLETIC PARTICIPATION[a]
(National Longitudinal Study of the High School Class of 1972, Five-Survey Respondents)

Percentage Distribution of Athletic Participation

Participation Level	Percentage
Athletic leader	10.0
Actively participate	34.5
Not participate	55.5
	100.0
	(12,821)
No data	(159)

[a]Recomposed table.

version, Table 13-5B, which is based on the three-category recode, we see that more than 25 percent of the respondents graduated from college within a seven-year period following high school graduation, another 36 percent had some college, and more than 37 percent had no college education. There are very few missing cases for this variable, which is particularly fortunate given that it is our dependent variable.

FIGURE 13-3

Bar graph of athletic participation.

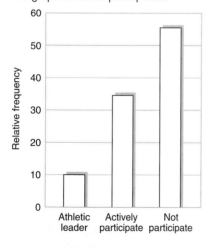

Examining the frequency distributions of these five variables gives us an overview of these data. We learn that the dataset is roughly half male and half female, and largely middle class in origins. The grade-point averages of these high school students are skewed toward the high end of the grading scale, with few students receiving grades of D (is this evidence of grade inflation?). Slightly fewer than half the students participated in athletics in high school. Finally, nearly two-thirds of the students attended college at some point in the seven years following high school, and one-quarter of them had received a college degree. We are now ready to move on to analyzing the relationships between these variables. Before we do this, however, let's consider the types of analytic tables we have just produced.

Recomposing Frequency Tables. Although the computer tabulates and presents all the information necessary for the univariate table, you need to reconvert this table into one that can be presented in your study. The computer tables offered in the text have had variable labels and variable category labels included (because they were requested and set up through the SPSS[x] program, which is explained in Appendix C). This makes them quite "readable." But you should not merely cut out these tables and paste them in your report. Instead, use the computer tables as guides to produce your own tables.

Your table needs to contain six things: (1) a complete title, (2) labels for the categories, (3) percentages presented consistently (either rounded off to whole numbers or left with one or two numbers to the right of the decimal), (4) the total percent at the bottom of the table, (5) the number of cases on which the percentages are based, and (6) the number of cases for which there are no data (the missing cases).

Tables 13-1B through 13-5B are recomposed versions of the computer-produced tables. Examine Table 13-3B, for instance. It includes all the information necessary to understand the table. The computation of the percentages can be understood

TABLE 13-4A

FREQUENCY DISTRIBUTION FOR HIGH SCHOOL GPA—COMPUTER TABLE

VAR229R HIGH SCHOOL GPA: FOUR CATEGORIES

VALUE LABEL	VALUE	FREQUENCY	PERCENT	VALID PERCENT	CUM PERCENT
A AND A-B	1.00	3959	30.5	30.7	30.7
B AND B-C	2.00	6322	48.7	49.0	79.6
C AND C-D	3.00	2496	19.2	19.3	98.9
D AND BELOW	4.00	138	1.1	1.1	100.0
	9.00	165	.5	MISSING	
	TOTAL	12980	100.0	100.0	

VALID CASES   12915   MISSING CASES   65

TABLE 13-4B

FREQUENCY DISTRIBUTION FOR H. S. GPA[a]
(National Longitudinal Study of the High School Class of 1972, Five-Survey Respondents)

Percentage Distribution of High School GPA

GPA	Percentage
A and A–B	30.7
B and B–C	49.0
C and C–D	19.3
D and below	1.1
	100.0[b]
	(12,915)
No data	(65)

[a]Recomposed table.
[b]Totals throughout are rounded.

because the number on which it is based is included (the *base*). The total size of the subsample can also be estimated from the table (it includes both the base number and the cases on which there were no data). Note that a brief description of the source of the sample and of the type of subsample presented appear in the title. The term *participation level* has been added to Table 13-3*B* as an appropriate heading for the range of categories offered. In this example, the percentage numbers include a decimal: this is generally the practice in research reports though the percentages may be rounded off to whole numbers in some studies.

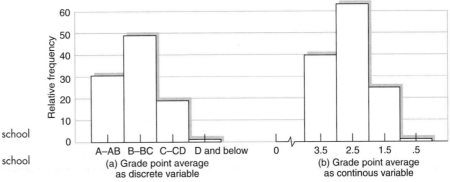

FIGURE 13-4
(a) Histogram of high school GPA (ordinal).
(b) Histogram of high school GPA (ratio).

Now let's examine the distribution for educational attainment, Table 13-5*B*. In this table, the title has been changed from the computer table since the recoding basically ignored the vocational training and concentrated on whether the subjects had attended college or not. *University/college* has been used in the title instead of just *college,* because such institutions are not synonymous, even though the term *college* is used to refer to both types of institutions. Furthermore, the year in which the question was asked (1979) has been

highlighted since, for many subjects, the highest level of educational attainment may not yet have been reached.

Statistics for Univariate Analyses

There are a number of statistical techniques for describing the distribution of a single variable, which will be fully explained in Chapter 15. The type of statistics that can be employed meaningfully will

TABLE 13-5A

FREQUENCY DISTRIBUTIONS FOR UNIVERSITY/COLLEGE ATTAINMENT—COMPUTER TABLE

VAR3281R EDUCATIONAL ATTAINMENT RECODE

VALUE LABEL	VALUE	FREQUENCY	PERCENT	VALID PERCENT	CUM PERCENT
ADVANCED DEGREE	1.00	344	2.7	2.7	2.7
4 OR 5 YEAR DEGREE	2.00	3110	24.0	24.0	26.7
GT 2 YRS, SOME VOC	3.00	1087	8.4	8.4	35.1
GT 2 YRS, NO VOC	4.00	1135	8.7	8.8	43.8
LT 2 YRS, SOME VOC	5.00	1329	10.2	10.3	54.1
LT 2 YRS, NO VOC	6.00	1090	8.4	8.4	62.5
NO COLL, SOME VOC	7.00	1616	12.4	12.5	75.0
NO COLL, NO VOC	8.00	3240	20.0	25.0	100.0
	9.00	29	.2	MISSING	
	TOTAL	12980	100.0	100.0	

VALID CASES   12951   MISSING CASES   29

VAR3281T EDUCATIONAL ATTAINMENT THREE CATEGORIES

VALUE LABEL	VALUE	FREQUENCY	PERCENT	VALID PERCENT	CUM PERCENT
COLL DEGREE OR MORE	1.00	3454	26.6	26.7	26.7
SOME COLLEGE	2.00	4641	35.8	35.8	62.5
NO COLLEGE	3.00	4856	37.4	37.5	100.0
	9.00	29	.2	MISSING	
	TOTAL	12980	100.0	100.0	

VALID CASES   12951   MISSING CASES   29

TABLE 13-5B

FREQUENCY DISTRIBUTION FOR UNIVERSITY/COLLEGE ATTAINMENT BY 1979[a]

(National Longitudinal Study of the High School Class of 1972, Five-Survey Respondents)

Percentage Distribution of Educational Attainment	
1979 Attainment	**Percentage**
College degree or higher	26.7
Some college	35.8
No college	37.5
	100.0
	(12,951)
No data	(29)

[a]Recomposed table.

depend on the *level of measurement* of the variable in question. For variables measured on a numerical scale, a broad array of statistical measures can be used to describe the central point of a distribution, the range of responses, and the frequency of each response. For variables measured with categories forming a nominal or ordinal scale—such as most of the variables in our athletic participation study—fewer statistics apply. Now that you have learned how to produce univariate tables, we will turn to the discussion of bivariate tables. These will be needed to test our hypothesis regarding athletic participation and educational attainment.

BIVARIATE ANALYSES

A Note on Terminology

Bivariate tables based on percentage distributions of one variable in relation to another can be referred to by a number of terms. Computer programs generally refer to them as *cross tabulations.* These are tables in which the categories of one variable are crossed with the categories of another to form a matrix type of table. Another

way of referring to these tables is to call them *cross-classification tables,* suggesting that one variable is being sorted in terms of the categories (or classification system) of the other variable. Finally, the term *contingency tables* is also widely used. This term stresses the relationship between the variables being studied, because the table shows how contingent (or dependent) one variable is on another.

Bivariate Tables for the Athletic Participation Study

By cross-tabulating different pairs of the five variables in our study of athletics and higher educational attainment, we will see how the variables are related to one another. Three types of bivariate relationships interest us. First, we want to see whether athletic participation is directly related to educational attainment (the association representing our major hypothesis). Second, we want to see whether grade-point average relates to educational attainment (an alternative hypothesis). Third, we want to examine whether there are important differences in the athletic participation of different subgroups (based on sex or social class) which might affect the association between athletics and educational attainment.

Does Athletic Participation in High School Relate to Post–High School Educational Attainment?   To examine this, we need to set up a cross tabulation between educational attainment (the dependent variable) and athletic participation (the independent variable). We will place the dependent variable at the left-hand side of the table to serve as the row variable and the independent variable at the top to serve as the column variable. (This can be requested from the SPSS[x] program; instructions on how to do so are included in Appendix C.)

Table Formats.   Table 13-6*A* presents the computer-prepared table showing the relationship between these variables; Table 13-6*B* gives a version of the table suitable for research reports. To begin

TABLE 13-6A

1979 EDUCATIONAL ATTAINMENT BY HIGH SCHOOL ATHLETIC PARTICIPATION—COMPUTER TABLE

```
C R O S S T A B U L A T I O N   O F ----------------------------------------------------
VAR3281T EDUCATIONAL ATTAINMENT THREE CATEGORIES
BY VAR241R HIGH SCHOOL ATHLETIC PARTICIPATION
-----------------------------------------------------------------------------------------
```

		VAR241R			
COUNT					
COL PCT		PARTICIP ATE AS L	PARTICIP ATE ACTI	NOT PART ICIPATE	ROW TOTAL
		1.00	2.00	3.00	
VAR3281T					
	1.00	520	1355	1558	3433
COLL DEGREE OR M		40.6	30.7	21.9	26.8
	2.00	487	1639	2469	4595
SOME COLLEGE		38.0	37.2	34.8	35.9
	3.00	274	1415	3076	4765
NO COLLEGE		21.4	32.1	43.3	37.2
COLUMN		1281	4409	7103	12793
TOTAL		10.0	34.5	55.5	100.0

with, reproductions of some of the actual computer tables made for the study will be presented so that you can familiarize yourself with how such tables look and see how to convert them to the types of tables presented in reports and publications. As we move along, however, only the recomposed tables will be presented, but you will understand how they were created.

In Table 13-6A, first examine the table setup. Note that the highest level of educational attainment is the first member of the set of categories (coded as 1), as is the highest level of athletic participation (being an athletic leader). Since the hypothesis states that the strongest athletic participants are likely to go the furthest in their education, the measures of each of these highest qualities are coded as 1, and the categories meet in the upper left-hand cell of the table. (A *cell* in a table is a position where two categories meet. Thus, Table 13-6A has nine cells.)

At the bottom of each column are the column base numbers on which the percentages are computed; these are referred to as *marginals*. For each

of these columns, the percentage of each category of the dependent variable (the row variable) appears in each cell. The percentages in the cells of the table can be totaled down each of the columns to 100 percent. The computer table includes as well a total column percentage, that is, the proportion of all cases in the table which are in that column. (Do you know what number would serve as the base for this column percent? It is the total table number, 12,793, which is at the base of the row totals.)

Recomposing Table 13-6A into Table 13-6B requires these changes:

- Adapting the title to say exactly what you want it to mean without any computer jargon or abbreviations.

- Putting in subtitles for each of the variables—at the upper left-hand side for the dependent variable and across the top for the independent variable. [Note that on the computer table only the variable number (VAR241R) is presented; on the final table, this computer name should be deleted.]

TABLE 13-6B

1979 UNIVERSITY/COLLEGE ATTAINMENT BY HIGH SCHOOL ATHLETIC PARTICIPATION[a]
(National Longitudinal Study of the High School Class of 1972, Five-Survey Respondents)

Attainment	Participation Level		
	Athletic Leader	**Active Participant**	**Did Not Participate**
College degree or higher	40.6%	30.7%	21.9%
Some college	38.0	37.2	34.8
No college	21.4	32.1	43.3
	100.0%	100.0%	100.0%
	(1,281)	(4,409)	(7,103)

[a]Recomposed table.

- Entering 100 percent at the bottom of each column to enable the reader to understand quickly how the table was "percentaged."
- Removing the code numbers of the categories, the variable numbers, the row totals (the row marginals), the table total, and the column total percents.

In the tables presented, only the column percents were calculated and presented in the cells because this is what had been requested from the computer (see Appendix C); row percentages and total percentages (based on the proportion of the total cases falling in each cell) could have been presented had they been requested in the SPSS[x] program.

Understanding the table. Looking at Table 13-6B, note that the differences in the column marginals are quite great (with over 7,000 cases in the Did Not Participate column and fewer than 1,300 cases in the Athletic Leader column). Yet percentaging allows you to compare these different columns by making each of them equivalent to 100. Again, we will follow the principle of "percentage down, read across" and compare the column distributions across each category of the independent variable.

Over 40 percent of athletic leaders completed a college degree, nearly twice the proportion of those who did not participate in athletics in high school

(21.9 percent). In the middle row, you see that the distribution narrows so that roughly similar proportions have completed some college, whatever their athletic participation level during high school. Looking at the bottom row, those who did not go to college, we see that the distribution widens again, but in a converse manner to the top row. Twice as many athletic nonparticipants had completed no college (43.3 percent) as athletic leaders (21.9 percent).

There is a steady increase in the proportion attaining a college degree among those with higher levels of athletic participation in high school (21.9 percent of those with no athletics, 30.7 percent of those with some athletic participation, and 40.6 percent of those who were athletic leaders graduated from college). These steadily increasing (or decreasing) percentages across a table between two variables show *monotonicity*. This means that higher levels of the independent variable are related incrementally to higher (or lower) levels of the dependent variable. (Of course, we would hope to find steady increases in the expected direction of the more athletic reporting higher levels of educational attainment, but we might find opposing evidence of a monotonic relationship between the two variables with steady decreases of athletic high school leaders completing college.) This search for patterns in the distributions (steady increases or steady decreases) would be a primary aim of the analysis of tables.

In some cases, it might also be useful to consider the differences between specific percentages in the first and last columns. Such high-low percentage differences are referred to as *epsilons*. In Table 13-6*B*, there is an 18.7-percentage-point difference between the college graduation rates of high school athletic leaders and nonathletes. Note that in the middle row, there is only a 3.2-percentage-point difference in completing some college between athletic leaders and nonathletes. But in the bottom row, the epsilon is 21.9 percentage points, similar to the size of the epsilon in the top row, though the cell location of the highest percentages is reversed. In short, an epsilon represents the differences between the percentages falling into extreme cells of a table.

We can conclude from Table 13-6*B* that there is a relationship between high school athletic participation and college attainment and that the more involved the student was in high school athletics, the more likely he or she was to have entered col-

lege and to have received a degree. But actually how important relative to other possible factors is high school athletic participation in attaining post–high school education? Wouldn't high school academic achievement be even more strongly related to post–high school educational attainment? The next set of tables will examine this.

Does Academic Performance in High School Affect Post–High School Educational Attainment?   We will repeat the exercise we did above presenting the computer table as Table 13-7*A* and a recomposed table as Table 13-7*B*. Comparing the column distributions in this table shows very strong differences in post–high school educational attainment for those with different academic achievement levels in high school. The proportion of A-level high school students who finish college is two and a half times larger than the proportion of those who do not attend. For students with GPAs of C and below, the proportion of those who

TABLE 13-7A

1979 EDUCATIONAL ATTAINMENT BY HIGH SCHOOL GPA—COMPUTER TABLE

```
C R O S S T A B U L A T I O N  OF -----------------------------------------------------
VAR3281T EDUCATIONAL ATTAINMENT THREE CATEGORIES
BY VAR229TH HIGH SCHOOL GPA: THREE CATEGORIES
-----------------------------------------------------------------------------
```

	COUNT COL PCT	VAR229TH			
		A and A- B 1.00	B and B- C 2.00	C and Be low 3.00	ROW TOTAL
VAR3281T					
COLL DEGREE OR M	1.00	1939 49.1	1341 21.3	164 6.2	3444 26.7
SOME COLLEGE	2.00	1185 30.0	2558 40.6	877 33.4	4620 35.9
NO COLLEGE	3.00	829 21.0	2409 38.2	1584 60.3	4822 37.4
	COLUMN TOTAL	3953 30.7	6308 49.0	2625 20.4	12886 100.0

TABLE 13-7B

1979 UNIVERSITY/COLLEGE ATTAINMENT BY HIGH SCHOOL GRADE-POINT AVERAGE (GPA)[a]
(National Longitudinal Study of the High School Class of 1972, Five-Survey Respondents)

| | GPA | | |
Attainment	A and A–B	B and B–C	C and Below
College degree or higher	49.1%	21.3%	6.2%
Some college	30.0	40.6	33.4
No college	21.0	38.2	60.3
	100.0%[b]	100.0%	100.0%
	(1,281)	(4,409)	(7,103)

[a]Recomposed table.
[b]Totals throughout are rounded.

do not attend is ten times larger than the proportion of those who graduate from college. B-level high school students are most likely to have attained some college but not graduated from college. This table strongly confirms the association between high school grades and college attainment.

Comparing Tables 13-6*B* and 13-7*B*, we can easily see that grades are more strongly related to college attainment than is athletic participation. This is hardly surprising, given that college attainment (like high school grades) depends on the ability to do academic work. However, it is interesting that the major differences in these tables show up in the comparison of C students with athletic nonparticipants. A student with a C-or-below average in high school is much less likely to complete college than one who is a nonparticipant in sports. In fact students with a GPA of C or less are much more likely not to have gone to college at all than are athletic nonparticipants. In summary, athletic leadership is almost as advantageous as a strong GPA in high school in its relation to acquiring a college degree; but nonparticipation in athletics does not have as negative an effect on educational attainment as a low high school GPA.

How Do Sex and Socioeconomic Origin Relate to High School Athletic Participation?   Since these tables will examine the independent variable in terms of groups to which the respondents belong, the tables serve as *subgroup comparisons.* The primary object of subgroup comparisons is to describe the differences between the groups. Our object here will be to analyze whether some types of students (or students characterized by different qualities) are more involved in athletics in high school. For these tables, only our recomposed tables will be presented.

Table 13-8 reports the cross tabulation for sex, and Table 13-9 reports the cross tabulation for social class origins. In Table 13-8, we see a strong relationship between being male and athletic participation. We find a 9-percentage-point difference in favor of the men among athletic leaders, a 17-percentage-point difference in favor of the men among active participants, and a 26-point difference in favor of the women among the nonparticipants. Clearly, the distribution of males and females in athletic activities in high school was different, with males much more likely to have participated. Figure 13-5 presents a bar graph comparing distribution of athletic participation levels by sex.

TABLE 13-8

HIGH SCHOOL ATHLETIC PARTICIPATION BY SEX

(National Longitudinal Study of the High School Class of 1972, Five-Survey Respondents)

Participation Level	Sex	
	Male	**Female**
Athletic leader	14.7%	5.7%
Active participant	43.5	26.2
Did not participate	41.8	68.1
	100.0%	100.0%
	(6,127)	(6,694)

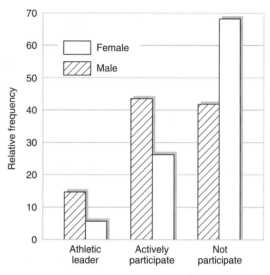

FIGURE 13-5

Bar graph of athletic participation by sex.

Socioeconomic status (SES) categories range from high to low. Since this categorization implies an order, we can analyze Table 13-9 in terms of monotonicity. When we compare the athletic participation of students from different social class origins, we can see distinctive differences. High SES students were more likely to have participated in athletics in high school and to have been leaders than medium or low SES students. There is a clear ordering between the groups such that athletic leadership and participation decline with each lower social class group. This is evidence of monotonicity in the relationship between social class and high school athletic participation.

If we compare the two tables on the influence of sex and social class on athletic participation in high school, we see that sex differences are somewhat greater than social class differences, though both factors are clearly related to differential athletic participation in high school. For our research prob-

TABLE 13-9

HIGH SCHOOL ATHLETIC PARTICIPATION BY PARENTAL SOCIOECONOMIC STATUS (SES)

(National Longitudinal Study of the High School Class of 1972, Five-Survey Respondents)

Participation Level	SES		
	High	**Medium**	**Low**
Athletic leader	13.0%	9.7%	7.8%
Active participant	38.5	34.2	31.2
Did not participate	48.6	56.0	61.1
	100.0%	100.0%	100.0%
	(3,155)	(6,170)	(3,488)

lem, what is now important is to consider how far these three background characteristics affect the relationship of high school athletics to college degree attainment. To examine this requires setting up trivariate tables. Before we do this, however, let us recapitulate the meaning of bivariate tables.

The Nature of Bivariate Relationships

A two-variable table tells you how one variable is related to another. It does not show whether one variable *determines* or *causes* the other, since other factors currently being ignored in the two-variable association may help to explain the relationship between the two being studied. However, it is useful to begin by first trying to understand the relationship between two variables. The best way to start is to consider the *direction of the relationship.*

What you want to look for is how much variation in one variable relates to variation in another. Are the cases that are categorized as high on one variable also high on the other? Or are they low on the other? If the first case is true (high is related to high, low is related to low), there is a *positive,* or *direct association* (relationship), between the two variables. If the second case is true, and those high on one variable tend to be low on the other, there is a *negative,* or *inverse association* (relationship). In either case, the relationship would be considered *linear* in that as the values of one variable go up, the value of the other will also go up (a positive association) or down (a negative association). (Looking for the direction of the relationship between two variables requires that the categories of each variable have some order. However, if one of the variables, such as sex, is measured at the nominal level, and therefore has no implied order, then this concept of the direction of the relationship does not apply.)

Positive and Negative Associations.   Whether a positive or negative association is considered strong or weak depends on your hypotheses about

the type of relationship you expected to find. In Chapter 15, statistical tests will be presented to test the strength of the relationship between variables. However, even a statistically weak relationship may nevertheless be considered important, depending upon what you had expected the relationship to be according to your theory or hypotheses.

In many tables, the pattern of relationship is less evident (*high* may be related to high, medium, *and* low; *low* may be related to low, medium, *and* high). In such an instance, the relationship is less clear-cut. If one variable is related to both high and low values of a second variable, then the relationship is not linear, but *curvilinear.* (Chapter 15 will show graphic examples of these.) One way to determine whether a table is positive or negative is to see whether more cases appear in the cells that cross the table diagonally. If the high categories have been coded as 1 for the computer and are in the upper left-hand corner, then the positive diagonal will go from the upper left-hand to the lower right-hand corner. Conversely, if the high categories are given the higher number codes, the highest code will appear above the upper right-hand cell, and the positive diagonal will go from the upper right-hand to the lower left-hand corner. Our discussion assumes that tables are set up where the high categories are coded as 1 and the positive diagonal runs from the upper left-hand corner to the lower right-hand corner.

If in a table you find more cases in the cells forming the positive diagonal, even though the cases are widely dispersed, this may be evidence of a *weak positive association* between the variables. If there are fairly large percentages along the negative diagonal, even though the cases are widely scattered across the cells, then the relationship would be called a *weak negative* one. Eventually, you must learn to read a table so quickly and carefully that you can *see* by its very appearance whether the associations are positive or negative. With experience, you will be able to do this with ease.

As mentioned above, how you set up your bivariate table may well determine whether the relationship you find will be positive or negative. If you expect (or hypothesize) that higher-class students are more likely to participate in athletics, then you should set up the table so that they will be given the code of 1 (and will be placed in the table in the upper left-hand cell). Likewise, strong participation should be given a 1. This causes the hypothesized association of higher class and strong athletic participation to converge in the upper left-hand cell of the table. Programs such as SPSS[x] allow you easily to recode the categories in your variables before carrying out your computer runs. This will enable you to set up your variables to test the hypothesis you want to test. Recall that in Table 13-6*A*, educational attainment had been recoded to make "college degree or more" category 1, and "athletic participation" had been set up so that "athletic leader" was category 1. We found that the larger percentages were in the upper left-hand and lower right-hand cells (along the positive diagonal).

Bivariate tables can also be analyzed in terms of the *strength of association* (or strength or relationship) between the two variables. Statistical tests indicate the degree of strength of the association. Chapter 15 presents statistical tests for the bivariate analyses presented in this chapter as well as correlation statistics appropriate for variables measured on numerical scales. Statistical material is in a separate chapter so students with varying exposure to statistics can concentrate on this subject, if they need more background.

The Issue of Spuriousness.   Even when you find a strong relationship between two variables, you cannot be certain that the one caused the other. A number of other phenomena may explain the relationship between the two variables being considered. One such explanation could be that the relationship between the two variables being examined has in fact come about because of a third, unexamined, variable. When this happens, the relationship between the two variables is said to be *spurious;* it is in fact caused by an unseen third variable. To test whether two-variable relation-

ships are spurious requires moving from the analysis of two-variable relationships to the analysis of three-variable relationships.

REVIEW NOTES

- Data analyses aim to test hypotheses or research questions posed in a study.
- Tables prepared to present the evidence need to be set up in such a way that the hypothetical relationship being studied can be easily examined. Careful attention must be given to forms of table presentation so as to facilitate an understanding of the evidence. Data analysis begins after the problem has been defined, an analytic model has been set up, the data have been secured, an appropriate sample (or subsample) has been selected, and the variables to be examined have been chosen.
- Univariate tables, those based on one variable, are the most elementary form of tables. One of the most common forms of univariable tables is a frequency distribution which shows the percentage breakdowns of the categories of a variable.
- Most quantitative data analyses are now carried out by computers, which can produce a great range of formats. However, for presentation in a paper or report, the researcher must recompose computer-generated tables so that they show clear and complete labels and numbers and exclude unnecessary information.
- Bivariate tables reveal the relationship of two variables to each other. They are also referred to as cross tabulations, cross classifications, or contingency tables.
- Bivariate tables allow for the testing of two-variable hypotheses.
- Table formats should facilitate the examination of the expected (hypothesized) relationship and should be presented in a consistent fashion throughout a study.
- Bivariate tables are generally set up so that the dependent variable is the row variable and ap-

pears to the left of the table; the independent variable is the column variable and appears at the top of the table. Then the table is *percentaged down* (the separate categories of the independent variable form the bases on which percentages of the dependent variable are given) and *read across* (so that the distributions on the dependent variable are compared across the subgroups of the independent variable).

- Positive associations are those in which the data show that those with high responses to the dependent variable have high responses to the independent variable, and those with low responses to the dependent variable have low responses to the independent variable. Negative associations occur where high responses on one variable are matched with low responses on the other. Positive associations generally support the hypothesis. These directional associations cannot be determined if the variables are nominal.

- Evidence of a strong relationship between variables may be caused by the unexamined effects of a third variable. When this is the case, the relationship is termed spurious.

KEY TERMS

bivariate table
cell
contingency table
cross classification
cross tabulation
epsilon
marginals
monotonicity
negative association (inverse)

positive association (direct)
spurious relationship
subgroup comparison
univariate analysis
univariate table

STUDY EXERCISES

1. Explain the evidence for monotonicity and calculate how large the epsilons are in Table 13-7. Compare the differences in monotonicity and the sizes of the epsilons in Tables 13-7 and 13-9.

2. Three test variables have been offered for consideration in analyzing the relationship between high school athletic participation and educational attainment beyond high school. Suggest two other variables that might be good ones to test, and defend your choices.

3. Diagram the relationships of the two new variables you selected in Exercise 2 with the bivariate relationship of high school athletic participation and post–high school educational attainment.

RECOMMENDED READINGS

1. Frost, Peter J., and Ralph E. Stablein: *Doing Exemplary Research,* Sage, Newbury Park, Calif., 1992. A collection of researchers' reflections on how they thought through and carried out their research analyses.

2. Riley, Matilda White: *Sociological Research: A Case Approach,* Harcourt, Brace, New York, 1963. This classic text, widely available in libraries, combines selections from various studies with discussions of the methodological techniques used and the analyses developed in these studies.

CHAPTER 14

Data Analysis II: Trivariate Analyses and the Elaboration Model

LOOKING AHEAD

Using the athletic participation and educational attainment analysis begun in Chapter 13, this chapter advances to three-variable (trivariate) tables. It also examines the elaboration model for explaining the influence of a third variable on a bivariate relationship.

INTRODUCTION

The primary object of this chapter is to help you become comfortable in setting up, reading, and interpreting three-variable or *trivariate tables.* We have already examined bivariate tables in Chapter 13. Bivariate tables can be used to support or challenge previously developed explanations, or theories. Once a third variable is entered into the analysis as a *control* or *test* variable, the relationship between the original two variables may well change. The manner in which these changes occur has been a subject of interest in the development of social science analytic methods. One well-known approach to studying the ways in which a third variable can alter the patterns of a bivariate relationship is referred to as the elaboration model, or paradigm. This chapter includes an examination of the elaboration paradigm.

We will return to the study we were developing in Chapter 13 on athletic participation and educational attainment and develop the trivariate tables needed to test our hypothesis. We will also show how such tables may be condensed for presentation in a report. Finally, we will use data from this study (as well as some other examples) to explain the elaboration paradigm.

TRIVARIATE ANALYSES

Adding a third variable to an analysis can make an enormous difference. As stated earlier, this third variable may be referred to as a *control variable.* This implies that you plan to examine a two-variable relationship, *controlling* for the possible effects of a third variable by looking at the two-variable relationship under each condition of the third, or control, variable. (Your purpose here may be to check for possible spuriousness between the dependent and independent variables.) The third variable in an analysis is also often referred to as a *test variable,* meaning that the analysis will test for the effects of the third variable on the two-variable association. The terms *test variable* and *control variable* can be used interchangeably.

A number of different terms are used to differentiate bivariate from trivariate tables (and bivariate from trivariate relationships). Sometimes the bivariate relationship is called the *original relationship* and the trivariate relationship, a *partial relationship.* This means that each partial table represents only part of the sample presented in the original table and that the sample has been divided among all the partial tables. For example, if the original table related athletic participation in high school to post–high school educational attainment and if a third variable, sex, were then used to "partial" the original relationship, there would be two partial tables, one relating athletic participation to educational attainment for men, the other relating the same two variables for women.

Bivariate tables can also be referred to as *zero-order tables,* meaning that they are at the lowest or most basic level, and trivariate tables can be labeled as *first-order tables,* which means that they are raised up to the next higher level. In this case, you could also have second-order, third-order, or higher-order tables where the zero-order table is subdivided (broken down, or partialed) first by one test variable, and then the first-order tables are broken down by a second test variable, etc.

Trivariate Tables for the Athletic Participation Study

In this section, we will examine our original relationship of athletic participation to educational attainment, controlling for a number of third variables. What this does is separate the dataset into the categories of the third variable and then cross-tabulate the two original variables.

How the Control Variables Might Affect the Original Relationship Between High School Athletic Participation and Educational Attainment. In Chapter 13, when the variables from the NLS study were selected, three variables were included as possible factors which might change the relationship between the independent variable, high school athletic participation, and the dependent variable, post–high school educational attainment. These three control variables were sex, socioeconomic status (SES), and high school academic performance.

Figure 14-1 diagrams the predicted effects of sex and social class background on the relationship of high school athletic participation and educational attainment. Because we predict that the effect of the independent variable on the dependent variable will vary under each condition of the control variable, we are expecting the control variable to interact in the original relationship between the independent and dependent variables. This is called an *interaction effect.* In terms of the interaction effect of sex, we expect athletic participation to be positively related to educational attainment for males, but we offer no prediction for females. In terms of the interaction effect of SES, we predict that athletic participation will strongly affect educational attainment for lower-class students and may affect middle-class students, but will not affect higher-class students.

High school grade-point average, or GPA (as an indicator of high school academic performance), could be an *intervening* factor between the independent variable, high school athletic participation, and the dependent variable, higher educational attainment. High school GPA could itself be affected by athletic participation, assuming that the attitudes instilled in athletic performance also encourage academic performance. In addition, high school athletes are often required to maintain a certain level of academic achievement. Thus, athletes are under greater pressure to maintain decent grades. (In some ways, this may seem contrary to our commonsense notion of athletes as less serious students. But since our plan is to compare athletes to all other high school students, not

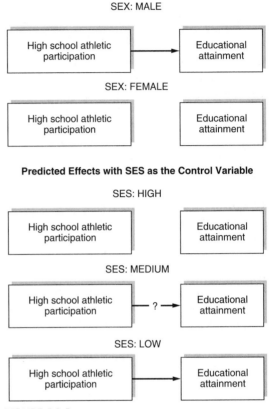

FIGURE 14-1
Hypothesized relationship between high school athletic participation and educational attainment, showing interaction effects of sex and socioeconomic status (SES).

just to the most academically able students, our hypothesized positive effect of athletic participation on final high school GPA seems reasonable.)

Figure 14-2 depicts the model with the addition of the intervening variable, GPA. We will want to explore what might happen to our original relationship between high school athletic participation and educational attainment if we take account of such different intervening conditions as having a high, average, or low GPA in high school. The forthcoming trivariate analyses will show what happens when each of the three factors (sex, SES, and high school GPA) is entered as a control variable. In each case, we will examine the

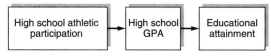

FIGURE 14-2
Hypothesized relationship among high school athletic participation, high school grade-point average (GPA), and educational attainment.

distribution of the dependent variable (university/college attainment) among the different independent variable (high school athletic participation) subgroups, then compare and contrast these differences under each category of the control variable. We will prepare separate bivariate tables for subsamples representing different categories of a control variable; then, while controlling (or testing) for the effects of the third, control (or test) variable, we will compare the original relationship with the partial relationships. Only part of the sample is considered in each of the subtables, which are referred to as *partial tables.*

What Happens to the Original Relationship of Educational Attainment and Athletic Participation When Sex Is Controlled?   Tables 14-1*A* and 14-1*B* present these partial tables. Let's first look at the computer tables. Notice that they are very similar to the bivariate computer tables except that, under the title, Table 14-1*A* (part 1) states:

```
CONTROLLING FOR..
   VAR1626 SEX VALUE = 1. MALE
```

This means that in this table only the males will be considered. Compare the number of cases in this table (6,112) to Table 13-6*A* (which had 12,793). Where are the other subjects? They are in the table for females, which has 6,681 subjects (6,112 + 6,681 = 12,793).

The table is read in precisely the same way as a bivariate table. The difference is that you want to compare this table for males to the one for females. If you compare the distribution of educational attainments across athletic types and then

contrast these differences in distributions for males and females, you can see that the distributions show greater variation for the males. This greater variation suggests that athletic leadership and participation are more strongly related to educational attainment for males than for females.

Now consider the percentage differences (or *epsilons*) between athletic leaders and nonparticipants for males and females. In the table for males, there is a 22-percentage-point difference between athletic leaders and nonparticipants in attaining a college degree; in the table for females, there is less than a 14-point difference. It would seem that being an athletic leader is more advantageous for men, in terms of achieving a college degree, than it is for women. It is still advantageous for women, but not as much.

We would conclude that the association between participation in high school athletics and post–high school educational attainment is slightly stronger for men than for women; however, both male and female athletes are more likely to have completed more higher education than nonathletes. We should recall that the relationship between sex and athletic participation (Table 13-8) had indicated a much greater tendency for males than females to participate actively in athletics and to be athletic leaders.

Now consider Table 14-1*B* (parts 1 and 2), which is the rewritten version of the computer tables. Again, these are set up in a way similar to bivariate tables. Note that it is good to present the partial tables side by side (or directly beneath one another) to facilitate comparisons between the tables. For the rest of the trivariate tables to be presented here, only the recomposed tables will be shown. (Remember, however, that each of these tables was drawn up on the basis of a computer table.)

Is Social Class Origin an Important Factor?
Table 13-9, which was the bivariate table of athletics and social class origins, indicated that athletic leadership and participation was more prevalent among the higher classes than the middle, and among the

TABLE 14-1A

1979 EDUCATIONAL ATTAINMENT BY HIGH SCHOOL ATHLETIC PARTICIPATION BY SEX— COMPUTER TABLE

C R O S S T A B U L A T I O N   O F   -
VAR3281T EDUCATIONAL ATTAINMENT THREE CATEGORIES BY VAR241R HIGH SCHOOL
ATHLETIC PARTICIPATION CONTROLLING FOR.. VAR1626 SEX VALUE = 1. MALE
- -

	VAR241R			
COUNT COL PCT	PARTICIP ATE AS L 1.00	PARTICIP ATE ACTI 2.00	NOT PART ICIPATE 3.00	ROW TOTAL
VAR3281T				
1.00 COLL DEGREE OR M	379 42.0	852 32.0	509 20.0	1740 28.5
2.00 SOME COLLEGE	353 39.1	981 36.9	925 36.3	2259 37.0
3.00 NO COLLEGE	170 18.8	826 31.1	1117 43.8	2113 34.6
COLUMN TOTAL	902 14.8	2659 43.5	2551 41.7	6112 100.0

C R O S S T A B U L A T I O N   O F   -
VAR3281T EDUCATIONAL ATTAINMENT THREE CATEGORIES BY VAR241R HIGH SCHOOL
ATHLETIC PARTICIPATION CONTROLLING FOR.. VAR1626 SEX VALUE = 2. FEMALE
- -

	VAR241R			
COUNT COL PCT	PARTICIP ATE AS L 1.00	PARTICIP ATE ACTI 2.00	NOT PART ICIPATE 3.00	ROW TOTAL
VAR3281T				
1.00 COLL DEGREE OR M	141 37.2	503 28.7	1049 23.0	1693 25.3
2.00 SOME COLLEGE	134 35.4	658 37.6	1544 33.9	2336 35.0
3.00 NO COLLEGE	104 27.4	589 33.7	1959 43.0	2652 39.7
COLUMN TOTAL	379 5.7	1750 26.2	4552 68.1	6681 100.0

TABLE 14-1B

1979 UNIVERSITY/COLLEGE ATTAINMENT BY HIGH SCHOOL ATHLETIC PARTICIPATION BY SEX[a]

(National Longitudinal Study of the High School Class of 1972, Five-Survey Respondents)

	Participation Level		
Attainment	**Athletic Leader**	**Active Participant**	**Did Not Participate**
Males			
College degree or higher	42.0%	32.0%	20.0%
Some college	39.1	36.9	36.3
No college	18.8	31.1	43.8
	100.0%[b]	100.0%	100.0%
	(902)	(2,659)	(2,551)
Females			
College degree or higher	37.2%	28.7%	23.0%
Some college	35.4	37.6	33.9
No college	27.4	33.7	43.0
	100.0%	100.0%	100.0%
	(379)	(1,750)	(4,552)

[a]Recomposed table.
[b]Totals throughout are rounded.

middle classes than the lower. Should we expect athletic participation to have a stronger educational payoff for the more advantaged classes? Table 14-2 (parts 1 to 3) offers the relevant comparisons.

What we need to do here is ask whether youths from every social class benefit equally from high school athletic participation. Again we will need to examine the distribution on the dependent variable (university/college attainment) across the categories of the independent variable subgroups, and then contrast these differences across the three categories of the control variable, social class. What we see for the higher SES students is that the distributions of educational attainment do not vary much by the level of athletic participation, though there is still a slight tendency for students who participated in high school athletics to be more likely to finish college. (Note that among the high SES group, ath-

letic leaders have no real advantage over those who have merely participated.)

For the medium and low SES groups, athletic leadership clearly relates to attaining a college degree, and athletic nonparticipation becomes much more highly associated with not attending college. In other words, athletic leadership seems to be a more powerful determinant of one's educational future among the middle and lower classes than among the higher classes. Clearly, this suggests that athletics have more significant educational consequences for less socially advantaged high school students. Students from more advantaged backgrounds seem to have other resources to compensate for not participating in athletics. We see this in the finding that higher-class students who were nonathletes in high school are almost as likely to be college graduates as those who were high school athletes. However, among the other two

TABLE 14-2

1979 UNIVERSITY/COLLEGE ATTAINMENT BY HIGH SCHOOL ATHLETIC PARTICIPATION BY SES
(National Longitudinal Study of the High School Class of 1972, Five-Survey Respondents)

	Participation Level		
Attainment	**Athletic Leader**	**Active Participant**	**Did Not Participate**
High SES			
College degree or higher	57.2%	56.5%	48.1%
Some college	35.0	34.2	37.0
No college	7.8	9.2	14.9
	100.0%	100.0%[a]	100.0%
	(409)	(1,212)	(1,531)
Medium SES			
College degree or higher	37.7%	25.0%	18.4%
Some college	38.8	40.8	37.7
No college	23.5	34.2	44.0
	100.0%	100.0%	100.0%
	(600)	(2,111)	(3,444)
Low SES			
College degree or higher	22.2%	13.1%	8.9%
Some college	40.7	33.4	28.5
No college	37.0	53.5	62.6
	100.0%	100.0%	100.0%
	(270)	(1,084)	(2,124)

[a]Totals throughout are rounded.

class groups, the nonparticipants are distinctly less likely to graduate from college.

What Happens When High School Academic Ability Is Controlled?   Table 14-3 (parts 1 to 3) examines the relationship of participation in high school athletics to attaining a higher education, while controlling for high school academic ability. Because we assume that athletic participation in high school may subsequently affect a student's overall high school grade-point average and because we assume that this high school GPA will then affect post–high school educational attainment, we are using high school academic

ability as an *intervening variable* between athletic participation and post–high school educational attainment.

We also expect that there may be an *interaction effect* of high school athletic participation and high school grades on post–high school educational attainment. In such a case, both GPA and athletic talent would be considered important factors in determining a student's educational future. We might consider them as alternative resources. For academically talented students, academic ability would be a primary resource in helping them to be accepted by and be successful at a college. For less academically talented students, athletic prowess would be a primary resource that would in some ways substitute for academic ability in determining access to and success in higher education.

In fact, Table 14-3 indicates that athletic leadership is associated with getting a college degree for all GPA groups, but this is especially true for high school students with B-level GPAs. Among the A students, as we saw in Table 14-3, nonparticipation only moderately reduces the proportion completing a college education. Among the C students or below, the proportion attaining college degrees is much lower, but here athletic leadership and participation are related to getting *some* col-

lege education. (Note that athletic leaders with C-or-below GPAs are as likely as those with B averages to spend some time in college, but they are much less likely to complete college.) In other words, athletic ability may be a substitute for academic ability in relation to who goes to college, but it is not a substitute for academic ability in terms of who will get a college degree.

Condensing Trivariate Tables

One of the objects of data analysis is to compress data—to restrict as much as possible the amount

TABLE 14-3

1979 UNIVERSITY/COLLEGE ATTAINMENT BY HIGH SCHOOL ATHLETIC PARTICIPATION BY HIGH SCHOOL GPA
(National Longitudinal Study of the High School Class of 1972, Five-Survey Respondents)

	Participation Level		
Attainment	**Athletic Leader**	**Active Participant**	**Did Not Participate**
GPA: A and A–B			
College degree or higher	57.0%	55.0%	44.2%
Some college	30.0	29.8	30.1
No college	13.1	15.2	25.7
	100.0%[a]	100.0%	100.0%
	(467)	(1,290)	(2,154)
GPA: B and B–C			
College degree or higher	35.6%	25.5%	15.9%
Some college	42.6	41.2	39.9
No college	21.8	33.3	44.3
	100.0%	100.0%	100.0%
	(620)	(2,292)	(3,328)
GPA: C and Below			
College degree or higher	16.9%	7.2%	4.6%
Some college	43.4	37.2	30.5
No college	39.7	55.6	64.9
	100.0%	100.0%	100.0%
	(189)	(811)	(1,586)

[a]Totals throughout are rounded.

of data it is necessary to present in order to make one's point—while at the same time maximizing the amount of information each table can give. For trivariate tables, this can often be done by presenting one category of the dependent variable in a table that cross-tabulates the independent variable with the test variable. Let's take the last set of trivariate tables and show how much of the information from the three tables can be condensed into one.

Suppose we are primarily interested in finding out which is more highly associated with attaining a college degree—athletic participation in high school or grades in high school. Specifically, this means we want to compare proportions of students with particular combinations of grades and athletic participation in high school who received college degrees. How can we show this in one table? Look at Table 14-4. This table presents the percentage of college graduates among those with certain combinations of grade-point average and athletic participation. Each cell gives the percentage of college graduates from each athletic participation group who had a particular GPA. Since the proportions of those who had some college or no college are not presented (as they were in Table 14-3), the columns in Table 14-4 do not add up to 100 percent.

Note that in this table the numbers (in parentheses) are from the columns of the trivariate table, so that you know the size of the group on which each of the percentages was based (for example, 57 percent of the 467 students who were athletic leaders and who had A-level averages attained a college degree within seven years). Here we see even more clearly what we reported above: that athletic leadership is more important for attaining a college degree among students with B-level GPAs (20 percent more of the athletic leaders complete college than nonparticipants) than for those with A-level averages. (This trend, though characterizing fewer students, is also seen for those with C-level GPAs.)

If a condensed table is prepared from variables with two categories, then it is easy for the reader to determine what the rest of the table would look like (by merely subtracting the percents shown in the table from 100 percent). In the example given, however, where the dependent variable has three categories, the original tables cannot be reconstructed from the condensed table; nevertheless, the condensed table reports on the most important category of the dependent variable (for an ordered variable, this might be the highest category) and indicates more succinctly the effects of the independent and control variables.

TABLE 14-4

CONDENSED TRIVARIATE TABLE OF ATTAINING A COLLEGE DEGREE BY HIGH SCHOOL ATHLETIC PARTICIPATION BY HIGH SCHOOL GPA
(Percentage Attaining College Degree within 7 Years of High School Graduation)

High School GPA	High School Athletic Participation		
	Athletic Leader	Active Participant	Did Not Participate
A and A–B	57.0	55.0	44.2
	(467)	(1,290)	(2,154)
B and B–C	35.6	25.5	15.9
	(620)	(2,292)	(3,228)
C and below C	16.9	7.2	4.6
	(18 9)	(811)	(1,586)

ELABORATION

A third variable may alter the relationship between dependent and independent variables in a number of different ways. Certain types of outcomes that can occur with the entry of a third variable into a bivariate relationship have come to serve as exemplary models for social analyses. These effects were studied first by Samuel Stouffer, a well-known social researcher whose studies of the U.S. Army were very influential in the development of social research after World War II (Stouffer, 1949). Stouffer's ideas were formulated and disseminated more widely by Paul Lazarsfeld, Patricia Kendall, Robert Merton, and others at the Bureau of Applied Research at Columbia University (see Kendall and Lazarsfeld, 1950). Perhaps the most widely used work applying the principles of elaboration to cross-tabular analysis has been Rosenberg's *The Logic of Survey Analysis* (1968).

These analytic models have been so influential in social science analyses that they are often referred to as the *elaboration paradigm.* For our purposes, what is important about elaboration is

that it is a way to try to explain what happens to two-variable relationships under the conditions of a third (test) variable. We will examine the different forms of the elaboration model using, in certain instances, the trivariate tables we have already discussed and, in other instances, some hypothetical results that might have occurred.

There are two factors to consider in an elaboration. The first is whether the third variable logically comes in a time sequence *before* the independent variable (in which case, it is *antecedent*) or whether it occurs *between* the independent and dependent variables (in which case, it is *intervening*). Figure 14-3 shows trivariate models with antecedent and intervening test variables as well as applications of these models where the variables from our study on athletic participation and educational attainment have been fit into the models.

The second consideration comes into play once the partial tables are formed. When the third variable is introduced, the relationships between the independent and dependent variable under the various conditions of the test variables may either

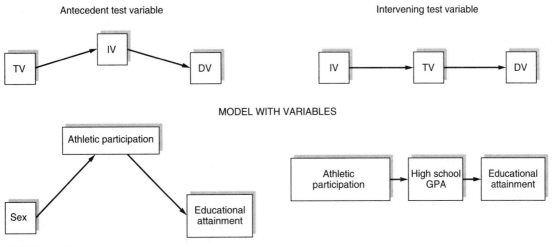

MODEL OF EFFECTS ON RELATIONSHIP OF INDEPENDENT (IV) TO DEPENDENT VARIABLE (DV) UNDER DIFFERENT CONDITIONS OF A TEST VARIBLE (TV)

Antecedent test variable

Intervening test variable

MODEL WITH VARIABLES

FIGURE 14-3
Trivariate models with antecedent and intervening test variables.

remain the same as in the original table or change. If the relationships between the dependent and independent variables remain largely the same in the partial tables, they represent a *replication*. If the relationships between the dependent and independent variables weaken in the partial tables, and the test variable is antecedent to the independent variable, the original relationship has been explained and is therefore considered *spurious*. (In this case, the antecedent variable would be an extraneous variable producing the spurious relationship.) Using the terms of the elaboration paradigm, such an occurrence is referred to as an *explanation*—i.e., the original relationship has been explained by an extraneous factor.

If the original relationship weakens, but the test variable was intervening between the independent and dependent variables, then the intervening factor has largely destroyed the original relationship. This form of elaboration would be called an *interpretation*. This generally means that both the independent and the dependent variables were related to the intervening variable, which is also the case in an explanation. Thus, when the sample is divided into the different categories "of the test variables, the partial relationships between the original variables will vanish" (Kendall and Lazarsfeld, 1950). In short, when the intervening test variable is used to stratify the sample, it serves to largely wipe out the relationship between the original two variables.

Finally, if the two partial relationships show different trends in comparison to the original relationship such that one partial relationship is stronger than the original relationship and the other is weaker, the results are referred to as a *specification*. What this implies is that under one condition of the test variable the relationship between the dependent and independent variables strengthened, while under another condition of the test variable it weakened or largely disappeared. In other words, the third variable *specified* the condition in which the original relationship is the strongest. Recall that this is also referred to as an *interaction effect*.

Using Sex as the Test Variable

Now we will try out our own elaboration analysis by returning to the athletic participation study to reexamine a few trivariate analyses to see what the partial relationships showed about the original relationship between high school athletic participation and college attainment. To do this, we will begin by carefully going through every step of a three-variable relationship, thinking through what we can learn at each step. Our first example will use sex as the test variable;[1] our second example will use high school grade-point average as the test variable.

Educational Attainment, Athletic Participation, and Sex.   We will return to our trivariate analysis of Table 14-1, which cross-tabulates educational attainment by athletic participation for males and females. This is the diagram we saw above in Figure 14-1. Clearly, sex is empirically antecedent to both variables in its time of designation (at birth). Before reexamining this table in the light of the elaboration model, let us first examine each of the bivariate relationships between the three variables in order to develop a thorough sense of how these variables relate to one another.

Sex and athletic participation.   Reconsider Table 13-8. Here we see that the proportion of males who are athletic leaders is more than double the proportion of females and that males are also active athletic participants much more often than females. In short, sex is related to athletic participation in high school.

Sex and 1979 university/college attainment.   Table 14-5 presents the association of sex and edu-

[1] One's sex can be empirically determined prior to one's athletic participation even if athletic participation does not directly *depend* on one's sex. Athletic participation in grade school, or a measure of athletic ability, would represent stronger examples of antecedent test variables for high school athletic participation (however, no such measures were included in the NLS surveys).

TABLE 14-5

1979 UNIVERSITY/COLLEGE ATTAINMENT BY SEX
(National Longitudinal Study of the High School Class of 1972, Five-Survey Respondents)

	Sex	
Attainment	Males	Females
College degree or higher	28.3%	26.4%
Some college	36.8	35.3
No college	34.9	38.3
	100.0%	100.0%
	(6,168)	(6,783)

cational attainment (not presented before). Here we see slight advantages for men among college degree recipients and among those with some college. The differences, however, are small—in the two- to three-point range—clearly not as large as sex differences in athletic participation in high school.

Athletic participation and 1979 university/college attainment. This is the original relationship as seen earlier in Table 13-6*B*. Reexamining it, we see again how athletic leadership and participation are strongly associated with attaining a college degree (twice the proportion of leaders as compared to nonparticipants have received degrees).

Determining Type of Elaboration

The three bivariate tables have indicated (1) that high school athletic participation fosters post–high school educational attainment, (2) that males are much more likely than females to participate in high school athletics, and (3) that males (among 1972 high school graduates) are only slightly more likely to receive college degrees within seven years of high school graduation than are females. A trivariate table must be examined to determine which type of elaboration the three-variable model represents.

Table 14-6 offers a condensed version of Table 14-1 in which the percentages presented in the cells represent the proportion of college degree holders among males and females with different levels of high school athletic participation. We see that among athletes, males are somewhat more likely to have degrees than females; but among nonathletes, females are slightly more likely to have degrees than males. For both sexes, athletic leadership is strongly associated with attaining a college degree. Since males benefit slightly more from it, this means that the original relationship between athletics and college education (as seen in Table 14-6) has been *specified*. In other words, the original relationship is greater when it is specified for men, lesser when it is specified for women. In short, the effects of high school athletic participation on attaining a college education in the 1970s can be specified as occurring more for men.

Let me stress that this is not a very *strong* specification. It would be stronger if the differences in the original relationship for men and women had been greater.[2] Suppose athletic leadership actually reduced the number of degree recipients for women as compared to nonparticipants. The specification would then be much more substantial. However, we have seen that by examining the original relationship under the different conditions of a third variable, sex, we learned more about the original association. This is precisely the point of elaboration.

Specification, as a form of elaboration, differs from other types of elaboration because it uses the test variable to examine under what conditions the original relationship is reinforced. As Rosenberg states, "The object of this procedure is clarification—clarification of the true value of the relationship" (1968, p. 131). Here, rather than finding that

---

[2]The differences between these partial tables might be considered by some to be so small that they would better exemplify a replication of the original relationship rather than a specification of it.

TABLE 14-6

CONDENSED TRIVARIATE TABLE OF ATTAINING A COLLEGE DEGREE BY HIGH SCHOOL ATHLETIC PARTICIPATION BY SEX
(Percent Attaining College Degree within 7 Years of High School Graduation)

	High School Athletic Participation		
Sex	**Athletic Leader**	**Active Participant**	**Did Not Participate**
Male	42.0	32.0	20.0
	(902)	(2,659)	(2,551)
Female	37.2	28.7	23.0
	(379)	(1,750)	(4,552)

the association between the original two variables disappears (or weakens) in the partial tables, you look for which attribute of the test variable *strengthens* the original association. You know you have found an example of specification when one of the partial tables (representing one condition of the test variable) increases the relationship between the independent and dependent variable, while the other partial table (representing another condition of the test variable) weakens the original relationship. What you are doing is *specifying* the conditions where the relationship is strong. For this type of elaboration, the test variable may be either antecedent to the independent variable or intervening between the independent and dependent variables.

Using GPA as the Test Variable

In this case, we want to examine carefully how a test variable which logically occurs after the independent variable, but before the dependent (that is, an intervening test variable) can affect the original association between the independent and dependent variables. As stated earlier, we are assuming that high school academic achievement (a student's cumulative GPA) will intervene in the relationship between athletic participation and post–high school educational attainment. By mak-

ing this assumption, we are proposing that athletic participation will affect high school GPA, which will then affect college attainment. Table 14-3 (and Table 14-4) presented the trivariate tables of educational attainment by high school athletic participation by high school GPA. In this case, we placed the GPA as intervening between the athletic activity and attaining a college education.

These tables indicated that the original relationship between athletic participation and educational attainment is strongest among the B students, less strong for the C students, and even weaker for the A students. What type of elaboration does this portray? It is not an *interpretation,* for the original relationship is not eliminated by the test variable. Instead, it is a *specification,* in that the test variable specifies the condition under which the original relationship is maintained—for the B and for the C-and-below students. Again, it is not a very strong specification. Recall, as in the last case, that it would be stronger had the trivariate tables shifted further from the original relationship. Imagine, for example, that the original relationship was very strong for the B students, while it was very weak for the C students, and that athletic leadership was even negatively associated with getting a college degree for the A students. Here, the evidence for a specification would have been much greater.

Replication

Let us consider what would happen if the last trivariate table for the three grade groups (Table 14-4) had been nearly the same in each case as the original relationship. This would mean that the original relationship had been *replicated* under different conditions. A replication can occur whether the test variable is intervening or antecedent. In other words, if within homogeneous subgroups of the test variable, the partial relationships between the independent and dependent variables remain very similar to one another and to the bivariate relationship, then the original relationship has been replicated.

A search for replications is often carried out on different samples. If you were using the NLS dataset on United States high school students, you might want to try to replicate these findings for Canadian students. Or, if you had data on students in one state, you might want to compare the results from that state to those from another. If the relationships under the new condition remain roughly

the same, you have a replication of your original findings.

Explanation

This form of elaboration raises the issue of spuriousness which we discussed earlier. The aim is to see whether the original relationship between the two variables can be explained away by the effects of an antecedent variable to which both variables are related. If such an effect could be established, it would mean that the antecedent test variable really explains why an association between the first two variables occurred. Table 14-7 gives a hypothetical example using the trivariate relationship of athletic participation, educational attainment, and sex (as in Table 14-1).

These hypothetical results could have occurred in Table 14-1. If they had, they would have explained away the original relationship between athletic participation and educational attainment. In other words, they would suggest that athletic

TABLE 14-7

EDUCATIONAL ATTAINMENT BY HIGH SCHOOL ATHLETIC PARTICIPATION BY SEX[a]

| | Participation Level | | |
Attainment	Athletic Leader	Active Participant	Did Not Participate
	Males		
College degree or higher	44%	40%	40%
Some college	35	35	30
No college	21	25	30
	100%	100%	100%
	Females		
College degree or higher	35%	33%	30%
Some college	35	33	30
No college	30	33	40
	100%	100%	100%

[a]Hypothetical data.

participation and getting a college degree are both strongly affected by sex. When you control for sex, you see that there is no relationship between athletics and post–high school college attainment. In Table 14-7, males are more likely to get college degrees, regardless of their athletic participation in high school; females are less likely to get degrees, whatever their athletic participation.

Given such findings, the original relationship would be considered spurious, because it would have been fully accounted for by the introduction of sex as a test variable. Since the sex of the student preceded high school athletic participation (and we are making the case here that athletic participation was heavily contingent on sex, though surely not completely contingent on it), this means that what was first seen in the original relationship really occurred because of the unexamined influence of sex differences.

Interpretation

As stated above, when the test variable is intervening and the partial relationships again largely or completely disappear, this is referred to as an interpretation. Hyman (1955) described interpretation as trying to determine "the process through which the assumed cause is related to what we take to be its effect" (p. 276). What this means is that we need to examine the intervening period between the time at which the independent variable had its effect and the time at which the dependent variable occurred. If we can select a factor that took place in the interim which might have altered the effect of the independent variable on the dependent variable, we would be able to interpret the original relationship. Figure 14-4, a diagram comparing *interpretation* to *explanation,* was first offered by Kendall and Lazarsfeld (1950).

In explanation, the test variable is antecedent to the *xy* relationship and affects each variable separately. In interpretation, the test variable is intervening between the *xy* relationship. Table 14-8 gives a hypothetical example using the inter-

vening variable of college entrance exam scores as the test variable. Keep in mind that in this example we have assumed that entrance exams intervene between athletic activity in high school and college attendance. If the time sequence between the independent variable and the test variable were unclear (that is, if you were not sure whether the test variable were intervening or antecedent), it would be impossible to distinguish between interpretation and explanation. In this case, the meaning of the relationship between high school athletic participation and attaining a college degree has been *interpreted* by college entrance examination scores.

Those with higher exam scores are more likely to attain college degrees, with high school athletic participation playing only a minor role; those with lower exam scores are less likely to attain a degree almost regardless of the level of their athletic activity in high school. In other words, if we stratify the sample into groups according to their college entrance examination scores, within these academically homogeneous groups, we find no strong relationship between athletic participation and educational attainment. The athletically active student will be no more likely to finish college than the athletic nonparticipant with similar academic ability. This means that if the partial associations between athletic participation and post–high school educational attainment disappear when students

FIGURE 14-4

Effects of a test variable (*t*) on the relationship between an independent variable (*x*) and a dependent variable (*y*). [Patricia L. Kendall and Paul F. Lazarsfeld, "Problems of Survey Analysis," in Robert K. Merton (ed.), Continuities in Social Research, Free Press, Glencoe, Ill., 1950, p. 157.]

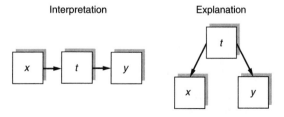

TABLE 14-8

EDUCATIONAL ATTAINMENT BY HIGH SCHOOL ATHLETIC PARTICIPATION
(By College Entrance Examination Scores[a])

Attainment	Participation Level		
	Athletic Leader	**Active Participant**	**Did Not Participate**
Entrance Exam: High Score			
College degree or higher	50%	48%	45%
Some college	25	30	30
No college	25	22	25
	100%	100%	100%
Entrance Exam: Midrange Score			
College degree or higher	35%	33%	30%
Some college	30	33	30
No college	35	33	40
	100%	100%	100%
Entrance Exam: Low Score			
College degree or higher	20%	20%	18%
Some college	48	45	42
No college	32	35	40
	100%	100%	100%

[a]Hypothetical data.

are subdivided into groups according to college entrance exam scores, we must conclude that the original relationship between athletics and educational attainment was interpreted almost completely by students' academic aptitude as measured by college entrance examination results.

In this example, we saw that when we looked at students grouped by their college entrance exam scores (those whose scores were high, midrange, or low), attaining a college degree was not affected much by their high school athletic achievement. The original relationship between high school athletics and college attainment has been interpreted by the level of academic ability indicated by college entrance examination scores received.

Suppressor and Distorter Variables

When an original relationship shows no clear association between the variables, this generally tends to dissuade the researcher from pursuing any further possible meaning in the relationship. However, numerous researchers have found that, in some instances, a zero-order association which is weak might become much stronger in the first-order tables when certain test variables are introduced. Rosenberg (1968) coined the terms *suppressor* and *distorter* control variables in order to account for the appearance of strong associations in the partial tables when the original table had shown only a very weak relationship.

Suppressor Variables.   One of the studies considered by Rosenberg was by Middleton (1963), who had hypothesized that black Americans would be more "alienated" than white Americans because their subordinate social status was a "disabling condition." For most of his measures of alienation, that is precisely what Middleton found. On the factor of "cultural estrangement," though, there was virtually no difference between white and black people. He discovered, however, that when education was entered as a test variable, white people among both the lower and higher education groups appeared to have higher cultural estrangement.

Thus the important differences between the races in their degree of cultural estrangement had been suppressed by the variable of education. By ignoring the factor of education in the original table, the relationship of race to cultural estrangement was *suppressed*. Once the partial associations were examined for the various educational groups, it was clear that race had an important effect on a sense of cultural estrangement.

In short, if you have a zero-order table which shows a very weak relationship, there might still be an important relationship between the two variables that is being suppressed by a third unexamined variable. In this case, finding that important third variable and examining its influence through trivariate analyses may help to uncover the original relationship.

Distorter Variables.   In certain instances, an original table of moderate strength may reverse itself to show the opposite relationship. Rosenberg gives the example of examining social class and attitudes toward civil rights. In Table 14-9, the original relationship between class and support of civil rights indicated that the working classes were slightly stronger supporters of civil rights than the middle classes (45 percent of the working-class respondents compared to 30 percent of the middle-class respondents had high civil rights scores). However, when the test variable of race was used to partial the original relationship, the opposite was found in the partial relationships—the middle classes appeared to be stronger supporters. This was especially true among the African-Americans (there was a 40 percent difference in the propor-

TABLE 14-9

SOCIAL CLASS AND ATTITUDE TOWARD CIVIL RIGHTS BY RACE[a]

Civil Rights Score	Middle Class	Working Class		
High	30%	45%		
Low	70	55		
Total percent	100%	100%		
Number	(120)	(120)		

	African-Americans		White Americans	
Civil Rights Score	Middle Class	Working Class	Middle Class	Working Class
High	70%	50%	30%	20%
Low	30	50	70	80%
Total percent	100%	100%	100%	100%
Number	(20)	(100)	(100)	(20)

[a]Hypothetical.

Source: Adapted from Morris Rosenberg, *The Logic of Survey Analysis,* Basic Books, New York, 1968, pp. 94–95.

tion of high scorers among the middle-class as compared to the working-class respondents but only a 10 percent difference in the proportion of high scorers among middle-class as compared to working-class white respondents).

How can you account for the change and strengthening of the relationship between social class and civil rights scores in the partial relationship tables? In this instance, race (which was the test variable) would have been *distorting* the original relationship between social class and civil rights attitudes such that when it was entered as a test variable, and the sample was subdivided into African-Americans and white Americans, a much stronger and different association between class and civil rights support appeared for the black respondents, and a weaker, though changed, relationship appeared for the white respondents. This is to say that in the partial tables it was the middle classes who had the larger proportions of high civil rights scores, the working classes the smaller proportions. Race, the test variable, had been a *distorter variable* in the original relationship.

Elaboration: What Does It Tell Us?

The reason why an understanding of the elaboration model is useful is that it makes you think carefully about (1) the temporal order of your variables and (2) the types of associations produced by your variables. In short, it is a way to push toward a causal explanation. Naturally, there may be more than a third variable affecting a relationship (and to study this possibility you need to employ multivariate techniques). Here I merely want to stress that understanding how a third variable may alter or replicate the original association noted will strengthen your logical abilities in discovering the interdependencies among variables.

REVIEW NOTES

- Trivariate analyses include a third variable which serves as a control or test variable for the hypothesis.

- Trivariate tables may be called first-order tables in contrast to zero-order bivariate tables. Trivariate relationships may also be referred to as partial relationships in contrast to the original relationship of the bivariate table.

- Condensed trivariate tables can be made by presenting the percentage of one category of the dependent variable in a cross tabulation of the independent and test variables.

- The elaboration paradigm offers explanatory models for trivariate analyses. When a third variable causes no change in the bivariate relationship, it represents a replication. When the original relationship weakens with the introduction of the test variable, it represents an explanation (if the test variable is antecedent to the independent variable) or an interpretation (if the test variable is intervening between the independent and dependent variables). If the partial relationships are stronger than the original relationship under certain conditions of the test variable, but weaker under other conditions, this represents a specification.

- When a weak original relationship becomes stronger in the partial relationship, this may be the result of the test variable serving as a suppressor variable. When a partial relationship reverses the association noted in the original relationship, this may be caused by a test variable serving as a distorter variable.

KEY TERMS

antecedent variable
condensed trivariate table
control variable
distorter variable
elaboration paradigm
explanation
first-order table
interaction effect
interpretation
intervening variable
original relationship
partial relationship

replication
specification
suppressor variable
test variable
trivariate table
zero-order table

STUDY EXERCISES

1. In the following five examples, indicate what form of elaboration (replication, explanation, interpretation, or specification) has been discovered.

   a. The negative relationship between knowledge of a foreign language and educational attainment disappears when the variable of whether English is spoken in the home is controlled.

   b. The relationship between the purchase of fluoride or nonfluoride toothpaste and the number of cavities of buyers disappears when the control variable of frequency of brushing is examined.

   c. The relationship between juvenile delinquency and whether the juveniles' mothers work strengthens if the mother-child relationship is negative and weakens if the mother-child relationship is positive.

   d. The association between the number of swimming medals won by suburban high schools as compared to urban high schools weakens when one controls for the presence of a swimming pool in the schools.

   e. The relationship between high expectations of parents for their children's achievement in mathematics and the children's mathe-

matical achievement noted in Japan occurs in the United States as well among children whose parents hold high expectations.

2. Consider the hypothesis "Catholics are more likely to support tax credits for private education than non-Catholics."

   a. Set up a bivariate table to test this hypothesis.

   b. Now add the control variable of presence of school-aged children. Set up the trivariate tables that would be needed to test for the effects of the control variable.

   Note: Be sure to set these tables up so that the dependent variable is the row variable and the independent variable the column variable. Also arrange the categories so that the hypothesized effect is being tested in the upper left-hand cell.

RECOMMENDED READINGS

1. Caplovitz, David: *The Stages of Social Research,* Wiley, New York, 1983. There are very good chapters on bivariate and multivariate analyses with further development of the elaboration model.

2. Merton, Robert K., and Paul F. Lazarsfeld: *Continuities in Social Research,* Free Press, Glencoe, Ill., 1950. An old, but widely available, classic reader on data analysis in the testing of hypotheses. The chapter on "Problems of Survey Analysis" by Kendall and Lazarsfeld gives excellent examples of the elaboration model.

3. Rosenberg, Morris: *The Logic of Survey Analysis,* Basic Books, New York, 1968. This comprehensive and clearly written exposition of survey analysis offers perhaps the best coverage of the elaboration model.

Elementary Statistics for Social Research

LOOKING AHEAD

This chapter shows how descriptive statistics can be used to summarize data and measure associations between variables. The chapter explains correlations and regressions, discusses the conditions appropriate for using inferential statistics, and describes the meaning and procedures for carrying out a chi-square test.

INTRODUCTION

S tatistics are needed in social research to improve our ability in describing and interpreting the meaning of large amounts of information. If you have information only on one item or on a few subjects, you can probably give an adequate description in words, citing central characteristics and qualities. Naturally, you may be wrong in your description of even one case, but you have the resources in terms of language to carry out the task. When you have information on 10,000 cases, it becomes much more difficult to describe this information in words. *Descriptive statistics* are tools which can enable you to describe large bodies of data in a summary fashion. The most common forms of descriptive statistics describe the central tendencies and variability of a set of data.

When your findings are from a probability sample, summary descriptions, or *statistics,* from these findings may be used to estimate the corresponding population parameters using certain assumptions about the distribution of the underlying population. Statistical procedures that allow you to *infer* from what you found in a representative sample to the whole population are called *inferential statistics.* Such statistics may be used to test hypotheses about the relationships that may exist within a population under study. Simply speaking, this is done by asking whether the patterns actually found in the sample data would differ from those in the population from which the data were drawn. Another branch of inferential statistics is estimation of the population parameters based on representative samples. As described in Chapter 6 (which discusses the normal curve and confidence intervals), a mean from a sample can be used to estimate the confidence interval in which the population mean would occur.

The main purpose of this chapter is to suggest statistical tests that would be helpful in some of the types of research projects described in this text. The purpose is to help you to become a useful "consumer" of statistics. For those of you with earlier statistics courses, most of these statistics will be familiar, and the material in this chapter can serve as a refresher session. For those of you without any prior course, this chapter will offer an introductory overview of certain statistical techniques commonly used in elementary social analyses. We will also raise issues that surround the use of statistics, such as what options are available, what the numbers mean in relation to the study, what assumptions are being made by the use of a particular test. When the mathematics are easy to understand, the statistical formulas will be given to help you get a clearer sense of what the statistic is actually representing. In other cases, statistical tests will be described unaccompanied by their formulas, which you could examine in an introductory statistics text if you wish.

USING AND MISUSING STATISTICS

Some statistical techniques useful in the analysis of data generated by the research methods explained in this text will be presented in this chapter. By applying a few commonly used statistical tests to the cross-tabular analyses which we have developed in our study on athletic participation and educational attainment, we can see how statistical tests can enhance our understanding of the data we have.

Nowadays, almost all statistics that are produced are generated from a computer. Thus, what we present in this chapter will be statistical tests produced by the statistical computer package program SPSS^x (described in Appendix C), which we have been using. Statistics are not only easy to use, but they are also easy to misuse. Computer programs will generate tables and accompanying statistical tests so readily that there is often a tendency to have the computer turn out a lot of statistics, whether or not your sampling design and the data you have collected are appropriate to these statistical tests.

All of us as researchers would like to be able to say that our findings are "statistically significant." In many situations the samples we draw, the kinds of data we have, and the measurement of our variables prevent us from being able to use certain types of statistical tests or require us to interpret the tests in a particular fashion. This concern for the appropriateness of statistics will be a central one in this chapter. Remember that a computer program (usually) cannot decide which types of statistics are appropriate for your study. *You* must make those decisions.

We shall begin by presenting a brief overview of certain statistics; then we will return to the athletic participation–educational attainment study to see what statistical tests might be used to describe our data and to test our hypotheses. Finally, we will examine a few other commonly applied statistical tests to see with what types of data they could be used profitably.

OVERVIEW OF STATISTICAL CONCEPTS AND MEASUREMENT

Measurement (described in Chapter 5) and sampling (described in Chapter 6) are central to the discussion of statistics. Measurement theory and sampling theory are two of the major branches of statistics. We will need to recall some of the information from these chapters as we lay out some of the central concepts and forms of measurement in statistics. Since this discussion will include only a few hand calculations of statistical tests, you might like to refer to an introductory statistics text for more detail.

Measures of Central Tendency

Recall from Chapter 5 that there are two types of measurement: categorical and numerical. Categorical measurement may have categories that are merely characterized by *distinctiveness,* in which case the measurement scale is referred to as a *nominal* scale; or the categories may be both distinctive and ordered, in which case the measure-

ment is referred to as an *ordinal* scale. Numerical scales may either be based on a true number scale with a meaningful zero point (such as age or weight), or they may only imply equal intervals between numbers but have no true zero point (characteristic of psychological tests, IQ scores, and temperature scales). The former types of scales are called *ratio* scales; the latter type, *interval* scales.

Numerical scales (both interval and ratio) may be used for *discrete* variables, that is, those which can take only whole numbers as values (such as number of children); or they may be used with *continuous* variables, that is, those which can be defined over intervals that have no breaks between all the possible values of the variable. In other words, a continuous variable can assume a countably infinite number of values (for example, time, height, weight). Furthermore, you can measure a continuous variable with a high level of accuracy (in decimals) depending on the type of measuring instrument you use.

There are three measures of central tendency. The *mean* represents the arithmetic average. If we add together every number representing each case in the sample (or population) and then divide this sum by the number of cases, the resulting arithmetic mean describes the center of the distribution. For this reason, cases at the extremely high end of the distribution or at the extremely low end will disproportionately influence the mean. In addition, if the cases are unevenly distributed, so that, for example, a large proportion are at one end, the distribution will be highly *skewed.*

Skew refers to an asymmetrical distribution of the data such that the data are not evenly spread around the central point. So when you consider the *skewness* of the distribution of data, you are looking for the degree to which the data are symetrically distributed in relation to their central point. When data are highly skewed, the mean will naturally be affected, and it will not serve so effectively as a measure of central tendency. In such an event, the *median,* which represents the centermost position in an ordered series of cases and largely ignores the skew of the distribution, might be the right choice as a measure of central tendency. The *mode* represents the most popular value (or position) in the distribution, the one representing the largest number of cases. Thus the mode is not sensitive to the spread of the distribution. Deciding which measure of central tendency to use will also depend upon the type of question you are interested in answering.

Let's say that the variable you are studying is the yearly income of the parents of a sample of 12 high school students, rounded off to the nearest thousand dollars. It is possible to compute the *mean* income by adding up all the incomes given by the respondents and dividing this number by the number in the sample. No specific order is required to compute a mean. However, the cases must be ordered to determine the median. An ordered list facilitates determining the mode as well (in order to see how many cases share the same

TABLE 15-1

DATA DISTRIBUTION FOR THE MEAN
Family Income ($N = 12$)

Unordered Data	Income Values ($)
Case 1	10,000
Case 2	12,000
Case 3	15,000
Case 4	24,000
Case 5	20,000
Case 6	8,000
Case 7	12,000
Case 8	10,000
Case 9	14,000
Case 10	21,000
Case 11	12,000
Case 12	18,000

Summed total: 176,000

Number of cases: 12

$\bar{x}$ = summed total ÷ number of cases

$\bar{x} = \$176,000/12 = \$14,667$

TABLE 15-2

DATA DISTRIBUTION FOR MEDIAN AND MODE
Family Income ($N = 12$)

Ordered Data	Income Values ($)
Case 6	8,000
Case 1	10,000
Case 8	10,000
Case 2	12,000
Case 7	12,000
Case 11	12,000
Case 9	14,000
Case 3	15,000
Case 12	18,000
Case 5	20,000
Case 10	21,000
Case 4	24,000

Median = midpoint
= (Case 11 + Case 9) ÷ 2
= ($12,000 + $14,000) ÷ 2
= $13,000

Mode = most popular value
= Cases 2, 7, 11
= $12,000

value). Tables 15-1 and 15-2 show, comparatively, the distributions of a set of cases for income data for ascertaining the mean, the median, and the mode.

The Mean.   The *mean* is a very useful statistic when a variable is based on a number scale, such as weight or income. It is often commonly computed for ordinal variables as well. As stated above, if the scale of numbers is not fairly evenly distributed, the mean will not be a good indicator of the central tendency of the distribution. In deciding whether to use a mean, consider carefully whether the variable you want to analyze is based on a type of measurement that can be represented by an arithmetic mean. (Remember that a nominal variable should not be represented by a mean.) If a mean is an appropriate descriptive statistic for the variable you are studying, you may also want to include information on the *dispersion* (or variation) of scores around the mean (this was described in Chapter 6). Ways to describe the range of scores (the most common being the *standard deviation*) will be described below.

The Median. In contrast to the mean's sensitivity to the whole range of values, the *median* reflects only the centermost case (or cases). The purpose of the median is to describe that case which falls exactly in the center of the range of cases (from high to low). The median is often preferable to the mean, where the distribution is skewed. In such a case, the centermost case—that is, the median—will better represent the central tendency of the distribution than will the mean. If the distribution contains an odd number of cases, then the centermost case will be easy to select as the median. (If there were 11 cases, the median would be the sixth, with 5 cases on either side.) In the example given, where there are an even number of cases (12), it would be easily computed as halfway between Case 11 and Case 9. Figure 15-1 depicts the median's position.

The median is somewhat more difficult to compute when you have grouped data, such as data distributed among income groups of below $10,000, $10,000 to $13,000, $13,001 to $16,000, etc. When data are grouped, each category represents a range of values. The median number for the range falls somewhere within the interval which contains the centermost value (median). There is a formula that will help you estimate where in the centermost group (let's say between $16,001 and $19,000) the actual median would fall.[1]

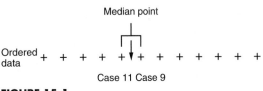

FIGURE 15-1
Establishing the median from the data in Table 15-2.

The Mode. This is the most easily determined measure of central tendency. It is merely the value which occurs most frequently in the full range of values. In Table 15-2, the mode was $12,000 because three cases were represented by that amount.

Measures of Variation

When you compute a mean, you have estimated a central position representative of all the data in your sample. What you have not done is consider how these data are distributed, how widely or narrowly they are dispersed, or how much variation there is across all the cases in the sample. Consider the average weight of students in a college class. Let's say you know that the average is 140 pounds. What you would not know was whether most of the students weighed close to the 140-pound mark, or whether they ranged from a very low to a very high weight, or whether the distribution was skewed (i.e., whether there were many weights above 140, with a few low ones keeping the average at 140). Measures of variation, or dispersion, which were described in Chapter 6, will again be briefly examined.

Types of Variation. Turning back to the cookie weight example in Chapter 6, Table 6-1 found the average (mean) weight of the 15 cookies to be 3.7 ounces. But how well did this average weight represent each of the individual weights of the cookies? To answer this question we need to compute the variance, a measure of the distribution pattern or range of individual cookie weights from the mean weight.

---

[1]Statistics texts generally show methods for computing a median from grouped data.

Variance is a way of measuring how far different units which have been used to establish a mean vary from the mean. The principle is that you take the difference between every measure and the average measure, square these differences, sum them, and then divide this sum by the number of measures considered. Thus, based on the data from the cookie weight example, in Table 6-1 (p. 144), you would proceed in this fashion:

$$\text{Variance} = \frac{\begin{aligned}(2.5 - 3.7)^2 + (3 - 3.7)^2 + \cdots \\ + (6 - 3.7)^2 + (3.5 - 3.7)^2\end{aligned}}{15}$$

$$= 1.29$$

In the case of the cookies, you are taking the differences in the weight of each cookie from the average weight, squaring these differences, adding all these squared differences up, and dividing by the number of cookies. This measure of variance tells us about the spread (or dispersion) of all the values of the different cookie weights from the average cookie weight. More commonly, the square root of the variance, called the standard deviation, is considered. In the above example, the standard deviation would equal 1.14 (which is the square root of 1.29).

Assuming a sufficient number of cases, you could plot distributions like the weight example on graph paper in which the vertical axis would indicate the number of individuals with each weight (the frequency) and the horizontal axis would show the scale of weights ranging from the lowest to the highest. Then if you plotted all the weights by placing dots on the graph appropriately, and if you connected the points on the graph, you would be likely to find a curved shape which was highest (had the most cases) around the point of the mean and then fell off as it moved away from the mean. This would resemble the bell-shaped curve, the *normal curve* described in Chapter 6. Recall that the more values you had, the greater the likelihood that the curve would come nearer to resembling the bell shape. However, you should remember that the bell-shaped curve does not occur in every distribution.

Distributions may, for example, have more than one high point. This might be true (for example) for the variable of length of college terms: for those on a semester system, the high point would be 15 weeks, with variations from 13 to 16; while for those on a quarter system, 10 weeks would be the high point, with variation from 8 to 11 weeks. When this is the case, the distribution is referred to as a bimodal distribution.

When variables are categorical, such as religion, line graphs are generally not used, though bar graphs (as we saw in Chapter 6) and pie charts are appropriate. In either of these types of graphs, percentages of the total characterized by a certain category are represented proportionately. More often, categorical variables are presented as *frequency distributions,* in which the percentages are given for each category of the variable. We have already examined many frequency distributions in Chapter 13. Tables 13-1 to 13-5 are examples of frequency distributions.

The Standard Deviation.   Recall from the cookie example that the standard deviation is the square root of the variance, that is, the mean of the squared differences between the values of each case in the distribution and the value of the mean. What the standard deviation tells you is how much *dispersion* (or spread) there is in the distribution of values in a sample: 68 percent of the cases fall within one standard deviation above and below the mean, 95 percent fall within two standard deviations, and more than 99 percent of the cases fall within three standard deviations above and below the mean. If you assume that the population from which the sample was drawn had a normal distribution, you can apply the standardized normal distribution, the *normal curve,* to your sample and thereby determine the range within which the population mean would likely fall.

The *standardized normal distribution,* the normal curve, has been very influential in the development of statistics. As we saw in Chapter 6, the normal curve is used to represent the sampling distribution of means from all possible samples of the same sample size drawn from a population. In most cases, of course, only one sample has been drawn. The standardized normal distribution has a mean of 0 and a standard deviation of 1. What is so useful about the normal curve is that it indicates the proportion of the values that will fall between the mean and so many standard deviations away from the mean. These standard deviation end points can serve as *confidence levels,* and the set of all values between the confidence limits, the *confidence intervals,* serve to indicate the range within which the mean of the population would be enclosed.

Range.   Various other measures are even easier to compute and can give you an indication of the dispersion of the frequencies. One of the simplest is the *range.* This is simply the distance between the highest and lowest points in a set of cases. Returning to the example of the range of weights among students in a class, if the lightest person in your class were 89 pounds and the heaviest person were 220 pounds, the range could be determined by subtracting 89 from 220, giving 131 pounds. In this example, the *maximum value* would be 220, and the *minimum value,* 89. Knowing the maximum, the minimum, the range, and the mean would tell you quite a lot about the variation of the distribution. What these statistics would not tell you is how closely the data were gathered about the mean or how widely and evenly they were dispersed. Because the range is very sensitive to extreme values (called *outliers*), its usefulness is limited. A better way to understand the dispersion of the data is to use the standard deviation. In addition, there are other measures of dispersion which determine the degree of skewness (or tilt) of the distribution.[2]

DESCRIBING RELATIONSHIPS BETWEEN VARIABLES

The choice of which statistical test to employ will depend on the level of measurement of the variables. Recall that when the variables are categori-

cal, the data represent the number of counts in each category (the number of Catholics, Protestants, and Jews related to the number of voters and nonvoters) rather than a set of values on a numerical scale (for example, age and IQ score). When both variables are ratio or interval measures (such as age and IQ score), correlations (such as Pearson's *r*) can be used; when the variables are categorical (religion and voting status), you can use other measures of association between the variables.

What will follow is a brief discussion of some of the more common types of statistical measures of association. In the cases where the statistical formulas are very simple to comprehend, these will be reviewed; where the formulas are more complex, they will not be presented. In any case, it would be useful to refer to an introductory statistical text if you wish to examine the mathematics of these measures.

MEASURES OF ASSOCIATION

A number of different statistical tests can be used to determine the strength, and sometimes the direction, of an association between variables. As stated above, the choice of tests to use depends on the level of measurement of the variables being considered. In some cases, it also depends on the number of categories in the variables being associated. The statistical tests suggested here are not the only ones available. By consulting a statistics text (a number of texts are listed in the Recommended Readings section at the end of this chapter), you will find other measures of association appropriate for variables with different levels of measurement.

Lambda (λ)

This easy-to-compute statistic is appropriate for nominal-level variables. It is based on the principle of being able to reduce the proportion of errors in the prediction of one variable by knowing the distribution of another. This principle of *proportionate reduction of error (PRE)* means that you are trying to assess whether knowing the distribu-

---

[2]Consult a statistics text for other measures of dispersion.

tion of the dependent variable in relation to the categories of the independent variable would enable you to reduce the errors in predicting the distribution of the dependent variable compared with predicting the variable distribution without any knowledge of the independent variable. Because this statistic is based on a simple formula, it will be presented and explained in Box 15-1 using the relationship of sex to participation in high school athletics as the example.

Lambda ranges from 0 to 1. If lambda were 0, there would be no reduction in error in predicting the distribution of the dependent variable if we knew the distribution of the dependent variable cross-classified with the independent variable. Conversely, if lambda were 1, your knowledge of the independent variable would allow you to predict accurately the dependent variable without making any errors. In the example (Table 15-3), a lambda of .164 indicates that something is gained (in terms of predicting the dependent variable) by knowing the distributions of the independent variable but that you are still unable, by knowing only the sex distribution, to reduce all the errors in the prediction of participation in athletics.

Yule's Q

This statistic is an appropriate measure of association for 2 × 2 tables. It is simply computed on the basis of the cross products of the cells of the table. Consider a 2 × 2 table in the following way:

Dependent Variable	Independent Variable	
	Present	**Absent**
Present	a	b
Absent	c	d

The formula for this statistic is

$$Q = \frac{ad - bc}{ad + bc}$$

In cross-classifications where there are more cases in which both the independent and dependent variables are present (cell *a*), or both the independent and dependent variables are absent (cell *d*), the product of the major diagonal (*ad*) will be greater than the product of the minor diagonal (*bc*). In this event Q will be positive, indicating a positive association between the independent and dependent variables. Conversely, in cross-classifications where there are more cases in which the dependent variable is present but the independent variable is absent (cell *b*), or in which the independent variable is present but the dependent variable is absent (cell *c*), the product of the *bc* diagonal will be greater than the product of the *ad* diagonal. In this event, Q will be negative. This is referred to as the *direction* of the association. If one of the cells has a 0, then the Q will equal 1. If either cell *a* or cell *d* is 0, the Q will be −1; if either cell *b* or cell *c* is 0, the Q will be +1. In the case of nominal variables where the two categories indicate no order, the direction of the Q may well be ambiguous (Davis, 1971, p. 49) or may not have meaning (Loether and McTavish, 1976, p. 202), but the magnitude of the Q may be used on its own.

Conventions for Setting Up 2 × 2 Tables. As you might recognize from the distribution of the four cells in a 2 × 2 table, if you set up your table so that the larger cell frequencies will appear in the *a* and *d* cells, you will have a positive relationship; conversely, if the *b* and *c* cells have the larger frequencies, then the Q will be negative. Your object is not to try to get a positive relationship but to test what you would *predict* to be the stronger relationship in the *a* and *d* cells. What you should do is set up your table so that the *a* cell in the upper left-hand corner will contain the combination of variable categories which you are interested in studying, which will test your hypothesis, or which you think will be associated more strongly. Then if it is the case that the *ad* diagonal is greater, the positive sign will confirm your prediction. On the other hand, if it is not the case (that is,

BOX 15-1

COMPUTING A LAMBDA

TABLE 15-3

PARTICIPATION IN HIGH SCHOOL ATHLETICS BY SEX

Participation in High School Athletics	Sex		
	Female	Male	Row Total
Have participated actively	2,632	4,384	7,016
Have not participated	5,758	3,234	8,992
Column total	8,390	7,618	16,008

If you had to predict whether a particular student was active or not active in athletics, and all the information you had was the distribution on the dependent variable (participation in athletics) which is portrayed in the row totals, then you would make more accurate judgments by predicting that students *have not* participated than that they *have*. In other words, if you predicted that students have not participated, you would make only 7,016 errors (as compared to 8,992 errors had you predicted that they have participated).

However, if you could make your predictions knowing as well the distributions of participation for males and females separately, for males you would predict they have participated actively and you would make 3,234 errors; for females you would predict they have not partici-

pated and you would make 2,632 errors. Knowing the distribution of participation by sex produces 5,866 errors (3,234 + 2,632) while knowing the distribution of only the dependent variable led to 7,016 errors. Thus the additional knowledge of the distribution of the independent variable (IV) reduced the errors by 1,150 (7,016 − 5,866). Lambda then equals 1,150 *fewer errors* divided by the 7,016 *total errors* [knowing only the distribution on the dependent variable (DV)].

The formula for lambda is

$$\frac{\text{Number of } \textit{fewer} \text{ errors knowing distribution of the DV within categories of the IV}}{\text{Number of errors knowing only DV distribution}}$$

In this example 1,150 ÷ 7,016 = .164.

if the *b* and *c* cells are greater), the negative sign will challenge your hypothesis.

Let me add that this way of setting up tables is merely a convention; sometimes the *a* cell is in the upper right-hand corner. The important thing is not to get confused when you see a cross tabulation or when you set up your own. If you are preparing your own tables, be consistent in how

you set them up so that you know which diagonal you are expecting to be greater. If you are reading tables created by others, be sure to look carefully to see how they have set up the tables before you try to interpret the meaning of a positive or negative sign. Table 15-4 gives two examples of the use of *Q*, one with ordinal variables, the other with nominal.

TABLE 15-4

COMPUTING YULE'S Q

For Ordinal Variables:[a] Importance of Money by Success

Having Lots of Money	Being Successful in My Line of Work	
	Very Important	Somewhat or Not Important
Very important	75	50
Somewhat or not important	25	50

$$Q = \frac{(75)(50) - (50)(25)}{(75)(50) + (50)(25)}$$

$$= \frac{3{,}700 - 1{,}250}{3{,}750 + 1{,}250}$$

$$= \frac{2{,}500}{5{,}000}$$

$$Q = +.50$$

For Nominal Variables:[a] English Course by Sex

Type of English Course Taken in College	Sex	
	Male	Female
Literature	40	75
Composition	60	25

$$Q = \frac{(40)(25) - (75)(60)}{(40)(25) + (75)(60)}$$

$$= \frac{1{,}000 - 4{,}500}{1{,}000 + 4{,}500}$$

$$= \frac{-3{,}500}{5{,}500}$$

$$Q = -.64$$

[a]Hypothetical data.

Describing the direction and magnitude of a Q.
James Davis (1971) offers a summary set of conventions for describing the strength and direction of Yule's *Q*. These statements, presented in the box, should help you to formulate your findings in words. Using Davis' terms to describe the examples in Table 15-4, you would state the following.

In the first example, it would be accurate to say

There is a substantial positive association between believing that being very successful in one's line of work is very important and believing that making lots of money is very important.

DAVIS' CONVENTIONS FOR DESCRIBING YULE'S Q

Value of Q	Appropriate Phrase[a]
+ .70 or higher	A very strong positive association
+ .50 to +.69	A substantial positive association
+ .30 to +.49	A moderate positive association
+ .10 to +.09	A low positive association
.00	No association
− .01 to −.09	A negligible negative association
− .10 to −.29	A low negative association
− .30 to −.49	A moderate negative association
− .50 to −.69	A substantial negative association
− .70 or lower	A very strong negative association

[a]*Correlation* and *relationship* are synonyms for association.
Source: James A. Davis, *Elementary Survey Analysis,* Prentice-Hall, Englewood Cliffs, N.J., 1971, p. 49.

For the second example, the following statement would be appropriate:

> There is a substantial negative association between sex (male) and taking a course in English literature.

These statements make clear the strength of the association, and they also describe the direction of it.

Goodman and Kruskal's Gamma (γ)

This is an extended version of *Q,* appropriate for larger than 2 × 2 tables when variables are ordinal in measurement. It will produce a statistic between −1 and +1. In this measure, the cross products must be extended to take into account every cell in the table. The sums of these cross products then become the terms in the gamma formula. Box 15-2 explains how it is computed.

Pearson's r

This statistic is referred to as a *product-moment correlation coefficient* or, more commonly, as a linear *correlation coefficient.* It can be used to determine both the strength and the direction of a linear relationship between two interval-scale variables. There is also a way to calculate the *statistical significance* of the *r* (not presented here) which tests whether the linear relationship between two variables measured by *r* exists in the population.[3] *Pearson's r* is a test of the null hypothesis that there is no linear correlation in the population (that $r = 0$). This statistic is commonly used in educational and psychological research where test scores are being correlated. For this reason, correlations were discussed in Chapter 5, when reliability and validity were described.

To use Pearson's *r,* a number of conditions must be satisfied. First, as already mentioned, both the variables should be interval or ratio variables such that it is meaningful to determine their mean. (It should be noted that researchers often use *r* with ordinal-level variables as well.) Second, it must be assumed that the relationship between these variables is *linear,* such that an increase in one variable will show a corresponding increase in the other (or a decrease in one will be paired with a decrease in the other) or an increase in one variable will be matched by a decrease in the other. This means that *r* tests for the *direction of a relationship.* The size of the *r* will indicate how strongly a pattern of variation (or change) in one variable is matched by change in another variable. Thus, *r* also tests for the *strength of relationship* between two variables.

For example, it would be assumed that students who achieve higher American College Test (ACT) scores (or SAT scores) would also have higher grades in high school. What this means is that you expect a positive linear relationship between ACT scores and high school grade-point average (GPA) or, conversely, that students who have achieved lower ACT scores would be expected to have lower grades. The matching of high with high and low with low would produce a posi-

---

[3]There are tests for the statistical significance of lambda and gamma as well.

BOX 15-2

COMPUTING A GAMMA

MODEL FOR A 3 × 3 TABLE

Dependent Variable	Independent Variable		
	High	**Middle**	**Low**
High	*a*	*b*	*c*
Middle	*d*	*e*	*f*
Low	*g*	*h*	*i*

In this table, the encircled set of cells (*aefhi*) take the role that cells *a* and *d* played in the calculation of Q. For gamma, you multiply each of these cells by elements to the right and under it (those on the positive diagonal), after eliminating its row and column, and then you add all these up:

$$Positive \text{ diagonal combinations} = a\,(e + f + h + i) + b$$
$$(f + i) + d\,(h + i) + e\,(i)$$

Then you consider the set of cells which will take the role of the *b* cell in the calculation of Q. You multiply each of these cells by elements to the left and under it (those on the negative diagonal), after eliminating the values in the same row and column:

$$Negative \text{ diagonal combinations} = c\,(d + e + g + h) +$$
$$b\,(d + g) + f\,(g + h) + e\,(g)$$

In other words, gamma is an extension of Q

in which the *ad* product is based on the sum of all the positive diagonal combinations and the *bc* product is based on the sum of all the negative diagonal combinations. As for Q, once the combinations are determined, the numerator is based on subtracting the negative combinations from the positive; the denominator is based on the sum of the positive and negative combinations. Thus the formula for gamma is:

$$Gamma = \frac{\left(\begin{array}{c}\text{Positive diagonal}\\\text{combinations}\end{array}\right) - \left(\begin{array}{c}\text{negative diagonal}\\\text{combinations}\end{array}\right)}{\left(\begin{array}{c}\text{Positive diagonal}\\\text{combinations}\end{array}\right) + \left(\begin{array}{c}\text{negative diagonal}\\\text{combinations}\end{array}\right)}$$

where the *positive* diagonal combinations replace the *ad* pair of the Q formula, and the *negative* diagonal combinations replace the *bc* pair from the Q formula. We will offer an example of the gamma statistic for tables from the athletics study below.

tive linear relationship. If the high school measure were absentee rates from school instead of GPA, we would expect that lower absentee rates would be matched with higher ACT scores and that higher absentee rates would be matched with lower ACT scores. This matching of high scores on one variable with low scores on another produces a negative linear association. Finally, you must have an adequate sample size in order to meet the assumptions for carrying out a correlation coefficient. As a rough guide, a sample size of 30 is usually acceptable.

A correlation coefficient can best be understood by examining the relationship of two variables on a *scattergram*. If you had only a single variable and you wanted to make the best prediction of an individual case, your best prediction (or guess) would be the mean for the variable. However, if you had a second variable and knew the values on the second variable for every value on the first variable, then you would have the information to make a scattergram and determine Pearson's *r*. Figure 15-2 presents a hypothetical scattergram of high school GPA with ACT scores. At a glance, you can see that the higher the high school GPA (the *x* value, the independent variable), the higher the ACT score (the *y* value, the dependent variable). Figure 15-2 clearly indicates that there is a linear relationship between high school grades and ACT scores and that this relationship is *positive* such that the higher the high school GPA, the higher the ACT score.

To understand this actual scattergram better, we need to consider the ideal relationships we would like to find if the variables were perfectly related and then compare these with relationships we are likely to find in the real world. Figure 15-2 shows a positive relationship between *x* and *y*. However, it is not a perfect relationship such that in every case a higher GPA is related to a higher ACT score. If there were a perfect correspondence between the two variables, the relationship would look like Figure 15-3, in which all scores would fall on the positive diagonal line. This is called a *direct* or *positive relationship*. In this case *r* would equal +1. If, conversely, for every increase in high school GPA there were a related decrease in ACT score, then there would be a perfect negative (or

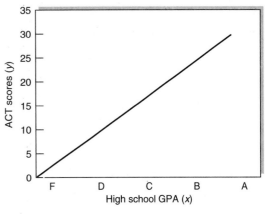

FIGURE 15-3
Direct relationship between *x* and *y*.

inverse) relationship between grades and college aptitude tests, and *r* would equal −1. This *inverse* or *negative relationship* is depicted in Figure 15-4. (Note that it would be very unlikely to find a negative relationship between GPA and ACT scores; it would be quite likely to find a negative relationship between high school absenteeism and ACT scores.) Figures 15-3 and 15-4 both show ideal linear relationships. As we saw in Figure 15-2, in real instances, there is almost always a wide scatter of points representing the position on the graph where the measure on one variable meets the mea-

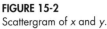
FIGURE 15-2
Scattergram of *x* and *y*.

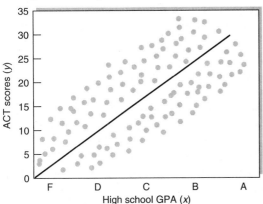

FIGURE 15-4
Inverse relationship of *x* and *y*.

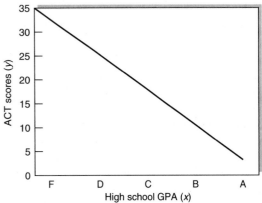

sure on the other. However, if there is a general tendency for an increase in one variable to be related to an increase (or decrease) in the other, the relationship would be considered linear.

There might also be a case where every value of the ACT occurred with equal frequency for every value of the GPA. This would mean that r would equal 0 and could have been produced from the scattergram in Figure 15-5. In such a distribution, the observation points are scattered in such an overall pattern that there appears to be no way to draw a diagonal line that would reduce the distance of the points to the line (or that would best fit the scatter of points; such a line is called the *best-fit line*). In this case, a horizontal (or vertical) line would be the best-fit line. This would indicate no linear association between the x and y. Note that in this case it would be impossible to predict an ACT score on the basis of the high school GPA. In Figure 15-2, if you knew a respondent's GPA, depicting the best-fit line relationship of GPA to ACT would enable you to predict the ACT score. We will turn to this topic in the following section on linear regression.

Finally, Figure 15-6 shows points clustered in a curved shape which represent a *curvilinear relationship*. This would mean that those with the high-level and low-level grades in high school had

FIGURE 15-5
No relationship between x and y.

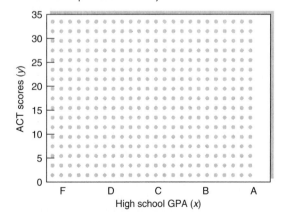

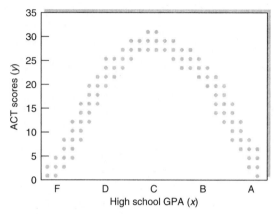

FIGURE 15-6
Curvilinear relationship between x and y.

the lowest ACT scores and that those with the middle-level grades, the highest ACT scores. While a curvilinear relationship is unlikely to occur for these two measures, there are variables that are likely to produce curvilinear relationships. An example might be the relationship between fertility rate and income. It has sometimes been shown that those with the highest and lowest incomes have the highest fertility, while those with middle-level incomes have the lowest fertility. In this case the curvilinear relationship would be the opposite of the one in Figure 15-6: it would be U-shaped with the high points on the two ends, the low point in the middle. Recall that one of the assumptions of r was that the relationship would be linear. Pearson's r cannot be used with variables that relate to one another in a curvilinear manner; there are, however, other statistics, such as *eta*, which can be employed when the relationship is curvilinear.

The best-fit line which you draw to come closest to all of the points on the scattergram uses the principle of least squares. The line represents one in which the *sum of the squared differences between the points on the graph and the line is the smallest possible.* It is important for you to understand that the r represents the degree of scatter around the line or the systematic explained variance that remains once the best-fit line between the variables is established. Thus *r* indicates how good the best-fit line is for predicting one variable from another. Box 15-3 describes the formula and mathematical procedures required to calculate Pearson's *r*. While it is tedious to compute an *r* by hand, the mathematical procedures are fairly easy to comprehend. By going through this computation, you can see that the product of the sum of the differences of the independent variable (*y*) from the mean independent variable (*ȳ*) and the sum of the differences of the dependent variable (*x*) from

the mean dependent variable (*x̄*) indicates the closeness of the pattern of responses of the independent variable to the dependent variable. In other words, we move toward the prediction of one variable from knowing the other.

In Table 15-5, statistics generated using the SPSS[x] program and the National Longitudinal Study of the High School Class of 1972 (NLS) dataset are presented. This computer table shows the Pearson correlation coefficient for VAR44 ACT scores by VAR229V, high school GPA. It is

BOX 15-3

COMPUTING A PEARSON'S *r*

The formula[a] for *r* is

$$r = \frac{\sum (x - \bar{x})(y - \bar{y})}{\sqrt{[\sum (x-\bar{x})^2][\sum (y-\bar{y})^2]}}$$

where x = the independent variable scores
　　　x̄ = the mean independent variable score
　　　y = the dependent variable scores
　　　ȳ = the mean dependent variable score

Thus *r* is calculated as the sum (Σ) of the difference of each independent variable score from the mean independent variable score, times the sum of the difference of each dependent variable score from the mean dependent variable score—this is the numerator—divided by the square root of the product of these same differences (x − x̄) and (y − ȳ) which have been squared.

　Use GPA and ACT scores as an example and follow steps 1 to 11.

1. Calculate the mean GPA and the mean ACT score.
2. Subtract every GPA (from every respondent in the study) from the mean GPA to determine the x − x̄ difference.
3. Sum these differences.

4. Subtract every ACT score (from every respondent in the study) from the mean ACT to determine the y − ȳ difference.
5. Sum these differences.
6. Multiply the sum of the x − x̄ differences (step 3) by the sum of the y − ȳ differences (step 5).

Now you have calculated the numerator!

7. Square the sum of the x − x̄ differences (square the results of step 3).
8. Square the sum of the y − ȳ differences (square the results of step 5).
9. Multiply the squared results of step 7 and step 8.
10. Take the square root of the product created in step 9.

Now you have calculated the denominator!

11. Divide the numerator by the denominator to calculate *r*.

[a]This is the mean deviation method, which is the traditional method for computing r. Social scientists often use more simplified methods, such as the raw score method, which can be examined in any statistics text (see Elifson, Runyon, and Haber, 1990).

TABLE 15-5

CORRELATION OF ACT SCORES AND HIGH SCHOOL GRADE-POINT AVERAGES—COMPUTER TABLE

```
P E A R S O N   C O R R E L A T I O N   C O E F F I C I E N T S
          VAR44
VAR229V    .4713
          ( 2710)
          P= .000
(COEFFICIENT / CASES) / 1-TAILED SIG)
" . " IS PRINTED IF A COEFFICIENT CANNOT BE COMPUTED
```

.4713, and would be written as $r = .47$. This means that there is a fairly strong relationship between high school grades and ACT scores among the high school class of 1972. Remember that the r signifies both the *direction* of the relationship between two variables and the *strength* of the relationship. The direction is indicated by the sign (but make sure you keep in mind how each variable was coded). In Table 15-5, since higher grade-point averages are related to higher ACT scores, the sign will be positive. Had higher grades been more strongly related to lower ACT scores, the relationship would be *inverse* and the sign would be negative.

Often Pearson's r is squared. It is then called r *squared* (r^2), or the *coefficient of determination.* This statistic, r squared, denotes the proportion of variance in one variable (the dependent variable) which can be explained by the independent variable. The r squared gives the *amount of variance explained* by the linear model. By subtracting r^2 from 1 ($1 - r^2$), you estimate the degree of error remaining. For Table 15-5, the r^2 between ACT and GPA would be .22. This means that 22 percent of the variance in ACT scores can be predicted from high school GPAs.

Is this considered a high, moderate, or low correlation? If only 22 percent of the variance is accounted for, then 78 percent remains unexplained. However, depending on your expectations, your hypothesis, and the other factors you think may be affecting the relationship, will help you to decide how to describe the correlation co-

efficient. For the correlation between high school grades and ACT scores, you have some evidence that the variance in the ACT scores has been partially explained by high school grades. If you were trying to decide what would be good predictors of ACT scores, you might examine the correlation coefficients from a number of different variables. In this way, you would be using r squared to select relevant predictor variables. For such purposes, consideration of the r squared helps you to better understand your observations. It assists you in understanding the empirical nature of your study.

REGRESSION ANALYSES

Linear Regression

We noted that Pearson's r, the correlation coefficient, indicates the amount of variance that remains once the best-fit line has been established. The *linear regression* equation expresses the relationship of the two variables x and y. Let's start with a simple example. Suppose the independent variable, x, is hours worked per day and the dependent variable y, is work hours per week. Now it is easy to set up the equation $y = 5x$. Table 15-6 presents the work hour data for seven employees. Were the weekly hours on the y axis of a graph and the daily hours on the x axis, you would easily see that the line drawn to connect dots representing each worker's weekly and daily hours (the *best-fit line*) would be a straight line.

TABLE 15-6

DAILY AND WEEKLY WORK HOURS OF A GROUP OF WORKERS

Worker	Weekly Hours (y)	Daily Hours (x)
Mary	42.5	8.5
Fred	37.5	7.5
Susan	40.0	8.0
Karen	45.0	9.0
Jack	40.0	8.0
Homer	35.0	7.0
Sarah	32.5	6.5

If you can recall from your algebra, the formula for a straight line is

$$\hat{y} = a + bx$$

in which x and y represent the independent and dependent variables whose values change from case to case, b represents the slope of the best-fit line that relates y to x, and a equals the value of y when x is zero (this is called the y intercept). In the example given, $y = 0$; therefore $a = 0$ and the linear regression equation is

$$y = 0 + 5x \qquad \text{or} \qquad y = 5x$$

For most pairs of variables, the y intercept has a nonzero value, either above zero (a positive y intercept) or below zero (a negative y intercept). The slope (b) refers to the amount of change in y expected from a change in x (or the ratio of the change in y to the change in x). If you know the values of a and b for a series of data on x and y, then for a new case in which you have data for the independent variable (x), you can predict the value of y. In our simple example $a = 0$ and $b = 5$. If a new employee, Sam, works four hours per day, we can predict his weekly hours:

$$y = 0 + 5(4)$$
$$y = 20$$

Multiple Regression

This widely used statistical technique is based on an extension of the linear regression model. In this case, instead of using one independent variable to predict a dependent variable, we use a number of independent variables ($x_1, x_2, x_3 \ldots$). This means that a one-dimensional line cannot be fit to the many x's with the y; rather, a three-dimensional best-fit model needs to be established. This is precisely what multiple regression analysis tries to do. The equation for a multiple regression with three independent variables is

$$\hat{y} = a + b_1 x_1 + b_2 x_2 + b_3 x_3$$

where $\hat{y}$ = the dependent variable's predicted value
  a = the y intercept
  b_1 = the slope of the first independent variable
  b_2 = the slope of the second independent variable
  b_3 = the slope of the third independent variable
  x_1 = the value of the first independent variable
  x_2 = the value of the second independent variable
  x_3 = the value of the third independent variable

The slope of b_1 indicates the change in the dependent variable y accounted for by an increase of one unit in x_1 if x_2 and x_3 are held constant; b_2 represents the change in y accounted for by one unit of change in x_2 if x_1 and x_3 are held constant. This suggests that the larger the b, the more its related x (the independent variable) helps to predict y (the dependent variable).

The b value is generally referred to as the *regression weight,* the *beta weight,* or just the b. The larger this number, the greater the weight of the variable in question in predicting the dependent variable. Hence one of the purposes of most regression analyses is to determine which independent variables have the highest weights associated with them (in other words, which independent variables lend more to the prediction of the dependent variables, or, more simply, which independent variables are better predictors of the dependent variable).

In addition, a researcher often wants to know how much all of the independent variables taken together can predict the dependent variable. This requires computing a multiple correlation coefficient, similar to Pearson's r for two variables, which is reported as R. Squaring this multiple correlation coefficient—R^2, or the *coefficient of multiple determinants*—produces a more useful measure. It indicates the percentage of variance in the dependent variable that has been explained jointly by the independent variables.

Because multiple regression is a complex mathematical procedure, such analyses are nearly always carried out by computer. For our purposes, we will conclude this discussion by presenting a regression analysis that Peter Rossi offered in his study on homelessness in Chicago (1989). This example shows how the b values for a set of independent variables can help in the understanding of an independent variable. One of Rossi's aims was to determine what factors favored individuals spending nights on the streets instead of in some form of alternative shelter.[4]

Table 15-7 presents these findings. The dependent variable (y) is reported in the title: "Percentage of Nights Spent on Streets." The independent variables are the 11 characteristics of the homeless listed in the left-hand column. The table presents b (that is, the regression coefficients or beta weights) for each of the independent variables, the intercept (or a value), the R^2 (or coefficient of multiple determination), and the N (or number of cases) on which the data are reported.

Let's begin by looking at the list of characteristics. Note that all but two are at the interval or

ratio level of measurement—"female" and "white" have been treated as dichotomous (or dummy) variables, with the presence of the characteristic given a 1 and the absence of the characteristic a 0. As described in Chapter 5 (n. 4), *dummy variables* are two category variables in which the presence of an attribute is coded as a 1, the absence as a 0. This means that any variable, whatever its measurement level, can be converted into a dummy variable. Categorical variables, set up so the presence of a characteristic = 1 and its absence = 0, are often used in regression analyses. Looking at the b column, you see that some of the values have negative signs, meaning that a decrease in that independent variable was related to an increase in the dependent variable. Some, with asterisks, report the statistical significance of the beta weights. Note that the larger the b—the closer the number is to ± 1—the more likely it is to be significant, though other factors, such as the order in which the independent variables are entered in the equation, also affect the likelihood that the weight is significant. The significance levels reported at the bottom of Table 15-7 refer to p as the probability that the population value is equal to zero.

We see that the best predictors of spending nights on the streets during a Chicago winter were a shabby appearance, incoherent behavior, and evidence of depression. Surprisingly, the less time the individual had spent in a mental hospital or detoxification center, the more likely that person was to spend nights on the streets. Finally, the negative sign for "female" indicates that being male was predictive of spending more nights on the streets (−.100 means that females spent 10 percent fewer, males 10 percent more nights on the streets). The variables without asterisks added some weight to the prediction of spending nights on the streets, but not to a significant degree.

The R^2 of .18 was significant, meaning that 18 percent of the variance in the percentage of nights on the streets was explained by the 11 independent variables in the regression equation. As Rossi concludes, "those who consistently use the streets and

---

[4]Rossi's book, addressed to a broad range of educated readers, presents only one regression analysis; all other data presentations are in percentages.

TABLE 15-7

PERCENTAGE OF NIGHTS SPENT ON STREETS REGRESSED ON CHARACTERISTICS OF THE HOMELESS
(Winter 1986 Only)

Characteristics	b
"Shabby and unkempt" interviewer rating[a]	.077[‡]
"Incoherent and confused" interviewer rating	.071[†]
Detoxification, mental hospital, or both[b]	−.075[*]
Depression scale	.014[†]
Psychotic symptoms scale	.000
Criminal justice experiences scale	−.029
Age (years)	.001
Female	−.100[*]
White	.045
Log of time homeless	.008
Worked sometime last month	−.006
Intercept	.021
R^2	.18[‡]
N	335

Note: Dependent variable is percentage of past seven days spent on streets or in public places.

[a]Number of negative ratings made by interviewer of respondent's appearance, neatness, dress, and cleanliness.

[b]Count of mental hospitalization and having been in a detoxification center.

[*]$p < .05$; [†]$p < .01$; [‡]$p < .001$.

Source: Peter H. Rossi, *Down and Out in America: The Origins of Homelessness,* University of Chicago Press, Chicago, 1989, p. 104.

public places are most likely to fit one of the stereotypes of the homeless as disreputable in appearance, incoherent in speech, and demoralized and depressed" (1989, p. 104). Rossi surmises that such individuals may feel more negative toward shelters, perhaps in response to rules of behavior which the shelters claim to enforce.

INFERENTIAL STATISTICS

While descriptive statistics are used to describe the association between variables as well as the distributions of single variables, inferential statistics are used to infer whether the relationships among the variables in the sample would be likely to recur in other samples drawn from the same population—that is to say, that they did not merely occur as a result of chance. You may never know exactly what the true values of the population characteristics (that is, the *parameters*) are on the basis of data drawn from a sample representative of that population. However, you can use rules of probability in selecting a sample that will allow you to make inferences from evidence on your sample to the probable characteristics in the population, with some degree of confidence.

To do this, you use hypothesis tests. What you will do is test the null hypothesis which is based on a logical assumption that there is no relationship (no association) between the two variables being studied in the population. Inferential statistics enable you to test this assumption. In other words, you are testing whether the relationship between the variables in the sample is sufficiently strong to warrant your rejecting the null hypothesis that in the population, the variables are independent of each other. This means that the relationship found in the sample is unlikely to have occurred by chance or, to put it another way, that the kind of relationship which might occur if only chance were operating would be highly unlikely to reappear were you to select other samples from the population.

Statistical Significance of *r*

You might want to use *r* (described above) to make a claim for the statistical significance of a relationship found. Again, it must be restated that for statistical significance to be determined, the assumptions for computing the *r* must be met. The probability that the size of the correlation coefficient which occurred in your sample happened by chance and that a correlation of similar magnitude or more extreme would be likely to be found if many other samples were drawn from the same population is the significance level of the test, sometimes called the *P* value. You are testing whether the magnitude of the *r* found in your sample could have occurred as a result of chance, assuming the null hypothesis that in the population from which you drew your sample, $r = 0$. (In the case of the population, the *r* should be written with the Greek letter rho —*P*.) When the sample size is very small, the probability that the *r* occurred by chance increases. Therefore, it may be unwise to suggest that a correlation coefficient from a small sample is statistically significant even if its value is quite large. Keep in mind that when a correlation is deemed to be statistically significant, this means that the *r* value in your sample is sufficiently large to infer that the null hypothesis (that the correlation in the population is 0) should be rejected.

It is generally accepted that an *r* of .10 is weak, while an *r* of .70 is strong. (However, with a large sample size, even a weak correlation could be statistically significant.) Between .10 and .70 is where most correlation coefficients occur in the

social sciences. As Simon and Burstein (1985, p. 325) suggest, in a field like economics, where time-series analyses of aggregate measures are examined (such as economic indicators), the correlations are high because the variables move together. On the contrary, in educational psychology, where the data represent cross-sectional measures of student ability or achievement in relation to educational programs or qualities of schooling, there is so much that is unaccounted for that correlations tend to be low. This reinforces the need to take into account the type of data you have and the time dimension the data represent, when deciding whether a correlation is strong or weak.

The Chi-Square (x^2) Test

This is one of the most widely used tests for statistical significance in the social sciences, when the variables under study are nominal or ordinal in measurement. The chi square simply tests whether there is any variation in the data different from mere chance variation. It tells you whether you can safely assume that there is some relationship (between the variables being studied) in the population from which your sample was drawn.

More formally, the *chi-square* (x^2) test is called a *test of independence.* It tests whether the row classifications (of the dependent variable) are related to, or affected by, different levels of the column classifications (the independent variable). It does not measure the strength of the relationship between the variables, but rather whether there is a significant relationship at all, whether the variation differs from chance.

Consider this example. Let's assume you were studying the association of political conservatism and sex. If there are 40 percent males and 60 percent females in the sample, and you assume no association between the variables, then 40 percent of the conservatives would be male, and 60 percent would be female. These would be the *expected values,* assuming independence between the variables.

Box 15-4 shows how to compute x^2. To determine the cell frequencies for the expected values

BOX 15-4

COMPUTING A CHI SQUARE (χ^2)

TABLE 15-8

POLITICAL CONSERVATISM AND SEX[a]

Expected Frequencies

Political Conservatism	Sex Male	Female	Total
Conservative	a (26)	b (39)	65
Not conservative	c (14)	d (21)	35
Total	40	60	100

Observed Frequencies

Political Conservatism	Sex Male	Female	Total
Conservative	3 5	30	65
Not conservative	5	30	35
Total	40	60	100

[a]Hypothetical data.

You can readily see by comparing the two parts of Table 15-8 that there are fairly large differences between the expected and observed frequencies. On the basis of this information, a χ^2 can be computed. The formula is

$$\chi^2 = \Sigma \frac{(\text{Observed frequencies} - \text{expected frequencies})^2}{\text{Expected frequencies}}$$

For the example given,

$$\chi^2 = \frac{(35-26)^2}{26} + \frac{(30-39)^2}{39} + \frac{(5-14)^2}{14} + \frac{(30-21)^2}{21}$$

$$= \frac{9^2}{26} + \frac{(-9)^2}{39} + \frac{(-9)^2}{14} + \frac{9^2}{21}$$

$$= \frac{81}{26} + \frac{81}{39} + \frac{81}{14} + \frac{81}{21}$$

$$= 3.1 + 2.1 + 5.8 + 3.9$$

$$= 14.9$$

in Table 15-8, you would merely take 40 percent of the total (65) and put that figure (26) in cell *a* (as seen in the parentheses). Cell *b* would then be the other 60 percent of the 65. Similarly, you would take 40 percent of the 35 to determine the *c* cell; the remaining 60 percent would be the *d* cell. These are the *expected frequencies.* Then you compare these expected frequencies to the actual observations, the *observed frequencies,* to determine how different they are. The chi square tests how far the expected values deviate from the observed values.

To determine whether the chi square is significant, you must compare your statistic to a table of critical values of chi square (see Appendix B).

You need one other number besides the computer chi square to determine its significance. This number is the *degrees-of-freedom* figure in the table. To compute the degrees of freedom (*df*) in a chi-square table, you take the number of rows minus 1 times the number of columns minus 1: $df = (r - 1)(c - 1)$. In Table 15-8, this would be $(2 - 1)(2 - 1) = 1$.

Turning to the chi-square table in Appendix B, we find that with 1 degree of freedom, a chi square of 14.9 would occur in fewer than 1 sample in 100 if there were no association between the variables (that is, if the null hypothesis were true and the finding were merely due to chance). In fact, 14.9 is much greater than the needed x^2 of 6.635 for the .01 level. We can therefore reject the null hypothesis and state that the hypothesis is statistically significant at greater than the .01 level ($p < .01$). This means that if 100 different samples were drawn from the population, in (at most) 1 of them the x^2 would be larger than 6.635, if there were no relationship between these variables in the population.

Statistical and Substantive Significance

Statistical significance tells us the degree of risk being taken in assuming that there is a systematic pattern or finding within the population. Statistical significance does not mean the same thing as

strength of relationship. Even if, as in the example in Table 15-8, you prove statistical significance, showing that there is a statistically significant relationship between the two variables, this does not mean that one variable causes another or explains its behavior. Note as well that chi square is always positive; it does not measure the direction of relationships. It only means that when the two variables are present, they occur in certain patterns.

If the sample is based on individuals, this indicates that certain individuals will be more likely to be characterized by certain combinations of characteristics than if the characteristics were distributed solely by chance. A significant chi square does not make such patterns necessarily interesting or theoretically significant. However, if no statistical significance is shown, perhaps you should not bother to explore the association more fully.

Statistical tests cannot establish the substance or meaningfulness of your findings. This requires a consideration of other matters: whether your findings meet the expectations set by the theory (here you would want to examine the size of your findings in the light of your hypotheses) and what relevance your findings have to other research in the field.

COMPUTERS AND STATISTICS

Although this chapter has shown you how to compute a number of statistical tests by hand (or with the help of a small calculator), most statistics computed today (and most of those you will be likely to compute) will be produced by a computer. Naturally, you must tell the computer what you want and therefore you must know what you want. Remember, a computer will compute anything you ask it to compute, but it won't decide whether or not it makes sense to do so. It will compute a x^2 for data from a nonprobability sample. It will compute an *r* for nominal variables or a lambda for interval variables. You must know what to ask for in order to have the computer assist your analysis, rather than let the computer simply grind out numerous statistical tests that are inappropriate for your data and for your sample. The object of this chapter has been to help you understand what is appropriate and necessary to particular types of studies.

You can get statistical advice from many sources. If you have had previous statistics courses, peruse your texts. Many excellent statistics books are comprehensible to those with only a basic knowledge of arithmetic. A number of titles are suggested at the end of this chapter. Your instructor will also have suggestions regarding which statistics would be appropriate for your study. Although many types of statistical tests have not been presented here, those shown in this chapter are particularly popular in social science analyses of survey data and for cross-classification tables. We will conclude this discussion of statistics by returning to our study of athletic participation in high school and educational attainment to see how we might have used some of these statistics to further our understanding of those data.

STATISTICAL TESTS IN THE ATHLETICS STUDY

We will return to our study of the effects of athletics on post–high school educational attainment to see how statistical tests can be applied to these data. Let's reexamine the primary bivariate table relating athletic participation and educational attainment (Table 13-6A). The table is offered again in this chapter as Table 15-9A, with a recomposed version in Table 15-9B, but now includes the statistics prepared by the computer when the data were run. We noted in Chapter 13 that the data supported the conclusions that there were (1) a strong trend favoring the attaining of a college degree among those who were athletic leaders, (2) some positive influence among those who participated actively, and (3) a much smaller likelihood of completing college among those who had not participated in sports at all in high school.

The Gamma.   In order to test the strength of this association between athletics and college at-

tainment, we will use a measure of association appropriate for variables measured at the ordinal level, namely, the gamma. As shown in the previous section, gamma is computed on the basis of products of positive diagonal cells minus negative diagonal cells, divided by the sum of these cross products.

Figuratively, gamma determines (1) how far the data cluster along the diagonals or (conversely) how widely dispersed they are across all the cells and (2) whether the data lie more along the positive than along the negative diagonal. If the data are more concentrated along the diagonals and in the cells beneath the diagonal, then the gamma will be larger. If the values are greater along the positive diagonal, the gamma will have a positive sign; if the values are greater along the negative diagonal, the gamma will have a negative sign. Note that in Table 15-9B, the gamma is .247 (or rounded to .25) and the sign is positive. This is a moderate-size gamma. Therefore, it could be said that there is a *moderate positive association* between athletic participation in high school and college attainment.

If we consider a trivariate table of the relationship of athletic participation and educational attainment by sex (Tables 14-1A and 14-1B, shown here as Tables 15-10A and 15-10B), we can compare gammas for two bivariate tables of athletics by attainment for both sexes. We see that the gamma for the males is .294 and for the females is .181. Comparing these gammas to the tables themselves, we can easily see that the differences in the rows between the high and low values (the epsilons) were greater for the men than for the women and that the positive diagonal cells have higher values in the table for men. In other words, there is a stronger positive association between active athletic participation in high school and post–high school educational attainment among men than among women. For men there is a moderate positive association; for women, a low positive association.

We can also take the trivariate table of the same relationship, controlling this time for grades

TABLE 15-9A

1979 EDUCATIONAL ATTAINMENT BY HIGH SCHOOL ATHLETIC PARTICIPATION—COMPUTER TABLE

```
C R O S S T A B U L A T I O N   O F   - - - - - - - - - -
VAR3281T  EDUCATIONAL ATTAINMENT THREE CATEGORIES
BY  VAR241R   HIGH SCHOOL ATHLETIC PARTICIPATION
- - - - - - - - - - - - - - - - - - - - - - - - - - - - - -

                      VAR241R
             COUNT
             COL PCT | PARTICIP  PARTICIP  NOT PART   ROW
                     | ATE AS L  ATE ACTI  ICIPATE    TOTAL
                     |   1.00  |   2.00  |   3.00 |
VAR3281T     --------+---------+---------+--------+
             1.00    |   520   |  1355   |  1558  |   3433
  COLL DEGREE OR M   |  40.6   |  30.7   |  21.9  |   26.8
                     +---------+---------+--------+
             2.00    |   487   |  1639   |  2469  |   4595
  SOME COLLEGE       |  38.0   |  37.2   |  34.8  |   35.9
                     +---------+---------+--------+
             3.00    |   274   |  1415   |  3076  |   4765
  NO COLLEGE         |  21.4   |  32.1   |  43.3  |   37.2
                     +---------+---------+--------+
             COLUMN     1281      4409      7103     12793
             TOTAL      10.0      34.5      55.5     100.0


CHI-SQUARE     D.F.      SIGNIFICANCE       MIN E.F.     CELLS WITH E.F. <5
----------     ----      ------------       --------     ------------------

372.96876        4          0.0000          343.756          NONE
          STATISTIC                    VALUE            SIGNIFICANCE
          ---------                    -----            ------------

GAMMA                              0.24732
NUMBER OF MISSING OBSERVATIONS =       187
```

TABLE 15-9B

1979 UNIVERSITY/COLLEGE ATTAINMENT BY HIGH SCHOOL ATHLETIC PARTICIPATION[a]
(National Longitudinal Study of the High School Class of 1972, Five-Survey Respondents)

	Participation Level		
Attainment	**Athletic Leader**	**Active Participant**	**Did Not Participate**
College degree or higher	40.6%	30.7%	21.9%
Some college	38.0	37.2	34.8
No college	21.4	32.1	43.3
	100.0%	100.0%	100.0%
	(1,281)	(4,409)	(7,103)

Gamma = .25
Chi square = 372.97; *df* = 4; *p* <.01

[a]Recomposed table.

TABLE 15-10A

1979 EDUCATIONAL ATTAINMENT BY HIGH SCHOOL ATHLETIC PARTICIPATION BY SEX—COMPUTER TABLE

```
C R O S S T A B U L A T I O N  OF   - - - - - - - - - -
VAR3281T  EDUCATIONAL ATTAINMENT THREE CATEGORIES
BY  VAR241R   HIGH SCHOOL ATHLETIC PARTICIPATION
CONTROLLING FOR.. VAR1626   SEX    VALUE =   1. MALE
- - - - - - - - - - - - - - - - - - - - - - - - - - -
                        VAR241R
            COUNT
            COL PCT  PARTICIP  PARTICIP  NOT PART    ROW
                     ATE AS L  ATE ACTI  ICIPATE    TOTAL
                       1.00      2.00      3.00
VAR3281T   --------+---------+---------+---------+
           1.00   |  379    |  852    |  509    |  1740
  COLL DEGREE OR M|  42.0   |  32.0   |  20.0   |  28.5
                  +---------+---------+---------+
           2.00   |  353    |  981    |  925    |  2259
  SOME COLLEGE    |  39.1   |  36.9   |  36.3   |  37.0
                  +---------+---------+---------+
           3.00   |  170    |  826    |  1117   |  2113
  NO COLLEGE      |  18.8   |  31.1   |  43.8   |  34.6
                  +---------+---------+---------+
           COLUMN    902      2659      2551      6112
           TOTAL     14.8     43.5      41.7      100.0
```

```
CHI-SQUARE      D.F.       SIGNIFICANCE          MIN E.F.      CELLS WITH E.F. <5

273.20421        4          0.0000              256.787           NONE
        STATISTIC                     VALUE            SIGNIFICANCE

GAMMA                                0.29359
```

```
C R O S S T A B U L A T I O N  OF   - - - - - - - - - -
VAR3281T  EDUCATIONAL ATTAINMENT THREE CATEGORIES
BY  VAR241R   HIGH SCHOOL ATHLETIC PARTICIPATION
CONTROLLING FOR.. VAR1626 SEX    VALUE =  2.   FEMALE
- - - - - - - - - - - - - - - - - - - - - - - - - - -
                        VAR241R
            COUNT
            COL PCT  PARTICIP  PARTICIP  NOT PART    ROW
                     ATE AS L  ATE ACTI  ICIPATE    TOTAL
                       1.00      2.00      3.00
VAR3281T   ---------+---------+---------+---------+
           1.00   |  141    |  503    |  1049   |  1693
  COLL DEGREE OR M|  37.2   |  28.7   |  23.0   |  25.3
                  +---------+---------+---------+
           2.00   |  134    |  658    |  1544   |  2336
  SOME COLLEGE    |  35.4   |  37.6   |  33.9   |  35.0
                  +---------+---------+---------+
           3.00   |  104    |  589    |  1959   |  2652
  NO COLLEGE      |  27.4   |  33.7   |  43.0   |  39.7
                  +---------+---------+---------+
           COLUMN    379      1750      4552      6681
           TOTAL     5.7      26.2      68.1      100.0
```

```
CHI-SQUARE      D.F.       SIGNIFICANCE          MIN E.F.      CELLS WITH E.F. <5

86.63457         4          0.0000               96.041           NONE
        STATISTIC                     VALUE            SIGNIFICANCE

GAMMA                                0.18120
NUMBER OF MISSING OBSERVATIONS =     187
```

TABLE 15-10*B*

1979 UNIVERSITY/COLLEGE ATTAINMENT BY HIGH SCHOOL ATHLETIC PARTICIPATION BY SEX[a]
(National Longitudinal Study of the High School Class of 1972, Five-Survey Respondents)

Attainment	Participation Level		
	Athletic Leader	**Active Participant**	**Did Not Participate**
Males			
College degree or higher	42.0%	32.0%	20.0%
Some college	39.1	36.9	36.3
No college	18.8	31.1	43.8
	100.0%	100.0%	100.0%
	(902)	(2,659)	(2,551)

Gamma = .29
Chi square = 273.20; *df* = 4; *p* < .01

	Females		
College degree or higher	37.2%	28.7%	23.0%
Some college	35.4	37.6	33.9
No college	27.4	33.7	43.0
	100.0%	100.0%	100.0%
	(379)	(1,750)	(4,552)

Gamma = .18
Chi square = 86.64 = *df* = 4; *p* <.01

[a]Recomposed table.

in high school (which was Table 14-3 and is here shown as Table 15-11). What we find here is a somewhat lower gamma among the A students (.21), a stronger gamma for the B students (.27), and a gamma of the same magnitude as for the bivariate relationship (.25) for the C students. In this case, all the gammas are in the moderate positive range and this indicates that high school grades do not dramatically alter the relationship between high school athletic participation and post–high school educational attainment.

The gamma from both of these sets of trivariate tables can be used to apply to the elaboration model. In the case of the test variable of sex, note that the gammas split in contrast to the bivariate gamma of .25 (for males it rose to .29, for females

it dropped to .18). This is a weak case of specification. And contrasting the gamma from the bivariate table with the gammas from the trivariate tables facilitates determining what type of elaboration is evident.

In the case where high school GPA was the test variable, the gammas stay within a closer range. For the B and C students, the gamma is nearly identical to the bivariate gamma (.25 and .26 compared to .25 for the bivariate). However, for the A students there is a drop in the gamma to .21. This signifies a weak specification, though one that is interesting. High school athletics are an important predictor of college attainment, but mainly for those students with lower high school grade-point averages. This suggests that the aca-

TABLE 15-11

1979 UNIVERSITY/COLLEGE ATTAINMENT BY HIGH SCHOOL ATHLETIC PARTICIPATION BY HIGH SCHOOL GPA
(National Longitudinal Study of the High School Class of 1972, Five-Survey Respondents)

Attainment	Participation Level		
	Athletic Leader	**Active Participant**	**Did Not Participate**
GPA: A and A–B			
College degree or higher	57.0%	55.0%	44.2%
Some college	30.0	29.8	30.1
No college	13.1	15.2	25.7
	100.0%[a]	100.0%	100.0%
	(467)	(1,290)	(2,154)

Gamma = .21
Chi square = 83.98; $df = 4$; $p < .01$

	GPA: B and B–C		
College degree or higher	35.6%	25.5%	15.9%
Some college	42.6	41.2	39.9
No college	21.8	33.3	44.3
	100.0%	100.0%	100.0%
	(620)	(2,292)	(3,328)

Gamma = .27
Chi square = 216.09; $df = 4$; $p < .01$

	GPA: C and Below		
College degree or higher	16.9%	7.2%	4.6%
Some college	43.4	37.2	30.5
No college	39.7	55.6	64.9
	100.0%	100.0%	100.0%
	(189)	(811)	(1,586)

Gamma = .25
Chi square = 77.0; $df = 4$; $p < .01$

[a]Totals throughout are rounded.

demically more able students, as we concluded in Chapter 14, may have alternative resources to bring to bear in college. In other words, such students can gain the rigor and responsibility from their academic efforts that they could have gotten from athletic training.

The Chi Square. The other type of statistical test that you might want to apply to these tables concerns hypothesis testing. We have been hypothesizing that athletic activity in high school is related to attaining higher levels of education after high school. But how can we know that the findings in our tables did not merely occur by chance? How confident are we that we can infer from our evidence based on the sample of 1972 high school graduates to the population of all high school graduates of that year?

To test this hypothesis statistically, we need to test the *no association,* or *null hypothesis,* namely, that there is no association between athletics in high school and post–high school educational attainment. Such a *hypothesis of indifference* predicts that there is no likelihood that the values we found in this sample would be similar to those found in another sample—that the finding in this sample was merely the result of chance. Recall from above that the chi square is affected by the size of the sample. With the NLS survey, which has a very large sample size, we would find that small differences between the expected and observed frequency tables will be significant.

Note that in Table 15-9*A,* for educational attainment and athletic participation, the $x^2 = 372.97$ with a significance level of 0.0000. That means that in no more than 1 in 10,000 times would a table such as Table 15-9*A* have occurred in a sample drawn from a population in which there was no association between these two variables. This is equivalent to saying that in only 1 in 10,000 times would the result be due to sampling error. This supposes that if numerous samples were drawn from the population of 1972 high school seniors, the probability of obtaining a chi square of this size (if there were no relationship in the population) is less than .00001. Such a table is therefore considered statistically significant at greater than .00001 (we will give the significance level as $p<$ .01). In such a case, we would reject the null hypothesis and accept that there is a relationship between athletics and educational attainment.[5] Note that chi squares of large magnitudes characterize trivariate Tables 15-10 and 15-11 as well.

---

[5]The chi square does not test for the significance of the relational pattern assessed by the gamma. Another test, not included here, examines the significance of gamma.

TABLE 15-12

BEING A TWIN BY SEX
With Presentation of Chi Square

	Sex	
"Are You a Twin?"	**Female**	**Male**
Yes	2.57%	2.35%
	(230)	(188)
No	97.43%	97.65%
	(8,706)	(7,828)
	100.00%	100.00%
	(8,936)	(8,016)

$x^2 = .83$; $df = 1$; $p < .36$ (not significant)

Now let's examine two variables that we would not expect to be related. Table 15-12 presents a cross tabulation from the NLS survey of being or not being a twin with sex. Here the chi-square test would be testing the null hypothesis that there is no association between being a twin and sex designation, which is what we would logically expect. Table 15-12 shows that the chi square for that association is very low (.83) and is not significant (.36). This means that the probability of this table occurring by chance would be 36 times in 100. In this case, the null hypothesis must be accepted, and we must conclude that sex and being a twin are independent of each other and therefore that the relationship in this table between being a twin and sex designation could well have occurred by chance.

Choosing and Using Statistics

This chapter has only provided some introductory material on the nature of statistics and a brief overview of a few commonly used statistical tests in social research. As in the use of anything, the way to be a good consumer is to both understand your needs and understand what options are available to meet your needs. Statistics can help you to summarize information on a lot of data; they can enable you to determine the strength of association between variables. In addition, for data which have been collected from a probability sample, statistics may be used for hypothesis testing to examine the assumption that the relationship found in your sample was not merely the result of chance and therefore that the variables are dependent on one another.

This chapter should have helped you to select which statistics are appropriate for your study and given you some guidance on what these statistical tests do and what they signify about your data. The material presented here is only a beginning, however. Your instructor, other statistics texts, and various computer package programs are all good sources to tap for other ideas in the selection and use of statistics.

REVIEW NOTES

- Descriptive statistics are tools that summarily describe large bodies of data.
- Inferential statistics are based on comparisons of summary descriptions (or statistics) from a probability sample to expected distributions in the population. Such tests allow for making inferences from the evidence in the sample to the unseen evidence in the population.
- The mean, median, and mode are measures of central tendency. The mean is the arithmetic average of a distribution of values; the median is the centermost position in ordered data; the mode is the most popular value in a distribution.
- The standard deviation is a measure of dispersion. It is based on the sum of the squared differences between the separate values of each case and the mean.
- The standardized normal distribution, or normal curve, is a model representing the variability in a population. It has a mean of 0 and a standard deviation of 1. It enables the establishing of confidence limits between the mean and one or more standard deviations above or below the

mean. The confidence intervals, between the limits, establish the range of the values that would need to be considered in order to account for the true population mean.

- Lambda is a measure of association appropriate for nominal variables.
- Yule's Q is an appropriate measure of association for 2×2 tables. Gamma is an extension of Q appropriate as a measure of association for ordinal variables.
- Pearson's r (Pearson's product-moment correlation, more commonly referred to as a correlation coefficient) is an appropriate measure of the strength and direction of relationships between interval-scale variables. The r^2 (r squared) denotes the proportion of variance in the dependent variable that can be explained by the independent variable.
- Multiple regression is a statistical technique for predicting a dependent variable using a best-fit model from a number of independent variables.
- The chi-square (x^2) test is an inferential statistic testing the null hypothesis of independence between two variables.
- Most statistical tests are now calculated by computers, but the researcher must select the appropriate statistics to be presented with a particular table.

KEY TERMS

best-fit line
chi square (x^2)
confidence intervals
confidence levels
curvilinear relationship
degrees of freedom
descriptive statistics
dispersion
dummy variable
frequency distribution
gamma (γ)
inferential statistics
lambda (λ)

linear regression
linear relationship
mean
median
mode
multiple regression
negative (inverse) relationship
normal curve
null hypothesis
parameters
Pearson's *r* (correlation coefficient)
positive (direct) relationship
proportionate reduction of error (PRE)
r squared (r^2) (coefficient of determination)
range
scattergram
skew
standard deviation
statistical significance
statistics
strength of relationship
variance
Yule's *Q*

STUDY EXERCISES

1. State which of the descriptive statistics described in this chapter (*Q,* gamma, lambda, or Pearson's *r*) would be appropriate to use to test the strength of relationship between the following variables:
   a. IQ score by age
   b. Have life insurance (does not have life insurance) by sex
   c. Race by religion
   d. Satisfaction with job by type of job (from professional to unskilled)
2. Consider the following table, based on a sample of 50 college students at Eatwell University, set up to examine the (exciting) hypothesis: "Students in the Liberal Arts and Sciences (LAS) College are more likely to eat in the cafeteria than students in the Business College." (The table contains the raw numbers.)

	College	
Eat in College Cafeteria	**LAS**	**Business**
Yes	7	19
No	18	6

   a. Fill in the column percents and the marginals (the row and column totals).
   b. Compute a lambda for this table. Write a one-sentence analysis of the meaning of the results.
   c. Compute a *Q* for this table. Write a one-sentence analysis of the meaning of the results.

RECOMMENDED READINGS

1. Anderson, T.W., and Stanley L. Sclove: *Introductory Statistical Analysis,* Houghton Mifflin, Boston, 1974. A statistics text that minimizes the use of formulas and explains subjects with ease.
2. Davis, James A.: *Elementary Survey Analysis,* Prentice-Hall, Englewood Cliffs, N.J., 1971. This very helpful small volume sets up cross-classification tables and explains how they are interpreted. Offers a very clear explanation of Yule's *Q.*
3. Elifson, Kirk W., Richard P. Runyon, and Audrey Haber: *Fundamentals of Social Statistics,* 2d ed., McGraw-Hill, New York, 1990. A clear, easy-to-understand statistics text which includes all the statistics most commonly used by social researchers. This text covers all the relevant mathematical formulas as well as offering a review of basic mathematical operations.
4. Johnson, Allan: *Social Statistics without Tears,* McGraw-Hill, New York, 1977. This text aims to help students understand how statistics are used, and what they mean, as they are presented in social research studies.
5. Wallis, W. Allen, and Harry V. Roberts: *The Nature of Statistics,* Free Press, New York, 1962. A classic discussion of the meaning of statistics.
6. Weinbach, Robert W., and Richard M. Grinnell, Jr.: *Statistics for Social Workers,* New York, Longman, 1987. An easily comprehensible discussion of various statistics, described almost totally in words (without formulas), using examples from the field of social work.

CHAPTER 16

Developing and Selecting Indexes and Scales

LOOKING AHEAD

This chapter covers how to build a simple index, recognize and develop different types of scales, and locate and select already developed scales.

INTRODUCTION

*T*his chapter will show how to introduce indexes and scales into a research analysis. A scale or an index generally represents a single complex concept, or construct, that combines multiple indicators into a common composite measure. The reason why scales and indexes are widely used in the social sciences is that many of the concepts which social researchers want to study cannot be measured with a single indicator. Concepts like authoritarianism, which we examined in Chapter 5, are too multidimensional to be measured with a single item. When such concepts are of interest, a scale or an index can be developed to try to incorporate the many facets of the abstract variable into a set of indicators representing its operational definition. As you know by now, indexes and scales are central to the subject of measurement in social research.

In this chapter, I will first describe the techniques for constructing some of the major types of indexes and scales. Because so many indexes and scales are already available, I will then suggest how to find and use these resources, which may serve your needs effectively. One advantage to using an available scale or index is that it will already have been studied on samples of subjects, and tests of its validity and reliability will also have been carried out.

You cannot assume, however, that because a scale has been published, it is totally free from problems. The amount of error that occurs in measuring a variable with a single indicator may be reduced when multiple indicators are used to measure a variable (as explained in Chapter 5). Nevertheless, issues of validity continue to plague many scale instruments even years after they have been developed and used extensively. Recall from Chapter 5 that although the F-Scale of authoritarianism has been used in a broad range of studies, thereby receiving widespread scrutiny, its validity has been seriously challenged. Does this mean that beginning social researchers should avoid scales or indexes? That is a matter of debate. Some would say yes: they would argue that social concept scales (like the F-Scale) are too "messy," too fraught with problems, to be worked with effectively. Others would defend scales and indexes, even though they are not problem-free, regarding them as effective devices to measure complex ideas.

For a beginning researcher, the value of developing an index or scale is that it forces one to consider carefully the concept underlying a variable and, if it is not unidimensional, to develop and select multiple indicators of the concept. In other words, developing and using scales and indexes is a very good exercise in conceptualization and measurement. If an already developed scale is to be used, the researcher should examine all available information on this scale and, especially, any efforts to test its reliability and validity.

Indexes and scales are relevant at two possible points in the research process. The first appropriate point is after the discussion of conceptualization, operationalization, and measurement, since index and scale development represent a more elaborate form of operationalization. The second time is after the data have been collected, at which point you might decide to combine several items into an index. In such a case, the index or scale development would occur at the analysis stage of the research process. However, if you do not consider indexes or scales during the planning stage of your study, you may not have the necessary items to create a composite measure later on. Furthermore, the conceptual issues surrounding the development of scales and indexes should be considered while the study is being designed (during the conceptualization and measurement stage of the study when the validity and reliability of measures are being considered). Because index construction depends on the use of bivariate tables, this chapter was placed here after bivariate tables had been introduced. The chapter will begin with a discussion of the characteristics and construction of indexes and scales.

BASIC DEFINITIONS

An *index* is a composite measure developed to represent different components of a concept. It is composed of a set of indicators that have simply been added together. Recall that Hirschi's Index of Delinquency (Chapter 2) was based on six indicators of delinquent acts that were combined into a single measure.

An index is much like a test score that you might receive on a multiple-choice test. Your score, the number of answers you got right, would be easily constructed by adding up your correct answers. This would be your index score. In some cases, your instructor might then average the grades (by adding up all the scores and dividing by the number of students who took the test): this would be the average index score for your class. If the instructor then ordered all the scores from the highest to the lowest, he or she could determine the *median* score (by picking out the score received by the student who was exactly in the middle between highest and lowest). Or the instructor may group scores into grade categories by breaking down the distribution into the highest group (perhaps the top quintile, or 20 percent) who are given A's, the second highest group (the second quintile, from 21 to 40 percent) who are given B's, and so on. These procedures are very similar to the manner in which an index would be constructed and the results analyzed.

The difference between an index and a *scale* is that a scale takes into consideration not only how each item is answered (right or wrong, true or false, liberally or conservatively) but also the patterns which the answers present. As an example, let's return to the multiple-choice test. Suppose your instructor wanted to know which question on the test was most often answered correctly (this would be the easiest item) and which question was least often answered correctly (this would be the hardest item). One logical assumption that could be made is that those individuals who answered the hardest question correctly would be more likely to have higher scores on the test as a whole. In other words, answering the hardest question correctly should be an indicator that the person had understood the material better (and possibly studied more) than if she or he had answered the easiest item correctly.

Assume that the instructor selected five items from the test which had been answered correctly by the following proportions of students: for the first item, 95 percent of the class; for the second, 75 percent of the class; for the third, 50 percent of the class; for the fourth, 25 percent of the class; and for the fifth, 5 percent of the class. (Note that the instructor would not want to pick an item on which everyone answered correctly or incorrectly, because such an item would not be a good differentiating item for any purpose since it would not record any variation.) From these five items, your instructor might want to determine the patterns of answers of those who correctly answered the hardest item, the second-hardest item, etc.

If the material examined on the test represented a cumulative body of knowledge, those who answered the hardest item correctly should have answered the other four easier items correctly; those who answered the hardest item incorrectly but answered the second-hardest item correctly should have the next three correct, and so on. Thus, a comparison of the actual pattern of responses with the expected pattern would tell you whether this was true in this particular case. In such a scale with a cumulative structure, knowing the toughest question subsumes knowing the next-toughest one. A scale like this is an example of a Guttman Scale, which will be discussed in greater detail below. Naturally, not all the respondents would answer questions in the assumed patterned order; the Guttman scaling technique offers a number of tests for determining how far the items you are looking at form an expected pattern.

Your instructor might also decide that the 50-item test was too long and wish to reduce the number of items in the test. This is one of the functions of scales; they enable you to reduce the amount of material asked and yet retain the conceptual components of the scale and the ability of the test instrument to differentiate. One way to reduce the number of items would be to get a group of judges to assign level-of-difficulty scores to each of the questions. Suppose that the judges were told to assign a 10 to the questions considered to be hardest, a 9 to the next-hardest questions, down to a 1 for the easiest questions. The instructor could then take all the items and see how the judges had rated them. Those items receiving all 10s, or mostly 10s and 9s, would be considered difficult questions. A few of these could then be selected for the shorter test. Then the instructor could look for items assigned 6, 7, or 8; those with the most scores in these categories might be selected as moderately difficult questions. Items scored as 5s might be considered neither difficult nor easy; those scored 3 or 4, moderately easy; those scored 1 or 2, the easiest. Remember that the instructor would select items on the basis of those on which the judges had indicated the most agreement. This procedure is a form of *Thurstone scaling,* which will also be described more fully below. A test that selected several questions from each of the five levels of difficulty should provide as good an indicator of the range of students' abilities as the longer test.

What these two types of scales have in common is that a comparison of the items is made in terms of some factor (their difficulty, for example). This attempt to figure out the patterns which make the best sense of the multiple items and their interrelations—what is referred to as the *intensity structure* of the scale—distinguishes scales from indexes, which are merely cumulative measures. However, both indexes and scales aim to reduce the number of items needed to represent the full meaning of the underlying abstract variable. This is the rule of *parsimony.* Now we shall turn to a consideration of the characteristics and construction of these composite measures.

CHARACTERISTICS OF INDEXES

Having looked at examples of how scales and indexes are regularly created for many purposes, we will turn to a more detailed consideration of the general qualities and construction of indexes. Indexes are sets of items that are drawn together because it is believed that the selected set of indicators will measure a concept more comprehensively and effectively than a single indicator would. In a survey, a set of questions might be included, rather than only a single question, as a better way to operationalize the particular concept under study. Very simply, the coded responses to the items would be added up (and then possibly divided by the number of items) to compose the index score. In short, an index combines indicators of the different dimensions of a concept into a multidimensional whole.

An Example: The Work Orientation Index

As a part of the National Longitudinal Study (NLS) of the High School Class of 1972, which we have used to set up our own data analysis for this text, the original researchers wanted to develop a measure of the importance that is placed "on the fulfillment of values associated with disparate roles" (Kanouse et al., 1980, p. 46). One of these roles was the work role. For a study of work values among high school students, the researchers needed to develop indicators that would measure how strong work values were among high school students. In the first place, they had to decide which work values were to be studied. In the second place, they had to figure out a way to measure work values.

The indicators they selected for the index addressed three dimensions of work values: occupational success, financial gain, and job security. These represented outward rewards gained from work rather than an internal appreciation of the work experience for its own sake. In other words, the NLS staff chose three indicators of extrinsic work values rather than intrinsic values. Three questions about the relative importance of occupational success, making money, and having job security were developed. Because the responses to the questions were posed in terms of the *impor-*

tance of these factors, the responses reflected the value which the respondent placed on these factors. (Had the responses, instead, included degrees of expectation for attaining these goals, the items would have been an indicator of work expectations—not work values.)

The researchers also gave their extrinsic work value index a name (something researchers commonly do). They called it the *Work Orientation Index*. This index was based on the average response (1 = "not important," 2 = "somewhat important," 3 = "very important") to three questions which asked each subject to rate

1. Being successful in my line of work
2. Having lots of money
3. Being able to find steady work

The term *orientation* suggests both that the subject has developed a sense of the meaning of work and that she or he has come to value certain aspects of it. As you read more about the Work Orientation Index, ask yourself whether you find the index convincing. Do the indicators seem to be measuring the concept of work orientation? (Does the index have face validity?) Are the items appropriate to a sample of high school–aged students? Would all the students understand the items clearly enough so that they would be likely to give consistent responses? (These questions relate to the *reliability* of the index.) Is the range of variation in extrinsic work values adequate to represent what would seem to be the range of such values in the real world? This is a question of validity. Is the title of the index a good one, or do you think it obscures what the items are actually measuring?

How to Create an Index. Suppose you came across the three work orientation items and wanted to build them into an index. On the one hand, an index needs to be based on items that represent indicators of the underlying abstract concept that you are trying to measure. If the concept is multidimensional, items representing different dimensions may not be strongly related to one another.

On the other hand, if the items are assumed to reflect similar dimensions of the concept (or the same dimension), then they are likely to be related to one another. However, the items should not be so closely related that a response to one would determine a response to another. Were this the case, one of the items would be redundant: in other words, it would add nothing more to the index. (Actually, however, this situation almost never occurs.)

In order to discover whether the three items are sufficiently related to form an index, but not totally correlated, the simplest procedure is to set up a number of bivariate tables (such as those described in Chapter 13) to relate the items to one another. Table 16-1 shows how these relationships might look, using the data from the NLS study for the three variables which were used to create the Work Orientation Index.[1]

Examine the relationships between the pairs of variables. Looking at the first part of the table you can see that among those respondents who thought that money was "very important," an overwhelming proportion chose success as "very important" as well. Those who thought that money was "not important" were less likely to attach great importance to success. Note that there is a 21-percentage-point difference between these two extreme groups. In the second part of the table, where the importance of steady work is compared to the importance of success, there is nearly a 40-percentage-point difference between the 91.3 percent who find steady work "very important" and success "very important" and the 52.2 percent who find steady work "not important" and success "very important." In other words, there is a strong relationship between finding both money and success

---

[1]While an examination of a series of bivariate tables is an appropriate way to study the interrelationships among a set of items, more commonly Pearson's *r* correlation coefficients are computed between each of the pairs of items and presented in a correlation matrix, where the *r* for every pair of items is positioned at the cross point of the two variables in the matrix.

TABLE 16-1

TWO-VARIABLE RELATIONSHIPS OF WORK ORIENTATION ITEMS

Success in Work	Money		
	Very Important	**Somewhat Important**	**Not Important**
Very important	92.4%	87.9%	70.9%
Somewhat important	6.7	11.6	25.7
Not important	.9	.5	3.4
	100.0%	100.0%	100.0%
N	(2,189)	(7,812)	(2,842)

Success in Work	Steady Work		
	Very Important	**Somewhat Important**	**Not Important**
Very important	91.3%	63.2%	52.2%
Somewhat important	8.3	34.3	31.1
Not important	.4	2.5	16.8
	100.0%	100.0%	100.0%
N	(10,034)	(2,481)	(322)

Money	Steady Work		
	Very Important	**Somewhat Important**	**Not Important**
Very important	19.6%	7.4%	10.6%
Somewhat important	63.9	52.4	30.4
Not important	16.5	40.2	59.0
	100.0%	100.0%	100.0%
N	(10,008)	(2,474)	(322)

important, and between finding both steady work and success important.

Let us also examine the third part of the table. Here we find only a 9-percentage-point difference between those who find steady work very important and money "very important" (19.6 percent) and those who find steady work "not important" and money "very important" (10.6 percent). (Note that much smaller proportions of respondents value making lots of money as "very important.")

However, if we compare the same proportions among those who believe money to be "somewhat important," we find a 33-percentage-point difference (63.9 percent as compared to 30.4 percent). The bivariate tables indicate that the success item is more closely related to the two other items of money and steady work than the latter two are related to each other.

Once you are convinced from your examination of the two-variable tables that there is sufficient association between the three pairs of variables, the next step is to set up a three-variable table (a trivariate table) to see how the variables interrelate. Table 16-2 presents such a table. Note that you must select one of the variables to be the one on which the percentages in each cell of the table will be given. We will select the success item, since that was the one with the strongest relationship to the two other items.

Table 16-2 shows that if you look at those for whom steady work was "very important" (column 1), the difference between the importance of money and the importance of success is 9 percentage points (94 percent minus 85 percent); if you examine those for whom steady work was "not important" (column 3), the difference of the importance of money to the importance of occupational success is 29 percentage points (73.5 percent minus 44.1 percent).

Comparing this to the relationship of success and money in Table 16-1 advances our knowledge about the interrelationships between the items. Knowing the response to the importance of steady work increases our understanding of the relationship of the importance of success to the importance of money. In short, it seems advantageous to have the three items in the index. If the differences in percentages had been smaller in the trivariate than in the bivariate tables, then it might indicate that the third variable was not contributing to the measure of work orientation.

Scoring an Index. In the index described above, if the scores on the three items (from 1 to 3 for each one) are cumulated, the range of scores is from 3 to 9. The scores should have a wide enough range to maximize the variation, but not be so dispersed that there are many empty points on the scale. Table 16-3 gives a frequency distribution of the Work Orientation Index; this, of course, is a univariate table of the variable, work orientation index. Note that the most common score (the mode) was an 8, the least common a 3. In short, for most high school seniors in 1972, success, steady work, and making money were very important.

An Appropriate Univariate Analysis for an Index. Since the Work Orientation Index is an interval measure which is continuous with many points on its scale, it is appropriate to use measures of central tendency and dispersion to describe the index. As described in Chapter 15, the measures of central tendency most commonly examined are the mean, the median, and the mode. Once a measure of central tendency is determined,

TABLE 16-2

THREE-VARIABLE RELATIONSHIPS AMONG WORK ORIENTATION ITEMS
(Percentage Who Believe That "Being Successful in My Line of Work" Is Very Important)

Importance of Having Lots of Money	Importance of Steady Work		
	Very Important	Somewhat Important	Not Important
Very important	94.0%	79.8%	73.5%
	(1,956)	(183)	(34)
Somewhat important	92.1%	69.0%	60.2%
	(6,395)	(1,295)	(98)
Not important	85.0%	52.6%	44.1%
	(1,649)	(993)	(188)

TABLE 16-3

INDEX SCORES FOR THE WORK ORIENTATION INDEX

Cumulative Score	Percent	N
3	.3	41
4	.9	113
5	4.5	580
6	9.6	1,225
7	22.3	2,850
8	48.0	6,144
9	14.4	1,838
Totals	100.0	12,791
No data		189

mean; three measures dealing with the dispersion of responses around the mean [the standard deviation, variance, and standard error (i.e., S.E. mean)]; two measures describing the shape of the distribution of responses as they might be pictured on a graph (i.e., kurtosis and skew); and three indicators describing the range of responses (i.e., the range, minimum score, and maximum score). The sum of all the scores is given, on which the mean is computed. Finally the number of missing cases is shown. In Chapter 15 some of these statistics were explained more fully.

Table 16-4 shows (1) that the mean score for WO72 is 7.5 (quite high); (2) that there is a standard deviation of 1.08, which points to a 68 percent confidence level that the population parameter would occur within the interval of approximately 1 point above or below 7.5 (in other words, between 6.5 and 8.5); and (3) that the minimum score was 3, the maximum 9, and the range (maximum to minimum) was 6. You can see that 189 respondents were missing from this variable (having given no response to one of the items). In summary, Table 16-4 offers different information describing the Work Orientation Index from that given in Table 16-3.

the next question to consider is how far the responses are closely clustered around the mean or are spread evenly from the highest to the lowest point on the index. Are the data skewed toward the upper ranges? Is there more than one peak in the data?

Most computer software programs offer you a very simple method to determine measures of the central tendency and dispersion of a continuous variable. In SPSS[x], the subprogram which generates these data is Condescriptive (which is more fully described in Appendix C). Table 16-4 presents output on the continuous variable of the Work Orientation Index (WO72). It includes the

What to Do about Missing Data. When there is missing information for a particular respondent (say that only two of the three items were answered), one solution is to exclude all respondents with any missing data from an index. This ap-

TABLE 16-4

DESCRIPTIVE STATISTICS FOR THE WORK ORIENTATION INDEX—SPSS[x] OUTPUT FROM CONDESCRIPTIVE

```
NUMBER OF VALID OBSERVATIONS (LISTWISE) =    12791.00
VARIABLE WO72       WORK ORIENTATION INDEX: 1972
MEAN           7.542      S.E. MEAN         .010      STD DEV        1.081
VARIANCE       1.169      KURTOSIS         1.300      S.E. KURT       .043
SKEWNESS      -1.054      S.E. SKEW         .022      RANGE          6.000
MINIMUM        3.00       MAXIMUM          9.00       SUM       96469.000
VALID OBSERVATIONS -      12791           MISSING OBSERVATIONS -       189
```

proach would produce the most reliable scale scores, since only those completing *all* items in the index would be included. However, this method can only be considered where not too many data are missing and where you have a sufficiently large sample size.

Another approach is to use the average score from the aggregated data on the relevant item to replace the missing data. In this case, the respondent's index score would be based on the two actual responses that were given and the one averaged score. A third way is to use the average score from the other items that the respondent has given. The advantage to this approach is that it maximizes the information already gained from the respondent. Finally, a method for replacing missing data is to give a randomly selected score for any missing response. Whatever system you decide to use to handle missing data, it should be followed consistently in every case.

Weighting an Index. You may either give the score from each item the same weight in the index or give certain items greater weight. Note that even when each item is given the same weight of 1, it is still weighted (by unity). Suppose you decided, for some solid theoretical reasons, that the success item was twice as important as the other two. You could then double that score before adding it to the other two, dividing the result by 4 (as if there were four items) to determine the index score. In general, unless you have some clear reason to do otherwise, you will give each item equal weight.

Testing the Validity of an Index

A variety of techniques are commonly used to test the validity of an index.[2] One is to set up an *item analysis* which cross-tabulates index scores to the separate items. To do this, you would set up bivariate tables in which the index is the indepen-

dent variable (across the top of the table) and the separate item is the dependent variable. Table 16-5 presents an item analysis of the three items making up the index in relation to the total index score.

Table 16-5 shows that high index scores of 7 and 8 were based more often on "very important" responses to the success and steady work items, with "somewhat important" for the money item. (Naturally, a top score of 9 required a response of "very important" to each item!) Low scores of 4 or 5 were more often based on "somewhat important" responses to the success item and "not important" responses to the money item. In terms of the steady work item, note that among those respondents with scores of 5, three-quarters gave a response of "somewhat important," and among those with scores of 4, nearly two-thirds gave a response of "not important." (Of course, the bottom score of 3 required that "not important" be selected for each item.) Thus the money item contributed the most to lower index scores and the success item, to higher index scores.

This suggests that the steady work item was the least important in determining the range of responses. One implication of this could be that you might consider dropping this item. If an index were composed of a larger set of items, and if some items contributed little to determining the range, or if one were related to the overall index score in an unexpected manner (those with higher scores were consistently low on this item), then you might consider excluding it. A primary ground rule for deciding whether to keep or drop an item would be a consideration of content validity: Is the item necessary in representing a critical domain of meaning in the concept? Another reason for dropping items may be to reduce the size of the scale. What an item analysis does is tell you the nature of the contribution that different items make in determining the overall index score.

In considering the internal validity of an index, such as the Work Orientation Index, you should remember that tests for criterion-related validity could be particularly relevant. Any number of fac-

---

[2]SPSS[x] has various subprograms that can be used to help determine the reliability and validity of an index or scale.

TABLE 16-5

ITEM ANALYSIS OF THE WORK ORIENTATION INDEX

	Total Index Scores						
	3	4	5	6	7	8	9
Importance of Success in Work							
Very important	0.0	0.0	14.3	47.4	81.4	98.3	100.0
Somewhat important	0.0	56.6	79.5	50.9	18.2	1.7	0.0
Not important	100.0	43.4	6.2	1.7	0.4	0.0	0.0
Importance of Having Lots of Money							
Very important	0.0	0.0	0.9	0.7	2.4	4.1	100.0
Somewhat important	0.0	7.1	8.1	37.7	48.4	95.9	0.0
Not important	100.0	92.9	91.0	61.6	49.2	0.0	0.0
Importance of Finding Steady Work							
Very important	0.0	0.0	2.6	20.4	66.6	97.6	100.0
Somewhat important	0.0	36.3	76.9	74.4	32.5	2.4	0.0
Not important	100.0	63.7	20.5	5.1	0.9	0.0	0.0
N	41	113	580	1,225	2,850	6,144	1,838

tors might serve as criteria of whether the Work Orientation Index is actually measuring what it purports to measure. It would be expected that those who work would have higher scores on the Work Orientation Index than those who do not and that those with higher-prestige occupations would have higher index scores than those with lower-prestige occupations. Another item that could be used as a criterion for validation would be income. It might also be assumed that those earning a higher income may have higher work orientation scores.

Since data on occupational characteristics would be based on subsequent post–high school experiences, such data could be used to establish the *predictive validity* (using a criterion that will be determined in the future) of the Work Orientation Index. The longitudinal character of the NLS data makes such a validity check possible. For evidence of *concurrent validity* (using a criterion measured at the same time as the index) in 1972, variables such as plans to attend college and occupational aspirations or expectations might have to be used. Validation may lead to a reappraisal of the index—the sense that it does not relate to (or predict) what it should. In such cases, you should consider redoing the index (possibly using some different items) or abandoning it altogether.

SCALES

As stated earlier, scales differ from indexes in that they take into account some qualities about the nature of the relationship of the separate items to each other. This is referred to as the *intensity structure* among the items. Because of this additional consideration, scales are more complex to devise. In this section, the most common forms of scales will be defined. Further, examples of actual scales will be described to show how the different types of scales work. Scales are not easy to develop, and they may create more error in measurement than a less complex instrument.

This section will give an overview of different types of scaling techniques without going into the measurement problems inherent in many types of scaling. Box 16-1 addresses major concerns in con-ceptualizing and building scales. If you plan to create your own scale, you will need to enhance your knowledge about the possible problems of a specific scaling technique, which is beyond the scope of this chapter. A variety of resources (reference books, scale instructions from already developed scales, evidence on validation and reliability of various scaling procedures) can be used to increase your knowledge of how to construct scales.

Remember that the most important aspect of developing a scale is to create items that measure

BOX 16-1

NUNNALLY'S THINKING ON MEASUREMENT SCALES

In his classic work on scaling, Nunnally offers a way to think about and assess scales. The most obvious way is to visualize a scale or think of its obvious physical characteristics—for example, a yardstick. However, most scales of attitudes or interests do not have such visible characteristics; therefore, a better approach in the social sciences is to develop scaling models based on assumptions (or axioms) "concerning how the data should appear when the measure is put to use" (1978, p. 27). If the data correspond to the assumptions for the model, then "the measure has scale properties specified by the model" (p. 27). Thus the criteria for the "goodness" of a scale come from the empirical data themselves.

Suppose you have never seen a yardstick but have developed a "yardstick scale," using the assumptions of the measurement employed by a yardstick, to develop a model for a ratio scale. You would then test whether the data generated by employing the yardstick model actually support the assumptions of a yardstick measure. As Nunnally says, "One could derive the scale properties of the yardstick from the model even if one had never seen one" (p. 27).

Nunnally stresses that the consequences of wrong assumptions about a scale (e.g., the intervals in the developed scale are different from the "real" intervals in the "real" scale, thus leading to imperfect measures) are not that serious. Scale results are usually reported as summary measures, such as means, and are used in statistical analyses in which differences in a scale mean are correlated with other variables. If the mean is slightly inaccurate, the correlations are only slightly altered (pp. 28–29).

Scales, Nunnally asserts, are established by *convention*. At one time the Fahrenheit scale was taken as *the* scale of temperature. Over time, new discoveries led to the development of the centigrade scale, which is now considered the more useful measure (p. 30). Each social scientist who works with a formal model of a scale helps to contribute to the effort of testing and refining scales which is necessary for the continued improvement of scaling.

Finally, it is important that a scale work well in practice. As Nunnally contends, "The usefulness (validity) of a measure is in the extent to which it relates to other variables in a domain of interest" (p. 32). Hence the best scales will lead to the simplest forms of relationships with other variables (p. 32).

Source: Jum C. Nunnally, *Psychometric Theory,* 2d ed., McGraw-Hill, New York, 1978, pp. 27–32.

what you are trying to measure (items that have face validity). In addition, these items should cover the various domains of content that the scale is purporting to represent; that is to say, the issue of content validity is an overriding one in scale development. Recall from the discussion of the F-Scale in Chapter 5 that the concept of authoritarianism is considered to have nine dimensions, each of which is operationalized into a set of questions serving as indicators. This is a *multidimensional* scale. In contrast, a scale may be composed of indicators representing a single dimension of a concept. This would be a *unidimensional* scale.

There is another option: use an already constructed scale. We will end with a discussion of the types of scales available to measure occupational status. Even when you select an already constructed scale, you should nevertheless understand how it was made. If you do not, you are likely to use it inaccurately and may find interpreting your results very difficult. The scale types discussed here are not all equivalent to one another. Some refer largely to how the variation in answers is set up. Others have to do with the type of items presented. Still others are distinguished by the responses given.

Likert Scales

Perhaps the most widely used form of scaling in survey research is one that sets up ordinal categories for degrees of agreement, generally including the five levels of "strongly agree," "agree," "disagree," "strongly disagree," and "don't know" (or "undecided"). These response categories are attached to a set of statements. Assuming that the responses to each statement are equivalent, you can assign scores of 1 through 5 (or 0 through 4), and can create an index by summing the scores and averaging them. Because the items are added up, a *Likert scale* is in some ways an index of items with consistently scaled response categories.

If there are many statements in the set, you may want to condense them in some way. One procedure is to create a total index of the items

and then carry out an item analysis (as described above) to see which items are most closely related to the index; you might then use these to form a smaller index. A more complex procedure is to carry out a *factor analysis*—a statistical technique which examines all the interrelationships between the various items to determine which sets of items are most strongly related. These sets of items are called *factors;* they serve as new dimensions of the concept being measured. (For a more comprehensive review of factor analysis, you will need to look beyond this text.)

The box shows how a large set of items on sex-role attitudes was reduced to two factors that were used as separate scales of sex-role attitudes in the National Longitudinal Study of the High School Class of 1972.

Semantic Differential Scale

Developed initially by Osgood, Suci, and Tanenbaum (1957), a *Semantic Differential Scale* offers bipolar positions (such as two adjectives: "active/passive") to a single stimulus (for example: "my mother"). The respondent is asked to rate the stimulus on a seven-point (or five-point) scale. Usually, as in the above examples, the bipolar items are adjectives; the stimulus, a reference to a person or persons. To review this, the bipolar adjectives might be "strong-weak," "happy-unhappy," "tense-relaxed," and the stimulus "I am." Somewhere between the bipolar extremes of these adjectives would commonly be a seven-point scale on which the subject must place the stimulus referent at a point which seems most appropriate.

The reason why the Semantic Differential Scale is useful is that a respondent may not always be sure how to describe in words exactly how intelligent or not intelligent, how timid or bold, or how happy or unhappy another person is. Placing the person on a scale running from one extreme to the other is easier. In some cases, instead of adjectives, brief statements are used at one end, their converse at the other. (Such a technique may be more useful in sociological studies

DEVELOPING TWO SUBSCALES FROM A 10-ITEM SCALE

Using a four-point Likert Scale of response categories, with 1 = "disagree strongly" to 4 = "agree strongly," Kanouse and his colleagues offered 10 statements:

A. A working mother of preschool children can be just as good a mother as a woman who doesn't work.

B. It is usually better for everyone involved if the man is the achiever outside the home and the woman takes care of the family.

C. Young men should be encouraged to take jobs that are usually filled by women (nursing, secretarial work, etc.).

D. Most women are just not interested in having big and important jobs.

E. Many qualified women can't get good jobs; men with the same skills have much less trouble.

F. Most women are happiest when they are making a home and caring for children.

G. High school counselors should urge young women to train for jobs which are now held mainly by men.

H. It is more important for a wife to help her husband than to have a career herself.

I. Schools teach women to want the less important jobs.

J. Men should be given the first chance at most jobs because they have the primary responsibility for providing for a family.

Using factor analysis, the researchers produced two factors from the 10 items. The first factor, which was labeled "traditional family priority," was based on the items B, D, F, H, and J.[a] These were the items that supported a woman's primary status as a homemaker who would recognize her economic dependence on her husband and would provide him with emotional support. The second factor, labeled "equal employment," was largely based on items C, E, G, and I. These were the items which confronted the issue of equalizing job opportunities between the sexes. What factor analysis provides are *scores* for each of the factors. These factor scores can then be used instead of the total score for the items. Alternatively, all or some of the items in the two factors could be used separately as indicators of the now differentiated concepts that they purport to measure.

[a]You might note that some of these items (such as J) are double-barreled; therefore "disagreement" might only refer to one aspect of the item. Clearly, when you choose a scale, you should be careful to look at the items comprising the scale to decide whether they meet the criteria for clear and unambiguous items.

Source: David E. Kanouse et al., *Effects of Postsecondary Experiences on Aspirations, Attitudes, and Self-Conceptions,* Rand, Santa Monica, Calif., 1980, pp. 118–119.

where social behaviors and social attitudes may be of greater concern than personality traits.) Furthermore, a study may contain more than one semantic differential, each with the same set of bipolar items, but with different subjects to apply them to. Then the ratings on each item can be compared.

Box 16-2 gives an example of the use of a Semantic Differential I used in a study I carried out on black and white college students at predominantly white colleges. Two other scales with the same set of bipolar items were rated in reference to the stimuli: "Most of my friends *not at this college* are" and "I am." Comparisons could then be made between the individual and his or her college friends or noncollege friends, and the college and noncollege friends could be compared as well.

The scoring of these scales uses the scale numbers. Let's first consider how you would score a single item. Note that each bipolar item comprises its own scale. Thus, by merely numbering the scale positions and recording the scale position for each respondent, you could determine an average scale position for the sample. If the stimulus were "I am", you could compare scale positions for different subgroups (men and women, first-year students and seniors, etc.).

Another type of scoring would involve creating subscores by grouping certain items on the scale. For example, the scale in Box 16-2 had many statements that measured some form of political activism (interested in social betterment, interested in trying to change the military involvement of the country, radical politically). Note that in some cases the radical-activist position was on the left-hand side of the scale; in others it was on the right-hand side. This reversal was done to reduce *response set,* which (you may recall from Chapter 7) was the propensity of respondents to mark down a set of answers in a consistent manner without seeming to pay heed to the meaning of the questions.

Let's go over how to score a Semantic Differential. You would first want to give numbers to the scale positions, putting a 7 at the radical end and going down to a 1 at the conservative end. Then

BOX 16-2

SEMANTIC DIFFERENTIAL SCALE IN THE STUDY OF COLLEGE STUDENTS

MOST OF MY FRIENDS *AT THIS COLLEGE* ARE:

Very interested in national and international affairs	Not at all interested in national and international affairs
Very interested in working toward social betterment of disadvantaged people	Not at all interested in working toward social betterment of disadvantaged people
Very interested in trying to change certain organizational structures and practices in America	Not at all interested in trying to change certain organizational structures and practices in America
Very interested in trying to change the military involvement of the country	Not at all interested in trying to change the military involvement of the country
Very interested in joining groups outside the college	Not at all interested in joining groups outside the college
Very interested in joining groups at the college	Not at all interested in joining groups at the college
Conventional in dress or appearance	Unconventional in dress or appearance
Conservative politically	Radical politically
Intellectual	Not intellectual
Critical of rules	Accepting of rules
Absorbed in academic studies	Not absorbed in academic studies
Absorbed in social life	Not absorbed in social life

whatever scores were marked for "Most of my friends" on these items could be added together and divided by the number of items in the scale. (Remember that you would not need to use all the items on the scale; you might want to consider those items that fitted together and formed a sub-scale within the total scale.)

A third way to score a Semantic Differential is to compare scores given to one response stimulus (let's say, "most of my friends at this college") to another stimulus, for example, yourself ("I am"). Considering the "absorbed in social life" item, if the respondent rated college friends as a 2 and him or herself as a 6, you would see that there is a 4-point difference. Sets of difference scores could be summed over all the items comprising the sub-scale (or the difference scores for a whole set of items comprising a Semantic Differential). Then the *median difference* score could be determined. In my study on black and white college students, this is how the Semantic Differential Scales were analyzed. Those students with scores at or below the median were considered to be identifying with their college friends; those with scores above the median were not identifying with their college friends. Note that this summing procedure is actually similar to index construction.

Bogardus Social Distance Scales

This is a scale that focuses on the distances between the ordinal items in the scale (Bogardus, 1959). It has been widely used to measure the attitudes toward ethnic groups, but it has also been employed to measure attitudes toward occupational, social class, and religious groups. It asks the respondent to think of the group to be rated in terms of the type of social interaction in which he or she would choose to engage with members of that group. The forms of social interaction vary in their degree of intimacy. Box 16-3 gives an example from Bogardus' original work.

This scale assumes that if you give assent to item 7, you would agree as well to items 6 through 1, and that if you agree to item 3, you would also agree to items 2 and 1. In other words, it assumes

a *cumulative* set of scores. One problem that critics have raised with this form of scale is that there is no way to determine the actual distance between the various points on the scale, and some points seem to be at a greater distance from the point next to them than others farther away. The scores, however, are treated as equidistant. Nevertheless, such a scale—and there are many versions—may be useful if you are studying attitudes toward groups of "others."

Thurstone Scales

Thurstone Scales are composed of items selected by judges as indicative of measuring some concept. The general procedure is that the researcher would amass a large number of items seemingly measuring a particular concept, for example, conservatism. Judges would be asked to classify each item, independently, on a scale of 1 to 11, from the strongest measure of conservatism to the weakest. Once the panel of judges has completed the classifying, the researcher determines an average score for each item from the average responses of the judges. Then a subset of items can be drawn, usually a few with scores from the very top to the very bottom of the scaled responses of the judges.

This means that the items selected relate to one another in such a way that the ones to which the judges gave higher scores presume agreement with the items given lower scores. Thurstone scaling is one of the earliest and best-known forms of scaling. However, it is very time-consuming, and it has been challenged by some methodologists as very problem-ridden. For these reasons, it is not often used today.

Guttman Scales

This form of scaling is similar both to the Bogardus Social Distance Scale and to the Thurstone Scale—the items have an inherent order such that some are considered more powerful measures of the concept and therefore subsume other, weaker measures. As usual, the best way to understand

BOX 16-3

A BOGARDUS SOCIAL DISTANCE SCALE

1. Remember to give your *first feeling reactions* in every case.
2. Give your reactions to each nationality as a group. Do not give your reactions to the best or the worst members that you have known,

but think of the picture or stereotype that you have of the whole group.

3. Put a cross in as many of the boxes as your feelings dictate.

Scoring Weights	Category	Mexicans	Vietnamese	Nigerians	Chinese
7	Close kinship by marriage				
6	In my club as personal chums				
5	On my street as neighbors				
4	Working alongside me in my occupation				
3	As citizens in my country				
2	As visitors only to my country				
1	Would exclude from my country				

Source: E. Bogardus, cited in John B. Williamson et al., *The Research Craft*, 2d ed., Little, Brown, Boston, 1982, p. 367.

this form of scaling is to consider an example. I will describe how I thought through my reasons for developing a scale and then how I carried out its construction and implementation.

In my research on black and white college students, I used changes in response to the *Autonomy Scale* to study the *effect* of college on students. In selecting the Autonomy Scale, I had to trace back the history of the development of this scale. I discovered that its origins lay in the work done on the study of authoritarianism, as described in Chapter 5. In fact, some of the Autonomy Scale items were taken directly from the F-Scale.

The Autonomy Scale had 43 items. I began by carrying out a factor analysis (referred to above) to determine the different dimensions in the scale. This produced three factors which I labeled (on the basis of the items that were most strongly represented by the factors) antiauthoritarianism, anticonventionalism, and open-mindedness. However, I also began to wonder whether persons who supported the third factor (open-mindedness) would also have supported the second and first factors, that is, whether the third factor subsumed the two earlier ones and whether people who supported the second factor were likely to have supported the first. In short, I wondered whether the factors represented stages in attitude development: whether you first subscribed to one set of attitudes before moving on to accepting a second set of attitudes.

It seemed possible that these were stages in the development of the autonomous personality. Theoretically, I developed a position in which each of the factors represented a stage further and further removed from authoritarianism. The first stage, antiauthoritarianism, suggested a negative reversal of authoritarianism, but in both cases attitudes toward the society are seen as imposed. For the authoritarian they are seen as positively imposed and for the antiauthoritarian, negatively imposed. Thus the antiauthoritarian repudiates authority while the authoritarian welcomes it. The second stage, anticonventionalism, suggested a questioning of the traditional order: society is not repudiated, but it is also not accepted unquestioningly. The individual seems to be trying to throw off values that are no longer relevant and to replace them with ones that he or she has reason to support. The third stage, open-mindedness, suggests an attitude toward society as open to many possibilities and toward individual conduct within society as relatively free from social constraint. The individual is beginning to see that he or she has possibilities and choices within the social order (Baker, 1976, pp. 630–631). While these seemed theoretically interesting, I needed a way to test for evidence to support the idea of the stages of nonauthoritarianism. [Let me add that although this is a special situation, it is often the case that, when you are trying to make sense of a complex measuring instrument (like the Autonomy Scale), the Guttman scales suddenly look interesting.]

To test for the stages of nonauthoritarianism, I created a Guttman type of scale.[3] First I selected the three items which had the strongest *weights* (or which contributed most to determining the factor) for each of the three factors: for *antiauthoritarianism,* a "true" response to the statement, "Society

puts too much restraint on the individual"; for *anticonventionalism,* "false" to "Every person ought to be a booster for his or her hometown"; for *open-mindedness,* "false" to "Nothing about fascism is any good." Then I examined the responses to these three items.

Table 16-6 gives the possible scores on the three items for both the scale and nonscale types. Scale types are those which represent the expected pattern: if you accept the open-minded item, you should accept the two earlier-stage items (if you accept the anticonventional item, you should accept the lower-level antiauthoritarian item as well). Nonscale types include any other possible pattern of response which diverges from the scale types.

As the table indicates, 56 respondents gave answers that were scale types and 44 gave nonscale responses. Various tests can be used to justify calling the items a Guttman Scale. I used the *coefficient of reproducibility* to see if the three items represented a Guttman Scale. It is based on the following formula:

Coefficient of reproducibility

$$= 1 - \frac{\text{number of errors}}{(\text{number of cases} \times \text{number of items})}$$

In the example, the number of errors (or nonscale types) was 44, the number of cases was 100, and the number of items was 3.

$$\text{Coefficiency of reproducibility} = 1 - \frac{44}{300}$$
$$= .853$$
$$= 85.3\%$$

This produced a coefficient of reproducibility of .85, which is below the .90 level suggested as evidence that a scale forms a true Gutmann Scale. The scale seemed to qualify only as a quasi-Guttman scale, one that is only fairly close to being a Guttman Scale. What I learned from this procedure is that there was some evidence of an ordering among the items I had distinguished as

---

[3]The example given is more precisely a summed index that has been tested to see how far it conforms to Guttman's criteria for setting up a scale.

TABLE 16-6

GUTTMAN SCALE OF THREE ITEMS FROM THE AUTONOMY SCALE

	Item				
	Social Restraint	**Booster**	**Fascism**	**Score**	**Number of Cases**
Scale types	1	1	1	3	18
	1	1	0	2	20
	1	0	0	1	7
	0	0	0	0	11
Total					56
Nonscale types	1	0	1	2	13
	0	1	1	2	10
	0	1	0	1	13
	0	0	1	1	8
Total					44

representing different dimensions of nonauthoritarianism, but the evidence was not conclusive.

This is only one way in which a Guttman Scale might be used. It is not an easy scaling method, and some methodologists believe that it is often misused. Nevertheless, if you want to determine the pattern of responses to a set of items and you suppose that the pattern suggests a set of stages that are ordered, then Guttman scaling may be worth considering. Guttman Scales need not be computed by hand, but may be carried out using computer package programs such as SPSS^x.

SELECTING ALREADY DEVELOPED INDEXES AND SCALES

Many of the most commonly measured variables in social research (for example, socioeconomic status) already have corresponding indexes or scales developed which you might use. In this section, I want to suggest the types of variables likely to have already available scales, and discuss how you might find these instruments.

Scales are very popular in both psychology and sociology. In order to measure complex psychological qualities, such as authoritarianism, anomie, or alienation, self-report statements cannot often be used (you can't really ask someone, "Do you feel alienated?"). Rather, sets of questions that tap various aspects of these complex measures must be developed. Most complex psychological concepts have been the basis for scales. Using the bibliographical resources discussed in Chapter 4 and looking for the concept name itself (authoritarianism, for example) would lead you to a vast number of references to articles in which this concept was studied.

The earliest articles and the titles of articles would tell you where the scale might first have been published. Remember that most scales, if they are popularly used, undergo revisions over time. The revised versions may shorten the scale, they may make it more applicable for different types of audiences (for example, children or non-Americans), and they may revise anachronistic items. For this reason, a revised version of a scale may serve your purposes better than the original. It is a good rule of thumb not to grab the first scale you find that you think might measure what you want. Instead, use this first scale as a reference point for finding earlier or later versions or for finding scales to which it has been correlated. You will want to examine quite a few scales before making a final decision. Above all, remember that the wording of the items must be appropriate for your population.

Excellent reference sources are available to help you find the right scale or index. Perhaps the most comprehensive is O. K. Buros (ed.), *Eighth Mental Measurements Yearbook* (1978). This reference work has six different types of indexes for finding scales (by name, by scale title, etc.). It briefly describes each scale, outlining its length and the types of factors involved; it suggests appropriate audiences for the scale and gives references as to where it can be found. Another excellent resource work is Delbert C. Miller, *Handbook of Research Design and Social Measurement* (1991). There are other reference works that are more specialized: for example, O. G. Johnson (ed.), *Tests and Measurements in Child Development: Handbook II* (1976).

Some volumes offer copies of the scales themselves. These include collections of attitudinal scales, such as Robinson and Shaver, *Measures of Social Psychological Attitudes* (1973), or M. E. Shaw and J. M. Wright, *Scales for the Measurement of Attitudes* (1967). For special types of scales and indexes, you might turn to Robinson et al., *Measures of Occupational Attitudes and Occupational Characteristics* (1969); Robinson et al., *Measures of Political Attitudes* (1968); or C. A. Beere, *Women and Women's Issues: A Handbook of Tests and Measures* (1979). Usually you need permission to use a scale, and sometimes there is a charge. It is normally acceptable to shorten a longer scale to meet your purposes, but if you do so, the validation and replication evidence that its authors developed will not apply to your shortened version.

Occupational and Socioeconomic Scales

Occupation is one of the central characteristics of individuals in modern society, and it is the primary factor in identifying the social status of individuals.

Thus a measure of occupational status is needed in many social research projects. Other factors such as geographic region, ethnicity, or age may also be important differentiating factors, but "What do you do?" is the one question in the United States which is most readily asked and is considered the primary measure of one's status. For this reason, the use of occupation as a primary social indicator is widespread. The problem with measuring occupation is that it is a nominal variable with numerous categories which have no inherent order. To be able to use it to rank individuals, you must place the occupations on a scale in some fashion to denote differences in their qualities.

Two different types of scales or indexes are usually used for this purpose. The first is an *occupational prestige scale,* such as the one developed at the National Opinion Research Center (NORC) by Paul Hatt and Cecil North in 1947 and revised by Robert Hodge, Paul Siegel, and Peter Rossi (1964); or the newer cross-nationally validated occupational prestige scale developed by Donald Treiman, the *Standard Scale* (1977). The other type is a *socioeconomic index* (SEI) based on indicators other than occupational prestige (such as income and educational attainment). The best-known example here is the Duncan Socioeconomic Index (SEI) (described in detail in Reiss, 1961). We will consider the NORC Prestige Scale, the Treiman Standard Scale, and the Duncan SEI.

Occupational Prestige Scales. The rationale for developing an occupational prestige scale is that individuals conceive of occupations as forming a ranked set of job categories; therefore, to establish such a scale only requires asking a large enough number of individuals to rank occupational titles and forming the composite scores these occupations receive into a scale. The original procedure used by NORC was to give the following statement to the subjects (Reiss, 1961, p. 19):

> For each job mentioned, please pick out the statement that best gives *your own personal opinion* of the *general standing* that such a job has.

1. *Excellent* standing.
2. *Good* standing.
3. *Average* standing.
4. *Somewhat below* average standing.
5. *Poor* standing.
X. I don't know where to place that one.

Many subjects were asked to rank the occupations. The ratings from each subject were converted into scores of 5 for "excellent," 4 for "good," etc. The "don't know" responses were excluded. For each occupational title, the percent of responses in each of the five categories was multiplied by the assigned score ("excellent" = 5, "good" = 4, etc.). These products were then summed and divided by 5 to yield an average score for each occupation. Box 16-4 shows how this was done.

There was also the issue of which job titles to give respondents to rate. Occupational titles are not easy to select; there are a number of problems. First, there are so many titles that it is difficult to make the selection; second, titles may be ambiguous ("engineer" or "supervisor" can refer to a vast array of actual jobs); third, individuals in the society may not use the same terms for each occupation; fourth, the use of titles changes over time. The revised versions of the original NORC Prestige Scales have had to readdress the issue of job titles. When the NORC Prestige Scale was revised in 1963 by Hodge, Siegel, and Rossi, a national sample was asked to rank 90 occupations (1964).

One of the surprising findings of these prestige studies was the degree of agreement among the respondents on the ranking of occupations. Evidence was accumulated over time that people throughout the world rated occupations similarly. Donald J. Treiman (1977) developed an international scale by taking scores from 509 occupational titles (which naturally varied among different languages and within languages between different cultures) in 60 countries where occupational prestige studies had been carried out and converting them into a standard score. This required using a somewhat complicated formula which compared the differences in means and

BOX 16-4

RANK-ORDER SCORING FOR THE ORIGINAL NORC[a] OCCUPATIONAL PRESTIGE SCALE

Suppose the title "carpenter" received the following percentages from respondents:

Excellent	= 20%
Good	= 30%
Average	= 20%
Below average	= 10%
Poor	= 10%

Each percentage would be multiplied by the assigned weighted scores, summed together, and then divided by 5.

$$\frac{(20 \times 5) + (30 \times 4) + (20 \times 3) + (10 \times 2) + (10 \times 1)}{5} = 62$$

Thus the occupational prestige score for "carpenter" would be 62. Note that if everyone ranked an occupation as "excellent," the score would be 100 [$(100 \times 5)/5 = 100$]; if everyone rated it "poor," the score would be 20 [$(100 \times 1)/5 = 20$].

[a]NORC = National Opinion Research Center.

standard deviations (see Chapter 15) of scores for occupations in each country to those in the United States. The result was that each occupational title was given a score between 0 and 100 (Treiman, 1977, pp. 166–167). One quality of Treiman's *Standard Scale* is that unit group categories (those used by the Census Bureau to categorize sets of job titles) are also given scores. This means that if you wanted to score only large categories ("managers" as compared to "clerical workers") you would have a numerical scale to use. Table 16-7 gives these group categories and their corresponding scores.

Duncan SEI. An alternative to an occupational prestige scale is a composite measure based on variables other than the level of prestige attributed to occupations. The most widely used of these scales is the Duncan Socioeconomic Index (SEI). This was developed to extend the effort begun in the Hatt-North Occupational Prestige Scale, which

had rated only a relatively small number of occupations on the basis of prestige. Otis Dudley Duncan and his associates wanted to scale a much larger number of occupations on the basis of income derived from the occupation and educational attainment normally held by those in the occupational group. The SEI ranges from 1 to 100.

In developing the SEI, stronger weights were given occupations (measured by income and educational attainment) that had higher prestige scores. In short, the SEI was created in such a way that it would be highly correlated to the NORC Occupational Prestige Scale. The SEI was applied to a very wide range of occupational titles. (For a detailed discussion of how the SEI was developed and how it compares with the North-Hatt Occupational Prestige Scale, see Reiss, 1961.)

Whether you should choose an occupational prestige scale or a socioeconomic index "is not at all obvious," as Treiman states (1977, p. 211). He suggests that a socioeconomic index should be a

TABLE 16-7

TREIMAN'S STANDARD SCALE[a]

Unit Group Categories	Standard Scale Score
Professional, technical	59
Managers, administrators (except farm)	53
Sales	39
Clerical	42
Craftsmen	39
Operatives (except transport)	32
Transport equipment operatives	30
Laborers (except farm)	21
Farmers and farm managers	41
Farm laborers and farm foremen	24
Service workers (except private household)	29
Private household workers	20

[a]Scores for unit group categories for the 1970 census, detailed occupational classification.

Source: Condensed from Donald J. Treiman, *Occupational Prestige in Comparative Perspective*, Academic Press, New York, 1977, pp. 306–314.

better measure of occupation if you are using occupation as an indicator of *resources* that might be transmitted intergenerationally or that might be considered as beneficial for some other end. Therefore, if you are doing a study of intergenerational mobility (let's say, how sons' careers compare to their fathers'), then the SEI might be preferable. On the other hand, occupational prestige seems to be a better indicator of career attainment, since it implies the subjective "rewards" gained by holding an occupation (1977, p. 212). Furthermore, Treiman argues that his scale is useful in the study of employed women, black workers, and other minority groups whereas income differences between these groups and white men make the SEI a less reliable measure for the former groups (1977, p. 212). Naturally, if you are using cross-national data, Treiman's Standard Scale is preferable, since it was built from a large set of studies from 60 different nations.

WHETHER TO USE AN INDEX OR A SCALE

This chapter has offered you some guidelines for constructing indexes and some information about types of scales and where you might find already developed scales. Socioeconomic indexes and occupational prestige scales have been described in detail to show you the range and types of scales available for measuring occupational status.

How useful a scale or index might be for your project will naturally depend on what you are planning to do. Social researchers vary in terms of the types of scales they are likely to use. Some of the differences in usage have to do with which branch of the social sciences one is working in— social psychologists are particularly fond of personality scales; sociological survey researchers almost always use occupational status scales. You should carefully consider what you are trying to measure in your study and decide whether a composite instrument would help you to achieve your goals. Remember that if you use an already constructed scale or index, evidence will be available concerning the validity and reliability of the scale. If you develop your own index or scale, you will have the creative experience of developing a measuring instrument of your own.

REVIEW NOTES

- An index is a composite set of indicators to measure a complex concept. The cumulative score on the indicators serves as the index score.
- A scale is a measurement instrument based on a set of indicators which have certain interrelationships to one another. These internal interrelationships are referred to as the intensity structure of the scale.
- Index construction involves developing empirical indicators to represent the dimensions of the concept, examining the interrelationships of the indicators, and selecting those which form the best composite measures.
- One way of validating an index is with an item analysis in which index scores are cross-tabulated (or cross-correlated) with responses to the separate items forming the index.
- Likert Scales are the cumulated scores from sets of statements (selected to represent a concept) to which ordinal responses ("strongly agree" . . . "strongly disagree") are given.
- A Semantic Differential Scale is based on ratings for a stimulus subject ("I am") on a five- or seven-point bipolar set of items (often adjectives). The cumulated ratings determine the scale score. Often a number of different stimuli are presented with the same set of bipolar items to enable comparisons.
- The Bogardus Social Distance Scale is an ordinal scale in which the kind and degree of social interaction the rater would allow with members of a specific group are determined. The social interaction items are assumed to be cumulative (for example, if you would agree to have your

daughter or son marry a member of the group, it is expected that you would have no objection to living next door to a member of that group).

• Thurstone Scales are based on items chosen by a multistage procedure in which (1) judges select items best representing a concept (or a particular quality of a concept) and (2) the researcher averages the scores of the judges and selects items on this basis.

• Guttman Scales are a means for determining whether respondents rate items in a cumulative fashion so that responses to some items appear to subsume responses to others.

• Many already developed indexes and scales are available to researchers. Numerous reference books describe these composite measures in detail. Socioeconomic indexes and occupational prestige scales are examples of widely used composite measures for determining socioeconomic status.

KEY TERMS

Bogardus Social Distance Scale
coefficient of reproducibility
Guttman Scale
index
intensity structure
item analysis
Likert Scale
occupational prestige scale
scale
Semantic Differential Scale
socioeconomic index (SEI)
Thurstone Scale

STUDY EXERCISES

1. Create index items to measure the concept of satisfaction with college that could be used in

a survey to be given to college students. Think of the dimensions that you would want to cover in this index, and develop one or more items to serve as indicators of each.

2. Review the five types of scales presented in the chapter and give a one-sentence description of each one.

3. Find one already created scale in the research literature. Briefly describe the scale and how it was developed. What evidence is there as to its validity? In what kind of a study might *you* want to include this scale?

RECOMMENDED READINGS

1. De Vellis, Robert F.: *Scale Development: Theories and Applications,* Sage, Newbury Park, Calif., 1991. This is a helpful and comprehensible guide on how to build your own scales (generating items, determining length, measurement format).

2. Mueller, Daniel J.: *Measuring Social Attitudes: A Handbook for Researchers and Practitioners,* Teachers College Press, New York, 1986. An easy introduction to the use of different scaling methods (Likert, Thurstone, Semantic Differential) with some helpful examples.

3. Miller, Delbert C.: *Handbook of Research Design and Social Measurement,* 5th ed., Sage, Newbury Park, Calif., 1991. Miller's fifth edition includes a good overview of types of scale construction and a section comparing socioeconomic scales. It also includes guides to social science data libraries, and scales on group structure, social indicators, community, social participation, leadership, job satisfaction, family and marriage, and personality measures.

4. Nunnally, Jum C.: *Psychometric Theory,* 2d ed., McGraw-Hill, New York, 1978. This classic work on the meaning of scaling discusses scaling models and the measurement of interests, values, and attitudes.

Presenting the Research Results

LOOKING AHEAD

This chapter discusses a variety of ways to present research results for papers, presentations, and publication and outlines the sections of a student research paper.

INTRODUCTION

*T*his chapter offers an overview of the various ways in which social research is presented to others. Social research, as described in Chapter 3, has a social purpose, a function. But if it is not disseminated, or shown to others, it can play no social role.

Naturally, there are very different publics for social research. You may be writing a research project paper for an undergraduate methods course, in which case your immediate audience will be your professor! You may be writing a research paper to be presented to an audience at a professional meeting or to be published in an academic journal. If you are funded by a grant, you may be writing a final report for the funding agency to tell them what you have found. Social research projects may also serve as the basis of a book. All the surveys and field studies detailed in Chapter 1 were finally developed into books. Often a research project is disseminated in several ways—as a paper presented at a professional meeting, in one or more published articles, and, possibly, also as a book.

The usual way of disseminating social research is through a research report. Whether it is written for a course paper or for an academic journal or conference, the general form of such a research paper is roughly the same. The principles for organizing such a research report will form the major section of this chapter.

FORMS FOR DISSEMINATING SOCIAL RESEARCH

When to Decide on the Form

Research projects vary in their purpose. If you are carrying out your project for a course, you know that it will culminate in a project paper to be handed in to the course instructor. If you are doing an evaluation research project for a particular agency, you know that you must prepare a report of your findings for the agency. If you have a research grant, you are obliged to prepare a final report for the granting agency. These types of projects have preresearch writing commitments. In such a case, the manner in which the project will be disseminated should guide the design of the project throughout. In Chapter 4, the outline for the research proposal was similar to an outline for the final research report.

Sometimes research projects are begun without a clear idea as to what the form of dissemination will be. This can sometimes lead to problems if, after finally deciding what the form of dissemination should be, you discover that your research data do not enable you to produce it. The flexibility of your project, in terms of how many types of disseminated products it might lead to, will depend on the size and focus of the project.

If you do a very tight little experiment with a small sample which tests a single hypothesis, you may be able to write only a single article to address its findings. If, however, you engage in an analysis such as Coleman's high school study, which comes from a large longitudinal study on which all the data are not yet collected, your writings from that one research effort may be numerous and go on for years. Such a comprehensive survey can be analyzed from so many different perspectives, since it contains so many different variables which can be manipulated in so many different ways, that it is not likely a single researcher can exhaust all the research analyses possible in that study. This is why such datasets become the bases for secondary analyses (as discussed in Chapter 10).

When you are working with a large dataset, or with numerous experiments, or with a complex content analysis, you must decide at some point precisely which subtopic within the larger project you plan to write about and what material from all that is available can be used to address it. In other words, with a large project, which will likely form the basis of a number of disseminated writings and presentations, you may not in the beginning have specified all the writings you plan from it; they may evolve over time. The problem with this type of planning is that often you may not have exactly the data you require to address each new idea for a paper. Then you will need to operate as a secondary analyst would—being willing to substitute a less perfect measure for a concept than you might have chosen if you had planned this particular paper before collecting the data.

Basic Ingredients Needed for a Research Report

If you look back to Chapter 4 on the 11 steps of a research project, you will see that we have reached the eleventh step. Before you write your research project, you must assemble four basic ingredients which come from different steps of the research effort:

1. *A clear topic.* Your topic must be precisely worked out in written form. It cannot be simply "Delinquency," or "Prejudice," or "Problems of Hispanic Children in Schools." All of these titles are too vague and unspecified. The topic must be posed in the form of a research question or a hypothesis.
2. *A review of other relevant evidence.* The background literature may well have been gathered together when the research was designed. It is likely that you will need to round out your review by going through the most recent journal articles relevant to your topic which have appeared since you began and by carefully considering whether the topic on which you are writing requires evidence from areas which you had not examined previously.
3. *A research design.* The research design is the

model which controls your project. In most cases, this design will have been formally worked out during the planning (or *proposal* writing) stage of your study. During the course of the research itself, the design may have undergone some changes. To write up the final project, you must clarify the precise model you worked from. If the study is being written for a class project paper, it may make sense to describe how the research design evolved over the course of the study; if it is being written for a more formal presentation or publication, then the final research design will be the one to present. A research design is primarily the model you propose to use to analyze the data; but it must also include the plans for measuring the major variables and collecting the data. In many cases, analytic designs can be best presented with diagrams, where variables are laid out with lines and arrows pointing their relationship to one another.
4. *Analyzed data.* The findings of your study reside in the analyzed data. Writing a report or paper on the data is often the very way in which the analyses are produced. Some researchers take notes on each table when it is examined; others merely select tables to discuss as they write the analysis.

From Research Project to Research Report

In addition to the four basic ingredients for the paper, you will need introductory, connective, and explanatory material to form the research project into a logical whole. The most critical explanatory material is the information on the methods used. This can include discussions of the form of data collection, the instruments used, the nature of the sample, and issues of conceptualization and measurement. These *structuring* ingredients vary more depending on the type of dissemination you are doing.

Types of Research Reports

Research Papers for Courses. These papers should include comprehensive discussions and evidence of the methods used. Since such papers are often completed to fulfill the requirements of a methods course, you must make it very clear to the instructor that you understand every one of the methodological steps which were taken to carry out the project. In my experience, students seem to have two problems in this regard. In the first place they often skip crucial steps by jumping over a procedure that was crucial to the study but which may be forgotten once subsequent steps were completed (a good example here might be the pretest). You should, therefore, keep a clear record of the steps in your research as you go along. In the second place, students often become too detailed about certain aspects of the research effort, describing them in so much depth that their discussion becomes repetitive and redundant (a good example here would be the coding).

Research papers for classes often require that the instruments for data collection, the raw data, frequencies for all variables, or other sorts of evidence of the data be presented in an appendix.

Presentation Before a Professional Audience. These papers often have a greatly reduced discussion of the methods used. Such papers must usually be highly focused to address a subtopic of the central research topic. The discussion of others' relevant research findings may be reduced to those bearing most directly on your findings. Presented papers emphasize the findings section since this is what will interest the audience most. In addition, such papers need to draw sharp conclusions to make sure the audience remembers what has been said. Not every study produces decisive findings, but you can often draw interesting conclusions even from a study with inconclusive findings. Your research may also have raised stimulating questions: What was the probable cause of the inconclusiveness? What type of future research pro-

ject might be able to produce more conclusive evidence on this topic?

Publication in Professional Journals. Such papers require the ability to write concisely. Because printing costs are high and journals tend to have page limits, the art of writing for journals is to be able to describe what is essential about your study in a very few words. The reader is often given references to help locate more explicit evidence (from the author, from a research organization, from another publication on the same research). Extensive appendices are rare, though sometimes certain elaborations of critical aspects of the methodological approach (e.g., how an index which served as the dependent variable was formed) are added. Because a published article becomes a part of the literature on this research subject, greater care must be taken to make certain that the evidence presented is without error, that the implications of the findings are the most rational and cogent that can be produced, and that the background literature supporting your project is the most relevant and current.

Papers Prepared for the Mass Media. The findings of many research projects are made available to the public through the mass media. Usually this occurs at a second stage, after the research was first disseminated through another form (such as being presented at a professional meeting or appearing in a book). Sometimes the reports of such research are very brief and may be written by reporters on the basis of reading or hearing your paper. The journalist may telephone you to discuss the evidence.

You may also prepare a written piece or article for a mass-media form. Here the details of your methods cannot be given, though the most central facts (the size of your sample, the types of individuals sampled) will be needed. What is often left out entirely is the background literature, how the concepts were measured, and how the data were collected. There is a tendency to report the findings as bold facts with the only qualification being some general information on the sample. When you prepare such material yourself, be sure to include the most critical information the reader will need in order to apply your findings. If your measure of work orientation could be translated as "commitment" but not as "job satisfaction," then make certain that it is described accurately. If your finding is that the nursing homes you studied were deficient in some manner, make certain that the types of homes you actually observed are described quite explicitly. If there are any strong reservations hanging over your findings—let's say that you have grounds for doubting that your control group was comparable to the experimental group, so that the findings you have presented may not be completely fair—put them in. The public is rarely turned off by reservations if they are stated simply and directly. You cannot overload a piece for the mass media with qualifications and reservations, but the most central ones may be slipped in without overburdening it.

If you are writing for a nontechnical audience, you will need to drop all the jargon used in the field. Phrases such as "random sample," "control group," and "participant observer," which may be understood by anyone with an undergraduate course in research methods, will probably mean nothing to most readers of a newspaper. All these phrases can be described in other ways: a random sample might be described as a "fair representation of the voters of James County," a control group as a "comparable group who were not given the treatment," a participant observer as "one who visits an organization both to collect information for a study and to offer consultation to the management." Note that these phrases tend to be longer, which explains why technical jargon is often developed.

Finally, if you are preparing a piece for dissemination in the mass media, you may need to consider what it is about your study that would be most fascinating to a lay audience. You may have a finding which is relatively minor in terms of your overall study but which should form the basis of your piece because it addresses an issue of wide public interest. For example, if, in addition to the topic of your primary research, you have interesting data on the attitudes of Catholics toward abortion or the elderly to changes in taxing social security, these additional data may well appeal to the public.

Dissemination in Book Form. A book is a much more ambitious form of dissemination. Books based on social research studies often follow the general outlines of a research article, which will be given below; but sometimes they vary quite substantially from such an article. If the book will contain quantitative data in tables, it will be necessary to explain the methods used early in the manuscript. However, if the book is based on a field study, the methods may be left for the end and may only appear in an appendix. In such a field study, the goal is to try to get the writing to "flow" in a manner somewhat like a novel; complex explanations of methodological techniques should not impede this objective.

Books are also written for different audiences. Most books based on social research studies are intended for other researchers, faculty, students, and members of the public who have a particular interest in the subject matter. However, sometimes a social research project is the basis of a book which will have an even wider audience. The wider the audience you hope to address, the less you should emphasize your methodological techniques. These details may be cited in notes or references so that professionally interested readers may consult them if they wish. The wider the audience you hope to address, the more explicitly and simply you need to state your findings. The wider the audience you hope to attract, the more you must relate your findings to issues of current relevance to the general public. This is why social research is often written to address current social policy issues. The public is rarely interested simply in whether you have supported or refuted some other researcher, a hypothesis, or an abstract theory.

Commissioned Research Reports. These may be prepared because you are fulfilling the obligations of a grant or a contract or because you are preparing a report for an agency or organization which hired you to carry out a study for purposes of evaluation or to formulate policy. In such cases, there is nearly always an earlier proposal which was prepared to secure the grant. Your primary obligation is to give the agency what you promised. Often this is all you give them, all that is really wanted. But agencies do not want just data. They also want analyses that back the data up. Sometimes you may offer analyses that diverge from the original directives of the proposal because you feel certain that these new directions are relevant to the needs and interests of the granting agency. When you do this, you should make clear that what you are analyzing was not proposed earlier.

If the project is being carried out for an organization so that its managers can make decisions on the basis of it, you should offer your policy suggestions at the end of the report (this was discussed in Chapter 11 on evaluation research). Don't feel that it is presumptuous of you to do so because you are not an employee of the organization. You are only doing what you were paid to do. You may well have some hesitations about your policy suggestions, in which case you should simply state them. Be bold about your suggestions, however. It is always better to be explicit and forceful, while maintaining some reservations, than to be so timid and wishy-washy that it is impossible for those receiving the report to know precisely what you have concluded.

Multiple Dissemination Modes

As stated earlier, any research project could produce a great variety of written materials for different audiences and in different formats. What is necessary for each piece of writing is that the relevant audience be considered and the proper format be used. Once an initial writeup of a project has been prepared for one purpose, others can be devised which take up different aspects of the findings or which address different audiences. Whoever the audience and whatever the subject, it is necessary

to cast the problem for the paper in such a way that the attention of the audience is caught. That's why you must know what audience you are writing to!

Papers for courses, journals, or presentations often address problems which diverge from the initial ideas that fostered the project in the first place. As findings are discovered, the original research problem may be recast to lead up to newly discovered, interesting findings. This does not mean that finding that your initial hypothesis was not supported by the data means that you should bury this evidence. Scientific research should not ignore disproving hypotheses. In some cases, your initial hypothesis may be of such interest and importance that people will want to know that it was disproved. Often, however, the hypothesis may not be a matter of any wide interest, and to base a paper on showing that it was disproved may make little sense. Such an exercise may be appropriate for a course paper, but would not meet the requirements of having sufficient interest for a professional audience.

Any research project may produce numerous written papers. First you must write the paper that meets your primary commitment. Once this is done, you can consider how else to disseminate it. Some of the papers you write from a piece of research may be ones that were never considered in the early design stages of the project.

CASTING THE PROBLEM OF THE PAPER

Every paper needs a primary focus, usually a specific problem. Naturally, problems may vary enormously. David Caplovitz suggested that most quantitative research projects have one of the following three foci: a dependent variable, an independent variable, or a special group (1983, pp. 391–398). In a *dependent variable study,* the problem is to understand why, how, and under what conditions the dependent variable occurred. In survey research projects, the object may be to determine those other variables which are most strongly related to, or predictive of, the attribute of the dependent variable in which you are interested. Let me emphasize this point. Suppose you are studying why students drop out of college or the self-concept of male and female first-graders. In each case, you are focusing primarily on one end of the variable: in the dropout study, your interest is in why students leave college, not in why they stay (which is the other end of the variable). In the self-concept study, you would be interested in high, positive levels of self-esteem (or if it were a longitudinal study, you might be interested in positive changes in self-concept) more than in average or low levels. Naturally, you could just as easily be interested in why students stay in college or in low self-concept. The important thing is that you know what end of the variable interests you so that your study focuses clearly on that end.

Dependent variable studies are often easy to diagram. The dependent variable generally comes at the end of a number of other possibly contributing factors. One truism which is often stated (but is still worth repeating) is that the more clearly defined and easier to understand the dependent variable, the better able the researcher is to keep the project on a clear course. I remember when I was a graduate student, I knew a young man studying why students dropped out of college. He surveyed a sample of first-year students, and then at the beginning of the next academic year he was able to determine which ones had dropped out. This was a precise dependent variable. (Either a student had or had not dropped out.) The focus of the study was very sharp. In contrast, my study on the weakening of authoritarianism was much more difficult to handle. How far did students need to move on the Autonomy Scale before I considered their authoritarianism to have weakened? Furthermore, the very concept of authoritarianism (or autonomy) was much fuzzier to begin with. So when you design your study, ask yourself if you have a clear, precise dependent variable as your focus. It will facilitate and clarify your analyses and help to keep you on a sure path to your conclusions.

The *independent variable study* tends to

compare one social context to another. The income maintenance experiment described in Chapter 1 and many of the evaluation research projects in Chapter 11 were focused on an independent variable. While such studies examine the outcome or effects of such social programs (income maintenance programs, Head Start, a federal law, or whatever), the primary interest is in the program or social enactment itself. Did it bring about the desired effect? Did it have any effect? Often in an evaluation program, there may be variation built into the independent variable itself. (In the income maintenance programs, a number of conditions varied—the level of support, the city in which the experiment took place, etc.) Here the interest is in determining which form of the social program seemed to be the most effective. Those who commission the evaluation want to know whether the social program works, and, if it does, which form of the social program works best.

Finally, Caplovitz identified the type of study which focuses on a *special population*. This is typical of anthropological studies of primitive tribes or of studies of a particular group of people, such as the men who "hung out" at Jelly's Bar and the homosexuals of Humphreys' (1970) research described in Chapter 3. In these studies there is no control group with whom the special group is being contrasted. Usually these studies are very descriptive; they try to give a complex view of the group in question.

ORGANIZING A STUDENT RESEARCH PROJECT PAPER

Whatever the central focus of your project, you will do best to set up an outline of the sections you plan to include in your paper. The following seven-point outline should be applicable to nearly all types of research methods approaches. You might want to refer back at this point to the 11 steps of a research project described in Chapter 4. These steps will be collapsed into the seven parts of the research paper.

I. General Statement of the Research Problem

This will serve as the introduction to the paper. You must state clearly and concisely what your problem is, what the general issue is that the study will address. This will cover step 1 of the research project: *defining the research topic.* You will want to write this first, but you are likely to return to it once the analyses have been written to make some changes in it. Remember that while you went into this project with a firm (let's hope) research problem in mind so that you might have written this general statement before you collected your data, the research problem may well have altered somewhat over the course of your project.

Here is where the type of focus your study has—whether it centers on a search for the determinants of a dependent variable, on an appraisal of a program or condition serving as the independent variable, or on a special group—will be addressed. Sometimes students are confused about exactly what they are studying. One might say, "I'm studying people who voted for Perot." Yet note that this could imply many different types of studies. Is the student studying the characteristics of those who voted for Perot in contrast to those who did not? Or is the student studying why Perot supporters voted for him? The general problem must be stated in such a way that the design of the study, the data collection, and the analyses make logical sense as a way to address this problem. The section defines the purpose of the study, the reason why you are carrying it out. If it is to explore, describe, or explain a problem, this must be stated in the beginning of the study.

II. Background of the Problem

Research problems do not fall ready-made from outer space. They grow from the ideas and findings of earlier studies, earlier observations of what we are studying. Therefore you must present these earlier findings. This is the background literature, or review of the literature, section which covers step 2 of the research project: *finding out what is known about the topic.* To find the most central and important studies which have laid the groundwork for your study is not a simple task. Naturally you must understand clearly what your primary focus is. If you are writing a dependent variable study, you will need to have reviewed research by others on the same variable.

Other studies on your topic may be numerous. In selecting which of these to include in your review, consider the following points:

1. How similar to your study is the other one in terms of the variables studied, the types of samples used, and the theoretical positions put forth?

2. How recent is the study? All things considered, a more recent study is more useful to you if it has been well done, because it should have taken into account earlier studies. This stems from the cumulative nature of science.

3. Are the researchers who carried out the study important sources of authority on the subject? This is the issue of reputation. As in all fields, social research has its stars. Certain researchers have an eminence and established reputation which makes their research more prominent than the work of lesser-known social researchers. Now this is a somewhat complex issue. That someone does not have a famous reputation does not mean that his or her work is not good. Another problem for a student is that you may be much less familiar with who is and who is not prominent in any given area. If you look through enough studies on your topic, however, you will find that certain researchers are cited repeatedly. These are surely the more prominent ones. You cannot be certain, however, that every citation is a good one. The only way to determine the quality of the reference is to examine the study itself and weigh it according to the canons of research techniques that you have learned. You will probably want to address the work of the most

central researchers in the field, whatever else you do; but do not neglect the work of other scholars that you think is important for your purposes.

There are also a number of *don'ts* for a literature review:

- *Don't* use articles from the mass media as if they were social research articles. Although you may get some statistical material or ideas from newspapers or popular magazines, you do not want to base your study on the writings of journalists. Theirs is a different field, a different way of collecting and presenting material.
- *Don't* include a study in your literature review simply because it addresses a topic similar to your own. Be critical. If you haven't learned anything of interest concerning your research project by reading the article, then don't use it.
- *Don't* simply use the abstract of the article or transfer the abstract into your paper almost verbatim. Read the article searching for those parts which are most relevant to your study and then report on this material. You will need to say a few general things about each study you report on, such as the general problem being studied and the type of sample used. Otherwise, use from an article the precise points you need; these are rarely found in an abstract!
- *Don't* automatically assume that if a piece of research studies a concept with the same name as the one you study, these concepts are directly comparable. Remember that how the concept has been operationalized and measured in each case may be so different that you are really dealing with two concepts bearing the same label with very little else in common. Be sure to explain how central concepts in the research which you are comparing to your study were measured in the study under review.

In writing the literature review, keep it well organized. Often such a review will have a number of subheadings indicating the various subareas of the study which are being addressed. For example, in writing an article on work orientation in women, my colleague Judith Bootcheck and I (Baker and Bootcheck, 1985) divided the literature review section into two major parts:

1. *The Changing Conception of Women's Work Orientation.* This section addressed the various conceptions of women's work attitudes which came to bear on what we termed *work orientation,* including earlier-developed concepts of *career aspirations, career expectations, career commitment, career salience, taste for employment.* The object of this section was to lay the groundwork for our use and operationalization of the concept of work orientation. It was the part of the literature review that focused on our dependent variable.
2. *Work Orientation in Women: Factors Related to Change.* This section addressed the various independent variables in the study. The subsections included (1) higher education, career preparation, and training; (2) marriage, motherhood, and singlehood; (3) sex-role ideology; and (4) characteristics of family of origin (mother's employment and social status). Under each of these sections, we reported on studies in which these factors were related to some quality of women's work orientation.

Literature review sections should be full of good, relevant material explained clearly and concisely. Remember that you are reporting on other work only because it will bear on your study. For this reason, literature review sections usually cannot be written until your analyses have been carried out so that you are certain what the variables of central import in your study are. However, many researchers prepare a preliminary draft of their literature review section following their search of the literature at the beginning of the project.

III. Design of the Study

This is where the formal statement of your specific research question or hypothesis is made. Generally you draw on ideas that were introduced first in

Section I on the general statement and developed in Section II on the background literature. Your paper should build in Sections I and II with a kind of crescendo to this Section III, where the problem you will be addressing in this paper is explicitly laid out.

It should be clear in most cases from the research question or hypothesis what type of study focus you have, what your primary dependent and independent variables will be. In some cases, diagrams of the research model are presented. The major concepts should be defined theoretically and explained operationally. This undertaking accomplishes step 3 of the research project: *clarifying concepts and their measurement.* The exact measurement of the central variables may not be presented until the analysis section, but a description of the operationalized variables and the research instruments which measured them should be offered. If you are addressing or testing a specific theory, this theory should be laid out and associated with your study objectives here in this section. Remember this is where it should be made clear whether the study was deductive (hypothesis testing) or inductive.

IV. How the Data Were Obtained

This is the section of your paper that tells the reader *how* you did the study. It is the central methods section. There are always two primary aspects to the design: the first is what you did to get the data (data collection); the second is from whom you got the data (the sample).

Data Collection Methods. The research method used to gather your data needs to be described carefully. In this section you must report how you *established an appropriate data collection method,* which was step 4 in your research project. No aspect of your method should be ignored in preparing this section, though some aspects may need to be mentioned only very briefly. The section should also include the type of instrument used. The general issues of operationalization, reliability, and validity should be highlighted in this

discussion. Thus this section of the written paper also describes step 5 of the research project: *the design of the research instruments,* which includes the *operationalized concepts.* The exact measurement of the central variables may not be presented until the analysis section, but a description of the operationalized variables should be offered. The section should describe the conditions under which the data were collected, the identity of the data collectors, the training of the data collectors, the type of pretesting done, and some evaluation of the data collection procedures so that any weaknesses may be considered in appraising the evidence.

How the Sample Was Designed. A detailed but concise description of the sample studied must be given. This was step 6 in our research project: *selecting a sample of subjects to study.* If you developed your own sample, you must compare your final sample to the one you hoped to obtain. Remember to offer a definition of the population from whom the sample was drawn. Don't make your sample sound better than it is. If you have collected your own data using a purposive sample, there is nothing wrong with that. Be forthright about what you have; this will strengthen, not weaken, your study. Sometimes tables are presented that summarize basic characteristics of the sample, such as sex distribution, work status, educational status, age, race, or other factors which are central to your study.

Ethical Issues. It is usually in the data collection and sample selection phases that the ethical issues arise. Were respondents deceived in any way? Was the role of the researcher covert? Did the data collection procedures or specific questions invade the privacy of others? How far had your subjects given an *informed consent* to their own participation in your study? There may be reasons to use some forms of deception or covert research activities, but you should know and state explicitly the ethical issues raised and how you tried to deal with them. You should explain how the confidentiality or anonymity of your subjects was preserved, if indeed it was. Addressing the ethical issues of your research will cover step 7 of your research proposal: *the purpose, value, and ethics of the study.* This section has covered the outcome of step 8 in the research project: *data collection.* Remember that for a survey research project, it is essential to report the *response rate.* Results of pretesting and refining the data collection procedures should be addressed if they affected the final data obtained.

V. Analysis of Data

This is the heart of your paper. Yet without the introductory materials in the earlier section, the reasons for the analysis and an understanding of what the data represent could not be reached. Don't just report "the facts." Remember that all facts must be interpreted, and it is the choice of interpretations (as well as the choice of facts) that will form the basis of the analysis. In order to analyze the data, you first had to accomplish step 9 of the research project: *processing the data.* However, these procedures are rarely elaborated in a paper, though they might be referred to in a methodological footnote or appendix. The written analyses cover step 10 of the research project: *analyzing the data.*

In quantitative studies, this section has the tables in it. These tables must be carefully planned so that they show the reader what he or she needs to be shown to understand the table. Tables must be well labeled and must be presented in a format which is conventionally used for that type of data. By looking at the presentation of other tables in studies similar to your own, you will develop a sense of how your tables should look. Remember that there are many different ways of presenting a cross tabulation; some styles are used more often in certain types of journals. But however they are set up, they must be readily accessible to others.

Quantitative studies often begin with a summary table offering some basic evidence on the frequency of the dependent variable in relation to

one or more other central factors in the study. Such a table may be a series of different frequency distributions strung together; in such a case, not all categories of each independent variable need to be presented. Tables then move across the analysis trying to address all the theoretical issues raised by the research problem. When multivariate analyses are used, such tables are often the last in a paper, since they serve to tie together all of the tables presented earlier.

In a field study, the analysis section offers the findings of the study in relation to the problem you set out to study. Since there are no hard, numerical "facts" to substantiate your position, you must present your findings in such a convincing manner that they are seen as fulfilling your research concerns.

Analysis sections need to be highly focused. Beware of a tendency to report every finding, to move from one point to the next without a clear sense of which findings are more important and more central to the purpose of your study. Don't let the analysis get out of hand: you must keep it in control by addressing *only* what is relevant to your research concern. Many of your findings, let's say from a survey, should not be reported. I am not urging you to throw out findings that seem insignificant but to be strict with yourself in deciding what is really important for your presentation and what is not.

If you are writing a course research paper testing a hypothesis, and your evidence does not support it, report that. Negative findings can be as interesting as positive ones. It is difficult, however, to write a paper on a nonexistent finding. It can be done. But it is also fair, and widely practiced, to reexamine your data for other potentially more interesting analyses.

VI. Discussion

Once you have presented your findings, you need to discuss them in more general terms, relating them back to what your expectations were when you designed the study. In other words, the discussion should relate the empirical findings back to the theory. This covers step 11 in the research project: *presenting the results.* Here, if a hypothesis is not proven, is the time to speculate on why this might be the case. Did the study address (or even challenge) a paradigm in the social sciences? Here, you may relate your major findings to those of others mentioned in the review of literature section. Did you corroborate their findings? Did your analyses offer different dimensions that now need to be considered in the discussion of this research topic? Make clear what is important, even memorable, about this study. Is there any method or finding of your research that might be profitably used by other researchers?

VII. Conclusions and Summary

What did this research project prove? Was the program evaluated effectively? What brought about change in the dependent variable? What was the central meaning of the environment studied in the field? What was the significance of the content analyzed? These are the questions you must ask yourself and answer for your reader in the conclusion of your paper. You might look back to Chapter 3 on the uses of social research for assistance. What in your study might be considered worthwhile and contributing to the field? Did your study address the changing nature of society? Did it have a dynamic quality in which institutions or individuals undergoing changes were examined? Were there implications in the findings of your study for current social policies or laws? Did your research lead to a deeper understanding of a social group, a condition, or an event? Such questions, if appropriate, might be addressed in your conclusions. In addition, suggestions for future research might be offered.

A brief summary of the study may come at the end of the paper, or in some cases, as in journal articles, it may be abbreviated as an abstract at the beginning. The summary will touch on all of the seven sections: stating the general problem; possibly referring to an important earlier finding; describing the research design; data collection and sampling procedures; analyzing the data; giving the central findings; and making a brief conclusion.

JUST BEFORE YOU FINISH A RESEARCH PROJECT

When you are nearly at the end of writing your research project, stop and consider some of the important issues that were discussed earlier in this book. Did the study support the rationale for doing the study in the first place? Now consider what was, in Chapter 3, suggested as one use of social research: Did the study make use of some experience of yours, some particular knowledge, so that you were able to capitalize on your strengths in the course of the research project? Often the quality of a research effort will represent a project which highlighted the strengths of its researcher. It often is the case, however, that a project may get bogged down in the areas of your weakness. It is in such situations that the research project itself becomes a teacher. You find you learn what you need to learn for the project.

In such a sense, doing research is a form of education, of growing, of trying to use your own strengths, and of improving your abilities. You've done a "scientific" study based on explanatory models and with empirical evidence. You were forced to be creative in this study because you had to figure out how to measure, to question, to organize, and to develop a new way of doing something. At the end of a course in research methods, students often say, "Whew! I never thought I'd make it." When you've finished your project, ask yourself what you've gained in the course of carrying out a research project. You may conclude that what you have learned is among the most valuable sets of skills and knowledge you've been exposed to. Now having thought about what you as a student or as a young researcher may have learned from doing a research project, ask yourself what you have contributed by doing your social research. Maybe you have in some small (or not so small) way added to what we know about how our society works. Thanks for doing social research.

REVIEW NOTES

- The basic ingredients for writing a research report are a clear topic, a review of the relevant evidence, a research design, and the analyzed data.
- The degree of detail in discussing the methods used will vary with the form of dissemination of the research project being prepared.
- Types of research papers that might be prepared include those written (1) to fulfill course requirements; (2) to be presented to professional or academic audiences; (3) to publish in professional and academic journals; (4) for popular journals, magazines, newspapers, television, or other mass-media forms; (5) in the form of a book; or (6) as a commissioned research report.
- Caplovitz proposed that all quantitative research projects have one of three foci: a dependent variable, an independent variable, or a special group. In a dependent variable study, the aim is to understand why, how, and under what conditions the dependent variable occurred. In an independent variable study, one social context is compared to another. In a special population study, usually based on qualitative data, the primary aim is to develop a careful description of the special population.
- A seven-point outline for a student research report should have the following sections:
  1. A general statement of the problem
  2. Background to the problem based on a review of the related literature
  3. The research model and design of the study
  4. How the data were obtained, including the data collection procedure, the method and success of the sampling procedure, a consideration of ethical issues, and the results of the data collection

  5. An analysis of the data
  6. A discussion of the findings
  7. The conclusion and summary

KEY TERMS

dependent variable study
independent variable study
proposal
special population study

STUDY EXERCISE

1. If your assignment for this term has been to prepare a proposal for a project or to complete a project, briefly show what you would include under each of the seven points of the research outline.

RECOMMENDED READINGS

1. Becker, Howard S.: *Writing for Social Scientists: How to Start and Finish Your Thesis, Book, or Article,* University of Chicago Press, Chicago, 1986. An engaging book on writing for academic purposes. Becker relates many of his own experiences as a researcher, writer, and editor. The book offers fertile suggestions to facilitate writing and to try to avoid the hangups (what to do if you can't say it just right, how to edit by ear). There is a good chapter by Pamela Richards on the need to take risks.
2. Richardson, Laurel: *Writing Strategies: Reaching Diverse Audiences,* Sage, Newbury Park, Calif., 1990. Covers science writing, literary devices, narrative, establishing authority and discovering a collective story.
3. Strunk, William, Jr., and E. B. White: *The Elements of Style,* Macmillan, New York, 1959. This is a classic work on writing that has been very influential among both academic and nonacademic writers.
4. Sociology Writing Group: *A Guide to Writing Sociology Papers,* 2d ed., St. Martin's Press, New York, 1991. This helpful volume was written by a group of teaching assistants, counselors, and writing tutors in the sociology and English departments at the University of California, Los Angeles. It is a practical guide

to preparing a paper based on a textual analysis or on library, field, or quantitative research.

5. Van Wagenen, R. Keith: *Writing a Thesis: Substance and Style,* Prentice-Hall, Englewood Cliffs, N.J., 1991. How to write up research, particularly in the social and behavioral sciences, is the subject of this volume. Writing a research introduction, results from various types of statistical analyses, discussion sections, and suggestions for improving writing styles are addressed.

6. Wolcott, Harry F.: *Writing Up Qualitative Research,* Sage, Newbury Park, Calif., 1990. This readily accessible guide to writing up field studies has many thoughtful suggestions for students.

Using a Library
for Social Research

INTRODUCTION

*I*n Chapter 4 there is a discussion of how to use the library to enhance your knowledge about a research topic. To do this effectively you must know the range of resources that are available to you and the best methods of accessing and utilizing those resources.

There are a number of very good overall guidebooks on how to use the library to help you carry out social research. The following useful guides cover a range of reference sources in social science disciplines as well as in the subject-oriented sociological fields: Pauline Bart and Linda Frankel, *The Student Sociologist's Handbook* (Random House, New York, 1986); Stephen H. Aby, *Sociology: A Guide to Reference and Information Sources* (Libraries Unlimited, Littleton, Co., 1987); and Patricia McMillan and James R. Kennedy, Jr., *Library Research Guide to Sociology* (Piernan Press, Ann Arbor, Mich., 1981). In a related area, Jeffrey G. Reed and Pam M. Baxter [*Library Use: A Handbook for Psychology* (American Psychological Association, Washington, D.C., 1992)] cover similar resources with examples from the field of psychology; they suggest methods of locating psychological tests and measures. For women's studies, see Susan E. Searing, *Introduction to Library Research in Women's Studies* (Westview Press, Boulder, Co., 1985), an annotated bibliography of traditional reference aids; and Elizabeth H. Oakes and Kathleen E. Sheldon, *A Guide to Social Science Resources in Women's Studies* (ABC-Clio Books, Santa Barbara, Calif., 1978), an evaluation of social science literature on women. This appendix will cover some of the most important resources in the field and will describe how to find and use them.

USING THE ONLINE/CARD CATALOG

The online (computer) or card catalog in a university or college library is a listing of all titles the library holds, indexed by author, title, subject, and in many cases key words (or words in the title). To find the correct subject heading for your topic, consult the *Library of Congress Subject Headings* (Library of Congress, Washington, D.C., 1992) located in the reference section of your library. Box A-1 gives some abbreviations the Library of Congress uses to help a reader narrow or broaden a topic search. If, for example, you were looking up the Coleman study in your college library, you would likely find it under such subjects as "Academic Achievement" or "High School Students—United States—Statistics." Similarly, if you looked under the subject heading "Juvenile Delinquency," you would find Hirschi's *Causes of Delinquency* (1969).

The field studies described in Chapter 1 were all the basis of books. If you do not know the name of the author of a specific study in your area of interest, then searching subject headings can be especially helpful. For example, Kanter's book *Men and Women of the Corporation* (1977) could be found under both "Organizational Behavior" and "Women—White Collar Workers." Under what topics would you find Anderson's study of Jelly's Bar? Some possibilities are "Small Groups—Case Studies" or "Social Status—Case Studies." These books will also be cataloged under their authors' names, but searching by subject will uncover other studies in the area you are interested in. Looking at current studies will often give you references to older classic studies.

Your library may also have access via computer to the online catalogs of other libraries. Books

for which you have a citation but which you cannot find in your library can generally be requested through interlibrary loan.

FINDING RELEVANT PRINTED MATERIAL

Book Reviews

One way to find books related to your topic of interest is to read book reviews. Many journals include reviews of books within that journal's field. *Contemporary Sociology* is a sociological journal devoted solely to book reviews. Books are grouped under the major subfields of the discipline. For example, Coleman's book would be reviewed under "Education" and Hirschi's under "Crime." However some books could fit into more than one category. Kantor's book could come under "Organizations" or "Gender" but in fact was reviewed in a symposium in the opening section of the journal. Other journals, such as the *American Journal of Sociology,* regularly include some book reviews.

If your topic relates to psychology, check for book reviews in *Contemporary Psychology.* For social work topics, book reviews may be found in *Social Work, Social Case Work, and Social Service Review.*

To find book reviews on topics of current popular interest, look for the *New York Review of Books* and the *New York Times Book Review,* a section of the Sunday *New York Times.* These national publications include social research books that have a wide public interest as well as the usual fiction reviews. Finally, both *Book Review Digest* and *Book Review Index* will tell you where

BOX A-1

LIBRARY OF CONGRESS SUBJECT HEADINGS: ABBREVIATIONS		
UF = Used For	NT = Narrower Terms	SA = See Also
BT = Broader Terms	RT = Related Terms	USE = Use Instead Of

BIBLIOGRAPHIES TO USE IN DEVELOPING A SOCIAL RESEARCH TOPIC

GENERAL

Bibliographic Index, Wilson, New York, 1938.

International Bibliography of Sociology, Aldine, Chicago, 1951.

London Bibliography of the Social Sciences, Mansell Information, London, 1929.

A World Bibliography of Bibliographies, 4th ed., Theodore Besterman (ed.), Societas Bibliographica, Lausanne, 1965; Alice F. Toomey, updated 1964–74, Rowan & Littlefield, Totowa, N.J., 1977.

SPECIAL TOPICS

Aging/Elderly

Abuse of the Elderly: Issues and Annotated Bibliography, Benjamin Schlesinger and Rachel Schlesinger, University of Toronto Press, Toronto, 1988.

The Black Aged in the United States: A Selectively Annotated Bibliography, Lenwood G. Davis, Greenwood, New York, 1989.

Crime and the Elderly: An Annotated Bibliography, Ron H. Aday, Greenwood, New York, 1988.

The Elderly in America: A Bibliography, Joan Nordquist, Reference and Research Services, Santa Cruz., Calif., 1991.

Families and Aging: A Selected, Annotated Bibliography, Jean M. Coyle, Greenwood, New York, 1991.

Women and Aging: A Selected, Annotated Bibliography, Jean M. Coyle, Greenwood, New York, 1989.

AIDS

AIDS Bibliography, U.S. Department of Health and Human Services, Bethesda, Md., 1988.

AIDS: Political, Social, International Aspects, Joan Nordquist, Reference and Research Services, Santa Cruz., Calif., 1988.

Crime and Delinquency

Capital Punishment in America: An Annotated Bibliography, Michael L. Radelet and Margaret Vandiver, Garland, New York, 1988.

Child Abuse and Neglect: An Information and Reference Guide, Timothy J. Iverson and Marilyn Segal, Garland, New York, 1990.

Citizen Involvement in Crime Prevention: A Selected Bibliography, 1982–1987, Verna Casey, Vance Bibliographies, Monticello, Ill., 1988.

Comparative Criminology: An Annotated Bibliography, Piers Beirne and Joan Hill, Greenwood Press, New York, 1991.

Criminal Justice Ethics: Annotated Bibliography and Guide to Sources, Frank Schmalleger, Greenwood Press, New York, 1991.

Domestic Violence: Spouse Abuse, Marital Rape, Joan Nordquist, Reference and Research Services, Santa Cruz., Calif., 1986.

Mass Murder: An Annotated Bibliography, Michael Newton, Garland, New York, 1988.

Native North Americans: Crime, Conflict and Criminal Justice: A Research Bibliography, Charles Horn and Curt Taylor Griffiths, Northern Justice Society, Buraby, B.C., 1989.

Pornography and Censorship, Joan Nordquist, Reference and Research Services, Santa Cruz., Calif., 1987.

Rape: A Bibliography, Joan Nordquist, Reference and Research Services, Santa Cruz., Calif., 1990.

Research on Men Who Batter: An Overview, Bibliography and Resource Guide, Edward W. Gondolf, Human Services Institute, Bradenton, Fla., 1988.

Terrorism, 1980–1990: A Bibliography, Amos Lakos, Westview Press, Boulder, Col., 1991.

Terrorism in the United States and Europe 1800–1959: An Annotated Bibliography, Michael Newton and Judy Ann Newton, Garland, New York, 1988.

Violence Against Women: A Bibliography, Joan Nordquist, Reference and Research Services, Santa Cruz., Calif., 1992.

Drugs and Alcohol

Children of Alcoholics: A Bibliography and Resource Guide, 4th ed., Robert J. Ackerman and Judith A. Michaels, Health Communications, Deerfield Beach, Fla., 1990.

Cocaine: An Annotated Bibliography, Carlton E. Turner, University Press of Mississippi, Jackson, Miss., 1988.

Native American Youth and Alcohol: An Annotated Bibliography, Michael L. Lobb and Thomas D. Watts, Greenwood Press, New York, 1989.

Substance Abuse I: Drug Abuse: A Bibliography, Joan Nordquist, Reference and Research Services, Santa Cruz., Calif., 1989.

Substance Abuse II: Drug Abuse: A Bibliography, Joan Nordquist, Reference and Research Services, Santa Cruz., Calif., 1990.

Ethnic Studies

Asian American Studies: An Annotated Bibliography and Research Guide, Hyungchan Kim, Greenwood Press, New York, 1989.

Black Adolescence: Current Issues and Annotated Bibliography, The Consortium for Research on Black Adolescence with Velma McBride Murry, G. K. Hall, Boston, Mass., 1990.

Black Females in the United States: A Bibliography from 1967–1987, Christine C. Iijima Hall and Brenda J. Evans, American Psychological Association, Washington, D.C., 1989.

Black Males in the United States: An Annotated Bibliography from 1967–1987, Brenda J. Evans and James R. Whitfield, American Psychological Association, Washington, D.C., 1988.

BorderLine: A Bibliography of the United States-Mexico Borderlands, Barbara G. Valk, UCLA Latin American Center Publications, Los Angeles, 1988.

Immigrant Women in the United States: A Selectively Annotated Multidisciplinary Bibliography, Donna Gabaccia, Greenwood Press, New York, 1989.

Selected Bibliography of Social Science Readings on Women of Color in the United States, Center for Research on Women, Memphis, Tenn., 1989.

Women of Color and Southern Women: A Bibliography of Social Science Research, Center for Research on Women, Memphis, Tenn., 1988.

Family Studies

Children and Adjustment to Divorce: An Annotated Bibliography, Mary M. Nofsinger, Garland, New York, 1989.

Families in Transition: An Annotated Bibliography, Judith DeBoard Sadler, Archon Books, Hamden, Conn., 1988.

Mothers and Mothering: An Annotated Feminist Bibliography, Penelope Dixon, Garland, New York, 1991.

Mass Media

Mass Media Sex and Adolescent Values: An Annotated Bibliography and Directory of Organizations, A. Odasuo Alali, McFarland & Co., Jefferson, N.C., 1991.

Television and Young People: A Bibliography of International Literature 1969–1989, Kurt Aimiller, K. G. Saur, New York, 1989.

Violence and Terror in the Mass Media: An Annotated Bibliography, Nancy Signorielli and George Gerbner, Greenwood Press, New York, 1988.

Religion

Social Science and the Cults: An Annotated Bibliography, John A. Saliba, Garland, New York, 1990.

The Sociology of Religion: An Organizational Bibliography, Anthony J., Blasi and Michael W. Cuneo, Garland, New York, 1990.

Women's Studies/Feminism

Bibliography on Southern Women, Center for Research on Women, Memphis, Tenn., 1989.

Eating Disorders: Feminist, Historical, Cultural, Psychological Aspects: A Bibliography, Joan Nordquist, Reference and Research Services, Santa Cruz., Calif., 1989.

BOX A-2 *(continued)*

Female Psychology: An Annotated Psychoanalytic Bibliography, Eleanor Schuker and Nadine A. Levinson, Analytic Press, Hillsdale, N.J., 1991.

Feminism and Women's Issues: An Annotated Bibliography and Research Guide, G. Llewelyn Watson, Garland, New York, 1990.

The Feminist Movement: A Bibliography, Joan Nordquist, Reference and Research Services, Santa Cruz., Calif., 1992.

The Feminization of Poverty in the United States: A Selected Annotated Bibliography of the Issues, 1978–1989, Renee Feinberg and Kathleen E. Knox, Garland, New York, 1990.

Feminist Research Methods: An Annotated Bibliography, Connie Miller, Greenwood Press, New York, 1991.

Women's Diaries, Journals and Letters: An Annotated Bibliography, Cheryl Cline, Garland, New York, 1989.

Women's Issues: An Annotated Bibliography, Laura Stempel Mumford, Salem Press, Pasadena, Calif., 1989.

A Women's Studies Select Bibliography: With a Third World Emphasis, Annette Knight, University of the West Indies, St. Augustine, Trinidad and Tobago, 1988.

to locate reviews of books from many different fields. *Book Review Digest* includes brief abstracts of the reviews.

Bibliographies

There are bibliographies at many levels: the broadest are bibliographies of bibliographies; next are bibliographies of broad disciplines; last and most narrow are bibliographies of specific fields or subjects. Some bibliographies are annotated, i.e., they offer a short abstract or description of each book. Others just give basic bibliographical information: author, title, publisher, publication place, and date. Box A-2 gives some examples of bibliographies—with a special emphasis on recent bibliographies—that may be available in the reference section of your library. Check with a reference librarian on where to locate bibliographies in your field of interest.

Encyclopedias and Handbooks

Encyclopedias define a field's key concepts and provide information on the major leaders in that field. Handbooks and annual reviews contain an edited collection of articles that provide an authoritative summary of a specific topic, including evaluations of theory and research. The essays address the most important subjects, methods, and problems currently being studied. When doing research, you want to consider older studies in the field as well as current studies and annual reviews to bring you up to date on current concerns. Box A-3 gives a selection of handbooks and encyclopedias covering various subfields.

Journal Articles

Most published sociological research appears in the form of journal articles. The best way to find articles relating to a topic that interests you is to look in one of the indexes listed below.

Indexes and Abstracts in the Social Sciences

Begin with the *Social Sciences Index* (New York, Wilson, 1974–), which was formerly the *Social Sciences and Humanities Index,* and before that

BOX A-3

HANDBOOKS AND ENCYCLOPEDIAS TO USE IN DEVELOPING A SOCIAL RESEARCH TOPIC

ENCYCLOPEDIAS

Encyclopedia of Alcoholism, Robert O'Brien and Morris Chafetz, Facts on File, New York, 1982.

Encyclopedia of Child Abuse, Robin E. Clark and Judith Freeman Clark, Facts on File, New York, 1989.

Encyclopedia of Drug Abuse, Robert O'Brien and Sidney Cohen, Facts on File, New York, 1984.

Encyclopedia of Feminism, Lisa Tuttle, Facts on File, New York, 1986.

Encyclopedia of Sociology, Macmillan, New York, 1991.

Harvard Encyclopedia of American Ethnic Groups, Stephan Thernstrom, Belknap, Cambridge, Mass., 1980.

International Encyclopedia of the Social Sciences, David L. Sills, Macmillan, New York, 1986.

Women's Studies Encyclopedia, Helen Tremey, Greenwood Press, New York, 1989–91.

HANDBOOKS

AIDS Crisis in America: A Reference Handbook, Mary Ellen Hombs, ABC-CIO, Santa Barbara, Calif., 1991.

Alcohol and Drug Abuse Handbook, Roland E. Herrington, W. H. Green, St. Louis, Mo., 1987.

Analyzing Gender: A Handbook of Social Science Research, Beth B. Hess and Myra Marx Ferree, Sage Publications, Newbury Park, Calif., 1987.

Child Abuse and Neglect: An Information and Reference Guide, Timothy J. Iverson and Marilyn Segal, Garland, New York, 1990.

Criminology: A Contemporary Handbook, Joseph F. Sheley, Wadsworth, Belmont, Calif., 1991.

Handbook of Aging and the Social Sciences, 3d ed., Robert H. Binstock and Linda K. George, Academic Press, San Diego, Calif., 1990.

Handbook of Clinical Social Work, Aaron Rosenblatt and Diana Waldfogel, Jossey-Bass, San Francisco, Calif., 1983.

Handbook of Consumer Behavior, Thomas S. Robertson and Harold H. Kassarjian, Prentice-Hall, Englewood Cliffs, N.J., 1991.

Handbook of Marriage and the Family, Marvin K. Sussman and Suzanne K. Steinmetz, Plenum Press, New York, 1987.

International Handbook on Race and Race Relations, Jay A. Sigler, Greenwood Press, New York, 1987.

Prostitution: An International Handbook on Trends, Problems and Policies, Nanette J. Davis, Greenwood Press, Westport, Conn., 1993.

The Student Sociologist's Handbook, 2d ed., Pauline Bart and Linda Frankel, General Learning Press, Morristown, N.J., 1976.

Women in Sociology: A Bio-Bibliographical Sourcebook, Mary Jo Deegan, Greenwood Press, New York, 1991.

---

the *International Index of Social Sciences and Humanities.* This index lists articles from social science journals under subject and author headings.

Sociological Abstracts, or "Soc Abstracts," as it is often called, is a primary index for sociology and related disciplines. After locating an article in the *Social Sciences Index,* you can turn to *Sociological Abstracts* to get a brief abstract of the article. You can also use the abstracts as a primary source for locating articles from 1,200 scholarly journals. Since 1986, *Sociological Abstracts* has indexed articles according to the *Thesaurus of So-*

ciological Indexing Terms, which provides an alphabetical list of subject headings. The *Thesaurus* also uses *historical notes* to help you in locating articles published before 1986.

If your topic is in the area of social psychology, you should look in *Psychological Abstracts.* This series is indexed according to the subject headings in the *Thesaurus of Psychological Indexing Terms.* For education topics, check ERIC (*Educational Resources Information Center*), which is divided into two resources: (1) CIJE (*Current Index to Journals In Education*) and (2) RIE (*Resources in Education*). CIJE provides subject and author access to articles from approximately 800 journals in education and related disciplines. RIE is an index to published and unpublished curriculum guides, research reports, conference proceedings, and other types of documents collected by ERIC. Many libraries also carry the microfiche that RIE indexes, usually filed by the ERIC document number found in the index. Both RIE and CIJE contain brief abstracts of the cited articles and use the *Thesaurus of ERIC Descriptors* as a source of subject headings.

If your topic is in criminology, examine *Crime and Delinquency Abstracts;* if it has to do with studies on children, look at *Child Development Abstracts and Bibliography;* if your topic concerns an area of social work, check *Social Work Research and Abstracts,* which indexes almost all social work journals and offers short abstracts of articles.

If you are unable to locate an article you are seeking in the *Social Sciences Index* or *Sociological Abstracts,* try the *Public Affairs Information Service* (PAIS), which indexes (in addition to journal articles) government publications, pamphlets, and reports of agencies; or try *Human Resources Abstracts,* which includes many abstracts of unpublished reports on social action programs, governmental and community programs, and printed materials.

If you are looking for earlier material, examine the *Combined Retrospective Index Set to Journals in Sociology, 1895–1974* (CRIS), which has indexed over 100,000 articles under 86 categories.

Using a Citation Index

Once you have found an article that interests you, another way to expand your search and locate other relevant articles is to use the *Social Sciences Citation Index* (SSCI). Citation indexes are based on the idea that published research in an area includes references to previously published papers which provided the basis for the new work. Therefore, if you can locate an important early article in the field, you should be able to identify later articles that cite that source. The SSCI provides complete coverage of approximately 1,400 journals, with selective coverage of a further 3,300 journals in the social sciences. It contains four main divisions: the Citation Index, the Source Index, the Corporate Index, and the Permuterm Subject Index.

To use the SSCI, take an article of central interest to you and turn to the Citation Index to find where the author has been cited. The citations are listed first by the journal and then by the author of the article. When you find the name of someone who cited your first author in a journal that may be relevant to your interests, turn to the Source Index to find the exact citation of that article (in this location, the affiliation of the author will be listed as well). Alternatively, if you do not have a specific article of interest to work from but you do have a specific subject of interest, you can start at the Permuterm Subject Index, which indexes significant words (key words) from articles. Under the subject of interest are various subcategories of subjects, each with one or more authors cited. From these authors turn back to the Source Index for a complete citation. SSCI takes some practice to use but in return offers a number of ways to locate articles in your area of interest.

The SSCI is a very expensive index, so not all libraries have this tool. If yours does not, ask a reference librarian to direct you to a library that does.

COMPUTER SEARCHES

So far we have mentioned a number of tools that you can use to identify literature in your field. If you have a topic that combines several different concepts, this type of search can be especially time-consuming. If your search is complex, conducting your search on a computer in a CD-ROM (compact disk read-only memory) or online database will make your task much easier.

Because many different CD-ROM and online databases are available, there are also many different search techniques. Most libraries that have these available will also have handouts or brochures on how to search the database, or you may ask a reference librarian. In beginning your search, you need to choose a database relevant to your subject and then structure your search strategy so that you will obtain the most relevant citations and abstracts.

In Box A-4 is a selected list of databases, some of which may be available in your library. Some of the databases are available only on CD-ROM and some only online on such services as Dialog or BRS After Dark. Some are available in both formats. Some libraries have other online services, for example, Lexis/Nexis (good for current events and newspaper articles) or CARL UnCover (a general index to about 10,000 journals across all disciplines). Check with a reference librarian to find out exactly what CD-ROM and online databases your library offers.

Once you have selected an appropriate database, follow these steps:

1. State your topic concisely (e.g., *health care of women in Southeast Asia*).
2. Write down the major concepts in your topic (e.g., *health care, women, Southeast Asia*).
3. Look up the major concepts in the thesaurus for your database. (For example, the thesaurus for Sociofile is the *Thesaurus of Sociological Indexing Terms.*)
4. Write down the terms from the thesaurus that define your topic. (Using the *Thesaurus of Sociological Indexing Terms,* they would be *Health Care, Females, Southeast Asia.*)
5. Write out your search statement using the connectors *and* or *or* between subjects (*i.e., Health Care and Females and Southeast Asia*).

If you do not retrieve enough articles, you can expand your search by eliminating one of your terms (e.g., eliminate *Females* from the above search). If you retrieve too many, you can narrow your search by adding another subject, restricting the search to a particular country (e.g., Thailand), or restricting it to articles published during a certain time period (i.e., only articles published after 1985).

Getting the Article

Once you have located a citation to a journal article you want, you need to see whether your library carries that journal. Either check your library's online or card catalog or ask a reference librarian whether the library has a bound list of its journals for you to look at. Recent issues of a journal may be displayed in a "Current Periodicals" section; earlier journals are generally bound in volumes and placed in the library stacks. If your library does not carry the journal you need, you can usually order it through interlibrary loan and it will be obtained from another library for you.

Dissertations

Doctoral dissertations are the result of original research, so they can be an important resource in the field of sociology. The advantage of looking at a dissertation based on social research is that the method—how the study was done—is usually delineated in quite a lot of detail. Dissertations may even refer to the problems encountered in trying to accomplish the aims of the study (such problems are rarely reported on in an article). Copies of most

BOX A-4

SELECTED DATABASES IN SOCIOLOGY

Database	Date	Subjects	Print Equivalent
Child Abuse and Neglect (Online)	Current	Child abuse and family violence	None
Dissertation Abstracts (online and CD-ROM)	1861–	All	*Dissertation Abstracts*
ERIC (online and CD-ROM)	1966–	Education	RIE/CIJE
Family Resources (online and CD-ROM)	1970–	Social sciences	None
PAIS (online and CD-ROM)	1972–	Political and social sciences	*PAIS International In Print*
PsychINFO (online)	1967–	Psychology	*Psychological Abstracts*
PsychLIT (CD-ROM)	1974–	Psychology	*Psychological Abstracts*
Social SCISEARCH (online)	1972–	Social sciences	SSCI
Social Sciences Index	1983–	Social and political sciences	*Social Sciences Index*
Sociofile (CD-ROM)	1974–	Social sciences	*Sociological Abstracts*
Sociological Abstracts (online)	1963–	Social sciences	*Sociological Abstracts*
SSCI (CD-ROM)	1981–	Social sciences	*Social Sciences Citation Index* (SSCI)

doctoral dissertations written in the United States are sent to *University Microfilms Incorporated* (UMI). UMI then microfilms the dissertations and lists them in *Dissertation Abstracts International* (DAI). UMI also sells hard copies of dissertations.

DAI is published in three parts: Part A, The Humanities and Social Sciences; Part B, The Sciences and Engineering; and Part C, WorldWide. Parts A and B include references to about 35,000 dissertations produced each year at American, Canadian, and British Universities. Part C includes dissertations from other countries. Dissertations are indexed under broad disciplines, and within those by subfields, so you would want to check the keyword index to locate dissertations in your subject area.

Copies of dissertations may be purchased from UMI, although this can be expensive. Some dissertations may be available through interlibrary loan, so check at your library. Some dissertations become published books, so you might want to also check in the reference book *Books in Print* under the author's name to see if a book on the dissertation material appears. (Remember, the exact title of the dissertation may not be used for the title of the book—book titles tend to be shorter than dissertation titles!)

Thanks to Jacqueline M. Borin of California State University, San Marcos, Library, who revised and enlarged this appendix.

TABLE OF RANDOM NUMBERS

10 09 73 25 33	76 52 01 35 86	34 67 35 48 76	80 95 90 91 17	39 29 27 49 45
37 54 20 48 05	64 89 47 42 96	24 80 52 40 37	20 63 61 04 02	00 82 29 16 65
08 42 26 89 53	19 64 50 93 03	23 20 90 25 60	15 95 33 47 64	35 08 03 36 06
99 01 90 25 29	09 37 67 07 15	38 31 13 11 65	88 67 67 43 97	04 43 62 76 59
12 80 79 99 70	80 15 73 61 47	64 03 23 66 53	98 95 11 68 77	12 17 17 68 33
66 06 57 47 17	34 07 27 68 50	36 69 73 61 70	65 81 33 98 85	11 19 92 91 70
31 06 01 08 05	45 57 18 24 06	35 30 34 26 14	86 79 90 74 39	23 40 30 97 32
85 26 97 76 02	02 05 16 56 92	68 66 57 48 18	73 05 38 52 47	18 62 38 85 79
63 57 33 21 35	05 32 54 70 48	90 55 35 75 48	28 46 82 87 09	83 49 12 56 24
73 79 64 57 53	03 52 96 47 78	35 80 83 42 82	60 93 52 03 44	35 27 38 84 35
98 52 01 77 67	14 90 56 86 07	22 10 94 05 58	60 97 09 34 33	50 50 07 39 98
11 80 50 54 31	39 80 82 77 32	50 72 56 82 48	29 40 52 42 01	52 77 56 78 51
83 45 29 96 34	06 28 89 80 83	13 74 67 00 78	18 47 54 06 10	68 71 17 78 17
88 68 54 02 00	86 50 75 84 01	36 76 66 79 51	90 36 47 64 93	29 60 91 10 62
99 59 46 73 48	87 51 76 49 69	91 82 60 89 28	93 78 56 13 68	23 47 83 41 13
65 48 11 76 74	17 46 85 09 50	58 04 77 69 74	73 03 95 71 86	40 21 81 65 44
80 12 43 56 35	17 72 70 80 15	45 31 82 23 74	21 11 57 82 53	14 38 55 37 63
74 35 09 98 17	77 40 27 72 14	43 23 60 02 10	45 52 16 42 37	96 28 60 26 55
69 91 62 68 03	66 25 22 91 48	36 93 68 72 03	76 62 11 39 90	94 40 05 64 18
09 89 32 05 05	14 22 56 85 14	46 42 75 67 88	96 29 77 88 22	54 38 21 45 98
91 49 91 45 23	68 47 92 76 86	46 16 28 35 54	94 75 08 99 23	37 08 92 00 48
80 33 69 45 98	26 94 03 68 58	70 29 73 41 35	53 14 03 33 40	42 05 08 23 41
44 10 48 19 49	85 15 74 79 54	32 97 92 65 75	57 60 04 08 81	22 22 20 64 13
12 55 07 37 42	11 10 00 20 40	12 86 07 46 97	96 64 48 94 39	28 70 72 58 15
63 60 64 93 29	16 50 53 44 84	40 21 95 25 63	43 65 17 70 82	07 20 73 17 90
61 19 69 04 46	26 45 74 77 74	51 92 43 37 29	65 39 45 95 93	42 58 26 05 27
15 47 44 52 66	95 27 07 99 53	59 36 78 38 48	82 39 61 01 18	33 21 15 94 66
94 55 72 85 73	67 89 75 43 87	54 62 24 44 31	91 19 04 25 92	92 92 74 59 73
42 48 11 62 13	97 34 40 87 21	16 86 84 87 67	03 07 11 20 59	25 70 14 66 70
23 52 37 83 17	73 20 88 98 37	68 93 59 14 16	26 25 22 96 63	05 52 28 25 62
04 49 35 24 94	75 24 63 38 24	45 86 25 10 25	61 96 27 93 35	65 33 71 24 72
00 54 99 76 54	64 05 18 81 59	96 11 96 38 96	54 69 28 23 91	23 28 72 95 29
35 96 31 53 07	26 89 80 93 54	33 35 13 54 62	77 97 45 00 24	90 10 33 93 33
59 80 80 83 91	45 42 72 68 42	83 60 94 97 00	13 02 12 48 92	78 56 52 01 06
46 05 88 52 36	01 39 09 22 86	77 28 14 40 77	93 91 08 36 47	70 61 74 29 41
32 17 90 05 97	87 37 92 52 41	05 56 70 70 07	86 74 31 71 57	85 39 41 18 38
69 23 46 14 06	20 11 74 52 04	15 95 66 00 00	18 74 39 24 23	97 11 89 63 38
19 56 54 14 30	01 75 87 53 79	40 41 92 15 85	66 67 43 68 06	84 96 28 52 07
45 15 51 49 38	19 47 60 72 46	43 66 79 45 43	59 04 79 00 33	20 82 66 95 41
94 86 43 19 94	36 16 81 08 51	34 88 88 15 53	01 54 03 54 56	05 01 45 11 76

Source: The Rand Corporation, *A Million Random Digits,* Free Press, Glencoe, Ill., 1955, pp. 1–3, with the kind permission of the publisher.

CHI-SQUARE DISTRIBUTION

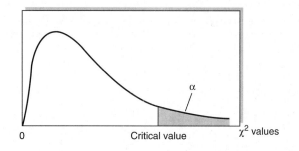

Degrees of Freedom (df)	Area in Shaded Right Tail (α)		
	.10	.05	.01
1	2.706	3.841	6.635
2	4.605	5.991	9.210
3	6.251	7.815	11.345
4	7.779	9.488	13.227
5	9.236	11.070	15.086
6	10.645	12.592	16.812
7	12.017	14.067	18.475
8	13.362	15.507	20.090
9	14.684	16.919	21.666
10	15.987	18.307	23.209
11	17.275	19.675	24.725
12	18.549	21.026	26.217
13	19.812	22.362	27.688
14	21.064	23.685	29.141
15	22.307	24.996	30.578
16	23.542	26.296	32.000
17	24.769	27.587	33.409
18	25.989	28.869	34.805
19	27.204	30.144	36.191
20	28.412	31.410	37.566
21	29.615	32.671	38.932
22	30.813	33.924	40.289
23	32.007	35.172	41.638
24	33.196	36.415	42.980
25	34.382	37.652	44.314
26	35.563	38.885	45.642
27	36.741	40.113	46.963
28	37.916	41.337	48.278
29	39.087	42.557	49.588
30	40.256	43.773	50.892

Example of how to use this table: In a chi-square distribution with 6 degrees of freedom (*df*), the area to the right of a critical value of 12.592—i.e., the α area—is .05.

Source: This table is abridged from Table IV of Sir Ronald A. Fisher and Frank Yates, *Statistical Tables for Biological, Agricultural and Medical Research,* 6th ed., Longman Group, Ltd., London (previously published by Oliver & Boyd, Ltd., Edinburgh), 1974. Reproduced with the permission of the authors and publishers.

Generating the Computer Tables in This Text Using the SPSS^x Computer Program

INTRODUCTION

*T*his is not a comprehensive introduction discussing how to use the statistical social science computer package program SPSS^x. Rather, this appendix will confine itself to describing how the computer tables in this text were prepared. In so doing, it will, in fact, offer the basic skills required in using SPSS^x. However, you must remember that the SPSS^x program is vastly more comprehensive than the material to be covered here. If you plan to use SPSS^x in analyzing your data, you will want to look at the large manual provided for this program and also at the introductory guide to using it. This appendix offers only a very simple first step in showing you what had to be done to produce the computer tables and statistics contained in this text.

What is SPSS^x? It is a very large computer package program in which complex computer procedures (which require from a computer programmer much time and ingenuity in preparation as well as a very sophisticated understanding of both computer programming and the computer languages needed to do programming) have been converted into fairly simple procedures that a person with no training in computer programming can carry out quite easily. For SPSS^x, you do not need to know BASIC, FORTRAN, or any other computer language. The SPSS^x statements are based on simple English commands that are easy to understand. All you need to do is learn the basic organization and principles of how SPSS^x operates, select which commands are appropriate for your analysis, and then use these commands exactly as SPSS^x requires them to be used. The computer does all the rest.

For starters, you must determine what version of SPSS^x is available to you. There are different versions of SPSS^x for mainframe computers and for personal computers. These versions, however, tend to use similar (often identical) commands and ordering principles. The version used in this text is SPSS^x VMS 4.5; and the computer on which the computer tables were prepared for this text was a VAX 11/780, which is a mainframe computer made by Digital Equipment Corporation.

In short, this is a very small "cookbook" on how I got the tables you see in this text. Even if you are planning to use a different computer program from SPSS^x or if you are not going to use a computer at all, this brief overview could be read as a way to see what the required ingredients are for using a comprehensive computer package program.

HOW SPSS^x COMMANDS ARE WRITTEN

There are two parts to every SPSS^x statement. The first part of each statement is the SPSS^x command or procedure statement; the second part is the specification of the data. The command statements are the ones that SPSS^x developed to tell the computer what type of procedure to perform; the specification statement is information about the data (which variables and which codes of variables) the user wants SPSS^x to process.

Converted into cookbook terms, you might say that the command statements would be GET FOOD ITEMS, CHOP, MIX TOGETHER, BROIL, TIME; and the specification statements would be 1 pound ground beef, 1 onion, 1 egg. To parallel SPSS^x statements, you would set up the cookbook material as shown in Table C-1A.

For an SPSS^x statement with three variables—sex (VAR1626), educational attainment (VAR3281), and athletic participation (VAR241)—you might have a statement as shown in Table C-1B. What this SPSS^x statement says is that

1. You are entering a data list with three variables which are located in specific places in the computer record (sex is in column or record position 1, etc.).

2. You want the computer to recode the values in the variable VAR3281 from eight values into three values, and then rename this new three-category variable VAR3281T. It should, however, preserve the unrecoded eight-value version of VAR3281.

3. You want the computer to give you frequency distributions for the three specified variables (that is, the count of cases falling into each category of the three variables) and the percentage distributions across the categories.

4. You want the frequency distributions to present a set of statistics which will include the median and the set of statistics that come with the command DEFAULT—the mean, standard deviation, minimum, and maximum. (You would need to look in the SPSS^x manual to see which statistics are available to be selected. I should add that asking for these statistics with the kinds of variables I use in the example would be quite meaningless, since they are two- and three-category variables, and the median and mean are more sensibly used with numerical variables.) This is a good time to stress the point that SPSS^x will carry out whatever types of requests you make regardless of whether they make sense for your data. The SPSS^x man-

TABLE C-1

GET FOOD ITEMS	1 lb. ground beef	1 onion	1 egg	
CHOP 1 onion				
MIX TOGETHER	1 lb. ground beef	1 onion	1 egg INTO hamburger	
BROIL hamburger				
TIME 10 mins.				*(A)*

```
DATA LIST /1
   VAR1626 1   VAR3281 2-3   VAR241 4
RECODE   VAR3281  (7,8=1)  (3 THRU 6=2)  (1,2=3)   INTO VAR3281T
FREQUENCIES   VAR1626   VAR3281T   VAR241
STATISTICS=MEDIAN DEFAULT/                                          (B)
```

ual does offer some discussions on the types of data that are appropriate to different analytic strategies.

ENTERING THE DATA INTO SPSS^X

In Chapter 13, the variables for the study of high school athletic participation and educational attainment were presented. How did these variables "get into" the computer? Very simply, they were *entered into* the computer using the data entry commands of the SPSS^X program.

If you had collected your own data and wanted to enter them into a computer using the SPSS^X program, you would use the DATA LIST command shown above in the example, the other command statements you wanted in your computer run, and then your last set of statements for entering the data. You would put a BEGIN DATA statement and enter the values for every variable in the file; then you would follow the last variable with an END DATA statement. Please check the SPSS^X manual for more extensive examples of how this is done.

In the computer tables shown in this text, the data were a part of a much larger dataset. I had purchased these data on a computer tape. Because these data were on the tape without any specifications as to how they would be processed by a computer, they formed a *raw data file*. Next I had to transform the raw data file into an SPSS^X *systems file*. The systems file would have all the variables required for the many different types of analyses I planned to carry out, set up in such a way that they were ready to be used by the SPSS^X program. The first step was to prepare a *command file*. The command file would include the selection of variables I wanted with the computer tape locations of each of these variables. Then, when this command file was run, it would create a systems file with the variables requested all there.

To explain the commands required to set up such a systems file from a large dataset is beyond

the scope of this discussion. However, once a systems file is set up, you no longer need to use a DATA LIST statement or to enter your data with BEGIN DATA . . . END DATA commands. Instead you use a FILE HANDLE statement to tell the computer what systems file you need from those stored in the computer, and then use a GET FILE command to tell the computer to get the necessary file so that it can be run on the computer. These commands would look like the following printouts:

TITLE   ATHLETIC PARTICIPATION STUDY

(This title would be printed at the top of each page of computer printout—this command is not necessary to run the program.)

FILE HANDLE *** NAME='******'

(The first set of three asterisks would actually be replaced by a brief name of the file, and the second set of six asterisks in the single quotation marks would be the full name.)

GET FILE=***

(This would repeat the short name following the FILE HANDLE command.)

LABELING THE DATA

Once the data have been entered into (or retrieved from) the file, you might want to put labels on all the variables you plan to use and on all the values of each variable. Thus, when your computer data are printed out, the variable labels will be printed out and the value labels will define the categories of each variable.

To do this you will use two command statements from SPSS^X: VARIABLE LABELS and VALUE LABELS. In our study of athletic participation, we had five variables. You can see how the VARIABLE LABELS statement for these five variables was set up:

VARIABLE LABELS	VAR1626	'SEX'
	VAR1070	'PARENTAL SOCIOECONOMIC STATUS'
	VAR229	'HIGH SCHOOL GPA'
	VAR241	'HIGH SCHOOL ATHLETIC PARTICIPATION'
	VAR3281	'EDUCATIONAL ATTAINMENT'

These variable labels commands connect the description in quotation marks (either single or double quotation marks are allowed) with the variable name (e.g., VAR1626) each time the computer prints out the variable.

For labeling the values, or categories, of each variable, use the VALUE LABELS command as follows:

VALUE LABELS	VAR1626	1 'MALE' 2 'FEMALE'/
	VAR1070	1 'LOW' 2 'MEDIUM' 3 'HIGH'/
	VAR229	1 'MOSTLY A' 2 'HALF A-B'
		3 'MOSTLY B' 4 'HALF B-C'
		5 'MOSTLY C' 6 'HALF C-D'
		7 'MOSTLY D' 8 'BELOW D'/
	VAR241	1 'NOT PARTICIPATE'
		2 'PARTICIPATE ACTIVELY'
		3 'PARTICIPATE AS LEADER'/
	VAR3281	1 'NO COLLEGE, NO VOC'
		2 'NO COLLEGE, SOME VOC'
		3 'LT 2 YRS COL, NO VOC'
		4 'LT 2 YRS COL, SOME VOC'
		5 'GT 2 YRS COL, NO VOC'
		6 'GT 2 YRS COL, SOME VOC'
		7 '4 OR 5 YEAR DEGREE'
		8 'ADVANCED DEGREE'

VALUE LABELS will associate the words in the single quotation marks with the numbers representing the categories of each variable.

DATA MANIPULATION STATEMENTS

SPSS^x offers various strategies for regrouping variables. One method is to combine the values of a variable by recoding the variable categories. The procedure is called RECODE.

Another way to manipulate variables is to carry out some mathematical procedure on a variable (for example, to multiply the variable by 100, which might be important if the variable were income; or to add 1900 to a variable, which might be useful if there were a two-digit variable for year of birth). This form of data manipulation is referred to in SPSS^x as COMPUTE. Another common way that COMPUTE is used is when a set of variables is added up to form an index.

Let's first consider how four of the five variables in the athletic participation study were recoded. Remember that when you want to do cross tabulations, having a large number of categories in a variable will produce a table with many cells. If you do not have many cases, you may have *empty* cells. Even where there are a very large number of cases, it is often preferable to reduce the number of values in a variable in order to sharpen the comparison groups.

Another reason to recode the values of a variable is to change their order. Recall that the value of 1 will be in the upper left-hand cell of the table. If you want that cell to represent the "high" category, but the "high" category was coded as 3 in your data, then you can reorder the value numbers to make "high" into a 1. I suggested that it is often preferable to set up a table so that your hypothesis can be tested in the upper left-hand cell. In other words, if you hypothesize that those students who were athletic leaders were more likely to attain the highest level of education, then both the category of "participate as leader" (in the athletic participation variable) and the highest-level college degree (in the educational attainment variable) should be recoded as 1.

Here are the recode statements set up for the variables in the athletic participation study:

```
RECODE    VAR1070   (MISSING=9) (1=3) (2=2) (3=1) INTO VAR1070R/
          VAR229   (MISSING=9)  (1,2=1)  (3,4=2)  (5 THRU 8=3)   INTO
          VAR229TH/
          VAR241   (MISSING=9) (1=3) (2=2) (3=1) INTO VAR241R/
          VAR3281   (MISSING=9) (8=1) (7=2) (6=3) (5=4) (4=5) (3=6) (2=7) (1=8) INTO
          VAR3281R/
          VAR3281   (MISSING=9)  (7,8=1)   (3 THRU 6=2)  (1,2=3)   INTO
          VAR3281T
```

Look very carefully at these recode statements. They show a logical set of operations. After entering the RECODE statement, you give the name of the variable to be recoded; then you put in parentheses exactly how you want the codes transferred. The equals sign virtually means "changes into." Thus (1=3) means "1 changes into 3." Note in each case a MISSING category is defined; this tells the computer what to do with cases where none of the categories has been given (see the discussion of MISSING VALUES below). Furthermore, in these examples, we created new recoded variables from the original variables by using the INTO statement; but we also retained the original variable. Thus, there would be VAR1070 where the "high" category would be coded as 3, and there would also be a VAR1070R where the "high" category would be coded as 1. By using the INTO command with the new variable, you have

the option of using the recoded version of the variable or the original variable. (Note that if you attach a SAVE FILE command at the end of your computer run, the new recoded variable will be saved.) Note also that at the end of each recode statement, there is a slash(/); this tells the computer that another variable to be recoded follows. After the last variable to be recoded, there is no slash.

Now let's consider where you might use a COMPUTE statement. In Chapter 16, when we were building the work orientation index from three questionnaire items in the National Longitudinal Study of the High School Class of 1972, we wanted to add together items measuring "importance of success in my line of work" (VAR313), "making a lot of money" (VAR315), and "finding steady work" (VAR317). Below is how such an index could be formed with SPSS^x.

COMPUTE
WO72 = VAR313 + VAR315 + VAR317

This statement creates a new variable, WO72 (meaning "work orientation index in 1972") to be equal to the combined values of the three variables. Since each of the three variables took the value of 3 = "very important," 2 = "somewhat important," or 1 = "not important," when the three variables are added together WO72 would have the range of values 3 through 9. In the computed variable, WO72, the numbers could not be so easily converted into words but would form a numerical scale from high scores (meaning that more 3s were given to the questions) to more moderate-level scores (where 2s were given) to low scores (where 1s were given).

The one other data manipulation statement which we will cover here is MISSING VALUES. This is a way of having the computer flag certain categories of a variable as *missing,* so that they will be left out of the data analysis. Generally, the number of missing cases is presented in some way in each data presentation. It is customary to code missing values of a variable as 9. If the variable is a two-digit variable, it is coded 99; a three-digit is coded 999. SPSS^x will flag up to three values in a variable as missing (such categories may have distinguished "no response," "not relevant," "don't know," or other types of responses that are not directly useful in the measurement of the variable in question). Below are the missing value statements entered for the variables we have so far discussed.

MISSING VALUES   VAR1070R, VAR229TH, VAR241R,
VAR3281R, VAR3281T (9)/
VAR313, VAR315, VAR317 (98, 99)

This tells the computer, as it carries out the statistical procedures, that it should ignore cases coded as 9 for six of the variables and that, in making the index, it should ignore categories coded 98 or 99. There was no MISSING VALUES statement entered for VAR1626 because it was known that there were no missing cases for the variable of sex (in other words, a sex designation was always present for each of the cases).

RELABELING RECODED VARIABLES

When you create new variables, they need new labels. This is true both for variable and value labels. Look through the changes in labels given to the recoded variables given in Table C-2.

LEARNING TO DO FREQUENCIES

SPSS^x has a number of subprograms which you can use to analyze your data. One of the easiest and most frequently employed is the FREQUENCIES program. As noted above, FREQUENCIES provides a count of the number of cases in each category of a variable and the percentage distribution of cases in each category of a variable. Tables 13-1*A*, 13-2*A*, 13-3*A*, 13-4*A*, and 13-5*A* show the results of running the FREQUENCIES program from SPSS^x. For example, the following command statements would be needed to produce the frequency tables from Chapter 13:

FREQUENCIES   VARIABLES = VAR1626   VAR1070R   VAR241R
VAR229   VAR3281R   VAR3281T

TABLE C-2

VARIABLE LABELS	VAR1070R	'PARENTAL SOCIOECONOMIC STATUS RECODE'
	VAR229TH	'HIGH SCHOOL GPA: THREE CATEGORIES'
	VAR241R	'HIGH SCHOOL ATHLETIC PARTICIPATION'
	VAR3281R	'EDUCATIONAL ATTAINMENT RECODE'
	VAR3281T	'EDUCATIONAL ATTAINMENT: THREE CATEGORIES'
VALUE LABELS	VAR1070R	1 'HIGH' 2 'MEDIUM' 3 'LOW'
	VAR229TH	1 'A AND A-B' 2 'B AND B-C'
		3 'C AND BELOW'/
	VAR241R	1 'PARTICIPATE AS LEADER'
		2 'PARTICIPATE ACTIVELY'
		3 'NOT PARTICIPATE'/
	VAR3281R	1 'ADVANCED DEGREE'
		2 '4 OR 5 YR DEGREE'
		3 'GT 2 YRS COL, SOME VOC'
		4 'GT 2 YRS COL, NO VOC'
		5 'LT 2 YRS COL, SOME VOC'
		6 'LT 2 YRS COL, NO VOC'
		7 'NO COLLEGE, SOME VOC'
		8 'NO COLLEGE, NO VOC'/
	VAR3281T	1 'COLLEGE DEGREE OR MORE'
		2 'SOME COLLEGE'
		3 'NO COLLEGE'

This brief statement is all that is required to produce these six distributions. However, you might have requested different types of distributions by putting a FORMAT statement after the VARIABLES statement; or you might have requested a HISTOGRAM or a BARCHART by so specifying. Furthermore, your frequency distributions could be accompanied by different statistical tests, if you requested these with a STATISTICS statement (as was shown in the first example in this appendix).

LEARNING TO DO CONDESCRIPTIVE

CONDESCRIPTIVE is a subprogram that gives you different types of measures of central tendency and dispersion (as were discussed in Chapters 6 and 15) without frequency distributions. This is a good subprogram to use with numerical variables that have many values (such as income or age). Table 16-4 shows the results from a CONDESCRIPTIVE program run for the variable WO72. To produce these results, the following data would need to be entered into the computer:

```
CONDESCRIPTIVE     WO72
STATISTICS         ALL
```

You can request fewer statistics by specifying which ones you want (check the SPSS^x manual). Note, in Table 16-4, that the CONDESCRIPTIVE data provide the number of valid observations and missing cases at the bottom of the table.

LEARNING TO DO CROSSTABS

This is one of the most popular subprograms in the SPSS^x program. It produces tables where one variable is cross-classified by another. There are three examples of tables produced by the CROSSTABS subprogram in SPSS^x in this text. These are Table 13-6A (reproduced in Chapter 15 with statistics added as Table 15-9A), Table 13-7A, and Table 14-1A (reproduced in Chapter 15 with statistics as Table 15-10A).

The following SPSS^x commands produced these tables. For Table 13-6A:

CROSSTABS	TABLES = VAR3281T BY VAR241R
OPTIONS	4

For Table 15-9A:

CROSSTABS	TABLES = VAR3281T BY VAR241R
OPTIONS	4
STATISTICS	1 8

For Table 13-7A:

CROSSTABS	TABLES = VAR3281T BY VAR229TH
OPTIONS	4

For Table 14-1A:

CROSSTABS	TABLES = VAR3281T BY VAR241R BY VAR1626
OPTIONS	4

For Table 15-10A:

CROSSTABS	TABLES = VAR3281T BY VAR241R BY VAR1626
OPTIONS	4
STATISTICS	1 8

The general principles for setting up these tables involve using the key word TABLES followed by an equals sign and then giving that variable first (before the BY) which you want to be the row variable in the table (the variable that will be to the left of the table) and the other variable second (after the BY) which you want to serve as the column variable (and which will be given at the top of the table). By convention, the dependent variable is set up as the row variable and the independent variable as the column variable; percentages are run accordingly.

The OPTIONS statement can request what numbers and percentages you want presented in the table: OPTIONS 4 produces column percentages, which are what you need if you set up the dependent variable as the row variable. If you do not use the OPTIONS statement, you will get only the number of cases in each cell printed on the table. The STATISTICS statement can be followed by a choice of different numbers referring to different statistical tests (check the SPSS^x manual for the range of tests available). In the example, the chi-square statistic was requested with the 1, the gamma statistic with the 8.

To produce trivariate tables, such as Table 14-1A, in which a cross tabulation of the dependent and independent variables is produced for every category of the third (control) variable, all you need to do is add another BY after the second variable, followed by the name of the third variable. (You could further break down the cross tabulations by a fourth variable by adding another BY with another variable.)

Although the examples given show each table produced by a different CROSSTABS statement, you can request multiple tables with one CROSSTABS statement. The example below shows how all the tables could be produced from a single CROSSTABS statement.

```
CROSSTABS     TABLES = VAR3281T BY VAR241R, VAR229TH/VAR3281T BY VAR241R
                      BY VAR1626
OPTIONS       4
STATISTICS    1   8
```

In this example, VAR3281T would first be cross-tabulated with VAR241R, and second with VAR229TH. Third, the trivariate tables would be produced. Note that the statistics are requested for each table. If they are not wanted, you need not use them.

LEARNING TO USE PEARSON'S *r*

The one other SPSS^x subprogram presented in this text, PEARSON CORR, will produce the Pearson's *r* Correlation Coefficient presented in Chapter 15 as Table 15-5. This is also very easily produced from a simple SPSS^x statement, as follows:

PEARSON CORR VAR229V WITH VAR44

Because Pearson's *r* requires that variables be at the interval level of measurement, the recoded version of VAR229 (VAR229V) was used where the GPAs were converted into scale scores of 0–4. VAR44 was satisfactory as it was since it was based on composite ACT scale scores.

This subprogram includes OPTIONS that can be requested (such as different ways to exclude missing data) and STATISTICS that can be requested (such as means, standard deviations, and number of missing values for each variable).

Once you are done with your computer run, you put in the statement FINISH. This informs the computer that the SPSS^x programming is over. On pages 462–463 you can see a reproduction of how these statements appear on the computer.

```
$SPSSX
FILE HANDLE *** / NAME = '******'
GET FILE = ***
VARIABLE LABELS    VAR1626  'SEX'
                   VAR1070  'PARENTAL SOCIOECONOMIC STATUS'
                   VAR229  'HIGH SCHOOL GPA'
                   VAR241  'HIGH SCHOOL ATHLETIC PARTICIPATION'
                   VAR3281  'EDUCATIONAL ATTAINMENT'
VALUE LABELS     VAR1626  1 'MALE' 2 `FEMALE'/
                 VAR1070  1 'LOW' 2 'MEDIUM' 3 'HIGH'/
                 VAR229  1 'MOSTLY A' 2 'HALF A-B'
                        3 'MOSTLY B' 4 'HALF B-C'
                        5 'MOSTLY C' 6 'HALF C-D'
                        7 'MOSTLY D' 8 `BELOW D'/
                 VAR241  1 'NOT PARTICIPATE'
                        2 'PARTICIPATE ACTIVELY'
                        3 'PARTICIPATE AS LEADER'/
                 VAR3281  1 'NO COLLEGE, NO VOC'
                         2 'NO COLLEGE, SOME VOC'
                         3 'LT 2 YRS COL, NO VOC'
                         4 'LT 2 YRS COL, SOME VOC'
                         5 'GT 2 YRS COL, NO VOC'
                         6 'GT 2 YRS COL, SOME VOC'
                         7 '4 OR 5 YEAR DEGREE'
                         8 'ADVANCED DEGREE'
RECODE  VAR1070  (MISSING=9) (1=3) (2=2) (3=1) INTO VAR1070R/
        VAR229  (MISSING=9) (1,2=1) (3,4=2) (5 THRU 8=3) INTO VAR229TH/
        VAR241  (MISSING=9) (1=3) (2=2) (3=1) INTO VAR241R/
        VAR3281  (MISSING=9) (8=1) (7=2) (6=3) (5=4) (4=5) (3=6) (2=7) (1=8)
                 INTO VAR3281R/
        VAR3281  (MISSING=9) (7,8=1) (3 THRU 6=2) (1,2=3) INTO VAR3281T
COMPUTE  WO72 = VAR313 + VAR315 + VAR317
MISSING VALUES  VAR1070R, VAR229TH, VAR241R,
                VAR3281R, VAR3281T (9)/
                VAR313, VAR315, VAR317 (98,99)
VARIABLE LABELS VAR1070R `PARENTAL SOCIOECONOMIC STATUS RECODE'
                VAR229TH   'HIGH SCHOOL GPA: THREE CATEGORIES'
                VAR241R    'HIGH SCHOOL ATHLETIC PARTICIPATION'
                VAR3281R   'EDUCATIONAL ATTAINMENT RECODE'
                VAR3281T   'EDUCATIONAL ATTAINMENT: THREE CATEGORIES'
VALUE LABELS  VAR1070R  1 'HIGH' 2 'MEDIUM' 3 'LOW'/
              VAR229TH  1 'A AND A-B' 2 'B AND B-C' 3 'C AND BELOW'/
              VAR241R  1 'PARTICIPATE AS LEADER'
                      2 'PARTICIPATE ACTIVELY'
                      3 'NOT PARTICIPATE'/
```

```
              VAR3281R  1 'ADVANCED DEGREE'
                        2 '4 OR 5 YEAR DEGREE'
                        3 `GT 2 YRS COL, SOME VOC'
                        4 'GT 2 YRS COL, NO VOC'
                        5 'LT 2 YRS COL, SOME VOC'
                        6 'LT 2 YRS COL, NO VOC'
                        7 'NO COLLEGE, SOME VOC'
                        8 'NO COLLEGE, NO VOC'/
              VAR3281T  1 'COLLEGE DEGREE OR MORE'
                        2 'SOME COLLEGE'
                        3 'NO COLLEGE'
FREQUENCIES   VARIABLES = VAR1626 VAR1070R VAR241R VAR229
                          VAR3281R VAR3281T
CONDESCRIPTIVE  WO72
STATISTICS  ALL
CROSSTABS  TABLES = VAR3281T BY VAR241R, VAR229TH/
                    VAR3281T BY VAR241R BY VAR1626
OPTIONS  4
STATISTICS  1,8
PEARSON CORR  VAR229V WITH VAR44
FINISH
```

REFERENCES

INTRODUCTION

Merton, Robert K.: "Notes on Problem-Finding in Sociology," in Robert K. Merton, Leonard Broom, and Leonard S. Cottrell, Jr. (eds.), *Sociology Today,* Basic Books, New York, 1959.

———— et al. (eds.): Reader in Bureaucracy, Free Press, Glencoe, Ill., 1952.

Mills, C. Wright: *The Sociological Imagination,* Oxford University Press, New York, 1959.

CHAPTER 1

Anderson, Elijah: *A Place on the Corner,* University of Chicago Press, Chicago, 1978.

Cohen, S., and L. Taylor: *Psychological Survival: The Effects of Long-Term Imprisonment,* Penguin, Harmondsworth, Middlesex, England, 1972.

Coleman, James S.: "Policy, Research, and Political Theory," The 375th Convocation Address, University of Chicago, December 18, 1979 (Published in the *University of Chicago Record,* 1980, pp. 78–80).

————, Thomas Hoffer, and Sally Kilgore: *High School Achievement: Public, Catholic and Private Schools Compared,* Basic Books, New York, 1982.

———— et al.: *Equality of Educational Opportunity,* U.S. Department of Health, Education, and Welfare, Washington, 1966.

Gottfredson, Michael R., and Travis Hirschi: *A General Theory of Crime,* Stanford University Press, Stanford, Calif., 1990.

Hirschi, Travis: *Causes of Delinquency,* University of California Press, Berkeley, Calif., 1969.

Horner, Matina: Sex Differences in Achievement Motivation and Performance in Competitive and Non-competitive Situations, unpublished doctoral dissertation, University of Michigan, 1968.

————: "Femininity and Successful Achievement: A Basic Inconsistency," in J. Bardwick, E. Douvan, M. Horner, and D. Gutmann (eds.), *Feminine Personality and Conflict,* Brooks/Cole, Belmont, Calif., 1970.

Kanter, Rosabeth M.: *Men and Women of the Corporation,* Basic Books, New York, 1977.

Lewis, Oscar: *Five Families: Mexican Case Studies in the Culture of Poverty,* Basic Books, New York, 1959.

McClelland, D., J. Atkinson, R. Clark, and E. Lowell: *The Achievement Motive,* Appleton-Century-Crofts, New York, 1953.

Mullins, Nicholas C.: *Theories and Theory Groups in Contemporary American Sociology,* Harper & Row, New York, 1973.

National Opinion Research Center: *High School and Beyond,* Chicago, 1980.

Tresemer, David W.: "The Cumulative Record of Research on Fear of Success," *Sex Roles,* **2**:217–236, 1976.

Whyte, William Foote: *Street Corner Society: The Social Structure of an Italian Slum,* University of Chicago Press, Chicago, 1955.

Wright, Sonia R., and James D. Wright: "Income Maintenance and Work Behavior," *Social Policy,* **6**:24–32, 1975.

CHAPTER 2

Atkinson, J. W. (ed.): *Motives in Fantasy, Action, and Society,* Van Nostrand, Princeton, 1958.

Bauman, Laurie J., Ruth E. K. Stein, and Henry Ireys: "A Framework for Conceptualizing Interventions," *Sociological Practice Review,* **2:** 241–251, 1991.

Bernard, Thomas J.: "Twenty Years of Testing Theories: What Have We Learned and Why?" *Journal of Crime and Delinquency,* **4**:325–347, 1990.

Eckberg, Douglas Lee, and Lester Hill, Jr.: "The Paradigm Concept and Sociology," *American Sociological Review,* **44**:937–947, 1979.

Gottfredson, Michael R., and Travis Hirschi: *A General Theory of Crime,* Stanford University Press, Stanford, Calif., 1990.

Hirschi, Travis: *Causes of Delinquency,* University of California Press, Berkeley, Calif., 1969.

Horner, Matina: Sex Differences in Achievement Motivation and Performance in Competitive and Non-competitive Situations, unpublished doctoral dissertation, University of Michigan, 1968.

Kanter, Rosabeth M.: *Men and Women of the Corporation,* Basic Books, New York, 1977.

Kuhn, Thomas S.: *The Structure of Scientific Revolutions,* 2d ed., University of Chicago Press, Chicago, 1970.

Merton, Robert K.: *Social Theory and Social Structure,* 3d ed., Free Press, Glencoe, Ill., 1968.

————: *The Sociology of Science,* University of Chicago Press, Chicago, 1973.

Mills, C. Wright: *The Sociological Imagination,* Oxford University Press, New York, 1959.

Mitroff, Ian: "Norms and Counter-Norms in a Select Group of the Apollo Moon Scientists: A Case Study of the Ambivalence of Scientists," *American Sociological Review,* **39**:579–595, 1974.

Mulkay, Michael: *Science and the Sociology of Knowledge,* Allen and Unwin, London, 1979.

Newton-Smith, W. H.: *The Rationality of Science,* Routledge and Kegan Paul, Boston, 1981.

Popper, Karl: *The Logic of Scientific Discovery,* Harper and Row, New York, 1968.

Rosenhan, D. L.: "On Being Sane in Insane Places," in Martin Bulmer (ed.), *Social Research Ethics,* Macmillan, London, 1982.

Wallace, Walter: *The Logic of Science in Sociology,* Aldine, Chicago, 1971.

Whyte, William Foote: *Street Corner Society: The Social Structure of an Italian Slum,* University of Chicago Press, Chicago, 1955.

CHAPTER 3

Bulmer, Martin: "The Merits and Demerits of Covert Participant Observation," in Martin Bulmer (ed.), *Social Research Ethics,* Macmillan, London, 1982.

Cassell, Joan: "Risk and Benefit to Subjects of Fieldwork," *The American Sociologist,* **13**:134–143, 1978.

Chronicle of Higher Education: "U.S. Has Barred Grants to Six Scientists in Past Two Years," **37** (42), July 3, 1991.

Chronicle of Higher Education: "U.S. Attorney Will Not Seek Indictment of Researcher Accused in 'Baltimore Case'," July 22, 1992, p. A7.

Cohen, S., and L. Taylor: *Psychological Survival: The Effects of Long-Term Imprisonment,* Penguin, Harmondsworth, Middlesex, England, 1972.

Erikson, Kai T.: "A Comment on Disguised Observation in Sociology," *Social Problems,* **14**:367–373, 1967.

Galliher, John: "Social Scientists' Ethical Responsibilities to Superordinates: Looking Upward Meekly," *Social Problems,* **27**:298–308, 1980.

Goffman, Erving: *The Presentation of Self in Everyday Life,* Doubleday, New York, 1959.

Humphreys, Laud: *Tearoom Trade,* Aldine, Chicago, 1970.

Katz, Jay: *Experimentation with Human Beings,* Sage, New York, 1972.

Merton, Robert K.: "Notes on Problem-Finding in Sociology," in Robert K. Merton, Leonard Broom, and Leonard S. Cottrell, Jr. (eds.), *Sociology Today,* Basic Books, New York, 1959.

Milgram, Stanley: "Some Conditions of Obedience and Disobedience to Authority," *Human Relations,* **18**:57–75, 1965.

New York Times: "Researcher Accused of Fraud in Her Data Will Not Be Indicted," July 14, 1992, p. B6.

Rosenhan, D. L.: "On Being Sane in Insane Places," in Martin Bulmer (ed.), *Social Research Ethics,* Macmillan, London, 1982.

Rosenthal, Robert, and Lenore F. Jacobson: *Pygmalion in the Classroom,* Holt, New York, 1968.

Rubinstein, J.: *City Police,* Farrar, Straus & Giroux, New York, 1973.

Shils, Edward: "Social Inquiry and the Autonomy of the Individual," in Martin Bulmer (ed.), *Social Research Ethics,* Macmillan, London, 1982.

Vidich, Arthur J., and Joseph Bensman: *Small Town in Mass Society,* Anchor, New York, 1960.

Wade, Nicholas: "I.Q. and Heredity: Suspicion of Fraud Beclouds Classic Experiment," *Science,* **194**:916–919, 1976.

Weinstein, Deena: "Fraud in Science," *Social Science Quarterly,* **59**:639–652, 1979.

CHAPTER 4

Adorno, T. W., et al.: *The Authoritarian Personality,* Harper & Row, New York, 1950 (Norton, 1969).

Almond, Gabriel A., and Sidney Verba: *The Civic Culture,* Princeton University Press, Princeton, 1963.

Babbie, Earl: *The Practice of Social Research,* 6th ed., Wadsworth, Belmont, Calif., 1992.

Coleman, James S., Thomas Hoffer, and Sally Kilgore: *High School Achievement: Public, Catholic and Private Schools Compared,* Basic Books, New York, 1982.

Cooper, Harris M.: *Integrating Research: A Guide for Literature Reviews,* 2d ed., Sage, Newbury Park, Calif., 1989.

Davis, James A.: *General Social Surveys, 1972-1988: Cumulative Codebook,* National Opinion Research Center, Chicago, 1988.

Heist, Paul, and George Yonge: *Omnibus Personality Inventory: Research Manual,* University of California, Center for the Study of Higher Education, Berkeley, Calif., 1968.

Hirschi, Travis: *Causes of Delinquency,* University of California Press, Berkeley, Calif., 1969.

Kanter, Rosabeth M.: *Men and Women of the Corporation,* Basic Books, New York, 1977.

Maccoby, Eleanor, and Carol Jacklin: *The Psychology of Sex Differences,* Stanford University Press, Stanford, Calif., 1974.

National Opinion Research Center: *High School and Beyond,* Chicago, 1980.

Simon, Julian L.: *Basic Research Methods in Social Science,* Random House, New York, 1969.

CHAPTER 5

Adorno, T. W., et al.: *The Authoritarian Personality,* Harper & Row, New York, 1950 (Norton, 1969).

Allen, Mary J., and Wendy M. Yen: *Introduction to Measurement Theory,* Wadsworth, Belmont, Calif., 1979.

American Psychological Association, American Educational Research Association, and National Council on Measurement in Education: *Standards for Educational Tests,* American Psychological Association, Washington, 1974.

Anderson, T. W., and Stanley L. Sclove: *Introductory Statistical Analysis,* 2d ed., Houghton Mifflin, Boston, 1986.

Bohrnstedt, George W.: "Measurement," in Peter H. Rossi, James D. Wright, and Andy B. Anderson (eds.), *Handbook of Survey Research,* Academic, New York, 1983.

Borgatta, Edgar F., and George W. Bohrnstedt: "Levels of Measurement: Once Over Again," *Sociological Methods and Research,* 9:147–160, 1980.

Bradburn, Norman M., and David Caplovitz: *Reports on Happiness,* Aldine, Chicago, 1965.

Brayfield, Arthur H., and Harold F. Rothe: "An Index of Job Satisfaction," *Journal of Applied Psychology,* 35:307–311, 1951.

Carmines, E., and R. Zeller: *Reliability and Validity Assessment,* Sage, Beverly Hills, Calif., 1979.

Chronbach, L. J., and P. E. Meehl: "Construct Validity in Psychological Tests," *Psychological Bulletin,* 52:281–302, 1955.

Department of Labor: *Dictionary of Occupational Titles,* 4th ed., Department of Labor, Washington, 1991.

Miller, Delbert C.: *Handbook of Research Design and Social Measurement,* 3d ed., McKay, New York, 1977.

Nunnally, J. C.: *Psychometric Theory,* New York, McGraw-Hill, 1967.

Srole, Leo: "Social Integration and Certain Corollaries: An Exploratory Study," *American Sociological Review,* 21:703–716, 1956.

Stevens, S. S.: "Mathematics, Measurement and Psychophysics," in S. S. Stevens (ed.), *Handbook of Experimental Psychology,* Wiley, New York, 1951.

U.S. Bureau of the Census: *Statistical Abstract of 1992,* Washington, 1992.

U.S. Department of Commerce: *Social Indicators III, Selected Data on Social Conditions and Trends in the United States,* Bureau of the Census, Washington, 1980.

Zeller, Richard A., and Edward G. Carmines: *Measurement in the Social Sciences: The Link Between Theory and Data,* Cambridge University Press, New York, 1980.

CHAPTER 6

Babbie, Earl: *The Practice of Social Research,* 6th ed., Wadsworth, Belmont, Calif., 1992.

Coleman, James S., Thomas Hoffer, and Sally Kilgore: "Cognitive Outcomes in Public and Private Schools," *Sociology of Education,* 55:65–76, 1982.

———, ———, and ———: *High School Achievement: Public, Catholic and Private Schools Compared,* Basic Books, New York, 1982.

Davis, James A.: *General Social Survey, 1972–1988: Cumulative Codebook,* National Opinion Research Center, Chicago, 1988.

Hirschi, Travis: *Causes of Delinquency,* University of California Press, Berkeley, Calif., 1969.

Kish, Leslie: *Survey Sampling,* Wiley, New York, 1965.

Levin, Jack: *Elementary Statistics in Social Research,* 3d ed., Harper & Row, New York, 1983.

McTavish, Donald G., and Herman J. Loether: *Descriptive and Inferential Statistics,* 3d ed., Allyn and Bacon, Boston, 1988.

National Opinion Research Center: *High School and Beyond,* Chicago, 1980.

Rand Corporation: *A Million Random Digits with 100,000 Normal Deviates,* Free Press, New York, 1955.

Slonim, Morris J.: *Sampling,* Simon and Schuster, New York, 1966.

Williams, Bill: *A Sampler on Sampling,* Wiley, New York, 1978.

Sudman, Seymour: "The Uses of Telephone Directories for Survey Sampling," *Journal of Marketing Research,* **10**:204–207, 1973.

——— and Norman Bradburn: *Response Effects in Surveys,* Aldine, Chicago, 1974.

Wallace, Walter: *The Logic of Science in Sociology,* Aldine, Chicago, 1971.

Warwick, Donald P., and Charles A. Lininger: *The Sample Survey: Theory and Practice,* McGraw-Hill, New York, 1975.

Wheatley, K. L., and W. A. Flexner: "Dimensions That Make Focus Groups Work," *Marketing News,* **22**:16–17, 1988

CHAPTER 7

Bradburn, Norman, and Seymour Sudman: *Improving Interview Method and Questionnaire Design,* Jossey-Bass, San Francisco, 1979.

Converse, Jean M., and Howard Schuman: *Conversations at Random: Survey Research as Interviewers See It,* Wiley, New York, 1974.

de Vaus, D. A.: *Surveys in Social Research,* Allen & Unwin, Boston, 1986.

Downs, Cal W., G. Paul Smeyak, and Ernest Martin: *Professional Interviewing,* Harper & Row, New York, 1980.

Groves, Robert M., and Robert L. Kahn: *Surveys by Telephone: A National Comparison with Personal Interviews,* Academic Press, New York, 1979.

Hirschi, Travis: *Causes of Delinquency,* University of California Press, Berkeley, Calif., 1969.

Kish, Leslie: "A Procedure for Objective Respondent Selection within the Household," *Journal of the American Statistical Association,* **44**:380–387, 1949.

Klineberg, Steven: Houston Area Survey, Houston, 1983, unpublished survey.

Riesman, David: "Some Observations on the Interviewing in the Teacher Apprehension Study," in Paul F. Lazarsfeld and Wagner Thielens, Jr. (eds.), *The Academic Mind: Social Scientists in a Time of Crisis,* Academic Press, New York, 1958.

Riley, Matilda White: *Sociological Research: A Case Approach,* Harcourt, Brace & World, New York, 1963.

Roth, Julius: "Hired Hand Research,' *The American Sociologist,* **1**:190–96, 1966.

Stewart, David W., and Pren W. Shandasani: *Focus Groups: Theory and Practice,* Sage, Newbury Park, Calif., 1990.

CHAPTER 8

Anderson, Barry F.: *The Psychology Experiment,* Brooks/Cole, Belmont, Calif., 1971.

Baron, James N., and Philip C. Reiss: "Same Time, Next Year: Aggregate Analysis of the Mass Media and Violent Behavior," *American Sociological Review,* **50**:347–363, 1985.

Berkowitz, Leonard, and Joseph T. Alioto: "The Meaning of an Observed Event as a Determinant of Its Aggressive Consequence," *Journal of Personality and Social Psychology,* **28**:206–217, 1973.

——— and Russell G. Geen: "Film Violence and Cue Properties of Available Targets," *Journal of Personality and Social Psychology,* **3**:525–530, 1966.

——— and ———: "Stimulus Qualities of the Target of Aggression," *Journal of Personality and Social Psychology,* **5**:364–368, 1967.

——— and Edna Rawlings: "Effects of Film Violence on Inhibitions against Subsequent Aggression," *Journal of Abnormal and Social Psychology,* **66**:405–412, 1963.

Campbell, Donald T., and Julian C. Stanley: *Experimental and Quasi-Experimental Designs for Research,* Rand McNally, Chicago, 1963.

Cook, Thomas D., and Donald T. Campbell: *Quasi-Experimentation: Design and Analysis Issues for Field Settings,* Houghton Mifflin, Boston, 1979.

Horner, Matina: Sex Differences in Achievement Motivation and Performance in Competitive and Non-competitive Situations, unpublished doctoral dissertation, University of Michigan, 1968.

Milgram, Stanley: "Some Conditions of Obedience and Disobedience to Authority," *Human Relations,* **18**:57–75, 1965.

Orenstein, Alan, and William R. F. Phillips: *Understanding Social Research: An Introduction,* Allyn and Bacon, Boston, 1978.

Orne, Martin T.: "On the Social Psychology Experiment: With Particular Reference to Demand Characteristics and Their Implications," in George H. Lewis (ed.), *Fist-Fights in the Kitchen,* Goodyear, Pacific Palisades, Calif., 1975.

Ostrum, Charles W.: *Times Series Analysis: Regression Techniques,* Sage, Beverly Hills, Calif., 1978.

Phillips, David: "The Impact of Mass Media Violence on U.S. Homicides," *American Sociological Review,* **48**:560–568, 1983.

Phillips, David P., and Kenneth A. Bollen: "Same Time, Last Year: Selective Data Dredging for Negative Findings," *American Sociological Review,* **50**:364–371, 1985.

Roethlisberger, F. J., and W. J. Dickson: *Management and the Worker,* Harvard University Press, Cambridge, Mass., 1939.

Rosenthal, Robert, and Lenore F. Jacobson: *Pygmalion in the Classroom,* Holt, Rinehart and Winston, New York, 1968.

—— and Ralph L. Rosnow: *The Volunteer Subject,* Wiley, New York, 1975.

CHAPTER 9

Anderson, Elijah: *A Place on the Corner,* University of Chicago Press, Chicago, 1978.

Bales, Robert F.: *Interaction Process Analysis: A Method for the Study of Small Groups,* Addison-Wesley, Cambridge, Mass., 1951.

——: *SYMLOG Case Study Kit,* Free Press, New York, 1980.

Becker, Howard S.: "Photography and Sociology," *Studies in the Anthropology of Visual Communication,* **1**:3–26, 1974.

Cloninger, Sally J.: The Sexually Dimorphic Image: The Influence of Gender Difference on Imagemaking, unpublished dissertation, Ohio State University, 1974.

Cohen, S., and L. Taylor: *Psychological Survival: The Effects of Long-Term Imprisonment,* Penguin, Harmondsworth, Middlesex, England, 1972.

Curry, Timothy J., and Alfred C. Clarke: *Introducing Visual Sociology,* Kendall/Hunt, Dubuque, Iowa, 1977.

Fetterman, David M.: *Ethnography Step by Step,* Sage, Newbury Park, Calif., 1989.

Freeman, Derek: *Margaret Mead and Samoa: The Making and Unmaking of an Anthropological Myth,* Harvard University Press, Cambridge, Mass., 1983.

Gold, Raymond L.: "Roles in Sociological Field Observations," in George J. McCall and J. L. Simmons (eds.), *Issues in Participant Observation,* Addison-Wesley, Reading, Mass., 1969.

Humphreys, Laud: *Tearoom Trade,* Aldine, Chicago, 1970.

Kanter, Rosabeth M.: *Men and Women of the Corporation,* Basic Books, New York, 1977.

Lewis, George H.: "Image-ing Society: Visual Sociology in Focus," paper presented to the Hawaiian Sociological Association, 1982.

—— and Jonathan F. Lewis: "The Dog in the Nighttime: Negative Evidence in Social Research," *British Journal of Sociology,* **31**:544–558, 1980.

Lofland, John: *Analyzing Social Settings: A Guide to Qualitative Observation and Analysis,* Wadsworth, Belmont, Calif., 1971.

Marshall, Eliot: "A Controversy on Samoa Comes of Age," *Science,* **219**:1042–1045, 1983.

McKinney, John C.: *Constructive Typology and Social Theory,* Appleton-Century-Crofts, New York, 1966.

National Park Service: *Film in User Analysis,* Project for Public Spaces, New York, 1979.

Parsons, Talcott: *The Social System,* Free Press, Glencoe, Ill., 1951.

Rosenhan, D. L.: "On Being Sane in Insane Places," in Martin Bulmer (ed.), *Social Research Ethics,* Macmillan, London, 1982.

Stasz, Clarice: "The Early History of Visual Sociology," in Jon Wagner (ed.), *Images of Information: Still Photography in the Social Sciences,* Sage, Beverly Hills, Calif., 1979.

Suchar, Charles S.: "Photographing the Changing Material Culture of a Gentrified Community," *Visual Sociology Review,* **3**:17–21, 1988.

Suelzle, Marijean, and Lenore Borzak: "Stages of Fieldwork," in Lenore Borzak (ed.), *Field Study: A Sourcebook for Experimental Learning,* Sage, Beverly Hills, Calif., 1981.

Wagner, Jon (ed.): *Images of Information: Still Photography in the Social Sciences,* Sage, Beverly Hills, Calif., 1979a.

——: "Avoiding Error," in Jon Wagner (ed.), *Images of Information: Still Photography in the Social Sciences,* Sage, Beverly Hills, Calif., 1979b.

Wax, Rosalie H.: *Doing Fieldwork: Warnings and Advice,* University of Chicago Press, Chicago, 1971.

Whyte, William Foote: *Street Corner Society: The Social Structure of an Italian Slum,* University of Chicago Press, Chicago, 1943.

Withall, John: "Assessment of the Social-Emotional Climates Experienced by a Group of Seventh Graders as They Moved from Class to Class," *Educational and Psychological Measurement,* **12**:440–452, 1952.

Zablocki, B.: *The Joyful Community,* Penguin, Baltimore, 1971.

CHAPTER 10

Alexander, Karl L., and Aaron M. Pallas: "Private Schools and Public Policy: New Evidence on Cognitive Achievement in Public and Private Schools," *Sociology of Education,* **56**:170–181, 1983.

Baker, Therese L., and Joyce A. Sween: "Synchronizing Post-Graduate Career, Marriage, and Fertility," *Western Sociological Review,* **13**: 69–86, 1982.

Bannan, Rosemary S.: "Briefing the Court: Dialectic as Methodological Perspective," *Journal of Contemporary Law,* **10**:121–139, 1984.

Berelson, Bernard: "Content Analysis," in Gardner Lindzey (ed.), *Handbook of Social Psychology,* Addison-Wesley, Cambridge, Mass., 1954.

Brewer, John, and Albert Hunter: *Multimethod Research: A Synthesis of Styles,* Sage, Newbury Park, Calif., 1989.

Cantor, David, and Kenneth C. Land: "Unemployment and Crime Rates in the Post–World War II United States: A Theoretical and Empirical Analysis," *American Sociological Review,* **50**:317–332, 1985.

Carey, James T.: "Changing Courtship Patterns in the Popular Song," *American Journal of Sociology,* **74**:720–731, 1969.

Chaffee, Steven H., George Gerber, et al.: "Defending the Indefensible," *Society,* **21**:30–35, 1984.

Coleman, James S., Thomas Hoffer, and Sally Kilgore: *High School Achievement: Public, Catholic and Private Schools Compared,* Basic Books, New York, 1982.

Davis, James A., and Tom W. Smith: *The NORC General Social Survey: A User's Guide,* Sage, Newbury Park, Calif., 1991.

Davis, Natalie Zemon: *The Return of Martin Guerre,* Harvard University Press, Cambridge, 1983.

Elder, Jr., Glen H.: *Children of the Great Depression,* University of Chicago Press, Chicago, 1974.

Fischer, David Hackett: *Growing Old in America,* Oxford University Press, New York, 1978.

Gerbner, George, et al.: "Cultural Indicators: Violence Profile No. 9," *Journal of Communication,* **28**:177–207, 1978.

——— et al.: "The 'Mainstreaming' of America: Violence Profile No. 11," *Journal of Communication,* **30**:10–29, 1980.

Gottschalk, Louis: *Understanding History,* Knopf, New York, 1950.

Hakim, Catherine: *Secondary Analysis in Social Research,* Allen and Unwin, London, 1982.

Holsti, Ole R.: *Content Analysis for the Social Sciences and the Humanities,* Addison-Wesley, Reading, Mass., 1969.

Horton, D.: "The Dialogue of Courtship in Popular Songs," *American Journal of Sociology,* **62**:569–578, 1957.

Kiecolt, K. Jill, and Laura E. Nathan: *Secondary Analysis of Survey Data,* Sage university paper 53, Sage, Newbury Park, Calif., 1985.

Office of Management and Budget: *Social Indicators,* Government Printing Office, Washington, 1973.

Rathje, William, L.: "Trace Measures," in Lee Sechrest (ed.), *Unobtrusive Measurement Today,* Jossey-Bass, San Francisco, 1979.

Riccobono, J., et al.: *National Longitudinal Study: Base Year (1972) through Fourth Follow-up (1979), Data File Users Manual,* National Center for Education Statistics, Research Triangle Park, N.C., 1981.

Schudson, Michael: *Discovering the News: A Social History of American Newspapers,* Basic Books, New York, 1978.

Sechrest, Lee, and Melinda Phillips: "Unobtrusive Measures: An Overview," in Lee Sechrest (ed.), *Unobtrusive Measurement Today,* Jossey-Bass, San Francisco, 1979.

Social Science Research Council Survey Archive: *Guide to the Survey Archives Social Sciences Data Holdings and Allied Services,* University of Essex, Essex, (n.d.).

U.S. Bureau of the Census: *Current Population Reports,* Government Printing Office, Washington.

———: *Statistical Abstract of the United States,* Government Printing Office, Washington, 1879–present.

U.S. Department of Commerce: *Social Indicators 1976,* Government Printing Office, Washington, 1977.

U.S. Department of Justice: *Uniform Crime Reporting Handbook,* Federal Bureau of Investigation, Washington, 1980.

————: *Criminal Victimization in the U.S., 1979,* Government Printing Office, Washington, 1981.

U.S. Department of Labor: *Employment and Training Report of the President,* Government Printing Office, Washington, 1980.

Webb, Eugene, Donalt T. Campbell, Richard D. Schwartz, and Lee Sechrest: *Unobtrusive Measures: Nonreactive Research in the Social Sciences,* Rand McNally, Chicago, 1966.

Williams, Gilbert A.: "Enticing Viewers: Sex and Violence in *TV Guide* Program Advertisements," *Journalism Quarterly,* **66**:970–973, 1989.

Wurtzel, Alan, and Guy Lometti: "Researching Television Violence," *Society,* **21**:22–30, 1984.

CHAPTER 11

Allen, Jr., Harris M., and David O. Sears: "Against Them or for Me: Community Impact Evaluations," in Lois-Ellin Datta and Robert Perloff (eds.), *Improving Evaluations,* Sage, Beverly Hills, Calif., 1979.

Andrews, Frank M. (ed.): *Research on the Quality of Life,* Survey Research Center, Institute for Social Research, University of Michigan, Ann Arbor, Mich., 1986.

———— and Stephen B. Withey: *Social Indicators of Well-Being: Americans' Perceptions of Life Quality,* Plenum, New York, 1976.

Brown, Lester R.: *State of the World 1991,* World Watch Institute Report, W. W. Norton, New York, 1991.

Campbell, Angus: *The Sense of Well-Being in America,* McGraw-Hill, New York, 1981.

Carley, Michael: *Social Measurement and Social Indicators,* Allen and Unwin, London, 1981.

Davenport, Barbara C., and Ronald L. Nuttall: "Cost-Effective Medicaid Mental Health Policies: Design and Testing," in Lois-Ellin Datta and Robert Perloff (eds.), *Improving Evaluations,* Sage, Beverly Hills, Calif., 1979.

Liu, Ben-Chieh: *Quality of Life Indicators in U.S. Metropolitan Areas,* Praeger, New York, 1976.

Naisbitt, John: *Megatrends: Ten New Directions Transforming Our Lives,* Warner, New York, 1982.

———— and Patricia Aburdene: *Megatrends 2000,* Morrow, New York, 1990.

Office of Management and Budget: *Social Indicators, 1973,* Government Printing Office, Washington, 1973.

Posavec, Emil J., and Raymond G. Carey: *Program Evaluation: Methods and Case Studies,* 3d ed., Prentice-Hall, Englewood Cliffs, New Jersey, 1989.

Scriven, Michael: "The Methodology of Evaluation," in R. W. Tyler, R. M. Gagne, and M. Scriven (eds.), *Perspectives of Curriculum Evaluation,* Rand McNally, Skokie, Ill., 1967.

Skellie, F. Albert, G. Melton Mobley, and Ruth E. Coan: "Cost Effectiveness of Community-Based Long-Term Care: Current Findings of Georgia's Alternative Health Services Project," *American Journal of Public Health,* **72**:353–358, 1982.

Terleckyj, Nestor E.: *Improvements in the Quality of Life: Estimates of Possibilities in the United States, 1974–1983,* National Planning Association, Washington, 1975.

U.S. Department of Commerce: *Social Indicators, 1976,* Government Printing Office, Washington, 1977.

U.S. Department of Health, Education, and Welfare: *Toward a Social Report,* Government Printing Office, Washington, 1969.

Weiss, Carol H.: *Evaluation Research,* Prentice-Hall, Englewood Cliffs, N.J., 1972.

Westinghouse Learning Corporation, Ohio University: *The Impact of Head Start: An Evaluation of the Effects of Head Start on Children's Cognitive and Affective Development,* U.S. Department of Commerce, Washington, 1969.

World Bank: *World Tables 1991,* The Johns Hopkins University Press, Baltimore, Md., 1991.

Yin, Robert K.: *Case Study Research: Design and Methods,* rev. ed., Sage, Newbury Park, Calif., 1989.

Zimring, Franklin E.: "Firearms and Federal Law: The Gun Control Act of 1968," in Gene V. Glass (ed.), *Evaluation Studies Review Annual,* Sage, Beverly Hills, Calif., 1976.

CHAPTER 13

Otto, Luther B., and Duane F. Alwin: "Athletes, Aspirations, and Attainments," *Sociology of Education,* **42**:102–113, 1977.

Riccobono, John, et al.: *National Longitudinal Study: Base Year (1972) through Fourth Follow-up (1979), Data File Users Manual,* National Center for Education Statistics, Washington, 1981.

CHAPTER 14

Hyman, Herbert: *Survey Design and Analysis,* Free Press, Glencoe, Ill., 1955.

Kendall, Patricia L., and Paul F. Lazarsfeld: "Problems of Survey Analysis," in Robert K. Merton (ed.), *Continuities in Social Research,* Free Press, Glencoe, Ill., 1950.

Middleton, Russell: "Alienation, Race, and Education," *American Sociological Review,* **28**:973–976, 1963.

Rosenberg, Morris: *The Logic of Survey Analysis,* Basic Books, New York, 1968.

Stouffer, Samuel A., et al.: *The American Soldier,* Princeton University Press, Princeton, N.J., 1949.

CHAPTER 15

Davis, James A.: *Elementary Survey Analysis,* Prentice-Hall, Englewood Cliffs, N.J., 1971.

Elifson, Kirk W., Richard P. Runyon, and Audrey Haber: *Fundamentals of Social Statistics,* 2d ed., McGraw-Hill, New York, 1990.

Loether, Herman J., and Donald G. McTavish: *Descriptive and Inferential Statistics: An Introduction,* Allyn & Bacon, Boston, 1976.

Rossi, Peter H.: *Down and Out in America: The Origins of Homelessness,* University of Chicago Press, Chicago, 1989.

Simon, Julian L., and Paul Burstein: *Basic Research Methods in Social Science,* 3d ed., Random House, New York, 1985.

CHAPTER 16

Baker, Therese L.: "The Dimensions of Nonauthoritarianism," *Journal of Personality Assessment,* **40**:626–634, 1976.

Beere, C. A.: *Women and Women's Issues: A Handbook of Tests and Measures,* Jossey-Bass, San Francisco, 1979.

Bogardus, E.: *Social Distance,* Antioch Press, Yellow Springs, Ohio, 1959.

Buros, O. K. (ed.): *Eighth Mental Measurements Yearbook,* Gryphon Press, Highland Park, N.J., 1978.

Hodge, Robert W., Paul M. Siegel, and Peter H. Rossi: "Occupational Prestige in the United States, 1925–63," *American Journal of Sociology,* **70**:286–302, 1964.

Johnson, O. G. (ed.): *Tests and Measurements in Child Development: Handbook II* (2 vols.), Jossey-Bass, San Francisco, 1976.

Kanouse, David E., et al.: *Effects of Postsecondary Experiences on Aspirations, Attitudes, and Self-Conceptions,* Rand, Santa Monica, Calif., 1980.

Miller, Delbert C.: *Handbook of Research Design and Social Measurement,* 5th ed., McKay, New York, 1991.

Nunnally, Jum C.: *Psychometric Theory,* 2d ed., McGraw-Hill, New York, 1978.

Osgood, C. E., C. J. Suci, and P. H. Tannenbaum: *The Measurement of Meaning,* University of Illinois Press, Urbana, Ill., 1957.

Reiss, Albert J.: *Occupations and Social Status,* Free Press, Glencoe, Ill., 1961.

Robinson, J. P., R. Athanasiou, and K. B. Head: *Measures of Occupational Attitudes and Occupational Characteristics,* Survey Research Center, Ann Arbor, Mich., 1969.

———, J. G. Rusk, and K. B. Head: *Measures of Political Attitudes,* Survey Research Center, Ann Arbor, Mich., 1968.

——— and P. R. Shaver: *Measures of Social Psychological Attitudes,* Survey Research Center, Ann Arbor, Mich., 1973.

Shaw, M. E., and J. M. Wright: *Scales for the Measurement of Attitudes,* McGraw-Hill, New York, 1967.

Treiman, Donald J.: *Occupational Prestige in Comparative Perspective,* Academic Press, New York, 1977.

Williamson, John B., et al.: *The Research Craft,* 2d ed., Little, Brown, Boston, 1982.

CHAPTER 17

Baker, Therese L., and Judith A. Bootcheck: "The Relationship of Marital Status and Career Preparation to Changing Work Orientations of Young Women: A Longitudinal Study," in A. Kerckhoff (ed.), *Research in Sociology of Education and Socialization,* vol. 5, 1985.

Caplovitz, David: *The Stages of Social Research,* Wiley, New York, 1983.

Humphreys, Laud: *Tearoom Trade,* Aldine, Chicago, 1970.

GLOSSARY

accretion measures   *Unobtrusive measures* of accumulated *physical traces* of social behavior (e.g., garbage, graffiti).

aggregate data   Data on large numbers of subjects showing a common characteristic. *Existing statistics* are a source of aggregate data.

anonymity   Assurance that subjects' identities will not be disclosed in any way.

antecedent variable   A third variable in a trivariate analysis that logically comes in a time sequence before the independent variable.

anthropology   A discipline focusing on the nature of human culture in which field research is the primary method of study.

applied research   Research for which one of the primary rationales is that the study may have some practical use. See *basic research.*

archival research   A method of studying organizations or societies, based on the collected records they have produced.

attrition   The loss of members of a sample, usually as a result of their refusal to respond or the researcher's inability to contact them.

bar graph   A graph on which categories of a variable are presented on the horizontal axis and their frequencies are presented on the vertical axis. The height of each bar represents the frequency of each attribute of a variable. The bars have gaps between them on the scale. See *histogram* and *frequency polygon.*

basic research   Research whose primary rationale is to contribute to systematic knowledge in a discipline. See *applied research.*

best-fit line   The line that would best reduce its distance to all points in a *scattergram.*

bivariate table   A two-variable table.

Bogardus Social Distance Scale   A scale used to measure attitudes toward ethnic, occupational, or religious groups or social class.

brute empiricism   Accumulating facts and information (without interpretation) as if this material were the sole means of establishing explanations. See *positivist.*

case studies   Observational studies of a single environment (an organization, a neighborhood, a public place). Field research is often based on a single case study.

case study protocol   A written plan based on a comprehensive outline of how the case study will be carried out. It should include an overview of the entire project, the field procedures, questions to be answered in the study, and a guide for preparing the final report.

categorical variables   Variables made up of sets of categories that do not represent a numerical measure. See *mutually exclusive categories* and *exhaustive categories.*

cathode ray tube (CRT)   A display monitor of a computer.

cell   In a cross-classification table, the position where two categories meet. In a 2 × 3 bivariate table, there will be six cells.

central processing unit (CPU)   The data processing component of a computer's hardware.

chi-square (χ^2)   An inferential statistic testing the *null hypothesis* of independence between two variables.

classical experiment   A *true experiment* in which a pretest is given to both the experimental and control groups, the experimental group is "treated" with the independent variable, and both groups are given the posttest.

classical test theory   The theory that if a test (or measure) is repeated over and over again, errors will tend to cancel each other out over time. See *random measurement error.*

closed-ended question   Questions in a questionnaire that force the respondent to select from a list of possible responses (often called *forced-choice* question).

clusters   *Heterogeneous groups* (such as schools, other institutions, blocks) selected at the first stage of a *multistage cluster sample.* See *primary sampling unit.*

codebook   A list of variables showing where they can be found and what decisions were made in setting up and recoding them.

coefficient of reproducibility   A test to determine whether a set of items form a *Guttman Scale.*

coercion of subjects   Forcing subjects to participate in a study which may be inconvenient or detrimental to them. Subjects may be in a "captive" situation (prisoners) or unable to defend their interests (children).

cohort studies   Studies based on a longitudinal study design in which the subjects are grouped by their ages for comparative purposes. The groups are sometimes referred to as generations.

community impact assessment   Evaluation research that tries to determine how a policy might affect a community.

computer-assisted telephone interviewing (CATI) An interviewing technique in which the interviewer uses a computer to select telephone numbers, reads the interview questions off the screen, and enters the responses.

concepts   Formally developed ideas that a researcher may seek to operationalize.

conceptualization   The process of forming and reforming concepts to make them useful and measurable in social research.

concurrent validity   A form of *criterion-related validity* in which the criterion to test the validity of the variable is measured at the same time as the variable itself.

condensed trivariate table   A three-variable table in which the percentage of one category of the dependent variable is presented in a cross tabulation of the independent and test variables.

confidence intervals   The range of values within which a population parameter (e.g., the mean of the population) would be expected to fall on a *normal curve*.

confidence levels   Probability estimates that a population parameter would fall within a particular confidence interval.

confidentiality   A promise to restrict knowledge of the identities of research subjects to the researcher and staff members.

constant   A measure that shows no variation.

construct validity   A form of validity testing in which hypotheses generated from a concept are tested, and the results of these tests are correlated with the original concept.

content analysis   A research technique that describes in an objective, systematic, and quantified manner the content of a body of communication.

content validity   The most basic form of validity testing in which the measure of a concept is examined in light of its meaning. See *face validity* and *sampling validity*.

contingency question   Question in a survey that depends on the responses to earlier questions or which has questions dependent on it.

contingency table   A table that cross-tabulates two variables. Also called a *cross classification* or *cross tabulation.*

continuous variables   Variables measured on a numerical scale which has an infinite number of points.

control group   The comparison group in an experiment who are not exposed to the experimental treatment.

control variable   The third variable in a trivariate analysis. The relationship between the dependent and independent variables is examined under each condition of the control variable. See *test variable.*

convenience sample   A nonprobability sample composed of subjects available and willing to participate.

cost-benefit analysis   An assessment of whether the benefits of a program or social strategy are worth the costs.

covert research   Carrying out research without the knowledge or consent of those being studied or by misrepresenting the role of the researcher.

criterion-related validity   A test of validity in which a variable under examination is correlated with another variable to which it should logically be related. (For example, college grades could be a criterion for testing the validity of college entrance examination scores.)

criterion variable   This is another name for a *dependent variable*. It is the criterion measure for determining whether the *predictor variable* brought about its expected effect.

cross-classification   A table that cross-tabulates two variables.

cross-sectional   Data gathered at one point in time.

cross tabulation   A table that presents one variable classified by another. A *cross-classification,* or *contingency, table.*

curvilinear relationship   A curved *best-fit line* indicating that an increase in the value of one variable is not related to an increase in the value of another.

database management program   A software program offering a structured approach to data entry, thereby reducing the likelihood of data entry errors and allowing storage on one or multiple files for later retrieval. Programs may include menus customized to facilitate different data collection instruments, multiple follow-ups, etc.

deductive method   A method in which hypotheses are logically derived from theories.

degrees of freedom (*df*)   In a chi-square table, *df* are determined by the formula $(r - 1)(c - 1)$ in which $r =$ number of rows in the table and $c =$ number of columns. The *df* is then used in conjunction with the computed *chi-square* statistic to determine significance level using a chi-square table.

demand characteristics   Inadvertent cues conveying the experimental hypothesis to subjects in such a way that they may try to cooperate in validating the experimental hypothesis. This undermines the *internal validity* of the experiment.

dependent variable   The variable in an experiment or survey that is affected, or subject to being affected, by the independent variable.

dependent variable study   A study that investigates why, how, and under what conditions change in a dependent variable occurred.

descriptive statistics   Summary numerical descriptions of large bodies of data, most commonly stating the central tendencies and variability of given variables or the relationship between variables.

dimensions   In conceptualization and measurement, dimensions refer to the different qualities of a concept. Indicators to measure each dimension are sought. A concept may have one (unidimensional) or more (multidimensional) dimensions. See *indicator*.

discrete variables   Variables measured on a numerical scale in which each point on the scale represents a whole number.

dispersion   The degree of variation of scores around the mean. This is measured by the *standard deviation*.

disproportionate sampling   A sampling design which deliberately increases the sample size of some subgroups (for example, minority groups) so that there will be a sufficiently large number of subgroup members in the study for the purposes of analysis. See *weighting*.

distorter variable   A third variable that reverses a relationship originally observed between two other variables. Controlling this third variable eliminates the distortion seen in the original relationship.

double-blind experiment   The practice in true experiments of having neither the subjects nor the experimenter know which subjects are in the experimental or control groups.

dross numbers   These are telephone numbers that for one reason or another do not lead to households. In telephone surveys, the ratio of good to dross numbers is about one to five.

dummy variable   A two-category variable, in which "1" represents the presence of an attribute and "0" represents its absence. In any statistical analysis in which variables based on numerical scales are required (such as regression analysis), categorical variables can be converted into dummy variables.

ecological fallacy   Using evidence from a group level of analysis to reach conclusions about individuals.

edge coding   A form of precoding on questionnaires in which the codes for computerizing the data are printed on the edge of the instrument across from the questions.

elaboration paradigm   An exemplary model to explain certain types of outcomes that can occur with the entry of a third variable into a bivariate relationship. The outcomes are called replications, explanations, interpretations, or specifications.

elements   The individual *units* composing a sample, usually individual persons.

empirical   Based on observable evidence.

empirical generalizations   Formed out of observations in the research process; the search for *regularities*. See *scientific model*.

epsilon   High-low percentage differences between the first and last columns in a *cross tabulation*.

erosion measures   *Unobtrusive measures* of wear or use.

ethnography   The observational description of a people or some other social unit.

evaluation research   Research to measure the effectiveness of a social program or institution.

exhaustive categories   Categories that cover all the potential range of variation in a variable.

existing statistics   Created statistical data that are available to researchers for analysis.

experiment   A research method that seeks to isolate the effects of an independent variable on a dependent variable under strictly controlled conditions.

experimental group   The group in an experiment that is exposed to the experimental treatment. See *control group*.

experimental mortality   Loss of subjects in an experiment over time. This is a potential cause of *internal validity* problems.

ex post facto design   An after-only evaluation research design where pretesting is not possible.

external validity The generalizability of an experiment to other settings, other treatments, other subjects.

face-to-face interview A method of administering a survey in which an interviewer questions an interviewee using a structured set of questions. See *interview schedule.*

face validity A form of *content validity*; a careful consideration and examination of the measurement instrument is made in order to determine whether the instrument is measuring what it purports to measure (sometimes called armchair validity).

factorial design The design of an experiment in which more than one independent variable is being measured.

field experiment An experiment taking place in a real-world environment, where it is more difficult to impose controls.

field research A research method based on careful observation of behavior in a natural social environment.

focus group A small group of individuals drawn together to express views on a specific set of questions in a group environment. This method may serve a number of functions in social research: as a starting point for developing a survey, to recognize potential problems in a research design, or to interpret evidence.

follow-up procedures The methods of following up nonrespondents to mail questionnaires to increase *response rate*. Methods include sending postcard reminders, sending second questionnaires and requests, and telephoning to solicit cooperation or to get the responses over the telephone.

formative evaluation An evaluation of a program in process, information from which will be used to reform or improve the program. See *summative evaluation.*

frequency distribution The distribution of cases across the categories of a variable, presented in numbers and percentages.

frequency polygon A graph, representing the same data from numerical variables as a histogram, which substitutes the midpoints of each histogram bar with dots which are then connected with lines to indicate the shape of the distribution. See *histogram* and *bar graph.*

full disclosure The practice of making all evidence generated and analyzed in the course of scientific research available to the relevant scientific community. This means that negative and insignificant findings should be presented as well as positive findings.

gamma (γ) An extension of the statistic *Yule's Q,* appropriate for ordinal variables.

Guttman Scale A form of scale with a cumulative structure such that responses to some items subsume responses to others. Tests for the degree of cumulativeness in the scale are carried out (see *coefficient of reproducibility*).

hard copy The printed output of a computer.

hardware The computer equipment itself, made up of input mechanisms, storage capacities, central processing unit (CPU), and output mechanisms.

Hawthorne effect When subjects in an experiment produce the expected experimental effect without being exposed to the experimental treatment (they are affected by merely being in the experiment itself). A Hawthorne control group, exposed to a meaningless treatment, is often added in an experiment.

heterogeneous groups In sampling, clusters which are usually formed as established groups (e.g., students in schools, residents of blocks) and are heterogeneous in their composition (contain individuals who vary in sex, race, etc.). See *clusters* and *multistage cluster sampling.*

histogram A graph depicting the frequency distribution of a numerical variable with bars which have at their centermost point the value being presented. The edge of each bar is halfway to the next value and touches the next bar. See *frequency polygon* and *bar graph.*

historiography The writing of history, which involves the imaginative reconstruction of the past from the surviving data.

history as actuality The whole history of the past including what can never be fully known.

history as record The study of what can be known of the past through the surviving record.

homogeneous groups In sampling, strata formed by sets of individuals who share certain characteristics (sex, race, age, etc.). See *strata* and *stratified sample.*

hypotheses Conditional statements, relating the expected effects of one variable on another, that can be subject to testing.

independent variable The variable, in an experiment or survey, that exercises an effect on a *dependent variable.*

independent variable study A study in which one social group or context is compared to another.

index A composite measure developed to represent different components of a concept.

indicators Observable phenomena that can be used to measure dimensions of a concept.

inductive method Reasoning from particular cases to more general theories.

inferences In probability theory, the object is to be able to make accurate guesses (or inferences) from evidence gathered on a relatively small probability sample to a much larger population. See *inferential statistics* and *probability sample.*

inferential statistics Statistics that allow a researcher to draw conclusions regarding the general population from the findings of a representative sample drawn from that population.

informed consent This is achieved when subjects in a research study comprehend its objectives, understand their level of *confidentiality,* and agree to cooperate.

institutional review board Committees in institutions where scientific research is being carried out who review the research methods to be sure that the rights of human (or animal) subjects are being protected.

intensity structure The patterns that make best sense of the multiple items in a *scale,* and their interrelationships.

interaction effect The tendency for a third variable to interact with the independent variable, thereby altering the relationship of the independent variable to the dependent variable. This means that the relationship between the independent and dependent variable will vary under different conditions of the third variable.

internal validity The extent to which an experiment actually has caused what it appeared to cause.

intersubjectivity The shared perceptions of individual observers. The greater the intersubjectivity, the greater the validity and reliability of the observations.

intervening variable A third variable in a trivariate study that logically falls in a time sequence between the independent and dependent variables.

interview schedule A set of questions with guided instructions for an interviewer to use in carrying out an interview.

invasion of privacy A possible abuse in social research, in which rights of privacy have been ignored. Must be weighed in relation to the public's right to know. See *informed consent.*

item analysis A test for validity of an *index* in which a cross tabulation of total index scores to separate items making up the index is examined.

judgmental sample A *nonprobability sample* composed of subjects judged to be relevant to the needs of the study.

laboratory experiment An experiment taking place in a laboratory setting, where it is possible to maintain a large number of controls.

lambda (λ) A statistical measure of association appropriate for nominal variables.

levels of measurement There are four commonly defined levels for measuring variables: *nominal,* for distinct categories with no order; *ordinal,* for ordered categories; *interval,* for numerical scales with mathematically defined intervals between points on the scale, but no true zero point; and *ratio,* for numerical scales with mathematically defined intervals and a true zero point.

Likert Scale A widely used scaling device that includes ordinal categories of agreement to a set of items for which the scores are summed and averaged.

linear regression A statistical analysis which represents the best-fit line between two variables. See *best-fit line* and *linear relationship.*

linear relationship Indicated by a diagonal *best-fit line* in a *scattergram,* a linear relationship shows that an increase (or decrease) in one variable is related to an increase (or decrease) in the other.

longitudinal data Data gathered over time.

longitudinal designs Studies based on longitudinal data include *trend studies,* in which data are compared across time points on different subjects; *cohort studies,* in which data on subjects from the same age cohort are compared at different points in time; and *panel studies,* in which the same subjects are compared across time points.

mail survey A survey consisting of a self-administered questionnaire, instructions, and a request for participation sent out through the mail to a selected sample. See *questionnaire.*

mainframe computer A large computer which can run many different kinds of jobs simultaneously and which can be accessed either through terminals near the computer or through remote job entry from other locations.

marginals The row totals that appear to the right of a *cross tabulation* and the column totals that appear at the bottom of each column. They are the base numbers on which the percentages in each cell of the table are calculated.

matching An experimental procedure in which subjects to be placed in the experimental group are matched with subjects possessing similar characteristics in the control group. This is not equivalent to *randomization in assignment to groups* required for *true experimental designs.*

matrix questions Sets of questions in a questionnaire that use the same set of response categories.

maturation A potential cause of internal validity problems in an experiment, due to the subjects getting older between the pre- and posttests, becoming more experienced, more (or less) intelligent, or physically strong.

mean The arithmetic average determined by adding up the quantities of each unit in a distribution and then dividing by the number of units.

measurement A process in which numbers are assigned according to rules of correspondence between definitions and observations.

measurement error Error which is unavoidably introduced into measurement in the process of observing a phenomenon. An observed measure (or score) is therefore based on the true score plus or minus the error. In social research this error may necessarily be great because of the crudity of the instruments used in measuring social phenomena.

median A measure of central tendency that represents the midpoint in a distribution of ordered data.

microcomputer (personal computer) A small computer in which the terminal, the screen, and the processing unit are located together.

mode A measure of central tendency that represents the most frequent value in a distribution.

modem A device that connects a terminal to a *mainframe computer,* often by means of a telephone hookup.

monotonicity Steady increases (or decreases) across the cells of a cross tabulation, indicating that an increase (or decrease) in the independent variable is related to an increase (or decrease) in the dependent variable.

multiple methods Using more than one research method, each with different strengths, to better approximate an ideal method and to create more generalizable evidence so as to better test the theories underlying the research.

multiple regression A statistical analysis which extends the linear regression model, relating one dependent variable to more than one independent variable. The influence of each independent variable can be computed separately, holding constant the influence of all other independent variables; the relative weights of each independent variable can then be determined. The combined effects of all the independent variables on the dependent variable can also be determined. See *linear regression.*

multistage cluster sampling A form of *probability sampling* in which *clusters* are selected first and then members of the clusters are selected at a second stage.

mutually exclusive categories Categories of a variable that must be distinct from one another.

natural experiment An experiment that has not been brought about by the efforts of the experimenter, but has naturally occurred in the real world, and is being selected out for study by the experimenter.

negative evidence In a field study, the nonoccurrence of expected events, an occurrence which is not reacted to, or one which is distorted in its interpretation or withheld from analysis.

negative (inverse) relationship A type of relationship between two variables in which cases that are *low* on one variable are *high* on the other. See *positive (direct) relationships.*

nonequivalent control group A control group which was not selected on the basis of random assignment. Usually created as a rough comparison group to participants in a social intervention program being evaluated. See *ex post facto design.*

nonprobability sample A sample based on a method for selecting nonprobability sample subjects that is not based on the rules of probability.

nonsampling error Mistakes in the data due to errors such as those caused by respondents' misunderstandings, the interviewer's incorrect entries, or faulty transcribing of the data by coders. See *sampling error.*

normal curve A frequency curve with a characteristic bell-shaped form. The distributions of continuous variables approach this curve as samples are repeated or as sample sizes increase.

null hypothesis A logical assumption that there is no relationship between the two variables being studied in the population. This assumption can be tested with *inferential statistics.*

numerical variables Variables measured on a numerical scale.

objective social indicators Aggregate measures of some actual occurrences or behaviors (such as high school dropout rates, average family income). See *subjective social indicators.*

observation   The primary work of science. In social research, various methods are used to facilitate observation for its measurement, recording, and analysis.

observer-as-participant   A field researcher who is primarily an observer of the field but participates to some degree in another informal role. See *participant-as-observer.*

occupational prestige scale   A *scale* that assigns scores to occupations on the basis of prestige rankings established at various times in the United States and other countries.

ongoing evaluation   Evaluation research carried out over the course of a social intervention program to assess its progress while in operation. See *preprogram evaluation.*

open-ended question   Question in a questionnaire that allows the respondent to answer in his or her own words.

operationalization   The process of figuring out how to measure *concepts* using empirical evidence.

oral history   History based on verbal accounts instead of written records.

original relationship   The bivariate relationship representing the base-level association between a dependent variable and an independent variable. See *partial relationship* and *bivariate table.*

panel studies   Based on a longitudinal study design in which the same group of respondents is followed up over time for comparative purposes.

paradigm   The set of presuppositions on which scientific activity is built; the body of theories, ideas, models, test cases, and values shared by a scientific community; and the specific scientific accomplishments (exemplars) that influence future scientific activity.

parameters   The true values of population characteristics, which may only be inferred from the descriptions of these values in a sample.

partial relationship   The relationship of two variables for the partial group category of a third variable.

participant-as-observer   A field researcher who serves as a participant in the field being studied. This means that the researcher has some role (or job) in the field setting other than observer. See *observer-as-participant.*

participant observation   A method of doing *field research* in which the researcher participates in a role in the field (for example, as a consultant) at the same time as the field observations are being collected.

Pearson's *r*   Referred to also as a *correlation coefficient* or more formally as *Pearson's product-moment correlation*; it is a statistical measure of the strength and direction of relationships between interval scale variables.

physical traces   *Unobtrusive measures* which include the examination of unintentional erosion and accretion of products of human origin or endeavor.

plagiarism   The incorporation of the work of one person into the presentation of work of another, without citing the source.

policy research   Social research from which findings are used to defend or refute various policies at the local or national level.

population   The collection of all elements (either known or unknown) from which a sample is drawn. In a *probability sample,* the population consists of the *elements* in the *sampling frame.*

positive (direct) relationship   A type of relationship between two variables in which cases that are *high* on one variable tend to be *high* on the other, and cases that are *low* on one variable tend to be *low* on the other. See *negative (inverse) relatonship.*

positivist   One who strives to accumulate facts as the sole means of establishing explanations.

posttest   In an experiment, measuring the effect of the experimental treatment. The results are often compared to a *pretest.*

posttest-only control group design   A more streamlined *true experimental design* in which neither the experimental nor the control group is subject to a pretest and both are administered a posttest.

precoded questionnaire   Coding information that is included on the questionnaire instrument itself. This facilitates transferring the data to a computer.

predictive validity   A form of criterion-related validity in which the measure being examined is correlated with a criterion which the measure should predict. See the example given in *criterion-related validity.*

predictor variable   Another name for the *independent variable*; it is the variable on which a prediction can be based. See *criterion variable.*

preexperimental designs   These are experimental designs that do not meet all the criteria for a true experiment. They include the one-shot case study, the one-group pretest-posttest design, and the static-group comparison.

preprogram evaluation   Evaluation research initiated before a social intervention program is established to anticipate possible effects of the program. See *ongoing evaluation.*

pretest   A base-line measure in an experiment that can be compared with the postexperimental treatment test, the *posttest.*

pretesting   A strongly recommended procedure in survey research in which the instrument is given to trial subjects.

primary sampling unit   In a sample to be drawn in more than one stage, the primary sampling units are the groups specified (*strata* or *clusters*) to be drawn first, the *secondary sampling unit*, the units to be drawn second, etc.

primary sources   Written materials historians use based on records of eyewitnesses to events.

probability proportionate to size (PPS) sampling   A selection method used in cluster sampling to select strata within clusters that are proportionate to their size.

probability sample   A sample designed according to the rules of probability, which allows a determination of how likely the members of the sample are to be representative of the population from which they were drawn.

proportionate reduction of error (PRE)   A ratio of the number of prediction errors when the researcher has no information about the independent variable to the prediction errors when the researcher has information about the independent variable. See *lambda.*

proposal   See *research proposal.*

purposive sample   A form of *nonprobability sample* in which the subjects selected seem to meet the proposed needs of the study.

quality-of-life (QOL) studies   *Social indicators* studies that report the average quality of social life in a nation or large social environment.

quasi-experimental designs   Experimental designs where some experimental conditions required for a true experiment (often the *randomization in assignment* of subjects to groups) cannot be carried out. See *regression discontinuity* and *time-series experiment.*

questionnaire   A written set of questions used to survey respondents. See *mail survey.*

quota sample   A form of nonprobability sample in which subsamples are selected from clearly defined groups.

random-digit dialing (ROD)   A computerized method of selecting telephone numbers randomly for a telephone survey.

random measurement error   Measurement errors incurred in the process of observing phenomena. Because some of the errors will be higher than the true measure and some lower, over an infinite number of repeated measures such errors would cancel one another out. See *classical test theory.*

random numbers   Sets of randomly determined numbers generated from a computer program or from a published random number list. See *simple random sampling (SRS).*

randomization in assignment to groups   Procedures for placing subjects randomly in the experimental or control group in a true experiment.

range   The distance between the highest and lowest point (the minimum and maximum value) in a distribution of cases.

rationale   The reasons why a particular subject of study and a particular method for carrying it out may have value or purpose.

raw data   Data before they have been processed.

reductionism   The tendency to reduce complex social phenomena to a single cause. A common example is psychological reductionism, which uses individual personality traits to explain the behavior of groups.

regression discontinuity   A *quasi-experimental design* usually set up to study the effects of a program or treatment on a group that needs and gets it, as compared with a group that does not.

regularities   Repeated patterns seen in data.

reliability   The degree to which a measurement procedure produces similar outcomes when it is repeated. Tests for reliability include measures of stability (test-retest reliability) and measures of equivalence.

research proposal   The written plan to guide a research project.

response   In an experiment, the effect that is produced by the experimental stimulus. Equivalent to the *dependent variable.*

response rate   The proportion of the sample that returns questionnaires. Response rates for mail questionnaires can be increased by using *follow-up procedures.*

response set   The tendency in answering a survey to give the same responses to different questions. This can be reduced by switching the positive and negative direction of the response choices.

rights of human subjects   The right of subjects of research to be protected from physical or psychological abuse and to be helped to maintain their privacy and their good reputations.

r squared (r^2)   Also called the *coefficient of determination*. The square of *Pearson's r*. It denotes the proportion of variance in the dependent variable that can be explained by the independent variable (or the amount of *variance* explained by the linear model).

running descriptions   These are types of field notes that include concrete descriptions of events, people, statements, and conversations seen and heard in the field.

sample   A set of selected subjects for study drawn according to some principles of sampling.

sampling distribution of the sample mean   This is the distribution of means from repeated samples from the same population. The greater the number of samples drawn, the more closely this distribution approximates a normal curve.

sampling error   In a *probability sample,* this is the variability of a mean of the sample from the mean of the population. See *nonsampling error.*

sampling frame   A list of all the *elements* in a population from which a *probability sample* may be drawn.

sampling validity   A form of testing for the *content validity* of the measure of a concept by looking to see if the measure includes a fair representation (or sample) of the various domains of meaning within the concept.

scale   A composite measure of a concept, based on some aspect of the *intensity structure* of the interrelationships between items in the scale. See *Bogardus Social Distance Scale, Likert Scale, Guttman Scale, Thurstone Scale.*

scattergram   A graph on which the values of one variable measured on the vertical axis have been plotted in relationship to the values on the other variable on the horizontal axis. See *best-fit line.*

scientific ethos   Norms or institutional imperatives governing the behavior of scientists which protect the integrity of the scientific enterprise. Merton defined four primary norms: universalism, communism, disinterestedness, and organized skepticism.

scientific model   Includes theories and observations, generalizations, and specifications. See *deductive method* and *inductive method.*

secondary analysis   A research method in which data from an earlier study (often a survey) are used as the basis for a new study.

secondary sampling unit   In a sample to be drawn in more than one stage, the secondary sampling units (strata or clusters) to be drawn second. See *primary sampling unit.*

secondary sources   Written materials which describe or interpret some past event either close to the time it occurred or in later years.

selection effect   Differences noted among respondents from different organizations (*clusters*) which are explained not as the result of what the organization did, but because of factors on which selection to the organization was based.

Semantic Differential Scale   A bipolar scale allowing for graduated intermediate response to a stimulus referent.

serendipity factor   A term used to describe the unanticipated ways in which tests of hypotheses from one theory can sometimes lead to the development of quite unrelated theories.

simple random sampling (SRS)   A method of *probability sampling* in which *elements* in a *sampling frame* are numbered and then drawn into the sample if they match the *random numbers* selected from a random number list.

skew   Assymetry in the distribution of data, or the degree to which the distribution is not evenly spread around the central point.

snowball sample   A form of nonprobability sample in which the researcher selects a few subjects who possess the qualities being studied, then asks these subjects to generate the names of others, who are in turn asked to generate names of others.

social desirability   The tendency of respondents to respond to potentially threatening (sensitive) questions in such a way as to make themselves look better.

social indicators   Measures of aggregate social conditions that are of interest to a society as a way of evaluating the overall state of that society.

socioeconomic index (SEI)   A scale that assigns ranks to occupations on the basis of income, educational attainments, and prestige of those who hold the occupations.

software   Programmed instructions that tell a computer what to do.

Solomon four-group design   The most comprehensive type of *true experimental design* in which both experimental and control groups are pretested and posttested.

special population study   A study (usually based on qualitative data) the primary aim of which is to develop a careful description of a special population.

sponsorship Financial or official support for research often received from organizations, agencies, or foundations. It is important to make this sponsorship known in the cover letter of a questionnaire or in an interview.

spurious relationship A strong relationship between two variables that disappears when the relationship is examined under the controlled conditions of a third variable. This means that the unseen influence of the third variable caused the original strong relationship between the dependent and independent variables.

standard deviation The square root of the variance; this commonly used measure indicates the degree of *dispersion* of all the values in a distribution from the mean value.

statistical regression The tendency in an experiment for those scoring at the extremes in the pretest to move to more middle-range scores on the posttest. This occurs because the extreme scores are more subject to error than the middle-range scores. It can cause a problem of *internal validity* in an experiment because the greater change in the scores of the extreme scorers may be falsely registered as an effect of the experimental treatment.

statistical significance The likelihood that the magnitude of the statistical association shown in a sample would be found consistently if repeated samples were drawn from the same population. In other words, the likelihood that the association observed is not the result of chance or error.

statistics Tools allowing summary descriptions of large bodies of data. When data are from probability samples, statistics can be used to estimate corresponding population parameters. See *descriptive statistics* and *inferential statistics.*

stimulus In an experiment this is the *independent variable,* designed to bring about a *response.*

strata The *homogeneous groups* selected from which a *stratified sample* will be drawn.

stratified sample A form of probability sampling in which a *sampling frame* is divided into one or more *strata* (sex, grade) from which the sample is drawn using simple random or systematic sampling strategies.

strength of relationship The degree of relationship between the two variables in a bivariate analysis.

subgroup comparisons When the independent variable represents a group to which the subjects belong, the object of the analysis can be a comparison of the differences in the dependent variable between the subgroups.

subjective social indicators Aggregate social measures of the attitudes and perceptions of individuals (e.g., job satisfaction, a sense of well-being). See *objective social indicators.*

summative evaluation A type of evaluation which summarizes the effects of a program after it is completed. See *formative evaluation.*

suppressor variable A third variable that strengthens an originally observed weak relationship between two other variables. Controlling this third variable eliminates the suppression.

survey research A research method that analyzes the responses of a defined sample to a set of questions measuring attitudes and behaviors.

system file A transposed raw data file in which the variables have been set up according to the requirements of a software program. Contains both the data and the necessary commands from the computer software program.

systematic sampling A form of probability sampling in which every *n*th element is selected into the sample, following a random start.

tampering with results An abuse in scientific research in which results may be altered or fabricated, often to have the evidence match preestablished hypotheses.

telephone survey A survey administered over the telephone, requiring somewhat different techniques from a mail survey or a face-to-face interview. See *computer-assisted telephone interviewing (CATI)* and *random-digit dialing (RDD).*

test variable The third variable in a trivariate analysis. A variable under whose conditions the strength of the relationship between the dependent and independent variables can be tested. See *control variable.*

theories Proposed explanations for a set of coordinated occurrences or relationships.

Thurstone Scale A scale composed of items selected by judges as indicative of measuring some concept.

time-series experiment A quasi-experimental design used when there is a large set of already collected data indicating rates over time. The experimenter examines the effects of an event (e.g., a new law) occurring at some point in time and studies changes in the rates before and after the event.

trend studies Based on longitudinal study design in which similar data collected in different years (and from different subjects) are compared.

triangulation   Drawing together multiple types of evidence gathered from different sources using different methods of data collection.

trivariate table   A three-variable table.

true experimental designs   These are designs organized in such a way as to meet the criterion for an experiment (that an independent variable be related to change in a dependent variable) and at the same time to address most successfully the potential problems of invalidity. They include the *classical experiment*, the *Solomon four-group design*, and the *posttest-only control group design*.

typology   The forming of a set of types based on a model, often developing out of a search for polar opposites.

unit   This is another term for the *elements* in a sample.

units of analysis   The social entities whose characteristics are the focus of study. In social research these may include individuals, groups, programs, organizations and institutions, larger communities (nations), or cultural artifacts.

univariate analysis   Analyses of single variables, such as frequency distributions or analyses of central tendencies, such as mean, median, or mode.

unobtrusive measures   The study of physical traces, archives, and observations without participation, generally used as a supplementary source of data in a research project.

validity   Tests for determining whether a measure is measuring the concept which the researchers think is being measured. See *content validity, criterion-related validity,* and *construct validity.*

variable   A measure on which differences in response can be established.

variance   A way of measuring how far different units which have been used to establish a mean vary from the mean. See *standard deviation.*

verstehen   The understanding of social action, the objective of field research.

visual sociology   This term refers to a branch of sociology in which social action is studied by photographing or filming social environments and the people who inhabit them.

weighting   A method used in probability sampling to give adequate emphasis to subgroups of disproportionate size or to cancel out the effects of differential response rates.

Yule's Q   A statistical measure of association appropriate for 2×2 cross-classification tables.

ACKNOWLEDGMENTS

QUOTATIONS

Pages 28, 29: Anderson, Elijah, *A Place on the Corner,* University of Chicago Press, 1978. Reprinted from Elijah Anderson, *A Place on the Corner,* by permission of the University of Chicago Press, © 1978 by the University of Chicago. All rights reserved.

Page 32: Kanter, Rosabeth, *Men and Women of the Corporation,* Basic Books, Inc., 1977. Reprinted from p. 233, *Men and Women of the Corporation* by Rosabeth Moss Kanter. Copyright © 1977 by Rosabeth Moss Kanter. Reprinted by permission of Basic Books, Inc., Publishers.

Pages 125, 127, 128: Zeller, Richard, and Edward G. Carmines, *Measurement in the Social Sciences: The Link between Theory and Data,* Cambridge University Press, 1980, excerpts from pp. 79, 81, 82, 100. Copyright © 1980. Reprinted by permission of Cambridge University Press.

Pages 194, 195: Converse, Jean, and Howard Schuman, *Conversations at Random,* John Wiley & Sons, Inc., 1974, pp. 27, 50. Copyright © 1974. Reprinted by permission of John Wiley & Sons, Inc.

Page 245: Kanter, Rosabeth, *Men and Women of the Corporation,* Basic Books, Inc., 1977. Reprinted from p. 295, *Men and Women of the Corporation* by Rosabeth Moss Kanter. Copyright © 1977 by Rosabeth Moss Kanter. Reprinted by permission of Basic Books, Inc., Publishers.

BOXES

Box on How an Income Maintenance Plan Works on page 24: Adapted from Wright, Sonia R., and James D. Wright, "Income Maintenance and Work Behavior," *Social Policy,* volume 6, pp. 24–32; © 1975 by Social Policy Corporation. Used by permission.

Box 2-1 on page 53: Adapted from Laurie J. Bauman, Ruth E. K. Stein, and Henry Ireys, "A Framework for Conceptualizing Interventions," *Sociological Practice Review,* volume 2, pp. 241–251; © 1991 by the American Sociological Association.

Box 2-2 on page 62: Adapted from Douglas Lee Eckberg, and Lester Hill, Jr., "The Paradigm Concept and Sociology," *American Sociological Review,* volume 44, pp. 925–937; © 1979 by the American Sociological Association.

Box 3-1 on page 76: "Researcher Accused of Fraud in Her Data Will Not Be Indicted," July 4, 1992. Copyright © 1992 by The New York Times Company. Reprinted by permission.

Box 3-1 on page 76: "U.S. Attorney Will Not Seek Indictment of Researcher Accused in 'Baltimore Case'," David L. Wheeler, volume 38, July 22, 1992, p. A7. Copyright 1992, *The Chronicle of Higher Education.* Reprinted with permission.

Box 3-2 on page 77: "U.S. Has Barred Grants to 6 Scientists in Past Two Years," David L. Wheeler, volume 37, July 3, 1992, p. A1, A6–A7. Copyright 1991, *The Chronicle of Higher Education.* Reprinted with permission.

Box on Validating the Measure of Happiness on page 126: From Norman M. Bradburn and David Caplovitz, *Reports on Happiness,* Aldine, Chicago, 1965. Adapted from pp. 15–17 and 21 by permission of the author.

Box 6-4 on page 164 and Box on Questions to Measure Self-Reported Delinquency Acts on page 173: From Travis Hirschi, *Causes of Delinquency,* University of California Press, 1969, excerpts from p. 256 and pp. 35–37. Copyright © 1969, The Regents of the University of California.

Box on Closed- and Open-Ended Forms of the Same Question on page 181: Donald P. Warwick and Charles A. Lininger: *The Sample Survey: Theory and Practice,* McGraw-Hill, © 1975. Reprinted from pp. 135–136 by permission of McGraw-Hill, Inc.

Box 7-3 on page 193: Converse, Jean, and Howard Schuman, *Conversations at Random,* John Wiley & Sons, Inc., 1974, pp. 12–13. Copyright © 1974. Reprinted by permission of John Wiley & Sons, Inc.

Box on The Unfolding Method on page 197 and Box on The Numbered Scale Method on page 198: Groves,

Robert M., and R. L. Kahn, *Surveys by Telephone,* Academic Press, © 1979. Adapted by permission of Academic Press, Orlando, Florida.

Box on Orenstein and Phillips on How Not to Confuse Random Assignment with Random Sampling on page 225: Orenstein, Alan, and William R. F. Phillips, *Understanding Social Research: An Introduction,* Allyn and Bacon, 1978. Copyright © 1978 by Allyn and Bacon. Reprinted by permission.

Box on Looking for Negative Evidence in the Field on page 248: Lewis, George H., and Johnathan F. Lewis, "The Dog in the Nighttime: Negative Evidence in Social Research," *British Journal of Sociology,* volume 31, © 1980, pp. 544–558. Adapted by permission of Routledge.

Box 9-1 on page 252: McKinney, John C., *Constructive Typology and Social Theory,* Appleton-Century-Crofts, © 1966, p. 169. Adapted by permission of Irvington Publishers, Inc.

Box 10-2 on page 269: Adapted from Gilbert A. Williams, "Enticing Viewers: Sex and Violence in *TV Guide* Program Advertisements," *Journalism Quarterly,* volume 66, 1989, pp. 970–973 with permission of Association for Education in Journalism and Mass Communication, publisher of *Journalism Quarterly.*

Box on the Lyrics of Dusty Springfield and Neil Simon on page 271: Reprinted from James T. Carey, "Changing Courtship Patterns in the Popular Song," *American Journal of Sociology,* volume 74, pp. 720–731, 1969, by permission of the University of Chicago Press, © 1969 by the University of Chicago. All rights reserved.

Box 11-1 on page 291: Adapted from F. Albert Skellie, G. Melton Mobley, and Ruth E. Coan, "Cost Effectiveness of Community-Based Long-Term Care: Current Findings of Georgia's Alternative Health Services Project," *American Journal of Public Health,* volume 72, pp. 353–358, 1982, by permission of the American Public Health Association.

Box 11-2 on page 295: Weiss, Carol H., *Evaluation Research: Methods of Assessing Program Effectiveness,* p. 46. Reprinted © 1972 by permission of Prentice-Hall, Englewood Cliffs, New Jersey.

Box 11-3 on page 297: Posavac, Emil J., and Raymond G. Carey, *Program Evaluation: Methods and Case Stud-*

ies, 4th ed., © 1992, pp. 36–40. Adapted by permission of Prentice-Hall, Englewood Cliffs, New Jersey.

Box 11-4 on page 303: Posavec, Emil J., and Raymond G. Carey, *Program Evaluation: Methods and Case Studies,* 3d. ed., © 1989, pp. 289–293, 294-299, 300–308, 309–315, 316–320. Adapted by permission of Prentice-Hall, Englewood Cliffs, New Jersey, and the author.

Box 11-5 on page 306: Reprinted by permission of Warner Books/New York from *Megatrends: Ten New Directions Transforming Our Lives.* Copyright © 1982 by John Naisbitt.

Box 11-6 on page 308: Adapted from Ben-Chieh Liu: *Quality of Life Indicators in US Metropolitan Areas,* Praeger, New York, 1976, pp. 57, 60, 64, 68, 75–77. Used by permission of Midwest Research Institute, Kansas City, Missouri.

Box on Davis' Convention for Describing Yule's Q on page 385: Davis, James A., *Elementary Survey Analysis,* © 1971, p. 49. Adapted by permission of Prentice-Hall, Inc., Englewood Cliffs, New Jersey.

Box 16-1 on page 415: Nunnally, Jum C., *Psychometric Theory,* 2d ed., McGraw-Hill, © 1978. Adapted from pp. 27–32 by permission of McGraw-Hill, Inc.

Box 16-3 on page 420: Bogardus Social Distance Scale, cited in John B. Williamson et al.: *The Research Craft: An Introduction to Social Research Methods,* 2d ed., 1982. Reprinted by permission of Scott Foresman/Harper.

FIGURES

Figure 2-3 on page 50: From Travis Hirschi, *Causes of Delinquency,* University of California Press, 1969. Reprinted from Figure 2 on p. 153. Copyright © 1969, The Regents of the University of California.

Figure 2-4 on page 54: Reprinted with permission from: Wallace, Walter L., *The Logic of Science in Sociology* (New York: Aldine de Gruyter). Copyright © 1971, Walter L. Wallace.

Figure 5-2 on page 131, Figure 5-3 on page 131, and Figure 5-5 on page 132: Reprinted from Anderson, T. W., and Stanley L. Sclove: *Introductory Statistical Analysis,* 2d ed., Houghton-Mifflin, Boston, 1986, pp. 29, 45, 39. Copyright © 1986 by The Scientific Press. Reprinted with permission of the author.

Figure 14-4 on page 370: Reprinted from Kendall, Patricia L., and Paul F. Lazarsfeld, "Problems of Survey Analysis," p. 157, in Robert K. Merton, ed.: *Continuities in Social Research,* Free Press, 1950. Copyright © 1950 by The Free Press, copyright renewed 1978. Reprinted with the permission of The Free Press, a Division of Macmillan, Inc.

TABLES

Table 2-1 on page 51 and Table 2-2 on page 52: From Travis Hirschi, *Causes of Delinquency,* University of California Press, Berkeley, 1969. Reprinted from Table 9 on p. 69 and Table 19 on p. 91. Copyright © 1969, The Regents of the University of California.

Table 8-1 on page 215: Berkowitz, Leonard, and Russell G. Geen, "Stimulus Qualities of the Target of Aggression," *Journal of Personality and Social Psychology,* volume 5, pp. 364–368, 1967. Copyright 1967 by The American Psychological Association. Adapted by permission of the publisher.

Table 8-2 on page 217: Phillips, David, "The Impact of Mass Media Violence on U.S. Homicides," *American Sociological Review,* volume 48, pp. 560–568, © 1983 by the American Sociological Association.

Table 15-7 on page 393: Rossi, Peter: *Down and Out in America: The Origins of Homelessness,* 1989. Reprinted from Peter Rossi, *Down and Out in America: The Origins of Homelessness,* by permission of the University of Chicago Press, © 1989 by the University of Chicago. All rights reserved.

Table 16-7 on page 425: Treiman, Donald J., *Occupational Prestige in Comparative Perspective,* © 1977, Academic Press. Adapted from pp. 306–314 by permission of the publisher and author.

Table of Random Numbers on page 451: Reprinted from pages 1–3 of *A Million Random Digits with 100,000 Normal Deviates* by The Rand Corporation (New York: The Free Press, 1955). Copyright 1955 and 1983 by The Rand Corporation. Used by permission.

Table on Chi-Square Distribution on page 452: I am grateful to the Literary Executor of the late Sir Ronald A. Fisher, F.R.S., to Dr. Frank Yates, F.R.S., and to Longman Group Ltd., London, for permission to reprint an abridged version of Table IV from their book *Statistical Tables for Biological, Agricultural and Medical Research* (6th edition, 1974).

INDEX